Economics of Family Law
Volume I

Economic Approaches to Law

Series Editors: Richard A. Posner
Judge, United States Court of Appeals for the Seventh Circuit and Senior Lecturer, University of Chicago Law School, USA
Francesco Parisi
Professor of Law, University of Minnesota Law School, USA

A full list of published and future titles in this series is printed at the end of this volume.

For a list of all Edward Elgar published titles visit our site on the World Wide Web at
www.e-elgar.com

Economics of Family Law
Volume I

Edited by

Margaret F. Brinig

Fritz Duda Family Chair in Law
Notre Dame University, USA

ECONOMIC APPROACHES TO LAW

An Elgar Reference Collection
Cheltenham, UK • Northampton, MA, USA

Published by
Edward Elgar Publishing Limited
Glensanda House
Montpellier Parade
Cheltenham
Glos GL50 1UA
UK

Edward Elgar Publishing, Inc.
William Pratt House
9 Dewey Court
Northampton
Massachusetts 01060
USA

A catalogue record for this book is available from the British Library

Library of Congress Control Number: 2006937374

ISBN: 978 1 84542 439 8 (2 volume set)

Printed and bound in Great Britain by MPG Books Ltd, Bodmin, Cornwall

Contents

Acknowledgements

The editor and publishers wish to thank the authors and the following publishers who have kindly given permission for the use of copyright material.

Cambridge University Press for excerpt: Steven L. Nock and Margaret F. Brinig (2002), 'Weak Men and Disorderly Women: Divorce and the Division of Labor', in Antony W. Dnes and Robert Rowthorn (eds), *The Law and Economics of Marriage and Divorce*, Chapter 10, 171–90.

Duke University School of Law for article: Saul Levmore (1995), 'Love It or Leave It: Property Rules, Liability Rules, and Exclusivity of Remedies in Partnership and Marriage', *Law and Contemporary Problems*, **58** (2), Spring, 221–49.

Elsevier for article: Allen M. Parkman (1998), 'Why are Married Women Working So Hard?', *International Review of Law and Economics*, **18** (1), March, 41–9.

Journal of Law and Economics and the University of Chicago for article: Gary S. Becker and Kevin M. Murphy (1988), 'The Family and The State', *Journal of Law and Economics*, **XXXI** (1), April, 1–18.

Journal of Legal Studies and the University of Chicago for articles: Elisabeth M. Landes and Richard A. Posner (1978), 'The Economics of the Baby Shortage', *Journal of Legal Studies*, **7** (2), June, 323–48; Stéphane Mechoulan (2006), 'Divorce Laws and the Structure of the American Family', *Journal of Legal Studies*, **35**, January, 143–74.

Louisiana Law Review for article: Margaret F. Brinig and Steven L. Nock (2004), 'Marry Me, Bill: Should Cohabitation Be the (Legal) Default Option?', *Louisiana Law Review*, **64** (3), Spring, 403–42.

Michigan Law Review Association for article: Brian H. Bix (2001), 'How to Plot Love on an Indifference Curve', *Michigan Law Review*, **99** (6), May, 1439–54.

MIT Press Journals and the President and Fellows of Harvard College and the Massachusetts Institute of Technology for article: George A. Akerlof, Janet L. Yellin and Michael L. Katz (1996), 'An Analysis of Out-of-Wedlock Childbearing in the United States', *Quarterly Journal of Economics*, **CXI** (2), May, 277–317.

Oxford University Press for articles: Margaret F. Brinig (1990), 'Rings and Promises', *Journal of Law, Economics and Organization*, **6** (1), Spring, 203-15; Douglas W. Allen (1992), 'What

Does She See in Him? The Effect of Sharing on the Choice of Spouse', *Economic Inquiry*, **XXX** (1), January, 57–67.

Jennifer Roback Morse for her own article: (1995), *The Development of the Child*, Prepared for the Liberty Fund Symposium: The Family, the Person and the State, March, 1–40.

Springer Science and Business Media for article: Margaret F. Brinig and Michael V. Alexeev (1995), 'Fraud in Courtship: Annulment and Divorce', *European Journal of Law and Economics*, **2** (1), March, 45–62.

University of Chicago Press for article: Shelly Lundberg and Robert A. Pollak (1993), 'Separate Spheres Bargaining and the Marriage Market', *Journal of Political Economy*, **101** (6), 988–1010.

Virginia Law Review and Copyright Clearance Center for articles: Elizabeth S. Scott and Robert E. Scott (1995), 'Parents as Fiduciaries', *Virginia Law Review*, **81** (8), November, 2401–76; Amy L. Wax (1998), 'Bargaining in the Shadow of the Market: Is There a Future for Egalitarian Marriage?', *Virginia Law Review*, **84** (4), May, 509–672.

In addition the publishers wish to thank the Marshall Library of Economics, University of Cambridge, UK and the Library of Indiana University at Bloomington, USA, for their assistance in obtaining these articles.

Introduction

Margaret F. Brinig

Although economists have studied other fields of law for many years – particularly contracts and corporate law – family law was virtually neglected until Gary Becker's pioneering work in the early 1970s (Becker, 1973, 1974). Since then, the field has received significant attention not only from his disciples but from economists at the Universities of Michigan (for example, Weiss and Willis, 1985, 1993), Washington (for example, Lundberg and Pollak, 1993; Allen, 1992) and Tel Aviv (Ben-Porath, 1982). However, except for the article by Landes and Posner (1975, Chapter 2; Volume I) on adoption, which received its share of negative attention (Cohen, 1987, Chapter 2; Volume II; Wiegers, 1992; Wagner, 1990; Sunstein, 1994; Mahoney, 1988), it was only fairly recently that the economic insights about the family crept into the consciousness of law professors.

Adding economics to the social science tools of psychology and sociology has only enriched the family law discourse. No-fault divorce, with its concomitant property distribution, has made at least a rudimentary understanding of economics important to the practitioner who now must assess the value, and marital share, of closely held family corporations and advanced degrees earned during a marriage. Further, economics can provide a framework for studying the important but otherwise undisciplined rules that pertain to family life.

This is not to say that the two disciplines of economics and law have maintained a perfect discourse. There are several reasons for the rather patchy communication that has occurred so far. Economists have what lawyers perceive as an irritating habit of simplifying. While this usually does not matter at all (and usefully explains much that goes on in the world, as Milton Friedman noted (1935, 1971)), sometimes looking at only one part of a complex picture completely distorts the results. Further, and fortunately for law professors, economists who do not have legal training tend not to be able to read cases and statutes with the same understanding lawyers possess. They therefore may miss subtleties, may misread results, may not be aware of recent developments, or may simply rely on others' sometimes inaccurate characterizations of what the law provides.

Another problem, which is described elsewhere as imperialism (Brinig, 2005), plagues both houses. Economists assume that everything can be assumed quite well in models that ought to work. When scholars try to describe what husbands and wives or parents are maximizing in their families, it may not be wealth or even personal utility, but something more like intimacy or, for their children, flourishing (Brinig, 2000). The problems of power and dominance that are at least on the periphery of discussions of criminal law take more of a front seat in the family, where gender and specialization have always been central (Nock, 1999). Lawyers, on the other hand, frequently assume that law can control and shape behavior to a far greater extent than it usually does. Some academics (e.g. Wardle, 1991) have noted that too much was expected of no-fault divorce, for example – that though it was supposed to end the acrimony of divorce, it merely redirected much of it to the other incidents of divorce, and particularly child custody and support. Sometimes, too, lawyers are shortsighted in missing the economic insight that one legal change may well lead to results in quite another, perhaps unanticipated, area.

Behavioral economics, while it certainly adds to the complexity of studying family law, may usefully explain some of the seemingly intractable problems. For example, Baker and Emery (1993) wrote some years ago that changes in law could not have too much impact ex ante because, for engaged couples, their over-optimism bias precluded any of them from expecting their marriage might end in divorce, or even if it did, from their spouse refusing to pay support. This same optimism arguably justifies the skepticism with which judges and legislators view premarital contracts, especially very one-sided ones,[1] though generally speaking individualized, ex ante contracting is much favored. Perhaps an even more persuasive problem for neoclassical economic treatment of families is the psychological insight that an exchange mentality (Hansen, 1991), or what Axelrod (1984) would call the tit-for-tat strategy that encourages cooperation in repeat-player games, may actually destroy family relationships. Cohabiting relationships are more like exchange relationships than are marriages, and these non-marital arrangements are much less stable and otherwise produce fewer good results than marriage (Brinig and Nock, 2004, Chapter 4; Volume I). What seems to be needed is an unconditional love, one without expectation of (at least immediate) payback (Brinig, 2000). Whether achieving this state is likely over the long run without what law and sociology both call the 'institution of marriage' poses an important policy question in the United States and elsewhere.

For many years, an obstacle to dialog between law and economics has come from the selection of attorneys into the family law bar. Before no-fault divorce, and to some extent even since then, the attorneys who specialized in family practice have been even more innumerate than the profession in general – they have been the people who were willing to be tarnished by an extremely sordid set of cases and/or plagued by people at some of the most emotional, and least rational, times in their lives. They filled roles as if they were the least savory of criminal defense lawyers or social workers and counselors and hand-holders (Brinig, 2000). This professional group was not likely to be enamored with the theory or the mathematics demanded by economic analysis. To some extent this picture of the divorce lawyer has changed over the past 50 years, though not many would call them the neurosurgeons or rocket scientists of the legal profession. While they still must deal with irate and seemingly irrational clients at times, many modern divorce practitioners must also deal with complex business valuations or concepts of human capital.

There is still not enough good empirical work being done in family law, and that dearth may lead to legislative mistakes (Brinig, 2002). When policymakers do see a study that is in any way credible, they are likely to overreact and assume that what the study showed is applicable to everyone and at any time. Thus mandatory arrest of domestic abusers suggested by one controlled study carried out in Minneapolis (Sherman and Berk, 1984) has become the law in many jurisdictions even though later studies (even by the same lead researcher) in other cities have showed that arrest may cause more rather than less recidivism by the abuser (Sherman *et al.*, 1992). Similarly, one study in Texas of 'immunity' for mothers who left newborns at hospitals has created numerous copycat laws[2] even though later work has shown no decrease in the number of infanticides. Studies for and against same-sex parenting have been criticized by lawyers on both sides of the debate as being too small or having inadequate controls or not asking the right questions (Wardle, 1997; Ball and Pea, 1998) and Brinig and Alexeer's discussion of fraud during courtship (Chapter 6, this volume). In fact, since there had been no legal same-sex marriage in the United States until *Goodridge* v. *Dept. of Public Health*,[3] there can be no real test. And even a 20- or 30-year longitudinal study in Massachusetts (much less Canada,[4] The Netherlands,[5] Belgium,[6] Spain[7] or South Africa,[8] which all have relatively recent legislation allowing same-sex marriage) might be hard to extend to other jurisdictions.

Most economic analysis of family law has drawn heavily on the economic analysis of contract law, which possesses its own quite respectable tradition. But even the long-term relational contract fails to capture what is going on in families. In addition to the qualifications discussed earlier, and particularly the exchange-relationship problem, there are usually, if not always, third-party externality dimensions to family problems. Many of these involve children, who possess their own utility functions and who are legally (and actually, for many years) incapable of making good decisions. At divorce or in cases of child welfare, particularly, their interests and those of their parents may be quite different or opposing. Scholars need some other way to describe what is going on: the firm is a helpful, if incomplete, analogy.

Further, many of the relationships, and particularly marriage and adoption, involve third-party interests of the general public. For that reason they are substantially regulated, and even private attempts to contract around basic duties will be to no avail.[9] For example, arguably people ought to be able to contract for more stringent divorce grounds than the no-fault ones generally available (Scott and Scott, 1998). Yet even people who sign covenant marriage contracts in states allowing for them are not bound to divorce only on the basis of fault or a long waiting period if they travel to neighboring states. The case law that exists suggests that they will not have to pay financial penalties for doing so, either. (They can, and do as a matter of fact, also divorce in the covenant marriage states using no-fault grounds without revealing their covenant marriages.) Perhaps this is because we conceive of the right to divorce under no-fault terms as inalienable, like a thirteenth amendment right, so that any attempt to marry under a more stringent regime, even in a covenant-marriage-permitting state, smacks of unconstitutional conditions.

Similarly, validly married couples who contract before marriage to remove responsibility for child support or to allocate child custody cannot enforce these provisions at divorce. Payment of child support is an absolute duty under state statutes, and especially if the custodial parent would otherwise need public assistance, cannot be completely bargained away (see, for example, Iowa Code 565:1). Child custody must be determined at divorce in the child's best interests, and these cannot be known at the time of marriage, particularly if the child is not even conceived at the time.

Other family contracts that might be enforced (but that are not) involve agreements (sometimes even written ones) for domestic services taking place during marriage (Silbaugh, 1996), or what might be called 'child' or 'parenting' services taking place at any time. The household services contract cases are more numerous and more academics have written about them. From a macroeconomic viewpoint, unpaid household labor constitutes a very large share of GNP, sometimes estimated at upwards of 40 percent. Feminist scholars have argued for years that this both devalues 'women's work' and places wives at a comparative disadvantage in the labor market, let alone upon divorce, or, still more frequently, widowhood (for example, Staudt, 1996). Some courts have reasoned that marriage intrinsically involves reciprocal duties of support, whether in cash or kind, so there is no additional consideration to support such a promise (In re Marriage of Graham, 574 P.2d 75, 77 (Colo. 1978); *Kirksey* v. *Kirksey*, 8 Ala. 131 (1845) (gratuitous promise)). Only when one spouse has breached the original marriage agreement (through grounds for divorce) may the other spouse collect 'damages' (Landes, 1978; Brinig and Carbone, 1988). Alternatively, and to return to the 'exchange relationship' discussion above, we do not enforce these household agreements, because they are so tied up with the respective identities of husband and wife. The reciprocal of turning 'labor into love,' as Katherine Silbaugh (1996) puts it, involves dealing with incommensurables, commodifying just as surrogacy arguably commodifies childbearing. From a more normative, sociological viewpoint (using words of fewer syllables), turning a marriage relationship into a web of discrete, enforceable contracts destroys the trust that is at its core even more than requiring the business corporation to treat every internal dealing as a separate contract destroys the value of the firm (Levmore, 1995, Chapter 14; Volume I). As an exception, courts have recognized some ability to recover for discrete investments in our spouse's career upon divorce, whether through 'reimbursement alimony' or division of goodwill. These concessions recognize a particular type of contract exchanged by husbands and wives when they typically have not accumulated a lot of property: if you will support me and tolerate a lower standard of living while I finish professional school and establish practice, I promise that I'll work to earn enough so we can live much better (or you can finish your own education) once I get through (Brinig and Carbone, 1988; Parkman, 1995).

Parenting- or child-services questions usually come up as third-party beneficiary problems when teenagers seek to enforce the portion of their divorced parents' separation agreements involving child support or college education (*Drake* v. *Drake*, 455 N.Y.S.2d 420 (N.Y. App. Div. 1982). These children are typically named in the agreements and would seem to be 'direct, intended' beneficiaries. So why are they disabled from suing? We can understand why our children should not be able to sue us if we fail to provide them with the latest levels of 'Halo 2' computer game even if they did take out the trash, do their homework, clear the table, or complete whatever other chores we assigned. Parenting is messy, complicated work and involves difficult questions of guidance and discipline. We need to 'maintain control of the family exchequer' (*Wright* v. *Wright*, 191 S.E.2d 223 (Va. 1972)) and may not have the $50 to plunk down. We may think our child needs fresh air more than more time playing video games or be worried that that game's violence would transmute into hitting the dog when annoyed. The deals parents make when divorcing are complicated and messy as well. The custodial parent is providing services the noncustodial parent (in terms of guidance and discipline as well as laundry and cooking) doesn't provide, as well as, typically these days, giving financial support. If there is more than one child involved, allowing a single emancipated child to sue may well mean less for the sibling – even, in less fortunate homes, less heat or even less food. Further, despite Congressionally mandated child-support guidelines, child support is still one strand of a convoluted, multi-faceted deal.[10] If one thread gets pulled, the remainder may no longer make sense and the custodial parent may come up on the short end. This is less true for the college education expenses or the requirement that a parent maintain health or life insurance for the child's benefit, and many cases allow children to sue for these (ALR, § 4).

As children, we also have at least a moral obligation to support our parents when they are no longer self-sufficient. Some state statutes (and the Napoleonic Code, Art. 205) specifically require this, at least if the parents are destitute. As medicine improves and we live longer and longer past retirement, live longer and longer in dependent conditions, and Social Security is threatened, we can expect many more cases where the younger generation is held accountable on the implied promise to support the older in return for what was provided during childhood. Like the spousal domestic services, this may well extend beyond financial support and into physical care. Legal enforcement of this implied contract may change the nature of parenting, or the way we relate to our parents as adults, or the assumptions we make in investing in our children's human capital.

Despite all these qualifications, some really good economic analysis of family law enriches the field. While the papers selected for inclusion do not represent more than a small portion of what has been published (and no consideration has been given to what may have been done in languages other than English), they certainly convey the flavor and some of the exciting ideas that have surfaced over the past 30 years. The questions posed by the authors included in this book are well worth pursuing by the next generation of academics.

The two volumes are divided roughly into four parts. Before Marriage and Parenthood (Volume I, Part I), deals with alternatives to marriage, particularly cohabitation and births outside marriage, as well as with courtship and premarital contracting. Parenting and Being Married (Volume I, Part II), as its title suggests, deals with the analysis of marriage and child rearing. It focuses on the division of labor between spouses, on the problems of combining work and parenting, on the role of parents, and on the division of responsibilities between family and state. Divorce and the Divorce Process (Volume II, Part I) includes some of the rather overwhelming literature on the effects of no-fault divorce, as well as some of the works on the incidents of marriage: alimony, property division and child custody. With Intergenerational Families (Volume II, Part II), the collection concludes with some works on intergenerational transfers and the elderly.

Before Marriage and Parenthood includes an essay by Nobel Laureate George Akerlof and others (Akerlof, Yellin and Katz, 1996, Chapter 1; Volume I) on the results of effective birth control and legalized abortion. Contrary to one's first intuitions, the authors posit that these technological changes in fact produced more births out of wedlock as women who would otherwise have insisted on marriage if confronted with unplanned pregnancy could no longer afford to do so. Elisabeth Landes and Richard Posner's (1975) famous essay on deregulation of the adoption market is here, as well as Brinig's (1990, Chapter 3; Volume I) essay on the use of engagement rings as bonding devices when legislatures removed tort liability for broken engagements. Brinig and Nock's (2004, Chapter 4; Volume I) socioeconomic analysis of the difference between cohabitation and marriage appears in this part, together with Stéphane Mechoulan's (2006, Chapter 5; Volume I) analysis of the effect of unilateral (no-fault) divorce on couples' willingness to marry and bear children and Douglas Allen's (1992, Chapter 7; Volume I) essay on the relationship between marriage rules and what Becker (1991) calls 'assortative mating'. Part I concludes with Amy Wax's (1997, Chapter 8; Volume I) discussion of why a truly egalitarian marriage is unlikely because of the relative (and changing) bargaining positions of men and women before and during marriage.

Parenting and Being Married Part II, begins with three essays on the role of parents. The first, by Nobel laureate Gary Becker and Kevin Murphy (1988, Chapter 9; Volume I) treats the division of responsibilities between state and parent as an efficient delegation of what parents would otherwise do themselves. Elizabeth and Robert Scott (1995, Chapter 10; Volume I) extend this idea by suggesting that law treats parents like other legal fiduciaries, possessed of great power and responsibility, to be curbed only if they are no longer worthy of trust, here because they abuse or neglect the child. Jennifer Roback Morse (2001, Chapter 11; Volume I) treats parenting from a different perspective, explaining how parents form their children's utility functions, and, at various stages, set the boundaries within which they may act. The next section includes essays on being married. Nock and Brinig (2002, Chapter 12; Volume I) explain how the division of labor in the family, long postulated by Gary Becker (1974, 1991), works out in marriages in which both spouses are working in the paid labor force. It turns out that the most egalitarian marriages (at least as far as the number of hours spent on household tasks goes) are not the most stable, and that the actual jobs that lead to marital stability are those traditionally assumed by men. Like the Scotts' (1995, Chapter 10, Volume I) paper, Brian Bix (2001, Chapter 13; Volume I) treats marriage and parenting through an economic lens in his extensive literature review. Saul Levmore (1995, Chapter 14; Volume I) analogizes corporate and family exit rules, explaining why spouses, like corporate managers, cannot sue each other during the ongoing relationship. In the final section Lundberg and Pollack (1993, Chapter 15; Volume I) model the marriage in distress as one in which the spouses revert to traditional gender roles in order to minimize criticisms while limiting their own investment in the relationship. Finally, Allen Parkman (1998, Chapter 16; Volume I) argues that in states with easier divorce rules women have spent more time in the labor force in order to protect themselves should divorce occur.

Divorce has perhaps received the most attention from students of the family. Accordingly, this book includes a number of papers on divorce and on the incidents of marriage. Volume II begins with a classic: Becker, Landes and Michael's (1977, Chapter 1) theory about why couples divorce. In many cases, due to incomplete searches for good marital partners, couples discover that the costs of divorcing and returning to the single state are lower than any gains they have in the less than satisfactory marriage. Lloyd Cohen's important paper (1987, Chapter 2; Volume II) begins with Becker, Elisabeth M. Landes and Robert T. Michael (1977) but adds the provocative theory that women and men invest most and profit most from marriage at different points in their life cycle: women invest most and profit least at the beginning of marriage. For men, the investment occurs later in the marriage while the profit comes earlier. Successful men can therefore extract quasi-rents from their wives and, sometimes, leave them for younger and more desirable women. The next three papers develop the debate on whether no-fault (or what economists call 'unilateral') divorce has caused a rise in divorce rates. Elisabeth Peters (1986, Chapter 3; Volume II) argues that under the Coase Theorem, there should be very little if any increase in divorces, but that as states moved to no-fault systems the consequences would come out in changes in property distribution and alimony. Using the same data set, Douglas Allen (1992, Chapter 4; Volume II) argues that when regional differences are taken into account, there is in fact an increase (and that there should be one because of the substantial transaction costs associated with divorce). Leora Friedberg (1998, Chapter 5; Volume II), using the same and different data, but a model of 'no-fault' that takes into account fault-based rules for property and alimony allocation, does show an increase in divorce rates. Brinig and Allen (2000, Chapter 6; Volume II) and Weiss and Willis add children to their models of the divorce process. Brinig and Allen show empirically that expectations about child custody determine which spouse files for divorce. Weiss and Willis (1993, Chapter 7; Volume II, 1985, Chapter 8; Volume II) demonstrate in their earlier piece that transfers among divorced couples do not seem to vary much due to the divorce regime, but do vary with custody and visitation patterns. Their second piece explains that many divorced fathers are reluctant to pay child support because they are unable to monitor either their children or the way their former wives allocate the support money. Allen Parkman (1995, Chapter 9; Volume II) provides a basis for awarding a divorcing spouse a share in the other spouse's professional degree or other career enhancement on the basis of the contribution made to the other's human capital. Elisabeth Landes (1978, Chapter 10; Volume II) provides the economic rationale for alimony as a recoupment of losses suffered because of the marriage and investments made in the household rather than one's career.

The final part, Intergenerational Families, enlarges the consideration of families to the extended, or multi-generational family. First, John Langbein (1988, Chapter 11; Volume II) details how inheritance rules and expectations have changed from the time in which wealth was held primarily in real property to modern times, when it consists largely of human capital. James Buchanan (1983, Chapter 12; Volume II) also discusses inheritance, but in term of rent-extraction from potential benefactors and (sometimes unwanted) rent-seeking from potential heirs. Brinig and coauthors (2004, Chapter 13; Volume II) conclude with a public-choice empirical paper on the promulgation and enforcement of elder abuse legislation and regulations.

Notes

1. For one recent example, see *In re Marriage of Bonds* 24 Cal.4th 1, 99 Cal.Rptr.2d 252, 5 P.3d 815 (2000) (abrogated by West's Ann.Cal.Fam.Code § 1612).
2. http://www.ncsl.org/programs/cyf/slr268.htm.
3. 798 N.E.2d 941 (Mass. 2003)
4. (S-38, enacted July 28, 2005)
5. Wet wan 21 December 2000, Stb. 2001, nr. 9 (Neth.) (providing for the 'Opening up of Marriage for Same Sex Partners'. Translated into English in Text of Dutch Act on the Opening Up of Marriage for Same-Sex Partners (Kees Alaaldijk trans.) in Legal Recognition of Same Sex Partnerships App. II, at 455, 455–56(Ribert Wintemute and Mads Andenaes eds., 2001)
6. 'Law of 13 February 2003 opening up marriage to persons of the same sex and modifying certain provisions of the Civil Code'.
7. Jennifer Green, 'Spain Legalizes Same-Sex Marriage: Prime Minister Makes Unexpected Speech Backing Law Termed "Unjust" by Church', *Washington Post*, Friday, 1 July 2005, A14.
8. *Fourie and Another* v. *Minister of Home Affairs and Others*, Supreme Court of Appeal, 30 Nov. 2004) (opinion limited to common law marriage).
9. (See, for example, Uniform Premarital Agreement Act §8 (b) provides, 'The right of a child to support may not be adversely affected by a premarital agreement.')
10. Think of Lon Fuller, 'The Forms and Limits of Adjudication', 92 *Harv. L. Rev.* 353, 393–400 (1978), who wrote about polycentrism in his discussion of Mrs. Timkin's will giving valuable paintings to two art museums 'in equal shares'.

References

Allen, Douglas W. (1992) 'What Does She See in Him?' The Effect of Sharing on the Choice of Spouse. *Economic Inquiry*, **30**(January): 57–67.

Allen, Douglas W. and Brinig, Margaret F. (2005) 'Bargaining in the Shadow of Joint Parenting', submitted to *Journal of Law and Economics*.

American Law Reports, (1970–2004) 'Right Of Child To Enforce Provisions For His Benefit In Parents' Separation Or Property Settlement Agreement', 34:1357.

Axelrod, Robert (1984) *The Evolution of Cooperation*, New York: Basic Books.

Baker, Lynn. A. and Emery, Robert E. (1993) 'When Every Relationship is Above, Average: Perceptions and Expectations of Divorce at the Time of Marriage', *Law and Human Behavior*, **17**, 439–50.

Ball, Carlos, and Pea, Janice (1998) 'Warring with Wardle: Morality, Social Science, and Gay and Lesbian Parents', *University of Illinois Law Review*, 253–339.

Becker, Gary S. (1973) 'A Theory of Marriage, Part 1', *Journal of Political Economy*, **81**(4): 813–46.

Becker, Gary S. (1974) 'A Theory of Marriage, Part II', *Economics of the Family*, Theodore W. Schultz (ed.) Chicago: University of Chicago Press.

Becker, Gary S., et al. (1977) 'An Economic Analysis of Marital Instability', *Journal of Political Economy*, **5**(6): 1141–87.

Becker, Gary S. (1991) '*A Treatise on the Family*', Cambridge: Harvard University Press.

Ben-Porath, Yoram (1982) 'Economics and the Family – Match or Mismatch? (Review)', *Journal of Economic Literature*, **20**: 52–64.

Brinig, Margaret F. (2000) '*From Contract to Covenant: Beyond the Law and Economics of the Family*', Cambridge, Mass.: Harvard University Press.

Brinig, Margaret F. (2002) 'Empirical Work in Family Law', *University of Illinois Law Review*, **2002**(4), 1083–1110.

Brinig, Margaret F. (2005) 'Some Concerns About Applying Economics to Family Law', in *Feminism Confronts Homo Economicus: Gender, Law and Society*, 450–67. Martha A. Fineman and Terence Dougherty, eds., Ithaca, N.Y.: Cornell University Press, 2005).

Brinig, Margaret F. and Allen, Douglas W. (2000) '"These Boots Are Made for Walking": Why Most Divorce Filers Are Women', *American Law and Economics Review*, **2**(1): 126–69.

Brinig, Margaret F. and Carbone, June (1988) 'The Reliance Interest in Marriage and Divorce', *Tulane Law Review*, **62**, 855–905.

Brinig, Margaret F. et al. (2004) 'The Public Choice of Elder Abuse Law', **33**, *Journal of Legal Studies*, 517–47.

Buchanan, James (1983) 'Rent-Seeking, Noncompensated Transfers and the Rights of Succession', *Journal of Law and Economics*, **26**, 71–84.

Cohen, Jane Maslow (1987) 'Posnerism, Pluralism, Pessimism', *Boston University Law Review*, **67**:105–75.

Cohen, Lloyd (1987) 'Marriage, Divorce and Quasi-Rents: Or "I Gave Him the Best Years of My Life"', *Journal of Legal Studies*, **16**: 267–304.

Friedberg, Leora (1998) 'Did Unilateral Divorce Raise Divorce Rates? Evidence from Panel Data', *American Economic Review*, **88**: 608–27.

Friedman, Milton (1935, 1971) 'The Methodology of Positive Economics', reprinted in *Essays In Microeconomics*, **23** (William Breit and Harold M. Hochman, eds), Chicago: University of Chicago Press (2nd edn).

Fuller, Lon L. (1978) 'The Forms and Limits of Adjudication', *Harvard Law Review*, **92**, 353–409.

Hansen, Gary L. (1991) 'Moral Reasoning and the Marital Exchange Relationship', *Journal of Social Psychology*, **131**: 71–81.

Landes, Elisabeth M. (1978) 'Economics of Alimony', *Journal of Legal Studies*, **7**: 35–63.

Langbein, John N. (1988) 'The Twentieth-century Revolution in Family Wealth Transmission', *Michigan Law Review*, **86**: 722–50.

Mahoney, Joan (1988) 'A Essay on Surrogacy and Feminist Thought', *Journal of Law, Medicine & Health Care*, **16**: 81–88.

Nock, Steven L. (1999) '*Marriage in Men's Lives*', Oxford, UK: Oxford University Press.

Parkman, Allen M. (1995) 'Human Capital as Property in Celebrity Divorces', *Family Law Quarterly*, **29**: 141–69.

Peters, H. Elizabeth (1986) 'Marriage and Divorce: Informational Constraints and Private Contracting', *American Economic Review*, **76**(3): 437–54.

Scott, Elizabeth S. and Scott, Robert E. (1998) 'Marriage as Relational Contract', *Virginia Law Review*, **84**(7): 1225–1334.

Sherman Lawrence W. *et al.* (1992) 'Crime, Punishment and Stake in Conformity: Legal and Informal Control of Domestic Violence', *American Sociological Review*, **57**: 680–90.

Sherman, Lawrence W. and Berk, Richard A. (1984) 'The Specific Deterrent Effects of Arrest for Domestic Assault', *American Sociological Review*, **49**, 261–72.

Silbaugh, Katharine T. (1996) 'Turning Labor into Love: Housework and the Law', *Northwestern University Law Review*, **91**: 1–86.

Staudt, Nancy (1996) 'Taxing Housework', *Georgetown Law Journal*, **84**: 1571–1647.

Sunstein, Cass R. (1994) 'Incommensurability and Valuation in Law', *Michigan Law Review*, **92**:779–861.

Wagner, William Joseph (1990) 'The Contractual Reallocation of Procreative Resources and Parental Rights: The Natural Endowment Critique', *Case Wesern Reserve Law Review*, **41**:1–202.

Wardle, Lynn D. (1991) 'No-Fault Divorce and the Divorce Conundrum', *Brigham Young University Law Review*, 1991: 79–142.

Wardle, Lynn D. (1997) 'The Potential Impact of Homosexual Parenting on Children', *University of Illinois Law Review*, 1997: 833–98.

Weiss, Yoram and Willis, Robert (1985) 'Children as Collective Goods in Divorce Settlements', *Journal of Labor Economics*, **1**:268–92.

Weiss, Yoram and Willis, Robert (1993) 'Transfers Among Divorced Couples: Evidence and Interpretation', *Journal of Labor Economics*, **11**: 629–79.

Wiegers, Wanda A. (1992) 'Economic Analysis of Law and "Private Ordering": A Feminist Critique', *University of Toronto Law Journal*, **42**:170–206.

Williams-Mbengue, Nina (2001) 'A National Center for State Legislatures, Analysis of State Actions on Important Issues: *Safe Havens for Abandoned Infants*', 2001 NCSL State Legislative Report No. 26(8). http://www.ncsl.org/programs/cyf/slr268.htm (last visited 29 July 2005).

Part I
Before Marriage and Parenthood

A
Outside Family Institutions

[1]

THE
QUARTERLY JOURNAL
OF ECONOMICS

| Vol. CXI | May 1996 | Issue 2 |

AN ANALYSIS OF OUT-OF-WEDLOCK CHILDBEARING IN THE UNITED STATES*

GEORGE A. AKERLOF
JANET L. YELLEN
MICHAEL L. KATZ

This paper relates the erosion of the custom of shotgun marriage to the legalization of abortion and the increased availability of contraception to unmarried women in the United States. The decline in shotgun marriage accounts for a significant fraction of the increase in out-of-wedlock first births. Several models illustrate the analogy between women who do not adopt either birth control or abortion and the hand-loom weavers, both victims of changing technology. Mechanisms causing female immiseration are modeled and historically described. This technology-shock hypothesis is an alternative to welfare and job-shortage theories of the feminization of poverty.

I. INTRODUCTION

When Daniel Moynihan wrote his famous report, *The Negro Family* [U. S. Department of Labor 1965] the black out-of-wedlock birth rate was 24 percent. Twenty-five years later this

*The authors thank Michael Ash, Halsey Rogers, and Neil Siegel for excellent research assistance. They are grateful to Lawrence Katz, John Baldwin, Nancy Chodorow, Curtis Eaton, Pierre Fortin, Claudia Goldin, Bronwyn Hall, Eugene Hamill, Joseph Harrington, Richard Harris, Elhanan Helpman, Edward Lazear, Ronald Lee, Richard Lipsey, Mark Machina, Carl Mason, Hajime Miyazaki, Preston McAfee, Daniel McFadden, James Montgomery, Fraser Mustard, Peter Nicholson, James Rauch, Christina Romer, David Romer, Paul Romer, Andrew Rose, Nathan Rosenberg, Edward Safarian, Andrei Shleifer, Tamara Springsteen, Judy Stacy, Jame Wilcox, Michael Wolfson, and anonymous referees for invaluable comments. They thank the Canadian Institute for Advanced Research and the National Science Foundation under research grant number SBR-9409426 for generous financial support. Janet Yellen is Governor of the Federal Reserve System. The views in this paper are those of the authors and do not represent the opinions of the Federal Reserve System.

The Quarterly Journal of Economics, May 1996.

rate, defined as the percentage of births to unmarried women, had more than doubled, to 64 percent. Over the same period the white out-of-wedlock birth ratio experienced yet faster growth—albeit from a lower-level—more then quintupling, from 3.1 percent to 18 percent.[1] Rising out-of-wedlock birthrates are of social policy concern because children reared in single-parent households are more likely to be impoverished and to experience difficulties in later life.[2]

A major role in the increase in out-of-wedlock births has been played by the declining practice of "shotgun marriage." Until the early 1970s it was the norm in premarital sexual relations that the partners would marry in the event of pregnancy. The disappearance of this custom has been a major contributor to the increase in the out-of-wedlock birth ratio for both whites and blacks. In fact, about three-fourths of the increase in the white out-of-wedlock first-birth ratio, and about three-fifths of the black increase, between 1965–1969 and 1985–1989 are explicable by the decrease in the fraction of premaritally conceived first births that are resolved in marriage. By that we mean that if the fraction of premaritally conceived births resolved by marriage had been the same from 1985 to 1989 as it had been over the comparable period twenty years earlier, the increase in the white out-of-wedlock birth ratio would have been only a quarter as high, and the black increase would have been only two-fifths as high.[3]

---

1. The simultaneous rise of out-of-wedlock births and other forms of social/economic distress such as crime, drug abuse, and poverty, especially in black urban ghettos, well documented by Anderson [1990], Wilson [1987], and others, is consistent with Moynihan's gloomy predictions.

2. A substantial literature documents that single parenthood results in a variety of adverse consequences for children (see, for example, Manski, Sandefur, McLanahan, and Powers [1992]).

3. The data for this calculation are taken from retrospective marital and fertility histories of the Current Population Survey, with a shotgun marriage defined as one occurring within seven months prior to the birth of the baby. The data are described in the Appendix. The CPS fertility supplements were first used to estimate shotgun marriage ratios by O'Connell and Moore [1980] and O'Connell and Rogers [1984]. The proportion of the change in out-of-wedlock births due to the change in the shotgun marriage rate is calculated as follows. If oow_t and oow_{t+1} are the fractions of out-of-wedlock births, $bcoow_t$ and $bcoow_{t+1}$ are the fraction of births conceived out-of-wedlock, and sr_t and sr_{t+1} are the shotgun marriage rates at t and $t + 1$, respectively, then the formula for the change in the out-of-wedlock birth ratio due to the change in the shotgun marriage ratio is $((1 - sr_{t+1})bcoow_{t+1} - (1 - sr_t)bcoow_{t+1})/(oow_{t+1} - oow_t)$. The denominator is the change in the out-of-wedlock birth ratio. The first term in the numerator is the fraction of out-of-wedlock births at $t + 1$. The second term is what the fraction would have been at $t + 1$ if the shotgun marriage ratio had been the same at $t + 1$ as at t. The difference between the first and the second term of the numerator is the change in the out-of-wedlock birthrate due to the change in the shotgun marriage rate.

Ethnographic studies describe shotgun marriage in the late 1960s. For example, Rubin [1969], who studied working-class whites in San Francisco in the late 1960s, found that courtship was brief and quite likely to involve sexual activity. In the event of pregnancy, marriage occurred. One of her subjects expressed the matter succinctly and with the absence of doubt with which many social customs are unquestionably observed: "If a girl gets pregnant you married her. There wasn't no choice. So I married her." The norms regarding pregnancy and marriage were apparently much the same among blacks, although perhaps with greater ambiguity and more doubt since out-of-wedlock birthrates for blacks were much higher than for whites.[4]

For whites the shotgun marriage ratio began its decline at almost the same time as the advent of female contraception for unmarried women and the legalization of abortion. In the late 1960s and very early 1970s, many major states including New York and California clarified their laws regarding abortion (significantly prior to Roe v. Wade in January 1973). At about the same time it became easier as well as more common for unmarried people to obtain contraceptives. In July 1970 the Massachusetts law prohibiting the distribution of contraceptives to unmarried individuals was declared unconstitutional in the landmark case Eisenstadt v. Baird. (See Garrow [1994, p. 457].) This paper will explain why there might be a link between female contraception and the legalization of abortion and the declining shotgun marriage rate.

Why should there be such a link? Both the advent of female contraception and the legalization of abortion are analogous to technical change: each has shifted out the frontier of available choices. While the morality of using these options generates heated debate, family planners have viewed female contraception and abortion as welfare-improving for women: they have made women free to choose. But technological innovation creates both winners and losers. A cost-saving innovation almost invariably penalizes producers who, for whatever reason, fail to adopt it. The hand-loom weavers of Britain in the early nineteenth cen-

---

4. Thus, in the very poor Pruitt-Igoe public housing project in St. Louis, Rainwater [1970] reports, "marriage is considered the most attractive solution [to an unwanted pregnancy]." But the custom of marriage, at least in Pruitt-Igoe, was not unquestioned, for Rainwater also observes: "But it [marriage] is not automatic; shotgun weddings are to be carefully considered, because if the couple is not compatible, they are not likely to stay married."

tury are the classic illustration of this point. In the case of female contraception and abortion, women who want children, and women who, because of indecision or religious conviction have failed to adopt the new innovations, have lost disproportionately.[5] Technological change may also benefit those who are not directly affected. For example, the development of yield-increasing varieties of wheat will lower wheat prices and benefit consumers. Analogously, in the case of female contraception and abortion, men may have been beneficiaries. Finally, it is conceivable that technological innovation could even harm those who choose to implement it. For example, if wheat is inelastically demanded, the availability of a new variety that costlessly increases yields will benefit consumers; but the returns to farmers will decline as long as they plant the same wheat acreage.

The first task of this paper is to illustrate, through two theoretical models, how analogous mechanisms could operate with respect to increased availability of abortion and female contraception for women. These models will show how the legalization of abortion and the availability of female contraception could result in a decline in the competitive position of women relative to men—especially if they do not use contraception or abortion.

In the first model a decline in the cost of abortion (or increased availability of contraception) decreases the incentives to obtain a promise of marriage if premarital sexual activity results in pregnancy. Those women who will obtain an abortion or who will reliably use contraception no longer find it necessary to condition sexual relations on such promises. Those women who want children, who do not want an abortion for moral or religious reasons, or who are unreliable in their use of contraception, may want marriage guarantees but find themselves pressured to participate in premarital sexual relations without any such assurance. They have been placed at a competitive disadvantage: in this case analogous to farmers who do not switch to the new varieties of wheat. Sexual activity without commitment is increasingly expected in premarital relationships, immiserizing at least some women, since their male partners do not have to assume parental responsibility in order to engage in sexual relations.

---

5. According to the 1982 National Survey of Family Growth, mothers of children born out of wedlock in 1970 reported that 19 percent were wanted at the time; 65 percent were mistimed or neither wanted nor unwanted; 15 percent were unwanted. These numbers reflect the commonly perceived indecision of women giving birth out of wedlock and ambiguity as to whether the children are wanted or unwanted.

A second model illustrates another reason why the previous support system could have been eroded by the advent of female contraception and legal abortion. The fact that the birth of the baby is now a *choice* of the mother has implications for the decisions of the father. The sexual revolution, by making the birth of the child the *physical* choice of the mother, makes marriage and child support a *social* choice of the father. This second model explores how the decisions of the father depend upon the decisions and options of the mother. The logic of this model corresponds to what one contributor to the Internet wrote to the Dads' Rights Newsgroup: "Since the decision to have the child is solely up to the mother (see Roe v. Wade) I don't see how both parents have responsibility to that child. . . . When one person has the decision-making power, they alone have the responsibility to provide and care for that decision."

In this second model, out-of-wedlock birth is the consequence of a sequence of decisions: about male-female relationships, about sexual activity, about the use of contraceptives, about abortion in the event of pregnancy, and about marriage in the event of birth. This work extends that of Becker [1981] by incorporating out-of-wedlock births and the sexual participation decision into a rational choice framework.[6]

The major economic theories for increased out-of-wedlock births are based on changes in job availability (see Wilson [1987]) and changes in welfare incentives (see Murray [1984]),[7] but as will be discussed, empirically neither of these factors explains more than a small fraction of the change. The alternative hypothesis offered in this paper thus fills a void. In the absence of any better theory, despite econometric evidence to the contrary, the welfare theory serves as the primary rationale for reducing welfare support. However, if the rise in out-of-wedlock births is mainly due to technical change or has occurred for yet some further reason, currently envisioned cuts in welfare will fall far short of their proponents' expectations.

This paper offers theoretical reasons why the technological shock of abortion and female contraception may have played a major role in the rise of out-of-wedlock childbearing. If the simplest versions of our models totally explained the data, then arguably the repeal of abortion and the denial of female contra-

---

6. This paper also extends to premarital states the work on the distribution of returns between men and women in marriage. For a recent review see Lundberg and Pollak [1994].
7. These are the two main theories reviewed by Ellwood and Crane [1990].

ception to unmarried women could reverse this trend. But the change in sexual customs and the subsequent rise in out-of-wedlock births have been accompanied by a decline in the stigma attached to out-of-wedlock childbearing. Because there is no reason to believe that destigmatization is reversible, it does not follow that the prohibition of abortion or of the pill and other contraceptive devices to unmarried women would be effective in reducing out-of-wedlock births. Instead of decreasing out-of-wedlock childbearing, the denial of choice would, in all likelihood, further increase the number of out-of-wedlock births as women who would have obtained abortions or used contraceptives instead give birth to unwanted babies.

If Humpty Dumpty cannot be put back together again, what can be done? In the old days a private system of contracting between sexual partners insured that children received the financial and emotional support of two parents. Although the old system may be impossible to reconstruct, social policy can still create incentives that make it costly for fathers to abrogate parental responsibility for their offspring. Ellwood [1988] has suggested administrative ways of making fathers pay. Such a system would not only directly contribute to the well-being of children born out of wedlock, but it would also tax men for fathering such children, thereby offsetting at least partially the technology-shock-induced change in terms between fathers and mothers.

II. Basic Trends

Before presenting models of out-of-wedlock births, it is useful to describe some key facts concerning the magnitude and timing of out-of-wedlock births, total births, abortion, use of the pill, sexual experience as an indicator of sexual participation, shotgun marriage, and the living arrangements of children. These facts will serve as the relevant background both for the development of the models and for their interpretation. The Data Appendix describes the derivation of statistics dependent on our own calculations. Table I summarizes the trends in vital statistics, and Table II presents statistics concerning important decisions relating to women's fertility and childbearing histories.

Table III describes time series tests for jumps and changes in trends in the use of abortion and the pill, sexual participation, and the shotgun marriage ratio. All regressions were run in first-difference form after failure to reject unit roots in the underlying

OUT-OF-WEDLOCK CHILDBEARING IN THE U. S.   283

TABLE I
VITAL STATISTICS: BIRTHS, FERTILITY RATES, MARITAL STATUS, OUT-OF-WEDLOCK
BIRTHS

	1965–1969	1970–1974	1975–1979	1980–1984	1985–1989
Births (in thousands)[a]					
Total	3599	3370	3294	3646	3809
White	2990	2760	2660	2915	3001
Black	542	538	540	590	636
Birthrates per 1000 married women 15–44[b]					
White	119.4	103.6	93.1	94.5	90.2
Black	129.1[f]	110.3	93.3	90.6	84.5
Birthrates per 1000 unmarried women 15–44[c]					
White	12.7	12.6	13.7	18.9	24.1
Black	91.0[f]	94.6	85.5	81.7	84.4
Women married, 15–44 (in percent)[d]					
White	67.8	65.3	61.6	58.8	57.9
Black	55.9[f]	52.9	45.2	39.9	37.7
Men married, 15–44 (in percent)[d]					
White	60.9	58.7	54.9	52.1	51.4
Black	49.7[f]	46.5	42.1	36.8	35.6
Out-of-wedlock births (in 1000s)[a]					
Total	322	406	515	715	911
White	144	166	220	355	485
Black	189[f]	230	280	337	393
Percent of births out-of-wedlock[e]					
Total	9.0	12.1	15.6	19.6	23.9
White	4.8	6.0	8.2	12.2	16.1
Black	34.9[f]	43.0	51.7	57.1	61.8

a. *Source. Vital Statistics of the United States, 1989: Volume I—Natality,* Tables 1-76 to 1-79 and Current Population Series P-20.

b. *Source. Vital Statistics of the United States, 1989: Volume I—Natality,* Tables 1-77.

c. *Source. Vital Statistics of the United States, 1989: Volume I—Natality,* Table 1-76.

d. *Source.* Current Population Reports, Series P-20, *Marital Status and Living Arrangements and Marital Status and Family Status.*

e. *Source: Vital Statistics of the United States, 1989: Volume I—Natality,* Tables 1-77 and 1-78.

f. Based only on 1969 figures.

series, but not in their first differences. In each case we fit ARMA models to characterize the relevant time series processes including year dummies (the dummy in levels is 0 prior to the relevant year and 1 thereafter) to capture discrete changes in the level of a series at one or more dates or trend dummies (the dummy is 0 prior to the relevant data and increases by 1 per annum thereafter) to allow for changes in trends. In the case of abortion, use of

TABLE II

Experience of Unmarried Women: Sexual Participation, Use of Pill, shotgun Marriage, Living Arrangements of Children, and Adoptions

	1965–1969	1970–1974	1975–1979	1980–1984
Women age 16 with sexual experience (percent)[a]				
White	13.8	23.2	28.1	32.8
Black	35.0	42.3	50.8	49.9
Unmarried women using pill on first intercourse (in percent)[b]	5.7	15.2	13.4	NA
Abortions of unmarried women 15–44 (1000s)[c,d]	88	561	985	1271[h]
Per 1000 unmarried women 15–44	6.7	35.3	50.0	54.2
First birth shotgun marriage rate (percent)[e]				
White: marriage before birth	59.2	55.4	45.7	42.0
Marriage before first birthday	70.9	65.6	57.6	53.3
Black: marriage before birth	24.8	19.5	11.0	11.4
Marriage before first birthday	34.7	29.3	18.1	16.4
Children age 3 to 5 living with never married mother (percent)[f]				
White	NA	0.5[i]	1.5[i]	2.2
Black	NA	13.5[i]	23.4[i]	28.6
Children age 3 to 5 living with neither parent (percent)[f]				
White	NA	1.5[i]	1.9[i]	1.5[i]
Black	NA	5.0[i]	5.6[i]	6.5[i]
Adoptions (in 1000s)[h]	158	156	129[j]	142[j]
Through agencies	83	69	48[j]	51[j]
By individuals	75	86	81[j]	91[j]
Ratio of adoptions to out-of-wedlock births (in percent)	49.0	38.4	29.0[j]	19.8[j]

a. *Source.* Women in given year who had ever had intercourse from retrospective data in the 1982 National Survey of Family Growth.

b. *Source.* Women using pill on first intercourse by year from retrospective data in the 1982 National Survey of Family Growth.

c. *Source.* 1965–1972: abortions for women 15 to 44 from retrospective reports in the 1982 National Survey of Family Growth, adjusted for age truncation, adjusted to conform to the Alan Guttmacher series for years 1973–1981.

d. *Source.* 1973–1984: *Abortion Factbook: 1992 Edition*, Alan Guttmacher Institute, Table 3, pp. 176–177.

e. *Source.* Authors' calculations based on data from June 1980, 1982, and 1990 Fertility Supplements of the Current Population Survey.

f. *Source.* Current Population Reports, Series P-20, *Marital Status and Family Status*.

g. *Source. Adoption Factbook*. Washington, DC: National Committee for Adoption, 1989. Table 11, p. 99.

h. Figure for 1983 is the average of 1982 and 1984.

i. Adjusted for increased coverage after 1982. Children with neither parent includes those living in group quarters or not in families.

j. 1975 to 1979 is based on 1975 adoption survey; 1980 to 1984 is based on 1982 adoption survey.

the pill, and sexual participation, there was a jump in levels, rather than a change in trend, whereas in the case of the white shotgun marriage ratio there was a change in trend, rather than a jump in the series. The table reports our preferred specifications. Key findings concerning the presence and estimated magnitudes of changes in levels and trends are robust with respect to alternative specifications, including the inclusion of lagged dependent variables, further moving average and autoregressive errors, changes in the sample period, and alternative methods of construction of the underlying series.[8] Precise dating of shocks is typically more difficult for nonwhites than for whites. The reported benchmark equations pass standard tests for the absence of autoregressive errors and heteroskedasticity.

A. *Out-of-Wedlock Births*

The fraction of children born out of wedlock increased at an accelerated pace beginning in the middle 1960s, for both whites and blacks. This trend has continued almost to the present time. In 1970 there were about 400,000 out-of-wedlock births (out of 3.7 million total births); in 1990 there were 1.2 million out-of-wedlock births (out of 4.0 million total).

B. *Fertility and Marriage Rates*

The number of births per unmarried woman aged 15 to 44 roughly doubled for whites from the late 1960s to the late 1980s. In contrast, for blacks this rate declined by 5 to 10 percent over the same period. For both whites and blacks the fraction of unmarried women rose dramatically: by slightly more than 30 percent for whites and by slightly more than 40 percent for blacks. There were also rapid declines in the fertility rates of married women, by almost a third for blacks and a quarter for whites. The decline in the fertility rates of married women and the decrease in the fraction of married women contributed, along with the decline in the shotgun marriage ratio, to the rise in the out-of-wedlock birth ratio.[9]

C. *Abortions*

Abortions to unmarried women prior to legalization were fairly small in number; our estimates show them to be less than

---

8. See Akerlof, Yellen, and Katz [1994] for further details.
9. Nathanson and Kim [1989] have devised a decomposition that has shown the importance of decreasing marriage and increasing sexual experience for teenagers for the period 1971 to 1979.

TABLE III
TIME SERIES PROPERTIES OF ABORTION, USE OF PILL, SEXUAL EXPERIENCE, AND SHOTGUN MARRIAGE

Dependent variable	Years	Constant	Change in 1970 dummy	Change in 1971 dummy	MA(1)	AR(1)	AR(2)	Adjusted R^2
Change in abortions per 1000 women 15 to 44[a]								
White women	1960–1987	−0.013	10.90***	—	−0.60***	—	—	0.55
		(0.45)	(2.31)		(0.17)			
Nonwhite women	1960–1987	−0.170	6.24**	7.51**	0.40	−1.07***	−0.46**	0.55
		(0.28)	(2.87)	(2.86)	(0.29)	(0.22)	(0.17)	
Change in percentage of all women using pill on first intercourse[b]								
	1961–1980	−0.0038	9.60**	—	−0.96***	—	—	0.58
		(7.10)	(3.82)		(0.30)			
Change in percentage of 16-year-old women with sexual experience[c]								
White women	1955–1981	0.41	10.20***	—	−1.00***	—	—	0.40
		(0.97)	(3.58)		(0.12)			
Black women	1955–1981	0.21	—	13.63**	−0.94	—	−0.51***	0.45
		(1.29)		(6.27)	(0.15)		(0.15)	

TABLE III
(CONTINUED)

Dependent variable	Years	Constant	1968 change in trend dummy	MA(1)	Adjusted R^2
Change in first-birth shotgun marriage ratio[d]					
White women	1955–1989	0.0083 (0.0069)	−0.021** (0.0089)	−0.90*** (0.11)	0.48
Black women	1955–1989	−0.0037 (0.013)	−0.0057 (0.017)	−0.75*** (0.13)	0.40

a. *Source.* Abortions per 1000 women 15 to 44 from retrospective reports in the 1982 and 1988 National Survey of Family Growth, adjusted for age truncation, combined. See Data Appendix.

b. *Source.* Percent of women using the pill on first intercourse by year of first intercourse from retrospective reports in the 1982 National Survey of Family Growth. See Data Appendix.

c. *Source.* Percentage of 16-year-old women in the given year who had ever had intercourse from retrospective data in the 1982 National Survey of Family Growth. See Data Appendix.

d. *Source.* Authors' calculations based on data from the June 1980, 1982, and 1990 Fertility Supplements of the Current Population Survey. The dependent variable is the percentage of women who conceived their first child out of wedlock and married within seven months prior to the birth of the child. A child is considered to be conceived out of wedlock if the mother was unmarried eight months prior to the birth. See Data Appendix.

Standard errors are in parentheses. *Significance at the 10 percent level. **Significance at the 5 percent level. ***Significance at the 1 percent level.

100,000 per year in the late 1960s.[10] This compares with an annual average of 322,000 out-of-wedlock births from 1965 to 1969. Abortion, both in absolute and in relative terms, increased rapidly in the 1970s. From 1980 to 1984 abortions to unmarried women averaged more than 1.25 million, while out-of-wedlock births had risen to 715,000.

As shown in the preferred regression in Table III, there appears to have been a discrete abortion shock in 1970 just at the time of legalization of abortion in New York and the liberalization in California under the Beilensen Act. Many other states liberalized their abortion laws at about this time (see Luker [1984, p. 272]).

D. The Pill

Use of the pill by unmarried women on first intercourse became a significant factor in the 1970s. According to retrospective self-reports in the National Survey of Family Growth, use of the pill on first intercourse averaged 15 percent from 1970 to 1974, more than double the fraction of the previous five years. The preferred regression equation (reported in Table III) shows that a jump occurred between 1969 and 1970. Given the significant fraction of unmarried women using the pill on first intercourse, it is likely that a sizable fraction of all sexually active unmarried women were using the pill in the 1970s.

E. Sexual Experience

Our index of sexual experience—the fraction of women retrospectively reporting having had sexual intercourse prior to age sixteen—jumped in precisely 1970 for whites and possibly one year later for blacks as shown by the regression results in Table III. Due to greater noise in the black data than in the white data, however, this jump is more difficult to date for blacks.

F. Shotgun Marriage

The white shotgun marriage ratio began to fall in the late 1960s. In 1969 the first-birth shotgun marriage rate peaked at 0.61; by 1988 it had fallen to 0.35. There has been a similar fall in the black shotgun marriage ratio, beginning earlier, however, than the negative trend for whites. In the late 1960s the black shotgun marriage ratio was about 0.25; by the late 1980s it had

---

10. For a discussion of the accuracy of abortion statistics, see the Data Appendix.

fallen to about 0.085. If the shotgun marriage rate had remained at its 1965–1969 level, the rise in the out-of-wedlock first-birth ratio for whites would have been 85 percent smaller over the ensuing fifteen years, and 76 percent smaller over the ensuing twenty. The decline in the shotgun marriage ratio also played an important role in the increase in the out-of-wedlock first-birth ratio for blacks, although the corresponding contributions, 50 percent and 58 percent, respectively, are not as large.

G. Births and Abortion

There was a drop in births both to black and white teenage women in New York immediately following the legalization of abortion in New York in 1970. However, recent studies, which are discussed below, have surprisingly found a positive relation between teenage births and abortion availability.

H. Living Arrangements of Children

In the old days, prior to the 1970s, only a small fraction of children born out of wedlock were kept by mothers who never married. In contrast, today only a small fraction are put up for adoption or given to other relatives. Consider the disposition of the 360,000 out-of-wedlock children born in 1969, just before the technology shock. According to our own estimate, the mothers of 135,000 of these children married within the next three years.[11] Of the remaining 225,000 children, 65,000 were reported living with never married mothers three years later. Seventy thousand children in the 1969 cohort were reported in 1972 as living with neither parent, a figure that entails some double counting since not all of these children were born out of wedlock. These figures are roughly consistent with the high rate of adoption at the time. In 1969 there were 170,000 adoptions, including some children whose mothers had been married at the time of birth.[12] The frac-

---

11. We calculated an extended shotgun marriage ratio, defined as the fraction of births conceived out of wedlock resulting in marriage before the child's third birthday. Applying these rates to the number of out-of-wedlock births reported in Vital Statistics yielded estimates of the fraction of out-of-wedlock children whose mothers had married before the age of three.

12. Because of reporting error, double counting, and children whose mothers were married at the time of birth, the sum of adoptions, children living with neither parent, children living with never married mothers, and children with mothers who later married do not add to the total number of out-of-wedlock births. Four different sources of data were used, each with its own reporting error. The total number of out-of-wedlock births is from *Vital Statistics*. Estimates of the fraction of mothers who had married within three years of birth come from the Current Population Survey's Fertility Supplements, which contain retrospective questions regarding women's dates of marriage and birth dates of their chil-

tion of children kept by the mothers who had not married within three years was roughly 0.28.

In contrast, fifteen years later a much larger fraction of children born out of wedlock were kept by their mothers. In 1984 there were 770,000 of these births. We estimate that the mothers of 200,000 of these children were married within three years. Of the remaining 570,000 about 320,000 were reported living with mothers who had never married three years later, and there were 60,000 with neither parent. Annual adoptions had fallen to 105,000. The ratio of children living with never married mothers to those born out of wedlock whose mothers had not married had doubled to 0.56.

III. A RUDIMENTARY MODEL OF FEMALE IMMISERATION

We shall now present a rudimentary model of shotgun marriage. In this model, prior to sexual relations, women may or may not ask for a promise of marriage in the event of pregnancy. If they ask for such a guarantee, they are afraid that their partners will seek other relationships. When the cost of abortion is low, or contraceptives are readily available, potential male partners can easily obtain sexual satisfaction without making such promises and will thus be reluctant to commit to marriage. Thus, women who, in the absence of contraception and abortion, would not engage in premarital sexual activity without assurance of marriage will feel pressured to participate in uncommitted relationships once contraception and abortion become available. In this model the implicit or explicit promise to marry is viewed as an enforceable contract. Men will, if necessary, meet their prior commitments.

Prior to sexual relations a woman may or may not ask for an implicit or explicit promise of marriage in the event of pregnancy.

---

dren. The number of children living with never married mothers and the number of those with neither parent are from the annual March CPS surveys on living arrangements. Adoption statistics come from the National Committee for Adoption. The number of children in the one-year cohort living with a never married mother or living with neither parent was estimated as one-third of the children aged three to five in these respective categories. Those classified as living with neither biological nor adoptive parents correspond to the Census categories "living in households with neither parent" and "not in families." Both the series on children living with never married mothers and those living with neither parent were adjusted for the change in coverage in 1982. Of course, children with neither parent and adoptions include some whose mothers had been married at the time of birth. Adoptees also include children whose parents have remarried and have been adopted by a new spouse.

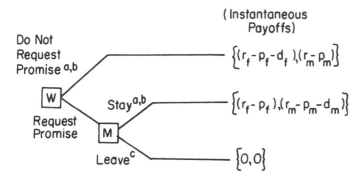

a. p_f takes on the two values $p_f^+ > 0$ and $p_f^- < 0$
b. with probability θ random mating occurs in the next period
c. with probability 1 random mating occurs in the next period

FIGURE I
Marriage Request Game Tree with Payoffs

We saw that 25 years ago among white working-class youths in San Francisco such a promise was the norm.[13] Our own survey (described below) of University of California at Berkeley undergraduates in the summer of 1994 suggests that today premarital sexual activity does not usually entail such a commitment.

A. Decisions in the Game

Figure I presents the tree for a simple game that focuses on the role of "competition" as it affects the choices of women whether or not to exact a promise to marry as a condition for premarital sexual activity. The decision of the woman is whether or not to ask for such a promise. If she asks for this assurance, she runs the risk that her boyfriend will exit. The basic decision for the man is whether or not to leave the relationship when such a guarantee is the prerequisite for sexual relations with his cur-

---

13. Luker [1991, p. 78] writes: "Yet even these statistics [on the growth of teen sexuality from the 1950s to 1979–1981] do not capture how profoundly different [current] teen sexuality is from that of earlier eras. As sources such as the Kinsey Report suggest, premarital sex for many American women before the 1960s was 'engagement' sex. The woman's involvement, at least, was exclusive and she generally went on to marry her partner in a relatively short period of time. Almost half of the women in the Kinsey data who had premarital sex had it with their fiances."

rent partner. We shall proceed to describe the payoffs to the woman and to the man.

B. Payoffs to the Woman

If the woman chooses to engage in premarital sex but does not exact the contingent marriage promise, she receives an instantaneous payoff $(r_f - p_f - d_f)$. p_f is the expected per period cost of pregnancy if there is a marriage promise prior to sexual relations. d_f is the expected per period additional loss if she does not obtain a promise of marriage from her partner. r_f is the per period value to her of her relationship with her partner. We assume that, if both parties have agreed to the relationship, then the relationship will continue in the next period with probability $1 - \theta$ and will terminate with probability θ. If the relationship terminates, there will be random pairing of available men and women in the next period. For tractability it is assumed that there are equal numbers of men and women.[14] The payoff to such a game will be v_f, the value of the game to this woman with random mating. In either event—if the woman begins a new relationship or if she continues the old—the future payoffs will be weighted with a discount factor γ.

To continue the discussion of the payoffs, if the woman asks for an assurance of marriage in the event of pregnancy, the man may then either remain in the relationship, or leave. If the man remains, the woman's payoff is $(r_f - p_f)$ in the current period. She keeps the relationship, whose per period return is r_f. She also continues to bear the potential costs of pregnancy, p_f, but without the extra costs of single motherhood because of the promise. Next period with probability $1 - \theta$ she will continue the same relationship with the same instantaneous payoffs, and with probability θ she will begin a new relationship with value v_f.

If the man leaves, the woman receives an instantaneous payoff of zero. She has forgone the relationship this period and, with it, the complications of a possible pregnancy. Next period she will begin another relationship whose expected value is v_f.

C. Payoffs to the Man

If the woman does not exact a promise prior to premarital sex, the man's instantaneous payoff is r_m, the per period value of

---

14. Other authors have emphasized that changes in the ratio of men to women will affect the equilibrium number of men who would rather marry than remain single. (See, for example, Willis [1994].)

the relationship. For convenience we assume that p_m, the man's pregnancy cost, is zero if he has not promised to marry the woman. As in the case of the woman, the relationship will continue with probability $1 - \theta$, and with probability θ the man will begin a new game with random mating of women seeking partners. The value of such a game to the man is v_m. If the woman exacts the promise and the man stays in the relationship, he receives an instantaneous payoff $(r_m - d_m)$. Again, with probability $1 - \theta$ the relationship will continue, and with probability θ he returns to the matching pool. Analogous to the notation for the woman's payoff, d_m is the expected per period cost of the promise of potential marriage. If the man leaves, in the next period he will begin a new game with value v_m. Of course, future returns are discounted by the factor γ.

D. A Simple Example

In principle, all of the payoffs, p_f, p_m, r_f, r_m, d_f, and d_m, have distributions across individuals. We shall make the minimal assumptions necessary to illustrate the earlier analogy with the hand-loom weavers. Such an illustration requires two types of women. One of these types will adopt the technologies of abortion or contraception or both when they become available, with a probable increase in welfare, while the other type will not adopt the new technologies and will consequently become impoverished. Men are all of the same type.

Women in this example fall into two classes depending on their expected costs of pregnancy. For a fraction α the expected cost of pregnancy is positive, denoted p_f^+. For these women pregnancies will be terminated by abortion if this option is available at sufficiently low cost. In order to model what we consider the norm in the old days, we shall assume that p_f^+ is not only positive but also less than r_f so that p_f^+ women would be willing to participate in sexual activity if their boyfriends promise to marry them. In addition, we shall assume that the sum $p_f^+ + d_f$ exceeds r_f so that, in the absence of contraception and abortion, p_f^+ women will not engage in sexual activity without an assurance of marriage.

In contrast to the women for whom a pregnancy without marriage would lead to a decrease in utility, we assume that there is a second group of women, a fraction $(1 - \alpha)$ of the population, for whom the cost of pregnancy, denoted p_f^-, is negative. We also assume that $r_f > p_f^- + d_f$, so that these women are willing to engage in premarital sex and bring the baby to term even without an assurance of marriage. d_f is also assumed to be positive. As a result, p_f^- women prefer a baby without a husband to neither baby nor husband, but, better yet, they would prefer both baby and husband.

While two types of women are necessary to illustrate the analogy with the hand-loom weavers, our example requires only one type of man. For simplicity, we shall assume that p_m is zero and that d_m, which is the same for all men, is positive but less than r_m. Men would prefer not to make a marriage promise, but they would be willing to do so if that is their only way to maintain their relationships.

E. The Equilibrium

We can now describe the equilibria in this model both before and after the technology shock. Before the technology shock it is clear that no woman with positive pregnancy costs will engage in sexual activity without a promise of marriage. There will always be an equilibrium in which women with negative pregnancy costs will also demand a promise of marriage before engaging in sexual activity. Indeed, this will be the unique equilibrium as long as α, the fraction of p_f^+ women, is sufficiently high. With α sufficiently high, even if *no* p_f^- women were demanding a promise of marriage, it would pay a man to stay with any p_f^- individual woman who decided to demand such a promise.[15] In this equilibrium p_f^+ women, who would be unwilling to bear children in the absence of marriage, demand a marriage assurance in the event of pregnancy, while p_f^- women, who would be willing to bear children even in the absence of marriage, demand the same, since they know the man will accept. For the man it is not worthwhile to seek another relationship because he would forfeit current utility and, ultimately, do no better.

Let us now see how this game and its equilibrium will be altered by the development of inexpensive and easily available contraception and abortion. Let us assume that the cost of abortion to p_f^+ women is less than the cost of pregnancy. For simplicity, let the cost of the abortion be zero. Empirically, the financial cost of an abortion is extremely low relative to the financial cost of raising a child. (Alternatively, we could assume that reliable con-

---

15. The man's stay/leave decision will be affected by the ratio of promise/do not promise women to be encountered in the random mating process. This ratio in the next period's random matching, however, will always be greater than $\alpha/(1-\alpha)$ since all p_f^+ women demand promises (of whom a fraction θ will be searching for new partners in the next period) and all the p_f^- women who are deserted by their partners and are therefore looking for new mates in the next period have decided on the demand-promise strategy.

traception becomes available.) With the advent of abortion a p_f^+ woman has no need to request a promise in the event of pregnancy. And even if she were to ask for such a promise, her partner would know that he would have no cost in fulfilling it, since the woman would obtain an abortion rather than bring the baby to term. The payoff to the p_f^+ women becomes r_f, with the payoff to the man in such a relationship, symmetrically, r_m. In this example, the new technology enhances the welfare of p_f^+ women and their partners.

Let us now consider the decision of a p_f^- woman and of her partner. This woman may ask for a promise of marriage, but if she does, her partner may leave. With abortion and the range of p_f^+ and d_f in our example, we know that the man will get r_m next period if he encounters a p_f^+ woman. Indeed, he will always leave if parameter values are such that the random mating of the next period yields him a p_f^+ woman with sufficiently high probability and if his disutility of marriage and discount factor are also sufficiently high. Under these conditions, the p_f^- woman therefore will not ask the man for a promise because she knows he would leave, and the man will stay in the relationship without making a commitment since he will not fare better elsewhere. The consequence is that after abortion and contraception become easily available, there is a new equilibrium in which no woman—even if she wants children and marriage—asks for a promise of marriage. In this equilibrium if any woman did ask for such a promise, her partner would leave, and she would lose the relationship. The p_f^- women, like the hand-loom weavers, suffer a reduction in welfare.[16]

16. If α, the fraction of p_f^+ women, is sufficiently low, there will also be equilibria in which all p_f^- women ask men to stay, and no man paired with such a woman will leave. In addition, in this very simple model there may be mixed equilibria with some women demanding marriage promises and other women forgoing them over a wide range of parameter values. This occurs, however, for an implausible reason. If a large number of p_f^- women ask men for marriage promises but a significant fraction of those men leave, disappointed p_f^- women who ask men for a promise to marry may dominate the random pairings in the next period. A high probability of encountering such a partner in the next stage of the game can be sufficient inducement for a fraction of the men to stay even when asked for a marriage commitment. This fraction of men staying will in turn be the incentive for some women to ask for a promise of marriage. We believe that this flooding of the random pairings with women asking for commitments after the technology shock is only a curiosum. For simplicity, we assumed that the exogenous probability of the relationship's termination, θ, did not depend upon the type of relationship between the couples. It seems reasonable, however, that the probability of a breakup is higher for couples in "uncommitted" relationships than for those in committed ones. As a result, with just a bit more realism, the equilibrium with no p_f^- women asking for marriage assurances is likely to be unique.

A slight modification of this example illustrates the possibility that all women, like the wheat farmers, could lose from implementing the new technology. Suppose that the advent of contraception/abortion decreases pregnancy costs without eliminating them. This may cause a switch from a unique equilibrium, with all women obtaining marriage commitments, to dual stable equilibria. In one equilibrium, as before, every woman obtains a marriage promise, and welfare is unchanged, but in the other equilibrium no woman obtains a marriage guarantee because each correctly foresees that such a demand would cause the breakup of her relationship. A move to this no-commitment trap is likely to reduce welfare for all women. In this example the gains from the advent of abortion and contraception accrue totally to the men.

Although we have used the model to analyze the effect of changes in abortion and contraceptive availability, other changes can easily be incorporated. Increases in welfare benefits payable only to single mothers will decrease the value of d_f, as will changes in the stigma of single motherhood. Better labor market opportunities for women, so that there is less dependence on male financial support, will likewise decrease the value of d_f. Higher wages for women will also increase the cost of pregnancy, p_f, because of the increased opportunity cost of own child care. Increased financial obligation by unmarried fathers for their biological offspring will increase p_m if the father does not marry the mother, and it will also decrease the value of d_m.

E. Isomorphic Model of Sexual Participation

Under a slight reinterpretation the previous game structure illustrates how increased competition may affect sexual participation. In this analogous model, women decide whether or not to engage in premarital sex at all, and men then decide whether to remain in relationships without sexual activity. This model is isomorphic to the previous one, with participate/do not participate substituting for promise/do not promise. Before the technology shock abstinence would be the norm for all women. After the technology shock those women who would use contraception or would be willing to obtain an abortion in the event of pregnancy or both engage in premarital sexual activity. However, those women who are not willing to use contraception or obtain an abortion will also engage in sexual activity, since they correctly fear that if they abstain their partners would seek satisfaction elsewhere. The advent of contraception and abortion used by others may result in an unwanted increase in sexual participation for those who reject the new technology.

IV. Sexual Participation, Abortion, and Shotgun Marriage

The previous section illustrated the consequences of competition in games with only one major decision. In reality, however, shotgun marriage is the outcome of a sequence of decisions: about premarital sexual activity, abortion, and marriage. In this section we model this sequence of decisions, with one significant change from the previous game. In that model the promise to marry was considered enforceable. In contrast, we now assume the man's willingness to marry just prior to the birth of the child depends upon a comparison of his own cost of getting married with his perception of the cost to his partner of becoming a single mother.

The previous model showed that advances in reproductive technology could lead to the immiseration of women through increased competition. The model in this section illustrates another mechanism whereby the technology shock could lead to the feminization of poverty. In the old world, before the sexual revolution, women were less free to choose, but men were expected to assume responsibility for their welfare, an expectation that was more often fulfilled than breached. Nowadays women are freer to choose, but men are affording themselves the comparable option. In the model we present, the man reasons: "If she is not willing to obtain an abortion or use contraception, why should I sacrifice myself to get married?" This model accurately predicts a decline in shotgun marriage: with abortion readily available, many relationships that previously ended in shotgun marriages now end in abortion. When, instead, the woman carries the baby to term, the man can also rationalize remaining single. The model also realistically predicts a decline in the fertility rate (see Wilson and Neckerman [1986]) and an increase in the out-of-wedlock birthrate. However, as shall be discussed later, we think that the factors emphasized in the last section are probably more important empirically in explaining the increase in out-of-wedlock births in the United States.

A. Description of the Model

Figure II is a tree diagram showing the sequence of decisions and their payoffs for a couple deciding whether or not to initiate

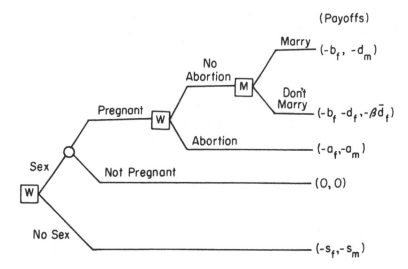

FIGURE II
Sequence of Decisions and Payoffs Confronting a Couple
Initiating a Sexual Relationship

a sexual relationship.[17] We omit from this model the value of the relationship to the woman and the man, r_f and r_m, respectively, but we shall describe in greater detail than in the previous model the sequence of decisions that each partner faces and then the payoffs attached to the various outcomes. In the beginning, the woman decides whether or not to initiate a sexual relationship with her partner. If she decides to have sex, there are potential future consequences. With probability q the woman becomes pregnant. This probability obviously depends on whether or not the partners use contraception, but for simplicity we ignore contraception and take q as fixed. If the woman becomes pregnant, we assume that she next chooses whether or not to have an abortion. If she chooses not to have an abortion, her partner must then decide whether or not to marry her (and she has to decide whether or not to marry him). Interestingly, a model in which the woman chooses whether or not to use contraception, rather than to obtain an abortion, is exactly isomorphic and yields results analogous to those obtained in the present model.

17. The same decision tree is used by Lundberg and Plotnick [1990, p. 247] in their study of the effects of state policies on pregnancy, abortion, and marriage.

The payoffs corresponding to each path of the tree determine the equilibrium outcomes of the game, including the shotgun marriage rate. We first describe the payoffs to the woman and then to the man.

B. Payoffs to the Woman

For notational convenience we shall normalize the payoffs so that the woman's payoff if she engages in sex and does not become pregnant is 0. If she decides to forgo the relationship entirely, her payoff is $-s_f$. If the woman agrees to the sexual relationship and a pregnancy occurs, she has the further choice of whether or not to obtain an abortion. The financial and emotional cost of the abortion to the woman is a_f, so her payoff if she chooses an abortion is $-a_f$. If she does not choose to have an abortion, there are two possibilities: either her partner marries her, or she is left as a single mother. We let b_f be the cost of having a child even if she does get married, so that her payoff as a married mother is $-b_f$. In contrast to our previous model, we assume for simplicity that b_f is positive for all women, so that no women want children, even with marriage. If she does not get married, there is an additional cost (both financial and emotional) in the amount d_f, so that her payoff in this state is $-b_f - d_f$. (For simplicity, we assume that $d_f > 0$ so that all women prefer marriage to single motherhood. With $d_f < 0$, a woman prefers single parenthood to marriage to the partner, and the game tree must include the woman's decision whether or not to marry as well.)

C. Payoffs to the Man

We normalize the man's payoffs by assuming that the reward from sex is 0 if no pregnancy occurs. Assuming that the man gains enjoyment from sex equal to s_m, his payoff if the woman chooses not to initiate a sexual relationship is $-s_m$. In the event of a pregnancy the man's payoff depends on whether or not the woman chooses an abortion and, if not, whether the man marries her. To allow for the possibility that the woman's choice of an abortion may be costly to the man, we denote the man's payoff in the event that the woman chooses an abortion as $-a_m$. If the man's partner chooses not to abort, the man's payoff depends on whether or not he marries her. We assume for simplicity that marriage imposes a cost of d_m on the man, so that his payoff if he marries is $-d_m$. Survey research by Marsiglio [1988] suggests that the major costs which men attach to forming households with their partners as a consequence of unplanned pregnancy stem from the loss of interaction with friends and inability to date other women. Men also strongly believe that they would be required to obtain steady work. But to explain why men may nevertheless marry, we assume that there is also a cost to be borne in the event that the man fails to marry the mother of his child. We let this cost depend on the concern of the man with his partner's (and child's) well-being as reflected in the parameter β and on the amount of suffering that the man expects to impose on the woman by his failure to tie the knot, denoted $\overline{d_f}$, where $\overline{d_f}$ is the mean value of d_f in the population of women who choose not to have abortions following unplanned pregnancies. The man's payoff is thus $-d_m$ if he marries the woman and $-\beta\overline{d_f}$ if he does not. An important assumption is that the man's feeling of guilt depends on $\overline{d_f}$ and not on the woman's own d_f, which we assume is unobservable. The importance of guilt as a motive for marriage is consistent with Marsiglio's findings. In the words of one respondent: "I wouldn't want to marry my girlfriend but since it was *my fault* I couldn't leave her in the cold" (italics added).

D. A Simple Example

In principle, virtually all of the payoffs along the tree differ among individuals, and therefore should be characterized by a joint distribution in the population. However, a simple example illustrates how the decline in the cost of abortion can induce a rise in the out-of-wedlock birthrate. We shall analyze the outcomes of this game in the simple case in which women differ only with respect to their values of d_f, the disutility of being single—rather than married—mothers, and men differ only with respect to d_m, the disutility of marrying. We assume that for all women, d_f is uniformly distributed from 0 to $D_f^{\max}$. Because there is the possibility that some women—those with high values of d_f—may not engage in sex at all, the distribution of d_f for pregnant women may not occur over this entire range. We let D_f denote the maximum value of d_f for those women who engage in sex, with the possibility of pregnancy. We assume that d_m is uniformly distributed from 0 to D_m. The remaining parameters are assumed to be the same for all individuals. These include a_f, the cost of abortion; b_f, the cost of having a child; β, the man's degree of empathy; s_f and s_m, the returns to sex for the woman and man; a_m, the man's distaste for abortion; and q, the odds of pregnancy. This simple model allows a surprisingly rich description of the interactions between the woman's decision and the man's.[18]

E. Equilibria of the Game

If the cost of abortion is less than the cost of single motherhood, this game has a trivial solution: all pregnant women obtain abortions. Since in this case there are no births whatsoever, we focus on the more relevant case in which $a_f > b_f$. In this instance the frequency of abortions, legitimate births, and out-of-wedlock births depend on parameter values.

With $a_f > b_f$, the game contains a basic simultaneity: abortion is sufficiently costly that any pregnant woman would prefer to carry her baby to term if she could be sure that her partner would marry her. But men differ in the disutility of marriage (d_m). Some will, and others will not, marry partners who forgo abortion. Thus, the woman's decision whether or not to abort depends on her perceived probability that the man will marry her if she carries the baby to term. For a given probability of marriage, those women with d_f in excess of a critical value, d_f^{crit}, choose to abort. For these women the disutility of single parenthood is too high to risk bearing a child. In contrast, women with d_f below d_f^{crit} carry their babies to term, gambling on the prospect that, having decided against abortion, their partners will legitimate the child. These decisions of the women determine the average d_f of those women choosing not to abort. This value is $\bar{d}_f$; with the uniform distribution assumed, $\bar{d}_f = d_f^{crit}/2$. The higher the probability of marriage, the higher is d_f^{crit}.

18. Pairs for whom (d_f, d_m) are not in the positive orthant will reveal their true values of d_f and d_m prior to the abortion decision and therefore will separate themselves from the game that we are describing here. The minimum values of d_f and d_m at 0 correctly reflect the information structure of the game for pairs of men and women for whom $d_f > 0$ and men for whom $d_m > 0$. If the woman has a negative value of d_f, she has no reason not to reveal it to her partner prior to the abortion decision since she does not want to marry him in any case. She should then make up her mind whether or not to have a baby dependent upon whether $a_f > b_f$ or $a_f < b_f$ independent of the man's decision. If the man has a negative value of d_m, then he should reveal that to his partner prior to the abortion decision. If d_m is negative and d_f is positive, the couple should reveal their information and then get married if the woman does not prefer an abortion. The game we have described will take place, however, if both d_f and d_m are greater than 0. If $d_m > 0$, the man wants the woman to believe that d_m is as large as possible to maximize her willingness to obtain an abortion. Similarly, if $d_f > 0$, the woman wants the man to believe that d_f is as great as possible so he will marry her. In such a situation neither the man's statements about his value of d_m nor the woman's statements about her value of d_f are credible. In these circumstances our model correctly assumes that the man and the woman know the distribution of d_f and d_m, but not their values for their specific partners.

Simultaneity arises because the probability of marriage depends in turn on d_f^{crit}. The higher is d_f^{crit}, the more likely it will be that men will marry women who choose to forgo abortions. The decision of the men whether or not to marry, given their own distaste for it, depends on the perceived cost to their partners of single parenthood. Men marry if $d_m < \beta \bar{d}_f$. With d_m uniformly distributed from 0 to D_m, the odds of marriage, F, for women choosing not to abort is $\beta \bar{d}_f / D_m$. We assume that men have no information concerning the actual d_f of their partner but they do have an accurate assessment of the mean value of d_f of women choosing not to abort. Thus, their decision is positively conditioned on their estimated value of $\bar{d}_f$.

The rational expectations equilibrium requires that $\bar{d}_f$ must be the actual mean value of d_f of those women choosing not to abort. In consequence,

$$(1) \qquad \bar{d}_f = d_f^{\text{crit}}/2.$$

Provided that d_f^{crit} is below its ceiling of D_f, it will be determined so that the marginal woman with $d_f = d_f^{\text{crit}}$ is exactly indifferent whether or not to abort. The payoff if a woman chooses abortion is $-a_f$, and the payoff if the woman chooses not to abort is $-b_f$ with probability F (which is $\beta \bar{d}_f / D_m$) and $-b_f - d_f$ with probability $1 - F$ (which is $1 - \beta \bar{d}_f / D_m$). The value of d_f^{crit} such that the woman is exactly indifferent to getting an abortion satisfies the equation,

$$(2) \qquad \frac{b_f \beta \bar{d}_f}{D_m} + (b_f + d_f^{\text{crit}})\left(\frac{D_m - \beta \bar{d}_f}{D_m}\right) = a_f.$$

In the internal solution in which the limits on the value of d_f^{crit} are not binding, we can express $d_f^{\text{crit}}/2$ as a function of $\bar{d}_f$:[19]

$$(3) \qquad \frac{d_f^{\text{crit}}}{2} = \frac{a_f - b_f}{2(1 - \beta \bar{d}_f / D_m)}.$$

Equation (3) is a "reaction function" that shows how the decision of women whether or not to abort depends on the mean value of d_f. As $\bar{d}_f$ rises, the odds of marriage rise, and thus d_f^{crit} rises, inducing more women to forgo abortion.

The equilibrium in this subgame is determined by the re-

---

19. If $(a_f - b_f)/(1 - \beta \bar{d}_f / D_m) \geq D_f$, then the limits on d_f^{crit} are binding, and $d_f^{\text{crit}} = D_f$.

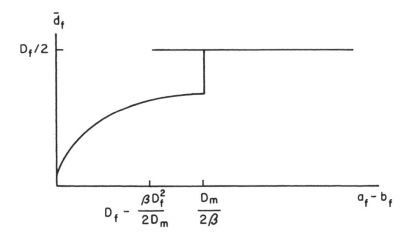

FIGURE III

The Relationship between the Cost of Abortion and the Mean Disutility of Single Parenthood among Women Who Bear Children Conceived out of Wedlock

quirements that (1) and (3) be simultaneously satisfied. The solution sets are somewhat complex, largely because of ceilings and the possibility of multiple equilibria when D_f is sufficiently large, but the nature of the solutions can be summarized by a graph, which plots the equilibrum value(s) of $\bar{d}_f$ as a function of $a_f - b_f$.

Figure III shows that as the cost of abortion, a_f, falls, with the cost of bearing a child (b_f) constant, the equilibrium value of $\bar{d}_f$ will fall. A decrease in the cost of abortion raises both the abortion rate and the out-of-wedlock birthrate. With abortion less costly, the fertility rate is lower for sexually active women. With fewer women choosing to carry their babies to term, the mean disutility of single parenthood among women choosing to bear children declines, and there is a consequent decrease in the marriage rate (F). The out-of-wedlock birthrate therefore rises.

For each equilibrium plotted in Figure III, the welfare (payoffs) to women and to men can be easily calculated. Three comparative static results are obtained if we restrict our attention to "internal equilibria." First, as the cost of abortion falls, women who do not refrain from sexual activity and who will not obtain an abortion if they become pregnant will lose out, because their probability of marriage will decline. Second, the expected value of welfare for all women may rise, or decline, dependent on the distribution of women's attributes. Third, as long as the parameter a_m (the man's own disutility of abortion) is sufficiently low, men's welfare will rise with a decline in the cost of abortion.[20]

The model may be expanded to include AFDC payments which are paid only to single mothers. The simplest way in which to incorporate such payments is to let the payoff to the woman in the event of single motherhood be equal to $-b_f - d_f + w$, where w is the level of AFDC payments. The payoff to the man who does not marry, in this case, is $-\beta(\bar{d}_f - w)$. The effect of decreased stigma to out-of-wedlock birth is identical in the model to an increase in benefits to unwed mothers.

G. The Decision to Engage in Premarital Sex

Our discussion so far has focused on the determinants of fertility and out-of-wedlock births for those women choosing to engage in premarital sex. Following the game tree in Figure II back to its initial node, we can also analyze the determinants of the original decision: whether or not to engage in premarital sex. A decrease in the cost of abortion or increased availability of contraception is likely to result in an increase in premarital sexual activity.

V. Discussion of Models and Experience in the United States

Neither of the leading economic theories, the welfare theory and the jobs theory, nor a third to be described, the mix effect hypothesis, is capable of explaining either the magnitude or the timing of the change in out-of-wedlock births. In contrast, the technology shock explanation, particularly when realistically

---

20. In addition to "internal" equilibria with a positive abortion rate, equilibria are also possible with $\bar{d}_f = D_f/2$, implying that no abortion occurs in spite of its availability. In such an equilibrium, there is, however, a positive out-of-wedlock birth rate. Figure III shows that this outcome may occur in two ways. (1) For costs of abortion in the range $\{b_f + D_f - (\beta D_f^2/2D_m) \le a_f \le b_f + D_m/2\beta\}$, there are dual equilibria. The two solutions correspond to the respective branches of equation (3)—one in which the ceiling on d_f^{crit} is binding, so that $\bar{d}_f = D_f/2$, and the other in which it is not, so that an internal equilibrium occurs. (2) For yet larger values of the cost of abortion, $(a_f > b_f + D_m/2\beta)$, the only equilibrium occurs with $\bar{d}_f$ at its ceiling of $D_f/2$. These solutions suggest that, as the cost of abortions fall, there may be discontinuous shifts in the levels of marriage and out-of-wedlock births. This discontinuity reflects the possibility of a rapid unraveling of men's willingness to marry due to their changing perception of the cost to women of their failure to do so—a process that may be triggered by a small change in the cost of abortion. Such a discontinuous fall in marriage and rise in out-of-wedlock births may in fact correspond to the abrupt decline in marriage and rise in the out-of-wedlock birthrates in the United States. These changes have occurred very rapidly in comparison with the usual sluggish pace of changes in family structure.

amended to include endogenous changes in stigma, is consistent with the facts documented in Section II concerning the magnitude and timing of changes in sexual participation, abortion, contraceptive use, shotgun marriage, and the living arrangements of children.

A. Welfare Theory, Jobs Theory, and Mix Effect

Despite their prominence in the literature, neither the welfare theory (see Murray [1984]) nor the job-shortage theory (see Wilson [1987]) can explain the size and timing of the increase in out-of-wedlock births. For example, Ellwood and Summers [1986] argue that AFDC could not have played a major role in the rise of out-of-wedlock births because AFDC rose a great deal in the 1960s and fell in the 1970s (when eligibility requirements also became more stringent), while out-of-wedlock births rose continually. Moffitt [1992, p. 29] reaches similar conclusions. He also finds that the effects of welfare benefits estimated with cross-section and panel data are too small to account for more than a very small fraction of the rise in the out-of-wedlock birth ratio.

Wilson's joblessness hypothesis has also been questioned. Mare and Winship [1991, p. 194], using cross-section data, estimate that at most 20 percent of the decline in marriage rates of blacks between 1960 and 1980 can be explained by decreasing employment. Jencks [1992, p. 133] has noted that the decline in the fraction of married unemployed black men aged 30 to 44 between 1960 and 1980 was only slightly higher (13 percent) than the decline in the fraction of married employed black men (11 percent).[21] In confirmation of these suspicions, Wood [1995] estimates that only 3 to 4 percent of the decline in black marriage rates can be explained by the shrinkage of the pool of eligible black men.

A third theory, which we term the mix-effect hypothesis, posits a relationship due to selection between the legalization of abortion and the out-of-wedlock birthrate. If anything, this theory fares worse than either the joblessness theory or the welfare theory. According to the mix-effect hypothesis, the shotgun marriage rate might have declined following the legalization of abortion because the type of couples who would have been especially likely to marry in the event of a premarital pregnancy prior to legalization would have been especially likely to obtain an abortion and avoid shotgun marriage after legalization. (O'Connell

21. Also see Lerman [1988].

and Rogers [1984] suggest this explanation for the decline in the shotgun marriage ratio.) Akerlof, Yellen, and Katz [1994] test for such an effect through cross-section regressions of an individual's probability of terminating a premarital pregnancy by abortion after legalization on that individual's predicted probability of shotgun marriage in the pre-abortion era. Education, which would be correlated with a tendency to plan ahead, and measures of religious practice (Catholic/non-Catholic, rate of attendance at services) were included in the various prediction equations.[22] Given the robust absence of any significant, positive association between the odds of shotgun marriage and abortion, it is unlikely that the mix effect played any serious role in the decline in shotgun marriage.

In sum, the failure of the job-shortage theory, the welfare theory, and the mix-effect hypothesis leaves a void in explaining the increase in out-of-wedlock births.

B. Relative Magnitudes of Technology Shock and Out-of-Wedlock Births

The models of the previous section have shown why the total impact of abortion and female contraception on the out-of-wedlock birthrate could have been positive—contrary to the natural supposition that the direct effects of abortion and contraception would dominate by reducing the number of unwanted out-of-wedlock babies. If the change in abortion and the use of female contraception were all quantitatively large relative to the number of births and relative to the number of unmarried women, it would then seem plausible that the technology shock could have been a very significant factor causing the large rise in out-of-wedlock births.

As we documented in Section II, both the use of the pill and the increase in the number of abortions were indeed very large relative to the numbers of unmarried women and out-of-wedlock births. The use of the pill at first intercourse by unmarried women jumped from 6 to 15 percent in just a few years, and the number of abortions to unmarried women, which were less than half the number of out-of-wedlock births in the 1960s, grew tenfold, or more. Indeed, the number of abortions grew yet faster than out-of-wedlock births over the 1970s so that, by the end of the decade, unmarried women had 75 percent more abortions than out-of-wedlock births.

22. For details see Akerlof, Yellen, and Katz [1994].

The technology shock hypothesis thus meets the test that changes in the use of the technology are of sufficient magnitude to be a potential propagator of the subsequent and very substantial changes in out-of-wedlock births and family structure—provided that the effect has the right sign.

C. The Technology Shock Explanation for Rising Out-of-Wedlock Childbirth

A very simple theory, which builds on the models of the previous sections, suffices to explain not only the increase in the out-of-wedlock birthrate but also the related changes in family structure and sexual practice. According to this theory, the legalization of abortion, starting in the late 1960s, induced a large fraction of unmarried women, who were willing to obtain an abortion if pregnant, to engage in premarital sexual relations while forgoing the promise of marriage in the event of a premarital conception. Similarly, the invention of the pill and increased availability of contraception enhanced the willingness of unmarried women to participate in uncommitted, premarital sex by reducing the odds of a pregnancy in the first place. The technology shock thereby triggered the behavioral shifts depicted in our two static models. Women who wanted to bear children were immiserized because their competitive position, and thereby their ability to bargain for the marriage guarantee, deteriorated, as in our first model. Moreover, their partners' degree of empathy and willingness to marry after the fact, may also have declined once it was apparent that the woman herself was unwilling to obtain an abortion. This causation mechanism is illustrated by our second model.

The technology shock hypothesis, like Wilson's job shortage theory, relates the increase in out-of-wedlock childbearing to a decline in the supply of eligible males. However, this decline occurs because there are fewer men who are willing to get married, and not just because there is a shortage of jobs. The technology shock theory explains the reduced marriage rates of both educated men with low unemployment and uneducated men with high unemployment. The technology shock model also predicts, and our survey results described below confirm, a decline in intimacy between sexual partners, since relations are likely to be short term, reinforcing the unwillingness to marry.

The technology shock theory suffices to explain why there was such a large rise in the rate of retention of children born out of wedlock. In the old days, if the woman wanted a child, she was typically able to exact a promise that the man would marry her.

Thus, most premaritally conceived first births (about 60 percent for whites and 35 percent for blacks by our tabulations) resulted in marriage before the birth of the baby who was then, of course, kept by the woman. If the woman did not get married soon after the birth of the baby, the chances were less than 30 percent that the child would be kept. In the new world, however, after the legalization of abortion, there were two reasons why the baby would more likely be kept. First, unmarried women who wanted children would find it increasingly difficult to make (and also to enforce) a contract in which marriage was promised in the event of pregnancy. Since these women wanted children, they would naturally keep them. Furthermore, because women who would not want to keep a child born out of wedlock had easy access to contraception and the option to abort an unwanted pregnancy, a greater fraction of the children born out of wedlock would be wanted. It is then no surprise that, despite the very large rise in sexual participation, the number of agency adoptions was halved from 86,000 to 43,000 in the five years following the introduction of abortion, or that 1970, the year of our shock, was the peak year for adoptions.

The question remains why the decline in the shotgun marriage ratio, following the technology shocks of the early 1970s occurred gradually over time rather than abruptly and all at once. For example, the time series results reported in Table III indicate a significant change in the shotgun marriage trend for white women beginning around 1968. Starting in the late 1960s, the white shotgun marriage ratio began a long and steady decline.

There are two different factors that probably account for the gradual decline in the white shotgun marriage rate. The first is simply that, in reality, shifts between equilibria take time to complete. The second, complementary factor, is that the stigma associated with out-of-wedlock motherhood has declined endogenously.

Focusing first on the transition between equilibria in our models, it is easy to appreciate why such moves would, in actuality, be gradual. Consider, for example, the attitudes of p_f^- women in the first "immiserization model"—those who would bring the baby to term with or without marriage—and their male partners. It would most likely have taken time for men to recognize that an implicit or explicit promise of marriage in the event of a pregnancy was too high a price to pay for sexual relations because men could fare better elsewhere. It may also have taken time for women to perceive the increased willingness of men to move if such marriage promises are demanded. As new expectations formed, social norms readjusted, and the shotgun marriage rate declined, albeit gradually. In the end, however, men who wanted sexual activity but did not want to promise marriage in case of pregnancy, were neither expected nor required to do so.

A second, important reason, why the decline in the shotgun marriage ratio occurred gradually, rather than abruptly, relates to stigma. Declining stigma of out-of-wedlock childbirth was a natural, endogenous consequence of the technology shock. A decline in stigma, represented in both models by a decrease in d_f, further reinforced the technology-driven causes for the decline in shotgun marriage and increased retention of out-of-wedlock children.

As we have documented, the norm of premarital sexual abstinence all but vanished in the wake of the technology shock. With premarital sex the rule, rather than the exception, an out-of-wedlock childbirth could no longer serve as a sign that society's sexual taboos had been violated. The stigma attached to out-of-wedlock childbearing thus gradually but, ultimately greatly, eroded. A reduction in d_f in our first model augments the willingness to engage in uncommitted premarital sex. In our second model, a reduction in d_f is an additional factor working to reduce the pressure on fathers to do their duty in the case of an unwanted pregnancy. Since out-of-wedlock childbirth no longer resulted in social ostracism, literally and figuratively, shotgun marriage no longer occurred at the point of the shotgun. Reduction in stigma provides an additional reason why women who, in previous times would have put up their baby for adoption, chose to keep the baby instead. As we have seen, in 1970 most children whose mothers did not get married in the first three years after their birth were put up for adoption (commonly by relatives). In contrast, by the late 1980s about two-thirds of these babies were kept by the mothers.

There can be little doubt that the stigma of out-of-wedlock childbearing has declined enormously. Even the name of the phenomenon has been changed over the last fifteen years: children born out-of-wedlock are no longer referred to as "illegitimate." The willingness of officials to ask, and of citizens to answer, questions about out-of-wedlock childbearing is a further indicator of the decline in stigma. For example, in the CPS fertility supplement, retrospectively questioned white mothers revealed 32 percent higher rates of out-of-wedlock first births when queried in 1990 than when queried ten years earlier (1980) about the very same births.[23] In former times high school students would quit school in the event of pregnancy. In 1958 the high school completion rate of mothers who became pregnant at seventeen or younger was 19 percent. By 1986 it was 56 percent. In 1972 Federal law made it illegal for schools to expel students for pregnancy or parenthood. The *New York Times* has described the transformation of attitudes underlying these changes:

> In the "old days" of the 1960s, 50s and 40s, pregnant teenagers were pariahs, banished from schools, ostracized by their peers or scurried out of town to give birth in secret. Today, pregnant teen-agers are even beginning to be viewed by their peers as role models. No longer are they shunned or ridiculed, but supported and embraced in their decisions to give birth, keep their babies, continue their education and participate in school activities [Williams 1993, p. C1].

A final paradox that requires explanation is why the black shotgun marriage ratio began to fall earlier than the white ratio and exhibits no significant change in trend around 1970. Here, welfare may play a role. For women whose earnings are sufficiently low that they are potentially eligible for welfare, an increase in welfare benefits has the same effect on out-of-wedlock births as a decline in the stigma to bearing a child out of wedlock. The difference in eligibility between whites and blacks and the patterns of change in welfare benefits—rising in the 1960s and falling thereafter—may then explain why the decline in the black shotgun marriage ratio began earlier than that for whites. That blacks will be more affected by changes in welfare benefits than whites goes almost without saying because of their lower incomes. Ellwood [1988, p. 201] has calculated that a full third of black children will live in poverty more than 70 percent of the time, in contrast to only 3 percent of white children. As a result, the rise in welfare benefits in the 1960s may have had only a small impact on the white shotgun rate but resulted in a significant decrease in the black shotgun marriage rate.

---

23. These mothers may have had different recall bias in 1990 than in 1980 because of the lapse of time, but that recall bias would most likely have resulted in an increased number of forgotten children which would have decreased the number of out-of-wedlock births rather than increased them.

D. Survey Results

Our technology shock theory posits two distinct mechanisms whereby the shotgun marriage norm eroded. The first model emphasizes the role of the new technologies in increasing the willingness of women to participate in uncommitted premarital sex. The second emphasizes the diminished sense of responsibility of men to care for women who have passed up available contraception and abortion options. Our guess, based partly on the qualitative results of a survey we conducted of University of California at Berkeley undergraduates, is that the first mechanism is more important than the second. We attempted to see whether students would agree with the logic of the second choice model regarding the effect of abortion availability on a man's responsibility to marry his partner.

Students were asked to gauge the responsibility of a man to marry his sexual partner in two vignettes: one in which abortion is "easily available" and another in which abortion is "illegal, as it was in this country until the 1970s."[24] They were also asked to explain the reasoning underlying their responses. Differences in students' ratings of responsibility with and without easily available abortion had the expected sign, but were on average small—only 1.2 points on a scale of one to ten—a particularly surprising result given that the questionnaire had been designed to elicit such a reaction. In this sense, students implicitly conceded the logical point that abortion should have an impact on their responsibilities. Interestingly, however, not a single student volunteered any explanation whatever of the *difference* in his or her answer to the two different vignettes. In other words, no student commented on the availability of abortion as a factor governing the responsibility for marriage. Instead, students focused on the *level* of responsibility. The most common explanation, offered by both male and female respondents, was that the man is responsible to the child but not to the pregnant woman. Many emphasized the *financial* responsibility of the man for the child. Others explained

---

24. The first vignette concerned Michael, aged 20, and Sharon, aged 19, each of whom earns $15,000 per year and is a department store clerk. After going out with Michael for a year, Sharon becomes pregnant. Michael makes it clear that he would prefer not to get married and that he wants Sharon to get an abortion. Abortions are easily available in their area, but Sharon says she would like to get married and wants to bring the baby to term. The second vignette is exactly the same as the first vignette except for the conditions under which abortion can be obtained. Rather than being "easily available," on the contrary, "abortion is illegal, as it was in this country until the early 1970s."

that a forced marriage was likely to end in an early divorce, so that the child would suffer more in a shotgun marriage than if born out of wedlock. Perhaps this folk wisdom is right. Nevertheless, such a response implicitly assumes that the couples in the vignettes—who had been going out together for a year and were clearly sexually intimate—would not be compatible. Consider the difference between Rubin's [1969] description of sexual and social mores in San Francisco 25 years earlier. Such a couple would surely have been considered sufficiently compatible to have gotten married even if the man had preferred to remain single. Indeed, sexual relations would have involved an implicit promise of marriage if the woman had become pregnant. We believe that the worldview of these UC Berkeley students in the summer of 1994 fits well with the description of behavior in our first model, in which unmarried partners have no commitment to marriage if a baby is the outcome of their sexual relations.

The students are probably a good gauge of the social mores regarding expectations of couples at the present time. If such questions had not arisen in a respondent's personal experience, he/she would still surely have heard numerous discussions of such matters. The respondents' implicit lack of enthusiasm for the second model as an explanation for the decline in shotgun marriage, however, should be viewed with some caution. An appreciation of social expectations regarding sexual and marital conduct five years prior to their own birth is likely to require unusual historic perspective, especially since those customs have, in fact, changed very greatly.

F. Recent Studies of the Relation between Abortion and Motherhood

Several recent studies have examined the relationship between abortion availability and births with surprising conclusions which support the basic tenet of this paper that the availability of abortion influences behavior, especially through sexual participation. If births decline less than one for one with the advent of abortion, then sexual participation or contraceptive use must be influenced by the availability of abortion. Jackson and Klerman [1993] and Levine, Trainor, and Zimmerman [1995] have shown that state restrictions of Medicaid funds for abortions have been associated with *declines* in birth rates. Kane and Staiger [1996] found that teen birthrates increase in a county when the distance to the nearest abortion provider declines.[25] These studies thus show that births decline at a much lower rate than one to one with the number of abortions.

VI. CONCLUSION

Over the last 25 years disturbing trends have occurred in the United States (and other Western countries as well). Just at the time, about 1970, that the permanent cure to poverty seemed to be on the horizon and just at the time that women had obtained the tools to control the number and the timing of their children, single motherhood and the feminization of poverty began their long and steady rise. As a result, United States poverty rates have been stubbornly constant for the last quarter century.

It is important to understand why these changes in family structure have occurred. Quantitative work by economists and sociologists suggests strongly that the magnitude of these changes is simply too great to be explained by the increase in welfare eligibility and benefits (which occurred in the 1960s and not the 1970s). Nor can it be explained by the decline in jobs for the less educated. Despite the lack of ambiguity from econometric work, misperceptions persist. On the right it is commonly believed that welfare did it, and on the left, that the deterioration of male jobs is the culprit.

There is, in consequence, a need for another explanation. That other explanation, which is also popular, centers on the vague notion that single parenthood increased because of a change in attitudes toward sexual behavior. This paper endorses that view, and attempts to explain the mechanisms whereby those changes in sexual and marital customs occurred. Although doubt will always remain about the ultimate cause for something as diffuse as a change in social custom, the technology shock theory of this paper does fit the facts. The new technology was adopted quickly and on a massive scale. It is therefore prima facie plausible that it could have accounted for a comparably large

---

25. These new results are particularly surprising in view of earlier studies that showed declines in teenage birthrates following the legalization of abortion—a decline in teenage birthrates in New York City after statewide legalization (see Joyce and Mocan [1980]) and a differential decline in out-of-wedlock birth ratios in states that legalized abortion in the late 1960s and early 1970s (see Sklar and Berkov [1974]).

change in marital and fertility patterns. The timing of the changes also seems, at least crudely, to fit the theory.

From a policy perspective, attempts to turn the technology clock backward by denying women access to abortion and contraception is probably not possible, and even if it were possible, it would almost surely be both undesirable and counterproductive. In addition to probably reducing the well-being of women who use the technology, along with that of men, such measures could lead to yet greater poverty. In the new equilibrium in which sexual abstinence is rare and the stigma of out-of-wedlock motherhood is small, denial of access would probably increase the number of children born out of wedlock and reared in impoverished single-parent families. On the contrary, efforts should be made to ensure that women can use the new technologies if they choose to do so. Finally, if the technology shock theory of this paper provides the correct explanation for the rise in single motherhood, cuts in welfare, as currently proposed, would only further immiserize the victims. Such cuts would have little impact on the number of out-of-wedlock children while impoverishing those already on welfare yet further. Instead, administrative measures, such as those suggested by Ellwood, to make fathers pay, deserve serious policy consideration.

DATA APPENDIX

Abortion, Sexual Experience, and Use of Pill

The time series on sexual experience, use of the pill, and abortion are derived from the 1982 and the 1988 panels of the National Survey of Family Growth. These surveys interviewed a nationally representative sample of women 15 to 44 of all marital statuses, with approximately 8000 respondents in each panel. Women were asked retrospectively about their fertility histories: pregnancies and their outcomes, infertility, contraceptive use, childbearing plans, adoption, sex education, and family composition.

Abortions were tabulated from answers to questions about the date of each pregnancy and its respective outcome, with the abortion series computed as the number of pregnancies terminated by that method. We used the age distribution of abortions in our data set and data from Vital Statistics on the age distribution of the population to impute the abortion experience of women under 45 who were omitted from the sample in prior years because of age truncation. A single series was constructed from the two panels by using the data from the 1982 panel for the period 1960 to 1972, an average of the data in the 1982 and 1988 panels for the period 1973 to 1981, and the data from the 1988 panel thereafter. The later panel was omitted from the pre-1973 series because of the importance of age truncation. This series was used to perform the time series tests reported in Table III. However, the NSFG contains considerable underreporting of abortion, in comparison with the complete tabulations from medical providers available from the Alan Guttmacher Institute after 1972. For example, from 1973 to 1982 the NSFG third and fourth panels reported only 31.3 percent of the abortions to unmarried women reported in the Alan Guttmacher Institute survey. The aggregate abortions statistics in Table II are based on the Alan Guttmacher data after 1972. Before 1973 the table uses abortions from the 1982 NSFG, adjusted for reporting error.

The fraction of women aged 16 with sexual experience was compiled from the 1982 panel of the National Survey of Family Growth from answers to the following two questions: "At any time in your life, have you ever had sexual intercourse?" If yes, women were subsequently asked: "When did you have sexual intercourse for the first time—what month and year was that? How old were you at that time?"

The series on the use of the pill is the fraction of unmarried women reporting using the pill on first intercourse by date of first intercourse from the 1982 panel.

Shotgun Marriage Rate

The shotgun marriage ratio, to recall, is the fraction of births conceived out of wedlock with marriage between conception and birth. To obtain an annual series and extended shotgun marriage ratios with marriage after the birth of the child, we followed the methodology of O'Connell and Moore [1980], O'Connell and Rogers [1984], and U. S. Department of Commerce [1991, p. 10, Table F]. The Fertility Supplements to the Current Population Survey taken in 1980, 1982, and 1990 asked women about the birth dates of their children and also their dates of marriage and divorce. The 1980 and 1990 surveys queried all women 15 to 65 about the first five births; the 1982 Supplement asked only about first births. The first birth shotgun marriage ratio is the fraction of *first* births taking place within seven months of marriage, where the

316   *QUARTERLY JOURNAL OF ECONOMICS*

mother was unmarried at the time of conception. We concentrate our analysis on first-births, since a first-birth is much more likely to be a defining event in a woman's life than a second (or subsequent) birth to an unmarried woman who is already a mother. The time series data used to estimate the change in trend in Table III are composite series consisting of the data from the 1980 and 1982 panels of the CPS Fertility Supplements up to 1979, and the 1990 panel thereafter. Because the shotgun marriage ratio estimated from the 1980 and 1982 CPS surveys for the exact same period as the 1990 CPS survey was 32 percent lower—presumably because of the decline in stigma attached to out-of-wedlock births—the entire pre-1979 series was adjusted upward to conform to the later reports concerning the same births.

UNIVERSITY OF CALIFORNIA AT BERKELEY AND THE BROOKINGS INSTITUTION
BOARD OF GOVERNORS OF THE FEDERAL RESERVE SYSTEM
UNIVERSITY OF CALIFORNIA AT BERKELEY

REFERENCES

Akerlof, George, A., Janet L. Yellen, and Michael L. Katz, "An Analysis of Out-of-Wedlock Childbearing in the United States," mimeo, University of California at Berkeley, 1994.
Anderson, Elijah, *StreetWise* (Chicago: University of Chicago Press, 1990).
Becker, Gary S., *A Treatise on the Family* (Cambridge: Harvard University Press, 1981).
Ellwood, David T., *Poor Support: Poverty in the American Family* (New York: Basic Books, 1988).
Ellwood, David T., and Jonathan Crane, "Family Change among Black Americans: What Do We Know?" *Journal of Economic Perspectives*, IV (1990), 65–84.
Ellwood, David T., and Lawrence H. Summers, "Poverty in America: Is Welfare the Answer or the Problem?" in *Fighting Poverty: What Works and What Doesn't*, S. Danziger and D. Weinberg, eds. (Cambridge: Harvard University Press, 1986).
Garrow, David J., *Liberty and Sexuality: The Right to Privacy and the Making of Roe v. Wade* (New York: Macmillan, 1994).
Jackson, Catherine A., and Jacob A. Klerman, "Welfare, Abortion and Teenage Fertility," mimeo, The RAND Corporation, 1994.
Jencks, Christopher, *Rethinking Social Policy* (Cambridge: Harvard University Press, 1992).
Joyce, Theodore, J., and Naci H. Mocan, "The Impact of Legalized Abortion on Adolescent Childbearing in New York City," *American Journal of Public Health*, LXXX (1980), 273–78.
Kane, Thomas, and Douglas Staiger, "Teen Motherhood and Abortion Access," *Quarterly Journal of Economics*, CXI (1996), 467–506.
Lerman, Robert I., "Employment Opportunities of Young Men and Family Formation," mimeo, Brandeis University, 1988.
Levine, Phillip B., Amy B. Trainor, and David J. Zimmerman, "The Effect of Medicaid Abortion Funding Restrictions on Abortions, Pregnancies and Births," NBER Working Paper No. 5066, 1995.
Luker, Kristin, *Abortion and the Politics of Motherhood* (Berkeley: University of California Press, 1984).
——. "Dubious Conceptions: The Controversy over Teen Pregnancy," *The American Prospect* (1991), 73–83.

Lundberg, Shelly, and Robert D. Plotnick, "Effects of State Welfare, Abortion and Family Planning Policies on Premarital Childbearing among White Adolescents," *Family Planning Perspectives,* XXII (1990), 246–75.

Lundberg, Shelly, and Robert A. Pollak, "Noncooperative Bargaining Models of Marriage," *American Economic Review,* LXXXIV (1994), 132–37.

Manski, Charles F., Gary D. Sandefur, Sara McLanahan, and Daniel Powers, "Alternative Estimates of the Effect of Family Structure during Adolescence on High School Graduation," *Journal of the American Statistical Association,* LXXXVII (1992), 25–37.

Mare, Robert D., and Christopher Winship, "Socioeconomic Change and the Decline of Marriage for Whites and Blacks," in *The Urban Underclass,* C. Jencks and P. E. Peterson, eds. (Washington, DC: Brookings Institution, 1991).

Marsiglio, William, "Commitment to Social Fatherhood: Predicting Adolescent Males' Intentions to Live with Their Child and Partner," *Journal of Marriage and the Family,* L (1988), 427–41.

Moffitt, Robert, "Incentive Effects of the U. S. Welfare System: A Review," *Journal of Economic Literature,* XXX (1992), 1–61.

Murray, Charles, *Losing Ground: American Social Policy 1950–1980* (New York: Basic Books, 1984).

Nathanson, Constance A., and Young J. Kim, "Components of Change in Adolescent Fertility, 1971–1979," *Demography,* XXVI (1989), 85–98.

O'Connell, Martin, and Carolyn C. Rogers, "Out-of-Wedlock Births, Premarital Pregnancies, and Their Effects on Family Formation and Dissolution," *Family Planning Perspectives,* XVI (1984), 157–62.

O'Connell, Martin, and Maurice J. Moore, "The Legitimacy Status of First Births to U. S. Women Aged 15–24, 1939–1978," *Family Planning Perspectives,* XII (1980), 16–25.

Rainwater, Lee, *Behind Ghetto Walls* (Chicago: Aldine, 1970).

Rubin, Lillian Breslow, *Worlds of Pain: Life in the Working-Class Family* (New York: Basic Books, 1969).

Sklar, June, and Beth Berkov, "Abortion, Illegitimacy, and the American Birthrate," *Science,* CLXXXV (September 13, 1974), 909–15.

U. S. Department of Commerce, *Fertility of American Women: June 1990,* Current Population Reports, Population Characteristics, Series P-20, No. 454 (Washington, DC: U.S. Government Printing Office, 1991).

U. S. Department of Labor, Office of Policy Planning and Research, *The Negro Family: The Case for National Action* (March 1965).

Williams, Lena, "Pregnant Teen-Agers Are Outcasts No Longer," *The New York Times,* Late Edition (December 2, 1993), C1.

Willis, Robert J., "A Theory of Out-of-Wedlock Childbearing," mimeo, University of Chicago and National Opinion Research Center, 1994.

Wilson, William J., *The Truly Disadvantaged* (Chicago: Chicago University Press, 1987).

Wilson, William J., and Katherine M. Neckerman, "Poverty and Family Structure: The Widening Gap between Evidence and Public Policy Issues," in *Fighting Poverty: What Works and What Doesn't,* S. Danziger and D. Weinberg, eds. (Cambridge: Harvard University Press, 1986), pp. 232–59.

Wood, Robert G., "Marriage Rates and Marriageable Men: A Test of the Wilson Hypothesis," *Journal of Human Resources,* XXX (1995), 163–93.

[2]

THE ECONOMICS OF THE BABY SHORTAGE*

*ELISABETH M. LANDES** and RICHARD A. POSNER****

INTRODUCTION

Although economists have studied extensively the efforts of government to regulate the economy, public regulation of social and personal life has largely escaped economic attention. With the rapid development of the economic analysis of nonmarket behavior, the conceptual tools necessary for the economic study of social (as distinct from narrowly economic) regulation are now at hand.[1] Nor is there any basis for a presumption that government does a good job of regulating nonmarket behavior; if anything, the negative presumption created by numerous studies of economic regulation[2] should carry over to the nonmarket sphere. An example of nonmarket regulation that may be no less perverse than the widely criticized governmental efforts to regulate imports, transportation, new drugs, bank entry, and other market activities is the regulation of child adoptions—the subject of this paper.

Sometimes natural parents do not want to raise their child; the typical case is where the birth is illegitimate. And in some cases where the natural parents do raise the child initially, their custody is later terminated for one reason or another—death or other incapacity, abuse, or extreme indigence. In either case—the unwanted infant or the abused, neglected, or abandoned child—there are potential gains from trade from transferring the custody of the child to a new set of parents. Where the new parents assume full parental rights and obligations over the child, one speaks of adoption; where they obtain simply a temporary custody (usually being partially compensated for their custodial services by the state), one speaks of foster care. An alternative to foster care in a home is foster care in an institution.

* Research for this study was supported by the Center for the Study of the Economy and the State at the University of Chicago. The authors wish to express their gratitude for comments received at workshops at the University of Chicago and the University of Lund.

** Charles R. Walgreen Postdoctoral Fellow, Graduate School of Business, University of Chicago.

*** Professor of Law, University of Chicago Law School.

[1] Particularly relevant here is the recent economic work on marriage and the family. See, *e.g.*, Economics of the Family (Theodore W. Schultz ed. 1974) (Nat'l Bureau Econ. Res.).

[2] See, *e.g.*, William A. Jordan, Producer Protection, Prior Market Structure and the Effects of Government Regulation, 15 J. Law & Econ. 151 (1972).

Ordinarily, potential gains from trade are realized by a process of voluntary transacting—by a sale, in other words. Adoptions could in principle be handled through the market and in practice, as we shall see, there is a considerable amount of baby selling. But because public policy is opposed to the sale of babies, such sales as do occur constitute a "black market." Recent hearings before the Senate Subcommittee on Children and Youth,[3] as well as a well-publicized indictment of baby sellers,[4] have brought into renewed focus the existence of the black market in babies. The hearings in particular constitute a rich if unsystematic source of data and opinions on the adoption problem, facilitating appraisal of a major and, we shall argue, probably misguided example of public regulation of nonmarket behavior.

Part I of this paper develops a model of the supply and demand for babies for adoption under the existing pattern of regulation and shows (1) how that regulation has created a baby shortage (and, as a result, a black market) by preventing a free market from equilibrating the demand for and supply of babies for adoption, and (2) how it has contributed to a glut of unadopted children maintained in foster homes at public expense. Part II explores the objections to allowing the price system to equilibrate the adoption market and argues that the objections do not justify the existing regulations though they might justify a more limited regulation of the baby market. In Part III we consider, in the spirit of the new economic analysis of the political process,[5] some of the reasons why the government has curtailed the operation of the market in this area. Part IV proposes a method of practical experimentation with introducing a market in adoptions. Parts III and IV are highly tentative. In the course of the analysis we attempt to sketch how the world would look if a free market in babies were permitted to come into existence. We also discuss, though much more briefly, the problem of foster care.

I. Disequilibrium in the Adoption Market

A. *The Baby Shortage and the Baby Glut*

Students of adoption agree on two things. The first is that there is a shortage of white babies for adoption; the second is that there is a glut of

---

[3] Adoption and Foster Care, 1975: Hearings before the Subcomm. on Children & Youth of the Senate Comm. on Labor & Public Welfare, 94th Cong., 1st Sess. (1975) [hereinafter cited without cross-reference as Adoption and Foster Care]. A further round of hearings on baby selling began on March 22, 1977 before the Criminal Justice Subcommittee of the House Judiciary Committee, in connection with a bill to make the sale of babies in interstate commerce a federal crime. See Chicago Sun-Times, March 3, 1977, at 55, col. 3. At this writing, those hearings are still going on, and none of the testimony given at them has yet been published.

[4] See New York Times, September 8, 1976, at 1, col. 4.

[5] See, *e.g.*, George J. Stigler, The Theory of Economic Regulation, 2 Bell J. Econ. & Management Sci. 3 (1971); Sam Peltzman, Toward a More General Theory of Regulation, 19 J. Law & Econ. 211 (1976).

black babies, and of children who are no longer babies (particularly if they are physically or mentally handicapped), for adoption. The dimensions of the problem are suggested in Table 1. The very high ratio of illegitimate black births to black adoptions suggests why there is no shortage of black babies for adoption.

Contrary to popular impression, Table 1 indicates that the increased availability of contraception and abortion has not perceptibly diminished the number of illegitimate births. A partial explanation may be that the availability of contraception and abortion, by reducing the risk of producing an unwanted child (but not to zero), has reduced the expected cost and hence increased the incidence of sexual intercourse outside of marriage. However, while the illegitimate birth rate remains high the availability of babies for adoption has declined, apparently because a larger proportion of parents of illegitimate children are keeping them.[6] This trend may be due to inexplicable (on economic grounds) changes in moral standards; or it may be due to the fact that the increased opportunities for women in the job market have made them less dependent on the presence of a male in raising a child. An additional feature is that, given the increased availability of contraception and abortion, an illegitimate baby is more likely than formerly to be a desired baby.

Students of adoption cite factors such as the declining proportion of illegitimate children being put up for adoption as the "causes" of the baby shortage. But such factors do not create a shortage, any more than the scarcity of truffles creates a shortage; they merely affect the number of children available for adoption at any price. At a higher price for babies, the incidence of abortion, the reluctance to part with an illegitimate child, and even the incentive to use contraceptives would diminish because the costs of unwanted pregnancy would be lower while the (opportunity) costs to the natural mother of retaining her illegitimate child would rise.

---

[6] Some indication of this is the recent decline in the ratio of illegitimate babies put up for adoption to illegitimate births, as shown in the following table (thousands).

	Babies Born[a] Out of Wedlock	Adoption of Babies[b] Born Out of Wedlock	Ratio
1957	183	48	.26
1960	225	60	.27
1965	292	88	.30
1970	399	110	.28
1971	402	101	.25
1972	404	N.A.	—
1973	407	77[c]	.19

[a] *Source:* Time of Transition, tab. 1-L, at 198. (Heather L. Ross & Isabel Sawhill eds. 1975).

[b] *Source:* U.S. Dep't of Health, Education, & Welfare, Nat'l Center for Social Statistics, Adoptions in 1971 (1973).

[c] This number is projected by a method similar to that used in Table 1, notes e and f. Thirty-eight states reported a total of 46,763 adoptions of out-of-wedlock children in 1973. These 38 states contributed 61% of out-of-wedlock adoptions reported in 1971.

TABLE 1
BIRTHS OUT OF WEDLOCK, ADOPTIONS, AND NONRELATIVE ADOPTIONS
BY RACE, 1957-1974 (thousands)

Year	Births out of Wedlock[a]		Adoptions[b]		Nonrelative Adoptions[b]	
	White	Nonwhite	White	Nonwhite	White	Nonwhite
1957	64[c]	119[c]	82.8	8.2	44.3	3.9
1960	83	142	96.3	10.7	52.6	5.2
1965	124	168	126.4	15.6	69.8	6.9
1970	175	224	154.0	21.0	78.5	10.7
1971	164	238	147.0	22.0	70.8	12.0
1972[d]	161	243				
1973[e]	163	244	125.1	22.8	48.87	11.6
1974[f]			110.6	24.5	37.9	11.5

[a] *Source:* Time of Transition, tab 1-L, at 198 (Heather L. Ross & Isabel Sawhill eds. 1975).

[b] *Source:* U.S. Dep't of Health, Education, & Welfare, Nat'l Center for Social Statistics, Adoptions in 1971 (1973). 1973 and 1974 data are reported in *id.*, Adoptions in 1973 and *id.*, Adoptions in 1974. The data for these two years are incomplete with only 38 and 41 states reporting, respectively. Note that these figures are not limited to adoption of babies born out of wedlock as in note 6 *supra.*

[c] Data are for 1955.

[d] Adoption data for 1972 were not sufficiently complete to permit calculation.

[e] Adoptions in 1973 are projected from available information. The 38 states reporting in 1973 were responsible for 76% of total adoptions reported in 1971 and for 73% of nonrelative adoptions reported in 1971. We project adoptions by race in 1973 by multiplying total adoptions reported in 1973 by 1/.76, and nonrelative adoption reported in 1973 by 1/.73.

[f] Adoptions in 1974 are projected from available data as described in note e to this table. The 41 states reporting adoptions in 1974 were responsible for 81% of total adoptions reported in 1971 and 76% of nonrelative adoptions reported in 1971.

The principal suppliers of babies for adoption are adoption agencies. Restrictive regulations governing nonagency adoption have given agencies a monopoly (though not a complete one) of the supply of children for adoption. However, while agencies charge fees for adoption, usually based on the income of the adoptive parents, they do not charge a market-clearing (let alone a monopoly-profit-maximizing) price. This is shown by the fact that prospective adoptive parents applying to an agency face waiting periods of three to seven years.[7] And the (visible) queue understates the shortage, since by tightening their criteria of eligibility to adopt a child the agencies can shorten the apparent queue without increasing the supply of babies. Thus some demanders in this market must wait for years to obtain a baby, others never obtain one, and still others are discouraged by knowledge of the queue from even trying. Obtaining a second or third baby is increasingly difficult.

The picture is complicated, however, by the availability of independent adoptions. An independent adoption is one that does not go through an agency. Most independent adoptions are by a relative, for example a stepfather, but some involve placement with strangers and here, it would seem, is an opportunity for a true baby market to develop. However, the operation

[7] Adoption and Foster Care 6.

ECONOMICS OF THE BABY SHORTAGE   327

TABLE 2
CHILDREN RECEIVING FOSTER CARE FROM PUBLIC AND
VOLUNTARY CHILD WELFARE AGENCIES, 1961-1972
(thousands)

Year	Total	Number of Children Receiving Foster Care Services		
		Public Agencies	Served by Public and Voluntary Agencies[a]	Voluntary Agencies
1961	244.5	133.3		111.2
1965	283.3	173.9		109.4
1970	326.0	226.0	57.0	42.2
1971	330.4	231.4	59.8	39.2
1972	319.8	223.4	61.4	35.0

Source: Numbers for 1961 and 1965 are derived from U.S. Dep't of Health, Education, & Welfare, Children's Bureau, Child Welfare Statistics, 1961 and 1965.
Numbers for 1970, 1971, and 1972 are derived from U.S. Dep't of Health, Education, & Welfare, Children Served by Public Welfare Agencies and Voluntary Child Welfare Agencies and Institutions, for 1970, 1971, and 1972.
[a] For the great majority of these children, the public agency was purchasing foster care from the voluntary agency.

of this market is severely curtailed by a network of restrictions, varying from state to state (a few states forbid independent adoption by a nonrelative) but never so loose as to permit outright sale of a baby for adoption.[8]

Just as a buyer's queue is a symptom of a shortage, a seller's queue is a symptom of a glut. The thousands of children in foster care revealed by Table 2 are comparable to an unsold inventory stored in a warehouse. Child welfare specialists attribute this "oversupply" to such factors as the growing incidence of child abuse, which forces the state to remove children from the custody of their natural parents, and the relatively small number of prospective adoptive parents willing to adopt children of another race, children who are no longer infants, or children who have a physical or mental handicap. No doubt these factors are important. However, some children are placed in foster care as infants and remain there until they are no longer appealing to prospective adoptive parents. We believe that the large number of children in foster care is, in part, a manifestation of a regulatory pattern that (1) combines restrictions on the sale of babies with the effective monopolization of the adoption market by adoptive agencies, and (2) fails to provide effectively for the termination of the natural parents' rights.

B. *A Model of the Adoption Market*

Here we present a simple analytical model of the adoption market as it exists today in the United States. Queues for some children (mainly white

[8] The relevant state laws are described in Note: Black-Market Adoptions, 22 Catholic Lawyer 48 (1976), and in Daniel R. Grove, Independent Adoption: The Case for the Gray Market, 13 Vill. L. Rev. 116 (1967).

infants) in the legal market, overstocks of others (older, nonwhite, or physi-cally or mentally handicapped children), and black-market activity in in-fants are all shown to be the result of the peculiar market structure in adoption that has been brought about by public regulation.

Whereas in 1957 only 53 percent of all nonrelative adoptions went through adoption agencies, in 1971 the proportion was almost 80 percent.[9] This would be a matter of limited significance from the economic standpoint if adoption agencies were both numerous and free from significant restrictions on their ability to operate as efficient profit-maximizing firms. The first condition is more or less satisfied but not the second. While agencies are generally not limited in the fees they may charge prospective adoptive par-ents, they are constrained to other inefficient restrictions. For example, they are constrained to operate as "nonprofit" organizations which presumably retards, perhaps severely, their ability to attract capital, and may have other inefficient effects as well.[10] The most significant restriction is the regulation of the price at which the agencies may transact with the natural parents. Adoption agencies that are also general child-welfare agencies must accept all children offered to them at a regulated price (but may place them in foster care rather than for adoption); and they may offer no additional compensa-tion to suppliers (the natural parents) in order to increase the supply of babies. The regulated price is generally limited to the direct medical costs of pregnant women plus (some) maintenance expenses during the latter part of the pregnancy. To be sure, agencies have some flexibility in the kinds of services they may offer the natural parents, such as job counseling, but they cannot thereby transfer to the natural parents anything approaching the free-market value of the child.

There are rough counterparts to such regulation in many explicit markets. Banks as a group have a monopoly of banking services, though most bank-ing markets contain several competing banks; the prices of banking services are unregulated (save for usury laws which are applicable to some bank loans); but banks are forbidden to pay a market-clearing price for an essen-tial input, demand deposits (corresponding to babies in the adoption mar-ket). Similar regulatory patterns are found in industries as otherwise diverse as taxi service and television broadcasting. Nevertheless the regulation of adoption has several peculiar characteristics reflected in our model: collusion among agencies, including market division (often along religious lines), is permitted; there exists a very close substitute for the good supplied by the

---

[9] See U.S. Dep't of Health, Education, & Welfare, Nat'l Center for Social Statistics, Adop-tions in 1971 (1973).

[10] In particular, it may lead the agencies to dissipate their profits in expenditures that reduce welfare—*e.g.*, unnecessarily intrusive inspections of the home of the adoptive parents.

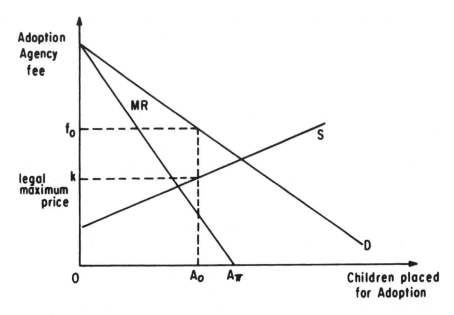

FIGURE 1

agencies—independent adoption; and the agency has, as mentioned, no power to refuse to take the children tendered to it.[11]

We begin by analyzing a monopoly model of the adoption market that would exist if agencies acted jointly as a monopolist (*i.e.*, if there were no competition among agencies or substitution in the independent-adoption markets and the agencies' only objective were to maximize economic profits). Agencies face a demand curve for children for adoption described by D in Figure 1. One can conceive of all families as being in the adoption market, with their location along the demand curve determined by the value they place on adopting a child. The supply curve of babies for adoption is described by S in Figure 1. It is assumed to be upward sloping. The supply curve reflects the transfer in wealth that natural parents would demand in exchange for giving up a child for adoption, and is determined by such things as the natural mother's direct and opportunity costs in carrying the child to term and any psychic costs she incurs by giving birth to a child she will not keep, over the direct, opportunity, and psychic costs of either having the child and keeping it or aborting it. For some women the supply price will

---

[11] This applies only to those agencies—the majority, however—that are general child-welfare organizations rather than solely adoption agencies.

be low, perhaps because of a strong aversion to abortion relative to giving up the child; for others the price will be high, perhaps because of high opportunity costs of bearing the child. At the legally prescribed maximum price that agencies may offer natural parents, A_o children will be placed with the agencies for adoption.

Abstracting from the administrative costs of placing children for adoption, it is clear that there is no marginal cost of children to the agencies in this model. In each period agencies have only a fixed cost of k times the number of children they must accept under the regulation, where k is the regulated price at which they must take any child tendered to them.[12]

Under these extreme assumptions the agency-monopoly would be willing to place up to A_π children, since marginal revenue from placing children is positive up to that number. However, the actual number of children the agency has to place may exceed or fall short of A_π. When the number of children it has, denoted by A_o in Figure 1, falls short of A_π, all the children will be placed for adoption. When A_o exceeds A_π, as in Figure 2, some of the children will be placed in foster care. The number placed in foster care will depend upon the cost to the agency of maintaining them there. The lower that cost is, the more children the agencies will place in foster care and the fewer they will offer for adoption. Clearly, if the cost to the agency of foster care is zero, because, for example, the state reimburses it for the full cost of maintaining children in foster care,[13] all of the children in excess of A_π will be placed in foster care and the number placed for adoption will never exceed A_π.

To be sure, if adoption agencies could price discriminate perfectly, children in excess of A_π would be placed in foster care only when the number supplied to the agencies at the regulated price exceeded the demand for children at that price. There is evidence that adoption agencies do price discriminate (though not perfectly): adoption fees are usually determined by, among other things, the income of the prospective adoptive parents.

What fee will the agency charge for the children placed for adoption? In Figure 1, which depicts the case where $A_o < A_\pi$, the profit-maximizing fee is f_0. In Figure 2, which depicts the case where $A_o > A_\pi$, the price will be somewhere between f_π and f_1, depending on the cost to the agency of maintaining the children in excess of A_π in foster care.

---

[12] Actually, there is some variation in this price, depending on the particular medical or maintenance costs incurred by the natural mother. This variation is immaterial to our analysis and will be ignored.

[13] In 1965, 41.6% of state and local foster care payments were for children living in foster family homes and institutions supervised or administered by voluntary agencies. This amounted to $95 million. We do not know what fraction of expenditures on total foster care provided by voluntary agencies was offset by this $95 million. See U.S. Dep't of Health, Education, & Welfare, Children's Bureau, Child Welfare Statistics (1965).

ECONOMICS OF THE BABY SHORTAGE   331

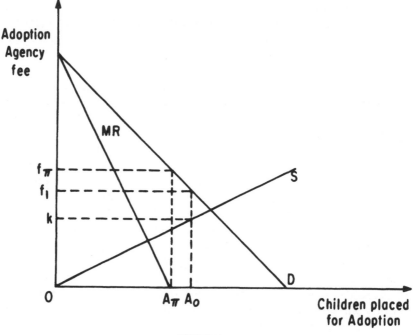

FIGURE 2

But such prices are not being charged by adoption agencies, the most telling evidence of this being the long queues that prospective adoptive parents must undergo to obtain a child through an agency even when they are willing to pay the agency fee. What constrains the agencies from charging f_0 in Figure 1? Probably not the fact that they are nominally nonprofit agencies: profits obtained in adoption activities could readily be used to support other activities in which these agencies engage. We suggest that the presence of competition from the independent adoption market may be one constraining force. This suggestion is consistent with the vigorous efforts by adoption agencies to restrict independent adoptions.

To understand how the presence of the independent market constrains the agencies, we must model the interaction between the agency and independent markets. To do this we make two assumptions: (1) Price in the independent market is determined competitively, and (2) babies available for adoption at any price are allocated in fixed proportions between the agency and the independent market depending on the costs of information in the independent market and the potential criminal and professional penalties from handling independent adoptions. Clearly, the assumption of fixed proportions is unrealistic; the proportion of babies in the agency market is presumably responsive to the price that could be obtained in the independent market relative to the supply price in the agency market. However, the assumption facilitates a graphic exposition of the model at only a small sacrifice of explanatory power.

Assuming for simplicity linear demand and supply curves, the market supply of children to the adoption market is described, as in Figures 1 and 2, by

$$S_M = e + gp.$$

The supply of children to be placed through agencies is a fixed fraction, γ, of market supply at the regulated price, k, which agencies may offer for children.

$$S_A = \gamma(e + gk) = A_O.$$

The supply of children to the independent market is also a fixed fraction, $1 - \gamma$, of market supply:

$$S_I = (1 - \gamma)(e + g(p_I - C_{IS})),$$

where p_I is the transaction price for children in the independent market, and C_{IS} represents the information and expected penalty costs that are incurred by suppliers to this market. Hence C_{IS} must be netted out of the gross supply price.

Market demand for adopted children is described, as in Figures 1 and 2, by

$$D_M = a - bp.$$

Demand in the independent market is assumed to be some fraction, δ, of market demand that is not satisfied through agency adoptions:

$$D_I = \delta(a - b(p_I + C_{ID}) - A_O),$$

where C_{ID} represents the information costs that must be incurred in order to obtain a child in the independent market. Hence C_{ID} must be included in the full price of independent adoption.

To complete the model, we assume that because of political considerations the agency may not charge a fee for adoption in excess of the full price paid for children in the independent market. We assume further (for simplicity of graphical exposition) that if the agency faces excess demand for children at that price, it will allocate its available children among its prospective parents so as to maximize consumer satisfaction (*i.e.*, among the highest-value bidders).

In equilibrium,

$$D_I = S_I,$$

and

$$p_I = \frac{\delta(a - bC_{ID}) - (1 - \gamma)(e - gC_{IS}) - \delta\gamma(e + gk)}{\delta b + (1 - \gamma)g}. \tag{1}$$

Assuming that the agency adoption fee is equal to the full price of independent adoption, the agency fee is

$$p_A = p_I + C_{ID} = \frac{\delta a - (1 - \gamma)(e - g(C_{ID} + C_{IS})) - \delta\gamma(e + gk)}{\delta b + (1 - \gamma)g}. \tag{2}$$

The queue facing the agency at this adoption fee can be determined from the difference between the total number of children demanded in the market at a full price of p_A and the total number supplied:

$$Q = D_M - S_M = \frac{(1 - \gamma)(1 - \delta)[be - \gamma g(e + gk) + g\delta(a - b(C_{IS} + C_{ID}))]}{\delta b + (1 - \gamma)g}.$$

This equilibrium is depicted in Figure 3. From our assumption that the agency allocates its available children among the highest-value bidders, demand in the independent market is represented by a linear demand curve D_I (in panel (b)) that is equal to a fraction δ of market demand in excess of agency supply. (The fraction of demanders who do not receive children in the agency market but appear as demanders in the independent markets will be a function of, among other things, the information and expected penalty costs of buying in the independent market.) This demand curve is gross of information costs. Assuming that the costs of information are the same for all demanders and are proportional to the number of children demanded, we can subtract the costs of search from D_I to get the net demand curve D'_I. The number of children adopted independently is determined by the intersection of D'_I and S_I.

From equation (2) it is clear that an increase in either the expected penalty or information costs of suppliers in the independent market or the information costs of demanders in that market would increase the equilibrium fee that agencies may charge. If an expected penalty equal to $f_0 - C_{IS} - C_{ID}$ were imposed on suppliers in the independent market, that market would vanish. It would reemerge, however, whenever the supply conditions of children shifted so that the (unconstrained) profit-maximizing agency fee exceeded f_0. Hence we predict that in times of relatively short supply of babies for adoption the private market will become more active and the agencies will agitate to have the restrictions on private placement tightened.

The above analysis is consistent with observed characteristics of the adoption market. It explains why agencies charge less than market-clearing fees in the face of baby shortages and why they agitate for stringent regulation of

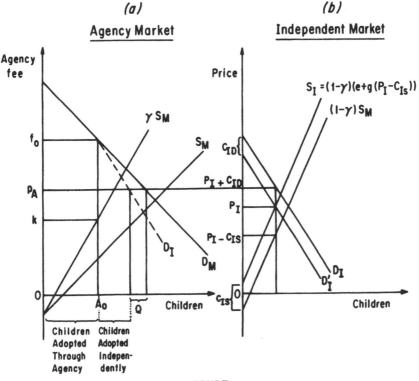

FIGURE 3

the independent market. The substantial costs of information in the independent market for both demanders and suppliers explain why there are queues at adoption agencies rather than simply a diversion of all unsatisfied demanders in the agency market to the independent market.

C. *The Effects of the Baby Shortage*

The baby shortage generates social costs in excess of the traditional welfare loss of monopoly. The counterpart to that loss would be the lost consumer surplus from sales not made at all because of the artificial unavailability of the product and is measured by triangle DBC in Figure 4. But assuming the nonprice rationing methods used by agencies to allocate children are random with respect to willingness to pay (rather than based on willingness to pay, as we assumed in Figure 3),[14] the loss in consumer surplus is the area

[14] This is a plausible assumption because length of time in the queue is presumably uncorrelated with income (it would be negatively correlated if the queue were "literal"—*i.e.*, involved real opportunity costs of time—but it does not).

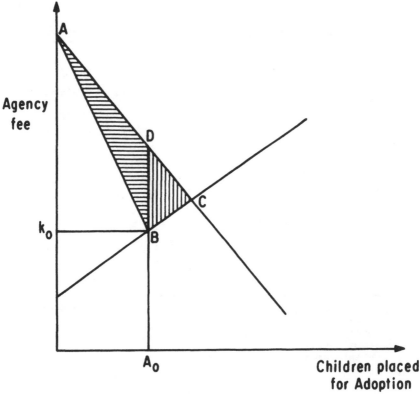

FIGURE 4

of the larger triangle ABC in Figure 4. To be sure, some of this loss is offset by the availability of children in the independent market, but the search costs in the independent market also represent a substantial social cost.

No effort will be made in this paper to quantify the social cost of the baby shortage (and hence of the governmental regulations that have generated it) or to measure its impact on the number of children adopted. However, the potential magnitude of the problem will be explored briefly.

A crude estimate of the potential size of the baby market can be obtained from a comparison of the fraction of married women who are childless throughout their married lives with the (much smaller) fraction of women who report, early in their marriage, that they do not intend to have any children. In 1975, 10.8 percent of white American women aged 50 or over who had ever been married were childless.[15] Many of these were childless by

---

[15] See U.S. Bureau of the Census, Statistical Abstract of the United States, 1976, tab. 75, at 56 [hereinafter cited without cross-reference as Statistical Abstract]. We limit our attention to

choice, but another statistic suggests that many were not: in 1975 only 4.4 percent of white American wives aged 18-24 *expected* to have no children.[16] The difference between these figures is some clue to the potential demand for babies that cannot be satisfied by natural means. Still another clue is the high cost (nominal, time, and risk) that childless couples incur in order to increase the probability of giving birth.

Of course, adopted children may not be a perfect substitute for natural children. The genetic characteristics of natural children are highly correlated with their parents' genetic characteristics, and this correlation could conceivably increase harmony within the family compared to what it would be with an adopted child.[17] Nevertheless, there is considerable substitutability between natural and adopted children and it might be much greater if better genetic matching of adopted children with their adoptive parents were feasible—as might occur, as we shall see, under free market conditions.

Given that the number of white marriages has averaged close to two million a year over the past decade,[18] about 130,000 married couples might be potential "buyers" in the baby market every year.[19] And this is probably an underestimate. Couples who have adopted children are not counted among the 10.8 percent of couples who are childless. More important, most natural parents want more than one child, and presumably the same is true of adoptive parents. This alone might double the 130,000 figure for potential demand. Offsetting this to some extent is the fact that some childless couples may not consider an adopted child a substitute for a natural child. But on balance it seems clear that the 37,000 white nonrelative adoptions a year (estimated in Table 1) fall far short of satisfying the potential demand.

In light of these statistics it may seem surprising that only about 17,000 nonrelative adoptions in 1971 (the last year for which adequate data are available)—a mere 21 percent—were independent rather than agency adoptions. Why do not a larger fraction of the potential demanders utilize the independent method, free from the restrictions that hamper the agency adoption process? The probable answer, already suggested, is that governmental restrictions on the fees that may be paid in an independent adoption artificially depress the net price of providing babies through this process. The result is to reduce the number of babies supplied below the free-

---

whites because, as mentioned earlier, there appears to be no shortage of black babies for adoption.

[16] Statistical Abstract, tab. 78, at 57.

[17] Cf. Gary S. Becker, A Theory of Marriage, in Economics of the Family, *supra* note 1, at 299.

[18] Statistical Abstract, tab. 97, at 68.

[19] This obviously crude estimate was obtained by multiplying the difference between the childless rate for older married women and the expected childless rate of younger married women by the number of marriages per year (whites only).

market level while simultaneously restricting the use of price to ration the existing, and inadequate, supply.

In independent adoption, normally the only payments that may be made are (1) compensation to the natural mother for her medical, and some maintenance, costs plus (2) compensation to the obstetrician and the lawyer for their professional (*i.e.*, medical and legal) services, excluding any search costs they may have incurred in arranging for the adoption. The included items represent only a part of the costs of producing and selling a baby. The major omitted items are (1) the opportunity costs of the natural mother's time during the period of pregnancy or hospitalization when she is precluded from working, over and above her maintenance costs, (2) any pain or other disutility of the pregnancy and delivery to her, (3) any value which she attaches to keeping the child rather than putting it up for adoption, and (4) the costs of search of the middleman—usually an obstetrician or lawyer—in locating and bringing together the supplier and demander.

In practice the constraints on full compensation to producer and middleman are less rigid than suggested. The difficulties of monitoring the fees and activities of the attorney, obstetrician, and natural mother enable these individuals to charge somewhat more than the technically permitted amounts without running any appreciable risk of punishment. This is why independent placement of babies for adoption (other than to relatives) is often referred to as the "gray market." However, the constraints placed on independent adoption are sufficiently stringent to prevent it from approximating a free market. Women have little or no incentive to put a child up for adoption rather than retain or abort it (since abortions are relatively inexpensive, and public assistance is ordinarily available to cover their medical expenses and maintenance costs regardless of whether they keep or give up the child). At the same time, the constraints on payment discourage the emergence of an effective middleman function to match up the prospective sellers and buyers—the middleman activity *per se* cannot be compensated. This is particularly serious in a market of this sort where the sellers and buyers tend to be geographically and socially remote, are not professional businessmen, do not participate in this market on a regular basis, and are dealing in a highly individualized commodity.

In these circumstances, the economist expects a black market to emerge. Some fraction—we do not know what—of the 17,000 independent adoptions are indeed black-market adoptions in the sense that the compensation paid either the natural parents or the middlemen, or both, exceeds the lawful limits.[20] However, the potential criminal and professional sanctions for the

---

[20] Regardless of how obtained—whether lawfully or in the black market—most babies are formally adopted and hence most black-market activities show up in the statistics of independent adoption. In some cases, however, where an adoption is arranged prior to the birth of the

individuals involved in baby selling not only drive up the costs and hence the price of babies (and so reduce demand) but necessarily imply a clandestine mode of operation. This imposes significant information costs on both buyers and sellers in the market, which further raise the (real) price of black-market babies to buyers and reduce the net price to sellers, as demonstrated in panel (b) of Figure 3.

The legally permissible compensation to the natural parents is unlikely to exceed $3,000.[21] However, prices for babies in the black market are alleged to range between $9,000 and $40,000.[22] To some extent these prices reflect search costs and other middleman expenses that would be found in a free market, but they may to a greater extent reflect the expected penalties suppliers face and the additional costs of search entailed by operating in a clandestine market.

A further consideration is that there will be more fraud in a black market for babies than in a lawful market, so fear of being defrauded will further deter potential demanders. In lawful markets the incidence of fraud is limited not only by the existence of legal remedies against the seller but also by his desire to build a reputation for fair dealing. Both the clandestine mode of operation of current baby sellers and the lack of a continuing business relationship between seller and buyer reduce the seller's market incentives to behave reputably. To summarize, we cannot, simply by observing the black market, estimate the market-clearing prices and quantities of babies in a lawful baby market.

The constraints on the baby market may also be responsible in part for the glut of children in foster care—and this quite apart from the possible incentives of adoption agencies to place children in foster care rather than for adoption. Since the natural parents have no financial incentive to place a child for adoption, often they will decide to place it in foster care instead. This is proper so long as they seriously intend to reacquire custody of the child at some later date. But when they do not the consequence of their decision to place the child in foster care may be to render the child unadoptable, for by the time the parents relinquish their parental rights the child may be too old to be placed for adoption. This would happen less often if parents had a financial incentive to relinquish their rights at a time when the child was still young enough to be adoptable.

The *total* effect of the baby-market constraints on the number of foster children is, to be sure, a complicated question. In particular, the limited

---

adopted child, the adoptive parents' name may simply be entered directly on the birth certificate, thus obviating any formal adoptive procedure.

[21] See Adoption and Foster Care 132, 139.

[22] See Adoption and Foster Care 160, 165-166, 175, 182; Chicago Tribune, March 22, 1977, sec. 1, at 3.

supply of desirable babies for adoption may lead some prospective adoptive parents to substitute children who would otherwise be placed in foster care. We suspect that this substitution effect is small, but in any event it is partly controlled by the agencies; they can manipulate the relative "prices" of infants and children residing in foster care by modifying the criteria for eligibility that must be satisfied by prospective adoptive parents.

II. OBJECTIONS TO A FREE BABY MARKET

The foregoing analysis suggests that the baby shortage and black market are the result of legal restrictions that prevent the market from operating freely in the sale of babies as of other goods. This suggests as a possible reform simply eliminating these restrictions. However, many people believe that a free market in babies would be undesirable. Representative of this point of view is the conclusion of a recent law-review note on baby selling:

> The black market in adoptions is a thriving business. Destructive of the best interests of parents, children, and society, such dealings in human flesh should be thwarted by strong, strictly enforced state laws and equally stringent barriers to interstate trade. . . . If state and federal governments show a determination to discover and punish black-market activities, this taint on civilized society can be removed.[23]

The objections to baby selling must be considered carefully before any conclusion with regard to the desirability of changing the law can be reached.

A. *Criticisms Properly Limited to the Black Market*

We begin with a set of criticisms that in reality are applicable not to the market as such, but only, we believe, to the *black* market. The first such criticism is of the high price of babies and the bad effects that are alleged to flow from a high price, such as favoring the wealthy.[24] This criticism of the use of the price system is based on the current prices in the black market. There is no reason to believe that prices would be so high were the sale of babies legalized. On the contrary, prices for children of *equivalent quality* would be much lower.[25]

The current black-market price is swollen by expected punishment costs which would not be a feature of a legalized baby market. In a legal and competitive baby market, price would be equated to the marginal costs of producing and selling for adoption babies of a given quality. These marginal

---

[23] Note, Black-Market Adoptions, *supra* note 8, at 69.

[24] See, *e.g.*, Adoption and Foster Care 11, 27.

[25] The importance of this qualification is emphasized at p. 341 *infra*.

costs include certain well-known items, such as the natural mother's medical expenses and maintenance during pregnancy and the attorney's fee for handling the legal details of the adoption proceeding, that are unlikely to exceed $3,000 in the aggregate. The question marks are the additional fees that would be necessary (1) to compensate a woman either for becoming pregnant or, if she was pregnant already, for inducing her to put the baby up for adoption rather than abort or retain it, and (2) to cover the search costs necessary to match baby and adoptive parents.

With regard to the first item (the natural mother's opportunity costs of adoption), the most important point to be noted is that these costs may be no greater than the cost savings to the adoptive mother of not undergoing pregnancy and childbirth herself. Adoption is a process by which the adoptive mother in effect contracts out one of the steps in the process of child production and rearing, namely the actual pregnancy and childbirth. The anxieties and inconveniences of pregnancy are a cost to the biological mother but a cost saving to the adoptive mother. Equally, all or most of the out-of-pocket expenses of the natural mother, including the obstetrician's fee, represent a cost saving to the adoptive mother. Therefore, at least as a first approximation, the only *net* cost of purchasing a baby in a free and competitive market should be the cost of the search, which would presumably be low.

Also, because the adoption agencies give substantial emphasis to the employment and financial situation of adoptive parents, a baby market might actually provide more opportunities for the poor to adopt than nonprice rationing does. If we are correct that the (acquisition) costs of babies in a lawful and competitive market would often be small, perhaps no more than the cost of an automobile, low-income families who would normally be considered financially ineligible by adoption agencies would be able in a free market to obtain a child.

Another prevalent criticism of the market, and again one that pertains primarily to the operations of the black market, is that fraud and related forms of dishonesty and overreaching pervade the market method of providing children for adoption. It is contended, for example, that the health of the child or of the child's mother is regularly misrepresented and that frequently after the sale is completed the seller will attempt to blackmail the adoptive parents.[26] Such abuses are probably largely the result of the fact that the market is an illegal one. Sellers cannot give legally enforceable guarantees of genealogy, health, or anything else to the prospective parents, and even the seller's adherence to the negotiated price is uncertain given the buyer's ina-

[26] Adoption and Foster Care 20-21.

bility to enforce the contract of sale by the usual legal procedures. Any market involving a complex and durable good (*i.e.*, one that yields services over a substantial period of time) would probably operate suboptimally in the absence of legally enforceable contracts or, at a minimum, regular, repetitive business relations between (the same) sellers and (the same) buyers. Both conditions are absent from the illegal baby market and this is the likeliest explanation for the number of complaints about the honesty of the sellers in that market.

To be sure, there are probably inherent limitations on the use of legal remedies to protect purchasers even in a legal baby market. For example, consideration of the welfare of the child might lead courts to refuse to grant rescission to a buyer as a remedy for breach of warranty (*i.e.*, allow him to return the child). And courts might be reluctant to order specific performance of a contract to put up a child for adoption. However, similar limitations are a traditional feature of remedies for personal-service contracts, yet do not appear to prevent effective enforcement of those contracts. Why should they do so in the case of baby sale contracts?

The foregoing analysis also enables us to place in perspective allegations that the sellers in the baby black market include a number of ex-convicts and other unsavory types and that the market reveals commercial "trafficking" at its ugliest.[27] An illegal market will naturally attract people who are less sensitive to the threat of criminal punishment than is normal and this group may include a large proportion of ex-convicts. But these characteristics of the market are an artifact of its illegality.

This analysis suggests a qualification to our earlier conclusion that legalizing the baby market would result in a reduction in the price of babies below the current black market level: the conclusion refers to a *quality-adjusted* price. The current illegality of baby selling reduces the benefits of transacting to the buyer by depriving him of the contractual protections that buyers in legal markets normally receive. Prospective adoptive parents would presumably be willing to pay more for a child whose health and genealogy were warranted in a legally enforceable instrument than they are willing to pay under the present system where the entire risk of any deviation from expected quality falls on them. Thus the effect of legalizing the baby market would be not only to shift the marginal cost of baby production and sale downward but to move the demand curve for adoptive children upward. Conceivably these movements could cancel each other out, resulting in no change from the current black-market prices, but even if they did consumer satisfaction would be increased. The same price would buy a higher-quality package of rights.

[27] Adoption and Foster Care 11, 159, 173.

B. *Criticisms of a Legal Market*

We now consider criticisms of baby selling that are applicable to a legal market rather than just to the present illegal market. The first is that the rationing of the supply of babies to would-be adoptive parents by price is not calculated to promote the best interests of the children, the objective of the adoption process.[28] This criticism cannot be dismissed as foolish. The ordinary presumption of free-enterprise economics is no stronger than that free exchange will maximize the satisfaction of the people trading, who in this case are the natural and adoptive parents. There is no presumption that the satisfactions of the thing traded, in most instances a meaningless concept, are also maximized. If we treat the child as a member of the community whose aggregate welfare we are interested in maximizing, there is no justification for ignoring how the child's satisfactions may be affected by alternative methods of adoption.

Very simply, the question is whether the price system would do as good a job as, or a better job than, adoption agencies in finding homes for children that would maximize their satisfactions in life. While there is no direct evidence on this point, some weak indirect evidence is provided in a followup study of independent adoptions which suggest that children adopted privately do as well as natural children. Witmer and her coauthors find that the distribution of I.Q. and a measure of school achievement, both at age 11, between children adopted privately and natural children of comparable socioeconomic backgrounds are virtually identical, although they also find that the adopted children did not perform as well on certain psychological tests as did the natural children.[29] It is true that some, perhaps most, independent adoptions do not involve price rationing, but the most important thing is that independent adoption involves a minimum of the sort of screening of prospective parents that the adoption agencies do. If children adopted without the screening seem nevertheless to do about as well as natural children, then one is entitled to be skeptical of the need for or value of the screening.

This conclusion is reinforced by the way in which adoption agencies screen. Agencies attempt to allocate children only to "fit" or caring parents. But after determining the pool of fit, or eligible-to-adopt, couples, they allocate available children among them on a first-come, first-served basis. The "fittest" parents are not placed at the head of the queue.

Further, and perhaps most important, agencies have no real information on the needs of a particular child they place for adoption beyond its need for

---

[28] Adoption and Foster Care 7.

[29] Helen L. Witmer, Elizabeth Herzog, Eugene A. Weinstein, & Mary E. Sullivan, Independent Adoptions: A Followup Study (1963).

love, warmth, food, and shelter. One cannot read from the face of a new-born whether he or she will be of above or below normal intelligence, or be naturally athletic, musical, or artistic. Hence agencies cannot be presumed to match these very real, if inaccessible, qualities of infants with the qualities of the adoptive parents any more effectively than a market would.

One valuable function agencies may perform is screening out people whose interest in having children is improper in an uncontroversial sense—people who wish to have children in order to abuse or make slaves of them. The criminal statutes punishing child abuse and neglect would remain applicable to babies adopted in a free market, but the extreme difficulty of detecting such crimes makes it unlikely, at least given current levels of punishment, that the criminal statutes alone are adequate. This may make some prescreening a more effective method of prevention than after-the-fact punishment. But the logical approach, then, is to require every prospective baby buyer to undergo some minimal background investigation. This approach would be analogous to licensing automobile drivers and seems as superior to the agency monopoly as licensing is to allocating automobiles on a nonprice basis.

Moreover, concern with child abuse should not be allowed to obscure the fact that abuse is not the normal motive for adopting a child. And once we put abuse aside, willingness to pay money for a baby would seem on the whole a reassuring factor from the standpoint of child welfare. Few people buy a car or a television set in order to smash it. In general, the more costly a purchase, the more care the purchaser will lavish on it. Recent studies suggest that the more costly it is for parents to obtain a child, the greater will be their investment in the child's quality attributes, such as health and education.[30]

A further point is that today some fetuses are probably aborted because the cost to the mother of carrying them to term and placing them for adoption exceeds the permissible return. In a free adoption market, some of the 900,000 fetuses aborted in 1974[31] would have been born and placed for adoption. If the welfare of these (potential) children is included in the calculation of the welfare of adopted children, both actual and potential, the heavy costs imposed on the market by adoption regulation may actually decrease child welfare.

Another objection to the market for babies is the alleged vulnerability of both natural and adoptive parents to overreaching by middlemen. Par-

---

[30] Gary S. Becker & H. Gregg Lewis, Interaction between Quality and Quantity of Children, in Economics of the Family, *supra* note 1, at 81; Gary S. Becker & Nigel Tomes, Child Endowments and the Quantity and Quality of Children, 84 J. Pol. Econ. S143-S162 (August 1976). Even critics of baby selling seem generally satisfied with the quality of the families who obtain children in the black market. See Adoption and Foster Care 13.

[31] Statistical Abstract, tab. 83, at 59.

enthood is thought to be so emotional a phenomenon that people cannot reason about it in the same way they reason about the goods and services normally traded in the market.[32] But many of those goods and services, such as medical care, also involve a strong emotional component, yet it has rarely been thought appropriate to exclude such goods from market exchange. And studies of marriage and procreation have shown that people in fact calculate in family matters, whether implicitly or explicitly, in the same way they do when purchasing ordinary goods and services.[33]

Other objections to legalizing the market in babies are more symbolic than pragmatic. For example, to accord a property right in the newborn child to the natural parents seems to some observers to smack of slavery.[34] But allowing a market in adoptions does not entail giving property rights to natural parents for all purposes. Laws forbidding child abuse and neglect would continue to be fully applicable to adoptive parents even if baby sales were permitted. Further, we are speaking only of sales of newborn infants, and do not suggest that parents should have a right to sell older children. The creation of such a right would require identification of the point at which the child is sufficiently mature to be entitled to a voice in his placement. However, the question is largely academic given the lack of any significant market for adopting older children.

Moreover, it is incorrect to equate the possession of property rights with the abuse of the property, even if the property is a human being. For example, a serious problem with foster care is the foster parents' lack of any property rights in the foster child. The better the job the foster parents do in raising the child, the more likely are the natural parents to reclaim the child and thereby prevent the foster parents from reaping the full fruits of their (emotional as well as financial) investment. This possibility in turn reduces the incentive of foster parents to invest in foster children, to the detriment of those children's welfare.

The antipathy to an explicit market in babies may be part of a broader wish to disguise facts that might be acutely uncomfortable if widely known. Were baby prices quoted as prices of soybean futures are quoted, a racial ranking of these prices would be evident, with white baby prices higher than nonwhite baby prices. One is reminded of Professor Tribe's objection to instructing the jury on the numerical probability implicit in the concept of proof beyond a reasonable doubt.[35] He argues that while the system of criminal justice would be unworkable if subjective certainty of guilt were re-

[32] See Adoption and Foster Care 12, 44.

[33] See studies in Economics of the Family, *supra* note 1.

[34] See Adoption and Foster Care 2–3.

[35] Laurence H. Tribe, Trial by Mathematics: Precision and Ritual in the Legal Process, 84 Harv. L. Rev. 1329 (1971).

quired, to acknowledge explicitly that people are convicted on less than such certainty might tear the social fabric. Similarly, anyone who thinks about the question will realize that prices for babies are racially stratified as a result of different supply and demand conditions in the different racial groups,[36] but perhaps bringing this fact out into the open would exacerbate racial tensions in our society.

Some people are also upset by the implications for the eugenic alteration of the human race that are presented by baby selling. Baby selling may seem logically and inevitably to lead to baby breeding,[37] for any market will generate incentives to improve the product as well as to optimize the price and quantity of the current quality level of the product. In a regime of free baby production and sale there might be efforts to breed children having desirable characteristics and, more broadly, to breed children with a *known* set of characteristics that could be matched up with those desired by prospective adoptive parents. Indeed, one can imagine, though with some difficulty, a growing separation between the production and rearing of children. No longer would a woman who wanted a child but who had a genetic trait that might jeopardize the child's health have to take her chances on a natural birth. She could find a very close genetic match-up to her and her husband's (healthy) genetic endowment in the baby market. However, so long as the market for eugenically bred babies did not extend beyond infertile couples and those with serious genetic disorders, the impact of a free baby market on the genetic composition and distribution of the human race at large would be small.

The emphasis placed by critics on the social costs of a free market in babies blurs what would probably be the greatest long-run effect of legalizing the baby market: inducing women who have unintentionally become pregnant to put up the child for adoption rather than raise it themselves or have an abortion. Some of the moral outrage directed against the idea of "trafficking" in babies bespeaks a failure to consider the implications of contemporary moral standards. At a time when illegitimacy was heavily stigmatized and abortion was illegal, to permit the sale of babies would have opened a breach in an otherwise solid wall of social disapproval of procreative activity outside of marriage. At the same time, the stigma of illegitimacy, coupled with the illegality of abortion, assured a reasonable flow of babies to the adoption market. Now that the stigma has diminished[38] and abortion has become a constitutional right, not only has the flow of babies to the (lawful) adoption market contracted but the practical alternatives to selling an unwanted baby have increasingly become either to retain it and raise

[36] See Table 1 *supra*.

[37] See Adoption and Foster Care 22-23.

[38] An economic reason for the diminution is suggested at p. 325 *supra*.

it as an illegitimate child, ordinarily with no father present, or to have an abortion. What social purposes are served by encouraging these alternatives to baby sale?[39]

The symbolic objections to baby sale must also be compared with the substantial costs that the present system imposes on childless couples, aborted fetuses (if they can be said to incur costs), and children who end up in foster care. In particular, many childless couples undergo extensive, costly, and often futile methods of fertility treatment in order to increase their chances of bearing a child. Some people produce unhealthy offspring (due to various genetic disorders) because of their strong desire to have children. And no doubt many people settle for childlessness because of the difficulties of obtaining an adopted child.

III. The Sources of Opposition to Baby Selling

Even though the benefits of free baby selling might well outweigh the costs, still it will come as no surprise to students of government regulation to find that there are well-organized interests opposed to an improvement in social welfare. The most vocal and organized opponents of the baby market are the adoption agencies. This is logical: we showed in Part I that both the supply of babies to agencies and agency revenues from adoption would be greater if the private market were regulated out of existence. Assuming that agencies would have no cost or efficiency advantage over private firms in an unregulated market, they would be reduced to operating at the competitive margin if such a market were permitted. They might even be competed out of the market.

To be sure, adoption agencies are generally not specialized in adoptions but engage in a variety of child welfare services—the primary one being foster care. Children placed in foster care are maintained at agency expense, although some fraction of the maintenance expenditures may be offset by government reimbursement. Today some 350,000 children are in foster care at an annual expense to the U.S. government alone of some $700 million.[40] Clearly, healthy infants and older, perhaps less healthy, children are substitutes in adoption, albeit imperfect substitutes. By obtaining exclusive control over the supply of both "first-quality" adoptive children and "second-quality" children residing in foster care but available for adoption, agencies are able to internalize the substitution possibilities between them. Agencies

---

[39] Cf. Raymond M. Herbenich, Remarks on Abortion, Abandonment, and Adoption Opportunities, 5 Philo. & Pub. Affairs 98, 103 (1975), proposing a tax credit for the natural parents to encourage carrying a fetus to term and placing the baby for adoption rather than aborting it.

[40] Opportunities for Adoption Act of 1977, S. Rep. No. 95-167, 95th Cong., 1st Sess. 17 (1977).

can charge a higher price for the children they place for adoption, thus increasing not only their revenues from adoption but also the demand for children who would otherwise be placed or remain in foster care at the agency's expense. Conversely, if agency revenues derive primarily from foster care, the agencies can manipulate the relative price of adopting "first-quality" children over "second-quality" children to reduce the net flow of children out of foster care.

The group that has the largest stake in the adoption agencies' net revenues is their professional personnel. If the principal effect of eliminating the agency monopoly in adoptions was to force agencies to operate at the competitive margin, it would surely reduce any rents now being received by agency personnel. Nor can it be argued that if baby selling were legalized the agency personnel would simply become the middlemen of the legal market; if the Securities and Exchange Commission were abolished, few of its personnel would become stockbrokers. One is not surprised that professional social workers' organizations have been strong proponents of governmental restrictions on nonagency adoptions.

Potentially allied to the agencies and the social welfare professionals who staff them in opposition to baby selling are those prospective adoptive parents who by virtue of their contacts and general sophistication are able to jump to the head of the queue or procure a baby easily in the (lawful) independent market, either way paying less than they would have to pay in a free market. The analogy is to the effect of usury laws in reducing the interest rate paid by the most credit-worthy borrowers.

The potential supporters of baby selling are difficult to organize in an effective political coalition. They consist of unborn babies, children in foster care, taxpayers (each only trivially burdened by the costs of foster care), and people who have only a low probability of ever wanting to adopt a baby, as well as couples currently wanting to adopt one. The members of this last group have the most concentrated interest in a free baby market, but they are relatively few and widely scattered at any given time.

IV. INTERIM STEPS TOWARD A FULL-FLEDGED BABY MARKET

We close by speculating briefly on the possibility of taking some tentative and reversible steps toward a free baby market in order to determine experimentally the social costs and benefits of using the market in this area. Important characteristics of a market could be simulated if one or more adoption agencies, which typically already vary their fees for adoption according to the income of the prospective parents, would simply use the surplus income generated by the higher fees to make side payments to pregnant women contemplating abortion to induce them instead to have the child and put it up for adoption.

This experiment would yield evidence with respect to both the demand and supply conditions in the adoption market and would provide information both on the value that prospective adoptive parents attach to being able to obtain a baby and on the price necessary to induce pregnant women to substitute birth for abortion. Follow-up studies of the adopted children, comparing them with children that had been adopted by parents paying lower fees, would help answer the question whether the payment of a stiff fee has adverse consequences on the welfare of the child.

Some states appear not to limit the fees that adoption agencies pay to natural parents. The experiment we propose could be implemented in such states without new legislation.

[3]

Rings and Promises

MARGARET F. BRINIG
George Mason University

1. INTRODUCTION

My mother had an engagement ring, but neither of my grandmothers did, although both my grandfathers were wealthy enough to afford them. Before 1930, diamond rings were certainly available. The South African diamond mines were discovered in 1880, and they soon replaced the rapidly disappearing supply of diamonds from India and Brazil (McCarthy). In fact, the first reported diamond engagement ring was given by the Emperor Maximilian to Mary of Burgundy in 1377 (Kunz: 234–35). Diamonds were associated in this country with engagement beginning in the 1840s, although they were at first given to men as well as women (Rothman: 161).

However, before the Depression, diamond rings were not considered a requisite for betrothal by most Americans. (Kunz: 230; Rothman: 161). What then made women rather suddenly demand diamonds on the occasion of their engagement, so that by 1945 the "typical" bride wore "a brilliant diamond engagement ring and a wedding ring to match in design?" (McCarthy: frontispiece).

I wish to acknowledge the thoughtful contributions of many colleagues, especially including Barry Adler, William Bishop, Steven Crafton, and Steven Eagle of the law faculty, and Michael Alexeev, Robert Tollison, and Jenny Wahl of the economics departments of George Mason University and St. Olaf's College. David Levy of George Mason gave invaluable help with the econometrics. Thanks is also owed to my research assistant, Laurie LaCorte, and three anonymous referees.

Journal of Law, Economics, and Organization vol. 6, no. 1 Spring 1990
© 1990 by Yale University. All rights reserved. ISSN 8756-6222

204 / JOURNAL OF LAW, ECONOMICS, AND ORGANIZATION VI:1, 1990

The diamond ring rapidly changed from a relatively obscure token of affection to what amounted to an American tradition. It is customary to explain such a shift in demand in terms of an increase in income, a change in relative prices, or a change in tastes. This assumes a stable legal setting—that contracts are enforceable. But if the enforceability of a contract is problematic, what formerly was a relatively costly (hence unused) form of private ordering may become more viable (Kronman: 5).[1] This paper looks at the change in America's demand for diamonds during the period 1930–1985, not as a Madison Avenue success story, but rather as a natural outgrowth of economic processes. The event beginning the movement toward diamond engagement rings was the abolition, with great fanfare, of a now relatively obscure cause of action called the "breach of promise to marry."

2. THE BREACH OF PROMISE ACTION

The breach of promise action entitled a woman whose fiancé had broken off their engagement to sue him in assumpsit for damages, including the actual expenses she had incurred in reliance on the marriage. She might also recover for her embarrassment, humiliation, and loss of other marriage opportunities.[2]

Until fairly recently, a woman's marriage was necessary to secure her social position. An "old maid" would not only be scorned because she was not attractive enough to snag a husband, but also would be disadvantaged because in later life she would not be secure financially (*Wightman v. Coates*, 15 Mass. 2, 2–4 (1918); Glendon: 31–32; Craik: 166–67; Grossberg: 36). Marriage was, as one writer noted, the "one career open to her," and once she had made her choice of husbands, the woman's "options were suddenly, irrevocably gone" (Rothman: 163; Brinig and Carbone: 872–74).

But there was more to the doctrine than this. Many, if not most, women

---

1. Other forms of property have been exchanged at engagement or marriage since antiquity. The dower gift of land or livestock by the bride's father would be returned by the man if the marriage was not consummated, but it did not belong to the woman in any event. Since the man could presumably marry his second choice, obtaining a like dower price, he would not be substantially damaged. She, however, might be precluded from marrying as well, and she might be precluded from marrying at all if she had lost her virginity (Jenks: 313). The transformation of agrarian forms of wealth to less tangible assets may be one reason why rings, as opposed to other gifts, became useful (Glenn, 1981). The breaking of a formal engagement, with return of property, was the type of "divorce" originally contemplated by Joseph in the Bible story when he was confronted by Mary's pregnancy (Matthew 1:19–20).

2. The early action for breach of promise to marry was within the jurisdiction of the English ecclesiastical courts, and in many cases the filing of the action resulted in specific performance of the marriage contract rather than an award of damages since the man was financially coerced into marriage to prevent the suit (Jenks: 303; Grossberg: 34). One of the reasons given in favor of abolishing the action was that these forced marriages ought not to be encouraged (*Fearon v. Treanor*, 272 N.Y. 268, 5 N.E.2d 815, 817 (1936); *Virginia Law Review*: 314; *Marquette Law Review*: 341).

who brought such actions had not only lost a husband, but also their virginity. Particularly during the period between the two world wars, a woman was expected to remain chaste until the time of her engagement (Kinsey, 1948a: 336, 1948b: 364; Gebhard and Johnson: 288). Once she was betrothed, however, sexual intimacy with her fiancé reportedly occurred nearly half the time (Kinsey, 1948a: 336; 1948b: 364). All this was well and good, but if the marriage never came about, she was irretrievably barred from offering an unblemished self to a new suitor[3] and suffered a loss in "market value" (Feinsinger, 1935a: 983). While a man could pretend inexperience, a woman's virginity or lack of it was a verifiable physical fact.[4] Because of the importance of premarital chastity, damages in breach of promise actions where seduction (intercourse) had occurred were far more substantial than in cases where no sexual intimacy was alleged (*Paul v. Frazier*, 3 Mass. 71, 73 (1807); Grossberg: 46–47). The trials themselves frequently became public spectacles because of testimony regarding the woman's previous chastity (or lack of the same).[5] By the beginning of the Depression, the breach of promise suit came to be regarded as legally sanctioned blackmail, a threat to marriage and the family (Grossberg: 62–63).[6]

In 1935, a legislator from Indiana sponsored a bill abolishing the heartbalm actions in that state (Byrnes: 94; *Marquette University*). Almost immediately thereafter, similar statutes were passed in most of the other major urban jurisdictions,[7] so that by 1945, sixteen states had eliminated breach of marriage promise.[8] Today, there are only scattered reported breach of marriage promise decisions from those few jurisdictions where the action remains viable.

3. *Bennett v. Beam*, 42 Mich. 346, 351 (1880); *Scharringhaus v. Hazen*, 269 Ky. 425, 107 S.W.2d 329 (1937); *Berry v. Da Costa* [1966] L.R., 1 C.P. 331); Cousens: 372.
4. One author notes that "our courts seem to demand only that the plaintiff be *virgo intacta*. All is a question of the condition of the flesh. The mind may be poisoned with filth, and the character hardened by ugly habits; in short, the spiritual hymen may have suffered many a breach, but if the physical one is not intact, the defendant will have no better alternative than to marry her or pay damages" (Brockelbank: 8).
5. *Van Houten v. Morse*, 162 Mass. 414, 38 N.E. 705 (1894); *Barrett v. Vander-Meulen*, 264 Ky. 441, 94 S.W.2d 983 (1936); *Baylor Law Review*.
6. There are relatively few appellate breach of promise cases that have been reported at any time. This might be because the action has never had a great deal of use. It is more probable, however, that in most cases there was no interesting legal question involved that was worth the various costs of an appeal to the defendant, that the case was "settled" by marriage of the parties either before a trial or after a verdict for damages, or that the very fact that the action existed deterred men from breaking engagements. For a discussion of the deterrent effect of laws regarding morality, see Devlin.
7. In 1935, in addition to Indiana, breach of promise actions were abolished in Alabama, Illinois, New York, New Jersey, Michigan, and Pennsylvania.
8. These states, with the year of legislation, are North Dakota (1877), Illinois (1935), Indiana (1935), New Jersey (1935), Pennsylvania (1935), Alabama (1935), New York (1935), Michigan (1935), Colorado (1937), Massachusetts (1938), California (1939), Maine (1941), Wyoming (1941), New Hampshire (1941), Nevada (1943), and Florida (1945).

3. DEMAND FOR DIAMONDS

At the same time the cause of action for breach of promise was being reconsidered, the diamond industry had faced a period of lessened demand and increased supply. For a few years following 1932, diamonds were stockpiled in Europe to prevent a glut on the market (Epstein, 1982a: 85–87). By the mid-1930s, DeBeers, the diamond-importing institution, was holding stocks valued at four times its annual sales (Koskoff: 272). New sources of diamonds had been discovered, particularly in the Soviet Union, and the price of diamonds had been in decline for some years (Koskoff: 272).[9]

There was not only a greater supply but also a reduced demand, for sales during the twenty-year period prior to 1939 declined by nearly 100 percent (Epstein, 1982b: 122–23). National advertising was thought of as "vulgar" before the Great Depression (Koskoff: 272), but in 1939, four years after the first states abolished the breach of promise action, DeBeers formed an alliance with a prominent New York advertising agency, Ayers, and prepared to release a significant advertising campaign focused on the slogan that "a diamond is forever" (Koskoff).

The advertising agency from the start aimed at a national market. One of its more successful techniques was exploitation of the burgeoning film industry: Hollywood stars were given large and conspicuous diamonds to wear off stage, and special scenes involving the presentation of engagement rings were introduced into popular movies after intervention by Ayers (Epstein, 1982b: 123–32), a notable example of which is the Mae West–Cary Grant classic *She Done Him Wrong*.[10]

The industry enjoyed a phenomenal success during the period following 1935, and by 1965, 80 percent of all brides chose diamond engagement rings (Ward et al.: 144). DeBeers attributed the changing market to the Ayers advertising campaign (Epstein, 1982b: 125–63), but, in fact, the market for diamonds began its growth four years before national advertising when the breach of promise action was first abolished in a significant number of important states. (North Dakota had abrogated breach of marriage promise actions

9. The diamond industry, which is represented by one importer, DeBeers (Epstein, 1982a: 23), has completely controlled the quantity of diamonds brought into the United States since its organization in South Africa in 1888 (Epstein, 1982a: 23; 1982b: 81). DeBeers therefore could meter the supply of diamonds, setting price according to the downward-sloping demand curve characteristic of a monopoly.

10. The sentiments of the heroine in that movie are echoed in the trial court's observations in *Goldstein v. Rosenthal*, 56 N.Y. Misc. 2d 311, 288 N.Y.S.2d 503 (1968): "When the burning blue white flames of romance died out, all that was left was the blue white diamond. The defendant does not wish to keep plaintiff's hand, but she does wish to keep his ring on her finger. In the words of the popular song: 'She took it off her finger, now it doesn't mean a thing.'"

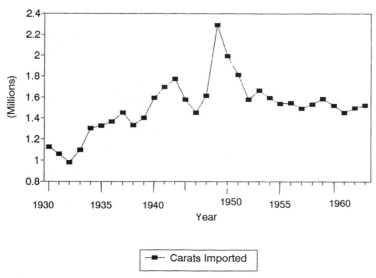

Figure 1. Diamond imports by year.

in the nineteenth century, but they were at least theoretically available in the other 47 states.[11])

The selection of states that abolished the action in the ten years following 1935 itself presents an interesting study. A glance at a map shows that they appear to have little in common: both urban and farm states, with an average per capita income approximating the norm for the period. What is interesting, however, is that the marriage rate in these states before abolition of the action greatly exceeded the contemporary national rate (67 percent of the United States marriages in 1935, with only 47.7 percent of the population). This suggests that the action for damages made people marry who otherwise would not. The scanty legislative history for the statutes abolishing breach of promise indicates that one motivation, and perhaps the primary one, may have been removal of a vestige of women's historic legal inferiority to men

---

11. In most of the discussion in the text, I have ignored the fact that North Dakota apparently has had a statute abolishing breach of promise since 1877. This may have been because it was one of the original "divorce mill" states, enjoying popularity for dissolution of marriage during the period 1871–99 (Jones: 25 (map), 33 (text)). As with Nevada, there may have been a corresponding rise in the marriage rate during that time. Unfortunately, the best statistical study (U.S. Bureau of the Census, 1968: Table 7, p. 28) does not contain any information about the Dakotas prior to 1890.

208 / JOURNAL OF LAW, ECONOMICS, AND ORGANIZATION VI:1, 1990

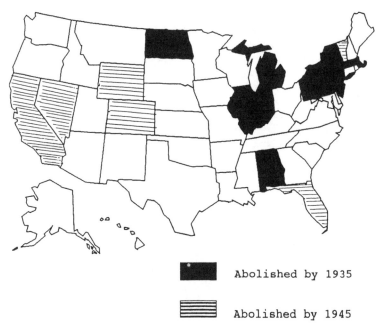

Figure 2. States abolishing breach of promise.

(Feinsinger, 1935a). States especially concerned with gender equality would therefore be expected to be the leaders in this reform, and some were involved at an early stage in the abolition movement. Other states abolishing breach of promise before 1945, including Nevada, Alabama, Florida, and Indiana, had always been important sources for migratory divorces.

4. EXPLAINING THE CHANGE IN DEMAND

The change in demand for diamonds can be studied empirically by analyzing the various factors that might have led to an increased desire for diamonds and observing what turns out to be the most significant. The dramatic increase in demand could be the result of a dramatic decrease in price. Or DeBeers' national advertising campaign could have caused the surge in popularity of diamonds.[12] This has certainly been the position taken by the industry (Epstein, 1982b). The hypothesis of interest here, the bond or

12. This does not explain the changes before 1939, the year when the Ayers agency assumed the DeBeers account.

pledge hypothesis,[13] is that the statutory changes abolishing the breach of promise action explain the increase in the demand for diamonds.

An alternative explanation is that Americans during and after the Depression began to prefer holding their portfolio in tangible assets that would be more secure than paper currency or bank deposits. In particular, it is possible that diamonds served an investment function during the uncertain financial climate of World War II. The thesis that investment patterns changed does not fit the more modern data, however, because the decline of interest in diamond engagement rings began before the relaxation in regulation of financial institutions that has led to Americans holding wealth in more liquid forms. In addition, advertising by the diamond industry should have tempered any trend toward the substantial use of diamonds for investment. One important component of the massive advertising campaign was designed to convince the public that diamonds could not be resold, and the DeBeers cartel has enforced this by threatening to cut off supply to dealers who bought diamonds back from purchasers (Epstein, 1982a: 25).

It is difficult, if not impossible, to get information about engagement ring sales fifty or more years ago, since even the large and well-known New York jewelers did not keep sales records by such categories at that time. A proxy for diamond sales in general, of which engagement rings were by all accounts the largest portion (Koskoff; Epstein, 1982b), can be found by examining the quantity of diamonds imported into the United States. However, even these figures become complicated by the emigration of most diamond cutters from Europe to the United States during the period 1938–40 (Historical Abstracts). Before this time, most diamonds used in engagement rings were cut in Europe and imported as cut diamonds. After this time, the cutting took place in New York, so that uncut diamonds of gem quality made up the majority of imports (Epstein, 1982b). My analysis therefore uses as a dependent variable a composite of figures reflecting cut gem quality diamonds before 1939 and uncut diamonds thereafter.[14] Independent variables to test

---

13. The utility of a diamond ring as collateral depends upon whether it belongs to the nonbreaching party. Even in Roman law, this was true in the case of engagement rings (*Tulane University*: 501). "The ring is a pledge to bind the contract to marry and it is given on the understanding that the party who breaks the contract must return it" (*Jacobs v. Davis*, [1917] K.B. 532). This conditional gift rule has survived the abolition of the breach of contract to marry in most states. See, e.g., *Bohn v. Lowe*, 146 Mich. App. 325, 379 N.W.2d 485 (1985); *Friedman v. Geller*, 82 Misc. 2d 291, 368 N.Y.S.2d 980 (1975); *Urbanus v. Burns*, 300 Ill. App. 207, 20 N.E.2d 869 (1939); *Gikas v. Nicholis*, 71 A.2d 785 (N.H. 1950); *Pavlicic v. Vogtsberger*, 390 Pa. 502, 136 A.2d 127 (1957); *Ruehling v. Hornung*, 98 Pa. Super. 535 (1939). Great Britain reaches a similar result by statute. Law Reform (Miscellaneous Provisions) Act 1970 (c.33) section 3(2).

Of course the reciprocal is true: a breach by the donor (man) would enable the donee (woman) to retain the ring. (*Sloine v. Levine*, 11 N.J. Misc. 899, 168 A. 849 (1933); *Notre Dame Lawyer*: 687).

14. The industry, which has kept detailed records of sales only for the last eight years and has been organized (through the Ayers agency) only since 1938, has no records by state, by

the hypotheses of interest are price (PRICE), advertising (ADSDUMMY),[15] the percentage of population living in states abolishing the action (PERCENT), and investment during World War II (WARDUMMY).[16] I also include as an explanatory variable the population of marriageable age (POP), as that surely will affect demand independent of the various hypotheses. Given the number of endogenous right-hand side variables in this demand equation, a system of equations—with dependent variables demand, price, and percentage of states with statutes abolishing breach of promise actions—was estimated by Three Stage Least Squares (3SLS).

The explanatory variables for the price chosen by DeBeers (PRICE) are the presence of the advertising campaign conducted by DeBeers (ADSDUMMY), per capita income (PCINC), and the stock of "used" diamonds (USEC).[17] The explanatory variables for the third equation, explaining which states abolished the breach of promise action, are the marriage rate (MARRIAGE), per capita income (PCINC), and a time series function (YEAR).

A Box-Cox study (Judge et al.: 555) of these equations revealed that they were not linear. Logarithmic transformations were therefore done on the non-dummy variables, and a 3SLS regression was performed on the transformed equations. The regression results are summarized in Table 1.

The data show that four factors explain much of the increase in the number of diamonds demanded in the period 1935–1960. The most important explanatory variable is the abolition of the breach of promise action. The standardized β coefficient of the bonding hypothesis variable is the largest at 0.52, and it is statistically significant. The population of marriageable age was also significant, with the second largest β coefficient of 0.36. The World War

---

merchant, or even by type of jewelry for these earlier years. The most reliable data come from *Navigation and Trade*, a journal available in the U.S. Department of Commerce library, and the original source for the Statistical Abstracts. These figures at least separate diamonds suitable for jewelry from those useful only in industry. Not even these figures are available for 1939, 1943, 1945, and 1947.

15. A dummy variable was included to represent the presence or absence of advertising because expenditures for the DeBeer's campaign are not available.

16. Because World War II might have made importation difficult or increased the desire to hold diamonds for investment purposes, a dummy variable for war/no war was put into the regression equation. Ruling out a more general investment hypothesis involves substantial data collection problems. One problem, again, is that the jewelry industry has no figures on jewelry sales during this period, and in any event, does not keep data for diamonds as opposed to other jewelry sold. Both gold and silver might have been used for secure investment as well as diamonds, but both are produced to some extent in the United States, so that import data do not account for the whole supply. Further, both precious metals are used industrially as well as for investment purposes. Government import figures separate gem-quality from industrial-type diamonds.

17. Since diamonds are a durable good, the stock of diamonds already sold should have an effect on price (Bulow). Although DeBeers' campaign was in part designed to convince the public that "diamonds were forever" and not to be resold, the stock of diamonds in the United States was also included as a variable.

Table 1. Regression Analysis (3SLS)

Variable	Coefficient	St. Error	T-Ratio	β
PRICE[a]				
ADSDUMMY	0.35772	0.11383	3.1425	0.53298
LOGPCINC	0.59504	0.12517	4.7538	1.2019
LOGUSEC	−0.19363	0.63622E-01	−3.0434	−0.85784
LOGCOMPOSIT[b]				
WARDUMMY	−0.87820	0.24987	−3.5146	−0.32495
ADSDUMMY	−0.19739	0.60364	−0.32699	−0.095013
LOGPERCENT	0.33977	0.11866	2.8635	0.51525
LOGPOP	2.4111	0.87293	2.7621	0.36042
LOGPRICE	0.86328	0.71901	1.2007	0.27891
LPERCENT[c]				
LOGMARR	4.3610	1.0878	4.0089	0.45748
LOGPCINC	0.076996	0.90321	−0.085247	−0.033133
LOG YEAR	218.43	103.23	2.1160	0.83156

Note: System R^2 = 0.9797; χ^2 −116.91 with 11 D.F.
[a] f(ADSDUMMY, LOGPCINC, LOGUSEC)
[b] f(WARDUMMY, ADSDUMMY, LOGPERCENT, LOGPOP, LOGPRICE)
[c] f(LOGMARR, LOGPCINC, LOGYEAR)

II dummy was almost as important as marriageable population (β = 0.33) and was also significant, although it is negatively related to diamond demand. This suggests that the hardships and absences of the war had a greater effect on demand than the desire to purchase diamonds as investment instruments. Although there is a fourth variable with a sizable β coefficient, price (β = 0.28), it is not statistically significant.[18] These results support the hypothesis that abolition of the breach of promise action created a need for a bonding device, a need fulfilled by the diamond engagement ring.

5. MODERN DEMAND FOR DIAMOND ENGAGEMENT RINGS

Another way of testing the hypothesis that diamond engagement rings serve as pledges is to see what happened to the demand for rings when social mores changed so that sexual intimacy was no longer confined to marriage and engagement.[19] Although from 1965 to 1980 real per capita income con-

18. The insignificance of the estimated coefficient shows that nothing can be assumed from the addition of price to the equation. To the extent that the positive sign means anything, it is suggestive of a series of positive supply points or the outward movement of the demand curve. As Table 1 indicates, the price of diamonds set by DeBeers was largely a function of its advertising campaign (raising the price), per capita income, showing that prices could be raised as people had more to spend on "luxury" goods, and the increasing stock of diamonds (negatively related).

The final endogenous variable, the abolition of the breach of promise action, was positively related to a state's high marriage rate and to the time trend variable.

19. This is not to say that there is no current relationship between permission for sexual

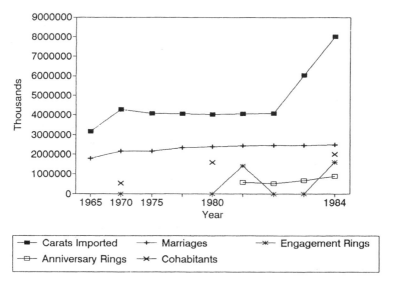

Figure 3. Modern trends.

tinued to increase, the demand for engagement rings leveled off and actually decreased for this more recent period, when cohabitation of nonmarried couples was no longer a curiosity (Koskoff: 273–74, 277).

There has been a recent decline in the number of marriages as more women enter the job market and more couples postpone marriage until education is complete and careers established (England and Farkas). However, since sexual activity by women is not so completely confined to marriage, the current need for a bonding device before consent to intercourse is greatly diminished. DeBeers has had to reach a new market: diamond ads of the late 1980s no longer show engagement rings, but rather diamond-studded wedding bands, anniversary rings, and other diamond jewelry. Ayers' statistics show that since 1980, and unlike the earlier period, engagement rings have never exceeded 20 percent of diamond jewelry sales (Ayers Research: 6–7).[20] Although diamond sales in general increased, the demand for

---

intercourse and the wearing of the engagement ring. Interestingly, Ayers, the public relations firm for the DeBeers organization, notes that the element of "surprise, even if it is feigned, plays the same role of accommodating dissonance in accepting a diamond gift as it does in prim sexual seductions: it permits the woman to pretend that she has not actively participated in the decision" (Epstein, 1982b: 138). A recent *Life* magazine ad for DeBeers is suggestively captioned "Want to Turn on the Heat?" (February, 1989).

20. Unfortunately, because no statistics were kept in the earlier period, one must rely on

engagement rings has changed, for the wearing of a diamond symbolic of engagement is no longer a prerequisite to premarital intimacy and because the cost to a woman of a broken engagement is no longer as significant.

6. CONCLUSION

Students of economics are told that demand curves shift outward because of changes in demographics or, less frequently, tastes. Becker and Stigler argued that, in fact, tastes are relatively constant: that any widespread human behavior can be explained by utility maximization (76). They illustrated their theory by discussing such "tastes" as those for addiction, custom and tradition, and advertising. Although they presented a sophisticated mathematical model, they did not attempt to test their hypotheses empirically. This is an empirical study that proves them as well as Kronman right: looking at one such change in tastes with a less than obvious economic explanation, I have found some evidence that engagement rings were part of an extralegal contract guarantee, so that the "ring is a pledge to bind the contract to marry and it is given on the understanding that the party who breaks the contract must return it" (*Jacobs v. Davis,* [1917] 2 K.B. 532).

The change in demand for diamond engagement rings may therefore be explained by an increase in need for such a bond because of the abolition of a cause of action for breach of marriage promise. My guess, having apparently found a reason for the change in demand for diamond engagement rings, is that many other mysterious demand changes could be accounted for as well, given some thought as to what the commodity might mean to consumers and some exploration of the legal or other changes of the time during which the demand change occurred.

REFERENCES

Ayers Research. 1987. *The Market for Diamond Jewelry—United States—1986.* New York: N. W. Ayers.

Baylor Law Review. 1965. "Comment: Breach of Promise to Marry," *Baylor Law Review* 51.

Becker, Gary, and George Stigler. 1977. "De Gustibus Non Est Disputandum," 69 *American Economic Review* 76.

Brinig, Margaret, and June Carbone. 1988. "The Reliance Interest in Marriage and Divorce," 62 *Tulane Law Review* 855.

Brockelbank, W. J. 1946. "The Nature of the Promise to Marry—A Study in Comparative Law," 41 *Illinois Law Review* 1.

---

qualitative evidence that engagement rings constituted the bulk of the diamond trade. Certainly the secondary sources believe that this is so (Epstein, 1982b; Koskoff, 1981). Further, the massive advertising directed at the market for diamond engagement rings suggests their importance to the industry.

214 / JOURNAL OF LAW, ECONOMICS, AND ORGANIZATION VI:1, 1990

Bulow, Jeremy. 1982. "Durable-Goods Monopolists," 90 *Journal of Political Economy* 314.

Byrnes, Jane. 1943. "The Illinois Anti-Heart Balm Law," 38 *Illinois Law Review* 94.

Cousens, Theodore. 1932. "The Law of Damages as Applied to Breach of Promise of Marriage," 17 *Cornell Law Quarterly* 367.

Craik, Elizabeth. 1984. *Marriage and Property.* Aberdeen: Aberdeen University Press.

Devlin, Sir Patrick. 1961. *Law and Morals.* Birmingham: Holdsworth Club of the University of Birmingham.

Ellman, Ira. 1989. "The Theory of Alimony," 77 *California Law Review* 1.

England, Paula, and Gary Farkas. 1986. *Households, Employment and Gender.* New York: Aldine Publications.

Epstein, Edward, 1982a. "Have You Ever Tried to Sell a Diamond?" *Atlantic Monthly* 23.

———. 1982b. *The Rise and Fall of Diamonds.* New York: Simon and Schuster.

Feinsinger, N. P., 1935a. "Legislative Attack on 'Heart Balm,'" 33 *Michigan Law Review* 979.

———. 1935b. "Current Legislation Affecting Breach of Promise to Marry, Alienation of Affections, and Related Actions," 10 *Wisconsin Law Review* 417.

Gebhard, Paul, and Alan Johnson. 1979. *The Kinsey Data: Marginal Tabulations of the 1938–63 Interviews Conducted by the Institute for Sex Research.* Philadelphia: Saunders.

Glendon, Mary Ann. 1981. *The New Family and the New Property.* Boston: Butterworths.

Grossberg, Michael. 1985. *Governing the Hearth.* Chapel Hill: University of North Carolina Press.

Jenks, Edward. 1913. *A Short History of English Law.* Boston: Little, Brown.

Jones, Mary. 1987. *An Historical Geography of Changing Divorce Law in the United States.* New York: Garland.

Judge, George, Carter Hill, William Griffiths, Helmut Luthepohl, and Lee Tsoung-Chao. 1988. *Introduction to the Theory and Practice of Econometrics.* New York: John Wiley.

Kane, Frederick. 1936. "Heart Balm and Public Policy," 5 *Fordham Law Review* 66.

Kinsey, Alfred, Wardell Pomeroy, and Clyde Martin. 1948a. *Sexual Behavior in the Human Female.* Philadelphia: Saunders.

———. 1948b. *Sexual Behavior in the Human Male.* Philadelphia: Saunders.

Koskoff, David. 1981. *The Diamond World.* New York: Harper & Row.

Kronman, Anthony. 1985. "Contracts in a State of Nature," 1 *Journal of Law, Economics, and Organization* 5.

Kunz, George. 1917. *Rings for the Finger.* Philadelphia: J. B. Lippincott.

Marquette Law Review. 1959. "Comment, Abolition of Breach of Promise in Wisconsin—Scope and Constitutionality," 43 *Marquette Law Review* 341.

McCarthy, James. 1945. *Rings Through the Ages.* New York: Harper and Brothers.

Notre Dame Lawyer. 1956. "Comment: Recovery of Antenuptial Gifts," 25 *Notre Dame Lawyer* 684.

Rothman, Ellen. 1987. *Hands and Hearts: A History of Courtship in America.* Cambridge, MA: Harvard University Press.

Tulane Law Review. 1950. "Note, Obligations—Breach of Promise to Marry, Art. 1934, La. Civil Code of 1870," 24 *Tulane Law Review* 501.

United States Bureau of the Census. 1987. *The Historical Abstracts.*

United States Department of Commerce, various years. *Navigation and Trade.*

United States Department of Health, Education and Welfare, 1968. *100 Years of Marriage and Divorce Statistics, United States, 1867–1967.*

Virginia Law Review. 1947. "Comment, Twelve Years with the 'Heart Balm Acts,'" 33 *Virginia Law Review* 314.

Ward, Ann, John Cherry, Charlotte Gere, and Barbara Cartlidge. 1981. *Rings Through the Ages.* New York: Rizzoli.

Wisconsin Law Review. 1935. "Comment, Current Legislation Affecting Breach of Promise to Marry, Alienation of Affections, and Related Actions," 10 *Wisconsin Law Review* 417.

[4]

Marry Me, Bill: Should Cohabitation Be the (Legal) Default Option?

Margaret F. Brinig[*]

Steven L. Nock[**]

> *Bill, I love you so, I always will, I look at you and see the passion eyes of May. Oh, but am I ever gonna see my wedding day?*
>
> *Oh, I was on your side, Bill, when you were losin'. I'd never scheme or lie Bill, there's been no foolin'. But kisses and love won't carry me 'til you marry me, Bill . . .*
>
> "Wedding Bell Blues," by Laura Nyro
Recorded by The 5th Dimension

INTRODUCTION

Are cohabitation and marriage similar enough to warrant similar legal treatment? Earlier public reports on cohabitation have focused on the question of whether cohabitation before marriage increases or decreases the divorce rate.[1]

But increasingly cohabitation is being proposed not as a testing ground for marriage, but as a functional substitute for it. The trend in family law and scholarship in Europe and Canada is to treat married and cohabiting couples similarly, or even identically.[2]

---

[*] William G. Hammond Professor of Law, College of Law, University of Iowa, and member of the New Jersey, Washington, D.C., Virginia, and Iowa bars. Ph.D., George Mason University, 1994; J.D., Seton Hall University, 1973; B.A., Duke University, 1970.

[**] Professor of Sociology, University of Virginia. Ph.D., 1976, Sociology with Distinction, University of Massachusetts, Amherst; M.A., 1975, Sociology, University of Massachusetts, Amherst; B.A., Sociology and Psychology, University of Richmond, 1972.

1. *See*, e.g., David Popenoe & Barbara Dafoe Whitehead, *Should We Live Together? What Young Adults Need to Know about Cohabitation Before Marriage: a Comprehensive Review of Recent Research* (Rutgers University National Marriage Project 2d ed. 2002) *available at* http://marriage.rutgers.edu/Publications/swlt2.pdf (visited March 31, 2004).

2. *See, e.g.*, Winifred Holland, *Intimate Relationships in the New Millennium: The Assimilation of Marriage and Cohabitation?*, 17 Can. J. Fam. L. 114 (2000); Miron v. Trudel, [1995] 2 S.C.R. 418, 13 R.F.L. (4th) 1; M v. H, [1999] 2 S.C.R. 3, 46 R.F.L. (4th) 32; Katharina Boele-Woelki, *Private International Law Aspects of Registered Partnerships and Other Forms of Non-Marital Cohabitation in*

404   *LOUISIANA LAW REVIEW*   [Vol. 64

In this country, the American Law Institute [ALI] recently proposed that, at least when it comes to the law of dissolution, couples who have been living together for a substantial period of time should be treated the same as married couples.[3] The ALI recommendations carry particularly intellectual weight, given they are the product of ten years of study by one of the most influential and mainstream voices on legal reform.

These legal and intellectual trends no doubt reflect in part the increasing prevalence of cohabiting couples including cohabiting families. Our best evidence (from 1991) indicates that twelve percent of cohabiting couples have a biological child together.[4] Births to cohabiting women now account for thirty-nine percent of all births to unmarried women.[5]

How will "institutionalizing" cohabitation, or treating cohabiting couples as if they were married, affect the couple, their children, and the well-being of marriage? These are the questions that need to be asked and answered, before courts, state legislators, policymakers, and scholars embrace legal proposals to treat cohabitation as a form of marriage.

Should law and social policy actively support the cohabitation option and if so, how? This could be accomplished by removing barriers to it. These might include laws against fornication,[6] sodomy,[7]

Europe, 60 La. L. Rev. 1063 (2000) (discussing recent statutory enactments giving legal status to nonmarital cohabitation between same or opposite-sex partners).

3. American Law Institute, Principles of Family Dissolution, Chapter 6 (2002).

4. Larry L. Bumpass, Andrew J. Cherlin & James A. Sweet, *The Role of Cohabitation in Declining Rates of Marriage*, 53 J. Marriage & Fam. 913 (1991).

5. Larry L. Bumpass & Hsien-Hen Lu, *Trends in Cohabitation and Implications for Children's Family Contexts in the United States*, 54 Population Stud. 29 (2000).

6. *See, e.g.*, Ga. Code Ann. §16-6-18 (2004); Idaho Code § 18-6603 (2004); Mass. Gen. Laws ch. 272, § 18 (2004); Minn. Stat. §609.34 (2004); Utah Code Ann. § 76-7-104 (2004); Va. Code Ann. § 18.2-344 (2004); N.C. Gen. Stat. §14-184 (2004); W.Va. Code §61-8-3 (2004).

7. *See, e.g.*, Ala. Code § 13A-6-65A (2004); Fla. Stat. Ann. § 800.02 (2004); Idaho Code § 18-6605 (2004); Mass. Gen. Laws ch. 272, § 34 (2004); Mich. Comp. Laws § 28.355/750.158 (2004); Minn. Stat. § 6509.293 (2004); Miss. Code Ann. §97-29-59 (2004); N.C. Gen. Stat. § 14-177 (2004); S.C. Code Ann. § 16-15-12 (2004); Utah Code Ann. § 76-5-403 (2004); Va. Code Ann. § 18.2-67.1; Ark. Code Ann. § 5-14-122 (2004); Ga. Code Ann. § 16-6-2 (2004); Kan. Stat. Ann. § 21-3505 (2004); Md. Code Ann. § 3-321 [Criminal Law] (2004); Mo. Rev. Stat. § 566.060 (2004); Okla. Stat. tit. 21, § 888 (2004); R.I. Gen. Laws §11-10-1 (2004); Tex. [Penal] Code Ann. § 21.06 (2004). Ryan Goodman points out that even if not enforced, laws against sodomy inhibit relationships and character. Ryan Goodman, *Beyond the Enforcement Principle: Sodomy Laws, Social Norms, and Social Panoptics*, 89 Cal. L. Rev. 643 (2001).

or cohabitation[8] and prescribing remaining legal differences in children's treatment based on their parents' marital state.[9]

Courts and legislatures in some jurisdictions have taken more affirmative actions to institutionalize and support cohabitation including establishing legal principles of "non-discrimination" between married and cohabiting couples and equalizing government benefits for formal and informal unions.[10] Government could remove

---

8. *See, e.g.,* Fla. Stat. Ann. § 798.02 (2004); Mich. Comp. Laws § 750.32 (2004) (if divorced) and § 750.335 (2004); Miss. Code Ann. § 93-5-29 (2004) (by divorced former spouse) and § 97-29-1 (2004); N.C. Gen. Stat. § 14-184 (2004); N.D. Cent. Code § 12.1-20-10 (2004); Va. Code Ann. § 18.2-345 (2004); W.Va. Code § 61-8-4 (2004) (lewd and lascivious); Mass. Gen. Laws ch. 208, § 40 (2004) (after divorce). *See also* Rehak v. Mathis, 238 S.E.2d 81 (Ga. 1977); Long v. Marino, 441 S.E.2d 475 (Ga. Ct. App.1994); Liles v. Still, 335 S.E.2d 168 (Ga. Ct. App. 1985); Hewitt v. Hewitt, 394 N.E.2d 1204 (Ill. 1979); Crawford v. City of Chicago, 710 N.E.2d 91 (Ill. App. Ct. 1999); Schwegmann v. Schwegmann, 441 So. 2d 316 (La. App. 5th Cir. 1984) (The court wouldn't even recognize agreements between cohabiting couples because of the underlying illegality of the relationship.); Zysk v. Zysk, 404 S.E.2d 721 (Va. 1990) (The court would not even allow a wife to sue her husband for the venereal disease she contracted from him while they were cohabiting.).

9. Though parents have the duty to support children regardless of marital status, in order for the child to be able to recover under a father's will, for example, some states require affirmative action on his or the mother's part. Levy v. Louisiana, 391 U.S. 68, 88 S. Ct. 1509 (1968). Sometimes states have gone out of their way to recognize "marriage" or "putative marriage" between children's parents in order to escape the hard distinction between legitimate and illegitimate children. Kasey v. Richardson, 331 F. Supp. 580 (W.D. Va. 1971). Unwed fathers have increasingly been granted at least the opportunity to "grasp the relationship" with their children; but this is their right, not the child's. Lehr v. Robertson, 463 U.S. 248, 103 S. Ct. 2985 (1983); Quilloin v. Walcott, 434 U.S. 246, 98 S. Ct. 549 (1978); Caban v. Mohammed, 441 U.S. 380, 99 S. Ct. 1760 (1979); Stanley v. Illinois, 405 U.S. 635, 92 S. Ct. 1221 (1972). *But see* Michael H. v. Gerald G., 491 U.S. 110, 109 S. Ct. 2333 (1989) (right belonged to adults in marriage relationship, not adulterous genetic father).

10. Some domestic partner legislation, and C-23 in Canada, does this. On Decmeber 19, 2000, the Dutch upper house of parliament passed the two bills that had been previously approved by the lower house in September 2000. *Upper House Approves Bill Allowing Same-Sex Marriages,* Justitie, *available at* http://www.justitie.nl/english//Press/Press_releases/archive/archive_2000/index. asp?ComponentID=42558&SourcePageID=191200. Effective April 2001, marriage and adoption in the Netherlands became open to both heterosexual and homosexual couples. *Id.* According to provisional figures from the Netherlands Central Bureau of Statistics, for the first six months same-sex marriages made up 3.6 percent of the total number of marriages—a peak of around six percent int he first month followed by around three percent int he remaining months,—about 2,100 men and 1,700 women in total. *Same Sex Marriage in the Netherlands,* word iQ, *at* http://www.wordiq.com/definition/Same-Sex_Marriage_in_the_Netherlands. It is rarer, but the civil union legislation in Vermont would be an example, for the duty of support during the relationship to be the same as in marriage. 2000 Vermont Laws P.A. 91, §§ 1202 *et seq.* Even in Norway, where about 25% of couples are

barriers to cohabitation for single mothers such as "man-in-the-house" welfare rules.[11]

The most radical view, espoused by some academics,[12] would abolish marriage as a legal institution (although it could of course remain a religious practice). In this view, the law should treat all family forms the same. The move towards recognizing same-sex marriage in Massachusetts has created surprising support for this view from some advocates of the traditional legal definition of marriage. Douglas Kmiec and Mark Scarberry of Pepperdine University recently urged that Massachusetts "temporarily get out of the new marriage business entirely," rather than offer same-sex couples marriage licenses.[13]

This essay evaluates (a) the weight of social science evidence on the extent to which, and the condition under which, cohabitation is the functional equivalent of marriage (b) the mechanisms, from a law and economics perspective, through which formal recognition of a relationship as a marriage may boost well-being, and (c) the likely consequences of blurring the legal distinction between formal and informal unions, as the ALI proposes.

Generally, we see too many problems with cohabitation defined as an alternative to marriage to believe that law and social policy

---

unmarried, "[U]nlike married couples, cohabiting couples have no legal responsibility to provide for each other." Truid Noack, *Cohabitation in Norway: An Accepted and Gradually More Regulated Way of Living*, 15 Int'l J. L, Pol'y & Fam. 102, 110 (2001). Compare the domestic partnership rules for medical insurance at the University of Iowa (available only to same-sex couples), which require mutual support. Student Health, University of Iowa *available at* http://www.uiowa.edu/~shs/ship.htm.

11. Aid to Families with Dependent Children (AFDC) historically worked to deny benefits to cohabiting indigent adults. King v. Smith, 392 U.S. 309, 88 S. Ct. 2128 (1968). This was on the theory that the cohabitant could support the indigent mother and children, so the government didn't need to. More recently, Temporary Assistance for Needy Families (TANF) payments have been structured to encourage marriage. Though married couples may receive temporary assistance, the second wage earner must be unemployed or disabled if the couple cohabits. Many states now terminate spousal support if the former wife cohabits with another—it would cease anyway if she remarried since the second spouse would assume the responsibility of supporting a needy wife. Wendell E. Primus & Jennifer Beeson, *Safety Net Programs, Marriage, and Cohabitation, in* Just Living Together: Implications of Cohabitation on Children, Families, and Social Policy 191, 197, 205 (Alan Booth & Ann C. Crouter, eds., 2002).

12. Martha Ertman, *Reconstructing Marriage: An InterSEXional Approach*, 75 Denv. U. L. Rev. 1215 (1998); Martha Fineman, The Neutered Mother, the Sexual Family, and Other Twentieth Century Tragedies (1995).

13. Quoted in Adam Liptak, *A Troubled 'Marriage': Core of Massachusetts Dispute is Tied to Traditional Exclusivity of the Word,*" N.Y. Times, Feb. 12, 2004, at A26.

should actively support this emerging family form.[14] Looking at the weight of social science evidence on marriage and cohabitation, this paper suggests what we believe is a middle ground: law and public policy should distinguish between cohabitation as a prelude to marriage (or a courtship strategy) and cohabitation as an alternative to marriage. The evidence, we suggest, points to many fewer problems with the former than the latter.[15]

I. THE FUZZY MEANING OF COHABITATION

Modern couples carry many hopes for the informal relationship. When they move in together, they may be holding a number of different expectations (and may differ even among themselves about the meaning of this step). Part of the reason we will argue for restraint in supporting cohabiting relationships when marriage is possible stems simply from this lack of individual and social meaning. Because we mean different things by cohabiting, there can be no community support through ritual.[16] Thus, "[c]ohabitation is an incomplete institution. No matter how widespread the practice, nonmarital unions are not yet governed by strong consensual norms or formal laws."[17] Couples may not even see the importance of the step they take in "just living together."[18] One or both members of a cohabiting couple may even cohabit (rather than marry) in order to

---

14. What about same-sex cohabitation vis à vis marriage? As a matter of social science evidence, until more jurisdictions legalize same-sex marriage, we cannot compare the consequences of marriage versus cohabitation for same-sex couples, although there are reasons for believing that some if not all of the benefits of formal marriage would apply to these couples. The benefits of domestic partnership or civil unions (or religious commitment ceremonies) for same-sex couples compared to more informal unions have not received adequate scholarly attention. Until more jurisdictions adopt same-sex marriage and other legal recognitions and more research is done, the case for public policies encouraging same-sex marriage and/or for ritualized public celebrations of commitment for these couples are generally made on other grounds.

15. *Atherley v. Atherley* suggests that the court start counting as "marital" property accumulated while engaged. 44 Cal. App. 3d 758, 119 Cal. Rptr. 41 (1975). Do some legislatures currently do this? *See also* Margaret F. Brinig, *Domestic Partnership: Missing the Target*, 4 J. of L. & Fam. Stud. 19 (2002). But see the new feminist pieces complaining about common law marriage. Ariela R. Dubler, *Wifely Behavior: A Legal History of Acting Married*, 100 Colum. L. Rev. 957, 1021 (2000); Barbara Stark, *Marriage Proposals: From One-Size-Fits-All To Postmodern Marriage Law*, 89 Cal. L. Rev. 1479 (2001).

16. Steven L. Nock, *A Comparison of Marriages and Cohabiting Relationships*, 16 J. Fam. Issues. 53 (1995).

17. Nock, *supra* note 16, at 74.

18. Just Living Together: Implications of Cohabitation on Families, Children and Social Policy (Alan Booth & Ann C. Crouter, eds., 2002).

side-step difficult disagreements about the meaning and future of
their relationship.

The lack of common definition of the term, either culturally or
empirically, also makes study of cohabitation difficult. How does
one phrase a survey question that would get at the complexity of
informal intimate unions (especially since perceptions may change
with time)? Some individuals who live together undoubtedly see
cohabitation as an alternative to marriage (perhaps because they
cannot marry; or sometimes because they don't see the need for
marrying, and sometimes because they see an overwhelming dark
side to the institution of marriage itself). In some couples, one or
both partners may see cohabitation as a prelude to marriage. One or
both may wish to cohabit simply because it is a convenient way to
live until the wedding or because, like the transition from dating to
going steady to "getting pinned" to engagement, living together
seems another stage in a deepening relationship.[19] Finally, a person
may cohabit to test the relationship: Can I live with this partner
without squabbling about cleanliness or sharing household chores?[20]
Will we still find each other sexually attractive lounging in
threadbare gym clothes? Can we really spend all our leisure time
together without being bored of one another?

II. IS COHABITATION THE FUNCTIONAL EQUIVALENT OF MARRIAGE? EVIDENCE FROM THE SOCIAL SCIENCES

However, we do know some empirical facts about cohabiting
couples as a result of research conducted since the mid 1980s. First,
there are growing proportions of them, particularly among African
Americans.[21] Second, the relationships themselves last a shorter
time than marriage, even if there are children.[22] Third, cohabitation

---

19. Pamela J. Smock and Sanjiv Gupta note that "evidence has recently begun
to emerge from both Canada and the United States that cohabitation's central
features have been changing fairly substantially over very short periods of time.
Pamela J. Smock and Sanjiv Gupta, *Cohabitation in Contemporary North America*,
in Just Living Together, *supra* note 18, at 53, 66. The most important implication
of these changes is that cohabitation has lost much ground as a precursor to
marriage. *Id.* The matter is complex, however. Although cohabitations appear to
be increasingly unstable and less likely to lead to marriage, there may be a growing
segment of cohabiting unions that do endure, with our without childbearing." *Id.*

20. Surprisingly, cohabiting men do the same amount of housework as married
men (on average 19 and 18 hours per week), while cohabiting women do 31 hours
of housework per week compared to 37 for married women. Smock & Gupta,
supra note 19, at 68-69.

21. Andrea G. Hunter, *(Re)Envisioning Cohabitation: A Commentary on Race,
History, and Culture*, *in* Just Living Together, *supra* note 18, at 41, 42.

22. Kathleen Kiernan, *Cohabitation in Western Europe: Trends, Issues, and*

followed by marriage (particularly when the couple cohabits without being engaged) leads to less stable marriages than marriages not preceded by living together.[23] Fourth, cohabiting couples experience a larger incidence of domestic violence than do married ones.[24] The Justice Department reports that "those who never married became violent crime victims at more than four times the rate of married persons."[25] Compared to married couples of the same duration (i.e., couples who have been together for the same length of time) those in informal (cohabiting) unions are less committed to their partnership (they see fewer costs should the relationship end), and report poorer quality relationships with one another and with parents.[26]

Scholars debate whether to view such findings as healthy adaptations to the constantly changing institution of marriage[27] or a sign of social decline and growing impermanence in the intimate lives of children and adults.[28] Still, there is little disagreement that cohabitation is still an informal union ungoverned by strong cultural beliefs and presumptions. As such, it is not a social institution; marriage is. In sharp contrast to cohabitation, marriage is surrounded by legal, social, and cultural beliefs about the broad contours of the relationship. This is the defining difference between legal marriage and informal cohabitation.[29] Thus, not only do scholars have difficulty pinning down the meaning of cohabitation, but (often) so do cohabitors themselves.

Implications, in Just Living Together, *supra* note 18, at 171; Smock & Gupta, *supra* note 19, at 59 ("Given the wide variation in data, samples, measures of marital instability, and independent variables, the degree of consensus about this central finding is impressive.").

23. Larry L. Bumpass & Hsien-Hen Lu, *supra* note 5; Susan L. Brown, *Child Well-Being in Cohabiting Families*, in Just Living Together, *supra* note 18, at 173; Kiernan, *supra* note 22.

24. Susan Brown & Alan Booth, *Cohabitation Versus Marriage: A Comparison of Relationship Quality*, 58 J. Marriage & Fam. 668 (1996); Jon Stets, *Cohabiting and Marital Aggression: The Role of Social Isolation*, 53 J. Marriage & Fam. 669 (1991); Jan Stets & Marta Stets, *The Marriage License as a Hitting License: A Comparison of Assaults in Dating, Cohabiting and Married Couples*, in Violence in Dating Relationships: Emerging Social Issues 89 (M.A. Pirog-Good and J.E. Stets, eds., 1989).

25. United States Department of Justice, Bureau of Justice Statistics, 2002 *available at* http://222.ojp.usdoj.gov/bjs/cvict_v.htm/marital.

26. Nock, *supra* note 16.

27. Martha A. Fineman, *Why Marriage?*, 9 Va. J. Soc. Pol'y & L. 239 (2001); Judith Stacey, *Good Riddance to "The Family": A Response to David Popenoe (in An Exchange on American Family Decline)*, 55 J. Marriage & Fam. 545-47 (1993).

28. Steven L. Nock, *Why Not Marriage?*, 9 Va. J. Soc. Pol'y & L. 273 (2001); David Popenoe, *American Family Decline, 1960-1990: A Review and Appraisal*, 55 J. Marriage & Fam. 527 (1993).

29. Nock, *supra* note 16.

The cohabiting relationship itself is qualitatively different from marriage[30] (This may be for some couples exactly what they wanted: an alternative to marriage.). Couples who cohabit, though they may boast of the strength of their love, as the song tells us,[31] express less interdependence than typical married couples.[32] The strong health effects seen by married couples—especially men, though women, too—are not as pronounced.[33] Sex is reportedly not as good, on average.[34] Fathers are less likely to stay involved with their children, or to support them.[35]

While we suspect that many of these undesirable features are not just "selection effects" but (at least in part) come from cohabitation itself, proving this thesis definitively is difficult. To begin with,

---

30. This set of effects is hard to sort out. Do couples cohabit because they are precisely the sort who are less likely to be dependent upon one another, or does causation work the other way?

31.
> I love you so, I always will
> And though devotion rules my heart, I take no bows,
> Oh, but Bill, you're never gonna take my wedding vows.

Laura Nyro, *Wedding Bell Blues* (Whether the couple in the song are cohabiting as opposed to just in love is unclear from the lyrics). See also the following statement from *Marvin v. Marvin*:

> On cross-examination, plaintiff testified that they were "always very proud of the fact that nothing held us. We weren't—we weren't legally married." After the breakup she declared to an interviewer: "We used to laugh and feel a great warmth about the fact that either of us could walk out at any time."

557 P.2d 106, 134 Cal. Rptr. 815 (Cal. 1976), (Opinion of the Trial Court on Remand, Superior Court of Los Angeles County) (1979).

32. In the United States, at any rate, social class, measured by educational attainment and economic standing, does much to determine those who cohabit rather than marry. Among 19-44 year old women, nearly 60% of high school drop-outs cohabited compared to less than 37% for college educated women. Bumpass and Lu, *supra* note 23, at 3; Smock and Gumpta, *supra* note 19, at 61-62.

33. Amy Mehraban Pienta, et al, *Health Consequences of Marriage for the Retirement Years*, 21 J. Family Issues 559 (2000). Brown & Booth, *supra* note 24; Brown, *supra* note 23.

34. Linda J. Waite & Karen Joyner, *Emotional and Physical Satisfaction with Sex in Married, Cohabiting and Dating Sexual Unions: Do Men and Women Differ?* in Sex, Love, and Health in America 239 (E.O. Lawrence & R.T. Michael, eds., 2001).

35. Wendy D. Manning, *The Implications of Cohabitation for Children's Well-Being, in* Just Living Together, *supra* note 18, at 121, 143. Shelley Lundberg and Elaina Rose suggest that although men respond with more work and higher wages at the birth of a child, they do so significantly more in response to births of sons than to the births of daughters. Shelley Lundberg and Elaina Rose, *The Effects of Sons and Daughters on Men's Labor Supply and Wages*, 84 Rev. Econ. & Stats. 251 (2002). The authors stated, "Our results are consistent with a model in which the gender composition of a couple's offspring affects the returns to marriage." *Id.* at 252. They found no difference in the effect of child gender on the labor market outcomes of mothers. *Id.*

studies in the United States simply haven't collected the right data.[36] Empirically, causation is difficult to tease out.[37] For example, did a particular couple cohabit (and then divorce) because they were less dependent on each other, or did the smaller degree of interdependence cause the instability (or both)? Or did the cohabitation produce some other effects that led to unhappiness, but in a case where divorce would have been practical only if the couple weren't dependent?

Because the meaning of cohabitation is difficult to establish and the consequences of cohabitation difficult to prove, the social policy implications have been the subject of considerable debate.

A. *Cohabitation as Courtship and Search*

Gary Becker[38] pioneered a discussion of courtship in terms of the search behavior that leads to what he called "assortative mating." This term implies that people sort themselves and others on some scale of desirability, finally choosing the most desirable person they can attract with their own attributes.[39] "Desirable" does not usually mean identical, however. In addition to the legal requirement that they be a man and a woman, each will seek out a mate who will be a complement—who will have strong points the other does not possess.[40] Young people usually begin the search for a mate after

---

36. Some questions that we would like answered in addition to those currently on the National Survey of Families and Households include:
> If you answered yes to whether you cohabited with your spouse prior to marriage, were you already engaged when you moved in together? Did you anticipate you'd be marrying even though you had made no formal pledge? What made you decide to get married? When did you decide to marry? Which of you first proposed getting married? Did you cohabit because you were unsure whether you wanted to marry (if ever cohabited with someone other than the spouse)? Why did your relationship end? Did you decide that you'd found out too many things about the other person, or about your relationship, to make a marriage work? Did you simply tire of each other? Did you receive any financial settlement from that other relationship? How did your relationship change when you got married?

37. Larry L. Bumpass & James A. Sweet, *National Estimates of Cohabitation*, 26 Demography 615 (1989); Neil G. Bennett et al., *Commitment and the Modern Union: Assessing the Link Between Premarital Cohabitation and Subsequent Marital Stability*, 53 Am. Soc. Rev. 127 (1988); William G. Axinn & Arland Thornton, *The Relationship Between Cohabitation and Divorce: Selectivity or Causal Influence?* 29 Demography 357 (1992); Bumpass & Lu, *supra* note 23; Smock & Gupta, *supra* note 19, at 59-60 (reviewing other studies).

38. Gary S. Becker, *A Theory of Marriage, in* Economics of the Family: Marriage, Children and Human Capital (Theodore W. Schultz, ed., 1974); Gary S. Becker, A Treatise on the Family 324-27 (Second ed. 1991).

39. Paula England & George Farkas, Households, Employment and Gender: A Social, Economic, and Demographic View 31-42 (1986).

40. Becker, *supra* note 38, at 327.

they have "played the field" for some time to discover what they want in a spouse and what they are worth to others.[41] They then date to find out enough about the other person to see whether he or she matches the characteristics that hypothetically would make a good marriage partner.[42] Finally, each attempts to convince the other party that he or she is capable of fulfilling the other's expectations. Engagement occurs when the expected utility from getting married outweighs the expected utility of remaining single and continuing the search.[43] The way in which people conduct these searches has varied through history.

At all times, courtship rituals have enjoyed major significance. Rituals are both forms of communications and instruments for the creation of meaning. They have always played a major role in courtship. In wealthy families at least (where parents arranged or strongly influenced children's mate choices), courtship involved an attempt by the two sets of parents to convince each other of the validity of an alliance. In ancient times, marriages could be repudiated if the intended did not conform to "specifications," such as virginity or fertility, that were needed to guarantee lineal descendants.[44] Presents were exchanged, and a dowry paid to cement the bargain.[45]

This practice of arranged marriage began to change as early as the twelfth century, when church reformers wrote that marital unions "should be contracted freely by the parties themselves, not by their parents or families." Increasingly affection, rather than property, now initiated the relationship.[46] In colonial America, the parents still had a role in approving the prospective son or daughter and in providing the necessary means of support for the new household, but the choice essentially belonged to the couple involved.[47]

Until the early twentieth century, American courtship was mainly carried on in the woman's home, with the suitor making a "call" upon her and her parents. The woman could elect whether or not he would be received, and could serve him tea or small sandwiches.[48] He

---

41.   Margaret F. Brinig, *Rings and Promises*, 6 J. L. Econ. & Org. 203 (1990).
42.   England & Farkas, *supra* note 39; Margaret F. Brinig & Michael Alexeev, *Fraud in Courtship: Annulment and Divorce*, 2 Eur. J. L. & Econ. 45 (1995).
43.   Becker, *supra* note 38, at 325.
44.   William Brundage, Law, Sex and Christian Society in Medieval Europe 453 (1987); Brinig, *supra* note 41.
45.   Edward Shorter, The Making of the Modern Family 55 (1975).
46.   *Id.,* at 21.
47.   John Demos, *The American Family in Past Time*, 43 Am. Scholar 422, 425 (1978).
48.   Beth Bailey, From Front Porch to Back Seat: Courtship in Twentieth Century America 17 (1988).

might escort her to church, if the relationship became serious, and he called upon her father to ask permission to marry before the engagement became formal. As historian Beth Bailey points out, the woman had little control over whether the man ever presented his card, signaling his wish to call upon her, but almost complete control over the progress of the courtship thereafter.[49]

With the advent of the automobile, courtship changed. It left the wife's home and increasingly took place in public. At first there was little "pairing off" during dates: at dances the woman sought to be "cut in upon" by a large number of men to show her attractiveness and popularity.[50] Her escort also wished her to be popular, since that enhanced his prestige in bringing her to the social event.[51]

Until fairly recently, a woman's marriage was necessary to secure her social position, so that the "old maid" would not only be scarred because she was not attractive enough to snag a husband, but also would be disadvantaged because in later life she would not be secure financially.[52] Marriage was, as one writer noted, the "one career open to her," and once she had made her choice of husbands, the woman's "options were suddenly, irrevocably gone."[53] The options may have been drastically limited even by a serious relationship short of marriage.

Particularly during the time between the two World Wars, a woman was expected to remain chaste until the time of her engagement. Once she was betrothed, however, sexual intimacy with her fiancé reportedly occurred nearly half the time.[54] If a marriage never came about, she was henceforth unable to offer an unblemished self to a new suitor,[55] and consequently she suffered a loss in "market value."[56] While a man could pretend inexperience, a woman's virginity or lack of it was considered a verifiable physical fact.[57]

---

49. *Id.*, at 21.

50. Willard Waller, *The Rating and Dating Complex*, 2 Am. Soc. Rev. 726, 730 (1937).

51. Bailey, *supra* note 48, at 26-31.

52. Mary Ann Glendon, The New Family and the New Property 31-32 (1981); Marriage and Property 166-67 (Elizabeth Craik, ed., 1984); Michael Grossberg, Governing the Hearth: Law and the Family in Nineteenth Century America 36 (1985).

53. Ellen Rothman, Hands and Hearts: A History of Courtship in America 162-163 (1987).

54. Alfred C. Kinsey, et al., Sexual Behavior in the Human Male 336 (1948); Paul Gebhard and Alan Johnson, The Kinsey Data: Marginal Tabulations of the 1938-63 Interviews Conducted by the Institute for Sex Research 20 (1979).

55. Theodore W. Cousens, *The Law of Damages as Applied to Breach of Promise of Marriage*, 17 Cornell L. Q. 367, 382 (1932).

56. Nathan P. Feinsinger, *Legislative Attack on Heart Balm*, 33 Mich. L. Rev. 979, 983 (1935).

57. W.J. Brockelbank, *The Nature of the Promise to Marry—A Study in*

After World War II, however, this mating practice changed. Although theoretically she was free to initiate a date, or to pay for it, during the latter part of the twentieth century most dating began with the man asking the woman "out" and financing the evening's expeditions.[58] Once the relationship became more serious, there was sexual intimacy in many cases. More than half the men reporting to Alfred Kinsey even before World War II said they had sexual intercourse during engagement.[59] And, since 1970, an increasing number of couples have been cohabiting prior to (or outside of) marriage. The National Center for Health Statistics reported in 1990[60] that forty-seven percent of women ages twenty to twenty-nine had cohabited, while Larry Bumpass[61] reports that forty-four percent of those marrying in the early 1980s cohabited first. As of Census 2000, fifty-two percent of marriages are formed from cohabiting relationships.[62] This more modern pattern of courtship gives the couple more opportunity to discover the good and bad characteristics of each other.

Indeed, attempts to formulate comprehensive theories of mate selection in the latter twentieth century incorporated such ideas about searching and matching as central elements. Murstein's[63] Stimulus-Value-Role theory, for example, argued that initial attraction (stimulus) is based on obvious personal attributes that tend to be matched (equal levels of education, physical attractiveness, styles of dress, preferences for recreation, etc.). Those who navigate this stage move on to the "value" stage during which information is obtained about basic orientations to such things as children, marriage, gender roles, and so on. Those who find each other's values compatible move on to the final "role" stage which provides information about styles of interaction in a relationship. Is one's partner insistent on having the final word in decisions? Does one's partner interact in compatible ways on important dimensions (decorum, centrality of work versus family, and so on)? Comparable attempts focused on the complementarity (or lack thereof) of each partner's needs (dominant

---

Comparative Law, 41 Ill. L. Rev. 1, 8 (1946).

58. Bailey, *supra* note 48, at 26-31.

59. Kinsey, *supra* note 54, at 336.

60. K.A. Loudon, *Advance Data from Vital and Health Statistics*, no. 194, Center for Health Statistics (1991). *See also* D'Vera Cohn, *Cohabiting Couples Are a Settled Bunch; Many Unwed Partners Own Homes, Have Children, Census Reveals*, Washington Post, Mar. 20, 1994 at B1.

61. Larry L. Bumpass, The Changing Significance of Marriage in the United States *in* The Changing Family in Comparative Perspective: Asia and the United States 63 (K. O. Mason, et. al., eds., 1998)

62. Bumpass & Lu, *supra* note 23.

63. Bernard Murstein, *Mate Selection in the 1970s*, 42 J. Marriage & Fam. 777 (1980).

partners were thought to pair with submissive, a nurturant individual will be attracted to someone who seeks nurturance, etc.).[64]

The later states of courtship induce significant reliance expenditures, meaning that these "serious" couples give up other opportunities for intimacy.[65] At the very least, the engaged person is removed from the marriage market for some period of time.[66] There may also be increasing specific investment in the other person: learning the favorite foods, establishing relationships with future in-laws, taking the other's career plans into account, beginning wedding preparations. If the reliance results in a marriage, there are weighty social and personal consequences.

B. Search and Fraud in the Marriage Market

Law and economics suggests that we examine the search process itself. When couples become engaged, they do not tell each other everything. Sometimes they misinform or fail to inform each other about important personal characteristics. When returning to the single state is more attractive than accepting the other spouse's true characteristics, the disappointed spouse may bring an action for annulment on the grounds of fraud.[67] Whether or not the action succeeds depends upon characteristics of the marriage market. Some of the incidence of fraud in courtship can be reduced through nonlegal means.

Historically, this often meant that one limited the search for a mate to individuals with good "reputations" within the relevant community. This provides the single person with a strong incentive to establish a good reputation. Such incentives are particularly important in small communities where "everyone knows everyone else."[68] In general, reputation will have less effect in a large urban

---

64. Robert F. Winch, Mate Selection: A Study of Complementary Needs (1958).

65. *Compare* The Beach Boys, *I Get Around* ("None of the guys go steady/cause it wouldn't be right/To leave your best girl home/ on a Saturday night...").

66. William Bishop, *Is He Married? Marriage as Information*, 34 U. Toronto L.J. 245, 258-59 (1984); Ellen Rothman, Hands and Hearts: A History of Courtship in America 162-163 (1987). However, on college campuses today, young people have apparently abandoned the dating approach in favor of more casual and less well-defined "hook ups." Norval Glenn & Elizabeth Marquardt. Hooking Up, Hanging Out, and Hoping for Mr. Right: College Women on Dating and Mating Today (2001). This may be, in part, because as the age of marriage has risen, college students are less likely to see themselves as participating in a "marriage market" search.

67. Brinig & Alexeev, *supra* note 42.

68. Bailey, *supra* note 48.

area, where one can conceivably take advantage of (cheat) any number of the members of the opposite sex without ever being discovered. Mechanisms have evolved, however, in which reputation or other signaling devices once again become important.[69] This is why there may be so much dating within particular organizations (university alumni clubs, church "singles" groups, sporting or exercise groups, or even computer dating services).[70] In circumstances where reputation is less effective in reducing fraud, other devices such as the "trial marriage" or cohabitation may be used. As England and Farkas note, premarital cohabitation is the search mechanism that provides the most relevant information about the performance of the other person as a marriage partner. Note also that such additional search mechanisms of course imply greater reliance expenditures than more traditional courtship behavior. Paradoxically, though, the selection of marriages that are preceded by cohabitation apparently includes some couples who are less committed to lifelong relationships, since these marriages end in divorce at a far higher rate than those not preceded by cohabitation.[71]

C. Cohabitation as a Search

Search before any kind of contract formation becomes complicated when there is asymmetric information between the parties, that is, when either or both can keep meaningful secrets from the other. Philip Nelson, writing in a more general contract context, distinguished between "search" goods and "experience" goods.[72] The qualities of the search goods can be examined in a short time or otherwise at low cost to the consumer, who can therefore make an inspection before purchase. (Think of the purchase of a tomato or a hair brush.) The qualities of the experience goods, on the other hand, cannot be ascertained until after purchase. (Nelson uses the example of a can of tuna fish.) Nelson predicts, among other things, that there

---

69. England & Farkas, *supra* note 39, at 41.

70. As Brinig's colleague Hillary Sale noted, however, too much "inbreeding" among those united by close bonds of group membership may result in a lack of information and, ultimately, a bad match because so much is taken for granted or assumed that ordinary inquiry may be foregone. For an application to law school hiring, see Theodore Eisenberg & Martin Wells, *Inbreeding In Law School Hiring: Assessing The Performance of Faculty Hired From Within*, 29 J. Legal Stud. 369 (2000).

71. Bumpass, Sweet & Cherlin, *supra* note 4. Cohabitation changes attitudes about domestic life. It reduces interest in marriage, and makes divorce appear more acceptable (net of attitudes prior to cohabitation.) Axinn & Thornton, *supra* note 37.

72. Phillip Nelson, *Information and Consumer Behavior*, 78 J. Pol. Econ. 311, 312 (1970).

would be fewer of each type of seller of experience goods, and that buyers would seek advice of others more frequently.[73] Darby and Karni[74] introduced an additional category of "credence" goods. The quality of these goods may not be easily determined even after the purchase.[75]

The "good" of the person you marry has the characteristics of all three categories of goods mentioned above. The experience good aspect of a marriage is, perhaps, its most important attribute for this paper. In the marriage context, as with the purchase of tuna fish, some things can't be known for certain until after the contract is made: for example, whether the other party desires (or is able) to have children, will be a good parent, will practice a particular religion, or generally will be interesting to live with.

However, there is a significant difference between marriage and Nelson's experience goods. At least in theory marriage is for life, and there will be no "repeat purchase" or "purchase of another brand." Also, the non-repetitive nature of marriage increases the importance of its credence goods aspect,[76] and perhaps provides some basis for distinguishing between dating (probably invaluable for marriages based upon love) and cohabitation (perhaps threatening to them). The search goods aspect of marriage is reflected in the fact that there are some things that a "diligent buyer" of marriage services can know, such as whether an admitted prior marriage was dissolved by death or by divorce. More obviously, we can know height and weight and facial characteristics. (Sociobiologists in fact

---

73. *Id.,* at 327.

74. Michael Darby & Edi Karni, *Free Competition and The Optimal Amount of Fraud in Contracts,* 16 J.L. & Econ. 67 (1973).

75. Darby and Karni write about situations involving service as well as sale of a particular good, where the buyer can't discern how much service was really needed even after the service has been performed. *Id.* For example, it may be costly or impossible for a surgery patient to find out after the fact if the removal of her appendix was warranted or not. *Id.*

76. In the marriage market, each party possesses complete information only about him- or herself. If one party is naive about what really goes on in marriage, whether it is about whether all wives put their husband's laundry away or all couples engage in some bizarre sexual practice, much of what Darby and Karni have to say about car sales and appendix operations can be applied in the marriage context. They suggest that one form of government intervention that may become necessary in situations involving commercial credence goods is occupational licensing. In marriage, there is at least some rough screening by the state through the marriage license, in which both parties swear to have the capacity to be married, that they are of the opposite sexes, and that each is of the appropriate age. There may also be a state requirement of blood testing to assure freedom from venereal diseases. (Illinois had such a requirement involving testing for the AIDS virus in 1988, during which the marriage rates in that state declined dramatically, and those in neighboring states rose as they took up the excess. Center for Health Statistics, *supra* note 60.).

assert that we find them attractive if they predict future health and success in childbearing.)[77] Fraud about such traits will not lead to annulment (although a spouse's disillusionment may result eventually in a divorce.)[78]

However, even when the couple becomes engaged, there are "secrets" that can only, if ever, be revealed after marriage. Becker, Landes, and Michael[79] note that divorce occurs when the new revelations make staying inside the marriage less desirable than resuming the single state.

Cohabitation might be expected to reveal some of these secrets, even if imperfectly. Those who share domestic space in a sexual relationship will likely learn about their partner's *personal habits* (cleanliness, fastidiousness, willingness, or desire to perform household chores such as laundry, timeliness in paying bills or preparing to go out, accuracy or diligence in taking telephone messages) and *tastes* (musical preferences, hobbies, feelings about pets, desired temperature in the dwelling, desired time together or apart, friends, and sleep habits). They are also likely to discover intimate personal characteristics (personal hygiene, medical practices, sleep habits, security fears, prayer behavior, religious beliefs, gender ideals). However, cohabitation is not typically associated with more stable marriages in the United States (even when it is in Europe). As we will develop, the search model may actually work for American couples, but it ignores the larger cultural context in which marriage and cohabitation exist. Marriage continues to be a distinct legal and social institution in America, unlike the case in Europe.

While United States data shows couples who live together are actually *more* likely to divorce than couples who marry directly, the European experience is different. The economic search model for cohabitation appears to work for European marriages in many countries, at least in so far as Kiernan points out, in some Western European countries, marriages preceded by cohabitation evidenced "little difference in the risk of dissolution of converted unions compared with direct marriages."[80] (Switzerland, Austria, and East Germany had lower rates of dissolution, or the difference was not statistically significant). Kiernan discusses the stages through which

---

77. Matt Ridley, The Red Queen: Sex and The Evolution of Human Nature 159-60 (1994).

78. It may be that courts are using the fact that the defect is discoverable when they assume that the spouse in fact *did* know of the defect prior to the marriage.

79. Gary Becker, Elisabeth M. Landes & Robert T. Michael, *An Economic Analysis of Marital Instability*, 85 J. Pol. Econ. 1141 (1977).

80. Kiernan, *supra* note 22, at 5, 16.

Sweden passed in recognizing cohabitation.[81] During the first state, cohabitation emerges:

> . . . as a deviant or avant-garde phenomenon practiced by a small group of the single population, while the great majority of the population marries directly. In the second stage, cohabitation functions as either a prelude to or a probationary period where the strength of the relationship may be tested prior to committing to marriage and is predominantly a childless phase. In the third stage, cohabitation becomes socially acceptable as an alternative to marriage and becoming a parent is no longer restricted to marriage. Finally, in the fourth stage, cohabitation and marriage become indistinguishable with children being born and reared within both, and the partnership transition could be said to be complete. Sweden and Denmark are countries that have made the transition to this fourth stage. At any time, cohabitation may have different meanings for the men and women involved.[82]

It is possible, of course, that for Western European nations, enough time has passed to move through these various stages. In the United States, where cohabitating couples were first counted in the 1970s, we may simply be at an earlier phase. It is equally possible that the social support given to cohabiting couples, particularly those with children, make these relationships attractive and possible to couples elsewhere where they would not be in the United States.[83] The Netherlands, at the beginning of 1998, instituted formal registration of partnerships for both heterosexual and homosexual couples and made legally registered cohabitation functionally equivalent to marriage (except that cohabiting couples do not have the right to adopt).[84] Denmark instituted legal registration of homosexual partnerships in the early 1990s.

---

81. *Id. See also* Jan M. Hoem & Britta Hoem, *The Swedish Family: Aspects of Contemporary Developments*, 9 J. Fam. Issues 397 (1988).

82. Dorien Manning, *The Changing Meaning of Cohabitation and Marriage*, 12 Eur. Soc. Rev. 53 (1996).

83. Chong-Bum An, Robert Haveman & Barbara Wolfe, *Teen Out-of-Wedlock Births and Welfare Receipt: The Role of Childhood Events and Economic Circumstances*, 75 Rev. of Econ. & Stat. 195 (1993); Robert Moffitt, *Incentive Effects of the U.S. Welfare System: A Review*, 30 J. Econ. Literature 1 (1992); Sara S. McLanahan and Irwin Garfinkel, *Single Mothers, the Underclass, and Social Policy*, 501 Annals Am. Acad. Pol. & Soc. Sci. 92 (1989); Peter Gottschalk, *AFDC Participation Across Generations*, 80 Am. Econ. Rev. 367 (1990).

84. Wendy M. Schrama, *Registered Partnerships in the Netherlands*, 13 Int'l J. Law, Pol'y & Fam. 315 (1999).

Alternatively, the reason that cohabitation is closer to marriage in Europe than in the United States is that in Europe marriage, *per se*, has been gradually and effectively deinstitutionalized. To the extent that marriage is no longer a legal status carrying differential privileges or obligations, and to the extent that such legal changes were in response to popular opinion, we may say that the cultural script that defined marriage as a distinct relationship has been rewritten to equate marriage and cohabitation. If marriage is treated in law and culture as the functional equivalent of cohabitation, it may no longer produce distinctive results. To the extent that this has happened (our impression is that it has in many Western European countries), cohabitation would be treated in law and custom as marriage. Alternatively, marriage would come to be viewed as one more alternative form of cohabitation.

Kiernan's work also points out the role of religiosity and parental divorce in predicting whether couples would marry directly or cohabit first:[85]

Proportions Married Directly According to Some Church Attendance Versus None Among Women Who Had Partnership and Were Aged Twenty to Thirty-Nine Years at the Time of the Survey[86]

	Some Church Attendance	Never Attends Church	% Reporting Never
Sweden	12	4	66
Norway	50	23	67
Finland	25	14	35
Great Britain	59	41	45
Switzerland	31	14	4
West Germany	32	14	77
East Germany	23	14	77
Spain	90	80	53
Italy	90	18	9

As in the United States, Kiernan found that Western European couples whose parents had separated or divorced were more likely to cohabit first rather than marry directly.[87] This was true for couples in Sweden, Finland, France, Austria, Switzerland, West and East Germany, Spain, and Italy.

---

85. Kiernan, *supra* note 22, at 12 & Table 1.3.
86. From *Id.* (from UN ECE Family and Fertility Survey (1992)).
87. *Id.*, at 13 & Table 1.4.

Controlling for age at first marriage, church attendance, and experience of parental divorce, Kiernan reports[88] that marriages preceded by cohabitation in Norway were more stable than those without cohabitation (while the difference was not statistically significant),[89] while for couples in Finland and Austria,[90] the risk of dissolution was greater,[91] but not statistically significant. In these countries at least, cohabitation appears to help some high-risk couples make better matches.

In Sweden, France, Switzerland, and the two Germanys, controlling for age at the time of marriage, religious attendance and parental divorce, first marriages that are also first unions are less stable than those preceded by prior cohabitation.[92]

However, in all the Western European countries surveyed, Kiernan reports that, controlling again for age at first marriage, church attendance, and experience of parental divorce, cohabitation without marriage was the least stable arrangement.[93] The differences are large (ranging from fifty percent more to more than six times more likely to dissolve). In Europe, then, cohabitation as a search process for marriage appears to "work." Cohabitation as an alternative to marriage, however, appears no more stable in Europe than in America.

Relative Risk of Partnership Dissolution According to Type of First Partnership for Women Aged Twenty to Thirty-Nine Years at the Time of the Survey

Country	Married	Cohabitated	Cohabitated Only
Sweden	1.00	1.5	3.96***
Norway	1.00	0.85	4.92***
Finland	1.00	1.12	3.44***
France	1.00	1.49**	6.04***

88. *Id.* at 15 & Table 1.5.

89. Norway had no information on parental divorce, so the only controls are for parental divorce and age at marriage. *Id.* Dorien Manting, suggests that the Netherlands, not included in Kiernan's chapter, will resemble Norway. Manting, *supra* note 82.

90. Austria had no control for religious attendance, so the only controls are for age at prior marriage and parental divorce. Kiernan, *supra* note 22.

91. The relative risk in Finland was 1.16, in Austria 1.24. *Id.* Kiernan used Cox proportional hazard models with the survival time being the duration of marriage to dissolution or censoring at the time of the survey. *Id.*, at 14.

92. France had no question on religion, so the only controls were for age at prior marriage and parental divorce. *Id.* In Sweden (1.58), Switzerland (1.28) and East Germany (1.38), the difference was significant at p < .05; while in France (1.63) and West Germany (1.42), the difference was significant at p < .01. *Id.*

93. *Id.*, at 17 & Table 1.7 (Model 2). Norway had no information on parental divorce and France and Austria had no question on religion. *Id.*

Austria	1.00	1.01	3.08***
Switzerland	1.00	1.11	4.84***
West Germany	1.00	1.38*	3.07***
East Germany	1.00	1.35*	1.55***

*** $p < 0.001$; **$p < .01$; * $p < .10$.

There are potential risks to using cohabitation as a mate selection strategy, however. Legally, the problem of trying to figure out whether a couple intended to marry when they first cohabited can be compared with a Virginia case dealing with intent to separate permanently at the time of separation. When both parties are sane, the law requires an intention to separate to commence the statutory "separate and apart" period required before divorce in some states. Thus, when the husband went overseas in connection with his employment, but wrote to an attorney two years later to institute divorce proceedings, the period of separation began at the later time, for "there must be proof of an intention on the part of at least one of the parties to discontinue permanently the marital cohabitation, followed by physical separation" without any cohabitation.[94] Many if not most couples probably changed their minds about the expected outcome of their relationship some time after moving in together. And sometimes only one individual may have had a change of expectation.

What happens to Western European couples who cohabit only to discover they shouldn't marry (and later find someone else)? If a failed search made through cohabitation produced no further costs than the waste of time and energy invested in the relationship, search theory would predict that the information gleaned about one's preferences would simply be kept for the next search. The research shows however that this doesn't seem to be what happens. Like a divorce, a "failed cohabitation" increases the risk of future relationship failure. For the next relationship, the partner who came from the failed cohabitation would already have cohabited prior to marriage even if this new relationship proceeded directly to marriage. The marriage would therefore have a lower rather than a higher chance of success. To our knowledge, this pattern has not been studied in the West European context. However, in repeated studies in the United States, a history of cohabitation (with another person or persons) that did *not conclude* in marriage is associated with higher rates of divorce.

III. THE USES OF COHABITATION: A THEORETICAL ANALYSIS

The studies of cohabitation in Europe focus on couples who transition from cohabitation to marriage. Absent empirical evidence

---

94. Hooker v. Hooker, 215 Va. 415, 417, 211 S.E.2d 34, 36 (1975).

one way or the other, we are unable to assert that a history of cohabitation with others would produce less stable marriages in Europe as it does in the United States. As we explain below, however, we suspect that it would (See chart on United States cohabitations, from the National Survey of Families and Households [NSFH]). Why?

Consider the search and hiring practices of law schools as an analogy. Most law schools hire "entry level" candidates who have graduated law school fairly recently and who show promise for succeeding in the academic world (as measured in class standing, law review editing, prestigious clerkships, writing during and especially after law school, and references by trusted academics who know them well). Since there are only short term contracts binding the school or candidate, we make an analogy to the engagement process. (It is exclusive for a "slot" and each candidate may only be full-time at one institution). After several years (varying from three or four to six) of short term appointments, the candidates apply for tenure. The vast majority of these are given tenure, or lifetime appointments (in our terms, like marriage). A few, however, are not successful on the teaching or especially the publishing front. If their institutions discover this early on, they may suggest that they find work elsewhere, or even arrange for fellowships or visits at other schools. By the sixth year, the American Association of University Professors [AAUP] rules require that a tenure decision be made or the applicant to receive a "terminal year's" appointment. Were the economists' search predictions true, the institution would simply hire another entry person to fill the slot, and the candidate would simply choose another law school that would better fit his or her needs.

Yet we know that tenure denials in fact inflict substantial costs on both the faculty member and the department involved. In this analogous situation, both sides will feel a loss of trust and more guilt or anger (or both) about what happened. To demonstrate, we conducted an unofficial and unsystematic survey of twenty American law schools where we knew that there had been tenure denials during the twelve year period of the *U.S. News and World Report* rankings of graduate schools. In each case, we know the ranking of the school at the time of the tenure denial, the ranking some years later (when any costs to reputation would have worked into the system), and the ranking of the school to which the candidate moved (ascertainable from the American Association of Law Schools Directory of Law Teachers). (Some of these people got out of law teaching altogether. These are not counted.) The average loss in rank by the tenure candidate from the original school to the new school was forty-three places, while the difference between the original school's rank in the last year of service to two years later was a loss of nearly one place.

While the first loss is not surprising (given the strong signal that there was a problem with scholarship or teaching), the fact that there's any loss in the original school's rank one might be.

While potential spouses are not "ranked" in the same way law schools are, they do occupy varying positions in the marriage market —as more or less desirable husbands or wives. A failed search in the marriage market (cohabitation that did not lead to marriage) may have similar consequences for ex-cohabitors as does a failed search in the law school hiring process. Both parties, that is, may experience a loss in attractiveness as potential spouses.

IV. MARRIAGE WITHOUT COHABITATION

Why might marriage work as well when *not* preceded by cohabitation? There are a number of reasons marriage might be more successful when the spouses did not cohabit first. One idea is that the couple saved sexual intimacy until marriage. Current estimates indicate that sixteen and three-tenths percent of men, and twenty and one-tenth percent of women are virgins at the time of their first marriage.[95] We do not know the percentage of marriages involving virgins among those who did not cohabit, though it would probably be higher.

V. MECHANISMS OF MARRIAGE

Marriage, unlike cohabitation, also signifies commitment to a decision to in some ways scrap one's individuality for a new identity and responsibilities.[96] At this point each spouse views the other as someone whose well-being must always be taken into account. Further (and obviously circular in a discussion of why marriage should be given legal protection), the marriage, in this respect like a corporation, becomes a legal person, an identity.

From a sociological perspective, cohabitation is not a social status, while marriage is. Once married, the same people on the outside (parents, friends, and employers) treat the couple differently. That difference may be a problem for couples who cohabit first, but it won't be for those who directly enter marriage.

If relationships are envisioned developmentally, we may expect that early experiences inform and influence subsequent ones. The evidence from the United States suggests that the early experiences

---

95. Edward O. Laumann, John H. Gagnon, Robert T. Michael & Stuart Michaels, The Social Organization of Sexuality: Sexual Practices in the United States 503 & Table 13.2 (University of Chicago Press 1994).
96. Steven L. Nock, Marriage in Men's Lives (1998); Nock, *supra* note 16.

of cohabitation may establish relationship trajectories that conflict with the expectations of legal marriage. The most obvious way in which American cohabitation might do this is by fostering greater individuality or independence while discouraging commitment. American cohabitors, in fact, are more independent, more egalitarian in who does what in the household, and less committed to conventional systems of beliefs about lifelong marriage. Marriage, on the other hand, is well defined in American culture and law[97] and the elements that constitute American marriages (pledge of lifetime commitment, dependency, childbearing, etc.) differ notably from the typical pattern observed among cohabiting couples.

Most heterosexual cohabiting couples fall into one of two groups. They may view themselves as on their way to marriage,[98] in which case the abolition of heartbalm actions[99] by legislatures and common law suggests a public policy to treat them differently from married persons.

Another set of couples affirmatively wishes to reject marriage.[100] As Canadian academic Nicholas Bala writes: "[t]he motivations for living together outside of marriage are complex, but these relationships frequently arise because one party (often the man) is unwilling to make the commitment of marriage and does not want to undertake the legal obligations of marriage."[101] The Comments to the American Law Institute's *Principles of the Law of Family Dissolution* note that Chapter Six on Domestic Partnerships "diminishes the effectiveness of that strategy" of avoiding responsibility.[102] To the extent that the goal of other chapters involving property distribution and "compensatory payments" is to encourage specialization between spouses and investment in the family,[103] applying the same principles to dissolving domestic

---

97. Nock, *supra* note 96.

98. Bumpass & Sweet, *supra* note 37, at 615.

99. For a review, see Margaret F. Brinig, *Rings and Promises*, 6 J. L. Econ. & Org. 203 (1990). The heartbalm actions typically involving engaged couples were breach of marriage promise and seduction. For a recent case discussion, see *Miller v. Ratner*, 688 A.2d 976 (Md. Ct. App. 1997).

100. Nicholas Bala, Review of From Contract to Covenant, 2 Isuma 1, 1 (2001) *available at* www.isuma.net/v02n02/bala/bala_e.shtml; Comment to American Law Institute, Principles of the Law of Family Dissolution, § 6.02, at 14 (2002) (hereinafter Comment to ALI).

101. Bala, *supra* note 100, at 1.

102. Comment to ALI, *supra* note 100, at 14.

103. Ira M. Ellman, *The Theory of Alimony*, 77 Cal. L. Rev. 1 (1989); June Carbone & Margaret F. Brinig, *Rethinking Marriage: Feminist Ideology, Economic Change, and Divorce Reform*, 65 Tul. L. Rev. 953 (1991); June Carbone, *Economics, Feminism, and the Reinvention of Alimony: A Reply to Ira Ellman*, 43 Vand. L. Rev. 1463 (1990); Jana B. Singer, *Alimony and Efficiency: The Gendered*

partnerships flies in the face of reality: cohabiting couples are less specialized than married couples, are less interdependent, and have far more embedded equality goals.[104]

On the other hand, couples can be in relationships featuring permanence, which encourages unconditional love. At this point we have what "looks like" a family: people who are committed to each other over the very long time horizon and who are giving to each other without an expectation of immediate return (or perhaps any return). In Steve Nock's terminology,[105] they are living in the past and future, in a world of debts and futures, rather than the present. At this point, society (the community, meaning the religious community, the state, and even extended families) will act to support the family.[106] There will be laws promoting families,[107] giving constitutional rights,[108] and protecting the entity from outside assault.[109] There will be benefits that flow from being in such a family[110] and obligations that "are the threads from which intimacy is woven."[111] The members of the family live in covenant.

Policy makers are unlikely to want to provide default rules for cohabitation that would encourage cohabitation as an alternative to marriage[112] then, since empirical studies show it is far less stable than marriage.[113] Further, the partners invest less in each other or in the relationship than they do if married. In other words, cohabitation does not promote "economic efficiency" in the same way marriage does. For example, when men marry, they do much better financially than if single or cohabiting,[114] presumably either because their wives "nag" them into more responsible behavior[115] or because women

---

Costs and Benefits of the Economic Justification for Alimony, 82 Geo. L.J. 2423 (1994); Elisabeth M. Landes, *Economics of Alimony*, 7 J. Legal Stud. 35 (1978).

104. Nock, *supra* note 16, at 508.

105. Steven L. Nock, *Turn-Taking as Rational Behavior*, 27 Soc. Science Res. 235, 239-41 (1998).

106. Margaret F. Brinig, *Troxel and the Limits of Community*, 32 Rutgers L.J. 733 (2001).

107. *Compare* Patricia A. Cain, *Imagine There's No Marriage*, 16 Quinnipiac L. Rev. 27 (1996).

108. *As in* Troxel v. Granville, 530 U.S. 57, 120 S. Ct. 2054 (2000).

109. For example, consider the household exemption from bankruptcy and the "family estate" or tenancy by the entireties that shields marital property from creditors.

110. Vermont Civil Union Legislation, 2000 Vermont Laws P.A. 91 (H. 847), § 1204(c).

111. Nock, *supra* note 105, at 243.

112. Comment to ALI, *supra* note 100, at § 6.02.

113. Bumpass, Sweet & Cherlin, *supra* note 4; Bumpass & Sweet, *supra* note 37, at 620-21.

114. Victor Fuchs, Women's Quest for Economic Equality 58-60 (1988); Nock, *supra* note 105, at 66, 143.

115. Linda J. Waite & Maggie Gallagher, The Case for Marriage: Why Married

contribute "backup" support that makes men's labor force participation more focused.[116]   Cohabitants are more likely than married couples to share household tasks relatively more equally, though still with less sharing and more gendered behavior than one would expect,[117] and to generally value gender equality.[118]

Cohabiting partners thus have less commitment to each other than do married spouses,[119] and are more likely to think in terms of short-term rather than long-term consequences.   In fact, cohabitation is usually an exchange relationship, which produces less satisfaction[120] than one taking an "internal stance"[121] central to a meaningful interpersonal relationship.   In marriage, a relationship centered upon short-run gains signals instability.[122]

Even the landmark cohabitation opinion, *Marvin v. Marvin*,[123] noted that "[l]est we be misunderstood, however, we take this occasion to point out that the structure of society itself largely depends upon the institution of marriage, and nothing we have said in this opinion should be taken to derogate from that institution." As a community, we in effect don't give the relationship trust, so why treat cohabitation as though we do? Brinig and Nock in their recent work have found that where young people grow up in areas where there is a higher percentage of divorced people, the males delay first marriages.[124]   In other words, one of the effects of a relatively high divorce rate seems to be a higher rate of cohabitation.   As noted earlier, American

People are Happier, Healthier, and Better Off Financially (2000); Linda J. Waite, *Does Marriage Matter?*, 32 Demography 483, 496 (1995).

116.   Margaret F. Brinig, *Property Distribution Physics: The Talisman of Time and Middle Class Law*, 31 Fam. L.Q. 93 (1997); Arlie Hochschild with Anne Machung, The Second Shift: Working Parents and the Revolution at Home (1989); Joan Williams, Unbending Gender: Why Family and Work Conflict and What to Do About It (2000).

117.   Sanjiv Gupta, *The Effect of Transitions in Marital Status on Men's Performance of Housework*, 61 J. Marriage & Fam. 700 (1999).

118.   Nock, *supra* note 105, at 16.

119.   *Id.*, at 53.

120.   Gary L. Hansen, *Moral Reasoning and the Marital Exchange Relationship*, 131 J. Soc. Psychol. 71 (1991).

121.   Milton C. Regan, Alone Together: Law and the Meaning of Marriage 24 (1999).

122.   *See* Steven L. Nock and Margaret F. Brinig, *Weak Men and Disorderly Women: Divorce and the Division of Labor*, in Marriage and Divorce: A Law and Economics Approach (Dnes and Rowthorn, eds., 2002).

123.   Marvin v. Marvin, 557 P.2d 106, 122 (Cal. 1976).

124.   Brinig & Nock, *supra* note 122, at 483 & Table 4. For an indication that this greater selectivity in marriage may be the reason for the decline in the divorce rate since 1991, see Stéphane Méchoulan, Department of Economics, Northwestern University, *Divorce Laws and the Structure of the American Family*, paper presented at the American Law and Economics Association Annual Meeting, May 7, 2000.

marriages entered into after cohabitation are less, not more stable, than those of couples who do not cohabit first.[125] Generally speaking, presence of a child increases union stability,[126] though boys apparently stabilize relationships more than do girl children.[127]

In sum, by using (as the ALI proposes) a default rule that is *not* what people would most likely agree to in advance, we force those who do not want this type of relationship into contract-mode, which is hard on the relationship (forcing over-planning)[128] and destroys "covenantal" thinking (as the parties focus on what they can get out of the venture and how long it will last). As those of us who read family law cases know, couples in committed relationships are unlikely to choose contracting.[129]

There is no requirement that *during* the relationship, cohabiting partners support one another or provide medical care.[130] They do not

---

125. Axinn & Thornton, *supra* note 37, at 161; John Ermisch & Marco Francesconi, *Cohabitation in Great Britain: Not for Long, But Here to Stay,* Journal of the Royal Statistical Society, Series A, vol. 163, Part 2, 153-172 (2000); Kathleen Kiernan, *Cohabitation in Western Europe,* 96 Population Trends 25, 30 & Table 7 (1999).

126. Bumpass, Sweet & Cherlin, *supra* note 4; Lee A. Lillard & Linda J. Waite, *A Joint Model of Marital Childbearing and Marital Dissolution,* 30 Demography 653 (1993); Linda J. Waite & Lee A. Lillard, *Children and Marital Disruption,* 96 Am. J. Soc. 930 (1991).

127. Aphra R. Katzev, Rebecca L. Warner and Alan C. Acock, *Girls or Boys? Relationship of Child Gender to Marital Instability,* 56 J. Marriage & Fam. 89 (1994).

128. Lenore J. Weitzman, *Legal Regulation of Marriage: Tradition and Change,* 62 Cal. L. Rev. 1169 (1974).

129. Some data from surveys of same-sex couples (who have very high incentives to contract) reveals that as of 1995 ten percent or less had written agreements. Information on Same-Sex Relationships (Self-Reported), Survey of 21,000 Couples Who Answered Website Questionnaire, *The Advocate* (1994-1995). Data for married couples is nearly impossible to obtain, since it will not be filed anywhere unless the marriage dissolves. By definition, then, we cannot know how often American couples write antenuptial contracts. Even if we were to survey individuals, the numbers writing antenuptial contracts would probably be too small to permit meaningful analysis. Further, those who rely on such contracts are so unrepresentative (and perhaps more inclined to divorce) that such a query would be tremendously expensive. It is impossible to rely on divorce records because those with antenuptial agreements may be more likely to divorce anyway. Therefore, any research on this issue would face daunting problems in establishing a causal connection. An article written in 1988 suggests that there are "more" such agreements than formerly. Sheryl Nance, *'Til Some Breach Doth Them Part,* Nat'l L. J., November 7, 1988 at 1.

130. This objection seems to be met, at least at a minimal level, by California's domestic partnership provisions, which apply to same sex couples and to persons over 62. Section 297 of the California Family Code allows registration of domestic partnerships in which partners must agree to assume joint responsibility for each other's "basic living expenses" and authorizes state and local employers to offer health care coverage and other benefits to domestic partners of employees and

enjoy the privileges of confidential communications[131] or tort immunities. They cannot hold property as a community or by the entireties. If one of them dies, the other does not have the benefit of intestacy laws (as would a putative spouse). Supporting children does not become a common enterprise because of the adults' relationship, [132]

---

requires health-care facilities to permit visits by a patient's domestic partner. Cal. Fam. Code § 297 (2000). See also Canadian C-23, the Modernization of Benefits and Obligations Act (2000), which amends Criminal Code § 215(1)(b) (Can.) to punish those who fail to provide necessaries to a common law partner. Denmark, through the Danish Registered Partnership Act, 1989; Norway, in the Norwegian Registered Partnership Act of 1991; Sweden (1995) and Iceland (1996), all have registered same-sex partnerships, which have almost all of the consequences of marriage.

The ALI Principles apply to family dissolution, not ongoing relationships. State laws presumably govern ongoing relationships. State laws limit requirements of support to married couples or parents of minor children. For example, Illinois Statutes Chapter 750, section 16/15 provides in sections a (1) and (b):

§ 15. Failure to support.

(a) A person commits the offense of failure to support when he or she:

(1) willfully, without any lawful excuse, refuses to provide for the support or maintenance of his or her spouse, with the knowledge that the spouse is in need of such support or maintenance, or, without lawful excuse, deserts or willfully refuses to provide for the support or maintenance of his or her child or children in need of support or maintenance and the person has the ability to provide the support; or

(2) willfully fails to pay a support obligation required under a court or administrative order for support, if the obligation has remained unpaid for a period longer than 6 months, or is in arrears in an amount greater than $5,000, and the person has the ability to provide the support; or

(3) leaves the State with the intent to evade a support obligation required under a court or administrative order for support, if the obligation, regardless of when it accrued, has remained unpaid for a period longer than 6 months, or is in arrears in an amount greater than $10,000; or

(4) willfully fails to pay a support obligation required under a court or administrative order for support, if the obligation has remained unpaid for a period longer than one year, or is in arrears in an amount greater than $20,000, and the person has the ability to provide the support.

(a-5) Presumption of ability to pay support. The existence of a court or administrative order of support that was not based on a default judgment and was in effect for the time period charged in the indictment or information creates a rebuttable presumption that the obligor has the ability to pay the support obligation for that time period.

(b) Sentence. A person convicted of a first offense under subdivision (a)(1) or (a)(2) is guilty of a Class A misdemeanor. A person convicted of an offense under subdivision (a)(3) or (a)(4) or a second or subsequent offense under subdivision (a)(1) or (a)(2) is guilty of a Class 4 felony.

131.   Milton C. Regan, *Spousal Privilege and the Meanings of Marriage*, 81 Va. L. Rev. 2045 (1995).

132.   What we mean by this is the following. If a couple marries, the stepparent may well have support obligations for the children of the spouse at least during the pendency of the relationship. *See, e.g.*, Wash. Rev. Code § 26.16.205 (2004):

and former cohabitant fathers seem to support less often than noncustodial fathers following divorce.[133]

A. Courtship and Expectations

More than men, American women initiate divorce,[134] and are the ones wanting the divorce,[135] even though they all too frequently end up in poverty following marital dissolution.[136] In fact, depression following divorce corresponds closely with being the spouse who did not want the marriage to end.[137]

Divorce might be taken to indicate a failure to satisfactorily conduct a marriage search since it typically occurs so early in the relationship. Recent national figures from the National Center for Health Statistics estimate that forty-two percent of first marriages

---

The expenses of the family and the education of the children, including stepchildren, are chargeable upon the property of both husband and wife, or either of them, and they may be sued jointly or separately. When a petition for dissolution of marriage or a petition for legal separation is filed, the court may, upon motion of the stepparent, terminate the obligation to support the stepchildren. The obligation to support stepchildren shall cease upon the entry of a decree of dissolution, decree of legal separation, or death.

N.D. Cent. Code § 14-09-09 provides:

a. Liability of stepparent for support. A stepparent is not bound to maintain the spouse's dependent children, as defined in section 50-09-01, unless the child is received into the stepparent's family. If the stepparent receives them into the family, the stepparent is liable, to the extent of his or her ability, to support them during the marriage and so long thereafter as they remain in the stepparent's family.

But see Wood v. Woods, 184 Cal. Rptr. 471 (Cal. App. 1982) (no requirement that stepparent repay country for AFDC). Whether this lasts beyond dissolution depends, under the Principles, upon whether the stepparent has become a de facto parent or parent by estoppel. Compare *Johnson v. Johnson*, 617 N.W.2d 97 (N.D. 2000) (parent liable under doctrine of equitable adoption), with *Bagwell v. Bagwell*, 698 So.2d 746 (La. App. 2nd Cir. 1997) (no obligation after divorce). But no such obligation exists for the child of a cohabitant.

133. Manning, *supra* note 35, at 143.

134. Margaret F. Brinig & Douglas W. Allen, *"These Boots Are Made for Walking": Why Most Divorce Filers are Women*, 2 Am. Econ. & L. Rev. 126 (2000).

135. Sanford L. Braver, Marnie Whitley, & Christine Ng, *Who Divorced Whom? Methodological and Theoretical Issues*, 20 J. Divorce & Remarriage 1 (1993).

136. Richard R. Peterson, *A Reevaluation of the Economic Consequences of Divorce*, 61 Am. Soc. Rev. 528 (1996); Greg G. Duncan & Saul D. Hoffman, *A Reconsideration of the Economic Consequences of Marital Dissolution*, 22 Demography 485 (1985); Ross Finnie, *Women, Men, and the Economic Consequence of Divorce: Evidence from Canadian Longitudinal Data*, 30 Canadian Rev. Soc. & Anthro. 205 (1993); Pamela J. Smock, *Gender and the Short-Run Economic Consequences of Marital Disruption*, 73 Soc. Forces 243 (1994).

137. We have shown this using data from the National Survey of Families and Households. Results are available from the authors.

will end in divorce. However, thirty-four percent of first marriages end in the first ten years (seventeen percent of first marriages end in the first five years.) Subsequent marriages have minimally higher rates of disruption at each year of duration.[138] Assuming that people are not systematically fooled,[139] we have thought of two possible reasons women might be willing to marry (and, relatedly, why they might divorce). One has to do with payoffs from marriage that differ between men and women. The other has to do with different views of courtship and what it predicts—or doesn't predict—about married life.

Although the expected value[140] of the payoff from marriage might be the same for men and women, the variance[141] in what they will experience may be different. In other words, both men and women usually hope for health, wealth, and happiness when they seek to marry.[142] (In fact, such good wishes are the staples of toasts at receptions.) Empirical data show that men receive the first two whether or not the third good wish is present.[143] There is a small

---

138. M.D. Bramlett, & W.D. Mosher, Cohabitation, Marriage, Divorce, and Remarriage in the United States, National Center for Health Statistics, Vital Health Statistics 23, Table 21 (2002).

139. People's rationality is a basic assumption of both micro- and macroeconomics. For example, if there is inflation, people will only adjust their spending momentarily, until they realize that their wages did not really increase relative to prices. *See, e.g.*, Milton Friedman, *The Role of Monetary Policy*, 58 Am. Econ. Rev. 1, 7-11 (1968); Edmund Phelps, *Money Wage Dynamics and Labor Market Equililibrium*, *in* Macroeconomic Foundations of Employment and Unemployment and Inflation Theory 124 (Edmund Phelps, ed. 1970).

140. Expected value is defined as the probability of something occurring times its value. The expected value of an asset of P currently worth $100 is calculated as follows:

> Say we want to know its expected rate in a year. There is an 80% probability that it will have a normal rate of return, and be worth $110. There is a 10% probability that it will do exceptionally well, and be worth $120, and a 10% probability that it will do badly, and be worth only $105. EV(P) = (.8 X $110)+(.1 X $120)+(.1 X $105) = $88+$12+$10.50 = $110.50.

See John von Neumann & Oskar Morgenstern, Theory of Games and Economic Behavior (1964).

141. Variance is defined as the sum of the squared deviances from the mean divided by one less than the total number of deviations. A small variance would indicate that most people would cluster tightly around the average value. A large variance would mean that the various outcomes would be widely spread. For example, if sample A included observations of 1, 2, 3, 4, and 5, and sample B 2, 3, 3, 4 and 3, the variance in sample A would be 2.5, while of sample B only .5. For a discussion of this concept, see Steven M. Crafton & Margaret F. Brinig, Quantitative Methods for Lawyers 293-95 (1994).

142. "What's Love Got to Do With It," Saturday Review, September/October 11 (1985).

143. Nock, *supra* note 16, at 14.

variance, therefore, in men's return from marriage. In a small number of cases, though, the marriage may be a disastrous mismatch.[144] For women, the second and third wish are tied together, and in fact the "wealth" is usually a derived benefit from the increase in her husband's wealth.[145] A man's private wealth, that wealth tied to his earning capacity, almost always increases when he marries, and particularly grows when he has children.[146] A woman's private wealth, that which is tied to her earning capacity, frequently decreases when she marries,[147] and almost always does so when the couple has children.[148]

Married men live longer, have more satisfying sex lives, participate more in beneficial social organizations,[149] and are physically and mentally healthier than their single counterparts. They receive these benefits even in low-quality marriages[150] (in terms of communication with their spouse or shared experiences with her or even desire to make her happy). Married women live longer,[151] have more satisfying sex lives, participate more in social organizations, and are healthier[152] than their single counterparts only in high quality marriages.[153] When they are unhappy in their marriage, women have more physical and emotional problems and consult mental health professionals more frequently than either single or divorced women.[154] But the wife in a good marriage is happier

---

144. Becker, Landes & Michael, *supra* note 79.
145. Fuchs, *supra* note 114, at 58-64.
146. Arlie Hochschild, The Time Bind: When Work Becomes Home and Home Becomes Work (1997); Suzanne Bianchi & Daphne Spain, *Women, Work and Family in America*, 51 Population Bull. 1 (1996); Gillian K Hadfield, *The Gender Gap in Compensation: Households at Work: Beyond Labor Market Policies to Remedy the Gender Gap*, 82 Geo. L.J. 89 (1993); Joyce P. Jacobsen, *The Effects of Intermittent Labor Force Attachment on Women's Earnings*, 118 Monthly Lab. Rev. 14 (1995).
147. Williams, *supra* note 116; Hochschild, *supra* note 146.
148. Fuchs, *supra* note 114, at 58-64.
149. *Id.* at 60-64; Nock, *supra* note 96.
150. Nock, *supra* note 96, at 14; Walter R.Gove et al., *Does Marriage Have Positive Effects on the Psychological Well Being of the Individual?*, 24 J. of Health & Soc. Behavior 122, 128 (1983).
151. Waite, *Does Marriage Matter?*, *supra* note 115.
152. Charlotte A. Schoenborn & Marie Marano, *Health Characteristics of Married and Unmarried Persons, Current Estimates from the National Health Interview Survey*, Series 10, No. 166 (1988); Lois Verbrugge & Jennifer Madans, *Women's Roles and Health*, 7 Am. Demographics 36 (1985).
153. Waite, *Does Marriage Matter?*, *supra* note 115, at 499.
154. Nadine Marks, *Flying Solo at Midlife: Gender, Mental Status, and Psychological Well Being*, 58 J. Marriage and Fam. 917 (1996); Martha L. Bruce & Kathleen M. Kim, *Differences in the Effects of Divorce on Major Depression in Men and Women*, 149 Am. J. Psychiatry 914 (1992).

than any other category of woman.[155] On another front, the most stable marriages of all are those in which the husbands perceive the unfairness of the housework and labor force situation for their wives, not those in which everyone perceives all divisions of responsibility as fair.[156] Thus, the woman sees a large variance from the returns to marriage. She may find herself in a disaster, a mediocre relationship in which she receives few rewards, or a glorious one in which the rewards overflow and she is appreciated.

Since the emotional success of the marriage has little to do with the man's payoff, and a great deal to do with his wife's,[157] it is not surprising that she will frequently be the one to break things off if it turns out that the marriage is not a happy one, despite producing material rewards.[158] Thus she is usually the one to file for divorce or seek separation, particularly if she can obtain custody of the children. According to Brinig and Allen, "[t]he proportion of wife-filed cases has ranged from around sixty percent for most of the nineteenth century to, immediately after the introduction of no-fault divorce, more than seventy percent in some states. Today, with some variation among states, it remains slightly above two-thirds."[159] Though she is less likely than he to repeat the marriage experience, she will be happier outside marriage than in an emotionally unsatisfying one. Women may thus seek marriage despite the fact that they may be less successful in finding Prince Charming[160] than their mates in finding Cinderella.[161]

The alternative explanation, one garnered from unscientific surveys of students (attending American schools) over the years, is that men and women think courtship is "about" different things. Men

---

155. Norvall D. Glenn, *Marriage on the Rocks*, 21 Psychol. Today 20 (1987); Norvall D. Glenn, *The Contribution of Marriage to the Psychological Well-Being of Males and Females*, 37 J. Marriage & Fam. 594 (1975); Norval Glenn & C.N. Weaver, *The Changing Relationship of Marital Status to Reported Happiness*, 50 J. Marriage & Fam. 317 (1988); G. Lee, K. Seccombe & C. Shehan, *Marital Status and Personal Happiness: An Analysis of Trend Data*, 53 J. Marriage & Fam. 839 (1991).

156. Nock & Brinig, *supra* note 122.

157. Women will divorce more often if they are highly educated and hold outside jobs, since by divorcing they have less to lose. Marilyn Manser & Murray Brown, *Marriage and Household Decision-Making: A Bargaining Analysis*, 21 Int'l Econ. Rev. 31 (1980); Suzanne Bianchi & Daphne Spain, *Women, Work and Family in America*, 51 Population Bull. 2 (1996).

158. Demie Kurz, For Richer, For Poorer: Mothers Confront Divorce 188-89 (1995).

159. Brinig & Allen, *supra* note 134, at 126-27.

160. Margaret F. Brinig, *In Search of Prince Charming*, 4 J. of Gender, Race & Justice 321 (2001).

161. These and following comments are drawn from patterns found in America. We know of no related work from Western Europe. Whether comparable generalizations would apply in that context, therefore, is speculation.

view courtship as a contest in which they triumph over other suitors.[162] Dating and courtship are therefore quite distinct from marriage, and the behavior in the early period need not have anything to do with that in marriage, when they are free to "be themselves." Cohabitation may be a time in which the conquest is not complete, in which their behavior is still not "normal."

The women in class, both married and unmarried, think that courtship is about successively revealing things about themselves to the men involved. They view the activities and the emotions involved with courtship as necessarily precursors to what will lie ahead in marriage. In terms of the economic explanation already given, courtship to women provides necessary information for their search. They regard courtship behavior as signaling what the man will be like as a husband.

Many of these women complained that their husbands changed after they married. Instead of being focused on their wives, they spent time with friends. Instead of being romantic, they wanted to just relax in front of the television when they got home from work. Instead of lengthy foreplay, they were interested almost immediately in intercourse. Many women felt that they'd been asked to shoulder the emotional work of the relationship, that they couldn't even get help with such simple matters as what to fix for dinner. Their husbands, who had been so spontaneously wonderful prior to marriage, were now much less interesting and more demanding creatures.

The men complained that what they'd thought of as discerning behavior before marriage they now saw as demanding. They didn't see why they should be expected to put on an act for their wives. They found it very difficult to figure out what their wives wanted from them because, they said, their own needs were simple compared to their wives'.[163] It's no wonder, if these differences in perceptions hold true among larger and broader samples than our own, that over forty percent of American marriages begun after 1980 may end in divorce in the next two or three decades. Perhaps, as one of us claimed some years ago, a good portion of courtship behavior is fraud.[164]

---

162. David M. Buss, *The Evolution of Human Intrasexual Competition: Tactics of Mate Attraction*, 54 J. of Personality & Soc. Psych. 616 (1988); Susan Sprecher, Quintin Sullivan & Elaine Hatfield, *Mate Selection Preferences: Gender Differences Examined In A National Sample*, 66 J. of Personality & Soc. Psych. 1074 (1994).

163. Deborah Tannen, You just don't understand: Women and Men in conversation (1991); John Gray, Men Are From Mars, Women Are From Venus: A Practical Guide for Improving Communication and Getting More out of Relationships (1992).

164. Brinig & Alexeev, *supra* note 42.

Many parents, ourselves included, may caution children against cohabiting. Parents, after all, are more likely to have grown up when cohabitation was stigmatized (or, at least, frowned upon). The generational difference in acceptability of cohabiting leads to a predictable problem. Those children who cohabit without their parents' approval lack an important form of social support.[165]

Goodman[166] shows that removal of stigmatizing laws can have an extremely beneficial effect on self-esteem and relationship quality even if the laws are seldom, if ever, enforced. This study (of the removal of sodomy laws in South Africa) indicates that removing the laws that still exist in many states[167] that tend to stigmatize cohabiting behavior might improve outside perceptions and cohabitants' feelings about their unions. This change has clearly occurred in Scandinavia, where there have been no laws prohibiting cohabitation for many years.

Professional baseball used to be followed by fans of particular teams (usually the home team).[168] Today, with free agency and thus no expected loyalty to a team, young people learning about baseball owe their allegiance to players rather than to teams. They will cheer for Jason Giambi whether he's an A or a Yank. A community finds it harder to be enthusiastic about a team or finds it brings people together, since the community can't count on continued success or presence of particular players. Roger Clemons, for example, has won notoriously high salary contracts from two different and very successful clubs: Boston, in 1991 ($5,380,250 a year for four seasons), and New York Yankees ($15.45 million a year for two seasons, in 2000). The average attendance at games, perhaps as a result at least in part, has decreased since the advent of free agency,[169] while the average salary has increased from $19,000 in 1967 to $1,895,630 in 2000 (Blum, 2000) and $2.3 million in 2002.[170] Free agency in baseball thus resembles the Scandinavian situation, where informal unions are sanctioned and treated as the same as marriages. But is there still a cost? What happens to the partners to trial

---

165. This may be changing with time. Most parents of 25 years olds today came of age as cohabitation was gaining in popularity. A large proportion grew up in the sexual revolution of the 1970s. Whether these historical experiences translate into more tolerant views of their children's cohabiting intentions or behaviors is not known. Our sense, however, is that most parents are relieved to learn that their children have decided to marry.

166. Goodman, *supra* note 7.

167. *See* sources cited, *supra* note 14.

168. Hal Bodley, *Free Agency Brought Big Changes*, USA Today, Dec. 22, 2000.

169. Thomas Heath, *Baseball Facing a Stop in Play: Familiar Problems Haunt Game as Threat of Strike Looms*, Washington Post, July 7, 2002, at A1.

170. *Id.*

marriages that don't work out? This data has never been collected systematically, but many studies would seem to lump these people with others who "cohabited before marriage," a group that has less successful marriage experiences. This we will turn to shortly.

The Canadian Supreme Court, in *M. v. H.*,[171] held that benefits granted to heterosexual cohabitants under the definition of "spouse" under the Family Law Act § 29, granting benefits to separating cohabitants who have lived together at least three years or who have a common child and have lived together in a relationship of some permanence, must be extended to same-sex couples as a matter of equality. In the legislation passed in 2000, C-23, the definition of "common law partner" for purposes of numerous federal benefits and obligations includes those in a conjugal relationship for one year or more. The Canadian Criminal Code § 215(1)(b) punishes those who do not furnish necessaries to the common law partner. The application of the benefits and obligations of domestic partnership law to ongoing relationships is a major difference from Chapter Six of the ALI Principles,[172] which do not impose a support obligation while the relationship continues. This is also a difference between Chapter Six and Vermont's Civil Union status[173] and implicitly the ALI (2002), both think that by imposing duties on separating cohabiting couples, men will not be discouraged from marrying. But they may miss the powerful evidence that men benefit powerfully from marriage, not cohabitation.[174]

PCT22. Unmarried-Partner Households and Sex of Partners[175]

Data Set: Census 2000 Summary File 2 (SF 2) 100-Percent Data

	United States	
Total:	105,480,101	
Unmarried-partner households:	5,475,768	
Male householder & male partner:		301,026
Male householder & female partner:		2,615,119
Female householder & female partner:		293,365
Female householder & male partner:		2,266,258
All other households:	100,004,333	

---

171. 2 S.C.R. 3 (1999).
172. Comment to ALI, *supra* note 100.
173. Bala, *supra* note 100.
174. Nock, *supra* note 96; Waite & Gallagher, *supra* note 115.

While increasing stability arguably may not be a value (if it's patriarchal or at the expense of happiness), it does increase the productivity of a couple. While increased productivity again may not be worth pursuing through private relationships, we do find persuasive evidence that stability is good for kids. Were cohabiting relationships stable, whether or not parents married would be a matter of indifference. As Wendy Manning notes, "[g]enerally, the marital status of biological parents does not have much impact on children's social well-being. Children in cohabiting-parent families have similar behavior and emotional problems as children in married-parent families."[176]

There are some differences in parenting behavior, however. Cohabiting parents are less likely to take their children on outings, and are less likely to read to their children under the age of six.[177] However, "[t]he disadvantage of being born to a cohabiting parent seems to emerge once the child and father live apart. Children born to cohabiting-parent families experience lower levels of nonresident father involvement for measures of visitation and child support payments than children born in a marriage."[178]

Further, cohabiting relationships are not stable. Children whose parent or parents cohabit are more likely to experience transitions in family structure. Graefe and Lichter[179] argue that "virtually all children in cohabiting-couple families will experience rapid subsequent changes in family status. For most, family reorganization involves forming married-couple families, but for a significant share, the dissolution of the parent's cohabiting relationship precipitates additional family transitions."[180] Thus, even if children in cohabiting unions have two parents, the possible problems posed by the instability of such unions are sufficient to caution us against encouraging such arrangements until we know more about how they affect children's lives.

Undoubtedly, cohabitation is increasingly popular in the United States and elsewhere. It has rapidly emerged as at least three things. First, for the majority of couples that marry (fifty-two

---

175. The table, taken from complete census data, is available by a search for "unmarried-partner" at http://factfinder.census.gov.

176. Manning, *supra* note 35, at 142.

177. Brown, *supra* note 23, at 184–85.

178. Manning, *supra* note 35, at 143; E. Mavis Hetherington et al., *What matters? What does not? Five Perspectives On The Association Between Marital Transitions and Children's Adjustment*, 53 Am. Psychol. 167 (1998).

179. D.R Graefe & D. T. Lichter, *Life Course Transitions of American Children: Parental Cohabitation, Marriage and Single Motherhood*, 36 Demography 205 (1999).

180. *Id.*, at 215.

percent during 1990-1994)[181] cohabitation is a prelude to marriage. Second, some young people elect to live in informal cohabiting relationships rather than marriage, even when children are involved. Finally, for a large and growing segment of previously married individuals, cohabitation substitutes for remarriage. While there is much to learn about the practice, it is safe to say that it has become an important option in the range of relationship possibilities in America and elsewhere. There is little evidence to suggest that cohabitation is superior to marriage in any measurable way.

At the moment, marriage and cohabitation exist as alternatives. As such, we have a situation much like housing tenure. Individuals have an option to rent or buy a residence. There are legal (financial) advantages to buying a home that are denied to renters. And presumably these benefits are recognized as legitimate by most Americans. Given what we know about marriage, isn't the same true with respect to intimate relationships? Even if marriage continued to convey some legal benefits, of what possible value is its abolition?

Still, certain forms of cohabitation may play a very useful and stabilizing role in our society. If our speculations about searching for a partner are correct, and if our interpretation of patterns in Western Europe are also correct, then for individuals who use cohabitation as part of a marriage search, cohabitation may lead to a better match between married partners. At the same time, there may be enduring consequences for individuals (and especially children) when cohabitations fail.[182] At least so long as marriage and cohabitation coexist as alternative regimes, the individual who has a history of failed cohabiting relationships faces greater chances of disruption should she or he decide to marry. Abolishing legal marriage will be a very difficult case to make in a society such as ours given the high degree of religiousness of most Americans.[183] We will do better by focusing on the connection between cohabitation and marriage, and studying the potential search benefits cohabitation may produce.

Given the centrality of marriage in our culture, and given the established and verified benefits it confers, any argument for

---

181. Bumpass & Lu, *supra* note 23.

182. In the same way that our society lacks a word for one's cohabiting partner (friend? partner? girl/boy friend?), we do not have a word for the breakup of such a relationship. Both are clear evidence of the lack of institutionalization of the practice.

183. Indeed, by comparison with other nations, America stands as one of the most religious in the world, no matter which measures one uses (church attendance, frequency of prayer, reliance on religion in making decisions, evangelizing, belief in God, belief in sin, etc.). George Gallup, Jr., & D. Michael Lindsay. Surveying the Religious Landscape: Trends in U.S. Beliefs (1999).

2004]   *MARGARET F. BRINIG & STEVEN L. NOCK*   439

abolishing it has its primary value in making us realize the vast and pervasive benefits that flow to the adults and children embedded in such an institution.

Table 1.   Relative risk of partnership dissolution according
           to type of first partnership for women aged twenty
           to thirty-nine years. Model 2 with controls for age
           at first partnership.

Country	Model 1	Model 2
Sweden		
Married Directly	1.00	1.00
Cohabitated-married	0.88	0.88
Cohabitated	7.73**	7.81***
Norway		
Married Directly	1.00	1.00
Cohabitated-married	0.70**	0.71**
Cohabitated	8.23***	8.69***
Finland		
Married Directly	1.00	1.00
Cohabitated-married	0.97	0.89
Cohabitated	4.91***	4.35***
France		
Married Directly	1.00	1.00
Cohabitated-married	1.20	1.15
Cohabitated	2.27***	2.01***
Austria		
Married Directly	1.00	1.00
Cohabitated-married	0.89	0.87
Cohabitated	5.12***	4.58***
Switzerland		
Married Directly	1.00	1.00
Cohabitated-married	1.01	1.03
Cohabitated	12.3***	12.9***
West Germany		
Married Directly	1.00	1.00
Cohabitated-married	1.21	1.15
Cohabitated	4.14***	3.83***
East Germany		
Married Directly	1.00	1.00
Cohabitated-married	1.08	1.07
Cohabitated	1.63***	1.55***
Great Britain		
Married Directly	1.00	1.00
Cohabitated-married	1.08	1.07
Cohabitated	10.5***	10.2***
Italy		
Married Directly	1.00	1.00
Cohabitated-married	1.52	1.48
Cohabitated	19.1**	16.8***

Spain		
Cohabitated-married	1.00	1.00
Married Directly	2.59***	2.52***
Cohabitated	18.71**	16.5***

Kathleen Kiernan, *Cohabitation in Western Europe*, 96 Population Trends 25, 30 & Table 7 (1999). Data based on Eurobarometer Surveys from 1996, typically several thousand respondents per country.

Table 2.   Life-table estimates of percentage of unions surviving three and five years after the birth of first child among women aged twenty to forty-five years according to type of first partnership.

Country	% surviving thirty-six months	% surviving sixty months	Number in the risk set
Norway*			
Married	97	94	1,677
Cohabitation	87	82	456
Cohabited/Married	98	95	131
Cohabited Only	79	71	325
Sweden*			
Married	96	93	817
Cohabitation	90	84	1,424
Cohabited/Married	97	94	493
Cohabited Only	84	75	931
Austria			
Married	97	94	2,161
Cohabitation	92	86	670
Cohabited/Married	98	96	246
Cohabited Only	86	71	424
Switzerland			
Married	97	95	2,191
Cohabitation	82	73	166
Cohabited/Married	95	86	65
Cohabited Only	64	53	101
West Germany**			
Married	95	91	873
Cohabitation	92	85	161
Cohabited/Married	97	91	45
Cohabited Only	89	80	116

Great Britain			
Married	96	92	1,242
Cohabitation	71	57	149
Cohabited/Married	90	75	43
Cohabited Only	61	48	106
Italy			
Married	99	98	2,677
Cohabitation	95	91	90
Cohabited/Married	-	-	31
Cohabited Only	93	82	59
Spain			
Married	99	98	1,540
Cohabitation	79	67	74
Cohabited/Married	-	-	16
Cohabited Only	71	51	58

From Kathleen Kiernan, *Childbearing Outside Marriage in Western Europe*, 98 Population Trends, 11, 19 & Table 11 (1999).

Data based on UN ECE European Family and Fertility Surveys and British Household Panel Survey, taken 1992-96.

[5]

Divorce Laws and the Structure of the American Family

Stéphane Mechoulan

ABSTRACT

This paper investigates the impact of no-fault divorce laws on marriage and divorce in the United States. I propose a theory that captures the key stylized facts of the rising then declining divorce rates and the apparent convergence of divorce rates across the different divorce regimes. The empirical results suggest that a shift from fault to no-fault divorce increased the odds of divorcing for those couples who married before the shift. The analysis further suggests that those couples who marry after the shift to a no-fault regime, in turn, sort themselves better upon marriage, which offsets the direct effect of the law on divorce rates. Consistent with that selectivity argument, after a switch to a no-fault divorce regime, women get married later in life. These results hold for the law that governs property division and spousal support. The law that governs divorce grounds does not seem to matter significantly.

INTRODUCTION

In the 1970s and early 1980s, the United States underwent what is commonly referred to as a "divorce revolution" (Weitzman 1985). Prior

STÉPHANE MECHOULAN is Assistant Professor of Economics, University of Toronto. I am greatly indebted to Margaret Brinig and Ira Mark Ellman. I also thank Joe Altonji, Gadi Barlevy, Gary Becker, Arie Beresteanu, Pierre-André Chiappori, Jacques Crémer, Dino Gerardi, Luojia Hu, Kathryn Ierulli, Ricky Lam, Steven Levitt, Dan Levy, Bruce Meyer, Dale Mortensen, John Panzar, Tomas Philipson, Imran Rasul, Emmanuel Saez, Chris Taber, Burton Weisbrod, and an anonymous referee, as well as seminar participants at the 10th American Law and Economics Association conference, and especially Eric Rasmusen, RAND, Ohio State, Duke, Université de Montreal, and University of Toronto for their helpful comments. I am grateful to Susan Arden, Ken Burdett, Nezih Guner, Elizabeth Peters, Eric Rapp, Arthur Stinchcombe, and Linda Waite for advice and encouragement at various stages of this research. Last, but not least, Ann Janda and Eanswythe Grabowski greatly helped me with my data work. Financial support from a Northwestern University Graduate Research Grant is gratefully acknowledged. All errors are mine.

[*Journal of Legal Studies*, vol. 35 (January 2006)]

144 / THE JOURNAL OF LEGAL STUDIES / VOLUME 35 (1) / JANUARY 2006

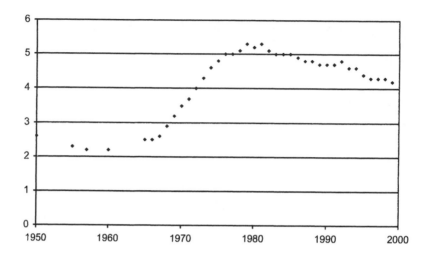

Figure 1. U.S. divorce rate per 1,000 population (National Center for Health Statistics 1950–2000).

to 1970, spouses typically either had to wait for a long period of time or had to prove that a fault had been committed in order to get a divorce. The reforms authorized spouses in most states to obtain a divorce by simply alleging a specific no-fault ground such as irreconcilable differences or irretrievable breakdown of the marriage. During the same period, about half the states adopted no-fault rules for property division and spousal support (henceforth referred to as "property").

Simultaneously, starting from the late 1960s, the divorce rate increased dramatically. It peaked in the late 1970s and early 1980s and has decreased slowly but continuously ever since (see Figures 1 and 2). In almost every state, divorce rates started to rise before the legal changes occurred, which has cast much doubt on the impact of these laws. The key is to address the potential endogeneity of divorce laws themselves and to disentangle the causation process: Were the new divorce laws at least partially a cause of the surging divorce rate? Did they accelerate the trend, if they did not create it? Or did they merely involve an upgrading of the legal texts, an adjustment to the common practice of courts and new attitudes regarding marriage?[1]

Divorce laws have received much attention lately. Gardiner et al.

---

1. In particular, there has been a growing acceptance of divorce within the U.S. population, especially in the presence of children; see, for example, Glenn (1991).

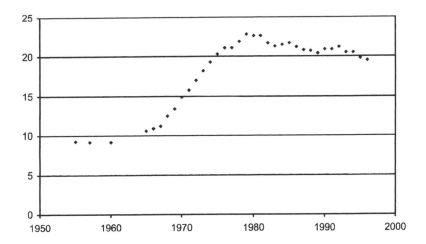

Figure 2. Divorce rate per 1,000 married women (National Center for Health Statistics 1950–2000).

(2002) provide an excellent overview of a wide range of state-level pro-family policies recently introduced in the United States, including the reintroduction of covenant marriages and the removal of marriage penalties in tax codes and Medicaid programs. A commonly expressed claim in support of a return to a fault rule is that the move to no fault caused the divorce rate to rise. One can add the arguments put forward by the fathers' rights movements, which take a strong position against no-fault divorce and its impact on custody of children (grandparents' groups make similar contentions) or the "supermom burnout" assertion that no-fault divorce has forced mothers to increase hours of work as a form of insurance against divorce. There is also a growing literature on the effect that no-fault divorce has had on the "culture" of divorce and the diminished social value placed on the institution of marriage (Dnes and Rowthorn 2002; Grossbard-Shechtman 2003).

Since the mid-1970s, a vast body of literature has sought to understand the effects of these divorce laws. After Peters's (1986, 1992; see also Allen 1992) seminal contributions, research focused on aggregate, state-level panel data to detect the impact of divorce laws changes on divorce rates.[2] There appears to be a consensus among scholars that no-

_____

2. See Brinig and Buckley (1998); Ellman and Lohr (1998); Gray (1998, which also uses Current Population Survey and Panel Study of Income Dynamics data); Friedberg (1998); Gruber (2000); and Wolfers (2003) to cite only recent studies that have appeared in the economics literature.

146 / THE JOURNAL OF LEGAL STUDIES / VOLUME 35 (1) / JANUARY 2006

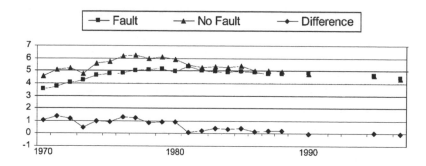

Figure 3. U.S. divorce rates by property regime (National Center for Health Statistics 1950–2000; U.S. Census Bureau 1999).

fault divorce produced a sudden burst in the divorce rate after the new laws were enacted. Yet there is still controversy around whether the changes were short-term or structural.[3]

The starting point of this analysis rests on the following observations: not only have aggregate divorce rates decreased since most of the legal changes were passed, but the average difference in divorce rates across different divorce regimes has been narrowing (Figure 3).[4] One should then also investigate why, since the early 1980s, divorce rates have decreased faster, on average, in states where fault is not considered for property.

To this end, the present contribution provides an empirical analysis of the underlying causation process between divorce laws, marriage, and divorce: the key extension on past literature is to consider that the changes in the laws may have different consequences depending on when marriages were contracted, that is, before or after the legal changes. In particular, this approach allows us to tell whether the divorce rate in any given regime is different for those married under different divorce laws.

The paper explores the hypothesis that spouses take the law into account and sort themselves differently according to which rule governs their possible future divorce. The main consequence is that the changes

---

3. Friedberg (1998) found permanent, structural effects. However, using the same data, Ellman (2000) and Wolfers (2003) questioned the robustness of those results.

4. Friedberg (1998) and Wolfers (2003) analyze this difference in difference, but their aggregate series stops in 1988, and therefore the bulk of the last divorces they analyze are for marriages contracted in the late 1970s and early 1980s.

in divorce laws did not necessarily translate into structural differences in divorce rates over time but rather more deeply into differences regarding match quality in marriage. Match quality, in turn, would affect the divorce rate and may thereby offset the effects of the change in the law. While the direction of the sorting is theoretically ambiguous, this study shows why a better match quality at the marriage stage is a consistent explanation for the patterns in the data described above. Such sorting would become apparent in the timing of marriage as well.

Using cross-sectional micro data from the June supplements of the Current Population Survey (CPS) (U.S. Department of Labor 1971–98), the findings first confirm that for couples who married before the changes in the law, there was a significant impact of no fault for property on divorce odds: this is referred to as the "pipeline effect" (that is, the increased divorce rate resulting from the divorces of couples whose marriages were falling apart but who did not divorce until the new law took effect). Most important, among individuals who have not experienced a change in property law since their marriage, the odds of divorce are found to not differ significantly between the two regimes: my interpretation is that the direct effect and the indirect offsetting effect (that is, better selection at marriage) cancel out. The law defining divorce grounds, in contrast, has a more limited impact on divorce probabilities. Further, there is evidence of a delay in marriage for women when fault is irrelevant for property decisions: ceteris paribus, a longer search also points toward better matching.

Consistent with the idea of adaptive behavior, I investigate both the overall average effect of no-fault divorce as well as its effect over time: the results suggest that those changes in the law that took place well after the first changes of the early 1970s still had some effect for those who married before those late changes. On the other hand, the selection effect is on par with other recent findings (Rasul 2003) and provides a clear economic rationale for the statistical argument, based on aggregate data, that no-fault divorce had only a short-run effect on divorce rates (Wolfers 2003).

As a caveat, it should be stressed that the use of CPS data is not without its problems: one does not know the migration history of the sample respondents, yet the American population is extremely mobile. Further, in most waves of the survey, divorcees do not report when they got divorced. Therefore, this study limits itself to individuals who married for the first time within a short time interval before their interview: this option bounds the error probability in assuming that respondents

148 / THE JOURNAL OF LEGAL STUDIES / VOLUME 35 (1) / JANUARY 2006

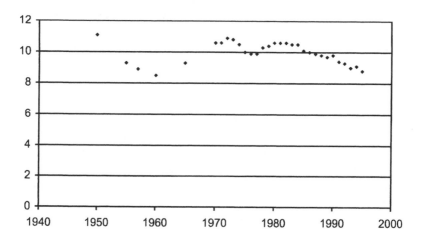

Figure 4. Marriage rates per 1,000 population (National Center for Health Statistics 1950–2000; U.S. Census Bureau 1999).

had not moved since their marriage and, most important, in classifying divorcees into one legal regime or the other. The divorce estimates obtained in the regressions cannot therefore be directly compared to those provided in Figure 3, which aggregate divorces per 1,000 population in each state and year. However, they should be seen as different angles of the same global picture. Put differently, this paper does not attempt to estimate the impact of divorce laws on divorce rates per 1,000 population. While it has been the object of past empirical research, this statistic is problematic: it aggregates divorces from marriages that were contracted under different legal regimes—thus mixing people with different incentive structures at marriage, as well as divorces from first marriages and remarriages. Therefore, these rates also indirectly capture the incentive effect of the legal changes on marriage and remarriage, making the identification of the impact of the laws on divorce per se very difficult. In particular, note that while overall marriage rates appear constant in the 1970s and 1980s (Figure 4), first-marriage rates have steadily decreased since the early 1970s (Figure 5): this is explained by the high number of remarriages, naturally following the increasing number of divorces over the same period.

Finally, it is important to emphasize that marriage vintage and endogenous selection effects in the "marriage market" by no means tell the whole story underlying divorce rate trends in the United States. That

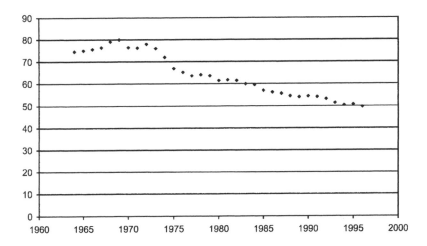

Figure 5. First-marriage rate per 1,000 unmarried women, 15 years and older (National Center for Health Statistics 1950–2000; U.S. Census Bureau 1999).

being said, any explanation must take into account the key empirical facts of rising then declining divorce rates and the apparent convergence of those rates across different divorce regimes.

The remainder of the paper is organized as follows. Section 2 provides further motivation for this research with a discussion of how to categorize divorce laws and with an overview of the existing literature. Section 3 describes the data; Section 4 presents the empirical methodology and sets out the results and interprets them; and Section 5 concludes the paper.

MOTIVATIONS AND LITERATURE ANALYSIS

Background

The concept of the divorce revolution covers a complex, multifaceted sequence of events, and there are detailed, excellent accounts of that story that focus on the now well understood causes of the movement and describe the actual changes that took place in the courts (see, for example, Jacob 1988; Parkman 1992).

In short, in the old system, proof of marital fault—defined differently in each state, but usually comprising adultery, desertion, or physical abuse, for example—or a long separation between spouses was required

150 / THE JOURNAL OF LEGAL STUDIES / VOLUME 35 (1) / JANUARY 2006

before a court would grant a divorce decree. Therefore, it was not uncommon for one spouse to endorse a bogus fault in court and to have friends commit perjury in order for a couple to be granted a divorce.

Several reasons for the divorce reform movement initiated in the 1970s can be advanced: to save the U.S. judicial system from a procedure that validated hypocrisy and led to condoning perjury, to allow obviously separated couples to formalize their status, and to grant divorces to permit remarriage. Also, it was felt that spouses could not reach efficient bargains under the old rules. Finally, a long-forgotten, original motivation was to encourage reconciliation through a less conflict-oriented procedure.

This reform movement resulted in various rules that made it possible for one spouse to obtain a divorce without citing a fault by the other spouse or having the other spouse's consent, for that matter. Some states abolished all fault grounds, whereas others added a no-fault provision (incompatibility, irreconcilable differences, or irretrievable breakdown of the marriage) to traditional fault grounds. This distinction will be not pursued in this work since fault is rarely used in practice when no-fault grounds have been added.[5] Finally, in states in which no such grounds were introduced, separation requirements were usually shortened. In the following, I define as having no-fault grounds only those states that have enacted specific no-fault statutes, even though there are other states that have not generally specified that a no-fault divorce may be granted after the spouses live separate and apart for some minimum period of time.[6]

Simultaneously, legislatures changed rules concerning the financial part of the procedure. However, it is important to note that property regimes changed in more than one way. The first one dealt with what was to be considered marital assets. Each spouse was now allowed to share in what had been available only in community-property states:

5. Fault still retains a role in bargaining and is still used about 10 percent of the time in states where both fault and no-fault divorce are available. I thank an anonymous referee for pointing this out.

6. All states now have some form of no-fault divorce. While divorce can be instantaneous for many fault grounds, a small number of states recognize a long waiting period of separation as the only no-fault ground for divorce. Other states require separation in addition to other no-fault grounds, or if the divorce is contested, one spouse can obtain a postponement. I do not count as having fault those states in which a no-fault divorce may not be granted if it is not agreed upon by both spouses and where separation alone may not be grounds for a no-fault divorce. This decision is disputable, however estimation results were not found to be sensitive to the classification of these states.

everything earned by either of them. This was a set of changes that theoretically benefited women at divorce. At the same time, many states also eliminated or greatly reduced permanent alimony. This was a set of changes that theoretically benefited men at divorce (see Fineman 1983, 1991). Almost simultaneously, many states barred the consideration of fault in asset division and spousal support settlements.[7] With regard to property regimes, this work focuses on that no-fault dimension.

An analysis of all the theoretical and empirical work on this issue would require a lengthy survey paper, and it is still a very intensive area of research. From a theoretical standpoint, a strict application of the Coase theorem implies that divorce laws should not influence divorce rates: theoretically, spouses could write a binding prenuptial agreement that would bypass any legal change.[8] Yet it seems fair to say that the assumptions of perfectly transferable utility and no transaction costs, on which the Coase theorem rests, are not realistic in the context of marriage and divorce.[9] In the empirical literature, the conclusions on whether a change to no-fault divorce resulted in higher divorce rates have been going back and forth—even though we observe a recent convergence. There is a consensus about the existence of a short-term increase in divorce rates immediately after the enactment of the no-fault regimes. I will advance here that there was also a structural behavioral effect and characterize which dimension of the divorce revolution was responsible for it.

Trends

Another point that needs to be emphasized is that divorce rates per 1,000 population have been decreasing since the early 1980s, as can be seen from Figure 1. The time series I prefer to focus on is the divorce rate per married woman, shown in Figure 2. But they exhibit similar trending

7. Almost always, the statutes making the first set of changes outlined above were also the ones that changed from fault to a no-fault regime for property. Also, those states that eliminated or reduced permanent alimony were usually those moving to a pure no-fault regime rather than adding a no-fault ground to the fault ones. I thank an anonymous referee for these remarks.

8. However, spouses in the United States cannot contract around grounds for divorce. An exception is the covenant marriage states, which allow spouses to choose between two state-sanctioned sets of grounds. I thank an anonymous referee for this point.

9. Grossbard-Shechtman and Lemennicier (1999) provide a comprehensive discussion of the transaction cost issue. Lundberg and Pollak (2001) and Murphy (2002) present models of household behavior in which limits on marital contracting lead to inefficient outcomes. Zelder (2002) provides a very good overview of the theoretical literature on household bargaining and the empirical evidence on the efficiency of household decisions.

152 / THE JOURNAL OF LEGAL STUDIES / VOLUME 35 (1) / JANUARY 2006

patterns, so looking at the former alone is not too misleading, provided the full time series is considered.

More puzzlingly, divorce rates have dramatically converged across regimes. Figure 3 depicts the divorce rates by property regime across time (note that rates for Nevada—the migratory divorce state—have been eliminated, as they are outliers, but adding them would actually reinforce the convergence pattern).[10] The number of states included in each series (fault and no-fault property) varied each time a state moved from a fault to a no-fault regime (the reverse never happened). A state that enacted no-fault laws in a given year was excluded when computing the average divorce rate of no-fault states that year. Thus, this figure is a picture without (most of) the so-called pipeline effect defined earlier. Excluding a state for more than 1 year to account for separation requirements would produce an analogous pattern. With a similar methodology, Rasul (2003) graphs divorce rates per married women using CPS data, separating those states that adopted "unilateral divorce" (in his terminology)[11] from those that did not, and obtains a very comparable picture.

This is a recent finding. However, we should concentrate on the trend and not on the magnitude of the divorce rates reported in Figure 3. Recall that this figure picks up divorce rates per 1,000 population,[12] and most important, as in Figure 2, it aggregates divorces from marriages that were contracted under different legal regimes. Therefore, the interpretation of those rates in isolation could be deceptive. But we know that the stock of marriages at high risk for divorce is composed of marriages with short tenure (the first 10 years of marriage, roughly speaking); so the divorces observed in no-fault states are increasingly coming from marriages contracted under no-fault rules, as we move forward in time.

Although standard demographic explanations can account, to some extent, for the patterns found in Figures 1 and 2,[13] the qualitative pattern

10. In Figure 3, the average divorce rates under each regime are calculated following Table A1.

11. "Unilateral" and "mutual consent" divorce are the terms fellow economists in this literature prefer to use. Sometimes they spell out the distinction between grounds and property, sometimes not.

12. The divorce rate per married woman is not available at the state level in the *Vital Statistics of the United States* (National Center for Health Statistics 1960–88).

13. For more on the aggregate compositional age effect on the marriage market, see, for example, Heer and Grossbard-Shechtman (1981), Grossbard-Shechtman and Granger (1998).

observed in Figure 3 is enough to tease out the main intuition that there are sorting, or selection, effects at the marriage stage that compete with the pure effect of no-fault divorce, and that intuition provides the key motivation of this work.

Interpretative Framework

In the Appendix, I construct a very simple interpretative framework that focuses on the change in the incentives to create high-quality matches and their consequences on divorce trends. It goes without saying that the issue is extremely complex, and it is very difficult to capture all the pieces of the puzzle; therefore, the framework abstracts from many interesting features that would make it appear more realistic.[14]

The model yields the following conclusions. (1) Ceteris paribus, people who married under a (broadly defined) fault regime are more likely to divorce after a shift to no-fault rules. (2) Given the pattern described in Figure 3, however, the model also implies that the match quality of those who marry under a new no-fault law should be higher than that of those who married under a previous, fault-based regime: this is a purely mechanical result. (3) Still, it is impossible to determine a priori if the higher selectivity of those married after a no-fault rule is passed would make the long-run equilibrium divorce rate lower under the no-fault regime than under the fault regime. It could be that, although more selective, the partners would not be selective enough to compensate for the higher probability of divorce generated by a no-fault rule. These three points are the subject of the empirical part of this work.

DATA

Sources

I use the June files of the CPS compiled as of 1971.[15] These data have the advantage that they provide some information on the marital history of the respondents. The number of observations is large, and this made the June CPS files a better candidate than the Panel Study of Income Dynamics.

Specifically, I use those waves that have information regarding the

---

14. A more sophisticated model of marriage markets that specifically examines the effects of divorce law liberalization on marriage market outcomes using the tools of search theory can be found in Rasul (2003).

15. From 1971 to 1998, years 1978, 1989, 1993, 1996, and 1997 are missing.

154 / THE JOURNAL OF LEGAL STUDIES / VOLUME 35 (1) / JANUARY 2006

state location of the respondent (most of them have such information). Almost no wave specifies the date of divorce, however, which makes impossible the use of a hazard regression model. Further, for questions pertaining to marriage duration, the universe was composed only of women in most waves. Unfortunately, no migration information is available in this data set, so one needs to work as if the respondent stayed in her state over the entire course of her history.[16] We also miss other information, such as who filed for divorce, whether both parties agreed to the divorce, and so on.[17]

For the divorce and marriage rates, I use *Vital Statistics* (National Center for Health Statistics 1950–2000) and the *Statistical Abstract of the United States* (U.S. Census Bureau 1999). Summary statistics are presented in Table 1. The legal dummy variables (no fault for grounds, no fault for property) are constructed on the basis of Table A1. It should be noted that there has been substantial controversy on how to categorize divorce laws, as can be seen from Ashbaugh Vlosky and Monroe's (2002) piece devoted to that single question. Certain states are inherently controversial when it comes to classifying them into a fault or no-fault category, especially because of separation requirements. The present paper does not claim to present a criticism-proof classification: what matters most is whether the results are robust to changes in those few states where a particular classification is debatable and for which different views have been held in the literature.

In this paper, I classify as having no-fault grounds only those states that have enacted specific no-fault statutes. For the law defining divorce grounds, I rely on Kay's (1987) scholarship, and for the law defining fault in property and alimony, I rely on a slightly modified version of Ellman's (1996) classification, itself very close to that used in Brinig and

---

16. There is a way to get a back-of-the-envelope calculation of the error probability in assuming an event in the respondent's history happened in the same location in which the respondent lives at the time of the interview. On the basis of calculations from the Panel Study of Income Dynamics on women with the same characteristics as those in the present work, 9 percent of the sample can be expected to migrate between states each year. So any event occurring x years before the interview can be assigned a crude $9 \times x$ percent error. Furthermore, given that the regional migration rate is much smaller (roughly half) than the state migration rate, and given that regions are quite homogenous regarding divorce and property laws, this error term is really an upper bound of the probability that the respondent moved from one regime to another.

17. Historically, women have filed for divorce in the majority of cases, and there has been no discernible change in this trend with divorce law liberalization (Brinig and Allen 2000). What this tells us about who initiated the divorce is of course less clear-cut.

Table 1. Summary Statistics

	Mean	SD	Min	Max
Table 2:				
Divorced by interview time (everyone)	.042	. . .	0	1
No-Fault Ground	.69	. . .	0	1
No-Fault Property	.38	. . .	0	1
Education	12.94	2.37	0	18
Time elapsed since marriage (months)	24.71	14.23	0	48
Marriage year[a]	79.34	5.5	67	90
Table 3:				
Divorced by interview time				
(nonsurprised)	.041	. . .	0	1
No-Fault Ground	.68	. . .	0	1
No-Fault Property	.37	. . .	0	1
Education	12.95	2.38	0	48
Time elapsed since marriage (months)	24.05	14.14	0	48
Marriage year[a]	79.54	5.4	67	90
Table 4:				
Age at first marriage (months)	275.26	58	166	977
No-Fault Ground	.69	. . .	0	1
No-Fault Property	.38	. . .	0	1
Education	12.9	2.38	0	18

[a] Marriage year dummies are included in the regressions.

Buckley (1998) and Friedberg (1998).[18] I have also used an alternative specification for the grounds dimension using Friedberg's classification.[19] Finally, as mentioned before, the no-fault property variable may capture other changes in property and alimony regimes that occured at the same time as the enactment of the no-fault statutes. Only the net effect is identifiable. Therefore, to be perfectly accurate, one may interpret this variable as the combination of these multiple changes.

18. The main differences are no irretrievable breakdown and no no-fault property statute found for Arkansas, no fault for property in New York in practice after 1980 (fault is excluded from consideration in equitable distribution except for egregious cases that shock the conscience of the court; see, for example, *Havell v Islam*, 301 A.D.2d 339 [2002]), and fault for property in Utah after 1987. I thank an anonymous referee for those last two corrections.

19. Specifically, I have used columns 1 and 4 in Friedberg (1998, pp. 612–13). Those states where a "no" appears in column 1 are uniformly coded as zero even if a date appears in column 4. Estimation results using this alternative classification are available upon request.

156 / THE JOURNAL OF LEGAL STUDIES / VOLUME 35 (1) / JANUARY 2006

Constructing the Sample

The sample pools cross sections of adult white female respondents between 1971 and 1990. The years 1975, 1984, 1991, and beyond were excluded because critical information was missing. Small states in year 1971, and to a larger extent in years 1973 and 1974, were identified only by their regions, so I dropped observations from them. Finally, my concern was to minimize the odds that a respondent might have moved to another state and, more important, become subject to a different divorce regime between her marriage and the time of the interview. A short marriage duration ensures that the location error will not matter too much. Therefore, I selected recently married women—specifically, I present here results for those who had married in the last 48 months before the interview: thus, on average, women are observed 2 years after marriage. The choice of 48 months is somewhat arbitrary, yet allows me to work with a large sample size with enough divorced respondents.

EMPIRICAL METHODOLOGY AND RESULTS

The econometric identification of the legal effects comes from the fact that many states changed their divorce laws during the period 1971–90 (see Table A1). More precisely, the identification comes from states in which one component of the law changed but not the other and, in states where both components changed, from those states in which the changes were not simultaneous. Table 1 shows that there are enough observations under different regimes for adequate identification. State dummy variables control for state fixed effects, year dummies control for time fixed effects, and I account for trend effects at the state level by using state × trend regressors (see, for example, Friedberg 1998). These variables should capture several evolutions in society that are unrelated to divorce law changes (such as greater opportunities for women in the workplace) and that may have an impact on the outcomes of interest. In particular, they will take care of any convergence in the definition of marital property and property division, regardless of the laws as they appear in the books. In the tables, No-Fault Ground indicates whether a state has introduced new no-fault grounds for divorce (such as irretrievable breakdown or irreconcilable differences) in addition to or instead of fault grounds or in addition to or instead of separation requirements, allowing, in theory, for a faster procedure. No-Fault Property indicates whether a state considers fault in the property settlement and support award.

I provide specifications with state controls only and state controls plus local trends at the state level. The comparison provides insight into the robustness of the parameters. The regressions that have local trend effects (columns 2 and 2' in Tables 2, 3, and 4) are the most meaningful and thus the ones on which to focus. I do not show specifications with no state fixed effects for clarity purposes.

We have observations on women who married before and after the changes. Yet those women who married before the changes, who were sampled after the law changes, and who declared themselves divorced might have divorced before the law changes. Therefore, the estimate of the impact of the divorce law on them is biased against finding a "surprise" effect. But we have no choice since we do not have the divorce date for most of the observations.

There are, therefore, for each legal dimension, two variables of interest: one for the surprised (married before the year of enactment of the change in their state) and one for the others (married after). The no-fault dummy for the surprised takes a value of one if the person was married under a fault-based regime and was sampled under no fault and zero otherwise. Conversely, for the nonsurprised the dummy takes a value of one if the person was married after the law changed to no fault and zero otherwise. Overall, 4 percent of the sample was surprised by no-fault property laws, while 5 percent was surprised by no-fault grounds.

In both cases, I investigate the following: as we move forward in time, how does the impact of the law change? For that purpose, I constructed the variables No-Fault Grounds × trend and No-Fault Property × trend.[20] The origin of the trend is the year of enactment of the first change for each legal dimension for all states (see Table A1) for the surprised and, if any, the year of enactment in each state for the others (that is, in the nonsurprised's states). The trend takes values (year of marriage − origin) for each observation. This way, I can measure whether the surprise effect dies out in states that implemented their change late. As for the nonsurprised, I can measure if the adaptation is immediate or gradual. The idea is that the equilibrium under the new

---

20. When simply using a dummy for the law, the dummy measures the average impact of the law over time. When using a dummy and a dummy × trend, the dummy measures the impact of the law at the time of enactment (it is purely an intercept) and the dummy × trend measures the impact of the law as it changes over time.

158 / THE JOURNAL OF LEGAL STUDIES / VOLUME 35 (1) / JANUARY 2006

law may not be reached immediately. In practice, we typically expect transition dynamics that are not purely a stock/flow composition effect— in other words, some kind of social learning. To be on the safe side, those who married or are sampled in the year of enactment of the law are dropped from the sample (but including them does not change the results considerably).

Formally, let $y_{i,s,t}$ for individual i in state s at time t take the value of one if an individual declares herself divorced and zero otherwise, $x_{l,i}$ are individual characteristics (education, marriage year, and time elapsed since marriage), and cov and so on are dummies that indicate whether the individual was surprised by the different legal changes.

In the regressions that investigate the evolution of the impact of the legal changes, $T_{(grounds/surprised)i,s,t}$, $T_{(grounds/nonsurprised)i,s,t}$, and so on, are the legal-change-specific trends described above, 1_s is a state s dummy, 1_t a year t dummy, $x_{grounds,s,t}$ and $x_{property,s,t}$ are the law dummies in state s at time t, and $\varepsilon_{i,s,t}$ is the error term that accounts for serial correlation within each state s and year t:

$$y_{ist} = 1 \quad \text{if } (\alpha_1 d_{(grounds/surprised)i,s,t} + \alpha_2 d_{(grounds/nonsurprised)i,s,t}$$

$$+ \ \alpha_3 d_{(grounds/surprised)i,s,t} T_{(grounds/surprised)i,s,t}$$

$$+ \ \alpha_4 d_{(grounds/nonsurprised)i,s,t} T_{(grounds/nonsurprised)i,s,t}) x_{grounds,s,t}$$

$$+ \ (\alpha_5 d_{(property/surprised)i,s,t} + \alpha_6 d_{(property/nonsurprised)i,s,t}$$

$$+ \ \alpha_7 d_{(property/surprised)i,s,t} T_{(property/surprised)i,s,t}$$

$$+ \ \alpha_8 d_{(property/nonsurprised)i,s,t} T_{(property/nonsurprised)i,s,t}) x_{property,s,t}$$

$$+ \ \beta 1_s + \gamma 1_t + l\delta_l x_{l,i} + \varepsilon_{i,s,t} > 0,$$

and $y_{i,s,t} = 0$ otherwise, where $\varepsilon_{i,s,t} \sim N(0, \sigma^2)$; $\forall$ i, s, t, i', s', t', $cov(\varepsilon_{i,s,t}, \varepsilon_{i',s',t'}) = 0$, and $cov(\varepsilon_{i,s,t}, \varepsilon_{i',s,t}) \neq 0$. In the regressions with local trends, an interaction term between state dummies and a time trend starting in 1971 (the first wave of the survey) is added.

Finally, in the divorce regressions (Tables 2 and 3), we should focus on the sign and significance of the estimates more than on their magnitudes. Recall that the observed divorces originate from marriages with short tenure. The driving hypothesis behind the estimations is that any effect found for such couples would hold for couples with longer marriage tenure, which cannot be studied here with sufficient precision because of the lack of migration history in the data. The dummy coefficients

Table 2. Probit Estimation: Change in the Law (June Current Population Survey Pooled Cross Sections)

	(1)	(1′)	(2)	(2′)
No-Fault Ground	−.002	−.018	−.002	−.002
	(.004)	(.016)	(.005)	(.014)
No-Fault Ground × trend		6×10^{-4}		6×10^{-4}
		(7×10^{-4})		(8×10^{-4})
No-Fault Property	.015	.067	.02	.069
	(.007)*	(.007)**	(.01)*	(.04)*
No-Fault Property × trend		-1.6×10^{-3}		−.001
		$(9 \times 10^{-4})^{+}$		(9×10^{-4})
Pseudo R^2	.067	.067	.073	.073

Note. The dependent variable is Divorced by Interview Time. The sample comprises white women married for the first time, for at most 48 months, between 1971 and 1990, for whom there was a change in the law between marriage and the interview (the surprised). Specifications: (1) No-Fault Ground, No-Fault Property, state dummies; (1′) No-Fault Ground, No-Fault Property, No-Fault Ground × trend, No-Fault Property × trend, state dummies; (2) No-Fault Ground, No-Fault Property, state dummies, state dummies × trend; (2′) No-Fault Ground, No-Fault Property, No-Fault Ground × trend, No-Fault Property × trend, state dummies, state dummies × trend. All specifications control for education, marriage year (dummies), time elapsed since marriage, and no-fault variables for both surprised and nonsurprised. For No-Fault Ground and No-Fault Property, no fault equals one, and fault equals zero; divorced equals one, zero otherwise. The coefficient reported is the discrete change dF/dx computed at the means of the data, where F is the cumulative distribution function of $N(0, 1)$. The t-test reported is that of the underlying probit coefficient being zero. See the text for details. Number of observations = 44,748. Robust standard errors that allow for arbitrary correlation within a state in any given year are in parentheses.

+ Significant at the 10% confidence level.
* Significant at the 5% confidence level.
** Significant at the 1% confidence level.

reported in the probit regressions represent the marginal effects of the law (that is, the discrete changes dF/dx, where F is the cumulative distribution function of $N(0, 1)$ and x the law dummy), restricted to the means of the data. The t-tests reported are those for the underlying probit coefficients being zero and are unrestricted. [21]

Analysis of the Surprise Effect

Although the estimation is done with both the surprised and the non-surprised, I present only the effects for the surprised here. The results

21. This explains a phenomenon familiar to Stata users, that in the case of dummy coefficients, the marginal effects can be reported as statistically significant despite seemingly too large standard errors.

160 / THE JOURNAL OF LEGAL STUDIES / VOLUME 35 (1) / JANUARY 2006

Table 3. Probit Estimation: No Change in the Law (June Current Population Survey Pooled Cross Sections)

	(1)	(1′)	(2)	(2′)
No-Fault Ground	.05	.004	4×10^{-4}	−.005
	(.004)	(.005)	(.006)	(.007)
No-Fault Ground × trend		.001		−.003
		(5×10^{-4})		(.001)*
No-Fault Property	.006	.01	.011	.008
	(.005)	(.005)*	(.009)	(.009)
No-Fault Property × trend		-9×10^{-4}		-5×10^{-6}
		(4×10^{-4})*		(.001)
Pseudo R^2	.069	.07	.075	.076

Note. The dependent variable is Divorced by Interview Time. The sample comprises white women married once, for at most 48 months, sampled between 1971 and 1990, for whom there was no change in the laws between marriage and the interview. Specifications: (1) No-Fault Ground, No-Fault Property, state dummies; (1′) No-Fault Ground, No-Fault Property, No-Fault Ground × trend, No-Fault Property × trend, state dummies; (2) No-Fault Ground, No-Fault Property, state dummies, state dummies × trend; (2′) No-Fault Ground, No-Fault Property, No-Fault Ground × trend, No-Fault Property × trend, state dummies, state dummies × trend. All specifications control for education, marriage year (dummies), and time elapsed since marriage. For No-Fault Ground, no fault equals one, and fault equals zero; for No Fault Property, no fault equals one, fault equals zero; divorced equals one, and zero otherwise. The coefficient reported is the discrete change dF/dx computed at the means of the data, where F is the cumulative distribution function of $N(0, 1)$. The t-test reported is that of the underlying probit coefficient being zero. See text for details. Number of observations = 42,474. Robust standard errors that allow for arbitrary correlation within a state in any given year are in parentheses.

* Significant at the 5% confidence level.

in Table 2, column 2, support the idea that for those women who married under a fault regime for property, a change to a no-fault regime was responsible for a significant increase in divorce odds. Another interesting aspect of the result is that the trend aspect is insignificant, despite the expected negative sign (Table 2, column 2′). This suggests that women who married after the first changes of the early 1970s in states that still retained fault did not fully anticipate that, in some cases, changes were about to occur there as well. A comparison of the average effect and of the immediate effect reveals that, not surprisingly, the early changes of the 1970s had a bigger impact.

On the other hand, we see that adding no-fault grounds to the statutes (whether supplementing fault grounds or supplanting them) seems to be irrelevant. This result is robust: specifications with no-fault grounds alone (that is, without the property variable), using the present classification or Friedberg's, would yield the same conclusion. Therefore, we can see that efforts to change that aspect of divorce alone bears little consequence. An interpretation is that collusion is not possible along the dimension of property: what one spouse gains is lost by the other; on the other hand, holding division of property constant, spouses who have reached an agreement have an interest in bypassing fault, with its higher transaction costs. Fault would then become ineffective, and, therefore, its change to no fault would become irrelevant.

Thus, these results offer an explanation for the sharp increase in divorce rates between the early 1970s and early 1980s. The second and probably most important piece of the puzzle is to determine what the reaction was of those who married after the legal changes.

Analysis of the Impact of the Divorce Laws on Couples Who Married after the Legal Changes

This analysis compares the divorce patterns of women who married before and after the legal changes, but the sample now excludes those women for whom the law changed between marriage and the time of the interview (the surprised). These results can be interpreted as the impact of the legal changes inasmuch as they were anticipated. The methodology is the same as above, except that there is now only one dummy for no-fault grounds and one for no-fault property.

Following the above notations,

$$y_{i,s,t} = 1 \quad \text{if } \alpha_1 x_{\text{grounds},s,t} + \alpha_2 x_{\text{property},s,t} + \alpha_3 T_{\text{grounds},t,s,t} x_{\text{grounds},s,t}$$

$$+ \alpha_4 T_{\text{property},t,s,t} x_{\text{property},s,t} + \beta 1_s + \gamma 1_t + l \sum \delta_l x_{l,t} + \varepsilon_{i,s,t} > 0,$$

and $y_{i,s,t} = 0$ otherwise, where $\varepsilon_{i,s,t} \sim N(0, \sigma^2)$; $\forall$ i, s, t, i', s', t', $\text{cov}(\varepsilon_{i,s,t},$ $\varepsilon_{i',s',t'}) = 0$ and $\text{cov}(\varepsilon_{i,s,t}, \varepsilon_{i',s,t}) \neq 0$.

Note that I present the results for the nonsurprised in a different estimation—after dropping out the surprised group. The reason for this is that some of the divorcees in the surprised group did in fact divorce before the legal change (since we do not know the divorce date); there-fore, there is no point in carrying this measurement error in the analysis of the nonsurprised group.

The nonsignificant coefficient on No-Fault Property in Table 3, col-umn 2, supports the selection hypothesis. In other words, an increase in selectivity by potential spouses leading to higher quality matches works as an indirect, offsetting effect of the divorce law changes. To account further for this idea, recall that I have selected respondents who had married in the last 48 months before the interview; the focus is on early

162 / THE JOURNAL OF LEGAL STUDIES / VOLUME 35 (1) / JANUARY 2006

divorces, which result from the worst matches on average. The more ill sorted the spouses are, the earlier they will find out about it and divorce. Therefore, if there is a sorting effect that prevents, to some extent, bad matches from being created in no-fault states, it will most clearly be reflected in early divorces.

The only unexpected result is the significant coefficient on the trend dimension of No-Fault Grounds. This result is not robust to using Friedberg's (1998) classification. One may interpret this trend effect as, for example, spouses making more "cooperative relationship-specific investments" (investments that affect only the noninvesting spouse's marital utility, such as reducing domestic violence) because no-fault grounds encourage such investments (Wickelgren 2005). However, while interesting in theory, this argument is still speculative.

The selectivity effect is likely to take many forms, most of them unobservable to the researcher. In the following section, I seek to detect it from an analysis of marriage patterns.

Analysis of the Incentive Effects of the Law at the Marriage Stage

The impact of no-fault divorce on age at marriage can be shown to be a priori ambiguous. However, from the analysis of the trends in divorce rates across property regimes (Figure 3), one may conjecture that selectivity became higher under no-fault regimes for property. The goal of this section is therefore to find some evidence of a selection effect at the marriage stage.[22]

Interestingly, age at first marriage has dramatically increased in the last 3 decades (Figure 6); therefore, I check here whether divorce laws can account for this phenomenon to some extent in the pooled cross-section sample. Of course, there is much evidence to suggest that age at first marriage for women has risen for a host of reasons. The regressions control for educational attainment (see Goldin 1992), but other causes for delaying marriage include, for example, access to modern contraceptives (Goldin and Katz 2002). Furthermore, changes in the age-sex composition of the population caused by the baby-boom generation may also lead to rising age at marriage for women. Quantifying all the prob-

---

22. A growing number of people in the United States never marry; in other words, marriage is not just delayed. Though first-marriage rates have been plummeting in the United States since the early 1970s (Figures 4 and 5), I could not find a significant impact of either aspect of divorce law changes on first-marriage rates. In a study on how no-fault laws affect marriage strategy, Rasul (2003) finds a very small effect on first-marriage rates and a stronger one for remarriage, on which I concur.

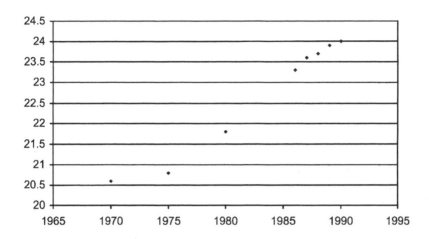

Figure 6. Median age at first marriage (women) (U.S. Census Bureau 1999)

able explanations for the rising age at first marriage is beyond the scope of this paper. Those trends are captured by the year dummies and state-specific trends in Table 4. In any case, they are independent of the adoption and timing of no-fault property regimes over the 1970s and 1980s.

Formally, defining A as being age at first marriage and following the notations defined above (I control only for education x now), I estimate

$$A_{i,s,t} = \alpha_1 x_{\text{ground},s,t} + \alpha_2 x_{\text{ground},s,t} T_{\text{ground},t,s,t}$$

$$+ \alpha_3 x_{\text{property},s,t} + \alpha_4 x_{\text{property},s,t} T_{\text{property},t,s,t}$$

$$+ \beta 1_s + \gamma 1_t + \delta x_i + \varepsilon_{i,s,t},$$

where $\varepsilon_{i,s,t} \sim N(0, \sigma^2)$; $\forall\ i, s, t, i', s', t'$, $\text{cov}(\varepsilon_{i,s,t}, \varepsilon_{i',s',t'}) = 0$ and $\text{cov}(\varepsilon_{i,s,t}, \varepsilon_{i',s,t}) \neq 0$.

From the empirical results in Table 4, we see that on average over the period, the impact of a no-fault regime for grounds regime is to decrease age at first marriage, although not statistically significantly,[23] while the effect of no fault for property is to significantly delay marriage.

---

23. This is also a robust result that holds using the law for grounds alone or using Friedberg's (1998) classification.

164 / THE JOURNAL OF LEGAL STUDIES / VOLUME 35 (1) / JANUARY 2006

Table 4. Ordinary Least Squares Estimation (June Current Population Survey Pooled Cross Sections)

	(1)	(1′)	(2)	(2′)
No-Fault Ground	1.41	1.12	−1.39	−1.71
	(1.45)	(1.46)	(1.49)	(1.52)
No-Fault Ground × trend		.25		−.14
		(.16)		(.4)
No-Fault Property	3.79	3.78	4.86	5.16
	(1.44)**	(1.46)**	(2.04)*	(2)**
No-Fault Property × trend		.306		.734
		(.149)*		(.382)+
Pseudo R^2	.165	.165	.166	.167

Note. The dependent variable is Age at First Marriage (in months). The sample comprises white women married for the first time, for at most 48 months, sampled between 1971 and 1990. Specifications: (1) No-Fault Ground, No-Fault Property, state dummies; (1′) No-Fault Ground, No-Fault Property, No-Fault Ground × trend, No-Fault Property × trend, state dummies; (2) No-Fault Ground, No-Fault Property, state dummies, state dummies × trend; (2′) No-Fault Ground, No-Fault Property, No-Fault Ground × trend, No-Fault Property × trend, state dummies, state dummies × trend. All specifications control for education and marriage year (dummies). For No-Fault Ground, no fault equals one, and fault equals zero; for No-Fault Property, no fault equals one, and fault equals one. Number of observations = 44,758. Robust standard errors that allow for arbitrary correlation within a state in any given year are in parentheses.
 + Significant at the 10% confidence level.
 * Significant at the 5% confidence level.
 ** Significant at the 1% confidence level.

Ceteris paribus, a no-fault rule for property should make marriage more risky for women.[24]

In the preferred estimation with state and state × trend controls (Table 4, column 2), the average effect of no fault for property laws is to delay first marriage by approximately 5 months—this result is very robust. The effect appears to be immediate since the trend effect is only weakly significant (Table 4, column 2′).

To summarize, my interpretation is that states provide little insurance against divorce when there is no fault for property: short of a third-party insurer (the state), women insure themselves by being more careful; hence, on average they put in a longer searching time. This follows the

---

24. For example, women are more at risk of falling below the poverty line if they get divorced, especially if they have children.

lines of Cohen's (1987) arguments.[25]

Finally, it can be verified that once education is controlled for, the impact of age at first marriage on divorce, although statistically significant, is small. Indirectly, this finding suggests that selectivity might operate at levels other than just age at marriage. Obviously, while we can measure searching time, we cannot observe search intensity.[26] As hinted previously, there are certainly more than just selectivity issues present in terms of people's strategic reaction to changes in divorce laws, not only at the marriage stage but also later. This deserves future research.

CONCLUSION

This paper has proposed a theory that intends to account for the patterns of divorce observed in the United States in the last 35 years. To summarize, this theory says that the divorce law changes introduced in the early 1970s affected the odds of divorce for those couples who married before these laws were passed. Such couples were more likely to divorce after a change in law from fault to no-fault divorce, and the key variable seems to be the law governing property division and spousal support. Once the first legal changes passed, many poorly matched couples who married before the changes in the law broke up, thus boosting the rate of divorce. The legal changes that appeared later still had some impact for those who had married under a fault regime. Most important, the effect of no-fault divorce was mitigated by those couples who reduced their probability of divorce through better sorting upon marriage. The main conclusion of the paper is that this better sorting decreased the probability of divorce by about as much as the institution of no-fault divorce increased it.

This selection effect is apparent since under no fault for property laws on average women marry when they are significantly older than are women in fault states. This work thus provides an explanation for the observed apparent convergence in divorce rates between fault and

25. Yet, I found that neither dimension of no-fault divorce significantly reduces first-marriage rates. This is based on a regression of first-marriage rates in states in which both bride and groom were residents of the state in which the marriage was registered, in at least 90 percent of cases, using the *Vital Statistics of the United States* (National Center for Health Statistics 1960–88). This regression is available from the author. Rasul (2003) finds a modest effect for the entire United States.

26. I also regressed race homogeneity and educational homogeneity within couples on the divorce laws, but the results were inconclusive.

166 / THE JOURNAL OF LEGAL STUDIES / VOLUME 35 (1) / JANUARY 2006

no-fault states over the last 20 years. It presents a consistent interpretation for the argument that the effects of unilateral divorce laws on divorce rates died out a decade after their introduction (Wolfers 2003). The results also expand on Weiss and Willis (1997), who found that couples married under unilateral divorce regimes are less likely to divorce than those married under mutual consent regimes, all else equal, despite living in a state with a more liberal regime, which reinforces the theory of selection into marriage.

This theory awaits being connected with other branches of research studying the consequences of divorce laws at other levels. For example, has the nature of marriage contracts changed? Has the welfare of divorced women decreased? Johnson and Skinner (1986), Peters (1986), Parkman (1992, 1998), and Gray (1998) argue, in different ways, that the divorce law changes have affected female labor-force participation rates. A recent study (Stevenson and Wolfers 2005) finds a significant decline in domestic violence and suicide following enactment of unilateral divorce laws, which is again consistent with the general argument presented in this work of better sorting as a consequence of no-fault divorce.[27] More research can be done along the same lines, for example, with the analysis of household specialization and provision of public goods. Another promising line of research is to look for the impact of divorce laws on features that signal assortative matching, such as religious homogamy (see Call and Heaton 1997).[28] Finally, the impact of no-fault divorce on children's outcomes is also under scrutiny (Gruber 2000; Johnson and Mazingo 2000). Murphy (1999) finds evidence that the average difference in child outcomes between children of married and unmarried parents has increased since 1960. This may reflect a compositional effect, that is, that the pool of surviving marriages are better on average. This would also be consistent with better selection into marriage over time, although the study did not specifically relate this pattern to the liberalization of divorce laws.

Finally, from a policy perspective, and without taking a stand on the welfare implications of no-fault divorce, the conclusions of this study show that divorce rates alone do not provide a justification for shifting back to fault-based divorce. In any event, this work predicts that if a

27. An alternative argument might be that no-fault divorce makes it easier for battered women to exit marriage because of lower transaction costs (and less fear of being penalized for leaving the marriage if the domestic violence cannot be proved). I thank an anonymous referee for this insight.

28. I thank an anonymous referee for this suggestion.

no-fault state switched back to a fault regime, the impact on divorce rates would be a spectacular drop in the short run because a strict law governing divorce would be applied to spouses who sorted under a no-fault regime. However, this victory would likely be short-lived.

APPENDIX: INTERPRETATIVE FRAMEWORK

In the following, I explore the implications of nontransferable utility. Although it must be acknowledged that a partly transferable utility might be more suitable, this polar case is useful in analyzing the consequences of adding transaction costs and imperfect foresight to the Coasian benchmark.

Setup

In a stylized way, a single person maximizes the value of marriage net of search costs over match quality. To capture the main idea, I will assume here that each female chooses an effort level first—which I occasionally refer to as selectivity—and that the matching technology is such that she is exogenously paired with, that is, married to, a male who has made the same search effort. Marriage is divided into time periods (1, 2, 3, and so on). For simplicity, suppose that divorcees do not marry singles.

Call q the probability that, at the end of each period of the marriage, nature reveals to a spouse that the match is a bad one, and think of q as a measure of search effort to find someone really compatible (hence, a higher q means lower effort); q indexes this probability under a fault regime. A fault regime is here defined as one in which a spouse cannot unilaterally leave the match, say, because it is too costly.[29] In other words, the single person's problem is interpreted as one in which he or she chooses a probability of being in a good match and then nature draws.

If nature reveals to one spouse that the other spouse is not suitable (with probability q), he or she always wants to divorce. On the other hand, if nature reveals to one spouse that the other spouse is suitable (with probability $1 - q$), he or she always chooses to continue in marriage.

Similarly, let p denote the probability that one spouse is willing to divorce in the no-fault regime after nature reveals the relevant information. In the no-fault case, if nature reveals to one spouse that the other spouse is not suitable (with probability p), he or she always wants to divorce. On the other hand, if nature reveals to one spouse that the other spouse is suitable (with probability $1 - p$), he or she always chooses to continue in marriage.

Nature tells the spouses whether the match is good or not at the same time, independently, so one spouse can be told that the match is good while the other

---

29. Therefore, in this formulation, the different dimensions of the law are lumped together, which is a crude simplification.

Economics of Family Law I

is told that the match is bad. Nature discloses whether the match is suitable at each period t of their marriage for all married couples and under both regimes. For simplicity, and without loss of generality, p and q are time invariant.

Recall that willingness to divorce is independent across spouses. Therefore, upon the revelation of match quality by nature in the fault regime, the probability that divorce occurs in each period of the marriage is q^2, since both spouses need to agree for the divorce to be granted. The probability that divorce occurs in the no-fault regime is $1 - (1 - p)^2$ because now only one spouse's decision is sufficient to get a divorce (and no transfers are possible).

These divorce probabilities correspond to the steady state under each regime. Note, however, that matches of the same quality can dissolve at different times: let us now turn to the transition dynamics when there is a regime change.

Transition Dynamics

We will see here why the short-run impact of no-fault laws is unambiguous while only the data can tell whether a no-fault regime increases selectivity or not. Yet even this is not enough to predict the long-run effect of no-fault laws on divorce rates.

After a switch in the law from fault to no fault, the composition of marriages in which the spouses decide to divorce is a mixture of those who married before the switch and of those who married after it. According to the assumptions above, we can state the following:

Proposition 1.   For those who married under fault and are not (yet) divorced, a no-fault regime increases the odds of divorce.

Proof.   The increase in the odds of divorce is simply $(1 - (1 - q)^2) - q^2 > 0$ for all q in $(0, 1)$.

The intuition is straightforward: no-fault laws allow parties in bad matches to get out of marriages unilaterally.

It should be clear that getting an unambiguous result on the long-term effect of a change in the divorce regime would require strong assumptions. At an intuitive level, one should be able to compare the ex ante value of marriage under each rule. In other words, ideally one should be able to compare the value of remaining married if willing to divorce (when the other party is not) and the value of being divorced against one's will (that is, when one would have preferred to remain married). However, it turns out that a simple accounting exercise can provide useful answers. I now make use of the dynamics of the above framework.

Call the fraction of spouses at time t who decide whether or not to continue in marriage (that is, when nature reveals to each spouse the suitability of the other) and who married after the switch, $a(t)$. It is straightforward to show that the weight of those who married after the law change is increasing with time, that is,

$$da(t)/dt > 0. \tag{A1}$$

Now the difference in divorce rates at any point in time after a switch from a fault to a no-fault regime is

$$\Delta(t) = [1 - a(t)][1 - (1 - q)^2] + a(t)[1 - (1 - p)^2] - q^2. \tag{A2}$$

This leads to the main proposition:

Proposition 2. Match quality is higher in no-fault states, $p < q$, if and only if the difference in divorce rates across regimes is decreasing over cohorts.

Proof. If the sign of the difference in difference is

$$\text{sign}\{d\Delta/dt\} = \text{sign}\{-[1 - (1 - q)^2] + [1 - (1 - p)^2]\} < 0, \tag{A3}$$

then since $f(x) = 1 - (1 - x)^2$ is increasing on $(0, 1)$, it must be that $p < q$.

Conversely, suppose $p < q$. Then, by the same argument, $\text{sign}\{-[1 - (1 - q)^2] + [1 - (1 - p)^2]\} < 0$. We can further state as an important corollary that the impact of no fault on divorce likelihood for those who married after the law was passed should be smaller than for those who married before its passage.

This simple framework provides a tentative explanation for the increase and then decline in the difference of divorce rates between fault and no-fault states over time and shows why looking at the effect of the law at a fixed point in time (or over a too-short period) would be misleading. Note, however, that this finding does not necessarily imply that divorce rates should equalize, nor does it rule out the possibility that divorce rates eventually will be lower in the no-fault regime, for that matter.

Table A1. Information Used to Construct Legal Dummy Variables

	Enactment of Specific No-Fault Provisions (Including Incompatibility)	No Fault for Property Division and Spousal Support
Alabama	1971	Fault
Alaska	1935	1974
Arizona	1973	1973
Arkansas	No (Ellman and Lohr: 1979)	Fault (Ellman and Lohr: 1979)
California	1970	1970
Colorado	1971	1971
Connecticut	1973	Fault
Delaware	1974 (Friedberg: no)	1974
DC	1977 (Friedberg: no)	Fault
Florida	1971	1986
Georgia	1973	Fault
Hawaii	1972	1960
Idaho	1971	1990
Illinois	1983 (Friedberg: no)	1977
Indiana	1973	1973
Iowa	1970	1972
Kansas	1969	1990
Kentucky	1972	Fault
Louisiana	No	Fault
Maine	1973	1985
Maryland	No	Fault
Massachusetts	1975	Fault
Michigan	1974	Fault
Minnesota	1974	1974
Mississippi	1976 (Friedberg: no)[a]	Fault
Missouri	1973 (Friedberg: no)	Fault
Montana	1975	1975
Nebraska	1972	1972
Nevada	1973 (Friedberg: no)	1973
New Hampshire	1971	Fault
New Jersey	No	1980
New Mexico	1973	1976
New York	No	1980 (Ellman and Lohr: fault)
North Carolina	No[b]	Fault
North Dakota	1971	Fault
Ohio	1974 (Friedberg: no)	Fault
Oklahoma	1953	1975
Oregon	1971	1971
Pennsylvania	1980 (Friedberg: no)[b]	Fault
Rhode Island	1975	Fault
South Carolina	No	Fault
South Dakota	1985	Fault
Tennessee	1977 (Friedberg: no)[a]	Fault
Texas	1969 (Friedberg: 1974)	Fault
Utah	1987 (Friedberg: no)	Fault (Ellman and Lohr: 1987)
Vermont	No	Fault

TABLE A1. *continued*

	Enactment of Specific No-Fault Provisions (Including Incompatibility)	No Fault for Property Division and Spousal Support
Virginia	No	Fault
Washington	1973	1973
West Virginia	1977 (Friedberg: no)	Fault
Wisconsin	1977 (Friedberg: no)[b]	1977
Wyoming	1977	Fault

Sources. Brinig and Buckely (1998); Ellman and Lohr (1998); Sepler (1981); Kay (1987); Freed and Foster (1977, 1979, 1981); Freed and Walker (1990); Friedberg (1998, pp. 612–13, cols. 1 and 4). Also Legal Research on LexisNexis (state codes and case law) and the expert scholarship of an anonymous referee. "Friedberg: no" may mean the state has no-fault grounds but includes or requires separation for a required length of time (compare column 2, pp. 612–13).

[a] Only if divorce is uncontested.
[b] Friedberg (1998) acknowledges ambiguity.

REFERENCES

Allen, Douglas W. 1992. Marriage and Divorce: Comment. *American Economic Review* 82:679–85.

Ashbaugh Vlosky, Denese, and Pamela A. Monroe. 2002. The Effective Dates of No-Fault Divorce Laws in the 50 States. *Family Relations* 51:317–24.

Brinig, Margaret F., and Douglas W. Allen. 2000. These Boots Are Made for Walking: Why Most Divorce Filers Are Women. *American Law and Economics Review* 2:126–69.

Brinig, Margaret F., and Frank H. Buckley. 1998. No-Fault Laws and At-Fault People. *International Review of Law and Economics* 18:325–40.

Call, Vaughn R. A., and Tim B. Heaton. 1997. Religious Influences on Marital Stability. *Journal for the Scientific Study of Religion* 36:382–92.

Cohen, Lloyd. 1987. Marriage, Divorce, and Quasi Rents; or, "I Gave Him the Best Years of My Life." *Journal of Legal Studies* 16:267–303.

Dnes, Antony, and Robert Rowthorn. 2002. *The Law and Economics of Marriage and Divorce.* Cambridge: Cambridge University Press.

Ellman, Ira M. 1996. The Place of Fault in Modern Divorce Law. *Arizona State Law Journal* 28:773–835.

———. 2000. Divorce. Working paper. University of California, Berkeley, School of Law.

Ellman, Ira Mark, and Sharon L. Lohr. 1998. Dissolving the Relationship between Divorce Laws and Divorce Rates. *International Review of Law and Economics* 18:341–59.

172 / THE JOURNAL OF LEGAL STUDIES / VOLUME 35 (1) / JANUARY 2006

Fineman, Martha Albertson. 1983. Implementing Equality: Ideology, Contradiction and Social Change. *Wisconsin Law Review* 4:789–886.

———. 1991. *The Illusion of Equality: The Rhetoric and the Reality of Divorce Reform.* Chicago: University of Chicago Press.

Freed, Doris J., and Henry H. Foster. 1977. Divorce in the Fifty States: An Outline. *Family Law Quarterly* 11:297–313.

———. 1979. Divorce in the Fifty States: An Overview as of 1978. *Family Law Quarterly* 13:105–28.

———. 1981. Divorce in the Fifty States: An Overview. *Family Law Quarterly* 14:229–47.

Freed, Doris J., and Timothy B. Walker. 1990. Family Law in the Fifty States: An Overview. *Family Law Quarterly* 23:495–608.

Friedberg, Leora. 1998. Did Unilateral Divorce Raise Divorce Rates? Evidence from Panel Data. *American Economic Review* 88:608–27.

Gardiner, Karen N., Michael E. Fishman, Plamen Nikonov, Asaph Glosser, and Stephanie Laud. 2002. State Policies to Promote Marriage: Final Report. Unpublished manuscript. Lewin Group, Inc., Falls Church, Va.

Glenn, Norval D. 1991. The Recent Trend in Marital Success in the United States. *Journal of Marriage and the Family* 53:261–70.

Goldin, Claudia. 1992. The Meaning of College in the Lives of American Women: The Past One Hundred Years. Working Paper No. 4099. National Bureau of Economic Research, Cambridge, Mass.

Goldin, Claudia, and Lawrence F. Katz. 2002. The Power of the Pill: Oral Contraceptives and Women's Career and Marriage Decisions. *Journal of Political Economy* 110:730–70.

Gray, Jeffrey S. 1998. Divorce-Law Changes, Household Bargaining, and Married Women's Labor Supply. *American Economic Review* 88:628–42.

Grossbard-Shechtman, Shoshana. 2003. *Marriage and the Economy: Theory and Evidence from Advanced Industrial Societies.* Cambridge: Cambridge University Press.

Grossbard-Shechtman, Shoshana, and Clive W. J. Granger. 1998. Women's Jobs and Marriage, Baby-Boom versus Baby-Bust. *Population* 53:731–52.

Grossbard-Shechtman, Shoshana, and Bertrand Lemennicier. 1999. Marriage Contracts and the Law-and-Economics of Marriage: An Austrian Perspective. *Journal of Socio-economics* 28:665–90.

Gruber, Jonathan. 2000. Is Making Divorce Easier Bad for Children?: The Long Run Implications of Unilateral Divorce. Unpublished manuscript. Massachussetts Institute of Technology, Department of Economics.

Heer, David M., and Amyra Grossbard-Shechtman. 1981. The Impact of the Female Marriage Squeeze and the Contraceptive Revolution on Sex Roles and the Women's Liberation Movement in the United States, 1960–1975. *Journal of Marriage and the Family* 43:49–65.

Jacob, Herbert. 1988. *Silent Revolution: The Transformation of Divorce Law in the United States*. Chicago: University of Chicago Press.

Johnson, John H., and Christopher J. Mazingo. 2000. The Economic Consequences of Unilateral Divorce for Children. Unpublished manuscript. University of Illinois at Urbana-Champaign, Institute of Labor and Industrial Relations.

Johnson, William R., and Jonathan Skinner. 1986. Labor Supply and Marital Separation. *American Economic Review* 76:455–69.

Kay, Herma H. 1987. Equality and Difference: A Perspective on No-Fault Divorce and Its Aftermath. *University of Cincinnati Law Review* 56:1–90.

Lundberg, Shelley, and Robert A. Pollak. 2001. Efficiency in Marriage. Working Paper No. 8642. National Bureau of Economic Research, Cambridge, Mass.

Murphy, Russell D., Jr. 1999. Family Values and the Value of Families: Theory and Evidence of Marriage as an Institution. Unpublished manuscript. Virginia Polytechnic Institute and State University.

———. 2002. A Good Man Is Hard to Find: Marriage as an Institution. *Journal of Economic Behavior and Organization* 47:27–53.

National Center for Health Statistics. 1950–2000. *Vital Statistics of the United States*. Vol. 3, *Marriage and Divorce*. Washington, D.C.: U.S. Government Printing Office.

Parkman, Allen M. 1992. Unilateral Divorce and the Labor-Force Participation Rate of Married Women, Revisited. *American Economic Review* 82:671–78.

———. 1998. Why Are Married Women Working So Hard? *International Review of Law and Economics* 18:41–49.

Peters, H. Elizabeth. 1986. Marriage and Divorce: Informational Constraints and Private Contracting. *American Economic Review* 76:437–54.

———. 1992. Marriage and Divorce: Reply. *American Economic Review* 82:686–93.

Rasul, Imran. 2003. Marriage Markets and Social Change. Unpublished manuscript. University of Chicago, Graduate School of Business.

Sepler, Harvey. 1981. Measuring the Effects of No-Fault Divorce Laws across Fifty States: Quantifying a Zeitgeist. *Family Law Quarterly* 15:65–102.

Stevenson, Betsey, and Justin Wolfers. 2005. Bargaining in the Shadow of the Law: Divorce Laws and Family Distress. Unpublished manuscript. University of Pennsylvania, Wharton School.

U.S. Census Bureau. 1999. *Statistical Abstract of the United States*. Washington, D.C.: U.S. Government Printing Office.

U.S. Department of Labor. Bureau of Labor Statistics. June 1971–98 (not all inclusive). Current Population Survey. Supplement, Fertility and Marriage History. Conducted by the Bureau of the Census for the Bureau of Labor Statistics. Washington, D.C.: Bureau of the Census (producer and distributor) 1971–98; Santa Monica, Cal.: Unicon Research Corporation (production and distributor of CPS utilities), 1999.

174 / THE JOURNAL OF LEGAL STUDIES / VOLUME 35 (1) / JANUARY 2006

Weiss, Yoram, and Robert. J. Willis. 1997. Match Quality, New Information, and Marital Dissolution. *Journal of Labor Economics* 15: S293–S329.

Weitzman, Lenore J. 1985. *The Divorce Revolution: The Unexpected Social and Economic Consequences for Women and Children in America.* New York: Free Press.

Wickelgren, Abraham. 2005. Why Divorce Laws Matter: Incentives for Non-contractible Marital Investments under Unilateral and Consent Divorce. Unpublished manuscript. University of Texas at Austin, Department of Economics.

Wolfers, Justin. 2003. Did Unilateral Divorce Laws Raise Divorce Rates? A Reconciliation and New Results. Working Paper No. 10014. National Bureau of Economic Research, Cambridge, Mass.

Zelder, Martin. 2002. For Better or for Worse? Is Bargaining in Marriage and Divorce Efficient? Pp. 157–70 in *The Law and Economics of Marriage and Divorce,* edited by Anthony Dnes and Robert Rowthorn. Cambridge: Cambridge University Press.

B
Choice of Spouse and Premarital Bargaining

European Journal of Law and Economics, 2:45–62 (1995)
© 1995 Kluwer Academic Publishers

Fraud in Courtship: Annulment and Divorce

MARGARET F. BRINIG
School of Law, George Mason University

MICHAEL V. ALEXEEV
Department of Economics, University of Indiana–Bloomington

Abstract

The possibility of fraud exists in any contract. Courts and custom allow some amount of fraud before voiding the contract. The same principles hold for marriage. This paper provides a comparative analysis of annulment and divorce, shows that there exists a socially optimal amount of fraud in marriage, and demonstrates how changes in the locale's divorce regime result in changing demand for annulments. While substitutability between annulment and divorce is limited, annulment is shown to become more valuable for introducing fault when the divorce regime shifts to no fault. As European nations harmonize their family laws, they should be conscious of this substitutibility.

1. Introduction

Marriage represents a (long-term) legal contract. In the Western countries, the laws governing dissolution of this contract have been evolving over time toward making it easier for each spouse to obtain a divorce. The ability of a spouse to prevent dissolution of a marriage constitutes a property right on the marriage. The legal evolution has been changing these property rights of the spouses (Posner, 1992; Rea, 1993). As Ronald Coase (1960) argues with respect to more conventional property rights, however, as long as transaction costs are relatively small, such changes affect distribution of wealth among the parties but do not affect the efficiency of outcomes (in this case, whether or not marriage will be dissolved) (Allen, 1992, 1990). This paper analyzes some of the effects of the progressive liberalization of divorce laws.

When couples are terminally unhappy and divorce is impossible, there are several solutions to their problems. The couple may separate, with the wealthier either disappearing[1] or paying support.[2] Another alternative is for one spouse to travel to another jurisdiction to obtain a divorce.[3] Finally, the couple might seek an annulment of their marriage or a legislative divorce, where that is permitted.[4]

A slightly more relaxed divorce regime permits divorces in cases where there is serious fault. If the spouse wanting to end the marriage is not the one at fault, divorce is relatively straightforward. However, if the party most wanting to exit the marriage does not have fault grounds, he or she may "buy the other out," inducing the reluctant spouse to manufacture grounds. This is called collusion (Wadlington, 1966; Walker, 1971). Other things being equal, an introduction of an additional option of fault divorce would reduce the incidence of other ways of dealing with an unhappy marriage (Parkman, 1992, p. 63; Allen, 1990, 1992).

The move to no-fault divorce regime, especially if it is accompanied by elimination of fault (or of alimony related to fault), may have some, presumably unintended, results of increasing the incidence of the "old" solutions to inviable marriages. One point of this paper is that the relatively obscure remedy of annulment can serve as a substitute for fault in divorce.[5]

We analyze fraud associated with marriage within a broader framework of fraud in contracts literature and test our results on the data for the United States. Although we concentrate on American statutes and cases, the analysis has implications for Western Europe. Divorce laws in Western Europe vary significantly between countries (Table 1). With the movement toward a United Europe, harmonization of laws, including family laws, becomes vitally important. This will change divorce laws of many countries. The changes are likely to be toward greater liberalization of divorce, perhaps eliminating fault or making it almost inconsequential for the outcome of property settlements. We hope that our analysis will improve understanding of the potential consequences of changes in the legal regime.

Table 1. Divorce laws in Western Europe.

Country	Divorce grounds	Fault in alimony	Citation
Austria	Fault and no fault	Guilty party pays alimony	
Belgium	Fault and no fault		Civ. Code 221 regulates support
Denmark	Fault and no fault[a]		Law No. 216, March 27, 1990
England	Fault and no fault[b]		Matrimonial Causes Act 1973; Family Proceedings Act 1984
Finland	No fault; unilateral		Law 16/4-1987
France	Fault and no fault	Yes (reprehensible)	Civ. Code Arts. 230–246
Germany	Fault and no fault if less than 1 year	Allows dominating reasons in equity plus need	Bugerliches Gesetzbuch, Secs. 1565–1587.
Greece	Fault and no fault[d]	No	Law 1329 of 15/18 February 1983
Ireland	None; judicial separation possible for fault grounds[e]		Judicial Separation and Family Law Reform Act 1989
Italy	Fault and no fault		Law 898 of December 1, 1970, as amended
Luxembourg	Fault and no fault	To successful plaintiff only	Civ. Code 230 and 231, 275.
Netherlands	Fault and no fault[g]	No	Civ. Code Art. 152
Norway	Fault and no fault		Act of May 31, 1918

Table 1. Continued.

Country	Divorce grounds	Fault in alimony	Citation
Portugal	Fault and no fault		Civ. Code Art. 1779
Spain	Fault and no fault		Law 30, July 7, 1981
Sweden[h]	Mutual consent and unilateral	No	Marriage Code of 1987
Switzerland	Fault and no fault[i]	Innocent only, Civ. Code 151	Civ. Code 137–42

a. According to Law 216 of March 27, 1990, "Before marriage both parties have to inform the authority granting the license as well as the other party, whether the party has or expects children with another man or woman." The *International Law Digest* (1993, p. DK-3) does not specify what happens if the party is not truthful.

b. According to *International Law Digest* (1993, p. ENG-10), the Matrimonial Cuases Act of 1973 provides that marriage is voidable for grounds including the fact that (c) either party did not consent due to duress, mistake, unsoundness of mind, or otherwise. Such actions must be brought within three years of marriage, and marriage will not be avoided where (b) petitioner led respondent reasonably to believe that he would not petition on discovery of grounds.

c. Annulment is governed by the law of February 20, 1946, as amended (Ehegesetz). Support is regulated as in case of divorce. Either party may sue at the court for dissolution of marriage in certain cases, especially in case of willful deceit, which does, however, not include misstatement about financial circumstances, unless such marriage is later ratified by the couple. Right to such action expires within one year from knowledge (*International Law Digest*, 1993, p. GER-10).

d. Annulment grounds are enumerated in Arts 1350–452, p. 1354, 1356–1357, 1359–1360, and 1362 of the Civil Code (*International Law Digest*, 1993, p. GRC-6).

e. The *International Law Digest* (1993, p. IRE-6) states that "Courts will in limited circumstances grant decrees of nullity thereby allowing re-marriage at law."

f. Annulment of civil or non-Catholic marriages is granted by civil courts, of Catholic marriages by Ecclesiastical courts in conformity with Lateran Treaty executed between Italy and Vatican of February 11, 1929. Grounds for annulment include (b) either spouse's consent having been extorted by use of violence or being result of an error in identity; (c) either spouse's impotence antecedent to marriage and unknown to other spouse.

g. The *International Law Digest* (1993, p. NTH-10) does not provide specific statutory sections. Annulment is available for "few causes" besides bigamy and incest (p. NTH-11).

h. It does not appear that annulment is available, but before a marriage license is issued, the couple must apply to the civil registry for an investigation to be made of obstacles to marriage. The application must be accompanied by their declaration in writing that no obstacles exist. *International Law Digest* (1993, p. SWE-8), citing the Marriage Law of 1987, did not state the effect of fraud in this process on the marriage.

i. Civ. Code 130, 131, provides that marriage is voidable by one of the spouses (2) for error, if the spouse declared consent to marriage but did not want to marry present spouse or was induced to marriage by error as to qualities of other spouse of such importance that defect renders married life unbearable; (3) for fraud, if spouse was fraudulently deceived with respect to honorability of other spouse by other spouse or by third person with knowledge and consent of latter and thereby induced to marry, or if sickness apt to greatly endanger own or descendant's health was concealed. . . . Property rights are treated as in divorce. Civ. Code 132–136 (*International Law Digest*, 1993, p. SWZ-12).

Because the annulment action may be unfamiliar to those readers who do not practice family law, we begin with a common law matrimonial arsenal. Section 3 provides a general

discussion of fraud in contracts and examines the nature of fraud occurring during courtship that results in marriage. Section 4 develops a simple model of fraud in marriage. This
model demonstrates the potential for fraud to be beneficial to both spouses and, perhaps,
socially. It also illustrates the possibility of substitution between annulment and fault in
divorce. This substitutability is tested on the U.S. data. Section 5 discusses common law
annulment cases in order to demonstrate the limitations of the use of annulment as a substitute
for divorce.[6] The final section provides brief conclusions.

2. The annulment action

An annulment was at first the only way (short of death) that a marriage could terminate.
It was a remedy granted by the ecclesiastical (church) court when it found an incapacity
to be married or to carry out the marital obligations. It was essentially a declaration that
no marriage had ever existed, and it freed either party to enter into another marriage relationship (Brundage, 1987, p. 453). When the common law became a part of the American
colonial jurisprudence, annulment jurisdiction was granted to the courts of chancery (since
there were no church courts in this country) (Phillips, 1988, pp. 134–135), but the old
grounds for annulment remained. Because of an increasing demand for ending "dead" marriages, jurisdictions with particularly strict divorce laws (such as New York, Illinois, and
California) expanded the concepts of fraud that had historically been used in annulment
cases. Even here, however, annulment was a less popular remedy than the collusive divorce
(*Project*, 1966; Wardle, 1991, p. 107). Like the divorce action, the annulment ends a relationship. but unlike a divorce, the annulment decree states that a marriage, legally speaking,
never existed.[7] Divorce can be thought of as analogous to an action for breach of contract
(or termination at will) (Brinig and Carbone, 1988), while annulment is more like a recision of contract. There are really two kinds of annulments; the decree of nullity, which
declares that purported marriages are void,[8] and the dissolution of marriage, which is for
voidable marriages.[9]

Marriages are void when they are prohibited by law or when there was an inability to
entertain any contract. Such marriages include those void for incest (marriages within the
prohibited degree),[10] polygamy (bigamy),[11] between two persons of the same sex
(sodomy),[12] between people so mentally retarded or mentally ill that they are incapable
of making a valid contract (idiocy or lunacy),[13] and marriage between persons at least one
of whom was so young as to be legally incapable of giving consent (nonage).[14] Although
children born of these marriages are legitimated by statute,[15] for all other purposes the
marriage never was.[16] Third parties can bring the "annulment" action, and there is usually
no ability to recover alimony[17] nor a distribution of property.[18] Almost all such annulments
are due to bigamy, usually because a first marriage was not validly dissolved before the
second was celebrated (Wadlington, 1990, pp. 141–144; *Project*, 1966).

The other type of annulment action, with which this paper is primarily concerned, concerns voidable marriages. These are marriages in which there was a defect in the contracting mechanism. Voidable marriages include sham marriages (for example, to gain admit-
tance to the United States as a nonquota immigrant),[19] fraudulent marriages, marriages
contracted under duress ("shotgun marriages"),[20] and marriages where minors did not have

the requisite parental consent.[21] These marriages are valid until the court declares them *void ab initio.* They therefore support not only legitimacy of children, but also in rem jurisdiction (jurisdiction based on the presence of the marriage in the state, as established by the residence and domicile of one of the spouses),[22] alimony (in most states),[23] and property distribution.[24] They operate in the same way as valid marriages to cut off the rights to alimony from a previous spouse.[25] A plurality of all annulments are for fraud. Even in 1966, when California revised its laws to include no-fault divorce, annulments represented fewer than 5 percent of all severance actions. Of these, 47 percent were based on fraud (*Project*, 1966).

A spouse may prefer annulment to divorce for several reasons. The action may be chosen by a spouse who would otherwise be forced to pay support or pay for medical expenses incurred during the marriage.[26] The spouse may think that a civil annulment may make a later ecclesiastical annulment less difficult.[27] An annulment may also be quicker than a divorce in a state requiring a waiting period before a divorce can be granted. Finally, as we shall discuss later, the annulment may be used as a device to circumvent a statute disallowing evidence of "marital fault" from entering into calculations of spousal support or property distribution.

3. Fraud in transactions of different types

Fraud in contracts occurs only when there is asymmetric information between the parties. The implications of fraud for behavior of the potential contracting parties depend on the nature of the informational discrepancy between them. Philip Nelson writing in another context distinguished between *search goods* and *experience goods* (Nelson, 1970, p. 312). The qualities of the search goods can be examined in a short time or otherwise at low cost to the consumer, who can therefore make an inspection before purchase. The qualities of the experience goods, on the other hand, cannot be ascertained until after purchase. (Philip Nelson uses the example of a can of tuna fish.) Nelson predicts among other things that there would be more monopoly among sellers of experience goods and that buyers would seek advice of others more frequently (Nelson, 1970, p. 327). Darby and Karni (1973) introduced an additional category of *credence goods*. The quality of these goods may not be easily determined even after the purchase.[28]

The "good" acquired through marriage has the characteristics of all three categories of goods mentioned above. The experience-good aspect of a marriage is, perhaps, its most important attribute for the topic of this paper. In the marriage context, as with the purchase of tuna fish, some things that can't be known for certain until after the contract is made: for example, whether the other party intends to have children, will be a good parent, will practice a particular religion, or generally will be interesting to live with. However, there is a significant difference between marriage and Nelson's experience goods. At least in theory marriage is for life, and there will be no "repeat purchase" or "purchase of another brand." This may be one reason for the legal intervention of annulment, like recision of the contract, in the case of marriage. Also, the nonrepetitive nature of marriage increases the importance of its credence-goods aspect.[29]

The search-goods aspect of marriage is reflected in the fact that there are some things that a "diligent buyer" of marriage services *can* know, such as whether an admitted prior marriage was dissolved by death or by divorce. Fraud about such traits will not lead to annulment (although a spouse's disillusionment may result eventually in a divorce.)[30]

There are also marriages in which there may be fraud but in which the deceived spouse will still be getting the person intended and the contract of marriage will be found valid. Typical of these situations are those involving assurances that one loves the other or will be faithful or even that one is a famous sports star.[31] In other situations there may exist some undiscoverable traits that are so much better than those the average person in the "marriage market" possesses that no annulment action would be filed despite the presence of fraud.

It is primarily in the first category of cases (the experience-good aspect), where fraud cannot be discovered at a reasonable cost prior to marriage, that the law offers the relief of annulment.

Gary Becker (1974) pioneered a discussion of courtship in terms of the search behavior that leads to what he called *assortative mating*. Young people usually begin the search for a mate after they have "played the field" for some time to discover what they want in a spouse and what they are worth to others. They then date to find out enough about the other person to see whether he or she matches the characteristics that hypothetically would make a good marriage partner.[32] Finally, each attempts to convince the other party that he or she is capable of fulfilling the other's expectations. Engagement occurs when the expected utility from getting married outweighs the expected utility of remaining single (Becker, 1991).

However, even when the couple becomes engaged, there are "secrets" that can only, if ever, be revealed after marriage. Becker, Landes, and Michael (1977, p. 1143) note that divorce occurs when the new revelations make staying inside the marriage less desirable than resuming the single state. These authors do not mention, however, that sometimes the misinformation or lack of information given during courtship vitiates the marriage contract itself. When returning to the *status quo ante* is more attractive than accepting the other spouse's true characteristics, the disappointed spouse may bring an action for annulment on the grounds of fraud.

Some of the incidence of fraud in courtship can be reduced through nonlegal means. To this end one may limit the search for a mate to individuals with good "reputation." This provides strong incentives to establish a good reputation. Such incentives are particularly important in small communities where "everyone knows everyone else" (Bishop, 1984, pp. 258–259; Rothman, 1987, pp. 162–163). In general, reputation will have less effect in a large urban area, where one could conceivably take advantage of (cheat) any number of the members of the opposite sex (Bailey, 1989). Mechanisms have evolved, however, in which reputation, or other forms of specific human-capital investment, becomes important (England and Farkas, 1987, p. 41). This is why there may be so much dating within particular organizations (university alumni clubs, church "singles" groups, sporting or exercise groups, or even computer dating services). In circumstances where reputation is less effective in reducing fraud, other devices such as the "trial marriage"[33] may be used. As England and Farkas note, premarital cohabitation is the search mechanism that provides the most relevant information about the performance of the other person as a marriage partner. Note also that such additional search mechanisms imply greater reliance expenditures than more traditional courtship behavior.

Despite the existence of nonlegal fraud-reducing devices, marital fraud does occur and it has to be dealt with by the legal system. Outside the marriage context, the law regulates fraud through the contractual devices of mistake, lack of meeting of the minds (fraud or lack of capacity), and unconscionability. Contracts can be rescinded or avoided if the parties, or either of them, *didn't* really understand what was involved, *couldn't* understand what was involved, or *shouldn't* be penalized because the bargaining power was so unequal and the results so unfair. In the case of marriage, the parallel remedy to rescission of contract is annulment, which declares the marriage void or voidable and decrees that from the beginning it legally has never existed.

The opportunity to commit fraud that could provide grounds for annulment in the future depends to a large extent on the customs of courtship in the society. The modern pattern of courtship gives the couple more opportunity to discover the good and bad characteristics of each other. Together with liberalized divorce laws that make release from bad (mistaken or mismatched) marriages fairly easy, one might expect to find a decrease in reliance on the annulment on grounds of fraud.

4. A model of annulment

This section sets up a model of fraud in marriage in the context of which we provide conditions for the willingness to engage in fraud and discuss when such fraud might be socially optimal.[34] Also, we demonstrate that, all other things being equal, inadmissibility of fault in divorce proceedings increases the likelihood of a spouse's asking for annulment instead of divorce.

We will use the following notation:

The potential future spouses are the expected utility-maximizing agents in the model. They are the potential spouses, with w being the future wife and h her husband;[35]

$x = (x_1, x_2)$ are true characteristics of the wife as a marriage partner;

$y = (y_1, y_2)$ are true characteristics of the husband as a marriage partner;

x_1, y_1 are the characteristics about which fraud sufficient for annulment may occur;

$\hat{x}_1$ is the value of the first argument of x that the wife reports to the husband prior to marriage;[36]

x_2, y_2 are the agents' characteristics that can be credibly communicated only after marriage and that cannot constitute the basis for annulment even if the other spouse has been misled about their true value. Both spouses realize this.

$W_t(y)$, $H_t(x)$ are the values of the utilities of marriage for wife and husband respectively as calculated at time t ($t = 0$ before marriage and 1 after marriage). Note that these utilities depend on the characteristics of the other spouse.

W_t, H_t are the opportunity costs of the marriage for wife and husband, respectively. They constitute the next best available alternative at time t. Note that W_1 and H_1 include the cost of marriage dissolutions, including the court costs and the results of division of marital property (and the custody of the children, if they are present) as the result of the annulment or divorce, as well as the change in the value of each spouse in the marriage market either because of the passage of time or because of the fact that they have been married.

$EW(.)$ and $EH(.)$ are the expected utility of marriage lasting a lifetime for wife and husband, respectively, evaluated at time 0.

$EW_{0,1}$ is the expected utility to the wife of staying in marriage from time 0 to time 1.

p is the probability (at time 0) that fraud is discovered at time $t = 1$.

π = the probability (at time 0) that h would want to remain in the marriage conditional on fraud having been discovered.

We assume that time 1 values are discounted whenever necessary.

Let us begin setting up a model of fraud prior to marriage with a set of simplifying assumptions describing the sequence of events in the model. At time 0 the following takes place: one of the agents—say, w—makes a decision to engage in fraud and carries out that decision. (We assume that h does not also engage in fraud—that is, that $\hat{y}_1 = y_1$.) The marriage takes place, and true values of x_2 and y_2 are revealed to h and w, respectively. At a later date (time 1), h discovers w's fraud with probability p and makes the choice of whether or not to file for annulment.

When will w engage in fraud by reporting an $\hat{x}_1 \neq x_1$? To begin with, w presumably wishes to be married to h, implying that

$$EW(y_1, y_2) > W_0. \tag{1}$$

Second, w must think that h would not want to marry her if he knew the true value of x_1 but that he would want to marry her if he thinks that $x_1 = \hat{x}_1$. In other words,

$$EH(x_1, x_2) < H_0, \text{ but } EH(\hat{x}_1, x_2) > H_0. \tag{2}$$

Third, w must expect to become better off due to fraud: w's expected utility after fraud must be greater than her expected utility without fraud. To begin with, there is a certain probability that w's fraud will never be discovered. Further, even if it is discovered, she knows that there are costs to bringing an annulment action that h may not wish to incur. Finally, she may believe that her x_2 values outweigh the difference between the true and reported values of x_1. In order to determine w's expected utility under some given amount of fraud, we have to determine the conditions under which fraud would cause dissolution of marriage. Dissolution would occur if fraud has been discovered and if at time 1

$$H_1(x_1, x_2) < X_1 \tag{3}$$

(recall that H_1 is the h's expected utility after dissolution through annulment of the marriage). Suppose that at time 0, wife attaches probability π to (3) holding at time 1. Recall that the probability of husband's discovering fraud is p. Wife will commit fraud if and only if her expected utility from engaging in fraud at time 0 is greater than W_o, or

$$\pi p (EW_{0,1}) + (1 - \pi p)(EW(y)) > W_0 \quad (4).$$

Less formally, wife may commit fraud expecting that husband will not discover her deception, or that even if he does, he will decide to remain married to her. Incidentally, W_1 is likely to be less than W_o because of court costs, loss of reputation due to the fraud being discovered, any tort damages husband could recover, and any alimony or property wife must give husband because the marriage existed, if only for a short time.

In order for a court to grant an annulment, there is a threshold value for the difference between $\hat{x}$ and x_1 that is independent of x_2. This may be seen from statements in the cases that the fraud must "go to the essence of the marriage" —that is, that it cannot concern a *de minimis* issue.

There should be more fraud as the probability of discovery decreases, as the costs of dissolution of the marriage decrease, and as the difference between the true value of x_2 and its expectation change relative to x_1.

Are there any circumstances where fraud committed by one agent results in improved welfare of both agents (Shavell, 1991)? First, this is likely to be the case if fraud is never discovered.[37] Second, both spouses may be better off even if the fraud has been discovered as long as h's expectations of the value of x_2 considerably underestimated its true value.[38] Formally, fraud that has been discovered might have been beneficial to both spouses provided that at time 0

$$EH(x_1, x_2) < H_0 < EH(\hat{x}_1, x_2) \text{ and } H_0 < H_0(x_1, x_2). \quad (5)$$

In other words, the negative effect of the difference between x_1 and $\hat{x}_1$ on the husband's utility must not offset the influence of the difference between the expected value of x_2 and its true value.

The social effect of fraud committed prior to marriage is somewhat more difficult to analyze. For example, it is not clear how to account for the changes in welfare of the couple's children if they exist. These children would not have been born if fraud did not take place. Even if there are no children, the possibly temporary marriage between w and h creates externalities that may be positive or negative. The social value of the fraud would depend on these externalities.

The model described above can also illustrate the relationship between annulment and divorce. Suppose the true value of x_2 is such that it provides grounds for fault divorce. Suppose also that fraud occurred prior to marriage—that is, x_1 is not equal to $\hat{x}_1$. (Sometimes this could also constitute grounds for fault divorce.) Assuming that transactions costs of an annulment are higher than those for fault divorce, the husband will file for fault divorce if (3) holds (if he is better off ending the marriage than staying in it). If fault is not admissible, then the husband would file for annulment if it offers a division of property that is more advantageous to him in expected terms than the no-fault divorce outcome.

Table 2. Dependent variable: Number of annulments ($R^2 = .252$).

Variable name	Estimated coefficient	Standard error	T-ratio 1001 DF
TREND	−0.033438	−0.0029586	−11.302
LOGMARR	0.78364	0.053362	14.685
NFDUMMY	0.14799	0.060831	2.4328
CONSTANT	−5.1956	0.14131	−36.767

Other things being equal, (1) there should be fewer annulments as it becomes easier to divorce at a fairly low cost,[39] and (2) there should be proportionately more annulment cases in those states or countries where fault cannot be brought into the divorce proceedings.[40] This should occur because when fault is eliminated, annulment is the only recourse for a person unhappy with the standard no-fault outcomes. In contrast, in a state or country allowing fault as well as no-fault divorces,[41] fraud before marriage might result in annulment, while divorce will be the remedy for unfulfilled expectations after the marriage takes place (when x_2 is known for sure, instead of probabilistically). In fact, if it is easier to prove fault in divorce rather than fraud prior to marriage, then some candidates for annulment may instead be tried (and dissolved) as fault divorces.

These predictions have been tested through an empirical study involving data on annulments for the years 1965 (before unilateral no-fault divorce was available in any state) to 1987 (when all states had at least some form of no-fault divorce). The pooled time series results are shown in Table 2.[42]

As we would predict, the number of annulments decreases with time (the variable TREND), as couples are able to dissolve their marriages through some reasonably expeditious type of divorce. The number of annulments increases significantly as the logarithm of the number of marriages (LOGMARR) increases because the number of couples who commit significant fraud increases. However, the number of annulments is (statistically) significantly higher in those states that have adopted a unilateral form of no-fault divorce (NFDUMMY), where no evidence of fault is admissible either to obtain a divorce or to allocate the marital resources. We suggest that this occurs because in these states spouses, on the margin, use annulments to place evidence of fault (fraud) before the court. They may do this either to vindicate their own sense of outrage (Wardle, 1991) or because they wish to deprive the other spouse of support or obtain it for themselves.

Annulment, however, represents a rather inflexible remedy that can be applied in a restricted number of situations. There is a consistent threshold value for the amount of fraud that triggers the annulment action (the necessary difference between $\hat{x}$ and x_1). We provide the following analysis for purposes of illustration of this threshold.

5. Analysis of annulment cases

5.1. Cases involving discoverable defects

Out of the 126 reported annulment cases used for this analysis,[43] thirty nine involved misrepresentations of social standing that the innocent party might have discovered prior to marriage through diligent search. Courts granted annulments in only twelve of these. All these successful cases were decided prior to no-fault divorce. They were therefore products of a time when the doctrine was expanded to its limit. Six of the twelve were New York cases involving concealment of a prior divorce at a time when the only ground for absolute divorce was adultery. The other cases involved "pregnancy by a negro porter," concealment of a trial for murder and conviction for petty larceny, concealment of pregnancy by another (two cases), and nondisclosure of four children of a prior marriage. All of these involve conduct that at that time was considered immoral and embarrassing.[44]

In some other cases where the true characteristics of the would-be spouse could or should have been known prior to marriage, the courts have been reluctant to grant annulments.[45] For example, in *Mistal v. Mistal*, 315 Mass. 308, 52 N.E.2d 418 (1943), the husband told the wife that he had tuberculosis but that it was only a mild case. Since they were married in the sanatorium, and the wife should have known that tuberculosis is usually severe, she had no grounds for complaint.[46] Similarly, when a fifteen-year-old girl said that she was eighteen in order to marry a man to get his Air Force allotment, there could be no annulment since there was no showing that she was unwilling or unable to perform her marriage vows. *Williams v. Williams*, 268 Ala. 223, 105 So. 2d 676 (1958).[47]

Another group of cases in which fraud is alleged, but is usually not a successful ground for annulment, is that in which the wife fraudulently tells her future spouse that she is pregnant with his child. Out of eighteen such reported cases, annulments were granted in only seven. All of these except one were decided after 1975, after which data the states have required child support by unwed fathers. In an age where premarital sexual behavior is commonplace, the rules may have been relaxed since the concern for the child's welfare is satisfied. Courts may now be saying that the identity of the father could only have been known after marriage (when the child was born) and therefore that the cases belong in the following "undiscoverable" fraud category. In the older cases, perhaps the main reason the husband cannot have the marriage annulled is that he has "unclean hands" because of his (illicit) intercourse with the woman prior to marriage.[48] As one of the newer cases says explicitly, the courts are "undoing" the old rule since it was unduly harsh. *Symonds v. Symonds*, 385 Mass. 540, 432 N.E.2d 700 (1982).

5.2. Cases where fraud is undiscoverable

Most successful annulment suits involve concealment of some fact that cannot be discovered until after the marriage takes place. In one group of cases, one or the other party conceals a desire not to have children until after the marriage ceremony. In each of the eleven cases read where the intent was proved to have existed prior to marriage, this concealment was grounds for annulment. In one of the more extreme of these cass, *Bruno v. Bruno*, 70 Misc. 2d 284, 334 N.Y.S.2d 242 (1972), the husband had to insist on intercourse without contraception, and the wife told others that she had had two abortions during the marriage. In the most recent case, *V.J.S. v. M.J.B.*, 249 N.J. Super. 318, 592 A.2d 328 (1991), the wife definitively wished no children, and the husband agreed before marriage not to have them. When he said he wanted them after the marriage and sought "unprotected" intercourse, the wife was able to get an annulment.

Twenty-two cases involved the unwillingness or inability of one spouse to consummate the marriage. This was grounds for annulment in all but two cases, which apparently involved proof problems. For example, in *In re Marriage of Danny and Pei-Lei-Li Liu*, 197 Cal. App. 3d 143, 242 Cal. Rptr. 649 (1987), the parties never had any intent to cohabit or consummate the marriage but wanted only to get a green card.[49] In *Kshaiboon v. Kshaiboon*, 652 S.W.2d 219 (Mo. Ct. App.), the husband concealed the fact that he lacked the physical and mental capability to engage in a normal sex life. The court allowed the wife to annul the marriage, saying that a sexual relationship is an essential element of a marriage.[50]

A last group of cases involves nondisclosure of religious preferences. This was grounds for annulment in nine of thirteen cases. Of the remaining four, three involved condonation after the true religious beliefs were discovered, although there would otherwise have been grounds for annulling the marriage. In the single case that reached the substantive issue,[51] the court held that refusal to have a religious wedding did not go to the essence of the marriage.[52] Perhaps the most famous of the cases allowing annulment is *Bilowit v. Bolitsky*, 124 N.J. Super. 101, 304 A.2d 774 (1973), where the deeply religious wife married her husband only because he maintained that he was an Orthodox Jew. An annulment was granted even though the marriage had been consummated because the fraud was "gross and far-reaching."[53]

From examination of the cases, it can be seen that the fraud that is undiscoverable and will vitiate the marriage promises is fraud that "goes to the essence." That is, it concerns an intent not to perform one or more of the terms of the marriage contract. Although it may not seem that marriage involves any concrete terms, in fact they are stated in the vows many couples exchange.[54] For example, the Book of Common Prayer of the Episcopal Church prescribes the ritual for the celebration of marriage as follows:[55]

> *N.*, will you have this woman to be your wife; to live together in the covenant of marriage? Will you love her, comfort her, honor and keep her, in sickness and in health; and, forsaking all others, be faithful to her as long as you both shall live?
>
> and
>
> In the Name of God, I, *N.*, take you, *N.*, to be my wife, to have and to hold from this day forward, for better and for worse, for richer for poorer, in sickness and in health, to love and to cherish, until we are parted by death. This is my solemn vow.
>
> *N.*, I give you this ring as a symbol of my vow, and with all that I am, and all that I have, I honor you, in the Name of the Father, and of the Son, and of the Holy Spirit.

These vows, although in archaic language, can be interpreted to mean that the couple intends to live together "until death," to support each other, to engage in sexual relations, to provide the bundle of goods and services that is called "consortium." Some ceremonies also state that the couple "will welcome the children God shall give them."[56]

Undiscoverable fraud that does not involve such "essential terms" is not grounds for annulment. Such fraud is interpreted in domestic relations cases as failing to "go to the essence of the marriage contract." Here the court may be setting a threshold value for the difference between the reported and actual characteristics. For example, *Avnery v. Avnery*[57] held that the fraud must be as to matters vital to the marriage relationship and must deceive the ordinarily prudent person. An extreme example of a court's willingness to say a marriage existed despite substantial concealment is *Husband and Wife*,[58] 257 A.2d 765 (Del. Super. 1969), where the wife concealed her narcotics addiction and convictions for narcotics possession. The court said that only her personal traits and moral character were involved. The fraud did not go to the essence of the marriage. In broader terms, such nondisclosure or misrepresentation may involve the type of bundling of more or less desirable goods frequently seen when a seller possesses substantial market power as in antitrust cases or restraints that are placed on property when it is sold (Butler, Lane, and Phillips, 1984; Natelson, 1990; Alexander, 1988).

When most people marry, they do not feel that their spouse is a perfect individual, even though they may not yet be aware of what the real flaws might be. Although the spouses can reduce overwhelming surprises by lengthy courtship, by living together prior to marriage, or by participating seriously in premarital counseling, they can never really completely know each other.[59] For those hidden deficiences that were not on the usual mental list of desirable or unacceptable characteristics, the law provides no relief through annulment.[60] Should the spouses discover eventually that the "bad" outweights the "good" in each other, the remedy is not annulment but divorce. For example, in *Heup v. Heup*[61] a woman sued her husband for divorce on grounds of cruelty. He countered with the claim that the marriage was voidable on grounds of fraud, that she had agreed before marriage to take birth control pills for one year and continued to take them thereafter. The court stated that there was no proof that *before marriage* she had intended to remain childless. She was granted a divorce on the basis of her testimony that, among other things, she has been "called a sinner" and criticized for parting her hair on the wrong side, painting her nails the wrong color, planting the wrong flowers in the garden, and eating crackers in bed.

6. Conclusion

Some amount of fraud is tolerated by spouses as they realize the other benefits of the person they have chosen to marry. Some is accepted because of the relatively high transaction costs of obtaining an annulment as opposed to a divorce. Some is found to be socially optimal by a court system that does not want to be concerned with *de minimis* mistakes. Some fraud is intolerable even under this constraint and results in annulment of a marriage.

Based on our model and an analysis of the data, we conclude that, other things being equal, the adoption of a regime in which fault is irrelevant in divorce contributes to an increase in the number of annulments. Annulment and fault divorce are substitutes in some cases, and, therefore, the elimination of fault divorce leads to an increase in the demand for annulment. This substitution, of course, is limited due to different requirements for annulling marriage and proving fault in divorce proceedings. Our analysis follows in the

Coasian tradition that predicts that so long as transactions costs are not prohibitive a change in the law (that is, a change in the initial assignment of property rights) at least to some extent would be circumvented by changed behavior of economic agents.

Acknowledgments

The authors wish to thank the Sarah Scaife and John M. Olin Foundations for research support and to acknowledge the helpful suggestions made by colleagues in George Mason Law School's workshop in law and economics as well as the editor and an anonymous referee.

Notes

1. This may have been the solution for many husbands in the days of the American and New Zealand frontiers (Phillips, 1988, pp. 435–436).
2. See, e.g., Brinig and Carbone (1988, p. 860), where the authors note that the duty to pay support after separation was a continuation of the husband's duty to support his wife during marriage.
3. In the United States, states like Nevada were (and still are) "divorce mills," where the rate of divorce is many times higher than that of other states. During the 1940s, this outmigration for divorce purposes spawned a series of Supreme Court cases, the most famous of which is *Williams v. North Carolina*, 317 U.S. 287 (1942). Ultimately the Court determined that so long as the migrating spouse became domiciled in the state permitting easier divorce, the divorce must be given full faith and credit in all other states.
4. See, e.g., *Maynard v. Hill*, 125 U.S. 190 (1888); see generally Phillips (1988, pp. 9–10, 71–77); Vernier and Hurlbut (1939).
5. Other things happen as well. There may, for example, be more spousal abuse, fewer childrenn, and fewer and later marriages (Brinig and Crafton, 1993; Cohen, 1987).
6. Because fault plays other roles in encouraging investment in marriage (Brinig and Carbone, 1988), discouraging opportunism (Brinig and Crafton, 1993; Cohen, 1987), choosing a purely no-fault regime is problematic. We suggest here that fault may well be introduced via the back door of annulment even if a no-fault solution is chosen.
7. See, e.g., *Gordon v. Pollard*, 207 Tenn. 45, 336 S.W.2d 25 (1969); *Flaxman v. Flaxman*, 57 N.J. 458, 273 A.2d 567 (1971).
8. See Va. Code § 20-38.1.
9. See Va. Code § 20-89.1.
10. See, e.g., *In re May's Estate*, 305 N.Y. 486, 114 N.E.2d 4 (1953); *State v. Sharon H.*, 429 A.2d 1321 (Del. Super. 1981).
11. See, e.g., *Buckley v. Buckley*, 133 Cal. App. 3d 927, 184 Cal. Rptr. 290 (1991).
12. See, e.g., *Baker v. Nelson*, 291 Minn. 310, 191 N.W.2d 185 (1971). See generally Comment, Constitutional Aspects of Homosexual's Right to Marriage License, 12 *J. Family Law* 607 (1972).
13. See, e.g., *Nicely v. Gardner*, 12 Va. Cir. 216 (City of Roanoke, 1988); cf. *Thomas v. Thomas*, 111 Ill. App. 3d 1032, 444 N.E.2d 826 (1983); *Edmunds v. Edmunds*, 205 Neb. 255, 287 N.W.2d 420 (1980).
14. *People v. Benu*, 87 Misc. 2d 139, 385 N.Y.S.2d 222 (1976).
15. For an extreme cse, see *Kasey v. Richardson*, 331 F. Supp. 580 (W.D. Va. 1971).
16. See, e.g., Va. Code § 20-89.1(a): "When a marriage is alleged to be void or voidable for any of the causes mentioned in §§ 20-13, 20-38.1, 20-45.1 or by virtue of fraud or duress, either party may institute a suit for annulling the same; and upon proof of the nullity of the marriage, it shall be decreed void by a decree of annulment.
17. Except in Maryland, which allows all marriages to be "divorced." *Clayton v. Clayton*, 231 Md. 74, 188 A.2d 550 (1946).
18. See, e.g., *Zaragliola v. Capriola*, 201 N.J. Super. 55, 492 A.2d 698 (Chan. 1985); *Mato v. Mato*, 12 Va. Cit. 153 (Spotsylvania Co. 1988).

19. See, e.g., *Mpirilis v. Hellenic Lines*, 323 F. Supp. 865 (S.D. Tex. 1969).

20. See, e.g., *Thomas v. Thomas*, 111 Ill. App. 3d 1032, 444 N.E.2d 826 (1983).

21. See, e.g., *Needham v. Needham*, 183 Va. 681, 33 S.E.2d 288 (1945).

22. See, e.g., Va. Code § 20-104; compare *Whealton v. Whealton*, 67 Cal. 2d 656, 432 P.2d 979, 63 Cal. Rptr. 291 (1967), and *Sacks v. Sacks*, 47 Misc. 2d 1050, 263 N.Y.S.2d 891 (1965) (void marriages).

23. See, e.g., Va. Code § 20-107.1.

24. See, e.g., Va. Code § 20-107.3.

25. See, e.g., *McConkey v. McConkey*, 216 Va. 106, 215 S.E.2d 640 (1975); *Flaxman v. Flaxman*, 57 N.J. 458, 273 A.2d 567 (1971).

26. See, e.g., *In re Marriage of Higgason*, 10 Cal. 3d 476, 516 P.2d 284 (1973) (but antenuptial agreement invalid to relieve duty of support during marriage); *Anonymous v. Anonymous*, 67 Misc. 2d 982, 325 N.Y.S.2d 499 (1971) (void marriage; no duty to pay for medical care even before annulment granted).

27. We were surprised to find that the percentage of a state's population that is Catholic was not significantly related to the number of annulments granted.

28. Darby and Karni (1973) write about situations involving service as well as sale of a particular good, where the buyer can't discern how much service was really needed even after the service has been performed. For example, it may be costly for a surgery patient to find out after the fact if the removal of her appendix was warranted or not.

29. In the marriage market, each party possesses complete information only about him- or herself. If one party is naive about what really goes on in marriage, whether it is about whether all wives put their husband's laundry away or all couples engage in some bizarre sexual practice, much of what Darby and Karni have to say about car sales and appendix operations can be applied in the marriage context. They suggest that one form of government intervention that may become necessary in situations involving commercial credence goods is occupational licensing. In marriage, there is at least some rough screening by the state through the marriage license, in which both parties swear to have the capacity to be married, that they are of the opposite sexes, and that each is of the appropriate age. There may also be a state requirement of blood testing to assure freedom from venereal diseases. Illinois had such a requirement involving testing for the AIDS virus in 1988, during which the marriage rates in that state declined dramatically, as those in neighboring states rose as they took up the excess (Loudon, 1991).

30. It may be that courts are using the fact that the defect is discoverable when they assume that the spouse in fact did know of the defect prior to the marriage.

31. As in *C. v. C.*, [1942] N.Z.L.R. 356. A new Utah case, *Haacke/Glenn v. Glenn*, 814 P.2d 1157 (Utah Ct. App. 1991), involves nondisclosure of a criminal record when the fiance was a lawyer whose job required access to such files. Because the felony record of her then husband put her employment in jeopardy, an annulment was granted. This case may be criticized because it involves a subjective determination of what is fraud "going to the essence" of marriage, and because the wife here, because of her employment, would have had more access than the average citizen to her prospective husband's criminal records. Perhaps the Utah court is, through this opinion, trying to increase good-faith reliance and trust by prospective marriage partners. Compare (Allen, 1992) regarding the importance of the idea of sharing in marriage to the choice of a mate.

32. With some traits, such as educational achievement, social class background, physical attractiveness, and personality type, the individual will seek a positive match. With others, such as earning ability and "household production" skills like cooking, the person's interest will focus on one whose attributes are complementary (England and Farkas, 1987, pp. 34–35; Becker, 1981).

33. The incidence of cohabitation has been rising dramatically since the mid-1960s (Loudon, 1991).

34. The model does not use continuous variables because fraud is typically of the discrete yes or no kind. One cannot, for example, be "half-married." In fact, when the conduct *can* be naturally represented by a continuous variable, such as with the amount of wealth a future spouse possesses, courts do not grant annulments. Because in our model the choice is among values of discrete variables, differential calculus is not used in the analysis. The analysis below, therefore, just sets out the restrictions that either are or are not satisfied.

35. We attach no significance to the symmetry between wife and husband in our setup. The roles could be reversed.

36. Either spouse could, of course, commit the fraud. In fact, in the reported fraud cases wives and husbands each bring the action about half the time.

37. Of course, even the fraud that has never been discovered by the defrauded spouse may indeed hurt that spouse without his or her knowledge. For example, suppose that *w* cannot have children but pretends that she can and that her inability to conceive is due to *h*'s infertility. Assume also that having children is highly important for *h*. Even if *h* believes *w*'s story, the fact remains that they do not have children, and *h* could have been better off marrying another person.

38. Recall that we assume that it is not possible for *w* to credibly communicate the true value of x_2 to *h* prior to marriage.

39. In fact, it has always been a more difficult process to obtain an annulment than to be granted a divorce, so long as the grounds for divorce existed. In this model, we are ignoring the fact that there are greater transactions costs in annulments than in divorces.

40. There should be more fault in such states because only a portion of it will be discovered and acted on by the deceived spouse. This, however, cannot be tested empirically with the available data.

41. Or at least taking fault into consideration in grants of alimony or in property distribution.

42. The regressions were run on the econometrics program SHAZAM (White, 1988).

43. More than a thousand were read, but many did not contain information regarding the type of fraud involved, or their statements about fraud were in dicta.

44. Interestingly, all except the last are categories of fraud specifically enumerated in some state statutes (i.e., Va. Code § 20-85).

45. This was certainly the rule in the older American cases (Schouler, 1870, p. 36): "*[C]aveat emptor* is the harsh but necessary maxim of the law. Love, however indispensable in an aesthetic sense, is by no means a legal essential to marriage, simply because it cannot be weighed in the scales of justice."

46. But compare *In re Marriage of Kathleen and John DeVille*, 45 Ore. App. 53, 607 P.2d 228 (1980), where wife was allowed to annul marriage where husband concealed his mental disability and inability to provide support at the time of the marriage, and she ended up supporting both of them.

47. See also *Picarella v. Picarella*, 20 Md. App. 499, 316 A.2d 826 (1974) (husband sixteen and one-half; wife knew this prior to marriage).

48. From the beginning, the American cases decreed that when a husband had premarital intercourse with his mate, there could be no fraud (Grossberg, 1985, p. 344 n.36).

49. See also *Pretlow v. Pretlow*, 177 Va. 524, 14 S.E.2d 381 (1941), where the wife apparently had no intent to consummate the marriage but wanted only to get the husband's property; and Cowhey v. Tator, 36 Ill. App. 3d 962, 344 N.E.2d 501 (1976), where the wife sought not only marriage but adoption of her three children by her wealthy spouse. Immediately after the marriage she showed that she had no intent to cohabit with him and moved to Colorado with her three children to move in with a ski instructor.

50. See also *Sites v. Johns Manville Products*, 2006 N.J. Super. 610, 503 A.2d 377 (1986) (physical and incurably impotence); compare *C. v. C.*, 158 Wis. 301, 148 N.W.2d 865 (1914), where a husband was allowed an annulment when his wife knew and failed to disclose prior to marriage that she had gonorrhea and that it was incurable.

51. *Wells v. Talham*, 180 Wis. 654, 194 N.W. 36 (1923).

52. This holding is contrary to a number of cases where there was a promise of a church ceremony following the civil one. See, e.g., *Babis v. Babis*, 45 Del. 496, 75 A.2d 580 (1950); *Brillis v. Brillis*, 4 N.Y.2d 125, 173 N.Y.S.2d 3, 149 N.E.2d 510 (1958); *Lamberti v. Lamberti*, 272 Cal. App. 2d 482, 77 Cal. Rptr. 430 (1969).

53. See also *State Compensation Fund v. Foughty*, 13 Ariz. App. 381, 476 P.2d 902 (1970) (husband professed Christianity when actually he was an atheist); *Wolfe v. Wolfe*, 62 Ill. App. 3d 498, 378 N.E.2d 1181 (1978) (wife showed husband a false death certificate for her former husband because she knew of his religious objections to remarriage following divorce).

54. If not, they are nevertheless implied by law. In this respect, marriage resembles a "standard form contract."

55. W. Va. Code § 48-1-12b prescribes a similar ritual for its civil ceremonies:

> N., wilt thou have this woman to be thy wedded wife, to live together in the bonds of matrimony? Wilt thou love her, comfort her, honor and keep her in sickness and health?
> (The man shall answer:)
> "I will." . . .
> (Then the judge shall ask the man to say after him:)

> I, N., take thee, N., to be my wedded wife, to have and to hold, from this day forward, for better, for worse, for richer, for poorer, in sickness and in health, to love, and to cherish, as long as life shall last, and thereto I pledge thee my faith . . . .
>
> (Then, if there be a ring, the judge shall say:)
>
> "The wedding ring is an outward and visible sign—signifying unto all, the uniting of this man and this woman in matrimony.
>
> (The judge then shall deliver the ring to the man to put on the third finger of the woman's left hand. The man shall say after the judge:)
>
> "In token and pledge of the vow between us made, with this ring, I thee wed."

56. The ceremonies including this term notably include the Roman Catholic Church. Where the vows exchanged do not include this term, it will be implied because of the centrality of child rearing in the marriage function.

57. 50 App. Div. 2d 806, 375 N.Y.S.2d 888 (1975); see also *Francis v. Francis*, VI Terr. Ct. 1985; *Emmons v. Emmons*, 34 App. Div. 2d 725, 312 N.Y.S.2d 117 (1970) (where husband misrepresented his financial status and fiscal responsibility, but the wife continued to live with him, there would have been no ground for annulling the marriage "even if the fraud had been material," and *Baird v. Baird*, 232 P.2d 348 (Nev. 1951) (misrepresentation that husband loved wife and wanted her happiness didn't go to the essence of the marriage).

58. See also *Woy v. Woy*, 737 S.W.2d 769 (Mo. App. 1987) (wife's lesbian activities and drug usage prior to marriage; she and husband cohabited for five years prior to marriage and had "fine" sexual relations before discovery).

59. Oliver Williamson, (1985, ch. 2) describes a bounded rationality that limits one's ability to acquire, retain, and use information.

50. See, e.g., the dissenting opinion in *Wolfe v. Wolfe*, 62 Ill. App. 3d 498, 378 N.E.2d 1181 (1978), or the cases in note 56, supra.

61. 45 Wis. 2d 71, 172 N.W.2d 334 (1969).

References

Alexander, Gregory. (1988). "Freedom, Coercion and the Law of Servitudes." *Cornell Law Review* 73, 883–905.

Allen, Douglas. (1990). "An Inquiry into the State's Role in Marriage." *Journal of Economic Behavior and Organization* 13, 171–191.

Allen, Douglas. (1992). "What's At Fault with No Fault?" Working paper presented at the Canadian Law and Economics Association Meeting, Toronto, September 25.

———. (1992). "What Does She See in Him? The Choice of Spouse." *Economic Inquiry* 30, 57–67.

Bailey, Beth. (1989). *From Front Porch to Back Seat: Courtship in Twentieth-Century America*. Baltimore: Johns Hopkins University Press.

Becker, Gary. (1974). "A Theory of Marriage." In T.W. Schultz (ed.), *Economics of the Family*. Chicago: University of Chicago Press.

Becker, Gary. (1991). *A Treatise on the Family* (2nd ed.). Cambridge, MA: Harvard University Press.

Becker, Gary, Elisabeth Landes, and Robert Michael. (1977). "An Economic Analysis of Marital Instability." *Journal of Political Economy* 5(6), 1141–1187.

Bishop, William. (1984). "Is He Married? Marriage as Information." *University of Toronto law Journal* 34, 245–262.

Brinig, Margaret, and Alexeev, Michael. (1993). "Trading at Divorce: Preferences, Legal Rules and Transactions Costs." *Ohio State Journal on Dispute Resolution* 8, 279–297.

Brinig, Margaret, and Carbone, June. (1988). "The Reliance Interest in Marriage and Divorce." *Tulane Law Review* 62, 855–905.

Brinig, Margaret, and Steven Crafton. (1993). "Opportunism in Marriage." Working paper, George Mason University.

Brundage, James. (1987). *Law, Sex and Christian Society in Medieval Europe*. Chicago: University of Chicago Press.

Butler, Henry, W.J. Lane, and Owen R. Phillips. (1984). "The Futility of Antitrust Attacks on Tie-In Sales: An Economic and Legal Analysis." *Hastings Law Journal* 36, 173–213.

Coase, Ronald. (1960). "A Theory of Social Cost." *Journal of Legal Studies* 3, 1–44.

Cohen, Lloyd. (1987). "Marriage Divorce and Quasi-Rents: Or, 'I Gave Him the Best Years of My Life.' " *Journal of Legal Studies* 16, 267–303.

Darby, Michael, and Eli Karni. (1973). "Free Competition and the Optimal Amount of Fraud." *Journal of Law and Economics* 16, 67–88.

England, Paula, and Gary Farkas. (1987). *Households, Employment and Gender.* New York: Aldine Press.

Grossberg, Michael. (1985). *Governing the Hearth.* Chapel Hill, NC: University of North Carolina Press.

"Comment: Constitutional Aspects of Homosexual's Right to Marriage License." (1972). *Journal of Family Law* 12, 607–634.

Loudon, K.A. (1991). "Advance Data from Vital and Health Statistics." No. 194. Bethesda, MD: National Center for Health Statistics.

Martindell-Hubbell. (1993). *International Law Digest.* Summit, NJ: Martindell-Hubbell.

Natelson, Robert. (1990). "Consent, Coercion, and 'Reasonableness' in Private Law: The Special Case of the Property Owners Association." *Ohio State Law Journal* 51, 41–88.

Nelson, Phillip. (1970). "Information and Consumer Behavior." *Journal of Political Economy* 78, 311–332.

Parkman, Allen. (1992). *No Fault Divorce: What Went Wrong?* Boulder, CO: Westview Press.

Phillips, Roderick. (1988). *Putting Asunder: A History of Divorce in Western Society.* Cambridge: Cambridge University Press.

Posner, Richard. (1992). *Sex and Reason.* Cambridge, MA: Harvard University Press.

Project of the Governor's Commission on the Family. (1966). Sacramento, CA.

Rea, Samuel. (1993). "The Economics of Divorce." Paper presented at the European Association of Law and Economics, Lund, Sweden, August.

Rothman, Ellen. (1987). *Hands and Hearts: A History of Courtship in America.* Cambridge, MA: Harvard University Press.

Shavell, Steven. (1991). "Acquisition and Disclosure of Information Prior to Economic Exchange." Working paper 24, American Law and Economics Association.

Wadlington, Walter. (1966). "Divorce Without Fault Without Perjury." *Virginia Law Review* 52, 32–87.

Wadlington, Walter. 1990. *Cases and Materials on Domestic Relations.* Westbury, NY: Foundation Press.

Walker, Timothy. (1971). "Beyond Fault: An Examination of Patterns of Behavior in Response to Present Divorce Laws." *Journal of Family Law* 10, 267–299.

Wardle, Lynn. (1991). "No-Fault Divorce and the Divorce Conundrum." *Brigham University Law Review* 1991, 79–142.

White, Kenneth. (1988). *Introduction to the Theory and Practice of Econometrics.* New York: John Wiley and Sons.

Williamson, Oliver. (1985). *The Economic Institutions of Capitalism.* New York: Free Press.

[7]

"WHAT DOES SHE SEE IN HIM?": THE EFFECT OF SHARING ON THE CHOICE OF SPOUSE

DOUGLAS W. ALLEN*

All husbands and wives share in the spoils of marriage. Sharing makes each partner a residual claimant and encourages spouses to provide marital inputs. However, because each spouse is only a partial residual claimant, each may be inclined to provide a "suboptimal" level of marital inputs. The choice of spouse influences the level of distortion, and under some circumstances the efficient mating is between individuals of equal value.

People tend to end up choosing partners of approximately their own social worth. Romantic choices appear to be a delicate compromise between one's desire to capture an ideal partner and one's realization that he must eventually settle for what he deserves.

Walster et al. [1978, 176]

I. INTRODUCTION

The literature on marriage, though for a long time exclusively concerned with the role of comparative advantage between husbands and wives, has begun to examine the institutional details that make a marriage different from other living arrangements such as those involving roommates and live-in servants. To this end, most of the work has focused on the role of the state in marriage.[1] Generally speaking, these papers have argued that a marriage generates potentially large transac-

tion costs, and that state regulation of *some* aspects of marriage is an economical method of reducing these costs. In the same spirit this paper examines the role of sharing in marriage. Sharing is common to all marriages and yet is not imposed by any third party. Sharing in marriage, as with sharing elsewhere, affects the behavior of those involved. In particular, it changes the incentives to provide inputs towards producing marital goods. The resulting change in behavior alters the value of potential marriages between different people, and therefore, the act of sharing influences the choice of spouse.

The issue of sharing is irrelevant in zero transaction cost household production models of marriage. When transaction costs are unimportant, any contract can achieve the same result, and so a marriage can easily be thought of as "a two-person firm with either member being the 'entrepreneur' who 'hires' the other at [some] salary."[2] Yet, if the choice of contract between a husband and wife was irrelevant, we should occasionally observe spouses hiring each other the way one hires a maid, gardener, cook, baby-sitter, gigolo or prostitute. That we do not, that we observe only sharing within a mar-

* Assistant Professor, Simon Fraser University. I would like to thank Tom Borcherding, Mike Caputo, Steve Ferris, D. Bruce Johnsen, Keith Leffler, Dean Lueck, Panos Nikolaidis, Tom Ross, Saul Schwartz, Gene Silberberg, and participants of the micro-workshop at the University of Washington for their suggestions and encouragement. The comments of Yoram Barzel, Kehhsiao Lin, Wing Suen, and three referees were particularly helpful. None of these people should share responsibility for any remaining errors.

1. See Allen [1990], Becker and Murphy [1988], and Cohen [1987], for examples.

2. Becker [1976, 216].

©Western Economic Association International

riage, suggests that transaction costs are not zero between spouses, and that sharing creates net benefits over other potential contracts between a husband and wife. In marriage, the Coase theorem doesn't hold.[3]

But is marriage not a case where transaction costs should be small? The literature on state intervention in marriage has argued that marriage can pose huge transaction costs. When a wife faces the threat of her husband leaving her after she has financed a medical degree, she takes actions to protect herself. When potential mates court one another they invest great amounts of time and effort towards measuring the other's attributes. When divorce laws change that put one sex at risk of exploitation, private methods of protection, such as postponing the age at marriage, occur. Becker and Murphy [1988] even argue that transaction costs can arise over dealings with immature, poorly funded, or even unborn children. In each case, transaction costs arise from efforts to prevent large involuntary transfers of wealth from one spouse to the other. Although the legal institution and formal status of marriage may be designed to take these kinds of transaction costs into account, the state is unable to mitigate the costs that arise over monitoring the day-to-day actions of each spouse. I argue that the share contract is used to police the numerous and often small decisions that a husband and wife continuously make.

In most marriage activities it is very costly for one partner to determine what the other has done or is doing. This difficulty arises because no one is omniscient and marital outcomes are influenced by husband, wife, and chance.[4] The separate inputs supplied by each towards a clean

house, a financial plan, a conversation, a child, and other marital activities are all but impossible to measure by the other because random variability distorts outcomes and prevents each partner from attributing outcomes to the other's inputs. Though observing a misbehaving child might rouse one's suspicions that the level or type of parental discipline has been inappropriate, this need not be the case since some children are naturally more disobedient than others, and the same child is sometimes docile and sometimes not. If a wife comes home from work and finds the house a mess, is this because the husband shirked his duty, or because "the phone just never stopped ringing." If a husband finds a dress receipt for $250, is he to believe his wife when she tells him that "everything else looked terrible, it was marked down 70 percent, and, besides, I bought it ages ago anyway." It's possible that the store had only one item in the wife's size and favorite color, and so it is almost impossible to prove her real motivation. Marriage is characterized by a countless number of situations for which the measurement of marginal products is difficult (is the husband a bad cook, or does the oven really have problems?), and direct payment for services rendered is too easily exploited. Although with any given activity it might be feasible to distinguish a spouse's action from bad luck, given the multitude of minor decisions in marriage it does not pay to measure marital inputs for all activities.

Although gains to cohabitation exist, the problems involved with each spouse monitoring the other prevent marriages from resembling fixed-wage or rental contracts. For wage or rental contracts to be feasible, measurement costs must not overwhelm the gains from concentrating ownership. In marriage, however, the measurement costs for wage or rental agreements seem enormous. Living together involves a myriad of minor tasks, each one often performed alone, and each

---

3. See Allen [1992] for statistical evidence that the Coase theorem does not hold in marriage.

4. Where chance is both random and its effect prohibitively costly to measure.

chore has many margins that could easily be manipulated to one's advantage.

Husbands and wives, though they submit to binding rules and are attracted to marriage to achieve the gains it allows, are still private maximizers. If a selfish spouse can gain at the expense of the other without getting caught or penalized, he or she will do so. Marriage vows, choosing a spouse that you love and who loves you, state laws regulating marriage and divorce, and moral and social pressure, are all attempts to mitigate selfish behavior in marriage, and I do not deny their importance—I simply wish to add sharing to the list. As a result of individual maximization, any spouse hired on a wage basis would take advantage of the other by providing fewer inputs to the marriage than is optimal.[5] Sharing reduces the losses caused by the improper input mix.

With sharing, each partner is a partial residual claimant and each polices his or her own behavior, although not to the extent a complete owner would.[6] Since each spouse's marginal decision to participate in marital activity is distorted, it is not possible to obtain the entire gains from trade realized in a zero transaction cost world. However, this loss is less than what would occur if the marriage resembled a wage contract or some similar arrangement that required direct measurement. A share contract reduces the loss resulting from neglected margins by creating an incentive for each spouse to curb his or her exploitative behavior.

In this paper I assume that sharing arises to best exploit marital gains from trade. *Taking sharing as given,* I argue that the usual constraints faced by young western couples lead to an optimal share of fifty-fifty. As a result, the model is consistent with the stylized fact that individuals usually marry others about as attractive, intelligent, educated, and socially desirable as themselves and subsequently share equally in the fruits and disasters of their union. Although people tend to avoid marrying others who have less to offer than themselves, the model indicates when contributions in marriage will not be equal and when spouses will not split fifty-fifty. The share model adds to Becker's explanation for divorce and explains some other stylized facts of marriage.

II. DETERMINING THE OPTIMAL SHARES

The Model

Given that husbands and wives share, the shares of household output must be determined. In both the real world and the next section, many partner combinations are possible. However, in this section a simple model is developed that determines an optimal share for *any* given couple; that is, the share that would arise for a random couple cast ashore on a desert island. As one might expect, for any given pairing, the optimal share depends on the relative productivities of each spouse, their responsiveness to changes in the share, and their next best alternatives—no single best share generally exists. However, it is necessary to examine this case before introducing competition among partners.

To examine this problem, I make the following assumptions:

(1) The actual share of output is observed at zero cost by both parties;

(2) Three goods exist: one shared (marital) good and two separate goods;

(3) There are no lump-sum transfers;

---

5. The input mix is sub-optimal in that it differs from what results from a joint wealth maximizing marriage. I define the loss of output from the incorrect input mix as the transaction costs of a particular union. This assumes that no direct monitoring takes place.

6. Eswaran and Kotwal [1985] justify the existence of sharecropping in agriculture on the same grounds. These transaction costs are not eliminated by the close proximity of one's spouse—keeping a close eye on the other is not always possible and is very costly.

(4) Inputs are endowed and divisible, with the endowment of inputs measured at zero cost prior to marriage, but the actual supply of inputs is not observable in production; and (required for section 2.2),

(5) The distributions of males and females, by quality, are identical.

In keeping with Becker's terminology related to divorce, the marital good is denoted Z.[7] The other goods are called separate goods and denoted S^h for the husband and S^w for the wife. The marital good requires both inputs and is shared for the reasons just mentioned—wage or rental contracts are too easily exploited. By assumption, though, both partners know ex post their own and their partner's actual consumption patterns. The marital good captures the gains from marriage—people get married to consume Z. The separate goods on the other hand, reflect an individual's available options when single. They are produced and consumed alone.

Perhaps an example will clarify the definition of a marital good. Suppose a husband and wife share (among a thousand other things) a car and agree to split its services 60–40. Each person provides difficult to measure inputs like checking the oil, driving safely, not riding the clutch, keeping the car clean, avoiding gravel roads, not slamming the door, and so on. What one spouse actually does with the car is unknown to the other and may never be known since any failure can be attributed to several sources, ranging from the manufacturer and vandals to children and poor luck. However, it may be easy to determine which partner uses the car the most and, indeed, whether one received 60

percent or not. Many goods in a marriage, such as children, a house, an investment, a meal, or a degree are such that the actual division of output is known, while the level of inputs provided by each for production are not. Goods that satisfy this condition are considered marital goods.

The production functions for these goods are given in equations (1)–(2).[8]

(1) $$Z = z(w, h, \alpha) + \varepsilon$$

(2) $$S^h = s^h(\overline{H} - h) + \varepsilon$$

and

$$S^W = s^w(\overline{W} - w) + \varepsilon$$

where $\overline{W}$ and $\overline{H}$ are the fixed, endowed levels of productive inputs for the husband and wife, respectively; h and w are the levels of inputs devoted towards producing the marital good; ε is a random error distributed over $(-\infty, \infty)$ with zero mean and constant variance; and α is a shift parameter for the wife's marginal product.[9] By assumption, all input endowments can be measured prior to the marriage and are fungible—production is independent of personality.[10]

I assume that each spouse is risk neutral and is concerned only with the total

---

7. Although sharing results from the fact that many marital goods are consumed, to analyze the effect of sharing it is sufficient to look at an aggregate good. Among other things, this assumes that all marital outputs are affected in the same way by increases in the productivity of either spouse. For more on this, see Becker [1976, 208].

8. Each production function z, s^h, and s^w has constant returns to scale with positive and diminishing marginal products. The error term in the production functions allows for the possibility of transaction costs, since it prevents either spouse from determining inputs from output levels. For simplicity the error terms are all distributed the same. See Allen [1991] for a further explanation of the conditions for transaction costs.

9. The role of α becomes important in the next section. A change in α shifts the woman's marginal product, but leaves the man's unaffected (i.e., $z_{h\alpha} = 0$. There may, however, still be a cross effect between men and women. For example, $Z = \alpha z_1(w) + z_2(w, h)$, is a possible formulation. Further, a change in α has no subsequent effect on the wife's separate good.

10. If $h_i = h_j$, then $Z(w_i, h_i) = Z(w_i, h_j)$. That is, if Bob is equal in productivity with Bill, Jane would be indifferent between them.

amount of his or her *own* consumption. Therefore, each individual's objective is to maximize his or her own expected wealth, given by equations (3) and (4).

(3) $E(W^w) = E\big[q[z(w, h, \alpha) + \varepsilon]$

$$+ s^w(\overline{W} - w) + \varepsilon\big]$$

(4) $E(W^h) = E\big[(1 - q)[z(w, h, \alpha) + \varepsilon]$

$$+ s^h(\overline{H} - h) + \varepsilon\big]$$

Here q is the share of marital good that goes to the wife. The solutions $\hat{w} = f(q, \overline{W}, \overline{H}, \alpha)$ and $\hat{h} = g(q, \overline{H}, \overline{W}, \alpha)$ come from maximizing expected private wealth, and they satisfy:[11]

(5) $qz_w(\hat{w}, \hat{h}) - s_w^w(\hat{w}) = 0$

(6) $(1 - q)z_h(\hat{w}, \hat{h}) - s_h^h(\hat{h}) = 0$

From equations (5) and (6) it is clear that if the wife gets all the marital good ($q = 1$), then she divides her inputs between Z and S^w, while the husband participates only in the production of S^h (i.e., $S^h = s^h (\overline{H})$). On the other hand, if $q = 0$, the husband supplies inputs for both goods, while the woman neglects her marital role. If the share to both the husband and wife is greater than zero, then both participate in producing the marital good.

In terms of obtaining a benchmark, it is worth looking at the cooperative solution (the zero transaction cost solution). Here, the objective is to maximize total expected wealth. Therefore,

(7) $E(Wealth) = E\left[W^h + W^w\right].$

And w^* and h^* satisfy:

(8) $z_w(w^*, h^*) - s_w^w(w^*) = 0$

(9) $z_h(w^*, h^*) - s_h^h(h^*) = 0$

Equations (8) and (9) state that for each individual the marginal product of the separate good and the marital good must be equal.[12]

If husband and wife maximize joint total wealth, h^* and w^* are used to produce the marital good and $(\overline{H} - h^*)$ and $(\overline{W} - w^*)$ are devoted to each respective separate good. If each maximizes his or her individual output, then $\hat{w}$ and $\hat{h}$ are used to produce the marital good. It must be the case that $\hat{w}$, $\hat{h}$ are less than w^*, h^* and, therefore, that the marginal product of each spouse is higher for the marital good than for the separate good when each spouse considers only his or her own welfare. The share contract is chosen to avoid expensive monitoring efforts, but the failure to completely compensate both parties also leads to dissipation. Figure 1 gives a geometric interpretation of the problem at hand.

The total deadweight cost (DWC) associated with a share of q to the wife equals the sum of the shaded areas. The marginal product curves z_w, z_h are drawn assuming each spouse supplies the optimal inputs h^*, w^*. The curves qz_w, $(1 - q)z_h$ are drawn assuming each spouse supplies the inputs $\hat{w}$, $\hat{h}$. This deadweight cost can be formally described as[13]

---

11. Where subscripts denote partial derivatives.

12. There is some intuitive appeal to the outcome of h^* and w^*. After all, if a marriage cannot be viewed as a cooperative venture, what can? In the model considered here, however, where measurement of performance is prohibitively costly, marriage is a non-cooperative game. If each person is concerned solely with his or her own consumption, then the level of sharing matters.

13. Where $h(0)$ means the amount of husband input into the marital good when $q = 0$.

(10) $DWC = z[h(0), w(1), \alpha]$

$\qquad - z[h(q), w(q), \alpha] + s^h[\hat{H} - h(0)]$

$\qquad - s^h[\overline{H} - h(q)] + s^w[\overline{W} - w(1)]$

$\qquad - s^w[\overline{W} - w(q)].$

Every potential share determines an input mix different from h^*, w^* and, therefore, a different deadweight cost. Keeping in mind we are considering only a random couple, they would choose q such that the deadweight cost is minimized.[14] The equilibrium share is the one that equates the marginal deadweight cost for each of the two inputs. That is, the share that minimizes the deadweight cost is the one that equates the two distances AB and CD (in Figure 1 these distances are not equal, and, therefore, the deadweight cost drawn is not the minimum one). Assuming the sufficient second-order conditions hold at the minimum, the implicit function theorem implies the solution $q = q^*(\alpha, \overline{W}, \overline{H})$ exists, where α is interpreted as a shift parameter of the woman's marginal product function for the marital good and measures the *relative* marital abilities of the two individuals in the production of the marital good, Z. The function q^* takes account of each individual's shirking in the production of the marital good and yields the share that *minimizes* the deadweight costs. In other words, q^* maximizes the value of a given marriage.

The share q^* depends on the productive characteristics of each spouse. Many sharing rules seem possible; that is, a random couple, tossed alone on a desert island could end up with almost any share. In the next section I argue that competition,

along with the assumptions made above, force individuals to choose an equally productive partner and share fifty-fifty.

Competition and Fifty-Fifty Sharing

What happens to the share q^* when the productivity of one spouse changes relative to the other's; that is, what are the signs of the first and second derivatives of q^* with respect to α? When, as is assumed here, the input of one spouse influences the marginal product of the other (i.e., $z_{wh} \neq 0$), then no unambiguous comparative static results are forthcoming. The rate of change of the share with respect to a change in productivity is ambiguous.[15] Thus, generally,

$$\partial q^* / \partial \alpha \gtrless 0$$

and

$$\partial^2 q^* / \partial \alpha^2 \gtrless 0$$

Unlike most situations in economics, this ambiguous second derivative leads to the interesting prediction that many marriages will share fifty-fifty. When each individual makes an equal contribution, the optimal share is fifty-fifty.[16] When

---

14. Assuming $0 < q < 1$, the necessary condition for a minimum of deadweight costs is,

(11) $0 = \left[s_h^h(\overline{H} - h(q)) - z_h(h(q),w(1),\alpha) \right] t_q$

$\qquad + \left[s_w^w(\overline{W} - w(q)) - z_w(h(0),w(q),\alpha) \right] w_q$

15. Substituting q^* into equation (11) of footnote 14 creates an identity, and therefore the marginal effect of a change in α on q^* can be calculated. Then,

$$q_\alpha^* = z_{wa} w_q / \Delta$$

where Δ is the determinant of the Hessian matrix and is positive by the second-order conditions for a minimum. The second derivative is also ambiguous. hang If $z_{wh} = 0$ then $w_q > 0$, and therefore $\partial q^* / \partial \alpha > 0$; however, $\partial^2 q^* / \partial \alpha^2$ is still ambiguous. The fifty-fifty result depends on the ambiguity of this second derivative, not on the sign of the first derivative.

16. From equations (5) and (6), if $z_w = z_h$, $s_w^w = s_h^h$, and $\overline{H} = \overline{W}$, then $\hat{w} = \hat{h}$, and $q = (1 - q)$. There, $q = .5$. For this result only the marginal values of these functions need to be equal in equilibrium. It does not imply that the functional forms are identical.

FIGURE 1
Optimal Allocation of Inputs in the Production of Martial Goods

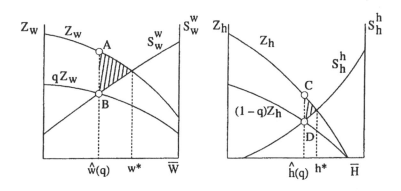

spouse makes an unequal contribution, the optimal shares will be unequal and *will not* equal the marginal products of each spouse. The only time q^* coincides with the share that appropriately compensates each party according to their marginal product is when each is equally productive and shares equally. This bears repeating: in most cases when, for example, a wife provides 60 percent of the inputs for marriage, 60 percent of the output is unlikely to be the optimal share. Further, if her contribution increases to 75 percent, the divergence between her share and contribution also increases.

Changes in the productivity of one spouse disproportionately change the share that minimizes the costs of sharing. Since it is assumed that the productivity of W and H are known before the marriage, *and* since no one will enter a marriage expecting to receive less than what he or she can receive elsewhere, a marriage between two vastly different people must have shares that fail to minimize the deadweight costs. More importantly, the larger the difference between potential

mates, the more expensive the proposed marriage becomes in terms of deadweight cost.[17] If each spouse receives a share that adequately compensates him or her (i.e., according to their respective marginal contributions) then the deadweight costs are not minimized, and if the deadweight

---

17. From equation (10), and by the Envelope Theorem, we have:

$$\partial DWC / \partial \alpha = z_\alpha(h(0), w(1), \alpha) - z_\alpha(h(q), w(q), \alpha)$$

A first-order Taylor series expansion of the second term around the point $h(0)$, $w(1)$ yields:

$$z_\alpha(h(q), w(q)) \simeq z_\alpha(h(0), w(1)) + z_{h\alpha}(0,1)[h(q) - h(0)]$$

$$+ {}_{w\alpha}((0,1)[w(q) - w(1)] + z_{\alpha\alpha}(\alpha - \alpha)$$

But $z_{h\alpha} = 0$ since α only affects the woman's marginal product directly. Therefore, since $w(q) - w(1) < 0$ and $z_{w\alpha} > 0$ it follows that $\partial DWC / \partial \alpha > 0$. As one spouse increases in productivity relative to the other, the total deadweight costs also increases. This makes sense. The reaction to a parametric change should be larger when both parties act as complete residual claimants than when they are only partially responsible.

costs are not minimized one partner will always be able to do better in another marriage. Thus competition among potential mates will force individuals to choose a spouse with equal productivity over the life of the marriage.

A marriage of two vastly different people may be expensive, but it may seem conceivable that an under-rewarded spouse is still better off than he or she is with a partner whose ability equals his or her own. For example, suppose a highly productive woman marries a man of minor means. Further, suppose the woman's contribution is 87 percent and the man's 13 percent; however, the optimal shares are 90 percent and 10 percent respectively. Although the man's share is "too small," could his actual return be greater than what he would receive in a fifty-fifty marriage with a woman equal to himself? It could be, but if it were, would this marriage exist? The answer is no. With constant returns to scale, the total gross value of all marital goods is highest with equal matching,[18] and since the minimum deadweight cost increases with increased differences in productivity,[19] the total net value of all marital goods will be lower when dissimilar people marry. Competition among potential spouses forces individuals to marry people with the same productivity, so that the shares are each .5 and total household output is maximized.[20] Since the pattern of mar-

riages is independent of personality and technology, there are no utility or technical reasons for diverse couples to join or remain together. As long as diverse partners remain together the total value of all marriages is not maximized. Competition for these unexploited gains from trade will force individuals to marry others of similar talent levels.[21]

Unequal Sharing

The result just reached will not hold for all share contracts. A crucial assumption required for the fifty-fifty result is that no lump-sum transfers occur. This absence of side payments forces the marginal and average shares to be equal. The marriage contract could, however, have taken the following linear form: $X + q\%$; that is, some amount of goods may be initially set aside for one particular spouse. This completely alleviates the problem of coinciding contributions with minimum deadweight costs, since the lump-sum payment can adjust for any shortfalls in compensation without interfering with marginal decisions. To the extent this happens with other sharing arrangements, shares other than fifty-fifty are expected. Thus, franchise agreements that have up-front money, contingency arrangements that provide for expenses, and agricultural share contracts that also share input costs

---

18. For a trivial example, let $A = 4$, $B = 9$ be two males, and $C = 4$, $D = 9$ be two females. Let $Z = w^{1/2}h^{1/2}$. With matched marriages AC and BD, total output is 13, while with mismatched marriages AD and BC, total output is 12.

19. See footnote (17).

20. This refers to one's productivity over the entire life of the marriage. The reason for treating marriage as a one-period, non-instantaneous game is because I am interested in the choice of spouse. It seems reasonable to assume that this is the first step in getting married, and that, therefore, all gains from trade are in the future. At any time during the marriage though, contributions will likely be unequal and arrangements will be necessary to deal with any problems that arise. See Cohen [1987] on this point.

21. Some find this result objectionable, citing marriages where the talents of one partner far outstrip the other's. In anticipation of this objection, consider the following: first, expected contributions are equal, not necessarily the actual ones. Second, the result cannot be tested by observing a subset of a married couple's attributes. For example, the observation that in many societies men marry women who are "inferior" or "beneath" them would seem to refute the result here. What is usually meant though, is that the man is better educated, taller, or whatever. That is, men are required to have a certain set of attributes. The women will have other attributes, and these attributes are predicted to be of equal importance within the marriage, although perhaps they are not as important socially. In any case, not all men can marry inferior women, since on average men and women have the same backgrounds. And, as I point out later, there are cases when unequal marriages are likely to occur.

should not be expected to always have fifty-fifty sharing splits.

What is the intuitive explanation for assuming no transfers and, hence, the fifty-fifty split? Consider the possibility of compensating a spouse with the Z good. Simply altering the share fails by the argument above. Just giving one spouse all of, say, the first Z produced and then sharing the rest will not work because the giving spouse is taxed 100 percent on the first unit. Since one cannot identify marginal products, the giving spouse shirks a great deal. Transferring separate goods will not work either. Recall that these goods reflect "single" activities and are likely to be non-transferable (a Saturday morning golf game) or not valued by the other spouse. Furthermore, having the overpaid mate transfer separate assets implies less time and inputs devoted to the marital good. In short, once a couple is married, additional separate goods cannot be created without reducing the amount of marital good. Transfers prior to marriage would solve the problem. However, it is likely that most young individuals marrying in the West will be too capital constrained. When transfers prior to marriage are possible, then it is possible for marriages to share in a proportion other than fifty-fifty.

An Explanation For Divorce

The fifty-fifty sharing model provides an explanation for why divorce is likely to occur when realizations deviate from expectations. In their seminal paper on marital instability Becker et al. [1977] argue that divorce largely results from mismatches caused by uncertainty. Much of their theoretical analysis considers variables that may influence either the expected gain from marriage or the chance of a mismatch. They hypothesize that when the expected gain is low or the chance of a mismatch is high, divorce is more likely. For example,

> ...men with relatively high earnings potential gain more from marriage than men with low earnings potential not only because of the higher level of their income but also because of greater gains from specialization within marriage, since their mates have a comparative advantage in specializing in non-market investments.
>
> Becker et al. [1977, 1146]

And,

> [If a matching trait is rare—such as very high or very low intelligence or an uncommon race or religion—extensive search costs would be greater because persons with average traits are more readily encountered in the marriage market.... Consequently, the probability of mismatches, and thus of marital dissolutions, would be greater with rare traits.
>
> Becker et al. [1977, 1150]

Becker et al. point out that a change in circumstances that favors one partner relative to the other does not immediately result in divorce, since it is possible to recontract. Divorce occurs only when the total wealth of remaining together is lower than the total wealth of the individuals when separated. In order for Becker's examples to work, however, a new and large unexpected alternative must present itself. The natural interpretation appears to be that as time passes, information regarding alternative spouses and occupations outside the marriage is gathered at near zero cost. This, although possible, seems unlikely when marriage tends to restrict one's ability to search for marital-like pleasures elsewhere. This rise in search costs makes it difficult to find a better mate. In addition, the degree of sunk investments by both spouses tends to increase over time, thereby reducing the incentive to find a new alternative arrangement.

The sharing theory presented above allows for a more plausible reason for marriage failure. It is not that the value of alternative partners increases, but that the value of marriage to the existing partners may decrease independently of others. According to this analysis, the key feature to predicting different divorce rates among broad classes of individuals still centers on mismatches; however, no one marries expecting a mismatch. Problems arise when either spouse turns out differently than was expected, causing the value of the marriage to fall. An unexpected change in one spouse may alter the efficiency of the marriage, even though the alternatives have not changed. Recontracting is usually a poor option for the same reasons why lump-sum transfers are difficult. Further, recontracting the share will necessarily lead to a marriage where the gains from the marriage are not fully exploited or the more productive spouse is undercompensated. In either case, breakdown occurs. Thus inter-racial and inter-religious marriages may have higher divorce rates because estimating marital productivities is more difficult, rather than because the chance of a better mate coming along is higher. The analysis presented here is consistent with Becker et al., but provides an additional mechanism for how uncertainty can lead to a dissolution.[22]

III. CONCLUDING REMARKS

Nothing in this clinical treatment suggests that love and emotion are absent from marriages. Rather, in holding such things constant, I have only exploited a single, though I think important, aspect of marriage.[23] It is often taken for granted

that people share equally in marriage. Here I've argued that equal sharing is the result of transaction costs and the efforts to mitigate them.

This paper contains no empirical evidence to support the model, but it does seem to conform to casual observation.[24] Consider a high-school romance, where anything more than skin-deep attraction is seldom involved. Is it not well known that the head cheerleader always chooses the football captain over the president of the chess club? And how often does one hear the comment, "I wonder what she sees in him"—implying that a superficial deficiency must be compensated for by some hidden redeeming feature. Also, the recent finding that men do less than half of the housework in two-income families is also consistent. Consider these excerpts from the *Seattle Times*:

> Janice Hogan, head of the Family Social Sciences Department at the University of Minnesota ... [said] ... "There really is a trend toward men doing more of the housework ... women are doing less .... My conclusion is there is less work being done at home.... The reason for the current state of untidiness is simple: Men ... have not picked up the slack.... The result is a rather unequal division.

> [August 11, 1987, F]

It may appear unequal, but to the extent that men have higher returns in the workforce, ceteris paribus , than women (due to their higher utilization rate), housework will mostly be done by women in households where both spouses work outside the home. Where wives earn more than their husbands, the household roles should reverse.

---

22. I would argue that the switch to no-fault divorce lowered the cost of divorce in the face of increased work force participation by women. With both spouses planning to work outside of the home, measuring marital inputs becomes more difficult, and hence fewer matches will continue to meet their fifty-fifty goal.

23. For example, Farrell and Scotchmer, in their introductory remarks on partnerships, assert that marriage involves equal shares with no side payments: "Marriage is an equal sharing, and we avoid making spouses' payoffs depend on their outside opportunities" [1988, 279].

24. An earlier version of the paper (available on request) attempted to exploit differences in state property laws to test the model here. Although the results were consistent with the proposition that first-time marriage partners share equally, the data did not allow confirmation of several key assumptions, and so the results are not reported.

Not all people marry someone who is expected to be an equal partner. When parents take part in the selection of their child's spouse, a pre-marriage transfer may take place, which may suggest a reason for dowries and bride prices. In societies where these are common, marriages will tend to have unequal partners. As the age at which one enters marriage increases, it seems likely that lump-sum transfers become more likely, and so fewer of these marriages that are otherwise unequal should split fifty-fifty. Similarly, second marriages should be less likely to split fifty-fifty since there is some possibility of a transfer, especially when children exist from a first marriage. So other shares are possible, but in general it seems that most first-time Western marriages are likely to succumb to the forces of a fifty-fifty split.

REFERENCES

Allen, D. W. "An Inquiry Into The State's Role In Marriage." *Journal of Economic Behavior and Organization* 13(2), 1990, 171–191.

_____. "What Are Transaction Costs?" *Journal of Research In Law and Economics*, 14, Fall 1991, 1–18.

_____. "Marriage and Divorce: A Comment on Peters." *American Economic Review*, forthcoming 1992.

Becker, G. *The Economic Approach to Human Behavior.* Chicago: The University of Chicago Press, 1976.

Becker, G., E. Landes, and R. Michael. "An Economic Analysis of Marital Instability." *Journal of Political Economy*, December 1977, 1141–88.

Becker, G. and K. Murphy. "The Family and the State." *Journal of Law and Economics*, April 1988, 1–18.

Cohen L. "Marriage, Divorce, and Quasi Rents; Or, 'I Gave Him The Best Years of My Life.'" *Journal of Legal Studies*, June 1987, 267–303.

Eswaran, M. and A. Kotwal. "A Theory of Contractual Structure in Agriculture." *American Economic Review*, June 1985, 352–67.

Farrel, J. and S. Scotchmer. "Partnerships." *Quarterly Journal of Economics*, May 1988, 279–97.

Walster, E., W. Walster, and E. Berscherd. *Equity: Theory and Research.* Boston: Allyn and Bacon, 1978.

[8]

VIRGINIA LAW REVIEW

VOLUME 84	MAY 1998	NUMBER 4

ARTICLE

BARGAINING IN THE SHADOW OF THE MARKET: IS THERE A FUTURE FOR EGALITARIAN MARRIAGE?

Amy L. Wax[*]

[*] Associate Professor of Law, University of Virginia School of Law. I wish to thank Anne Alstott, George Cohen, Anne Coughlin, Victor Fuchs, Marjorie Kornhauser, Paul Mahoney, Robert Pollak, Elizabeth Scott, Robert Scott, Peter Swire, Michael Trebilcock, George Triantis, Rip Verkerke, Steve Walt, Alan Wertheimer, and participants in faculty workshops at the Georgetown University Law Center, the University of Virginia, the John M. Olin series at the University of Toronto, the Center for Children, Families, and the Law at the University of Virginia, and a conference on The Future of Marriage in the 21st Century, sponsored by the Family Impact Seminar in Washington, D.C., for helpful discussions and comments. Blair Flynn and Shawn McDonald provided excellent research assistance.

INTRODUCTION

WOMEN'S quest for equality faces many obstacles. Perhaps the most important is conceptual. What do we mean by "equality for women?" How will we know when women have achieved equality with men?

This Article examines the issue of equality for women within an institution that is central to their fate and crucial to their prospects: marriage. As marriage rates decline and divorce rates rise,[1] the institution of marriage has become the focus of a polarized debate

---

[1] The divorce rate stands at about 50% of marriages, but has declined slightly in the past decade. See Arthur J. Norton & Louisa F. Miller, U.S. Dep't of Commerce, Marriage, Divorce, and Remarriage in the 1990's, at 1 (1992). Marriage rates have declined steadily over the past 25 years, and both men and women are marrying later. For example, in 1970, 88.4 men per 1000 over the age of 15 were married, but by 1988 that number had dropped to 57.4 men per 1000. See 3 U.S. Dep't of Health & Human Servs., Vital Statistics of the United States 1988: Marriage and Divorce 8, 9 tbl.1-7 (1996). Likewise, in 1975, 62.5% of 20- to 24-year-old women were married, but by 1990 that figure had dropped to 38.5%. See Norton & Miller, supra, at 3. For 25- to 29-year-old women, 87.2% were married in 1975, but only 69% were in 1990. See id. Between 1970 and 1988, the average age of first marriage for women rose from 20.6 to 23.7, and for men from 22.5 to 25.5. See U.S. Dep't of Health & Human Servs., supra, at 12 tbl.1-8. As matters stand, however, 90% of women are expected to marry during their lifetimes. See Norton & Miller, supra, at 4.

between, on the one hand, social conservatives who regard traditional marriage as an unalloyed boon and social good,[2] and, on the
other, feminist critics who view marriage as a patriarchal strait-
jacket that is antagonistic to women's interests.[3] This Article aims
to mediate between these extremes, arguing that both camps are
right, but for different reasons. Marriage presents women with a
paradox. Women greatly value marriage because it significantly
increases their well-being within society. But the fundamental
structure of the institution of marriage makes it almost impossible
for women to reap its benefits while maintaining their social
equality with men.

A review of the literature on the institution of marriage reveals a
striking imbalance: There is an enormous body of work on divorce
and marital failure, but relatively little on the anatomy of *successful* relationships. Some divorce scholars delve into marital dynamics in considering how some aspects of marital relations—
especially the division of labor, responsibility, and reward—may
affect the positions of the partners when marriage fails.[4] But there
is remarkably little sustained or systematic discussion of the reverse of that relationship: how extramarital prospects, or other
preexisting factors and partner attributes, might affect the allocation of effort and reward between spouses who are not contemplating divorce.

---

[2] See, e.g., David Blankenhorn, Fatherless America: Confronting Our Most Urgent
Social Problem (1995); Maggie Gallagher, The Abolition of Marriage: How We De-
stroy Lasting Love (1996); Barbara Dafoe Whitehead, The Divorce Culture (1997);
Karl Zinsmeister, Why the Traditional Family Will Never Become Obsolete, Am.
Enterprise, Mar.-Apr. 1997, at 28; Promises to Keep: Decline and Renewal of Marriage
in America (David Popenoe, Jean Bethke Elshtain & David Blankenhorn eds., 1996).

[3] See, e.g., Martha Albertson Fineman, The Neutered Mother, the Sexual Family
and Other Twentieth Century Tragedies (1995); Reva B. Siegel, The Modernization
of Marital Status Law: Adjudicating Wives' Rights to Earnings, 1860-1930, 82 Geo.
L.J. 2127 (1994); Joan Williams, Is Coverture Dead? Beyond a New Theory of Alimony, 82 Geo. L.J. 2227 (1994).

[4] See, e.g., Lloyd Cohen, Marriage, Divorce, and Quasi Rents; or, "I Gave Him the
Best Years of My Life," 16 J. Legal Stud. 267 (1987); Ira Mark Ellman, The Theory
of Alimony, 77 Cal. L. Rev. 1 (1989); Ann Laquer Estin, Economics and the Problem
of Divorce, 2 Roundtable 517 (1995); Michael J. Trebilcock & Rosemin Keshvani,
The Role of Private Ordering in Family Law: A Law and Economics Perspective, 41
U. Toronto L.J. 533 (1991). See generally Symposium on Divorce and Feminist Legal Theory, 82 Geo. L.J. 2119 (1994).

The lack of a comprehensive framework for understanding day-to-day relations within marriage has also led to serious blind spots in the analysis of women's fate within society as a whole.[5] A black box lies at the center of the elaborate explanatory structure that commentators and legal scholars have struggled to erect in the quest to understand the sources of women's predicament and to fashion policies that might improve their lot. By taking women's marital position—most notably, their weight of domestic responsibility—for granted in analyzing women's social standing and economic status, scholars have avoided the need to provide a fully satisfying or searching theory of why families operate as they do.[6]

This Article aims to lift the lid on the black box of marital relations and take a sustained look inside. It argues that there are good reasons—both empirical and theoretical—to believe that, on average, men and women share unequally in the benefits of marriage. What precisely does it mean to say that men and women are unequal within marriage? And what evidence supports this conclusion, once defined? This Article takes on these difficult questions using the tools and concepts of economic analysis. Part I examines the empirical literature that compares some aspects of the benefits and burdens of marriage for men and women and concludes that men typically gain a larger share of what marriage has to offer. Part II draws on game theory to model marriage as a bilateral, monopolistic bargaining relationship between rational ac-

---

[5] Sociologists have been most active in attempting to formulate theories to explain observed marital roles and decisionmaking, but they have failed to put forward a unified and comprehensive paradigm that fully accounts for existing patterns. See, e.g., Julie Brines, Economic Dependency, Gender, and the Division of Labor at Home, 100 Am. J. Soc. 652 (1994) [hereinafter Brines, Economic Dependency]; Julie Brines, The Exchange Value of Housework, 5 Rationality & Soc'y 302 (1993); Paula England, A Feminist Critique of Rational-Choice Theories: Implications for Sociology, 20 Am. Sociologist 14 (1989); Paula England & George Farkas, Households, Employment, and Gender: A Social, Economic, and Demographic View (1986); Paula England & Barbara Stanek Kilbourne, Markets, Marriages, and Other Mates: The Problem of Power, in Beyond the Marketplace: Rethinking Economy and Society 163 (Roger Friedland & A.F. Robertson eds., 1990); George Farkas, Education, Wage Rates, and the Division of Labor between Husband and Wife, 38 J. Marriage & Fam. 473 (1976).

[6] See, e.g., Anne L. Alstott, Tax Policy and Feminism: Competing Goals and Institutional Choices, 96 Colum. L. Rev. 2001, 2002 (1996) (observing, without trying fully to explain, that women take on a greater burden of domestic responsibilities); Cohen, supra note 4, at 285; Williams, supra note 3, at 2229.

tors in which husbands and wives engage in a process of allocating the benefits and burdens of married life under conditions of conflict—that is, where spouses' interests do not perfectly coincide and one partner's welfare can sometimes come at the other's expense. After proposing various possible standards for egalitarian marital relationships, Part II then adopts a working definition of egalitarian marriage. The analysis predicts that, although egalitarian marriage is possible in some cases, it will be the exception rather than the rule. Bargaining principles suggest that the deep structure of marriage is indeed "patriarchal" in the following sense: Although both partners benefit from marriage, men on average have more power in the relationship. That is, men are in a position to "get their way" more often and to achieve a higher degree of satisfaction of their preferences.

Parts II and III explore the sources of this power imbalance, examining both the structural features of the institution and the manner in which those features interact with the traits and preferences that men and women bring to marriage so as to strengthen men's bargaining position. Part IV reviews how the imbalance is worsened by a feedback process that parlays small and morally neutral differences between men and women into more pronounced marital and social disparities. It also discusses how the failure to see marriage as a paradigmatic bargaining relationship and to understand the dynamics of marital bargaining leads to fundamental misconceptions about the choices men and women make in marriage and in life. Specifically, the analysis demonstrates how, contrary to common wisdom, women's supposedly greater "taste" and skill for domestic and nurturing activities cannot fully explain observed patterns of behavior or divisions of labor and rewards of family life. Rather, a complete understanding of marital dynamics must take into account the inevitable conflicts that arise in any bargaining relationship between distinct, albeit loving, individuals and the role of power in resolving those conflicts. And, any explanation of men's and women's "choices" must confront women's relative lack of power to bargain for a different or a better deal.

Finally, Part V discusses possible solutions for bargaining imbalance between men and women in marriage. It discusses a number of devices that might help to mitigate the degree of imbalance, but concludes that all have their limitations and their price. Measures

to change the balance of power encounter formidable practical obstacles grounded in the nature of marriage as an exclusive, relational contract between parties who stand in different positions at
the outset. Many measures will not work well in the current legal
climate of no-fault divorce, and introducing fault creates as many
problems for women's bargaining position as it solves. And some
correctives may have problematic consequences because bargaining takes place in the shadow of markets—specifically, the labor
market and the marriage market. Attempts to change the balance
of power by regulating the marital relationship directly may have
the effect of deterring or delaying men's decision to marry or may
change the quality of mates women can obtain. These side-effects
may undermine or partially offset efforts to achieve marital balance.

This Article also asks what the future holds for egalitarian marriage, for families, and especially for children within marriages in
which men hold the balance of power and women fill multiple
roles. The number of married women with children entering the
workforce is rising steadily.[7] This trend has many positive effects

---

[7] See Barbara R. Bergmann, The Economic Emergence of Women 22-24 & tbl.2-3
(1986); Victor R. Fuchs, Women's Quest for Economic Equality 77 (paperback ed.
1990); Daphne Spain & Suzanne M. Bianchi, Balancing Act: Motherhood, Marriage,
and Employment Among American Women 147 fig.6.2 (1996); Claudia D. Goldin,
The Role of World War II in the Rise of Women's Employment, 81 Am. Econ. Rev.
741 (1991).

Most marriages now have two workers, and most married women work just to prevent an erosion of their family's standard of living. The economists Barry Bluestone
and Stephen Rose, using data from the Panel Study of Income Dynamics' examination of Michigan families between 1967 and 1989, have calculated that husband-wife
couples have increased their combined annual market work time an average of about
684 hours, or four months, of full-time work for that period. Barry Bluestone & Stephen Rose, Overworked and Unemployed, Am. Prospect, Mar.-Apr. 1997, at 58, 66.
That means that "[t]he typical dual-earner couple at the end of the 1980s was spending an additional day and [a] half on the job every week." Id.

Most families did not gain economically from the increased effort, which came
largely in the form of wives' time devoted to paid work. Indeed, most lost ground on
the measure of wage per hour of market labor during that 20 year period. Families
with spouses without a college degree gained no more than 4% in real earnings from
the extra effort, even though they put in between 11% and 18% more family hours of
paid work. See id. at 67 tbl. Those families actually experienced between an 11%
and 18% decrease in the "family" hourly wage. See id. Only college educated couples, who worked 16.6% more hours during that period, saw a gain of 13.6% in family
hourly wage, and a 32.5% increase in total real earnings. See id; see also Lawrence
Mishel, Jared Bernstein & John Schmitt, The State of Working America 1996-97, at
80-83 (1997) (noting wives' increasing contribution to family income from 1970-1992);

for women: It increases their security outside of marriage (i.e., after divorce) and adds to their leverage within that relationship. The evidence indicates, however, that the salutary effects of women's greater earning power are outweighed by other factors that impede women's ability to obtain a better deal within marriage. The result, paradoxically, may be that married women's increased workforce participation exacerbates the inequality in marital bargains. Women might bear the burdens of both family life *and* breadwinning, while obtaining fewer of the benefits than were sometimes forthcoming within more traditional relationships. Moreover, because women have generally served as children's principal champions within marriage and have been their main source of attention, the increased burdens placed on working women due to their bargaining weakness may well redound to children's detriment. Finally, this Article suggests that the structural persistence of marital inequality despite progress in other arenas poses an increasingly important threat to marriage as a social institution. As women become more disillusioned with their position within marriage, increasing numbers are seeking to end their relationships and are making fewer investments in them. This is also an unfortunate development for children and for society as a whole.

I. EGALITARIAN MARRIAGE: WHAT DOES THE EVIDENCE TELL US?

A. From Choices to Preferences

Any attempt to come up with a concept of equality within marriage must confront many of the same puzzles that plague attempts to define social equality in general. The central dilemma can be summarized: "equality of *what*?"[8] For the purpose of assessing marital equality, this Article employs a rational actor model and adopts a utility metric for measuring equality of welfare.[9] Although a utility-based concept might make some sense in theory, it is quite a different matter to detect deviations from the ideal in

---

id. at 93 (marshaling data to show that "in the 1980s families worked longer for less" and that "husbands' earnings declines were offset by wives' increases in both hours and earnings").

[8] Amartya Sen, Inequality Reexamined 1, 12 (1992); Ronald Dworkin, What is Equality? (pts. 1-2), 10 Phil. & Pub. Aff. 185, 283 (1981).

[9] See infra Part II.

practice. According to economic theory, individual preferences can only be inferred by reasoning backward from what individuals agree to do for a price or from the exchanges they are willing to accept. In the case of marriage, it is tempting to explain away any voluntary arrangements that do not appear to comport with one spouse's best interests with "fudge factors" of the necessary magnitude, such as altruism; interdependent utility functions; disparate spousal preferences, tastes, or skills; and other sources of intrinsic "psychic income."[10] The same rationalizations are available to explain general patterns that are systematically sex-skewed. If women usually specialize in housework and men in wagework, or if women agree to move for the husband's job more often than vice versa, these patterns can be attributed to some combination of economic and noneconomic satisfaction of each partner's self-interest, where those elements are assumed to differ systematically by sex in the population at large. What seems unequal can be rendered equal by positing hidden costs or benefits, or adjusting the subjective value of the apparent terms of the exchange. The burden of proving inequality is on the observer.[11]

---

[10] See Thomas F. Cotter, Legal Pragmatism and the Law and Economics Movement, 84 Geo. L.J. 2071, 2118-19 (1996) ("[V]irtually any behavior—no matter how ostensibly altruistic or irrational—can be viewed as consistent with the model of rational utility maximization."); Jeffrey L. Harrison, Piercing Pareto Superiority: Real People and the Obligations of Legal Theory, 39 Ariz. L. Rev. 1, 2 (1997) (noting that "'psychic income,' of which there is evidently an unlimited supply" is needed to explain those circumstances "in which norms and principles push people to do things that seem to make no sense if self-interest is the only goal"); Amartya K. Sen, Rational Fools: A Critique of the Behavioral Foundations of Economics Theory, 6 Phil. & Pub. Aff. 317, 335-36 (1977) (observing that rational actor models that can be adapted to try to take into account unselfish motives and altruistic impulses run the risk of explaining nothing by explaining *all* observed behavior as a manifestation of self-interest).

[11] While economists have shied away from analyzing marital allocation both because of the theoretical and methodological obstacles and because of their dominant interest in efficiency, sociologists have not harbored similar reservations. In testing the assumption that marriage short-changes women, researchers have examined, among other things, marital decisionmaking; control over wealth, income, and finances; and priority attached to each spouse's job or career goals. See Robert O. Blood, Jr. & Donald M. Wolfe, Husbands & Wives: The Dynamics of Married Living (1960); see also Belinda Fehlberg, Sexually Transmitted Debt 77-85 (1997) (reviewing the extent of sharing of a wide variety of resources and privileges between married couples across cultures and finding that "[i]nvariably, sociologists have concluded that women receive the lesser share"); Monica Biernat & Camille B. Wortman, Sharing of Home Responsibilities Between Professionally Employed Women

B. The Work-Leisure Gap

The divorce literature suggests that one place to look for women who are unequal within marriage might be the traditional role-divided relationship. Women who have invested in traditional domestic roles come away from divorce with far fewer resources than their husbands, and they suffer a decline in economic well-being and standard of living.[12] One might simply conclude that these

---

and Their Husbands, 60 J. Personality & Soc. Psychol. 844 (1991) (noting the traditionally unequal distribution of childcare responsibilities among professional couples and wives' greater self-criticism of their own domestic performance); Philip Blumstein & Pepper Schwartz, Money and Ideology: Their Impact on Power and the Division of Household Labor, *in* Gender, Family, and Economy: The Triple Overlap 261, 264-66 (Rae Lesser Blumberg ed., 1991) [hereinafter Gender, Family, and Economy] (attempting to measure spouses' "decision-making power," "leadership power," and "conciliation power," and to correlate these with spouses' market income); England, supra note 5, at 24 (reporting on studies determining that husbands on balance more often get their way); England & Kilbourne, supra note 5, at 165 (citing surveys concluding that husbands have more power than wives); Dair L. Gillespie, Who Has the Power? The Marital Struggle, 33 J. Marriage & Fam. 445 (1971) (examining multiple areas of marital decisionmaking and resolution of conflict); Gerald W. McDonald, Family Power: The Assessment of a Decade of Theory and Research, 1970-79, 42 J. Marriage & Fam. 841 (1980) (examining the sources of power in marital decision-making); Janice M. Steil & Karen Weltman, Marital Inequality: The Importance of Resources, Personal Attributes, and Social Norms on Career Valuing and the Allocation of Domestic Responsibilities, 24 Sex Roles 161 (1991) (determining that men overall have more say at home and less responsibility for children and the household). For a recent summary of studies relating to marital resource division, see Janice M. Steil, Marital Equality: Its Relationship to the Well-Being of Husbands and Wives 43-61 (1997).

Studies of financial arrangements among married couples suggest patterns of unequal control over spending, with men having greater unilateral discretion and decisionmaking power. For example, in one study in which most men were the primary, although not the exclusive wage-earners, the majority of husbands had "an apparently unquestioned right to personal spending money," whereas wives rarely made personal expenditures, and then not without consultation or consent. Carole B. Burgoyne, Money in Marriage: How Patterns of Allocation Both Reflect and Conceal Power, 38 Soc. Rev. 634, 648 (1990). Another study of family finances reveals that wives tend to be responsible for budgeting and spending only when "money is short [and] managing and budgeting become chores rather than a source of power within the household." Jan Pahl, The Allocation of Money and the Structuring of Inequality Within Marriage, 31 Soc. Rev. 237, 257 (1983). In both studies, the wife's marital contribution did not generally translate into an equal control over spending or an equal allocation of monetary resources to personal needs.

[12] See Ellman, supra note 4, at 5. See generally Lenore Weitzman, The Divorce Revolution: The Unexpected Social and Economic Consequences for Women and Children in America (1985) (examining the impact of economic decisions on spouses

wives were getting less from marriage than their husbands because when their marriages dissolve, they take away less. The post-divorce situation, however, does not necessarily imply an overall inequality of welfare during the course of the marriage. The factor of timing has to be taken into account: The conventional wife's investments (intensive domestic and childcare services) tend to be made early in the relationship, with the payoff (in economic security provided by her husband) expected late.[13] The extreme first performer element of this type of relationship gives rise to the potential for opportunistic defection but does not necessarily show that, in the absence of such defection, a traditional wife in a successful marriage gets less out of the marriage overall.[14]

---

and children involved in a divorce). Although Weitzman's groundbreaking study has come under attack and her data have been reanalyzed, subsequent studies support her basic conclusions. See Greg J. Duncan & Saul D. Hoffman, A Reconsideration of the Economic Consequences of Marital Dissolution, 22 Demography 485, 489 tbl.2 (1985) (finding that women's post-divorce income is 70% of their pre-divorce income while men's post-divorce income is 93% of their pre-divorce income); Ross Finnie, Women, Men, and the Economic Consequences of Divorce: Evidence from Canadian Longitudinal Data, 30 Can. Rev. Soc. & Anthropology 205, 218 (1993) (finding that women have post-divorce incomes that are 57% of their pre-divorce incomes while men have post-divorce incomes that are 82% of their pre-divorce incomes); Richard R. Peterson, A Re-Evaluation of the Economic Consequences of Divorce, 61 Am. Soc. Rev. 528, 532 (1996) (finding that women's standard of living fell 27% after divorce while men's standard of living increased 10%).

[13] See Cohen, supra note 4, at 287; Ellman, supra note 4, at 25-29; Trebilcock & Keshvani, supra note 4, at 552-53.

[14] For a discussion of the first performer problem, see infra Section IV.C. An alternative way to see the traditional wife's greater vulnerability after divorce as revealing something about her comparative well-being during marriage is to view her as bearing a disproportionate risk of loss during the life of the marriage. A traditional wife lacks the quality and type of "insurance" against the consequences of marital breakup that her husband typically enjoys. This relative lack of insurance may detract from her share of marital well-being. But the perception of imbalance in marital shares that stems from fewer hedges against insecurity depends crucially on assumptions about subjective preferences for risk and perceptions of probability of divorce, which vary from person to person. Looking at the overall risk of divorce will not do, because husbands and wives may not (and probably do not) judge their own risk of divorce as equivalent to that of the overall population. See Lynn A. Baker & Robert E. Emery, When Every Relationship Is Above Average: Perceptions and Expectations of Divorce at the Time of Marriage, 17 Law & Hum. Behav. 439, 443 (1993) (indicating that 100% of individuals about to marry reject the likelihood of their own divorce). Also, women may believe (not without justification) that their risk of divorce is at least partly within their own control so that they can take steps to reduce or minimize their own risk. The fact that many women may be wrong in their prospective assessment of their divorce risk suggests that many are in fact underinsured,

In fact, the traditional marriage is probably the least likely to provide persuasive evidence of marital inequality. The data on marital use of time, for example, indicate that men and women in traditional marriages, in which the division of labor is sharp, work similar hours and enjoy roughly similar amounts of leisure time.[15] This information provides little basis for asserting that the spouses in such relationships are not working equally hard on average, or that they do not enjoy equivalent well-being from the relationships overall. There is, of course, considerable individual variation from couple to couple. But the aggregate pattern makes it difficult to argue persuasively that the division of labor in such families is systematically unfair to one spouse, in the sense that one partner unceasingly gains at the expense of the other.

In contrast, the dual-earner couple[16] presents a more convincing story of marital inequality. There is good evidence of a systematic difference in the *total* number of hours worked—in both the paid and unpaid sectors—by each dual-earner spouse for the benefit of the household unit.[17] The average wife in a dual-earner couple de-

but this is perhaps better conceptualized as a form of market failure or information deficit rather than as evidence of a lopsided allocation of marital well-being.

[15] See Joseph H. Pleck, Working Wives/Working Husbands 30 tbl.2.1 (1985) (presenting data showing that husbands and housewives do similar amounts of work); Maximiliane E. Szinovacz, Changing Family Roles and Interactions, *in* Women and the Family: Two Decades of Change 163, 175 (Beth B. Hess & Marvin B. Sussman eds., 1984) (same).

[16] Empirical studies of working spouses have different criteria for inclusion of working couples into various categories for purposes of comparison. See infra note 18. For the purposes of this Article, a "dual-earner couple" is rather arbitrarily defined as one in which each spouse works for pay at least half-time (about 20 hours per week or more). This cutoff is unlikely to leave out many couples in which both partners do some work for pay: Because of discontinuities in the labor market's demand for part-time work (i.e., the paucity of jobs requiring less than a half-time commitment), it is not unreasonable to assume that most dual-earner families consist of spouses working at least half-time. See Francine D. Blau & Marianne A. Ferber, The Economics of Women, Men, and Work 223-24 (1986) (discussing problems with part-time employment opportunities); Rhona Mahony, Kidding Ourselves: Breadwinning, Babies, and Bargaining Power 210-11 (1995) (discussing reasons why part-time employment is rare); Spain & Bianchi, supra note 7, at 84 fig.4.2, 88 tbl.4.4, 151 fig.6.4, 152 tbl.6.4 (citing data indicating a steady increase in the number of employed women, especially women employed full-time); Maureen Perry-Jenkins & Karen Folk, Class, Couples, and Conflict: Effects of the Division of Labor on Assessments of Marriage in Dual-Earner Families, 56 J. Marriage & Fam. 165 (1994) (reporting that the majority of employed women are employed full-time).

[17] Work can be distinguished from leisure by a "third-party" criterion, which defines "work" as the production of goods or services that could be provided by another per-

votes significantly more time to work of one form or another (domestic or wage work) than does her husband. The difference in the number of hours spent working by members of dual-earner couples has been dubbed by sociologists the "work-leisure gap."[18]

---

son or economic unit without any utility loss to the consumer of those goods and services. See Katharine Silbaugh, Turning Labor into Love: Housework and the Law, 91 Nw. U. L. Rev. 1, 11 ("An activity is leisure rather than work if a person must do it herself to enjoy its benefits."). So "a person can eat a meal and enjoy its benefits whether she cooks it or whether someone else cooks it for her. A person cannot enjoy the benefits of reading a book unless she reads it herself. Thus cooking is work, and reading is leisure." Id. It should be apparent that some activities (e.g., childcare) mix work with leisure in supplying both fungible productive value and performer-specific consumption value. See discussion of childcare, infra note 117.

[18] There is a large body of empirical work that documents spouses' participation in domestic labor. For some of the most careful findings in the sociological literature, see Pleck, supra note 15. The data clearly show that "women perform more hours of work than men when paid and unpaid work is combined." Silbaugh, supra note 17, at 12; see Sarah Fenstermaker Berk, The Gender Factory: The Apportionment of Work in American Households (1985); Marion Tolbert Coleman, The Division of Household Labor: Suggestions for Future Empirical Consideration and Theoretical Development, in Gender, Family, and Economy, supra note 11, at 245, 248-49; Shelley Coverman, Explaining Husbands' Participation in Domestic Labor, 26 Soc. Q. 81, 93 (1985); Myra Marx Ferree, The Gender Division of Labor in Two-Earner Marriages, 12 J. Fam. Issues 158, 158 (1991); Heidi I. Hartmann, The Family as the Locus of Gender, Class, and Political Struggle: The Example of Housework, 6 J. Women Culture & Soc'y 366, 379 (1981); Suzanne Model, Housework by Husbands: Determinants and Implications, in Two Paychecks: Life in Dual-Earner Families 193 (Joan Aldous ed., 1982); Catherine E. Ross, The Division of Labor at Home, 65 Soc. Forces 816, 830 (1987); Beth Anne Shelton, Women, Men and Time: Gender Differences in Paid Work, Housework and Leisure 112 (1992); Joann Vanek, Household Work, Wage Work, and Sexual Equality, in Women and Household Labor 275, 277 (Sarah Fenstermaker Berk ed., 1980); Sara Yogev, Do Professional Women Have Egalitarian Marital Relationships?, 43 J. Marriage & Fam. 865, 868 (1981).

The work-leisure gap varies widely (from about 7-30 hours per week) from study to study, and depends on the size and type of population examined and the methods for measuring household responsibility. But the gap is uniformly observed and always favors the husband. See Berk, supra, at 8 (men do only 15% of housework); Pleck, supra note 15, at 56 (wives spend 3 more hours per day on "family work"); Shelton, supra, at 99 (15 hours per week on household labor); Susan M. Shaw, Gender and Leisure: Inequality in the Distribution of Leisure Time, 17 J. Leisure Res. 266, 274 (9 hours per week less leisure time for women); Szinovacz, supra note 15, at 175 (3½ hours per day); Yogev, supra, at 867 tbl.1 (11 hours per week for women without children and 30 hours per week for women with children). Most studies show that men and women generally perform different types of tasks, with women doing more routine, everyday, "low-control" work that cannot be put off; men take more sporadic, discretionary, or "high-control" jobs. See Rosalind C. Barnett & Caryl Rivers, She Works/He Works: How Two-Income Families Are Happier, Healthier, and Better-Off 179-82 (1996). In the area of childcare, women do more routine physical work and care while men do more play and education. See Scott Coltrane, Family

Man 79 (1996). Even when husbands' participation is relatively high, women tend to retain both control over and responsibility for making domestic decisions and insuring that household tasks are performed. See Helen J. Mederer, Division of Labor in Two-Earner Homes: Task Accomplishment Versus Household Management as Critical Variables in Perceptions About Family Work, 55 J. Marriage & Fam. 133 (1993). Although the trend over the past 25 years or so has been in the direction of husbands' taking on a greater share of domestic responsibility, this is largely explained by a reduction in the total number of hours women and families devote to children and domestic tasks rather than by an increase in the absolute amount of time men devote to these pursuits. See Pleck, supra note 15, at 31; Shelton, supra, at 145; Silbaugh, supra note 17, at 9; see also John P. Robinson & Geoffrey Godbey, Time for Life: The Surprising Ways Americans Use Their Time (1997) (arguing that male and female uses of time are converging, but basing this conclusion on data that do not focus precisely on marital status, employment of spouses outside the home, or the presence of children).

There are substantial methodological difficulties in gathering housework data. See Joanne Miller & Howard H. Garrison, Sex Roles: The Division of Labor at Home and in the Workplace, 8 Ann. Rev. Soc. 237, 239 (1982), on the methodological difficulties with research. For a review of methodological techniques for data collection and their problems, see Silbaugh, supra note 17, at 8 n.18. Studies of household labor have collected principally two types of data: time budgets (a form of diary kept by the subject) and survey questionnaires on the distribution of responsibility for various household and childcare tasks. See Glenna Spitze, Women's Employment and Family Relations: A Review, 50 J. Marriage & Fam. 595, 600 (1988).

Some studies either include childcare time or consider it separately, while some exclude it altogether. A review of studies of child-rearing practices reveals that "fathers on average are considerably less involved [with children] even when mothers are working." Eleanor E. Maccoby & Robert H. Mnookin, Dividing the Child: Social and Legal Dilemmas of Custody 26 (1992) (citing Michael E. Lamb et al., A Biosocial Perspective on Paternal Behavior and Involvement, in Parenting Across the Lifespan—Biosocial Dimensions 111 (Jane B. Lancaster et al. eds., 1987)).

Even when childcare time is excluded, employed women spend considerably more time on domestic tasks than men do, with time in housework outside of childcare correlated with number of children in the household. See Shelton, supra, at 100 (each additional child costs women on average six more hours per week of housework, and men one more hour). For excellent data on time in housework, as correlated with paid labor time, marital status, and number of children, showing that even women employed full-time (more than 40 hours per week) do about twice as much housework as men, see id. at 63-88; see also id. at 96-99 (showing through regression analysis that gender is an independent variable determining time spent doing housework, even after controlling for number of children, marital status, time in paid labor, education, and occupational status, though earnings were not included in the regression analysis). The gap carries through in the amount of time working men and women spend caring for children. Even controlling for total hours of paid work and unpaid housework (minus childcare), women have less leisure time than men. See id. at 139. Shelton attributes this gap to the extra time women spend on childcare. Id.; see Berk, supra, at 7; Pleck, supra note 15, at 50-51; Biernat & Wortman, supra note 11, at 855-58; Yogev, supra, at 867 tbl.1.

Although women on average engage in fewer hours of employment and earn less than their husbands,[19] many married women have achieved parity in number of hours and earnings from market labor.[20] But the work-leisure gap does not close significantly as women work more hours or earn more money.[21] Nor is it avoided by women in any social class.[22] This difference in the total work

---

[19] See Barnett & Rivers, supra note 18, at 178; Vanek, supra note 18, at 280. In 1993, almost half of mothers with children under 17 worked less than full-time, with 28% of women with children under six working full-time and year round. See Spain & Bianchi, supra note 7, at 147.

[20] Although women on average earn less than their husbands, working couples in which the wife makes an equal monetary contribution are increasingly common. In 1993, in a survey conducted by the Bureau of Labor Statistics, 48% of married women provided half or more of the family income, and fully 23% earned more than their husbands. See Tamar Lewin, Women Are Becoming Equal Providers, N.Y. Times, May 11, 1995, at A27. Married women who worked full-time contributed an average of 41% of family income. See id. Nine of ten women, whether employed or not, said that care of people in their families was their responsibility. See id.

[21] Studies on this issue consistently generated data showing that women do most of the domestic work even when the wife works for pay, and the gap does not disappear (although it narrows) when the wife's hours of paid work and amount of wage income approach or equal that of her husband. See Glenna Spitze, The Division of Task Responsibility in U.S. Households: Longitudinal Adjustments to Change, 64 Soc. Forces 689, 692-95 (reporting data from the National Longitudinal Surveys of the Labor Market Experiences of Young and Mature Women, compiled in the 1970s, showing that "women who earn 20 to 40 percent of couple income have the same decrease in tasks as those who earn over 40 percent"); see also Pleck, supra note 15, at 55-57 (questioning the empirical relationship between men's paid work time and domestic work time); Shelton, supra note 18, at 107 (showing that time in domestic labor is not significantly related to the ratio of spouses' earnings); Brines, Economic Dependency, supra note 5, at 682 ("[D]ependent husbands do less housework the more they depend on their wives for income."); Coverman, supra note 18, at 93 (surveying studies that found that wives' employment status had no effect on husbands' domestic participation); Farkas, supra note 5, at 482 (finding that wages were not a satisfactory explanation of the division of labor); Ferree, supra note 18, at 178-79 (noting that a one-to-one tradeoff of wages earned does not explain why women continue to do most of the housework); Mary Clare Lennon & Sarah Rosenfield, Relative Fairness and the Division of Housework: The Importance of Options, 100 Am. J. Soc. 506, 511-17 (1994) (finding in a sample survey of 13,000 couples that, although the women in dual-worker couples earned an average of 43% of the family income, they performed an average of about 68% of the domestic work); Model, supra note 18, at 202 (finding only slightly higher husband participation in couples with equal wages); Ross, supra note 18, at 821 (reporting on studies finding that "the ratio of husbands' [to wives'] earnings does not significantly affect the household division of labor").

[22] In fact, there is evidence that women with the most time-consuming and demanding jobs work the longest hours overall. Because husbands' hours of domestic labor appear consistently insensitive to wives' hours of work across the social spectrum, the hardest-working women tend to endure the largest work-leisure gap. Three

time of spouses in dual-earner couples gives rise to the notorious "double day" or "second shift" for women wage-earners.[23] Thus, the data indicate that in many homes there are periods when husbands are at leisure while wives work. The husband devotes the time freed up by the wife's efforts at home not to a form of produc-

---

studies show lopsided patterns among professional couples. Donna Hodgkins Berardo, Constance L. Shehan & Gerald Leslie, A Residue of Tradition: Jobs, Careers, and Spouses' Time in Housework, 49 J. Marriage & Fam. 381 (1987); Biernat & Wortman, supra note 11; Rebecca B. Bryson et al., The Professional Pair: Husband and Wife Psychologists, 31 J. Am. Psychol. 10 (1976).

Donna Hodgkins Berardo and co-authors define "dual-career" families as those in which "both spouses have high aspirations to achieve in the world of work" and take on demanding professional or managerial jobs in which they are called upon to perform tasks that "are highly productive or that carry great responsibility." Berardo, Shehan & Leslie, supra, at 382. In non-career dual-worker families, the jobs held by the spouses tend to be routine, demand fixed hours of work, or entail less independent responsibility. See Jane C. Hood, Becoming a Two-Job Family 183 (1983) (discussing the differences between "dual-career" and "dual-worker" families, and finding that only about 10% of dual-earner families fall into the former category).

Equality of earnings is more common among low-income, dual-worker families than among high-income families: Women's percentage of total household earnings generally increases as household income declines. See Spain & Bianchi, supra note 7, at 154 tbl.6.5. Most couples with equal earnings or job prestige are at the low-earning end of the scale. See Spitze, supra note 21, at 695 ("[W]ives who are the primary earner tend to have low-earning husbands rather than to be unusually high earners themselves."); Model, supra note 18, at 201-02 (finding that most equal-income families were in the low-income range). Nonetheless, higher-earning ("dual-career") wives spend somewhat less time in domestic pursuits than lower-earning women who work full-time ("dual-worker" wives). That pattern generally reflects dual-career wives' spending less time in domestic work than others, not their husbands' spending more. High-earning and well-educated wives still spend significantly more time doing housework than their husbands. See Shelton, supra note 18, at 70-72, 99, 107, 116. Thus, "[t]here is no evidence . . . that higher relative earnings lead incrementally to higher levels of interpersonal power" as measured by the ability to shift responsibility for domestic labor to the male partner in the marriage. Spitze, supra note 21, at 695. Rather, existing evidence quite decisively indicates that women rarely succeed in "buying their way out" of an unequal share of domestic responsibility by increasing their work commitment or earning power. See Berardo, Shehan & Leslie, supra, at 387; Biernat & Wortman, supra note 11, at 855-56; see also Yogev, supra note 18, at 868 (finding that work weeks of professional women with children were 29.7 hours longer than their husbands').

[23] See Arlie Hochschild, The Second Shift: Working Parents and the Revolution at Home (1989); Shelton, supra note 18, at 108. Women with children experience the greatest burden in the second shift, since they perform the majority of childcare and housework, and their housework burden increases with each additional child. See Shelton, supra note 18, at 104.

tion that benefits both parties,[24] but to leisure, a form of consumption that benefits mainly (if not solely) the consumer.

The work-leisure gap offers promise in the search for real-world evidence of inequalities in the distribution of marital welfare. Leisure, or discretionary time, is one marital resource available for distribution to individuals within the marital unit. Although leisure may sometimes have productivity-enhancing side-effects,[25] it functions primarily as a pure consumption good. As such, it carries positive utility for the person who enjoys it. Individuals surely vary in the degree to which they value leisure, but leisure is almost always considered valuable after a significant amount of paid work, which is the context in which the work-leisure gap among dual-earner couples appears.[26] Moreover, leisure is not a public good. Although couples can enjoy their leisure together (which can generate some extra joint utility in excess of each person's consumption value), each individual's period of leisure is enjoyed separately by that individual and can be enjoyed alone.[27] Because it is possible to exclude others from the enjoyment of one's discretionary time, leisure can be unevenly distributed within families and "hogged" by one or more family members. Furthermore, periods of leisure can be measured and compared by applying an objective metric (time). More leisure has greater value than less, although the law of diminishing returns applies.[28] Finally, there is no reason to believe that men's taste for leisure differs systematically from women's. Although men and women might differ in their preferences for different types of work and individuals might differ in their energy level and thus the intensity of their preferences for lei-

---

[24] See supra notes 18, 21, 22.

[25] See infra note 186 for a discussion of the "rejuvenation" and "flexibility" effects.

[26] Most people derive some "consumption value" or intrinsic satisfaction from paid work, with some—especially professionals with interesting or prestigious jobs—enjoying a considerable amount. These persons experience no sharp division between leisure and work because "free" time is often used for work-related activities. See supra note 17. That pattern is almost certainly the exception rather than the rule in the general population; the subjects in the work-leisure studies seemed to have little trouble distinguishing leisure time from work.

[27] There may be a small vicarious component in the enjoyment of leisure, but, assuming equal love between the spouses, that component should be shared equally by husbands and wives.

[28] See infra note 188.

sure, there is little evidence that either sex has a stronger desire for leisure as such.

The existence of the work-leisure imbalance in dual-earner families gives rise to two distinct questions. First, is the gap good evidence of marital inequality? The gap certainly seems to suggest sharp inequality, at least with respect to certain measurable components of intramarital effort and reward. The persistence of the gap over the past several decades has prompted one prominent scholar of family time use to comment that current arrangements assign "the cost of increased economic benefits the whole family enjoys thanks to the wife's employment to her alone."[29] Is there reason to believe that this scholar is correct—that women are bearing more of the costs and enjoying fewer of the rewards of the family's collective efforts? Second, if the imbalance in the allocation of effort and reward within families is real, why does it occur and why does it persist? Why do women acquiesce in arrangements that entail absolute sacrifice for them compared to other "deals" the family might adopt?

A number of stories can be told about the work-leisure gap that are consistent with more or less equality between spouses and that provide some explanation for women's voluntary acquiescence in this arrangement.[30] For example, it is commonly supposed that the wife will perform unpaid domestic services more efficiently—that is, at least cost per unit of output. If that were the case, allocating domestic responsibility mostly to the working wife might be Pareto-superior to a more even split, so long as the wife receives side-

---

[29] Joseph H. Pleck, Husbands' Paid Work and Family Roles: Current Research Issues, *in* 3 Research in the Interweave of Social Roles: Families and Jobs 251, 284 (Helena Z. Lopata & Joseph H. Pleck eds., 1983). If the baseline for comparison is the single breadwinner family of 25 years ago, the evidence indicates that the wife's employment often does not issue in "increased economic benefits" for the family. See supra note 7 (explaining that most families have not gained real income through increased extra hours of paid work, which have come in the form of wives' paid employment). Women's "break even" contribution to family earnings, however, must be offset by the cost of decreased time for domestic work, which must still be performed by someone despite women's paid employment. The evidence shows that it is women who are bearing a disproportionate amount of the costs of maintaining household services, with other family members enjoying the benefits of the maintenance of prior—or higher—income levels through women's paid employment. For further discussion, see infra Section IV.A.2.

[30] See infra Section IV.A.1.

payments from the extra surplus her efforts generate that are large enough both to cover her "extra" costs and to make her better off than under an arrangement of more equal sharing of responsibility.[31] But the bargaining model discussed in this Article shows that this is not the only, nor indeed even the best, explanation for these observed patterns. It is more likely that women go along with this regime because they lack the power to alter family life in their favor and to capture more of the gains of their efforts for themselves. By this account, observed patterns are consistent with a marked degree of inequality in the welfare of members of intact families.

II. A MODEL OF MARRIAGE: THE UNION OF RATIONAL UTILITY MAXIMIZERS

A. The Generation and Allocation of Resources in Marriage

Marriage can be modeled as a relationship between two people that generates a series of inputs and outputs. The process of generating those elements is bound up with allocation of burdens and rewards between mates and other family members. The model assumes that, in deciding how to allocate costs and benefits, household members behave as rational utility maximizers. They seek to increase their own individual well-being or satisfaction—their "psychic utility."[32]

---

[31] See infra Section IV.A.1 (discussion of side-payments).

[32] The concept of utility makes use of a subjective measure of overall well-being, in which each party's interests are defined in terms of psychological states: "pleasure, happiness, desire, preference satisfaction, and the like." Alan Wertheimer, Exploitation 207 (1996). On the rational utility maximizer model, see Cotter, supra note 10, at 2115; Harrison, supra note 10, at 2; Jeremy Waldron, Criticizing the Economic Analysis of Law, 99 Yale L.J. 1441, 1441-42 (1990) (distinguishing the "rational choice approach," which postulates "a type of human agent who seeks rationally to maximize the satisfaction of his own wants in a context where others are engaged in a similar enterprise, against a finite stock of resources" from the "economic analysis of law" which "seeks to characterize certain areas of law in terms of the pursuit of efficiency").

Much of the analysis in this Article takes men's and women's preferences as exogenous, or given. It also equates welfare or well-being with the maximization of utility, which in turn is understood as the satisfaction of "revealed preferences," while devoting little attention to the large body of research indicating that choice is subject to cognitive distortions that deviate from rationality. See, e.g., Judgment Under Uncertainty: Heuristics and Biases (Daniel Kahneman, Paul Slovic & Amos Tversky eds., 1982). The concept of utility used here is quite capacious, and can include the satisfaction of second-order preferences such as the desire to adhere to moral ideals and principles.

Applying the principle of rational utility maximization to individuals operating within the family, although a commonplace in the economics literature, meets resistance from those who believe that family life is not premised on self-regarding motives and that the principles governing family and market are, or at least should be, radically distinct.[33] But rational self-interest does not entail absolute selfishness: The model does not exclude altruism, love, or concern for other family members.[34] It is not inconsistent with the partial dependence of each spouse's individual well-being upon the well-being of other family members nor does it rule out a spouse's

---

The adoption of a streamlined model of rational choice is not meant to affirm its validity. For example, the analysis acknowledges that preferences bearing on the conduct of marriage appear to interact with social conventions and expectations in complex ways, see infra notes 161-163 and accompanying text, but does not seek to resolve the question of whether those preferences are the product of social experience or whether they are socially manipulable. The validity of the Article's main thesis—that women have less power to act on their preferences than men in marriage, whatever those preferences may be and however they are formed—does not depend critically on how welfare is defined or on whether preferences can be changed. Nor is it undermined by taking a very broad view of utility or "psychic income." See infra note 35.

For further discussion, see Susan Moller Okin, Justice, Gender, and the Family 165 (1989) (suggesting that the difference between men's and women's remarriage prospects are "socially constructed" and hence malleable; Amartya K. Sen, Gender and Cooperative Conflicts, *in* Persistent Inequalities: Women and World Development 123, 148 (Irene Tinker ed., 1990) (suggesting that women's greater involvement in the outside world may shape their expectations of household divisions); L.W. Sumner, Welfare, Happiness, and Ethics 66 (1996) (restating Sen's argument as the view that "[w]elfare cannot consist in utility . . . because an individual's tastes, ambitions, and aspirations are too malleable by processes of indoctrination, manipulation, and socialization"); Cass R. Sunstein, Naked Preferences and the Constitution, 84 Colum. L. Rev. 1689 (1984) (suggesting a preference-shaping function for law); Cass R. Sunstein, Social Norms and Social Rules, 96 Colum. L. Rev. 903 (1996) [hereinafter Sunstein, Social Norms] (same); see also Heidi Li Feldman, Harm and Money: Against the Insurance Theory of Tort Compensation, 75 Tex. L. Rev. 1567, 1580-94 (1997) (criticizing the notion that well-being or welfare is nothing more than subjective, experiential preference satisfaction); Robert A. Pollak, For Better or Worse: The Roles of Power in Models of Distribution within Marriage, 84 Am. Econ. Rev. 148, 151 (1994) (discussing preferences as endogenous or exogenous to distributional bargaining models).

[33] See infra Section IV.B.1.d; infra note 228.

[34] Nor does the concept of utility maximization rule out pursuit of the full range of nonmonetary and intangible goods that give marriage so much of its value. It also allows consideration of the various motives and sentiments that operate within the marital sphere. See Gary S. Becker, Accounting for Tastes 151 (1996) ("The interactions between husbands, wives, parents, and children are more likely to be motivated by love, obligation, guilt, and a sense of duty than by self-interest narrowly interpreted.").

taking vicarious pleasure in the other's happiness or satisfaction.[35] But the model does assume less than perfect altruism and, hence, a less than perfect coincidence between family members' interests. This means that there will be conflict within the relationship, not necessarily in the active sense of harsh words and recrimination, but in the sense that one spouse's well-being may sometimes come at the other's expense.[36]

---

[35] Another way to look at motivation within marriage is to posit that spouses always act out of self-interest, but that self-interest is sometimes advanced by the well-being of the partner, because spouses take vicarious pleasure in the others' satisfaction. That is, spouses' utility functions are partially interdependent, although the degree of interdependence may vary widely and in complex ways, depending on the characteristics of the individuals and the distribution of marital surplus goods. See Cotter, supra note 10; Sen, supra note 10.

[36] Thus, the model rejects Gary Becker's construct of the "altruistic head of household," which assumes away tradeoffs in well-being of family members by positing a household leader who automatically transfers resources to other family members to induce them to maximize the family's net utility. See Gary S. Becker, A Treatise on the Family (1981) [hereinafter Becker, Treatise]. In Becker's model, the family acts as a single decisionmaker, with the collective utility function effectively replacing the individual members' utility calculus as the determinants of behavior. See, e.g., Marilyn Manser & Murray Brown, Marriage and Household Decision-Making: A Bargaining Analysis, 21 Int'l Econ. Rev. 31, 31 (1980) (stating that a model such as Becker's "assumes that the two individuals who have formed, or are contemplating forming a household, pool their incomes and maximize a neoclassical household utility function").

Becker's "altruistic head" has been roundly criticized in the economics literature for failing to reflect actual family dynamics, for papering over real-life conflicts among family members, and for ignoring the differences between men's and women's fates within marriage. See Edward P. Lazear & Robert T. Michael, Allocation of Income within the Household 12 (1988) (noting that economic models that concentrate on the family unit, not the individual, divert attention away from the distributional issues of "what happens *within* the family"); see also Ann Laquer Estin, Love and Obligation: Family Law and the Romance of Economics, 36 Wm. & Mary L. Rev. 989, 996 (1995) (noting the tendency among economists, in the "absence of empirical knowledge about distributions within the family," to "assume that a family's resources are equally distributed among its members"). See generally Estin, supra (exploring the limits of economic theory as applied to family law); Beyond Economic Man: Feminist Theory and Economics (Marianne A. Ferber & Julie A. Nelson eds., 1993) (same); Marianne A. Ferber & Bonnie G. Birnbaum, The "New Home Economics": Retrospects and Prospects, 4 J. Consumer Res. 19 (1977) (discussing problems with Becker's model of household economics); Lazear & Michael, supra, at 1 ("[F]rom casual and personal observation, one knows that the household does not always distribute income or other resources evenly among its members.... Yet the myth persists in economic modeling of well-being and in many social policy contexts that once we know the level of resources available to the household, that is all we need to know."). By sidestepping household allocational issues, Becker's model does

B. Positive-Sum Marriage

A bedrock principle that can be derived from the rational self-
interest assumption is that couples will initially decide to marry
only when the marriage is a positive-sum or potentially Pareto-
superior arrangement: Each spouse expects to be better off married than he or she would be single[37] or married to another available person.[38] Moreover, each spouse must receive something over
and above the value of any positive investment that the person ex-
pends in maintaining the marriage—that is, each spouse in a viable
marriage must receive some form of compensation for his or her
contribution to the relationship. Finally, couples stay married as long
as each partner is better off than he or she would be if divorced.[39]

It follows that spouses will stick with a marriage only if it produces a marital surplus—in the form of potentially utility-enhancing
gains for each party—and only if each spouse receives some share
of the surplus.[40] How much and what kind of marital surplus will

---

have the virtue of avoiding the difficult conceptual exercise of comparing the well-
being of family members, which helps account for the paucity of attention to allocational issues in the economics literature. See supra notes 32-35 and accompanying text.

[37] See Becker, supra note 34, at 149 ("The point of departure of my work on the
family is the assumption that when men and women decide to marry, or have children, or divorce, they attempt to raise their welfare by comparing benefits and costs.
So they marry when they expect to be better off than if they remained single, and
they divorce if that is expected to increase their welfare."); Gary S. Becker, A Theory
of Marriage (pt. 1), 80 J. Pol. Econ. 813, 814 (1972) ("[S]ince marriage is practically
always voluntary, . . . the theory of preferences can be readily applied, and persons
marrying . . . can be assumed to expect to raise their utility level above what it would
be were they to remain single.").

[38] Since the decision to marry takes place on a marriage market, people will also
consider prospects for alternative matches, including the search costs and discounted
probability of making a comparable or superior marriage, in deciding when and whether
to marry. See, e.g., Gary S. Becker, Elisabeth M. Landes & Robert T. Michael, An
Economic Analysis of Marital Instability, 85 J. Pol. Econ. 1141, 1147-52 (1977).

[39] More specifically, each spouse's willingness to remain married is contingent upon
the marriage's offering more utility than the alternatives available upon giving up the
relationship, net of any losses and transaction costs occasioned by divorce.

In order not to complicate further an already complicated analysis of the basic elements of marital bargaining, this Article largely ignores information problems and
information costs, which figure prominently in actual decisions to marry or divorce, and
must be taken into account in any truly complete analysis of behavior in this area.

[40] The term "marital surplus" encompasses all utility-enhancing effects that would
not exist in the absence of the relationship. See Allan M. Parkman, No-Fault Divorce: What Went Wrong? 27 (1992) ("[T]he economic analysis of the decision

be produced? Decisions about the production side of marriage are inextricably bound up with the consumption patterns of the unit. That is because most marital decisions have implications for the distribution of both rewards and burdens to members of the household. The payoffs that result from the division of the marital assets are determined by the allocation of productive responsibilities as well as by the assignment to family members of resources for consumption.[41] Because inputs have costs, the costs will be borne by the person who makes a particular contribution to the unit. Although some of the outputs available to the marriage (such as market income generated during the life of the relationship) are liquid and easily divisible, outputs in the form of unpaid and in-kind services are not so easily transferable, but tend to redound to the fixed benefit of the family members for whom the services are performed. Thus, decisions concerning the specific contributions made by real-life marital partners can carry important distributional con-

---

to marry focuses on the parties' expectation that ... marriage will expand the 'commodities' available to them compared with those available if they remained single."); see also Becker, Treatise, supra note 36, at 15-21 (discussing surplus generated by specialization in the household). Marital partners invest resources in the form of material and intangible assets (such as previously accumulated wealth and talent) and productive labor at home and work. They reap gains in the form of increased utility from public goods, "own" children, economies of scale, and a host of intangible benefits (such as love, emotional support, companionship, and vicarious pleasure in the other's well-being) that are available for enjoyment and consumption within the unit. See Blau & Ferber, supra note 16, at 45-46 (discussing advantages of joint production and consumption, including economies of scale, public goods, externalities—or interdependent utility functions—and economic benefits of families); Becker, supra note 37, at 816 (noting that marriage produces market and nonmarket products, including such elements as "the quality and quantity of children, prestige, recreation, companionship, love, and health status"). Moreover, marriage appears to induce behavioral changes (harder work, sobriety, savings and investment, risk-averse strategies) and specialized activities and efforts that would not otherwise be expended. See Linda J. Waite, Social Science Finds: "Marriage Matters," Responsive Community, Summer 1996, at 26. Finally, there is added utility from coordination and cooperative effort in activities of daily life.

[41] The "total utility" that a marriage can generate—the sum of the utilities for the partners—is not a fixed quantity, but is a function of the actions and decisions of the partners, which can vary over a wide range. So the size of the marital surplus varies with the decisions as to its distribution. See Yoram Weiss, The Formation and Dissolution of Families: Why Marry? Who Marries Whom? And What Happens Upon Marriage and Divorce? 15 (Aug. 1993) (unpublished manuscript, on file with the Virginia Law Review Association) ("In general, associated with each marriage, there is a set of feasible actions. Each action yields an outcome which is the utility values (payoffs) of the two partners.").

sequences for family members, because they go a long way towards determining the allocation of in-kind costs and benefits.[42]

C. What Is Egalitarian Marriage?

1. Utility as the Metric for Egalitarian Marriage

Within the framework of the rational actor model, what counts as an egalitarian marriage? The popular conception of an egalitarian marriage seems to conform most closely to a partnership in which the spouses play quite similar roles.[43] I would term this type of role-sharing relationship an "equalitarian" marriage (as opposed to an egalitarian one). But a notion of marital equality that seeks more or less to match roles and externally observable contributions without regard to talents, preferences, or desires, is too rigid—and too narrow—to be useful. If a couple "shares everything," one partner may still feel (quite sensibly) that he or she is getting less than a truly equal share. A more theoretically useful way to measure input and output—and one that respects individual differences

---

[42] The utility derived by a family member from a productive contribution is the net sum of the separable costs and benefits to that person from engaging in production and consuming what is produced (which includes the pleasure of producing it). For example, if someone prepares a meal shared by everyone in the family, the cook bears the costs of cooking it alone while enjoying some of the benefits, whereas the others enjoy the rewards of a good meal without bearing the costs. To be sure, costs and benefits can be rearranged somewhat by means of "side-payments": the reallocation of other resources—including contributions in kind and money—to "compensate" for a contribution. See infra notes 135-136 and accompanying text (noting, among other things, that the possibility for side-payments will be limited by practical considerations in many relationships).

[43] One thinks of the family in which the husband and wife make similar investments in their human market capital and in "marriage-specific capital": Both husband and wife work at jobs of roughly similar status and demands, and both share in unpaid work and responsibility at home in roughly equal measure. See Hood, supra note 22, at 9 (defining the egalitarian marriage as one in which the "husband and wife share household, income-producing, and decision-making roles in roughly equal proportions"); Cynthia Starnes, Divorce and the Displaced Homemaker: A Discourse on Playing with Dolls, Partnership Buyouts and Dissociation under No-Fault, 60 U. Chi. L. Rev. 67, 126-27 (1993) ("In an egalitarian marriage, both spouses work full-time and each performs fifty percent of the household chores and childcare."); see also Linda Haas, Role-Sharing Couples: A Study of Egalitarian Marriages, 29 Fam. Rel. 289 (1980) (studying 31 role-sharing couples in Madison, Wisconsin).

For a discussion of a range of conceptions of marital equality, in part reflecting studies of couples' own ideas of "equality," see Steil, supra note 11, at 59-71.

in utility functions for various assets and resources[44]—makes use of the concept of psychic utility, both negative and positive, that lies at the heart of the rational actor model. The strength of this approach is that it is quite latitudinarian. It does not rule out the possibility that a quite even balance of psychic utility can prevail in highly role-divided marriages—including those with a conventional male breadwinner and female homemaker—as well as in relationships that conform more closely to the "equalitarian" model.

One problem with using utility as the currency for comparing spouses' positions is that utility is difficult to compare intersubjectively, especially in situations, such as marriage, in which utility functions can be expected to diverge.[45] It is possible to avoid

---

[44] See Wertheimer, supra note 32, at 223 ("Given differently shaped utility functions for different goods, the utility derived from transactions will vary considerably . . . .").

[45] See supra note 10. The welfare of family members—either absolute or relative—cannot be known without calculating utilities, but utilities are functions of preferences, and preferences are revealed only through "voluntary" choices. But choices only tell us whether a person believes that his or her welfare will be improved by the transition from one state to another among a limited range of options, and not whether her welfare compares favorably or unfavorably with another person's. Put another way, the fact that two people engage in an exchange that makes both better off tells us nothing about whether one is better off than the other. See Lazear & Michael, supra note 36, at 5 ("The value to the recipient of a transfer may not be the same as its value to the giver."); see also Richard A. Posner, The Economics of Justice 79 (1981) ("The 'interpersonal comparison of utilities' is anathema to the modern economist, and rightly so, because there is no metric for making such a comparison."); Wertheimer, supra note 32, at 222 (discussing the incommensurability of welfare); Harrison, supra note 10, at 2 (discussing the methodological limitations on interpersonal comparisons of utility); Sen, supra note 10, at 133, 147 (discussing interpersonal comparisons); Waldron, supra note 32, at 1456-57 (distinguishing between two objections to interpersonal comparisons of utility: "ontological"—which relates to the difficulty of finding a conceptual basis for expressing the difference between one person's well-being and another's—and "epistemic"—which concerns the problem of being "sure that we have chosen the right convention of comparability" and determining how "such a standard [is] to be applied in practice"). But see Robert A. Pollak, Welfare Comparisons and Situation Comparisons, 50 J. Econometrics 31 (1991) (suggesting that interpersonal utility comparisons are not incoherent and are a useful construct in some areas of welfare economics).

Marriage presents perhaps the most difficult case for interpersonal utility comparisons. The economic aspect of marital exchange is only one facet of a relationship with considerable noneconomic or intangible elements. Also, much of what family members "consume" or enjoy consists of public goods or of goods and services (both market and nonmarket) that generate consumption value for the producer. Family members also experience considerable "vicarious" utility from other members' well-being. These factors contribute to the difficulty of measuring and comparing the efforts and rewards of each partner to the marital exchange. See Lazear & Michael,

some—although not all—of the awkwardness of comparing utilities by introducing a normalized concept that does not directly require comparisons between persons: the utility each person would enjoy within a relationship relative to the maximum potential welfare available if all marital resources were allocated, and arrangements made, according to that partner's wishes. The benchmark notion of maximum potential welfare or utility would correspond roughly to the idea of each person consistently "getting his or her way" within the relationship. The concept of "percentage relative utility" can be defined as the ratio of each spouse's actual utility relative to that person's maximum potential utility. Each person's percentage relative utility can then be compared without worrying about differing utility functions.

2. Rival Conceptions of Marital Equality

Assuming that utility is the basic metric, and making use when appropriate of the concept of percentage relative utility to ease the problem of interpersonal comparisons, is it possible to describe marital arrangements that comport with an intuitive notion of what an egalitarian marital relationship would look like? Some alternative conceptions follow.

a. A "Substantive" Concept of Equal Division of the Marital Surplus

Each person's costs or inputs, measured as negative utility, are returned to him or her out of resources available to the marriage. Beyond that, resources (tangible and intangible) are divided so that each spouse achieves an equal net share of utility relative to that person's maximal utility. That is, each spouse enjoys an equal percentage relative utility.[46]

---

supra note 36, at 19-21 (noting difficulties in measuring intrafamily distribution of income and resources).

[46] If there is a simple one-for-one tradeoff, or linear relationship, then the egalitarian point will lie where each person receives half of his or her personal maximum possible utility—which corresponds to a 50 percent share of maximal utility for each. Where the relationship is not strictly linear—where, as in most viable marriages, there are public goods for sharing, or where the spouses experience vicarious utility due to altruism or caring—each spouse can simultaneously satisfy a greater percentage of his or her desires consistent with the other spouse receiving a similar "normalized" amount of utility. The greater the vicarious component (the more love

b. A "Procedural" Concept of Equality

The metric here is the input/payoff deal that would be negotiated if two people started from a hypothetical initial position of equal premarital baseline utility and identical negotiating skills,[47] with equal, and inferior, outside alternatives available to each (either no marriage at all, or an equal probability of an equally inferior alternative marriage for each). Under those conditions, it is not unreasonable to assume that the couple would agree to make equal contributions or efforts on behalf of the marriage (as measured in their own negative subjective utility) and to take equal shares of the output relative to each person's "best deal"—which once again amounts to equal percentage shares. Even if the spouses agreed to unequal inputs, they might still agree to an equal split once costs are covered (i.e., after costs are compensated to each contributor) which is equivalent to arrangement *(a)*.[48]

---

and sharing), the happier each person can be, and the more each will get of what he or she wants. The higher will be each person's percentage relative utility consistent with satisfying the egalitarian condition.

The definition of an egalitarian relationship advanced here is similar to that proposed by H. Peyton Young in his recent book, in which he defines an egalitarian bargain as one in which there is an "allocation of divisible property [such that] every claimant is indifferent between his portion and the same fraction of the entire property." H. Peyton Young, Equity: In Theory and Practice 148 (1994). Since the value of resources in our definition has already been translated into the metric of subjective utility, an egalitarian bargain would be one in which each person has gained the "same fraction" of the entire amount of utility available to him within the relationship. This would appear to satisfy Young's indifference principle. This definition also bears some resemblance to David Gauthier's "minimax relative concession" principle, which also seeks to equalize the gains of persons engaging in a bargaining relationship relative to the most favorable outcome available to each. David Gauthier, Morals by Agreement 136-56 (1986).

[47] See infra notes 145-151 and accompanying text.

[48] For why the ideal rational couple could be predicted to agree to an equal split once costs are covered, see infra notes 140-143 and accompanying text; see also Douglas G. Baird, Robert H. Gertner & Randal C. Picker, Game Theory and the Law 224 (1994) (suggesting that bargainers will split profits equally absent complicating factors).

c. An "Equal Gain" Concept of Equality

Each spouse gains the same utility (as a percentage of the maximum net utility) over premarital (i.e., unmarried) baseline utilities, where that baseline might be equal or unequal.[49]

* * *

Which of these rival suggestions—which may well fail to exhaust the possible list—best comports with our idea of egalitarian marriage? There is no need to make a definitive choice among the suggested options, because the major conclusions of this Article apply to all: By whatever measure we select, most marriages are inegalitarian.

This conclusion derives from applying bargaining theory principles to egalitarian conceptions of marriage as outlined above. The egalitarian models gauge marital equality on the basis of each spouse's utility inputs and outputs within a closed and private world of marital relations. They attempt to capture an ideal of reciprocity in which spouses match (subjective) effort with effort and (subjective) reward with reward. But bargaining theory teaches that the allocation of marital contribution and benefit will often deviate from equality as we define it. Distributions will be influenced in large part by factors other than and external to those that inform our intuitive concept of an egalitarian relationship, which looks to the value spouses give to and take from one another.

What are the factors that determine allocation and why do they matter? One is markets, which cast a shadow in which couples live and interact. This Article shows how markets for work and markets for mates put pressure on spouses to deviate from egalitarian conditions within marriage. The other key element is the deep structure of marriage. As explained below, marriage can be viewed as a bilateral and monopolistic bargaining game in which parties are relegated to self-help for the enforcement of any agreements within the ongoing relationship. External markets interact with that structure to constrain the deals struck by spouses with different preferences, tastes, and desires. Those constraints operate to undermine marital equality.

To illuminate these points, this Article adopts concept *(a)* above as a working definition of an egalitarian marriage.[50] Although this

---

[49] See infra Section II.D.3.a (discussing baseline premarital well-being).

definition has its flaws,[51] it nevertheless provides a useful basis for unpacking, identifying, and examining the host of forces that cause intramarital arrangements to deviate from the chosen, egalitarian baseline in directions that favor men or women, and what the social consequences of the deviations might be.

In applying the working definition, this Article will also adopt, for the purpose of exposition, the simplifying assumption that the utility inputs expended prior to marriage by the spouses to generate their initial contributions to married life are roughly similar, at least at the point of entering the relationship.[52] Although that assumption will obviously not apply to some real marriages (in that, for example, one person may have put more "psychic" effort into self-development or into the accumulation of assets brought to the marriage than the other), it is probably a safe one for the great majority of middle-class marriages in which personal, financial, and educational endowments more or less match at the outset.[53] Thus, the paradigmatic marriage is the marriage of persons who are roughly equally—and also moderately—endowed in attractiveness, education, wealth, property, and other resources and attributes that

---

[50] This concept—equal percentage shares net of effort expended—allows for transiently lopsided gains and investments. Transient imbalances often represent the most efficient strategy and should not be considered inegalitarian as long as the allocations balance out during the life of the relationship, whatever its duration.

[51] The model is overly simple because it fails to take account of the fact that each spouse's well-being is a function of changes in *marginal* utility that result from particular allocational shifts. But the marginal utility gains or losses from a particular allocational choice cannot be considered in isolation. Rather, utility effects are contextual and path dependent. The value of marital decisions for each spouse depends on the way things currently are, which in turn depends on prior decisions. For example, the effect on each partner of the birth of a child depends on the presence of other children and how their care has been arranged.

[52] As noted, compensation to each spouse for his or her effort expended on behalf of the union is taken into account in defining egalitarian marriage. The equality-of-inputs assumption means that, as a practical matter, spouses have expended roughly equal premarital effort (generating equal negative utility) in accumulating assets or cultivating endowments that are put to work to create value within the marriage. Those elements would include, for example, efforts expended on developing earning power through education or on accumulating tangible assets and property. See infra Section IV.B.2 (discussing problems that arise from the calculation of inputs and outputs to marriage, and the puzzle of how to treat "premarital endowments").

[53] This is especially true recently, due to the rise of educational assortative mating. See infra note 286.

are important within marriage.[54] Our model is Jane and Jim—the secretary married to the telephone lineman, the nurse married to the middle manager, or the computer repairman married to the college-educated housewife. How will these couples work out their marital relations?

D. *Marriage as a Bargaining Game*

The idea that marriage can be modeled as a bargaining game is not new. Scholars from various fields have recognized that game theory potentially provides an intellectually satisfying framework for addressing the problems of allocation within marriage, although none have undertaken a sustained and systematic analysis of the implications of the model for various aspects of domestic life, law, or public policy.[55] In addition, economists have created a number of theoretical and quantitative models of marital or familial relations as a form of bargaining game.[56] Those models provide the basic framework for the discussion here.

---

[54] This would appear to be a dubious assumption, given the salience in the popular imagination of the well-heeled, powerful older man marrying the toothsome younger woman of more modest means. But marriages in this mode are almost certainly a small minority of all unions in the population as a whole. Leaving aside the far right tail of the curve, where very wealthy or high status marriageable men are to be found, the differences in resources, attributes, and investments as between the sexes at the time of the typical marriage are probably not pronounced. There is, however, one caveat: A potential source of a small but perhaps not insignificant differential in endowments in the population as a whole is the age gap between husbands and wives. The fact that older persons tend to be better educated and to have accumulated more market and other types of capital may give husbands a slight edge. See infra note 104.

[55] The most sustained effort to take the model seriously as applied to marriage is Rhona Mahony's popular book. Mahony, supra note 16. A few legal scholars have also brought game-theoretic insights to bear on some aspects of family relations. Most notably, see Carol M. Rose, Women and Property: Gaining and Losing Ground, 78 Va. L. Rev. 421 (1992); Margaret F. Brinig & Steven M. Crafton, Marriage and Opportunism, 23 J. Legal Stud. 869 (1994); June Carbone & Margaret F. Brinig, Rethinking Marriage: Feminist Ideology, Economic Change, and Divorce Reform, 65 Tul. L. Rev. 953 (1991); Cohen, supra note 4; Gillian K. Hadfield, Households at Work: Beyond Labor Market Policies to Remedy the Gender Gap, 82 Geo. L.J. 89 (1993). Commentators in other disciplines have also made some use of bargaining principles in the context of broader discussions of family and gender issues. See, e.g., Okin, supra note 32; Bergmann, supra note 7, at 266-74; England & Farkas, supra note 5, at 53-54; J. Richard Udry, Marital Alternatives and Marital Disruption, 43 J. Marriage & Fam. 889 (1981).

[56] See, e.g., Theodore C. Bergstrom, Economics in a Family Way, 34 J. Econ. Literature 1903 (1996); Paul S. Carlin, Intra-Family Bargaining and Time Allocation, 7 Res.

1. The Exclusivity and Pooling Conditions: Marriage as Bilateral Monopoly

The bargaining model views a marital relationship as a bilateral monopoly that defines an arena of exclusive contribution as well as exclusive dealing. With respect to contribution and reward, it is necessary to define what the spouses bargain over. This Article assumes a "worldly goods"[57] or "pooling" condition under which each partner brings into the relationship, and places on the table for bargaining, everything each possesses at the time of marriage and everything generated through that person's presence or efforts during the life of the marriage. Nothing of value is initially held back or earmarked for exclusive use.[58] The parties' contributions

---

Population Econ. 215 (1991); Shelly Lundberg & Robert A. Pollak, Bargaining and Distribution in Marriage, J. Econ. Persp., Fall 1996, at 139 [hereinafter Lundberg & Pollak, Bargaining and Distribution]; Shelly Lundberg & Robert A. Pollak, Noncooperative Bargaining Models of Marriage, 84 Am. Econ. Rev. 132 (1994) [hereinafter Lundberg & Pollak, Noncooperative Bargaining Models]; Shelly Lundberg & Robert A. Pollak, Separate Spheres Bargaining and the Marriage Market, 101 J. Pol. Econ. 988 (1993) [hereinafter Lundberg & Pollak, Separate Spheres]; Manser & Brown, supra note 36; Marjorie B. McElroy, The Empirical Content of Nash-Bargained Household Behavior, 25 J. Hum. Resources 559 (1990); Marjorie B. McElroy & Mary Jean Horney, Nash-Bargained Household Decisions: Toward a Generalization of the Theory of Demand, 22 Int'l. Econ. Rev. 333 (1981); Robert A. Pollak, A Transaction Cost Approach to Families and Households, 23 J. Econ. Literature 581 (1985); Sharon C. Rochford, Symmetrically Pairwise-Bargained Allocations in an Assignment Market, 34 J. Econ. Theory 262 (1984); Sen, supra note 32, at 134-40.

[57] The "nothing held back" idea is neatly captured in this phrase, which appears in the Church of England marriage vows: "With this ring I thee wed, with my body I thee worship, and with all my worldly goods I thee endow . . . ." Book of Common Prayer (1886).

[58] Although strong conventions ordinarily create the expectation that members of a couple will throw all preexisting assets in the marital pot and make available all premarital as well as intramarital fruits of each partner's efforts for potential allocation within the family unit, this initial "pooling" or "worldly goods" condition does not always obtain in every marriage. For example, wealthy persons may sequester or otherwise set aside assets or wealth in a manner that makes those resources effectively unavailable to the other spouse and thus takes them permanently out of the pool of marital resources available for bargaining and allocation. For simplicity, however, this discussion adopts the pooling condition as a normative baseline.

The pooling condition should not be confused with household members' enjoying any particular share of resources including resources the other partner brings in. As discussed below, the share that each household member actually enjoys is the product of the outcome of a bargaining process that may allocate marital value in ways that increase welfare quite unevenly. For example, there is good evidence that men, women, and children do not always share equally in the wages that a breadwinner

include various resources and endowments that would exist regardless of the marriage (such as monetary income or mechanical ability)[59] as well as elements that are generated by virtue of the relationship. The latter elements comprise the marital surplus. Each spouse's income, for example, is not surplus to the partner who earns it. But marital surplus can be generated when each spouse enjoys public goods purchased with the other's income, or provides services or emotional satisfaction in exchange for a share of the other's income.[60]

These resources, and the costs of generating them, must be allocated among spouses during the life of the marriage.[61] The couple bargains over an array of choices concerning the balance of costs and payoffs for each spouse, deciding together who will make particular kinds of effort and who will enjoy certain rewards. The size and composition of the pool, and the payoffs to each spouse, are obviously not fixed, but depend on each partner's individual and

---

brings into the household, and that sharing patterns vary among couples. See, e.g., Silbaugh, supra note 17, at 44 & n.162; see also supra note 11 (citing findings by Pahl and Burgoyne that a wife's control over spending and allocation of monetary resources to personal needs is not dictated by her marital contribution).

[59] Tangible resources are not all that spouses may contribute to the relationship. They may also bring along such (initially) intangible assets as their developed human capital, earning power, financial acumen, capacity to love, talent for childrearing, family connections, extended family's security and conviviality, beauty, and winsomeness. Those personal attributes or abilities are then put to work within the relationship to generate more value, which includes but is not limited to "marital surplus" (which comprises the *enhanced* value that exists solely by virtue of the marriage). Those resources are then available for reallocation among family members. For further discussion of initial attributes of endowments, see infra Section IV.B.2.

[60] It should be apparent that the total "marital pool" as defined here is larger than the marital surplus, since the pool exists prior to any compensation for costs and includes some elements that partners would generate or enjoy whether they were married or not. Marital assets in the pool are available for surplus-generating investment (such as, for example, investing in a family business or in professional activities), for the creation of common goods, or for direct redistribution among family members.

[61] Allocations are assumed to be made between married couples. The interests of other family members (most importantly, children) are assumed to be represented by their parents within this model (although that representation is not perfect, since the overlap between parents' and children's interests—as with the interests of spouses—is not complete). In economic modeling of the family, children are often seen as adding to the marital surplus: They generate value as a "productive" output or, alternatively, add to the "consumption" value of their parents. See Becker, Treatise, supra note 36, at 7-8.

coordinated choices and actions.[62] There may be many different ways to arrange a family's affairs to effect a division—including an egalitarian division—with only some being the most efficient (i.e., generating the greatest possible total utility for all). In effect, there is always the possibility of expanding or contracting the pool of total resources available for distribution.

The marital bargaining process covers all sorts of issues and choices that extend well beyond the balance of productive effort and leisure, and the couple's use of time. Decisions relating to where to live; where and how much to work; what to buy; how much to spend, save, or invest; the priority given to the husband's and wife's careers; the conduct of sexual relations; the choice of friends; interactions with extended family; disciplining children; and myriad other matters are up for grabs within a relationship and are resolved on a daily basis in a continuous process of adjustment and readjustment, negotiation and compromise.[63] The resolution of those issues determines both the scope and composition of the marital pool and the marital surplus, as well as the well-being of each spouse.

The marital bargain also includes an exclusivity condition: Partners agree to go only to one another for certain types of resources and services. For the life of the marriage, certain "market" opportunities will necessarily be forsaken. The couple must decide on an allocation of most marital resources without direct recourse to a market pricing mechanism. These exchanges take place "off-market"; there is one buyer and one seller for a host of services and commodities. In deciding, for example, who shall get to take the children to the grocery store on Saturday and who shall play golf,

---

[62] For example, one partner may, through unilateral action—such as sexual infidelity—dramatically decrease the size of the marital surplus by simultaneously destroying marital capital and depriving the other spouse of much of the value of the marriage. See infra Section IV.A.3 (discussing sexual and fidelity issues).

[63] See Ira Mark Ellman, Should *The Theory of Alimony* Include Nonfinancial Losses and Motivations?, 1991 BYU L. Rev. 259, 292-302 (giving examples of complex marital compromises and "exchanges"); Carl E. Schneider, Rethinking Alimony: Marital Decisions and Moral Discourse, 1991 BYU L. Rev. 197, 207, 211-13 (same). Caution is also in order because the marital balance has a significant temporal component, which makes it difficult to keep accounts by taking a snapshot of some finite period. As suggested, see supra notes 12-14 and accompanying text, the relationship must be assessed over its entire duration before it can be said with confidence that there is a shortfall for one spouse or the other.

partners do not ordinarily go out on the general or "spot" market and suggest "purchase prices" to strangers to procure family services.[64] Rather, the understanding is that the tasks and rewards will be allocated within the family circle. In such circumstances, "price determination [is] ill-described by standard economic theory."[65] Each person must bargain with the other to decide who gets what. Finally, the enforcement of such a bargain is left to the parties. Courts will not enforce agreements between spouses intramaritally,[66] so there is no standing legal mechanism for remedying a breach of such an agreement so long as the partnership remains a going concern. Rather, recourse is had only to informal enforcement mechanisms, such as retaliation or other forms of self-help, which are largely—although not exclusively[67]—confined within the family unit.

2. Marriage as a Split-the-Pie Game

Under the rational choice paradigm, a couple marries if marriage offers a Pareto-superior result: Both parties must be no worse off by virtue of the union. But "embedded in all institutional arrangements that provide the opportunity for mutual gain is a bargaining game over relative shares."[68] The allocational possibilities that characterize marriage can be modeled as a two-person bargaining game of "split-the-pie." The key to the game is that a failure to settle on a mutually agreeable allocation will result in a reduction in welfare (a reduced payoff) for each bargainer. Without

---

[64] As noted, see infra notes 129 & 188, some families have recourse to the "cash solution" (that is, hiring household help) for a portion of family services, but those families are quite unusual. There are many key marital functions for which no market substitute can be found or where such a substitution (e.g., sexual services) would defy the core conditions of the relationship or be inimical to it.

[65] Eric Rasmusen, Games and Information: An Introduction to Game Theory 227 (1989).

[66] See Saul Levmore, Love It or Leave It: Property Rules, Liability Rules, and Exclusivity of Remedies in Partnership and Marriage, 58 Law & Contemp. Probs. 221, 225 (1995); Silbaugh, supra note 17, at 29 (discussing the legal taboo against intramarital enforcement of antenuptial agreements); see also Charles J. Goetz & Robert E. Scott, Principles of Relational Contracts, 67 Va. L. Rev. 1089 (1981) (discussing relational contracts generally).

[67] Social disapproval and other informal sanctions may play some, albeit a now diminishing, role. For a discussion of informal social norms, see infra Sections V.C, V.F.

[68] Jules L. Coleman, Markets, Morals and the Law 272 (1988).

agreement, both partners lose. This risk creates an incentive to come to a mutually satisfying agreement within the relationship.[69]

The condition that both partners must gain by agreement establishes the central constraint for a feasible bargain: The possible set of rational allocations within the bargaining relationship is limited by the alternatives available to each participant in the bargained-for agreement. Although proposed game-theoretic bargaining models of marriage differ in some particulars, they share the feature that the bargain struck will be some function of the consequences for each party of failing to reach agreement.[70] The alternatives awaiting the parties in the absence of a bargained-for agreement are variously known in game theory parlance as the "fallback alternative," "threat point," "threat advantage,"[71] "next best alternative,"[72] or "best alternative to a negotiated agreement."[73] The next best alternative is determined by the situation each party confronts in the absence of a negotiated agreement, and can include the option of forgoing any transaction at all or of transacting with another party. The value of each party's "threat point" (as determined by the next best alternative) reflects the potential value of an agreement for each party, which in turn determines each party's "reservation price." That price is equal to "the minimum threshold value that he or she is prepared to accept for entering into an agreement. A party gains from a transaction when he or she re-

---

[69] Baird, Gertner & Picker, supra note 48, at 220; Rasmusen, supra note 65, at 228. The analogy between marriage and "split-the-pie" is not perfect, because the latter assumes fungible, continuous, and infinitely divisible shares, and in marriage there may be some discontinuities of division. Such discontinuities, and other features of marriage such as the dominance of public goods, may sometimes make it quite difficult to bargain freely over "side-payments" to rectify imbalances of shares that may result, for example, from adopting a more efficient but lopsided allocation of productive effort. See infra Section IV.A.1.

[70] See Pollak, supra note 56, at 600 (reviewing proposed bargaining models of marriage).

[71] Wertheimer, supra note 32, at 67.

[72] See Pollak, supra note 56, at 600. There is some semantic confusion in the literature over whether the person with the better set of alternatives to an agreement has a "high threat point" or a "low threat point." I have chosen, as more intuitively sound, to describe the party with better outside alternatives as having a "high threat point." But see Mahony, supra note 16, at 44 (suggesting that the party to a marriage who has more alternatives—usually the man—has a lower threat point).

[73] See, e.g., Mahony, supra note 16, at 43; Howard Raiffa, The Art and Science of Negotiation 45 (1982); Wertheimer, supra note 32, at 211.

ceives more than the reservation price."[74] Each party's reservation price in turn fixes the magnitude of the bargaining surplus, which consists of the resources available for allocation between the parties through bargaining once each party's reservation price is met.

Each party's best alternative to an agreement is one of the factors that bear on each party's bargaining power. The term "bargaining power," although often used, is rarely understood or precisely defined.[75] In bargaining among rational, self-interested utility maximizers, bargaining power has a formal aspect and a behavioral one. Formally, threat points determine the limits of the negotiation set—the range of utility payoffs that each bargainer could rationally accept within the bargaining relationship.[76] That range is governed by a simple principle: If a party can do better outside the bargain than by striking a deal, he or she will not agree to a deal. Although the threat points set limits, they do not, in themselves, uniquely determine the precise arrangement within the negotiation set that will be selected by the parties. That selection is a matter for the two parties to work out, and a division will be arrived at through some kind of negotiating process for dividing up the bargaining surplus. Therefore, predicting or specifying the likely marital bargain and the respective payoffs to the players would require knowing something about the spouses' individual alternatives to striking a deal (the threat points), as well as something about their bargaining abilities and the determinants of the bargaining process.

---

[74] Wertheimer, supra note 32, at 211 (footnote omitted); see also Raiffa, supra note 73, at 45 (applying the reservation price).

[75] See Wertheimer, supra note 32, at 64-68 (discussing confusion surrounding "bargaining power"). The term is genuinely useful in the context of off-market, monopolistic bargaining games. Its meaning is far more ambiguous in the context of market transactions, where the terms of exchange and price are more closely fixed by aggregate supply and demand. See, e.g., Daniel J. Chepaitis, The National Labor Relations Act, Non-Paralleled Competition, and Market Power, 85 Cal. L. Rev. 769 (1997) (attempting to explore the concept of "market power" in the labor market).

[76] See Pollak, supra note 56, at 600. That negotiation set can include both Pareto-optimal and non-Pareto-optimal arrangements between the parties. See Mahony, supra note 16, at 38-48 (discussing suboptimal or "inefficient" marital deals).

3. "Threat Points" in Marriage

What determines the threat point of the partners to a marriage? The two competing game-theoretic models in the literature assume two different fallback positions that confront the couple if they fail to acquiesce in a mutually agreeable arrangement for the conduct of the marriage. Both fallback positions represent a loss of potential marital surplus and a reduction in the size of the pie or the pool available for distribution.

One possible fallback option for nonagreement is the breakup of the relationship—divorce.[77] That outcome risks loss for both parties of all benefits of the marriage. Another possible outcome is an uncoordinated or discordant living arrangement in which the partners are at odds, but remain married and continue to live together—the "harsh words and burnt toast" alternative.[78] The parties are worse off than if they agreed on how to coordinate their efforts, but may be better off than if they divorced. If they would be better off "at war" than apart, the threat points that effectively determine the parties' conduct are intramarital.

Since both partners to a potentially positive-sum marriage will lose if the marriage either dissolves through divorce, or degenerates into domestic strife, the partners have some incentive to come to an allocational agreement. Their incentives may not be the same, however. There is reason to believe that, on average, the fallback positions may differ significantly for husband and wife. Specifically, there is evidence suggesting that men will on average have better alternatives to a marital agreement—both inside and outside of marriage—than women.

a. Exit Options

The alternatives to getting married to a particular person are to remain single or to marry someone else. The alternatives to remaining married are to become single or marry again. In the words of one economist of family bargaining, the value of these alternatives is determined by the "extrahousehold environmental parameters" encompassing "every variable that affects how well each fam-

---

[77] See Bergstrom, supra note 56, at 1924.

[78] Id. at 1926; see also Lundberg & Pollak, Separate Spheres, supra note 56, at 1007 (discussing intramarital and extramarital threat point models).

ily member could do in the next best alternative outside of the family."[79] Variables include subjective preferences for being married or unmarried; the resources each member controls individually (most notably, market earnings and wealth); social and community ties and support; the sexual consequences of being unmarried; the costs or harms to third parties—most notably children—from divorce and how concerned the partner is about these harms; the amount of sunk cost or lost investment entailed by divorce; the social stigma and status consequences attached to being single or divorced; the legal rules that determine property divisions, alimony, and child support following the termination of marriage; and taxes and transfers conditioned on marital status (such as Aid to Families with Dependent Children ("AFDC") and other welfare payments). Related to all these elements is how a person who contemplates divorce would fare in the remarriage market.

Many of these variables operate in favor of men. Setting aside remarriage prospects, there is reason to suppose that single women may be less happy than single men within the unmarried state. That is, single women's baseline level of well-being may, on average, be lower than single men's. First, assuming an otherwise similar intensity of desire to marry, even young women at the peak of marriageability cannot afford to wait as long to get married, because their marriageability declines more rapidly than men's.[80] Thus, the cost of each additional period of being single is greater for women than men. This temporal factor alone introduces a difference in men's and women's average demand for marriage.

There are yet other reasons why women may, on average, be less satisfied being single than men. Many of the services that men once sought within marriage—"everything from sex to food preparation to old-age insurance"[81] as well as, in some cases, the production of "own" offspring[82]—are readily available outside of marriage or can be purchased on the open market. On the other hand, what

---

[79] McElroy, supra note 56, at 578.

[80] See infra notes 95-98 and accompanying text.

[81] Shirley P. Burggraf, The Feminine Economy and Economic Man: Reviving the Role of Family in the Post-Industrial Age 4 (1997).

[82] See Becker, Treatise, supra note 36, at 28-29 (discussing the importance of producing one's "own children" as a benefit of marriage); see also infra note 338 (discussing the demographics of out-of-wedlock birth rates and their relationship to men's extramarital well-being and willingness to marry).

women traditionally seek within marriage—emotional security, financial support, prestige, power, and a father's authoritative help and financial "sponsorship" for their children—are hard for women to obtain outside of marriage and generally cannot be purchased.[83] Moreover, factors like sex-specific differences in the costs and benefits of sexual variety or exclusivity may elevate men's baseline well-being relative to women's outside of marriage, at least under current social conditions.[84] Women's distaste for being single may also stem from women's need for a "protector": Single women may feel more threatened, vulnerable, lonely, or socially despised than single men.[85] Finally, labor market factors are influential. Women generally make less money than men, although there is evidence that the gap is closing rapidly for unmarried childless women as compared to men in comparable jobs.[86] Women's occupational choices differ from men's, which can result in somewhat lower earnings. Finally, discrimination against women in the job market may place important limits on women's earnings and career prospects compared to men's. Thus, women may start out less well off on the primary marriage market.

Women, notoriously, also do less well by divorce. Their labor market value is often impaired by marriage. Women generally make greater idiosyncratic, marriage-specific investments than men, and those investments often come at the expense of labor market opportunity costs.[87] Women also face direct loss of their marital investments, which function as sunk costs if a marriage dissolves.[88] Their preference for the custody of children imposes additional fi-

---

[83] But see infra Section V.E.3 for a discussion of the role AFDC plays in substituting for a husband's income and services.

[84] See infra Section IV.A.3 (discussing men's and women's attitudes and tastes with respect to fidelity and sex); infra note 338 (discussing recent changes in the availability of "respectable" premarital sex).

[85] See, e.g., Roberta S. Sigel, Ambition and Accommodation: How Women View Gender Relations 43-89 (1996) (surveying women's feelings of second-class citizenship, which some women may believe marriage will alleviate).

[86] See June Ellenoff O'Neill, The Cause and Significance of the Declining Gender Gap in Pay, in Neither Victim Nor Enemy 1, 7-8 (Rita J. Simon ed., 1995).

[87] See Cohen, supra note 4; Trebilcock & Keshvani, supra note 4; see also infra note 186 (discussing why women tend to start out making greater investments in domesticity).

[88] Women tend to specialize in nurturing and family work, whereas "men typically make fewer relationship-specific investments than women, accumulating instead resources which are as useful outside as within their current relationship." England & Farkas, supra note 5, at 55.

nancial burdens.[89] Men, in contrast, customarily make a greater investment in labor market capital, which is portable in the event of divorce. But, even if the sex differential in active marriage-specific investment could be completely eliminated—which is unlikely in the face of *other* sources of men's superior bargaining power[90]— men would still come out ahead. Given their relatively short reproductive lives, women bear a sex-specific "passive" opportunity cost that their husbands do not.

This leads us to perhaps the most significant difference in men's and women's fate outside of marriage, which lies in their currency on the remarriage market. On the assumption that marriage to a *suitable* partner generates surplus value for the pair to share over and above what each spouse can generate alone, remarriage to such a partner is by definition a more desirable option than remaining single. Indeed, the ability to remarry confers a bargaining advantage precisely because the opportunity to remarry can be very valuable. Remarriage has the potential to be a positive-sum game—that is, to produce a surplus for distribution to the participants. When there is a positive-sum game, everyone wants to play.

But not everyone gets to play. A woman's attractiveness and appeal to the opposite sex declines rapidly with age, causing a precipitous falling off of her remarriageability.[91] If her investment of her youth in her husband fails to yield future payoffs (because, for example, a marriage fails), that resource is effectively depleted.[92]

---

[89] See Robert H. Mnookin & Lewis Kornhauser, Bargaining in the Shadow of the Law: The Case of Divorce, 88 Yale L.J. 950, 979 (1979).

[90] See infra Sections III.C-D for a discussion of the interaction of roles and bargaining power.

[91] See Cohen, supra note 4, at 278-87. Divorce scholars have noted that "women lose value in the marriage market more rapidly than do men." Id. at 284. Ira Ellman notes that "[t]he more precipitous decline in the woman's sexual appeal" with age is exacerbated by its corollary, which is the age differential in marital partnerships. Ellman, supra note 4, at 43. He further observes that this "relatively universal and apparently intractable" male preference for marrying younger women is an important "noneconomic factor" (which nevertheless has economic consequences) that tends to exacerbate women's preexisting disadvantage upon divorce. Id. That factor operates to deprive many women of the benefits of remarriage.

[92] As Lloyd Cohen puts it, the wife experiences a "stochastic fall in value" during the life of the marriage, both because much of her active investment typically takes place during the early years of a relationship and because her passive currency on the remarriage market declines more rapidly. Cohen, supra note 4, at 288; Mahony, supra note 16, at 19-22.

In contrast, her husband's appeal is relatively unaffected by age, and is even enhanced somewhat by the human capital and earning power he accumulates during marriage.[93]

The loss of value of women on the marriage market as a function of age is driven by the social customs of male hypogamy (that is, men marrying down in age, education, and earnings) and female hypergamy (marrying up). These practices seem to be fueled by observed male preferences for marriage to young or younger women, and their aversion to partners of greater status, education, and ambition.[94] Female preferences may also play a role. Women seem not to mind marrying older men, and may positively prefer men of higher status and earnings.

But perhaps the most important factor driving remarriage patterns is the relatively shorter reproductive life of women compared to men. As women age, their capacity to bear additional children declines rapidly, whereas men can become fathers well into old age. Many prospective husbands, regardless of age, greatly value a woman's fertility.[95] This tends to diminish women's value on the remarriage market relative to similarly aged men's, and goes a long way towards explaining observed patterns of male hypogamy. The importance to the creation of unequal marital bargaining power of the difference in remarriage prospects grounded in the short reproductive life of women should not be underestimated. This pattern is ultimately driven by ineluctable biological facts.

Since the factors that disadvantage women all correlate with age, the end result is that divorced women on average find it harder than men to replace their mates, and these difficulties increase

---

[93] See Cohen, supra note 4, at 286-87; Ellman, supra note 4, at 43.

[94] See Cohen, supra note 4, at 281 (citing Jessie Bernard, The Future of Marriage 158 (1972)).

[95] Indeed, it is possible to construct an economic model that derives observed divisions of household labor solely from male-female differences in reproductive lifespan. The model posits a marriage market of fecund women and fertile men, and a post-divorce remarriage market in which all men and all previously unmarried women (but no divorced women), can remarry and have children. The model predicts that rational men and women will invest differentially in market and domestic human capital, respectively, based on the constraints introduced by these marriage-market assumptions alone. See Aloysius Siow, Differential Fecundity, Markets and Gender Roles, 106 J. Pol. Econ. 334 (1998).

sharply with advancing age.[96] Finding a replacement is made even more difficult by the likelihood that a woman will bring another man's children into her new family.[97] In contrast, the man's legacy from his first marriage—his earning capacity—is valuable "both in the marriage market and the commercial world." A man can "take much of the gain realized from his first marriage into a second and he can more easily find a replacement mate."[98]

Prospects for men and women outside of marriage are important to marital bargaining because the dissolution of the entire marital bargain as a going concern (i.e., divorce) always looms as a possible consequence of failure to agree. The relative importance of the divorce threat alternative to coming to mutual agreement, as compared to what partners face under conditions of marital discord, is difficult to assess, but surely depends in part on the costs of divorce. The current social and legal climate creates few external barriers to divorce, and provides for minimal redistribution among spouses following a marriage's dissolution.[99] The stigma of divorce

---

[96] Although remarriage is popular among both sexes, data gathered in the late 1980s indicate that the remarriage rate for women aged 35-44 is about two-thirds the rate for men, with the ratio dropping to less than one-half for women over 45. Barbara Foley Wilson & Sally Cuningham Clarke, Remarriages: A Demographic Profile, 13 J. Fam. Issues 123, 126 tbl.2 (1992); see also Weitzman, supra note 12, at 204 (reporting that divorced women under 30 have a 75% chance of remarriage, but women over 40 have only a 28% chance of remarriage).

Two other factors also affect the remarriage prospects of women. First, women with children remarry at a lower rate than women without children, regardless of age of divorce. Children have no effect on remarriage for men. See Larry Bumpass, James Sweet & Teresa Castro Martin, Changing Patterns of Remarriage, 52 J. Marriage & Fam. 747, 751-52 (1990); Helen P. Koo, C.M. Suchindran & Janet D. Griffith, The Effects of Children on Divorce and Re-Marriage: A Multivariate Analysis of Life Table Probabilities, 38 Population Stud. 451 (1984). Second, education is inversely correlated with the incidence of remarriage among divorced women. This relationship of education to remarriage does not obtain for men. See 3 National Ctr. for Health Statistics, U.S. Dep't of Health & Human Servs., Vital Statistics of the United States, Marriage and Divorce, 1988, at 41 tbl.1-32 (1996).

[97] See England & Farkas, supra note 5, at 57-58; see also supra note 96 (noting evidence that children depress a divorced woman's chance of remarriage).

[98] Ellman, supra note 4, at 44.

[99] Only two states require both spouses' consent to obtain divorce for breakdown of the marriage, and in 40 states one spouse may obtain a divorce over the other's objection after a separation of one year or less. See Elizabeth S. Scott, Rational Decisionmaking About Marriage and Divorce, 76 Va. L. Rev. 9, 17 n.23 (1990). The role of fault, if any, in the award of alimony and the division of property is more complex

has all but disappeared, at least insofar as it carries concrete occupational or financial consequences.[100] To be sure, there are lost
sunk costs and transaction costs from divorce for both parties,
which operate as internal restraints on divorce for many couples.[101]
But if staying married loses its intrinsic value to one partner—if
one partner faces an intramarital payoff that lies below his or her
reservation price—the law itself imposes few additional costs on
exiting the marriage. Thus, marital bargaining is informed by the
substantial possibility that the marriage will not last.

Because the ease or difficulty of obtaining a divorce is in large
part (although not exclusively) a function of the law of domestic
relations, all marital bargaining can be said to take place "in the
shadow of the law."[102] But because the law creates a right of easy
exit, and in many cases leaves both partners more or less where
they stood at the time the marriage dissolved, the law is perhaps
better described as a window. Through that window, two markets
cast their shadows upon bargainers: the labor market (which determines who can earn how much on his or her own) and the mar-

---

and varied. See Ira Mark Ellman, The Place of Fault in a Modern Divorce Law, 28
Ariz. St. L.J. 773, 781-82 (1996).

Although the law of domestic relations does effect some redistribution of marital
assets, it does not generally adopt the conventional contract measures—such as restitution, expectancy, or reliance damages—that govern the allocation of assets following an ordinary contract breach. Thus, post-divorce redistributive measures are
modest, at best, and routinely fall short of equalizing the parties' welfare following
divorce. See Ellman, supra note 4, at 49-53; Estin, supra note 4, at 559-60; Trebilcock
& Kevshani, supra note 4, at 551-60. Alimony is uncommon and temporary, see
Scott, supra, at 18, and although the law provides for the division of marital property,
there is little tangible property in most marriages. The most important marital assets
(such as human capital) are rarely reallocated. See Trebilcock & Keshvani, supra
note 4, at 552-53; Weitzman, supra note 12, at 269-78, 289-309; Williams, supra note
3, at 2250; see also Jana B. Singer, Alimony and Efficiency: The Gendered Costs and
Benefits of the Economic Justification for Alimony, 82 Geo. L.J. 2423, 2454-56 (1994)
(proposing income sharing alternatives).

[100] See infra Section V.F (discussing the social stigma surrounding divorce).

[101] These include accumulated marriage-specific investments, harm to children, costs
from liquidation, relocation, reordering of affairs, the psychological distress of breakup,
insecurity, search for a new spouse, and the violation of religious or other beliefs
about the permanence of marriage.

[102] Cf. Mnookin & Kornhauser, supra note 89 (suggesting how bargaining at divorce
takes place "in the shadow of the law").

riage market (which determines who will have the benefits of a new spouse).[103]

Because men generally have better options in these markets than women, the value of the right to exit from a marriage is on average greater for men than for women.[104] This means that where failure to agree increases the probability of divorce, men stand to lose less from disagreement than women. Not only is men's extramarital exit threat generally higher than women's, but the difference grows over time. And such would be the case even if men and women equalized patterns of wage and non-wage human capital investment and earning power, even if they did not have different preferences for children, and even if they did not have different absolute or comparative advantages (whether natural or acquired) in domestic and nondomestic pursuits. Because remarriage is quite valuable both financially and emotionally, all that would be required to generate a quite significant inequality in exit options is a difference in men's and women's currency on the marriage market with advancing age. That difference is a longstanding feature of the social landscape.

---

[103] With respect to the marriage market, the American marriage system has been described as involving an individual's "permanent availability" as a spouse, a system in which "every adult can be thought of as permanently available as a marital partner, regardless of the fact that the individual is presently married." Udry, supra note 55, at 889 (citing the work of Bernard Farber). Thus, each person

> continuously compar[es] his or her marital bargain with other marital bargains which he or she might be able to negotiate with other persons, and with his or her potential benefits from not being married at all. If an individual's present marital partnership is strikingly less favorable than the alternatives, he or she will opt for one of the alternatives if the cost of the exchange (barrier) does not obliterate the advantage to be obtained.

Id.

[104] Patterns of hyper- and hypogamy, which are more pronounced on the remarriage market, can give rise to systematic differentials in the labor market position of husbands and wives even in the absence of population-wide differences in men's and women's labor market prospects. The dual tendencies of women to marry somewhat older men and men to marry somewhat younger women leads to a systematic average gap in the ages of husbands and wives, a gap that can create a systematic differential in couples' earning power. See Ellman, supra note 4, at 43-44. As a general rule, persons with longer job market experience earn more, and older persons tend to have longer tenure on the job. This means that the combination of male hypogamy and female hypergamy carries with it a chronic initial gap in earning power as between couples, which would persist even if the average differences in wages and earnings for men and women in the economy were wiped out. This intracouple gap, even if modest, exacerbates the effect of the remarriage differential. See supra note 54.

b. *Intramarital Options*

Ultimately, the difference in men's and women's exit options is always relevant to bargaining because divorce defines the absolute outer limits of the scope for bargaining within an ongoing marriage.[105] Nevertheless, the immediate importance of "divorce bounds" to the actual bargaining process and the parties' bargaining power is minimized in the case where both parties anticipate that even forced togetherness is better than divorce. In that case, the threat point that actually matters to the couple and that will most immediately influence their conduct, is an intramarital one.

Just as with the exit threat, men's intramarital threat point can be expected to exceed women's. The "burnt toast and harsh words" model of marital interaction recognizes that there are times in every marriage when spouses will both be better off if they agree on a coordinated course of action.[106] In many cases, failure to agree

---

[105] See Lundberg & Pollak, Bargaining and Distribution, supra note 56, at 154 ("Individual rationality ensures that no individual will accept less than he or she would receive in the next best alternative and implies that the divorce bounds apply to all bargaining models, both cooperative and noncooperative.").

[106] This situation corresponds to a game-theoretic model of marriage created by Lundberg and Pollak, which they term the "separate spheres" model. Lundberg & Pollak, Separate Spheres, supra note 56. In that model, the threat point for an agreed-upon bargain—that is, the situation that would prevail in the absence of an agreed-upon allocation—is not divorce but a "noncooperative ... equilibrium within marriage." Id. at 992-93. The choices available to the spouses in the absence of agreement are given the game-theoretic designation of "noncooperative" situations. Id. The stable arrangements within this set—of which there are many—are designated "noncooperative equilibria." The bargain that is struck within the negotiation set created by the noncooperative equilibria (which function as threat points) is termed a "cooperative" agreement, and the model is designated a "cooperative model." Id. at 1007. The same authors have also created an alternative and so-called "noncooperative" model of marriage, which is a dynamic model predicting the outcome of repeated, costly offers and counteroffers by husband and wife who control different resources within marriage. See Lundberg & Pollak, Bargaining and Distribution, supra note 56, at 150; Lundberg & Pollak, Noncooperative Bargaining Models, supra note 56; see also Baird, Gertner & Picker, supra note 48, at 221 (describing dynamic or Rubinstein bargaining games).

The terminology that Lundberg and Pollak employ in their papers is unfortunate. The designations "cooperative" and "noncooperative" as they apply to game-theoretic agreements are terms of art referring to agreements that are, respectively, binding (i.e. externally enforceable) or nonbinding. See Rasmusen, supra note 65, at 29. As Lundberg and Pollak themselves acknowledge, however, it is probably inaccurate to refer to marital agreements as "cooperative" agreements in this sense, because there are no legal or other formal mechanisms for enforcing agreements during

will result in a less efficient arrangement than could otherwise be achieved by coordination of effort, as when failure to settle on one family dinnertime results in cold food for some family members. In other cases, failure to achieve a "meeting of the minds" on a mutual course of action will lead to a breakdown in the trust necessary to coordinate a *sequence* of contributions. That trust would ordinarily lead each party to put forward optimizing "best efforts" in anticipation of agreed-upon reciprocation.[107] Without coordination, some lesser degree of effort will be forthcoming, which will shrink the size of total output available to share.

In the absence of agreement, the intramarital threat point model assumes that one spouse decides how to go about his or her business without the other's consent, with each spouse independently choosing a "level of her private good and the public good that she supplies to maximize her own utility, subject to her budget constraint."[108] In this discordant or "uncoordinated" state, each spouse strategizes to inflict the most misery on the partner (as a spur to reaching agreement of some type) while doing the least damage to himself or herself in the process. The game-theoretic models sug-

---

the life of the marriage. There are only informal social sanctions and self-help. Lundberg & Pollak, Noncooperative Bargaining Models, supra note 56, at 133 (recognizing that marriage is best modeled as a noncooperative bargaining game). To reduce terminological confusion, the situation that prevails in the absence of mutual agreement—the "harsh words and burnt toast" situation—will be termed in this paper the "uncoordinated" or disharmonious marriage, and the bargain that would be struck against the background threat of such possible disagreement is termed the "coordinated agreement." Coordinated agreements, even though technically noncooperative (because externally unenforceable) nevertheless may be more efficient than uncoordinated behaviors, because they bring gains from mutually orchestrated actions.

[107] See, e.g., Goetz & Scott, supra note 66, at 1116-19 (discussing a "best efforts" convention as an informal way to optimize output in a long-term relational contract).

[108] Lundberg & Pollak, Bargaining and Distribution, supra note 56, at 148. As Lundberg and Pollak write:

> Within an existing marriage, a noncooperative [that is, uncoordinated] equilibrium corresponds to a utility-maximizing strategy in which each spouse takes the other spouse's strategy as given.... What distinguishes a noncooperative marriage from a pair of independently optimizing individuals? Joint consumption economies are an important source of gains to marriage, and even noncooperative family members enjoy the benefits of household public goods.... As one might expect, public goods are undersupplied in this noncooperative equilibrium, and there are potential gains to cooperation. Additional gains can be expected if coordination of individual contributions is required for efficient household production.

Lundberg & Pollak, Separate Spheres, supra note 56, at 993.

gest that there are many ways that spouses can arrange their affairs in the absence of marital harmony (that is, there are "multiple equilibria" for marital discord), depending on initial conditions or conventions.[109] Since many marital activities involve public goods and have secondary effects on the other spouse, each spouse inevitably benefits (or suffers) to a certain degree from the other's choices during the period of marital discord. As the examples above and discussion below show, however, the surplus loss from failure to coordinate may not fall equally on each partner.

Where both spouses are better off within the range of "uncoordinated equilibria"[110] than they would be if the marriage fell apart, then marital bargaining towards agreement will take place in the shadow of noncoordination or "marital warfare." The best alternative to agreement, which determines the negotiation set and the actual bargaining surplus, will not be divorce, but how miserable or well off each person will be in the uncoordinated state. That, in turn, will depend on how much deprivation and distress each spouse can inflict on the other without hurting himself or herself too much.

Do women suffer more from marital incoordination? The answer is not as clearcut as in the simple divorce threat-point model. As an initial matter, the spouse with more domestic responsibility stands to lose more because that party cannot withdraw his or her

---

[109] Lundberg and Pollak suggest that the range of intramarital threat points presented by the specter of an uncoordinated or warring household may be heavily affected by social conventions regarding appropriate sex roles. When family cooperation, coordination, and communication break down, people may fall back on well-worn roles in determining how to conduct themselves. See Lundberg & Pollak, Bargaining and Distribution, supra note 56, at 150-52. As the authors state, "[t]he existence of multiple equilibria in repeated noncooperative games and the need to choose among them suggest how history and culture might affect distribution within marriage." Id. at 151. Because there may be a "self-evident way to play" that is dictated by social conventions regarding "the rights and responsibilities of husbands and wives," what will often emerge without explicit bargaining or agreement is a division of labor based on traditional roles. Id. One glaring variation on marital disharmony is, of course, domestic violence, which can drastically lower the threat point of a woman's failure to acquiesce in her husband's wishes.

[110] The effect on actual bargaining of the uncoordinated equilibria represented by the potential for marital disharmony is complicated by the fact that there are multiple uncoordinated equilibrium conditions possible. Thus, whereas there is only one—or theoretically only one—divorce threat point, there are multiple intramarital equilibrium threat points generating different potential negotiation sets.

services (which generally produce public goods) without hurting himself or herself along with the other partner. The person who contributes cash or other tangible assets is in a better position to withhold benefits from the marital pool than the person who performs in-kind labor for the unit.[111] The difference, of course, is a matter of degree: Some domestic work is severable, just as "some monetary wealth must be shared in the form of housing" and other public goods.[112]

But these observations are not completely satisfying because they require assuming a division of labor as a starting point or background condition for deciding which bargainer stands to lose more. Ideally, the bargaining analysis should tell us how duties and benefits will be split. Its goal is to explain observed patterns of allocation, not to assume them. What determines the level of goods and services that each spouse will supply within the context of forced togetherness? Specifically, is there reason to believe that one party (the wife) might spontaneously supply the greater amount of public-goods producing domestic service, which then redounds to the benefit of her partner? Although the person who does more domestic work is less likely to withdraw that contribution in an uncoordinated situation than the person who contributes other resources, we still do not know why, in the absence of a bargained-for assignment, the wife will be performing the majority of those tasks. The answer could lie in a different preference structure concerning the costs and benefits of domestic labor for men and women.

c. The Parable of Neat and Slob

To explain how observed patterns come about, assume there are two law students—Neat and Slob—who are assigned as roommates. Suppose each would incur extreme financial liability for breaking the lease; it is so costly for each to get rid of the other (i.e., "divorce") that neither considers it. Neat cares more about cleanliness than Slob. Neat either is less averse to (that is, experi-

---

[111] As one scholar of housework has observed, the benefits of whatever housework is performed will, as a practical matter, be shared. That is because it often is not feasible to perform housework for oneself without providing a benefit to all members of the household. See Silbaugh, supra note 17, at 34.

[112] See id. at 35.

ences less negative utility from) cleaning the apartment, or derives greater positive utility from having a clean place to live, or both. Slob hates cleaning more—or cares less about having a clean apartment—than Neat. He nevertheless prefers a clean apartment to a dirty one and will clean it himself if it gets sufficiently dirty. The apartment is cleaned by an outsider on the weekend, but it gets progressively dirtier as the week wears on. Their respective preferences are such that Neat will clean the apartment on Tuesday, but Slob will not clean until Thursday. Neat and Slob neither coordinate their efforts nor bargain over allocation of labor. As a result, Neat cleans the apartment every Tuesday, and Slob, who studies while Neat cleans, reaps the benefits of the public good of the clean apartment.

If Neat and Slob are "forced" to live together and share public goods, their strictly rational and individually optimizing behavior will result in very lopsided costs and benefits to each member of the pair. If Neat gets fed up and decides to try bargaining with Slob—that is, tries to get Slob to take a larger share of the responsibility—the bargain he can hope to strike will be a function of how badly off Slob anticipates being if no agreement is reached. If they do manage to forge a compromise that shifts some work to Slob, Neat will be better off than before, and Slob will be worse off. Since Slob does not realistically anticipate being worse off in the absence of agreement than with one (because it is unlikely that Neat will make good on a threat to underperform), Neat will probably not get very far in his attempt to shift some responsibility to Slob.

The Parable of Neat and Slob shows how the marital game of "split-the-pie" can be transformed into a variation on the game of "chicken."[113] Here, each player is worst off if the task (cleaning) is not performed at all. And each is best off if the other player, and not he, performs it. Each prefers a compromise to doing all the work himself, but each prefers not doing it to a compromise. Slob's advantage can be attributed to the asymmetry of the hypothetical payoffs, which results from different costs and benefits to the parties either from performing the task or from enjoying the fruits of

---

[113] See Rasmusen, supra note 65, at 73-74 (describing the chicken game).

labor.[114] As the game is played out, the person with the most to lose from mutual nonperformance will more often end up performing the task, and the other person will free ride on the other's willingness to bear the costs.

Of course, this example is oversimplified, for it assumes rational actors who will not make good on threats that prove costly in a single round of a game. In reality, if Slob were a spouse he would have a somewhat greater incentive to agree on a compromise, because in marriage partners usually suffer additional costs from prolonged discord and lack of coordination, and intransigence on one issue can spill over into negotiations on others. Also, as discussed below, real-life bargainers might make good on disadvantageous threats because there might be plausible long-term strategic reasons for doing so.[115] Nevertheless, the basic principle illustrated by the example is quite pertinent: Where divorce is not a credible threat on the part of either spouse, the one who stands to lose more from the loss of a public good will suffer more in the absence of an express agreement. The spouse who can better tolerate an undersupply of a public good has less to lose from refusing to compromise.

It is quite possible that women care more about the sorts of public goods that are supplied to a marriage through unpaid domestic labor. For example, women may place a higher value on order and quality in domestic matters, may find domestic disorder more irksome, or may find the effort needed to bring about a high level of domestic order less onerous (because they mind doing housework less, they are more accustomed to doing it, or it carries less of a stigma for them).[116] Women's standards of childcare may also dif-

---

[114] A possible array of asymmetric payoffs to Neat and Slob is:

		SLOB:	
		STUDY	WORK
NEAT:	WORK	3, 8	8, 4
	STUDY	-3, 0	12, 2

For each roommate, the payoff is lowest when both study and no one works. It rises for each person to the maximum through the sequence of (1) doing the work alone, (2) sharing the work, and (3) having the other person do it. Neat gets a smaller payoff than Slob if the work is undone, but a larger payoff in all other situations.

[115] See infra note 153 (discussing failure to cooperate despite potential mutual gains).

[116] A number of feminist commentators have recognized the critical role of a marital dynamic that corresponds to a chicken game in the allocation of family responsibility.

fer from men's—for example, in their views of how much parental care children should get. The wish for children to have parental care is analogous to the desire for a clean apartment: The desire is to have it done, preferably at least cost to oneself. Absent that condition, however, it still proves worthwhile to do it oneself and bear the cost.[117] This is not inconsistent with the fact that men en-

---

See, e.g., Pat Mainardi, The Politics of Housework, *in* Sisterhood Is Powerful: An Anthology of Writings from the Women's Liberation Movement 447, 449 (Robin Morgan ed., 1970). Joan Williams describes a typical marital scenario in the following terms:

> Is it important to you to have a clean house? It's not to me: you clean it if it's important to you. You think it's important to pick the children up from school, go to the Halloween parade, be home before 7:00 p.m., spend extra time with the children during vacations, be a room parent, get involved with the PTA? I don't. But if you feel you must, then by all means do so.

Williams, supra note 3, at 2240 (footnotes omitted). Williams also quotes one male commentator who points out that "[o]verinvolvement with children may operate to discourage many husbands from fully sharing because they do not accept the ideology of close attention to children." Id. at 2240 n.56 (quoting S.M. Miller, The Making of a Confused Middle-Aged Husband, *in* Men & Masculinity 44, 50 (Joseph H. Pleck & Jack Sawyer eds., 1974)).

[117] The issue of how women in particular and parents in general regard unpaid domestic responsibilities is far more complex for childcare than for other domestic tasks. Most people would not ordinarily perform routine housework for its own sake, but only for its productive payoff. In contrast, the care of children has significant components of both work and leisure or, alternatively, of production and consumption value. See, e.g., Silbaugh, supra note 17, at 12.

Women may differ on average from men both in the degree to which they regard childcare as intrinsically enjoyable and in the degree to which they want their children to have more time with a *parent* as opposed to a nonparent (without necessarily wanting to provide it personally—as in, "I wish you would spend more time with the children, dear"). Both preferences—which are quite distinct, but are often conflated—will affect women's choices within a circumscribed set of options, but the choices that depend on the consumption value of childcare will not be influenced by bargaining strength or by the bargaining partner's choices. Childcare will be willingly supplied by the consumer as long as its consumption value holds out, compared to the benefits of other uses of time.

The component that predominates in childcare—whether work or leisure—can depend both on the circumstances in which childcare is performed, the specific childcare tasks at issue, and the peculiar preferences and tastes of the person caring for children. On the first of these, it has been noted that women and men care for children in different contexts, with women tending "to overlap the time during which they supervise children with shopping, laundry, or food preparation, while men tend to supervise children as their sole use of time." Id. at 12. There is evidence that men's childcare time is predominantly spent in play, while women take on a disproportionate share of routine care. See Pleck, supra note 29, at 261. Entertaining, teaching, and playing with children would appear to have more "consumption" value than dressing, bathing, feeding, and changing them, although it is unclear whether the

joy the fruits of domestic labor or reap the benefits of a well-cared-
for child. Nor is it inconsistent with women experiencing most
housework and much childcare as work—where "work" is defined
as an activity that, despite producing valuable benefits, one would
prefer, if given a choice, to have performed by someone else. Nevertheless, the prediction that women will do more of the work that
generates significant "positive" externalities for the family effectively creates divergent intramarital threat points, which will necessarily influence the agreements that couples will strike.[118]

III. The Bargaining Model and Egalitarian Marriage

This Article has identified several ways in which women's threat
points within marriage might differ on average from men's. In
short, men are generally better off premaritally, extramaritally, and
intramaritally. In light of the general observation that men tend to
have better alternatives to marital agreement than women, what
does bargaining theory have to say about the prospects for egalitarian marriage?

To answer this question, one must return to the observation that
the marital bargain is a function both of threat points (which fix the
negotiation set and the size of the bargaining surplus) and the
process of negotiation (which determines the allocation of the bargaining surplus). The most fundamental insight of the bargaining
model is that the alternatives to agreement that are available to
each partner limit how good a bargain the other partner can obtain;

---

sexes differ in their assessments of these activities. Finally, it may be the case that
men on average get less intrinsic satisfaction (or consumption value) from caring for
children, or that the positive marginal utility of the activity drops off more rapidly for
men than for women, so that the crossover from leisure to work happens sooner for
men. Thus, men may find a given amount of childcare responsibility more onerous
than women.

[118] There is yet another reason why women may be more reluctant than men to
withdraw their contribution to the marriage under conditions of marital discord, regardless of the nature of that contribution. When both spouses are better off at odds
than divorced, the wife is likely to be more cautious in choosing her strategy because
the husband's divorce utility will lie closer to his disharmonious intramarital utility
than will the wife's. That is because the husband's exit threat point will on average
be higher than the wife's, and this higher extramarital utility might tend to "crowd,"
or more closely shadow, the husband's intramarital utility in the event marital relations break down. If that is the case, the wife might be more wary about adopting a
strategy that inflicts too much unhappiness on her husband, because she might
"overshoot" and drive him away.

those alternatives set a lower limit on the share each spouse will rationally accept. This conclusion follows from the simple assumption that each bargainer seeks to maximize his or her own utility.[119] If we make the further assumption that the marriages that are contracted will run the full gamut of potential mutually advantageous relationships, then we can show that there will be some number of marital deals that will be inegalitarian. There will be some, however, that have at least the potential for equal division. Among those in which equality is at least a possibility, we can identify the conditions that tend to be conducive to equal, or more equal, allocations of well-being within marriage. Finally, we can apply additional principles that govern the actual conduct of bargaining to predict that, even among those relationships with the potential for equality, egalitarian deals will probably be the exception rather than the rule.

A. Is Egalitarian Marriage Possible?

To derive these conclusions, it is helpful to consider a more familiar commercial analogy of a typical long-term bargaining relationship. Imagine an agreement between a firm (say, IBM) and a supplier (designated S). After initially shopping around on the market, IBM and S agree to deal with each other because each considers the arrangement the best presently available. The units invested or brought to the relationship by each partner represent, in effect, all its worldly goods. All holdings and efforts are plowed back and made available for dividing between the partners. Assume that, as in marriage, there are no legal means for enforcing any deal for a division of proceeds, and assume that each unit of output brings an identical amount of utility to each party when distributed as a payoff to that party. Thus, units of output (utility) in-

---

[119] It should be obvious that if most marital partners can do as well or better, after accounting for transaction costs and sunk costs, by switching partners—that is, when "divorce bounds" are tight, see Lundberg & Pollak, Bargaining and Distribution, supra note 56, at 153-54—then there is little scope for bargaining within marriage. But bargaining models of marriage "are motivated by the assumption that, in at least some marriages, surpluses are large enough that their distribution is worth modeling." Id. at 154.

crease each partner's welfare to the same degree. (This assumption effectively makes utility payoffs equivalent to percentage shares.)[120]

Assume IBM and S have similar pre-deal "endowments," and both agree to invest 30 units of effort and/or assets in the relationship—so their initial negotiated inputs are the same. The deal is expected to generate a profit net of the 60 unit investment of 300 units (from 360 units *total* output). The parties enter the relationship with the knowledge that IBM has the potential to enter into an alternative deal with another company, S-1, which offers IBM a net payoff (in excess of input) of 200 units. S, on the other hand, faces a maximum anticipated net payoff of 50 from an alternative deal with a company called MS.

Negotiations conducted according to our egalitarian working definition—where both partners are equally well-off, net of costs, relative to a monopoly on the pie—would produce a deal in which the partners were left with equal payoffs net of investment. In this example, where inputs are equal, those payoffs are equivalent to an equal split of the profits from the deal. Each partner gets 150 units. (It is assumed for this discussion that each partner has already recouped its 30 unit investment out of total proceeds.)

The problem with the "egalitarian" solution, however, is that it is not a feasible one for this relationship. IBM would never rationally agree to such a division, because it could do better elsewhere. If such a "solution" to any bargaining problem were demanded, IBM would seek out the partner from whom it could anticipate a share of 200.[121] IBM must receive at least 200+ units net payoff to make the deal worthwhile. For purposes of the ensuing discussion, the type of bargain in which an egalitarian division is not one to which both partners could rationally agree will be designated as a relationship that is *never egalitarian* ("NE"). See Figure 1.

---

[120] For a discussion of egalitarian marriage as equal percentage shares, see supra Sections II.C.2.a, II.C.2.c.

[121] Similarly, if IBM were offered less than 200 units by S as an inducement to enter into the relationship in the first place, IBM would decline. Of course, the share IBM would receive from an alternative deal is to some degree speculative, since that deal would also presumably be subject to the condition that any allocation that is agreed upon before the fact is unenforceable. It is assumed that IBM has sized up the situation—including anticipated total payoffs to itself and the quality of S-1's respective outside options—and feels relatively certain that the payoff from the outside deal will be greater than that produced by an egalitarian division with S.

Figure 1. "NE" Bargain

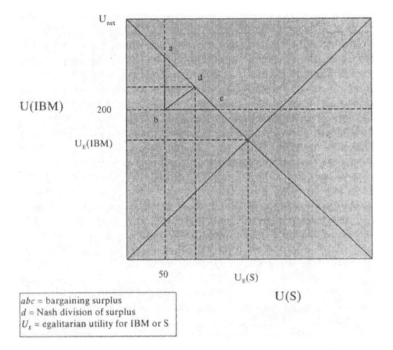

abc = bargaining surplus
d = Nash division of surplus
U_ε = egalitarian utility for IBM or S

The only realistic bargaining options for IBM and S are those that take into account the alternatives available to the partners outside the relationship—the potential partnerships between IBM and S-1, and S and MS. Because IBM and S can receive outside, net of investment, 200 units and 50 units respectively, that is the minimum each can be expected to accept from the current bargain. Once the two have received their minimum demands, there are 50 units up for grabs (300 - (200 + 50)). That is the bargaining surplus. Assuming that the units are infinitely divisible, there is theoreti-cally a limitless number of ways to split the 50 units between the parties, each of which would allow the parties to maintain the rela-tionship consistent with rational self-interest. None of those, how-

Egalitarian Marriage

ever, coincide with the egalitarian division, which requires each to receive 150 units.

Suppose the bargaining surplus were to be split equally; each party would receive 25 additional units.[122] IBM would take away a net payoff of 225 (200 + 25), and S would net 75 (50 + 25). That division diverges quite markedly from the egalitarian relationship described above. That divergence is a function of the size of the bargaining surplus—that is, the amount of joint gains available for division after each partner has received its reservation payoff. The better the outside alternatives for one partner or the other—the closer the alternatives approach the maximum possible payoff for each within the relationship—the smaller the bargaining surplus. For purposes of the example, however, it is important to see that it is not the fact that one partner has invested more in the relationship that is driving the inequality (since each partner's investment is the same). Rather, it is that something better than an egalitarian payoff awaits one partner outside the relationship. That party's superior prospects are the sole obstacle to equality in this relationship.

But, holding the outside alternatives constant, the bigger the size of the pie—corresponding to the pool for allocation—the bigger the bargaining surplus. The importance of the size of the pie—which corresponds here to the partnership proceeds—to the possibility for an egalitarian split is illustrated by modifying the example. Assume now that the deal generates a joint net payoff of 600 units, instead of 300. If the alternatives available to IBM and S on the market remain constant, then the egalitarian rule of division outlined above would generate a different result. Under an egalitarian rule of division, both partners receive total payoffs, net of their 30 unit investment, of 300 units. In contrast with the example above, this egalitarian split might satisfy both partners. Each will receive more than its expected alternative payoff (200 for IBM, and 50 for S). To be sure, the egalitarian deal described here would not coincide with an equal split of the bargaining surplus—the latter

---

[122] This would correspond to the so-called Nash bargaining solution to "splitting the pie" consisting of the 300 unit payoff. See Rasmusen, supra note 65, at 229-31 (discussing Nash bargaining solutions to the split-the-pie game, in which parties take an equal portion of the bargaining surplus); see also McElroy & Horney, supra note 56 (calculating a Nash solution to a cooperative bargaining game of household allocation); infra Section III.C (discussing Nash bargaining solution).

arrangement would necessarily be better for IBM, the partner with the best outside alternative.[123] The important point for now, however, is that the existence of a large enough profit, which has the effect here of generating a bigger bargaining surplus, allows for the possibility of conducting an egalitarian relationship consistent with both partners' rational self-interest. Such a relationship will be designated as *potentially egalitarian* ("PE"). See Figure 2.

Figure 2. "PE" Bargain

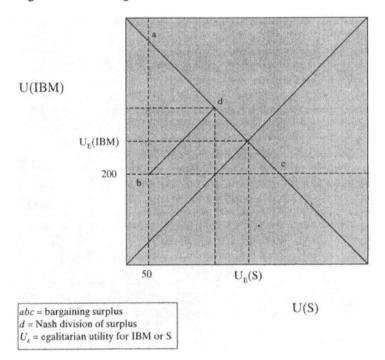

abc = bargaining surplus
d = Nash division of surplus
U_E = egalitarian utility for IBM or S

---

[123] If the bargaining surplus of 350, which is calculated by subtracting the sum total of the value of each party's outside alternatives from the 600 unit total proceeds, or 600 - (200 + 50), were to be split equally (yielding 175), then IBM would enjoy a net payoff from the deal of 375 (200 + 175) and S would enjoy 225 (50 + 175).

1998]   *Egalitarian Marriage*   565

B. Factors Affecting the Potential for Equality

Because maintaining such a relationship would benefit both parties, it can be predicted that there will be a considerable number of NE marriages—those within which equality of percentage shares of welfare is impossible because inconsistent with one person's (typically, the husband's) rational consent to continue within the relationship. But there will also be many PE relationships—those in which an egalitarian allocation is possible.

What can be said about PE marriages? Those are relationships in which there are enough resources available for sharing between the spouses to permit each to receive equal percentage utility, or to get their way to the same extent, without making the relationship less desirable (net of transaction costs) than alternatives available to either party.

A simplified paradigm using parameters relevant to marital division suggests that the potential for equality is greatest where the woman's or man's contribution (or marriage-specific investment) in the present marriage is small, or the man's specific investment in any alternative to the marriage is large relative to the investment in the current marriage and the man's expected payoff outside the marriage is small.[124]

---

[124] Assuming units of utility are normalized interpersonally, this would mean that the marital surplus (MS), which is the sum of payoffs net of costs, must be greater than twice as much as the next best alternative for the spouse with the best alternative to an agreement, assumed here to be the husband. That best alternative is designated as TH (or husband's threat point). Therefore: $MS/2 > TH$.

MS is assumed to be some function of the wife's income $I(W)$, the husband's income $I(H)$, and all other resources generated within or contributed to the marriage (R), net of each partner's contribution, which is the total utility expended to generate all monetary and nonmonetary resources and other potential benefits accruing to the unit. Those contributions are designated as $C(W)$ (wife's contribution) and $C(H)$ (husband's). The latter factors are assumed to have negative value. For simplicity, children's efforts are ignored, and their value and consumption included in R. The husband's threat point is assumed to be a function of his income $I(H)$ and his expected utility from divorce—the best alternative awaiting him outside the marriage. That alternative is represented by some cumulative function of the husband's income plus any additional expected payoff outside the marriage, $A(H)$ (which takes into account the probability of remarriage, and its attendant benefits), minus a term representing the total effort the husband must expend outside of marriage, $CA(H)$. A PE marriage, then, is one in which:

$$MS\ (I(W),\ I(H),\ R,\ C(H),\ C(W)) > 2TH\ (I(H),\ A(H),\ CA(H)).$$

In general, any large divergence in the spouses' prospects outside the marriage, from whatever source, makes equality in marriage less likely. For example, the paradigm reveals that the difference between spouses' earned incomes affects the possibility of an egalitarian marriage. The more the husband's income exceeds the wife's, the less likely is the possibility of an egalitarian allocation. As the husband's earnings rise relative to the wife's, his extramarital position relative to hers improves. To be sure, the husband's high earnings tends to enlarge the pool of assets to bargain over, which favors equality. But that effect will be offset by the elevation of the husband's relative exit threat, which tends to move the egalitarian point outside of the negotiation set. As the wife's income rises to the level of the husband's, the wife's exit advantage is bolstered, which decreases the size of the bargaining surplus.[125] But this reduction makes it more likely that an egalitarian allocation will fall within the feasible negotiation set. In sum, for a fixed amount of total income, and a fixed size of the marital pie, there is more room for equality as incomes converge. Concomitantly, the more unequal the incomes (in favor of the husband), the smaller the possibility, *ceteris paribus*, of an equal split.

All else, however, is not always equal. In the equation, the size of the marital surplus also affects the possibility for an egalitarian split. The marital surplus includes those resources that owe their existence to the marriage. The size of the marital surplus is determined by the amount of resources available for allocation within the marriage, and the amount of resources available for division affects the possibility of equal division, as the IBM/S example demonstrates. Holding constant the parties' threat points or alternatives to agreement, a larger marital surplus translates into a larger bargaining surplus. The larger the pool of resources available for division, the greater the possibility of equal division.

MS increases as I(W), I(H), and R rise and C(H) and C(W) fall. TH increases as I(H) and A(H) rise and CA(H) falls. This indicates that the possibility of an egalitarian marriage is more likely when the following factors are large: R, I(W), and CA(H). It is less likely when the following factors are large: I(H), C(W), C(H), and A(H).

[125] Bargaining theory predicts that equal spousal incomes, all else being equal, will destabilize marriage by reducing the space for possible bargaining. This effect would be independent of the absolute level of income for each. See Lundberg & Pollak, Bargaining and Distribution, supra note 56, at 148.

In considering the factors that affect the potential for marital equality, it is helpful to divide marriages into two types, recognizing that the latter includes a variety of relationships: traditional marriages and dual-earner marriages. Traditional marriages are uniform at least insofar as the spouses take on conventional sex roles; the husband is the breadwinner, and the wife works solely in the domestic sphere. In dual-earner marriages, on the other hand, the husband and wife both work for pay. Dual-earner marriages are quite varied, with the continuum anchored by relationships in which both spouses earn roughly comparable incomes and spend roughly comparable amounts of time at paid work.

Which type of marriage is more likely to be compatible with egalitarianism? The answer is not at all obvious. For traditional marriages, there are two conflicting sets of factors at work. The sharp disparity in earned income tends to raise the husband's threat point relative to the wife's, pushing the negotiation set away from equality. Offsetting that asymmetry, however, are factors that tend to increase the net marital surplus, or the utility for sharing among family members.

One important factor determining the size of the surplus is the degree of concern that each spouse has for the other and, thus, the degree of vicarious utility each spouse gains from the other's satisfaction. The performance of an unpaid service can generate benefits of various kinds. If the spouse who performs a task (say, cooking a meal) gets vicarious satisfaction from the other's enjoyment (which is above and beyond any consumption value from eating the food) then the total utility generated by a particular quantity of effort will rise, and this will add to the marital surplus. Increasing the marital surplus increases the marital pool (or size of the pie), which increases the possibility, *ceteris paribus*, for an equal split of relative satisfaction. This indicates that the possibility for equality may be enhanced by active love, caring, and altruism within marriage. Moreover, the more the cook enjoys cooking, the greater the contribution to the net marital surplus, because the effort costs the cook less.[126] Either way, the possibility of equality is increased.

---

[126] In the foregoing calculation, this reduces the value of C(W) for the cook, rather than directly adding to the value of R. See supra note 124.

Today, women are not forced to adopt the role of traditional wife. They have a spectrum of choices. It follows that women who elect conventional roles may comprise a self-selected and unrepresentative sample of all women. Women who stay home may thus have a greater than average taste for domestic work or may derive more than average satisfaction from nurturing or from rendering direct services to others. At a given level of service provided for family members, a woman of this type may experience a higher level of well-being, and comparatively less of her well-being will come at other family members' expense. Putting marital caring to work through domesticity may decrease the degree to which one spouse's utility is directly traded off with the other's.[127]

---

[127] As the economist Yoram Weiss puts it, altruism can have the effect of "reduc[ing] the range of disagreement. That is, the parties, if they had power to determine the outcome unilaterally, will choose actions which are relatively close." Weiss, supra note 41, at 19.

It is possible to overstate the difference between women who choose to work for pay and those who choose to work exclusively at home. One can speculate that there has been an evolution over time in the "utility profile" of women who choose to stay home full-time to care for their children. See, e.g., Danielle Crittenden, Turning Back the Clock, Women's Q., Autumn 1996, at 6, 6-7 (comparing the "old traditionalist"—who places greater emphasis on housekeeping and catering to husbands—to the "new traditionalist"—who is primarily focused on attentive childrearing). One at-home mother, in describing her motivation for staying home, has asserted that at-home moms "look upon housework the same way everyone else does: as a tedious necessity. Our real job . . . is caring for and teaching our children." Pauline A. Connole, Letter to the Editor, Mother, Not Housekeeper, Wash. Post, Jan. 29, 1997, at A20. This suggests that most variation among women will currently be observed, not in utility functions for homemaking tasks, but in preferences for time with children and views about the importance of intensive parental attention.

There are other reasons to exercise caution in advancing generalizations about working and stay-at-home women. The taste for domesticity is only one component of the decision whether to work for pay. That decision is also influenced by such factors as the market wage a woman can command (which is in turn based on educational, geographic, and economic factors) and the direct and opportunity costs of going out to work (such as transportation, childcare, taxes, clothing, possible decreased quality of household production, and psychic costs of separation from children). Moreover, the so-called "bargaining squeeze," see infra Section IV.C, describes the perpetuation of role divisions that does not depend on pronounced differences in preferences, but requires only that there be some small initial inequality in responsibility for household work. As that analysis reveals, women's choices may be as imperfect a guide to the magnitude of their differences with each other as they are to their differences with men, because choices are a complex function of many factors that include the power to "get one's way." Nonetheless, where economic and social factors bearing on the costs and payoffs of work are similar, different women will still make different choices. These could turn on variations in the "taste for domesticity" or for caring

Of course, a working woman serves her family by earning income and may get considerable consumption value from her work, just as the housewife does from hers. This would appear to complicate a comparison between the payoffs different women receive from the range of services they provide their families. By definition, however, some considerable part of the yield from paid work is not part of marital surplus. Although marriage makes possible the purchase of public goods and enjoyment of economies of scale, most of the paid work would presumably be done, and the income enjoyed by the earner, regardless of marital status.[128]

Some comparison is possible, however, because even in dual-earner families domestic services must somehow be performed. The foregoing analysis provides reason to believe that domestic services provided in dual-earner families generate less utility than equivalent services within traditional households. That is not just because the dual-earner provider—usually the wife—probably gets less consumption value and less vicarious pleasure from providing domestic services than a housewife. It is also because the services are provided under conditions that may increase their cost of production, and probably decrease their quality.[129] The housewife's

---

work carried on within a private sphere, as compared to the taste for the kinds of work available for pay.

Finally, to assert that housewives may get greater enjoyment from "doing for others" than working women is not to imply that dual-earner marriages lack love or caring. Rather, the difference may lie in the choices of how, and to what degree, to "put love to work" in direct service to others. Many husbands who do not do any housework surely consider themselves "loving." The ways in which they choose to exercise their caring tendencies—if at all—will be affected by other tastes and preferences, as these play out under bargaining constraints and in the face of more or less material scarcity. See infra note 133.

[128] Marriage may induce spouses—especially men—to work harder and earn more. That increment in earnings will count as part of the surplus. See Linda J. Waite, Does Marriage Matter?, Presidential Address to the Population Association of America 6 (Apr. 8, 1995) (transcript on file with the Virginia Law Review Association) (discussing the increased earnings of married men); Jane Waldfogel, Understanding the "Family Gap" in Pay for Women with Children, J. Econ. Persp., Winter 1998, at 137, 143 (describing as "well-established" the fact that married men earn more than single men); Waite, supra note 40, at 28-30 (noting, in addition to other benefits, the higher household wealth among most married individuals, compared to unmarried ones).

[129] Because the housewife spends more time overall on housework, she may be able to generate gains from specialization for each additional hour of work and provide a higher quality product for a given amount of effort. For dual-earner spouses who must perform domestic tasks in off-work hours, the specialization function is far

first and last hours of effort go into providing household services. Domestic services provided by wage earners require greater effort, and cost more, because that effort is added to many hours of paid effort.[130] Moreover, the housewife's first and last hours of effort go into direct service to others, and they bring her vicarious pleasure. Even if the working wife enjoys doing for others as much as the housewife, fewer of her total working hours are spent in hands-on caring or nurturing activities. Consequently, she gets less of the extra vicarious satisfaction from her efforts (although this effect may be mitigated somewhat by the housewife's diminishing returns in vicarious satisfaction with each hour of work). Finally, the pace and pressure of domestic work are greater for wage earners, who may attempt to complete each task in a shorter period of time. The frantic working wife's preparation of dinner, squeezed into half an hour, may come at greater cost (and produce a less tasty meal) than the housewife's two hours spent in unhurried preparation. In sum, a housewife/breadwinner arrangement, other factors being equal, may produce a larger marital pie than a comparable dual-earner arrangement by wringing larger positive utility gains from the sum total of activities (wage plus non-wage production) that all households must conduct.[131]

---

shallower, and the quality of the product is probably reduced. This is another way of saying, as Gary Becker has asserted, that housewives are more efficient producers of domestic services than members of working couples. See Becker, Treatise, supra note 36, at 21-32.

This does not exclude the possibility, as already discussed, see supra note 64, that the most efficient arrangement for some couples—especially the high earners—is to hire household help. One of the criticisms of Gary Becker's economics of the household is that he takes too little account of the gains from specialization by women through the hiring of paid help and contracting out of services. See Bergmann, supra note 7, at 260 (discussing the "cash-paying" solution); Margaret F. Brinig, Comment on Jana Singer's *Alimony and Efficiency*, 82 Geo. L.J. 2461, 2471 (1994) (noting that Becker and others "assume it is not 'efficient' to hire someone else to do the wash or clean the house").

[130] The more that responsibility is exclusively placed on one member of the couple, the steeper the increase in costs for an equal amount of work. See infra note 188 (discussing diminishing returns on work and leisure as each person moves towards relative monopoly on each).

[131] The main objection to this conclusion would stem from the observation that the dual-earner wife's efforts in the market also contribute to the well-being of others: She earns money that can be invested in public goods or other items for family members. But that is just a direct measure of the production value of her work. Working to provide goods for the enjoyment of oneself and others, and getting vicarious pleasure from others' enjoyment of those goods (or services provided in lieu of them)

If traditional role-divided couples do indeed come out somewhat ahead, as speculated, in generating utility from comparable effort, Gary Becker's "altruistic head of household" model[132] is turned on its head. To the extent there may be greater gains to traditional households, it is the altruism of the household caretaker—usually a woman—that makes those marginal gains possible.[133] That larger pie will tend to offset the inequality-producing influence of the disparity between incomes. It does not follow, however, that the cause of egalitarian marriage would be advanced by moving women back into the home since the equalizing effect is only partly dependent on the mechanics of division of labor. It is also a function of the idiosyncratic preferences and tastes of those who feel comfortable

---

are conceptually distinct. The latter can be added to the former, but need not be. Still, a working wife may take "extra" vicarious pride in providing materially for her family, in a way that may at least partly offset the loss of vicarious pleasure in forgone nurturing work.

[132] See supra note 36 (discussing Becker's model).

[133] This discussion does not entail the conclusion, nor does it require the assumption, that women generally are more altruistic than men, or that housewives are more altruistic than working women. (It also does not rule out, however, that both propositions might be true.) See infra Section IV.B.1 (discussing lessons of bargaining theory). It is necessary to distinguish here between altruism as a general trait (which is the tendency or capacity to enjoy contributing to others' well-being) and the specific ways in which altruism is actually brought to bear. The gender role conventions surrounding the conduct of marital relations; women's possibly average greater taste for domestic activities and hands-on, unmediated caretaking; and the power balance created by the bargaining relationship may all combine to push women of altruistic bent to express their altruism through direct service to family members—what is commonly referred to as "nurturing." The point is that nurturing is not the same as altruism. Rather, nurturing is one form that altruism can take.

Performing domestic services and being responsible for caring for others within the family is still costly for the caretaker, man or woman. It thus generates some negative utility. The person with more power in the family (generally the husband) will thus do less caretaking, even if that person is more altruistic than the average person and even if more altruistic than his or her spouse. Second, altruistic persons may choose very different avenues for expressing their concern for others, depending on interests and tastes that have nothing to do with altruism as such. (Ralph Nader could be said to be altruistic, but he might not make a very good housewife.) Expressing altruism through domesticity may carry different appeal for the average man and woman, and thus the private domestic realm may in fact provide fewer opportunities to men than to women to act on their altruism in preferred ways.

Finally, there are strong social conventions that make domestic activity generally more costly to men than women. See infra Section IV.A.1. The existence of these factors explains why the fact that family caretakers are usually women is not necessarily inconsistent with the proposition that men and women are equally altruistic.

in traditional female roles. Increasing the number of housewives who hate domesticity will not generally make marriage more equal.

The foregoing discussion reveals a broader point: The more love, the more the possibility for equality. When spouses care about each other, there is more overlap in their utility functions. One spouse's satisfaction automatically increases the other's happiness, at least to some extent. Where there is little altruism and little satisfaction in the other person's happiness, the spouses move closer to a zero-sum game in which one person's gain is the other's loss. The most efficient marriages may be those in which there is not just caring, but *active* caring. In such relationships, there is an even more pronounced divergence from strict linearity in the tradeoff of utilities because one or both spouses find happiness engaging in activities that directly increase the well-being of the other. This increases the effective size of the marital surplus. And the greater the surplus, the greater the room for equality as compared to a relationship marked by a more linear zero-sum tradeoff. Active caring can sometimes transform an NE deal into a PE one. See Figure 3.

Figure 3.

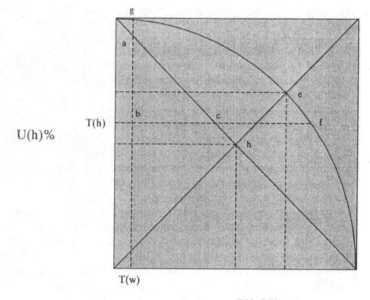

U(h)%

T(h)

T(w)

U(w)%

T(h) and *T(w)* = threat points of husband and wife
U(h) and *U(w)* = utility of husband and wife
abc = bargaining surplus for zero-sum deal
gbf = bargaining surplus for non-zero-sum deal
e = egalitarian split for non-zero-sum deal (which lies within negotiation set for that deal, gbf)
h = egalitarian split for zero-sum deal (which lies outside negotiation set for that deal, abc)

Two other factors merit further discussion, as they affect the possibility for an equal split of resources between the parties. The first is monetary income. As has already been suggested, the greater the income, the greater the quantity of marital resources available for division between the parties.[134] More income buys more goods,

---

[134] See supra Section III.B.

both public and private, which add to utility for both parties. But apart from the effects on the size of the pie, greater wealth also increases the practical potential for side-payments: Because not all assets are tied up in shared public goods, some of the surplus generated by one spouse's extra efforts can be kicked back in monetary form for that spouse's discretionary use.[135] Because having two earners tends to make couples financially better off, the income factor will tend to foster equality among dual-earner couples (especially the more affluent), thus offsetting somewhat the surplus-enhancing effects of role division.[136]

The final point to be gleaned from the bargaining paradigm is the importance of the cost of outside alternatives relative to the cost of the current marriage for the spouse with the best alternatives, which is assumed to be the husband. If remarriage is an important alternative, this suggests that the prospects for egalitarian marriage are minimized if the marriage market is dominated by women who demand few marriage-specific investments from men—as when, for example, men are generally expected to take on a small share of domestic responsibility and can devote themselves to paid work and leisure.[137] If most women demand little marriage-specific investment—whether from adherence to convention, poor bargaining power, or just plain personal preference—then it becomes more difficult for a few women to hold out for a lot more from men without pushing these men closer to their threat point or beyond and past their reservation price. This suggests that each woman's marital bargain can never be entirely independent of the marriage that other women are willing to make. Wives must bargain in the shadow of the market in a double sense—not just with the knowledge of the availability of potential rivals for their hus-

---

[135] See supra note 42 (discussing side-payments).

[136] The foregoing discussion should not suggest that having both spouses work for pay could never be the more efficient arrangement overall. See Becker, supra note 34, at 151 (acknowledging that both spouses working for pay may be an optimal arrangement as "families [become] smaller, divorce more common, and earning opportunities for women improve[]"); see also Brinig, supra note 129, at 2469-73 (creating a model to demonstrate how a dual-earner arrangement could be the most efficient for some couples).

[137] Under the relationship described by the equation supra note 124, the chance for an egalitarian split decreases when $CA(H)$ (a term that includes the husband's alternative marriage-specific input) becomes small absolutely and small relative to $C(H)$ (which includes a component of the husband's current marriage-specific input).

bands' affections, but also of the availability of rivals willing to offer a more favorable deal.[138]

C. The Influence of the Bargaining Process

Up to this point, the discussion has focused on whether and when egalitarian marriage is possible. We can predict that some rational, self-interested individuals will contract marriages that are unequal—those relationships will never be egalitarian (NE). But what of the remaining unions? Bargaining theory teaches that just because an egalitarian split is possible does not mean it will occur. The discussion in this Section is concerned with the likelihood that equality will be realized and with the conditions that will tend to foster or impede it.

If we take as given each party's reservation price and thus the negotiation set (that is, the possible set of bargains that are consistent with rational self-interest), what determines which bargain within that range will be struck? Game theorists have attempted to identify the factors that influence the actual allocation of shares in situations that require "splitting a pie." In predicting the outcome of real-life bargaining, idealized games can only take one so far. There is a large experimental literature suggesting that bargainers often deviate from the behaviors predicted from models based on perfect rationality and complete information. Social scientists have used empirical data to add richness to their models in an attempt to predict what real people will do.[139] Because there are so many psychological variables, analysis of the bargaining process has remained speculative and inexact.

The earliest models of how utilities would be divided within a feasible negotiation set were static and highly theoretical: They did not attempt to play out an actual bargaining sequence of alternat-

---

[138] See infra Sections V.C-D, V.E.2 (discussing the relationship between marital bargaining and "deals" available on the marriage market).

[139] See, e.g., Margaret A. Neale & Max H. Bazerman, Cognition and Rationality in Negotiation (1991); Raiffa, supra note 73, at 44-65; Rasmusen, supra note 65, at 227-43 (summarizing attempts to model real-life, dynamic bargaining process); Martin Shubik, Game Theory in the Social Sciences 395-98 (1982); Colin F. Camerer, Progress in Behavioral Game Theory, J. Econ. Persp., Fall 1997, at 166; Alvin E. Roth, Bargaining Experiments, *in* The Handbook of Experimental Economics 253 (John H. Kagel & Alvin E. Roth eds., 1995) (summarizing research on bargainers' behavior in various simulated bargaining games).

ing offers and counteroffers, but rather sought solutions that satisfied certain simple conditions and were stable in that no player
would have a rational incentive to deviate from his choices. The
most famous of these is the Nash bargaining solution. Under that
scenario, two players called upon to split a pie will divide the bargaining surplus—as delimited by each bargainer's threat point or
reservation price—down the middle, so that each has an equal share.[140]

The equal-split-of-bargaining-surplus solution, although a theoretical construct not meant as a "predictive exercise,"[141] has enormous intuitive and normative appeal as a "solution" to a vast
range of bargaining problems. It is also useful for understanding
the concept of bargaining power, and the factors that influence it.
Bargaining power is reflected in one party's ability to procure a
particular share of the bargained-for resources. Bargaining power
is in part a function of threat advantage—which determines the
feasible negotiation set—but it is also a function of a party's ability
to maneuver the other into accepting a proposed position within
the negotiation set. While there is no *a priori* reason to believe
that real-life bargaining will result in parties' adopting the Nash
solution—an equal split of the bargaining surplus—that solution
can be used as the starting point for gauging the influence of factors that might give parties an advantage in real-world bargaining.[142] It is not implausible to assume that an equal split of the bar-

---

[140] See supra note 122 (outlining a Nash solution for the IBM/S game); Baird, Gertner & Picker, supra note 48, at 21-23; Rasmusen, supra note 65, at 229 ("Nash's objective was to pick axioms that would characterize the agreement the two players
would anticipate making with each other."); Shubik, supra note 139, at 200, 240
(defining a Nash equilibrium point for noncooperative games and comparing a Nash
solution to those of two alternative models). The idealized Nash bargaining solution
was originally proposed for the so-called cooperative bargaining game. A cooperative game, as already noted, see supra note 106, is one in which the parties can make
enforceable and binding agreements as to payoffs (or in which a payoff division is
imposed by fiat "from above"), as opposed to a noncooperative bargaining game in
which any agreement is not binding in the sense that there is no externally imposed
penalty for defecting from it. Many of the principles discussed herein, however, apply also to noncooperative bargains—those enforced solely through self-help.

[141] Sen, supra note 32, at 133 n.14.

[142] Alan Wertheimer describes the Nash solution as one to which rational actors
would consent in a bargaining problem that is "fully described by a set of possible
outcomes in terms of the agent's utilities and by a 'threat point' or no transaction alternative." Wertheimer, supra note 32, at 218-19 n.24. He explains that "[t]he rational bargaining view of fair transactions is *not* a pure procedural view.... To the

gaining surplus should result if the parties possess perfect information and if all the factors that might affect the conduct of the bargaining are in balance as between them. In this sanitized setup, the
allocation of the cooperative surplus will be a straightforward reflection of the "relative strength of the parties' threat advantages."[143] Put another way, starting from a theoretical position of
an equal division of a bargaining surplus in a typical split-the-pie
game, the ability of one party to persuade the other to deviate from
that position is likely to reflect some bargaining advantage other
than that conferred simply by the lower limit on what each bargainer will rationally accept.

In the PE case, the egalitarian split lies within the feasible negotiation set. As the IBM/S example illustrates, an equal split of the
bargaining surplus will not precisely coincide with an egalitarian
division of overall payoffs if the parties' threat points differ at all.
The Nash solution will favor the person with the better outside alternatives. See Figure 4.

---

contrary. It attempts to identify the terms on which *fully* rational parties *would*
agree." Id. at 218-19 n.24. The conception, however, has a procedural analogue: It
can be used to describe a bargain that would be struck if the influence of factors that
might confer procedural advantages—including strategic or psychological advantages that
affect the negotiating process—are either absent or are evenly matched on both sides.

The Nash bargaining solution does not represent the only attempt to provide a de-
terminate answer to the bargaining "division problem" for rational actors. See Jules
L. Coleman, Risks and Wrongs 37 (1992) (distinguishing the division problem from
the compliance problem in constructing schemes for rational cooperation). For example, David Gauthier maintains that rational bargainers should, or would, abide by
the principle of "minimax relative concession," which seeks to minimize the difference in utility as between the bargainers relative to each person's best bargain.
Gauthier, supra note 46, at 137; see also Wertheimer, note 32, at 219 (describing
Gauthier's theory). Whether this theory is predictive or normative, however, is not
entirely clear. The Nash solution can be viewed as predictive only in the most ideal
sense. It predicts the bargain that would result if all factors that affect bargaining behavior and bargaining strength (except threat point) are taken out of the equation or
are set equal on both sides. In effect, it tells us what would happen if a person bargained with his *Doppelgänger*.

[143] Coleman, supra note 142, at 273.

Figure 4.

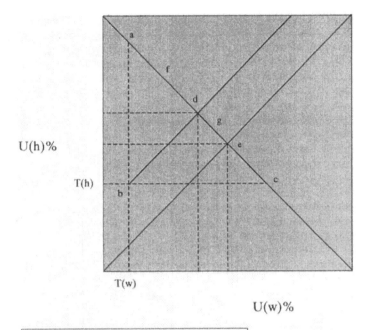

T(h) and *T(w)* = threat points of husband and wife	
abc = bargaining surplus	
d = Nash solution	
e = egalitarian split	
see text for *f* and *g*	

Thus, if the parties have different threat points but otherwise do not differ on traits and elements that confer actual bargaining advantage, they still will not have an egalitarian marriage. The outcome of their bargaining process will be point *d* (equal division of bargaining surplus utility), rather than point *e* (equal percentage net utility). The greater the divergence in their threat points, the more the actual bargain struck will deviate from the egalitarian ideal.[144]

These observations suggest that even if men and women bargained the same way within a potentially egalitarian relationship, the benefits of marriage would on average go disproportionately to men. This effect would be due *solely* to factors that enhance men's extramarital and intramarital threat advantage: most importantly, men's higher extramarital utility, better remarriage prospects, and longer reproductive life; less importantly, their greater earning power and their somewhat different preference set for providing and enjoying domestic and child-oriented "public goods." These factors alone explain the lion's share of men's bargaining advantage.

But there is reason to believe that the realities of the negotiating process only worsen the imbalance. A number of strategic and psychological factors have the potential to affect negotiating skills or to confer bargaining advantage. It has been suggested that women and men are not equally effective negotiators because they may differ systematically in various ways that determine the ability to strike a favorable bargain within the parameters that fix the negotiation set. These include "toughness, patience, perceptiveness,"[145] risk averseness,[146] tolerance for conflict, aggressiveness, "taste for cooperation,"[147] the differential concerns raised by the

---

[144] As Figure 3 illustrates (convex frontier), the less complete the tradeoff in the party's well-being (i.e., the more "caring"), the closer the Nash solution will be to the egalitarian ideal. This illustrates the principle that love tends to promote equality.

[145] See Wertheimer, supra note 32, at 64.

[146] There is a striking paucity of research supporting the frequently encountered assertion that men and women differ in their preferences for risk. Among the behavioral evidence that is commonly cited is male predominance in the incidence of criminal behavior, auto accidents, accidental death, and substance abuse. See, e.g., Bureau of Justice Statistics, U.S. Dep't of Justice, Sourcebook of Criminal Justice Statistics, 1996, at 380 tbl.4.8 (Kathleen Maguire & Ann L. Pastore eds., 1997) (presenting sex ratio of arrests for criminal offenses); National Highway Traffic Safety Admin., U.S. Dep't of Transp., Traffic Safety Facts, 1994, at 95 fig.23 (1995) (presenting data on sex ratio of involvement in motor vehicle accidents).

[147] Commentators have attempted to capture women's purportedly inferior negotiating ability in various ways, only some of which go more narrowly to negotiating ability as characterized herein. See, e.g., Rose, supra note 55; see also England, supra note 5, at 25 (asserting that women more often operate on a "connective model" that "takes both one's own and a connected other's utility as roughly of equal importance, regardless of who is in a stronger bargaining position," whereas men more often "see[] self-interested behavior as natural, and take[] advantage of being in a 'power-over' bargaining position when it occurs"); England & Kilbourne, supra note 5, at

presence of "hostages" (such as children),[148] the availability and willingness to use credible commitment strategies or first-mover advantages,[149] the sense of entitlement and notion of fairness,[150] and the time-dependent costs of disagreement.[151]

These factors are quite diverse and have disparate roles in the bargaining process. Moreover, there are a number of possible ways to conceptualize these elements and their effects on the conduct of bargaining and its outcome.[152] This is not the place for a comprehensive analysis of all factors that could possibly affect the conduct of bargaining. For the purposes of this Article, the best way to analyze the problem of weakness in the negotiating process is to focus on some of the general elements that might affect the psychology of bargaining over the allocation of resources within the bargaining set. The psychology of marital bargaining is critically affected by three closely related phenomena that determine how hard each partner will press his or her bargain: (1) the relative potency of defection threats, (2) the sense of entitlement, and (3) the endowment effect. In one way or another, these factors reflect how marital bargaining takes place in the shadow of the market. Each brings to bear the influence of extramarital market conditions and values upon the conduct of negotiations within the private, off-market relationship of marriage.

171-78 (discussing men's and women's possible difference in perception and use of power); Mahony, supra note 16, at 34 (arguing that the widely held perception that women have a stronger desire for cooperation puts women at a bargaining disadvantage); Rose, supra note 55, at 423 (discussing how perceptions of women's taste for cooperation may help put them at a disadvantage in acquiring property).

[148] See England & Kilbourne, supra note 5, at 172-73; Mnookin & Kornhauser, supra note 89, at 966-68; Rose, supra note 55, at 445.

[149] See Mahony, supra note 16, at 48-51 (noting that the marital partner with the higher status or the more demanding job can more persuasively assert the difficulty of taking on domestic responsibilities); see also Baird, Gertner & Pickner, supra note 48, at 43 (discussing first mover advantage in dynamic models of bargaining games); Rasmusen, supra note 65, at 35 (same).

[150] See infra note 164 and accompanying text.

[151] Another important factor that can influence bargaining is access to information about payoffs and preferences. For discussion of the importance of information in the conduct of bargaining, see Colin F. Camerer & George Loewenstein, Information, Fairness, and Efficiency in Bargaining, in Psychological Perspectives on Justice: Theory and Applications 155 (Barbara A. Mellers & Jonathan Baron eds., 1993).

[152] For example, some may be viewed not as going precisely to bargaining "strategy," but rather as affecting the utility value of the outcome of the bargain itself. See supra note 147; infra Section IV.B.2.

The first factor—the relative potency of defection threats—depends on the parties' respective alternatives to an agreement. In addition to fixing the parties' reservation prices, the alternatives also have a distinct effect on the psychology of bargaining: The party with the best alternatives has the more credible threat of walking away if the other party fails to cooperate. That is true even if both parties stand to gain from the proposed agreement, and thus would not rationally abandon it.[153] The result of this strategic advantage is that the party with the less desirable outside options will often be more reluctant to drive a hard bargain or more willing to make concessions, for fear that the other party will call the deal off.[154] If a wife has more to lose from marital discord or

---

[153] As long as both parties stand to gain by agreeing rather than failing to agree on a bargain, a rational actor's threat of defection or noncooperation is not strictly credible, even if that party has comparatively less to lose. See Gauthier, supra note 46, at 185; Sen, supra note 32, at 135 & n.21 (noting that "there are some very basic difficulties with any theory of threats, since it has to deal with situations *after* the bargaining has failed" when "the threatener has no obvious interest in carrying out the threat").

Nevertheless, different threat points can be expected to influence the conduct and outcome of actual bargaining because the danger of failure to reach an agreement is not illusory in real life. As Alan Wertheimer points out, "there is no reason to assume that just because both parties will gain from any division of the social surplus, they will find their way to such an agreement, just as there is no reason to assume that because both parties will gain from the cooperative solution to the prisoner's dilemma, they will both cooperate." Wertheimer, supra note 32, at 237. One reason a positive-sum deal may not go through is that refusal to cooperate can be part of a larger successful strategy; carrying out holdout threats helps parties enhance their credibility and discourages the other party's taking advantage in iterative bargaining situations. Thus a strategy that is a short-term loser may be a long-term winner. See Coleman, supra note 142, at 273; Robert H. Frank, Passions Within Reason: The Strategic Role of the Emotions, *in* 2 Applied Behavioural Economics 769, 774 (Shlomo Maital ed., 1988). But regardless of whether it confers tactical advantage, "breakdown" is always possible between real people, who are not always strictly rational. Thus, the "breakdown position" can be expected to influence the conduct of bargaining. See Sen, supra note 32, at 135 ("The breakdown position indicates the person [sic] vulnerability or strength . . . . If, in the case of a breakdown, one person is going to end up in more of a mess . . . , that is going to weaken that person's ability to secure a favorable outcome."); see also Henry Sidgwick, The Methods of Ethics 288 (7th ed. 1962) ("[I]n bargaining the less willing has the advantage.").

[154] This analysis applies where the relevant "threat point" is intramarital noncooperation as well as abandonment of the marriage. As already noted, see supra Sections II.D.3.b-c, men's intramarital threat point tends to be higher than women's. In cases where the husband's intramarital threat utility exceeds his extramarital threat advantage, the intramarital threat advantage will be especially high. In such cases, however, we can expect that the man's divorce threat advantage will more closely shadow his intramarital threat utility. That is, the distance between the average

her husband's displeasure, she will take that into account in deciding how adamantly to press her case. She must also consider the cumulative effect of dissatisfaction. A man will not divorce his wife solely because she insists he take the kids when he would rather play golf, but his forgone fun will make him disgruntled, and multiple instances of disgruntlement have a way of adding up to "I don't love you anymore." Marital bargaining can thus be said to proceed in the shadow of the market not just in the sense that each spouse's fallback position is influenced by labor market earning power and remarriage market prospects, but also because awareness of relative fallback positions in turn inhibits or emboldens each partner in the conduct of negotiations.

The second factor—the spouses' sense of entitlement to a share of rewards available from the relationship—is critically influenced by perceptions of the value of each sex's contributions and activities. As a general matter, men's contributions are considered more valuable than women's just because they come from men.[155] Experimental subjects of both sexes will rate a woman's contribution or performance lower than a man's, even when it is objectively the same.[156] Women themselves tend to undervalue their own contributions and to allocate less of a reward to themselves for a fixed amount of effort. Specifically, "when asked to split rewards between themselves and a partner," women tend to "take less reward for themselves and give more to their partners than men do," even when performance and inputs are objectively equivalent.[157] In ex-

man's extramarital and intramarital threat advantages is likely to be smaller than the average woman's. In cases where both spouses are better off fighting than splitting, a woman may nevertheless be more wary of antagonizing her spouse because the smaller margin for error presents a greater danger of overshooting and driving him to initiate divorce. In general, real life bargaining is bedeviled by imperfect information and there is always uncertainty regarding the conditions that will push the other person "over the limit." That uncertainty always makes the weaker party more cautious.

[155] See Cecilia L. Ridgeway, Interaction and the Conservation of Gender Inequality: Considering Employment, 62 Am. Soc. Rev. 218, 221 (1997).

[156] See Shelley E. Taylor, A Categorization Approach to Stereotyping, *in* Cognitive Processes in Stereotyping and Intergroup Behavior 83, 101 (David L. Hamilton ed., 1981) (describing experiments in which test subjects rated remarks lower in quality and cogency when made by a woman than when the same remarks were made by a man).

[157] Brenda Major, Gender, Justice, and the Psychology of Entitlement, *in* Sex and Gender 124, 126 (Phillip Shaver & Clyde Hendrick eds., 1987) [hereinafter Major, Justice]; see also Alice H. Eagly, Sex Differences in Social Behavior: A Social-Role Interpretation 111 (1987) (noting several experimental studies in reward allocation that demonstrate "a tendency for women to underpay themselves"); Kay Deaux,

perimental situations in which women and men were offered the same reward to complete assigned tasks, "women worked significantly longer, did more work, completed more correct work, and worked more efficiently than men."[158]

That women's contributions to the family are often denigrated in the minds of family members can be attributed not just to the devaluation of women's efforts generally, but also to the nature of what women contribute. There are two possible reasons why lesser value is attached to women's efforts. First, as a portion of total input to the family, more of women's than men's contributions are in the form of domestic services. Those services are associated with femininity. Activities considered feminine are consistently regarded as less worthy and valuable than activities considered masculine.[159] This valuation is reflected in—and perhaps reflects—the relative market value of traditionally masculine and feminine jobs. The value attached on the market and elsewhere to traditional female tasks is likely to influence the exchange value of domestic services in marital bargaining.

Second, the partner who performs more household work (typically, the woman) is necessarily providing more off-market and in-kind services to the family unit. Although there is a market for domestic services in general, the actual services a woman provides personally to the family are not openly traded or priced. In contrast, more of men's contributions come in the form of money and other tangible assets generated on the market. What happens in bargaining if the contributions of each party differ in this way—that is, some are market and some are off-market services or commodities? What determines the relative values? The answer hinges

---

From Individual Differences to Social Categories, 39 Am. Psychol. 105, 106 (1984) (describing experiments suggesting that women "predict[] a lower performance for themselves than men"); Brenda Major, Gender, Entitlement, and the Distribution of Family Labor, 49 J. Soc. Issues 141, 142-43 (1993) [hereinafter, Major, Entitlement] (tying women's tendency to take fewer rewards for effort to men's and women's sense of entitlement); Steil & Weltman, supra note 11, at 177 (citing empirical evidence that women tend "to seek less for themselves than comparable men making comparable contributions" within the marital relationship).

[158] Major, Justice, supra note 157, at 135.

[159] See Mary Anne C. Case, Disaggregating Gender from Sex and Sexual Orientation: The Effeminate Man in the Law and Feminist Jurisprudence, 105 Yale L.J. 1 (1995) (describing how activities and forms associated with femininity have lower cultural status and value).

upon another important sense in which bargaining takes place in the market's shadow: Parties may import market values into the bargaining process by allowing external criteria to influence the perception of appropriate bargaining concessions and demands. The market influences how parties value contributions that are of different types and thus are difficult to compare, if only because the market provides a ready measure of value. What does not come from the competitive market will appear less valuable than a contribution that is market-priced. Thus, the person whose contribution is in-kind and off-market—that is, the person whose contributions come largely in the form of direct and marriage-specific services to the family circle—will be deemed to contribute less than the person whose contribution comes largely in the form of money or other tangible assets.[160]

---

[160] A number of commentators have attributed the devaluation of women's contributions to the family economy to the tendency to discount "off-market" or "unpriced" contributions and to exaggerate the worth attached to contributions in the marketplace. Barbara Bergmann has described the importation of "a market idea of fairness into family life," whereby a family member with higher earnings will "buy himself out of spending certain hours doing housework," regardless of other measures of contribution or value. Bergmann, supra note 7, at 271. Amartya Sen calls the strong tendency to discount the value of nonmarket internal contributions in favor of more easily measurable (and externally priced) contributions from the marketplace the "perceived contribution response." Sen, supra note 32, at 137. He adds that

> [t]he nature of "perceived contribution" to family opulence has to be distinguished from the amount of *time* expended in working inside and outside the home. Indeed, in terms of "time allocation studies," women often seem to do astonishingly large amounts of work even when the so-called "economic" contribution is *perceived* to be relatively modest. The perception bias tends to relate to the size of the direct money earning rather than to the amount of time and effort expended . . . .

Id. at 139-40 (citations omitted). Sen describes how notions of "exchange entitlement," which are pegged to market value, produce the result that women are unable "'to see [their] work as a value-producing work.'" Id. at 144 (quoting Maria Mies, Lacemakers in Narsapur: Indian Housewives Produce for the World Market 173-74 (1982)). A greater market role can boost bargaining power by giving a woman "(1) a better breakdown position, (2) possibly a clearer perception of her individuality and well-being, and (3) a higher 'perceived contribution' to the family's economic position." Id. Finally, Shirley Burggraf describes the market invisibility of a woman's customary contribution to the family, which comes largely in the form of opportunity cost and value added to children. That invisibility fuels a pervasive tendency to take women's domestic contributions for granted and to discount their value. See Burggraf, supra note 81, at 16.

Finally, marital negotiations are heavily influenced by an "endowment effect," which pegs the exchange value of bargainers' offers to a preexisting status quo.[161] In this respect, women are hurt by the fact that bargaining rarely takes place on a clean slate. In the generic, idealized split-the-pie game, parties come to the table without a history of preexisting allocations and without preconceptions about the shares to which they are entitled. Real-life marital bargaining deviates from this ideal by taking place in the shadow of powerful cultural expectations for men and women in marriage. The conventional role divisions in marriage—in which men invest more heavily in market labor while women take on more domestic responsibility—make the worth of each spouse's contribution depend on a baseline in which the spouses either perceive themselves as possessing a presumptive entitlement or as seeking to acquire such an entitlement. The bargaining process then proceeds through a set of exchanges in which spouses propose concessions or demands that may alter the conventional baseline. If men see themselves as entitled to certain services, and women see themselves as duty-bound to provide them, then any woman who seeks to shift responsibility for those services onto her husband must purchase that shift through larger concessions than would be necessary from a neutral baseline. Likewise, men will demand greater concessions before they will consent to take that responsibility upon themselves.[162] Moreover, because individuals are generally

---

[161] See Cotter, supra note 10, at 2113 ("An endowment effect is said to arise when the price I would demand to sell something already in my possession is greater than the price I would be willing to pay to acquire that same thing if I did not already have it."); see also id. at n.188 (citing sources in the experimental social science literature concerning the psychology of endowment effects); Jeffrey L. Harrison, Egoism, Altruism, and Market Illusions: The Limits of Law and Economics, 33 UCLA L. Rev. 1309, 1358-61 (1986) (noting the implications of endowment effect research for the economic analyses of law); Herbert Hovenkamp, Legal Policy and the Endowment Effect, 20 J. Legal Stud. 225 (1991) (suggesting applications of the endowment effect to the formulation of law and policy); Cass R. Sunstein, Behavioral Analysis of Law, 64 U. Chi. L. Rev. 1175, 1179-81 (1997) (discussing behavioral manifestations of "loss aversion" as a form of endowment effect); Russell Korobkin, Note, Policymaking and the Offer/Asking Price Gap, 46 Stan. L. Rev. 663 (1994) (discussing the implications of the endowment effect for entitlement allocation policies).

[162] See Sigel, supra note 85, at 190 (commenting that "men expect to *receive* at home but to *give* at work . . . [whereas] the woman also gives at work, [but] she has to give at home as well"). Focus groups conducted by Sigel among 650 dual-earner families provide evidence of a significant endowment effect influencing men's perception of

observed to have different preferences for the risks of gains and losses, the endowment effect, like the quality of fallback options, can also influence the adamancy with which negotiating partners press their case. In experimental situations, "players are more willing to risk disagreement when bargaining over possible losses than when bargaining over possible gains."[163] Since greater sharing of a wife's traditional responsibilities represents a loss for the husband relative to the baseline, he is likely to resist concessions more firmly than his wife (who stands to gain) will insist upon them.

In practice, these three effects—"threat potency," entitlement, and endowment—all result in a wife's efforts counting for less than a husband's in any bargaining situation. The person who believes he has brought "more" into the relationship will think he deserves a better deal and will push for one. Even if contributions are objectively similar (for example, in representing an equal investment of time), the person who is viewed as bringing "less," feeling unworthy, will grant larger concessions or refrain from demanding more. Thus, a shared perception of the lesser worth of a woman's efforts—whether in the labor market or at home—will generally lead women to reduce their bargaining demands and men to increase theirs, causing women to lose out in situations that turn on hard bargaining. If "a wife's hour is not worth as much as a husband's hour, her dollar is not worth as much as his, her education and training count for less, and her attitudes carry less weight when spouses are negotiating,"[164] it is hardly surprising that women will

---

working women's contributions to the family. In general, men focused on the costs of their wives going out to work, and saw the extra income generated by their wives' employment as a mixed blessing. Id. at 163-64. This perception depended on men comparing their dual-earner existence to a more traditional baseline arrangement. The endowment effect created by that baseline allowed husbands to see their wives' income as earned at considerably greater sacrifice to the family than their own and to discount the value of that income accordingly. Thus, although husbands viewed their wives' earnings "as helping provide for the comfort of the family," id. at 164, and admitted "enjoy[ing] the higher standard-of-living their wives' employment facilitate[d]," id., they mentioned many drawbacks. Among these were decreased wifely attention, decline in quality of services, loss of the prestige and pride in the exclusive breadwinner role, and (for the more affluent) a loss of simplicity of lifestyle and an increase in consumerism from the availability of more disposable income. Id. at 163-65.

[163] Camerer, supra note 139, at 172; see also Sunstein, supra note 161, at 1179-81 (discussing behavioral evidence that an individual's displeasure from losses tends to exceed the pleasure from equivalent gains).

[164] Ruth Milkman & Eleanor Townsley, Gender and the Economy, *in* The Handbook of Economic Sociology 600, 614 (Neil J. Smelser & Richard Swedberg eds.,

come away with less of the bargaining surplus, and that the resulting bargains will deviate from the egalitarian ideal.

If women even partly share in the perception that their contributions are worth less, this carries important implications for the real-life conduct of marital relations. Bargainers' subjective perceptions of fairness can directly affect bargaining behavior. Women who think they have received a fair shake may simply cease trying to get more (even if they would be happier with a larger share).[165] But if willingness to press harder is a component of

---

1994). The effects described might also help to explain reports that many women, including those who are objectively overworked relative to their husbands, do not perceive their situation as inequitable or unfair. In the words of one researcher, many employed mothers express "a surprisingly high level of satisfaction with an objectively unfair situation." David H. Demo & Alan C. Acock, Family Diversity and the Division of Domestic Labor, 42 Fam. Rel. 323, 328 (1993). There is a voluminous literature reporting on field studies in which husbands and wives are asked whether they believe marital responsibilities are allocated fairly. In many, although not all, more than a majority of both men and women consistently reply that the division is fair. But cf. Sigel, supra note 85, at 36, 96-100 (finding that more than 80% of 650 women in sample focus groups expressed dissatisfaction with household division of labor). Even though women do complain about "overload" and even though women who receive more help from husbands at home are generally happier, most wives profess to be satisfied with less than a 50/50 split in responsibility or the balance of work and leisure.

For a comprehensive review of the literature on perceptions of fairness, see Perry-Jenkins & Folk, supra note 16; see also Biernat & Wortman, supra note 11 (discussing the results of interviews with 139 married couples regarding their attitudes about home and work life); Sampson Lee Blair & Michael P. Johnson, Wives' Perceptions of the Fairness of the Division of Household Labor: The Intersection of Housework and Ideology, 54 J. Marriage & Fam. 570 (1992) (analyzing factors in wives' perceptions of the fairness of the division of household labor); Bryson et al., supra note 22 (studying dual-career families); Hochschild, supra note 23 (examining the division of household responsibilities between wives and husbands in two-job couples); Emily W. Kane & Laura Sanchez, Family Status and Criticism of Gender Inequality at Home and at Work, 72 Soc. Forces 1079, 1095-96 (1994) (discussing perceptions of gender inequality at home and at work); Lennon & Rosenfeld, supra note 21 (investigating the sources and consequences of employed wives' perceptions of fairness in the division of housework); Major, Entitlement, supra note 157 (attempting to explain the perception of justice despite objective imbalance as stemming from women's sex-based perceptions of lesser deservingness and entitlement as well as the intrinsic value attached to being male); Steil & Weltman, supra note 11 (describing the effects of resources and personal attributes on the perceived importance of careers and sharing responsibilities at home).

[165] Alternatively, women's resignation may represent sour grapes or an adjustment of expectations to what women think they can get. See Jon Elster, Sour Grapes: Studies in the Subversion of Rationality 109-40 (1983); Sen, supra note 32, at 126; Sunstein, Social Norms, supra note 32; see also Hochschild, supra note 23, at 258-62

bargaining power, it might be possible for women to increase their share simply by being more insistent. This strategy might work precisely because where bargainers come to rest within the negotiation set is largely a matter of subjective perceptions of value and worth. There is no inexorable requirement that a particular contribution within a closed bilateral monopolistic system must carry any fixed exchange value within the relationship. There is no reason why income must translate into marital power more readily than domestic work, or why "women's fertility, child rearing, emotional work, and housework are somehow less of a contribution than men's earnings."[166] These relative values are a matter of psychology, not economics; bargainers in an off-market relationship that generates a bargaining surplus are not price-takers. There is no competitive market, with many buyers and sellers, where aggregate supply and demand curves meet to dictate price.[167] Thus, "exchange" values within a bargaining relationship are not the product of microeconomic forces generating an objective metric of value that is beyond the influence of individual actors.[168] On the contrary, the "value" of a particular contribution is a matter of the allocation each party can force the other to accept, which in turn is determined by volatile processes of negotiation and renegotiation. Once the negotiation set and bargaining surplus are fixed (by factors that do in part reflect the external market value of the parties' holdings and contributions), there is no reason, outside the perceptions of the parties, for the party who happens to be male, or whose primary contribution is monetary, to have a strategic advantage. The advantage proceeds from the bargainers' choice to honor the metrics of a market external to the bargaining process. That choice is far from inevitable, because the values bargainers attach to any deal are not fixed by any outside force.

(suggesting that women cease to press for change in their domestic situation principally because they realize they lack the power to obtain a better bargain).

[166] England & Kilbourne, supra note 5, at 165.

[167] See Rasmusen, supra note 65, at 227.

[168] The market price is generally impervious to individual choices or will. That does not mean, however, that people must adhere to the market price in day-to-day transactions involving market commodities. There is nothing to stop persons from selling or buying something for less or more than its market price if they can find a trading partner to join them in their folly. Finding someone to go along is the challenge. The market at least provides an objective measure of valuation to which those transacting business can refer.

On the other hand, just because some factors conferring bargaining advantage are "in the head" does not mean that they are easy to change. For one thing, there are two players to the marital bargaining game, and spouses' interests in adjusting the valuation of marital contributions are clearly divergent. Even if a woman successfully fights the psychology of her own devaluation and fear of loss, she must still negotiate to "get her way." But that introduces yet another factor that may impede women's bargaining success. That women at times seem to obtain objectively smaller shares can be fully explained by a combination of entitlement, endowment, and "threat potency" effects. But women's smaller share is often attributed to women's being more deferential, accommodating, or conflict-averse.[169] The latter can also be reconstrued as reflecting the utilities attached to the spoils of bargaining when set off against the psychic "transaction costs" of obtaining those spoils. As Jeffrey Harrison has put it, "one could say that the accommodations of others or the avoidance of conflict is something from which [a woman] derives utility."[170] A worse deal only looks worse because personal transaction costs have not been factored in. On this view, the problem with the "soft negotiator" is not that she does not press hard enough for what she wants. Rather, she just does not want it enough.[171]

The possibility of reinterpreting what can be viewed as tactical weakness as simply reflecting the "utility of the bargain" means that the status of the factors that are said to affect bargaining strategy is necessarily more ambiguous than those that determine the negotiation set. But, as already noted, the "softer" party's personality and strategies are not the only ones at stake. Men's tendency to attach little importance to women's efforts is as critical to the

---

[169] See, e.g., Harrison, supra note 10, at 7-9; see also id. at 8 ("[A]n accommodating person dealing with a non-accommodating person will likely receive a smaller share of the gain from the exchange."); see generally Rose, supra note 55 (discussing the importance of women's putative conflict-averseness in bargaining over property).

[170] Harrison, supra note 10, at 7.

[171] That cannot be the whole story, of course. A deferential bargainer will, in the long run, find herself with fewer objective resources, and she will have less to bargain with at a future time when there is something that she dearly wants and she is willing to shed any scruples against "hard bargaining." See, e.g., Rose, supra note 55 (describing how women fail to accumulate tangible bargaining chips in the form of property over the course of a long-term relationship).

outcome of the process as women's tendency to denigrate their own contributions. If a woman's firmer belief in her own deservingness were reflected in greater boldness and higher expectations at the bargaining table, she still might not succeed if her husband did not share her views. *Both* parties' expectations are critical to the outcome of bargaining. Of course, one could argue that this is only appropriate: One cannot expect men to give up value for what they regard as worth less. Does this reflect a tactical advantage, or is it just a matter of men's being true to their own utility profiles? The difficulty of resolving this question makes it hard to know whether and how much the strategic considerations discussed in this section can be said to influence equity, or deviations from equity. There is always the possibility of reframing considerations that seem to reflect the psychology of bargaining as simply reflecting the value of the underlying bargain itself.

The foregoing discussion focuses on why women might make greater concessions in one-on-one bargaining than they really *need* to. But, there is some evidence of movement in the opposite direction: that women's sense of fairness or equity is increasingly working to place limits on the concessions that they are willing to make, even to the point of leading to the rejection of some bargains that otherwise appear better than no bargain at all. There is, for example, evidence from behavioral game theory that parties will sometimes "irrationally" reject positive-sum bargains if they believe they are being taken advantage of.[172] In noniterative situations (like marriage) where the strategic advantages of establishing a reputation as a "hard bargainer" by rejecting a favorable deal are not apparent,[173] the decision to divorce a spouse who insists upon lopsided bargains can be explained as reflecting an independent "taste for equity," which factors revulsion against unfairness into

---

[172] See Rasmusen, supra note 65, at 229; Roth, supra note 139, at 266-74 (attempting to explain the rejection of profitable offers in some "ultimatum game[s]" as manifesting a preference as to "relative share[s]" or "fairness," or as advancing strategic retaliatory or credibility-enhancing goals); see also supra note 153.

[173] Marriage is still most commonly entered into only once or twice in a lifetime, and a reputation for having called a previous spouse's bluff may well make it somewhat harder to find a new "trading partner." Although discarding a spouse as a strategic move probably has few tactical advantages, driving a hard bargain within the context of a particular marriage might.

the utility function.[174] Regardless of whether the rebellion against bargains perceived as lopsided is seen as a tactical choice or as a shift in the perception of costs and benefits, it may help account for the observation that most divorces are initiated by women, even though marital breakup leaves most women objectively worse off (and worse off than their husbands).[175]

D. Hard Bargaining and Dual-Earner Couples

If we accept that some of the factors discussed in the foregoing Section may operate to cause marital deals to deviate from equity in favor of men (rather than to change the way we calculate equity), the payoffs of the actual bargains struck would diverge from the egalitarian ideal to the wife's detriment even more than those struck from bargaining equipoise.[176] There may be additional countervailing forces, however, that act selectively to moderate these sources of women's putative bargaining disadvantage. By some—although not necessarily all—external measures of well-being, traditional role-divided marriages are more egalitarian than dual-worker marriages: Specifically, conventional housewives' hours of

---

[174] See Harrison, supra note 10, at 5-9 (discussing ways to conceptualize, or incorporate into utility calculus, the observed "irrationality" of behavior in experimental ultimatum games); id. at 9 (suggesting that, as a matter of simple economics, "as soon as a potential contracting party develop[s] a sense of compensatory justice that prevents the making of the bargain, the bargain is not one that would have enhanced the position of both parties in the first place"). But see Wertheimer, supra note 32, at 239 n.75 (questioning whether the preference for fair deals is best analyzed as a "psychic utility gain[]" from fairness).

[175] See Ira Mark Ellman & Sharon Lohr, Marriage as Contract, Opportunistic Violence, and Other Bad Arguments for Fault Divorce, 1997 U. Ill. L. Rev. 719, 731 n.44 (stating that it is often difficult to determine whether wives or husbands are instigating a divorce, but noting polls that reveal that "between the early 1970s and the late 1980s, a majority of divorced persons shifted from reporting that their divorce was the husband's idea to reporting that it was the wife's"); see also Paul DeWitt, Breaking Up Is Hard to Do, Am. Demographics, Oct. 1992, at 53, 56. Data from the first half of the century indicate that the tendency of wives to initiate most divorces is not a recent trend. From the 1920s to 1950, women sought almost three-quarters of all divorces and annulments nationwide. See J. Herbie DiFonzo, Alternatives to Marital Fault: Legislative and Judicial Experiments in Cultural Change, 34 Idaho. L. Rev. 1, 6 (1997) (citing Paul H. Jacobson, American Marriage and Divorce 121 tbl.58 (1959)). For further discussion of how the bargaining paradigm helps explain patterns of initiation of divorce, see infra Section IV.C.

[176] This divergence is represented in Figure 4 by point *f*. Supra p. 578.

work more closely match their husbands', whereas employed women generally work significantly longer hours than their husbands overall.[177] As already discussed, the traditional wife's sources of bargaining weakness (large marriage-specific investment and market opportunity cost leading to reduced outside earning potential) might be partly offset by the utility-enhancing effects of the housewife's specialized efforts and preferences.[178] If housewives do get more of what they want, however, the one important reason may be the strong conventions that dictate that, in carrying most of the domestic load without contributing earned income, a woman has done all that is expected of her—that is, she has done her fair share. Although breadwinner husbands may theoretically be in the position to extract more from the marriage—by demanding an even higher level of services, or effectively monopolizing all the discretionary income, or dictating all major family decisions—social taboos may prevent the more powerful person in a traditional marriage from really pressing the bargain to unseemly limits. Thus, the actual bargain in many traditional marriages may be skewed even closer to the egalitarian point than even a bargaining surplus split would allow.[179] That equality would not reflect real equality of bargaining power, but rather a form of grace or gift conferred in the shadow of social expectations regarding the proper balance within the family. Nonworking wives can thus achieve an actual though uneasy equality of well-being within an ongoing marriage. Nevertheless, they do not hold power equal to their husbands'. Their equality is provisional, in the sense that it depends both upon men's forbearance and upon forestalling divorce.

In dual-earner couples, in contrast, social conventions governing the division of labor will tend to accentuate rather than mitigate inequality. When a woman brings in some portion of the family income, however large, there is no perception that she has done all that is expected. Quite the contrary. In this situation, there are fewer normative checks on a husband's full use of his bargaining power to negotiate for a more favorable deal and powerful incentives for him to do so. The result will be, at the very least, a failure

---

[177] See Pleck, *supra* note 15, at 62-63; Szinovacz, *supra* note 15, at 175; see also *supra* Section I.B (discussing the work-leisure gap among dual-worker couples).

[178] See discussion *supra* Section III.B.

[179] See point *g* in Figure 4, *supra* p. 578.

to mitigate the deviation from equality that would otherwise result from the host of other factors creating imbalance. The foregoing analysis helps explain why women's economic gains in the workplace have not translated into gains at home.[180] Although market earnings increase bargaining power, other factors supervene to undermine parity in dual earner families. This suggests that the future of egalitarian marriage is not bright and grows dimmer as married women engage in more and more paid work to generate needed income for the family.[181]

IV. INEQUALITY OF BARGAINING POWER: THEORY AND REALITY

A. *Equality in Practice?*

The marital bargaining paradigm and the working definition of egalitarian marriage used in this analysis beg many questions. These questions are both theoretical and practical. The theoretical objections center on issues of baselines (the starting point for measuring equality in the working definition of egalitarian marriage), metrics (the currency in which equality is measured), and the choice and treatment of variables such as preferences, norms,

---

[180] This conclusion is buttressed by data collected by the economist Victor Fuchs which suggest that the bargains married women have struck with their husbands have generally become less favorable in recent years. Using data from a number of sources, Fuchs found that in 1960 men on average worked longer hours than women (including hours of wage and non-wage domestic work). Fuchs, supra note 7, at 78 tbl.5.1. By 1986, that trend had reversed, and women worked more hours. Id. Fuchs also calculated an index of effective income per hour of work (paid and unpaid) for all men and women, and for married men and women, using an assumption of equal sharing of marital income. He found that the ratio of married women's to men's effective income per hour of work declined steadily from 1960 to 1986, dropping more than 10% in that interval. Id. at 82. The 1986 ratio was still slightly greater than parity, however, which may represent the influence of the traditional couples in the mix. (Unfortunately, Fuchs lumped together dual-earner and sole breadwinner couples, thus limiting the usefulness of his data for this Article's purposes.) Fuchs attributed the decline in the sex ratio of effective income to "the increased burden of work on women who took paid jobs but still had substantial responsibilities at home." Id. at 82. Although the ratio is not a complete gauge of well-being by any means, it does provide one good measure of women's economic status relative to men's, which reflects women's effective access to the pool of marital income. That access may serve as one indicator of women's relative bargaining power.

[181] See supra note 7 (discussing the importance of women's earnings to maintain their families' standard of living over time).

and social conditions that are taken as exogenous in setting up the bargaining model and in defining egalitarian marriage.

Even if the basic elements of this framework are accepted, those disinclined to believe that marriage is an engine of sex-based inequality are not without argument. It is one thing to posit a theoretical framework that predicts inequality of bargaining power in marriage, and another to assert that marriage often produces real-life inequality in fact. It can be argued that a truly complete accounting of all the costs and benefits of marriage for both sexes will produce a version of marriage that is, in practice, much more balanced. Indeed, alternative stories can be told to suggest that married men are in fact operating quite near their reservation price for the relationship, while women are not.[182] The purpose of this Part is to examine some of these possible accounts.

1. The Drudge Wife and the "Efficient" Household

Consider the example of a household that the social science data suggest is fairly common: Husband and wife engage in roughly similar hours of paid work and make significant, although not necessarily equal, contributions to family income, but the wife performs most of the domestic labor; she acts as a "drudge wife." Each hour of household work is costly to the performer.[183] But the work also generates positive utility, in the form of the production of services performed. Assume the couple shares in this positive utility in various degrees.[184] Suppose that, all else being equal, the wife has a modest absolute advantage in domestic productivity.[185]

---

[182] See, e.g., S.A. Lloyd, Family Justice and Social Justice, 75 Pac. Phil. Q. 353, 367-68 (1995) (offering three hypothetical marriages in which labor is unequally divided between spouses—with the greater burden resting with the wife—and attempting to reinterpret these as creating just allocations of burdens and benefits).

[183] That is, it generates "intrinsic negative utility" for the person who performs it. This function takes into account the inherent pleasure or consumption value (if any) of actually performing the work minus the cost of the effort expended. The sum of these two factors is assumed to be negative.

[184] Differences in shares may result from different preferences for public goods (such as a clean house) or because some of the tasks are performed for the benefit of one person only (such as ironing a husband's shirts).

[185] This may be because she generates more utility when she performs the tasks (she does a better job) or because she dislikes performing these tasks less than her husband does (although her performance is still costly for her).

Why does the wife consent to act as a drudge wife? On the assumptions here, the lopsided division of domestic responsibility is Kaldor-Hicks efficient for the unit as a whole if we compare it to an arrangement in which some of the domestic labor is reallocated to the husband (a so-called "sharing" arrangement). The drudge-wife produces a greater quantity of gains for the spouses to share. The problem with that explanation, as we have seen, is that it does not tell us whether or how those gains are divided. Our impulse is to assert that the wife must be capturing enough of a share of the extra gains to make her effort worthwhile. That is, the arrangement must be Pareto-superior to any alternative division of responsibility within the family, despite the extra costs imposed upon the wife, or she would not consent to it. This could occur in two ways. The drudge-wife scenario could be intrinsically Pareto-superior to alternatives (such as "sharing").[186] Or it could be made Pareto-

---

[186] How, despite appearances, might the wife be better off doing all the work? There are several possible stories to tell. There are two sources of positive utility for the wife: her share of the benefits of her labor, and the intrinsic consumption value from performing it (which can include vicarious pleasure in others' consumption of her services). On the negative side of the ledger are the costs of her effort (which factor in her degree of distaste for housework, which may on average be less than her husband's) and the opportunity cost of forgone leisure or other activities. Least plausible as an explanation for why wives do more is the possibility that a wife enjoys doing all the household work so much that her positive consumption value outweighs any extra negative utility or leisure opportunity costs she incurs. More credibly, the wife might have an absolute productivity advantage in domestic tasks, and her direct share of the yield from the larger pie, even without side-payments, might effectively compensate her for the extra net costs of taking on more work (which, due to differences in distaste for housework, might be somewhat less than her husband's costs under an even-split arrangement). In both of these scenarios, the wife takes on the extra tasks "voluntarily"—that is, because she herself comes out ahead by doing them. Put another way, if given the choice, she would choose these arrangements over an ostensibly more even split of responsibility.

The working wife's taking on the lion's share of domestic responsibility might also increase household productivity overall in another way: by increasing her husband's earning power. If the wife garners a great enough share of that increased earning power (which is by no means assured, see discussion infra Section IV.B.1.a) she may come out ahead despite her "extra" effort over the baseline of an equal split. The sources of increased earning power might include a rejuvenation effect, whereby the extra leisure men enjoy enables them to work harder and perform better on the job. If the husband earns more than the wife, the enhancement of family income from rejuvenation might be greater for the man than the woman. Similarly, the flexibility that freedom from domestic responsibility affords a man may have a significant impact on earning power by allowing him to be available to respond to unpredictable work demands and contingencies. Such flexibility may be more valuable to the fam-

superior by a redistribution of the surplus through side-payments. In exchange for the wife's greater contribution of time, the husband might cede to her enough of a share of the surplus generated by the wife's more productive efforts, in the form of other tangible or intangible benefits, to cover the wife's costs and make her better off overall than if she reduced her own effort at his expense.

Although these scenarios are no doubt apt depictions of some relationships, there are important reasons to doubt that they account for most observed instances of drudge-wife households. First, the example takes for granted that the arrangement is Kaldor-Hicks efficient because the wife has an absolute advantage in all domestic labor—an assumption that is problematic at best, and especially problematic in the case of dual-earner couples.[187] Even if

---

ily in the hands of men either because men's earning power is greater for equivalent jobs or because male jobs tend to require more flexibility or greater commitment. Alternatively, perhaps employers reward men's extra commitment at a higher rate. Even if such sex-linked effects were eliminated, however, it is not clear that two persons, each with half as much flexibility as a traditional husband, could equal the earning power of one person who has a monopoly on the ability to respond to employer demands. On the perils of trying to combine paid work with domestic labor, see Hochschild, supra note 23; Edward J. McCaffery, Slouching Towards Equality: Gender Discrimination, Market Efficiency, and Social Change, 103 Yale L.J. 595 (1993); Williams, supra note 3.

An additional factor that makes it costlier, to both men and women, for men to substitute domestic responsibility for leisure is that disgrace attaches in our society to men who take on tasks or roles that are associated with femininity. See Case, supra note 159, at 3; see also supra Section III.C (discussing the devaluation of traditionally feminine activities). This intangible stigma is compounded by more concrete reputational or signaling costs that may adversely affect a man's occupational position or prospects, with financial ramifications for the entire family. Even leaving aside the possible financial effects, a wife may refrain from attempting to press her husband into domestic service because she prefers not to be married to an uxorious man—either because she cares about how her husband appears to others or because he will appear less attractive to her.

Finally, a comparison based solely on duration of work time—the metric of marital contribution that implicitly underlies concern over the work-leisure gap—does not take into account the intensity of work effort, work-related stress, and the subjective unpleasantness of work. It can be claimed that men on average "work harder" or are subjected to more stress on the job, and that the "extra" work women do at home barely makes up for this in the cost-benefit calculus.

[187] Discussions of the allocation of wage work and domestic effort between spouses are often dominated by images conjured up by Becker's efficiency model, in which women are assumed to have both a "natural" absolute advantage as well as a comparative advantage over men in domestic pursuits compared to wage work. See Becker, Treatise, supra note 36, at 22 (discussing comparative advantage); Bergmann, supra note 7, at 266-67 (summarizing Becker's theory of comparative advantage);

that is the case, however, a drudge-wife arrangement will not necessarily be more efficient in every case than a more even split of responsibility.[188] Second, it is unclear what husbands are system-

---

Blau & Ferber, supra note 16, at 37-45 (describing the simple neoclassical model of family specialization and exchange); Hadfield, supra note 55, at 96 (discussing Becker's theory); Isabel V. Sawhill, Economic Perspectives on the Family, 106 Daedulus 115, 118-20 (1977) (summarizing Becker's theory of comparative advantage); Jana B. Singer, Alimony and Efficiency, 82 Geo. L.J. 2423, 2429-34 (1994) [hereinafter Singer, Alimony and Efficiency] (describing efficiency justification for alimony). For a critique of the comparative advantage argument, see Hadfield, supra note 55, at 96-98.

Becker's comparative advantage argument for household specialization is premised on a one-for-one tradeoff between the hours worked by husbands and wives in market and nonmarket sectors, in which the husband's time freed up by the wife's domestic labor is plowed into productive wage work, and vice versa. That model is consistent with both spouses' devoting equal time to work and enjoying an equal amount of leisure, and it does not directly address the efficiency or other consequences of a significant disparity in work and leisure time.

As we have seen, many dual-earner households deviate from Becker's premises. In many households, a spouse's work in one sector does not always come at the expense of work in the other. Rather, it comes at the expense of that spouse's leisure. Becker's model simply does not tell us how "optimizing" spouses should, or would, allocate the distribution of work and leisure hours in excess of the observed "matched hours" of labor, when one person is substituting consumption for work. See supra Section I.B.

[188] There are a number of factors that could tend to reduce the efficiency of a "drudge-wife" situation relative to sharing. A bedrock assumption of Gary Becker's analysis is that women are more productive in the domestic sphere. See Becker, Treatise, supra note 36, at 22-23. But Becker's "separate spheres" analysis assumes that the first and last hours of women's work are in the unpaid sector, and that men's and women's efforts are roughly matched. When women work for pay, the first hour of domestic work comes after many hours of paid work. That places her household effort on the steep part of the curve where the cost of putting in additional hours rises rapidly. Moving tasks to a flatter part of the curve can be expected to reduce costs overall. Thus, the total costs of distributing tasks more evenly between two working people may well be less than the total costs incurred by overloading one person with most of the responsibility.

Furthermore, the marginal value of leisure rises as the number of hours of work performed increases. Thus, the first hour of leisure after eight hours of work is worth less than the first hour after twelve, which means that, *ceteris paribus*, the consumption utility to the dual-earner unit will be greater when the leisure is shared than when it is monopolized. See Blau & Ferber, supra note 16, at 47 ("[L]eisure is likely to be more highly valued by the partner who has less of it.").

As already noted, see supra note 129, the gains attributable to specialization in domestic work are also greatly attenuated (and the quality of the product much reduced) when one spouse must squeeze domestic tasks into off-work hours rather than perform them as her primary activity. This attenuation argues for more sharing among working couples. Of course, it might also argue for wives' avoiding paid work altogether. But see Brinig, supra note 129, at 2472-73 & tbl.I (explaining why, con-

atically giving their wives—or what benefits women are systematically enjoying—to make up for the extra work the wives are doing across the board.[189] Third, although these accounts mitigate

---

trary to Becker, dual-earner families are sometimes more efficient than traditional breadwinner families).

Finally, for some couples—for example, where both spouses can command a high enough return on the labor market—the most efficient arrangement might be to hire household help. See Bergmann, supra note 7, at 260 (describing the "cash-paying" alternative to housekeeping); supra note 129. Only about 15% of couples use any in-home paid help at all, which suggests that the "cash-paying" solution is not efficient for most couples, and thus matters little to our analysis here. See Bergmann, supra note 7, at 263 tbl.11-2.

[189] See supra note 186. For example, monetary side-payments will largely be confined to those affluent families in which most resources are not consumed in meeting basic needs and husbands have access to discretionary income that can be "kicked back" to the wife to make in-kind efforts worthwhile. In most families, however, money is short, so most transfers must be in-kind. The only way the husband can "compensate" his wife is by giving up his leisure or by making other concessions. (Some of those concessions might be sexual. See infra Section IV.A.3.)

Also, both the rejuvenation and flexibility arguments lose their force unless men's freedom from responsibility raises total marital income (compared to the income under the sharing arrangement) enough to convince the woman, given her individual and joint shares, to agree to do most of the work. Such circumstances are most likely familiar only to upper-income bracket couples, for whom the nature of employment puts a steep premium on round-the-clock availability. See, e.g., Williams, supra note 3, at 2236 (describing the "dominant family ecology" of high status professional jobs, where the ideal worker can be away from home for more than twelve hours each day). Finally, the claim that men work at more stressful jobs is difficult to support empirically, as it is grounded in highly subjective preferences and requires a generalization over a range of diverse experiences. To the extent that there are durable measures of work-related stress, however, the evidence suggests that persons in low status, low control, or humdrum jobs experience more stress; it is women who are more likely to hold such jobs. See Spain & Bianchi, supra note 7, at 90-96 (discussing occupational trends of women); Shirley Fisher, Control and Blue Collar Work, in Job Stress and Blue Collar Work 19, 44 (Cary L. Cooper & Michael J. Smith eds., 1985) (concluding that "the blue collar worker should incur more distress at work"); Ben C. Fletcher, The Epidemiology of Occupational Stress, in Causes, Coping and Consequences of Stress at Work 3, 21-24 (Cary L. Cooper & Roy Payne eds., 1988) (citing studies that found higher levels of strain and stress among those in low occupational positions); Mahony, supra note 16, at 14-17 (discussing occupational sex segregation).

The main problem with the conclusion that some variation on the drudge-wife arrangement is Pareto-superior to sharing is that it fails to account for the sex bias in the data: Not only does the work-leisure gap in every study uniformly favor the husband on average, but it also does so in every family. It is exceedingly rare to find specific couples in the samples for whom the work-leisure gap is reversed. See sources cited supra notes 18, 21 . Thus, the suggestion that money—or nonmonetary concessions—will routinely be used by one spouse to "compensate" the other for the extra effort represented by the work-leisure gap only begs the question of why wives are virtually never observed to use money or intangible concessions to compensate

the apparent inequalities of the drudge-wife situation, none provides any *guarantee* that the work-leisure imbalance will leave the
wife as well off as other family members who benefit from her efforts.[190] On the contrary, there is a more compelling scenario: that
a drudge-wife situation is Pareto-*inferior* to sharing—that is, it entails an absolute loss for the wife, with or without side-payments.
The bargaining paradigm explains why this scenario is not just
plausible but likely to occur in many cases: The wife consents to do
more because she lacks the bargaining power to get a better deal.
Thus, acting as a drudge is not, for the wife, Pareto-superior to
sharing (or, for that matter, to a number of marital arrangements
the couple could "rationally" adopt). Rather, it is better for the
wife than the prospect of losing her husband. And although the
husband who shares might also be better off doing half the work
than losing his income-producing wife, his greater bargaining
power allows him to avoid facing that choice.

2. Married Women's Labor Market Choices

The previous discussion suggests a diversity of answers to a question that has long engaged economists (and others): What determines whether and how much a married woman decides to work
for pay?[191] The evidence suggests that married women who enter
the workplace shoulder a greater burden of work than women who

---

the husband for taking on more responsibility. Even if women are on average better
at performing domestic tasks, it is difficult to believe that working women are so *uniformly* more domestically productive than their husbands, or that the flexibility or
rejuvenation effects are so *uniformly* more valuable for men, that a reversed pattern
is never more efficient for *any* family. Finally, the most powerful objection to such
models is that there is simply no intramarital mechanism to *ensure* that, even if an
unequal division of labor produces a surplus, enough of that surplus will find its way
back to the wife to make her extra effort better *for her* than a more equal division of
responsibility.

[190] For example, there is no guarantee that the husband's putative extra earnings
due to the wife's greater domestic efforts will be distributed in the same manner. Indeed, existing evidence on the distribution and control of marital income suggests
that, even when women make a significant contribution to family income, the husband still maintains greater control over discretionary spending and family finances.
See supra note 11; infra note 220.

[191] See, e.g., Shelly Lundberg, Labor Supply of Husbands and Wives: A Simultane-
ous Equations Approach, 70 Rev. Econ. & Stat. 224 (1988); David Shapiro & Lois B.
Shaw, Growth in the Labor Force Attachment of Married Women: Accounting for
Changes in the 1970s, 50 S. Econ. J. 461 (1983); James P. Smith & Michael P. Ward,
Time-Series Growth in the Female Labor Force, 3 J. Lab. Econ. 59 (Supp. 1985).

work exclusively at home. Certainly in some cases a woman may judge that the "positive utility" she enjoys from working for pay outweighs the greater burdens. The sources of such utility can include the woman's share of a larger family income; her vicarious interest in her children's greater economic well-being; her expected long-term payoff from career investment; the value of insurance against marital breakdown; the bargaining power gains from improving her extramarital prospects and contributing family income; and the psychological and social benefits of occupational endeavor and career advancement. Of the items on this list, the value of insurance against eventual marital breakup probably looms especially large in light of current divorce rates and may go a long way towards explaining many women's apparently costly labor market choices. But that factor will not necessarily explain all wives' decisions to work.[192]

It is tempting to assume that no wife will go out to work unless working makes her *personally* better off. (Many women are motivated by their desire to make their children better off, but such desire counts in the present model as a personal gain in the wife's welfare.) If a married woman is better off *not* working, why would she ever go to work? This question should be answered in light of evidence of ambivalence towards fathers and mothers in married-couple households both working full-time for pay. The data suggests that some working mothers would like to work fewer hours or not at all.[193] It is possible that women who say they would like to

---

[192] For an article that finds a correlation between women's labor market participation and the availability of no-fault divorce, see Allan Parkman, Why Are Women Working So Hard?, 18 Int'l Rev. L. & Econ. (forthcoming 1998) (on file with the Virginia Law Review Association). Parkman finds that "living in a no-fault divorce state results in married women having four and a half hours less leisure and approximately the same amount of additional time devoted to work." Id. (manuscript at 11). He speculates that the increase in paid employment "is motivated by a desire for personal insurance against the potential costs of divorce rather than to increase [the] family's welfare." Id. (manuscript at 13). Nevertheless, women still "continue to provide substantial hours of domestic work" so as to "make their marriage attractive to their husband." Id.

[193] In a survey conducted by the Independent Women's Forum in 1996, only 13% of a random sample of male and female voters stated that both parents working full-time was their "ideal balance between work and family," and 36% of respondents said that one parent should stay home full-time. See Karl Zinsmeister, Indicators: Home Life & Life Work II, Am. Enterprise, July-Aug. 1997, at 16. Yet the majority of mothers of children under 17 work full-time. See supra note 19.

work less are not focusing on *net* benefits. Rather, they are focusing selectively on, and expressing regret over, the cost side of the
ledger, which includes less time with their children and work overload, while selectively ignoring the compensating benefits (money,
family power, relief from boredom) they receive from outside
work. Perhaps what they are truly expressing is a desire for the
benefits without the costs.

It is possible to imagine an entirely different explanation for this
regret or ambivalence, informed by a scenario in which the woman's
gains from working do not outweigh the personal costs to her: In
that case, a housewife's move into the workforce will cause her to
be *net* worse off within the marriage. A woman might work because her husband and family want more money—they want a bigger pie and believe her working will get them one—and she lacks
the power to refuse them. But, as the bargaining model shows, a
bigger pie does not necessarily translate into a bigger slice for the
person who works to expand the pie. Indeed, depending on that
person's bargaining position, she may find herself in a worse position.

How might this come about? Assume that a wife and husband
agree that the family needs more money. They are faced with a
dilemma: If the wife works, who will care for the children and run
the home? These responsibilities, the couple might understandably
resolve, will be adjusted after the wife begins her job. Assume,
however, that they are never adjusted after all, or at least not
much. The woman finds herself with more responsibility and less
time. Her share of the family's larger income simply does not
make up for her personal utility losses. Once she adjusts to this
crunch (by delivering fewer or shoddier domestic services or delivering services less efficiently), the household may indeed be better
off as a unit than before. But it may be worse off.[194] Regardless of
whether the pie is larger or smaller (that is, whether the bargaining
frontier moves out or in compared to the alternative of a single
breadwinner household), the new equilibrium bargain may place
the woman in a worse situation than she was in before. If there are
net gains to the unit, most of those gains may go to other family
members, with "assignment of the cost of increased economic

---

[194] See supra Section III.B on the indeterminacy of efficiency consequences of wives
working for pay.

benefits the whole family enjoys thanks to the wife's employment to her alone."[195] And even in the absence of net gains, the restriking of the bargain may shift the allocation of existing family resources away from the wife and towards other family members. In particular, the wife's paid labor may benefit the husband at the expense of others in the household. The husband may spend more of his income on personal pursuits, leaving his wife to pay household expenses previously paid out of his earnings alone.[196] And he may not mind the lower quality or increased disorder resulting from his wife's diverted energies, especially if those costs fall mainly on the children. Thus, despite a husband's rueful attention to the costs of his wife's working,[197] and *even if* the family unit might be worse off as a whole, a husband might actually want his wife to continue working because *his* gains outweigh *his* costs. This explains why women might work even though they really do not want to (in the sense that they would personally be better off if they did not). Their husbands want them to, and their husbands have the power to get their way.[198]

In the same vein, however, bargaining theory also explains why some women might not work even though they do want to. Suppose that a woman's going out to work would increase net returns to the household unit as well as make the woman, individually, better off. Assume further that the husband perceives that his wife's working for pay would make him individually worse off. He would

---

[195] Pleck, supra note 29, at 284.

[196] See infra note 220 (describing how men's greater bargaining power enables them to force their wives to spend their earnings on the household while allowing men to sequester some portion of their own earnings for personal spending).

[197] See supra note 162 and accompanying text (indicating that men are aware of and express regret over the costs of wives working).

[198] Although he overstates his case and erroneously assumes that all married women who work are the "victims" of husbands who force them to do so, the conservative writer David Gelernter is not too far off the mark when he writes that

> the typical husband would *always* have been happy to pack his wife off to work; he had no need of Betty Friedan to convince him that better income in exchange for worse child care was a deal he could live with. Society used to restrain husbands from pressuring their wives (overtly or subtly) to leave the children and get a job. No more.

David Gelernter, Why Mothers Should Stay Home, Commentary, Feb. 1990, at 25, 28; see also Maggie Gallagher, Enemies of Eros 45-48 (1989) (noting evidence that men increasingly are insisting that their wives work); David Gelernter, Drawing Life 90-98 (1997) (same).

then resist her decision to work. His greater bargaining power in the relationship, and the threat of his alienation or defection, might result in the wife's staying at home.

Finally, a housewife may recognize that working for pay could potentially carry some positive gains for her. But she might lack the bargaining power to force a reallocation of household responsibility that would make going out to work a net positive rather than a net negative move for her. If she could get other household members to change their ways, working would be worthwhile for her. But since she lacks the leverage to do so, she will find herself net worse off by going into the workforce and will choose to forgo the positive benefits of working that she might otherwise enjoy.

In sum, the wife's decisions about whether or how much to work are very much a function of her bargaining power within the marital relationship. And without an account of the reality of bargaining position, our understanding of workforce participation and other aspects of family decisionmaking must be incomplete. Side-payments and simple preferences can only be part of the story. Bargaining power is an essential part of the explanation for existing patterns. Husbands (and wives), like all "negotiators," will not compensate others for what they can take by threat. The insight that bargaining power affects distribution allows us to state what by now is obvious: Families can make adjustments towards efficiency—or, for that matter, towards inefficiency—in which one partner loses something, then loses more, and still more again. That the losing partner sticks around anyway should not surprise us. The loss of the bargain in its entirety would be even worse.

3. Love, Fear, and Fidelity

Those who would object to the suggestion that spouses enjoy unequal welfare might also point to the impossibility of knowing the dominant motives that operate when one spouse's choices appear largely to vindicate the other's interests. The divorce threat model posits that the person with the worse fallback options will be influenced to some extent by the fear of the other partner's defection, with its consequences of diminished extramarital prospects and disproportionate loss of marriage-specific investments. Thus a wife will sometimes (and more often than her husband) do what is worse for her personally or what she does not want to do because she fears the long-term consequences of getting her way in the short term. But how does one distinguish between striking a seemingly disadvantageous bargain out of a self-interested fear of defection, and engaging in the same activities out of love or an unalloyed interest in the welfare of others? A woman may be

> interested in the welfare of her husband for his own sake, because she loves him, and for the sake of her children, because she loves them. She may therefore want to make a sacrifice for her husband or her children that is in the nature of a gift.... Or the point can be put differently. One might say that her utility is immediately increased by giving her husband or children a gift, so that the wife is getting an immediate return on her investment in the form of the gratification that comes from giving the gift.[199]

The gift story is undoubtedly true in many cases, and the bargaining framework does not rule out pure generosity as an important motive in family life. Furthermore, husbands as well as wives undoubtedly give gifts in many forms. Working husbands, after all, give by allowing family members to share in their earned income.[200] But working women choose to give in that form, too. So why do women systematically give so much more than men in the form of domestic effort or work time? If altruism without expectation of reward dominates in the marital calculus, its effects ought to balance out by sex, in the absence of a theory as to why they do not.[201]

---

[199] Schneider, supra note 63, at 212; see also Melvin Aron Eisenberg, The World of Contract and the World of Gift, 85 Cal. L. Rev. 821, 823 (1997) (defining a gift as "a voluntary transfer that is made, or at least purports to be made, for affective reasons like love, affection, friendship, comradeship, or gratitude, or to satisfy moral duties or aspirations like benevolence or generosity, and which is not expressly conditioned on a reciprocal exchange").

[200] As previously suggested, see supra Section III.D, there is evidence that some men give gifts in the form of voluntary "forbearance" to press as hard a marital bargain as they might—although it is suggested that love does not carry the full freight here and that forbearance is confined largely to circumstances in which social conventions are on a woman's side.

[201] Although women may choose more often than men to express their altruism towards their families by providing direct domestic services, working women have obviously not chosen this as their primary mode of contribution. Unless women are generally more altruistic than men (as opposed to simply different in how they choose to channel altruism), it is not easy to explain observed patterns of effort and reward. See supra note 133.

Yet another way in which the typical snapshot of the utility/ disutility balance within marriage may be deceptive is in discounting or overestimating the value of certain elements of the marital bargain for men or women. For example, there may be subjective, hidden costs to men—and, more tentatively, benefits to women— from marriage that flow from the conventional expectation of sexual fidelity. Men and women may place a different value on sexual variety—a difference that could have biological roots.[202] Men may experience the sexual exclusivity expected within marriage as more of a burden, while women may gain more from sexual continuity and security.

There is yet another way in which average differences in men's and women's sexuality might have implications for bargaining power within marriage. Although the "law of sexual scarcity" for men has eased somewhat in recent years—in that it has become easier for men to find sexual outlets outside of marriage[203]—the greater urgency of male sexuality may mean that controlling access to sex within marriage is a more potent bargaining tool in the hands of women than of men. Certainly, sexual withholding is sometimes mentioned (although rarely written about) as a unique source of women's power in marriage, and it is tempting to conclude that it serves as a counterweight to male advantage in other sources of power. But the tactical advantages of sexual withholding for women are almost certainly minimal. First, a wife who deprives her husband of sex may also deprive herself. Second, sexual withholding is a risky strategy because it may induce extreme dissatisfaction, or even anger, in men.[204] Like sexual infidelity, it may destroy "marital capital" wholesale, dramatically reducing the value of the marriage for the other partner in a manner that is often difficult to calibrate or control. Thus, it represents a potentially high risk strategy that is as likely to lead to divorce as to a viable

---

[202] See David M. Buss, Evolution and Human Mating, 18 Harv. J.L. & Pub. Pol'y 537, 544 (1995) (discussing evidence of male desire for sexual variety); Robert Wright, The Moral Animal: The New Science of Evolutionary Psychology 33-92 (1994) (same).

[203] See supra Section II.D.3.a; infra note 338.

[204] See, e.g., David M. Buss, Conflict between the Sexes: Strategic Interference and the Evocation of Anger and Upset, 56 J. Personality & Soc. Psychol. 735 (1989) (reporting, based on responses to theoretical questionnaires, that sexual withholding by wives elicits most extreme expressions of anger and dissatisfaction from husbands).

bargaining advantage. Finally, because relatively little is known about the conduct of marital sexual relations (apparently one of the last taboos), it is unclear whether, in actual fact, male sexual deprivation within marriage is a greater problem—and female withholding a more common tactic—than female sexual deprivation and male lack of interest. Also, many women may be neither willing nor able to engage effectively in this ploy.[205]

The expectations of marital exclusivity and fidelity, goes the argument, can more plausibly be seen as adding more to the cost or minus side of the marital ledger for men, thus decreasing the sum total of their intramarital well-being. This cost to men must be subtracted from the other resources and benefits they enjoy in the net utility calculus. When the psychic disutility of sexual fidelity is added to what men otherwise get from marriage (and the psychic utility of sexual security perhaps taken into account for women), there is less inequality in men's and women's share of marital utility than meets the eye. By this analysis, the fidelity differential does not exacerbate inequality, but reduces it.

But there is an alternative way of viewing the effect of the fidelity factor. Negative utility attached to fidelity within marriage can alternatively be viewed as positive utility attached to the opportunities for sexual adventure outside it.[206] By raising men's premarital or extramarital threat point or reservation price relative to women's, enhancing these opportunities narrows the possibility for equality in the distribution of the other resources of marriage, and potentially *exacerbates* the problem of inequality of shares. Men would demand an even greater share of the net pool within marriage to bring them above their reservation price for entering into marriage in the first place. Because men's compensating share must come

---

[205] Douglas Allen and Margaret Brinig argue that whether the willingness to accommodate the other partner sexually, or the threat not to, can serve as a bargaining chip for one spouse depends on the spouses' relative level of interest in and demand for sex within the relationship. They speculate that the relative level of interest changes during the course of the relationship as a function of each spouse's age, with men's demand for sex generally exceeding women's during the earlier and later periods of marriage, but women's exceeding men's during the middle period. According to their analysis, a lower demand for sex creates a "property right" that can be traded away for other concessions or to forestall divorce. See Douglas W. Allen & Margaret Brinig, Sex, Property Rights, and Divorce, 5 Eur. J.L. & Econ. 211 (1998).

[206] See discussion infra Section V.F on changes in social conventions regarding premarital and extramarital sex.

out of other elements of the bargain that are up for grabs, the fidelity differential will drive inequality in other spheres.[207]

What is the best way to understand the fidelity factor? The analysis that treats men's relative preference for sexual variety as tending to produce inequality rather than equality in marriage relies upon a framework similar to that evident in the egalitarian convention: It views persons' prospects outside the relationship as external to, rather than as built into, the concept of an egalitarian marriage. This view is critically dependent on accepting a particular baseline for measuring equality of welfare. In addition to incorporating assumptions as to baseline, the framework put forward here also depends on adopting a utility metric and accepting a role for certain tastes or preferences as contributing to, or detracting from, equality.[208] Is this approach justified, or are there better ways to assess the balance of marital relations?

B. Equality in Theory?

1. The Lessons of Bargaining Theory: Egalitarian Marriage as Heuristic

To understand marriage as a bilateral bargaining relationship is to position it within a category of interactions taking place in widely varying social contexts. The puzzles posed by these relationships have much in common.[209] There are no universally

---

[207] The British antifeminist author Geoff Dench sees the exchange value of male fidelity as central to the explanation of observed patterns of effort and reward in male-female relationships. According to Dench, "on the issue of sexual possession most men feel no less and probably much more, trapped than women do. Men would say that it is they who are 'giving' most in a relationship which requests mutual fidelity." Geoff Dench, Transforming Men 228 (1996). Elsewhere he states that "[i]t may well be that most women are still prepared to carry a double load of domestic work, in return for male fidelity." Id. at 229.

[208] See discussion infra Section IV.B.2.

[209] For a general discussion of these issues in the context of bargaining generally and off-market monopolistic bargaining in particular, see Coleman, supra note 142; Wertheimer, supra note 32; Young, supra note 46; Gauthier, supra note 46; Harrison, supra note 10; see also Christine Jolls, Contracts as Bilateral Commitments: A New Perspective on Contract Modification, 26 J. Legal Stud. 203 (1997) (examining settings in which nonmodifiable contracts might enhance contractors' welfare); Edward B. Rock & Michael L. Wachter, The Enforceability of Norms and the Employment Relationship, 144 U. Pa. L. Rev. 1913 (1996) (examining the coexistence of self-enforcing systems of norms and state-enforced contracts); J. Hoult Verkerke, An

agreed-upon principles for fair transactions and no unproblematic criteria for equality of bargaining power within exclusive long-term relationships,[210] just as there is no uncontested theory of a just or equitable society as a whole.

Empirical Perspective on Indefinite Term Employment Contracts, 1995 Wis. L. Rev. 837 (offering an empirical investigation of bargaining for just cause protection).

[210] A complete treatment of the question of whether marriage is exploitative is far beyond the scope of this Article. Nonetheless, the characteristics of marriage explored herein would suggest at least the possibility of an affirmative answer for some who have attempted to define exploitative relationships. For example, Alan Wertheimer and Joel Feinberg have argued that mutual gains from a relationship are not inconsistent with a claim of exploitation, and coercion and duress are not necessary concomitants. Wertheimer, note 32, at 251 (citing Joel Feinberg, Harmless Wrongdoing 176 (1988)).

The philosopher David Miller suggests that there are two criteria for an exploitative transaction:

> First, the transaction must typically be more advantageous to the exploiting party and less advantageous to the exploited party than some benchmark transaction which we use (tacitly or explicitly) as a point of reference. Second, the actual transaction must have come about through some special advantage which the exploiter enjoys, upon which he capitalizes to induce the exploited to engage in this relatively less beneficial exchange.

David Miller, Exploitation in the Market, *in* Modern Theories of Exploitation 149, 156 (Andrew Reeve ed., 1987). If equal shares of welfare is the benchmark, and if better extramarital prospects constitute a "special advantage," then marriage could be exploitative. Both criteria, however, stand in need of further justification.

From the point of view of marriage as a form of relational contract, resolving the question of whether marriage is exploitative requires deciding whether changes in the marital status quo that are induced or motivated by the possibility of the other spouse's defection are to be regarded as valid or legitimate modifications. The answer to that question may partly turn on whether the ongoing agreement not to abandon the marriage is to be regarded as fresh consideration for the other party's otherwise unremunerated concessions. How that question is resolved may, in turn, depend on whether there is some basis for deciding that the promise not to abandon the marriage is a constitutive part of the agreement to marry in the first place. It is on the last point that claims that marriage is inherently exploitative potentially founder. Under the domestic law in operation in most states, which permits partners to call the contract off without incurring the types of penalties that would ordinarily be appropriate for a breach of contract for continued performance, there is little basis for inferring that either partner has made a formal *legal* promise to remain in the marriage indefinitely. For this reason, one partner's agreement to stay on would appear sufficient to support any sacrifice on the part of the other spouse. Thus, any claim that concessions motivated by the fear of defection, or concessions extracted by the threat of defection, are exploitative must find support in the realms of convention, morality, or social understanding. See, e.g., Eric Rasmusen & Jeffrey Evan Stake, Lifting the Veil of Ignorance: Personalizing the Marriage Contract, 73 Ind. L.J. 453 (1998); Elizabeth S. Scott & Robert E. Scott, Marriage as a Relational Contract, 84 Va. L. Rev. (forthcoming Nov. 1998).

The idealized criteria for an egalitarian relationship suggested in this Article include a utility metric and a benchmark of equal maximum percentage utility. Equality of division is measured from a baseline marital pool that employs a "worldly goods" assumption. The partners bargain over everything they have, with nothing held back. For the most part, their preferences and tastes are taken as exogenous—although not all preferences have the same status within the egalitarian model.[211]

As suggested in the previous Section, the framework advanced here—especially in its use of the working definition of an egalitarian relationship—is concededly vulnerable to challenge in a number of respects. Before engaging in further discussion of the problematic aspects of the analysis, however, it is best to review the strengths of the bargaining model in general and of combining that model with a notion of egalitarian marriage in particular. This analytical framework powerfully illuminates certain fundamental principles of allocation between family members that would otherwise be unexplored or poorly understood. What have we learned from the discussion so far?

a. The Fallacy of Compensatory Exchange

First, the bargaining analysis adopted here decisively scotches the notion that a viable marriage is one in which each partner must be as well off, or gain as much from marital transactions, as the other. One spouse can start out better off outside the marriage and once married continue to be better off.[212] Indeed, it is precisely be-

---

[211] See infra discussion Section IV.B.2.

[212] This point requires recognition of the difference between baseline utility or well-being, and gains therein. Attempts can be made to compare baselines or, alternatively, utility gains as between persons. Here, the argument is that men's higher extramarital baseline confers the ability to bargain for larger increments in utility over baseline. Put another way, because women have a greater desire to be married, they get less of what marriage has to offer. An analogy can be drawn to the relationship between an unemployed subsistence factory worker and a business owner. The unemployed worker's baseline well-being is extremely low. Precisely because of his dire straits (which make him desperate to raise his baseline well-being, even if only slightly), his bargaining position is weak. He is willing to accept quite a low wage (which represents his portion of the productive surplus generated by his work for the owner). The owner, who starts out from a higher baseline, is in a far better position to do without the worker than the worker is to do without him. This gives him the leverage to garner the lion's share of the productive surplus. It is tempting to conclude that for

cause the better-off spouse (in general, the husband) starts out ahead that he can garner the lion's share of what the relationship has to offer. The more favorable baseline confers bargaining strength, which translates into ownership of a greater portion of the gains. The coupling of a higher baseline with greater gains for men helps explain the seeming paradox of the folk wisdom that women often appear relatively eager, and men relatively reluctant, to marry despite evidence that marriage boosts men's well-being more than women's.[213]

---

someone who starts out with a lower baseline well-being, the marginal utility of a single quantum of sought-after benefit or resource will be greater for that person. Indeed, Alan Wertheimer seems to accept this assumption. See Wertheimer, supra note 32, at 64-70. Although this may be true for *money* (which has diminishing utility as the level of *wealth* rises), it is not necessarily true of other types of resources. The marginal utility of a particular asset or benefit transferred to a person bears no necessary relation to the baseline utility from which that person starts out. See, e.g., John C. Harsanyi, Interpersonal Utility Comparisons, *in* The New Palgrave: Utility and Probability 128 (John Eatwell, Murray Milgate & Peter Newman eds., 1990); see also Steven Croley & Jon Hanson, The Non-Pecuniary Costs of Accidents: Pain-and-Suffering Damages in Tort Law, 108 Harv. L. Rev. 1785, 1814-16 & n.103 (distinguishing between baseline utility and increments in utility and explaining that it is possible for persons with lower levels of well-being to experience smaller marginal utility gains from receiving certain quantities and types of resources). In any event, the ways in which the amount of utility gained from a fixed allocation of resources might relate to baseline starting points has little to do with the posited disparities in marital well-being, which are based on differences in utility that assume no particular distribution of resources. Rather, those disparities are simply a function of the initially better-off spouse's ability to bargain for a greater share of utility from the pool.

[213] See Linda J. Waite & Glenna D. Spitze, Young Women's Transition to Marriage, 18 Demography 681 (1981); see also Waite, supra note 40. Married men are notably better off than single men on measures of physical and mental health, life expectancy, occupational success, and earning power. The difference between married and single women on these parameters is far less pronounced. This pattern may reflect men's ability to garner the lion's share of the marital surplus when marriage does occur.

Men's large gain in well-being from marriage makes their supposed reluctance to marry seem puzzling, but that reluctance may be explained by men's higher "baseline," which in turn is attributable to men's far longer reproductive life and the availability of extramarital substitutes for much of what men seek from marriage. See supra Section II.D.3.a. The lack of urgency that men seem to feel about marrying, despite its benefits for them, may also reflect the nature of many of marriage's benefits for men. Married men are healthier and earn more, but those gains are long-term and cumulative. Because it is hard for the individual on the threshold of marriage to appreciate and assess these effects, men may tend to overestimate the benefits of remaining single, while underestimating the benefits of getting married.

Bargaining theory also helps explain why men might fear divorce less than women though marriage is a better deal for them. Bargaining theory predicts that men would value *being married*, whereas women would value *staying married*. Even if men gained disproportionately from any "positive-sum" relationship, they would still typically place a lower value than their wives on the particular marriage they happen

Bargaining analysis also cautions against indulgence in what might be termed the fallacy of compensatory exchange. As the discussion of the drudge-wife scenario demonstrates,[214] it is tempting to assume that any marriage that is a viable going concern will consist of a series of Pareto-superior intramarital deals or exchanges in which no partner loses ground over time, and all compromise takes place from a starting point in which both spouses share equally in surplus-producing decisions. Without this condition, what reason would the partners have to consent to any specific marital sub-deal?[215] But this is obviously all wrong. In the evolution of any marriage, one spouse's contribution need not be matched by the other's, and one spouse can lose ground absolutely compared to where that partner, or the other, started out within the relationship. All that is required for the marriage to remain feasible as between rational actors is that the deal struck be better for both partners than calling the deal off. This is perfectly consistent not only with one partner being chronically locked into a worse position than the other, but with her position relentlessly deteriorating over the course of the marriage.[216]

---

to be in presently because they have a better chance of finding a replacement mate. Women would place a higher value on any existing marriage, because their chance of finding a replacement is smaller (and grows ever smaller with time).

[214] See supra Section IV.A.1.

[215] This type of logic appears to inform Ira Ellman's landmark article on alimony, in which he takes the position that alimony should not take into account the balance of costs and benefits incurred during the life of the marriage. Ellman, supra note 63. Ellman writes that "a spouse who finds the intact marriage unsatisfactory, because the 'current exchange' seems unfair or for any other reason, has the option of leaving the marriage." Id. at 280. He goes on to assert (somewhat contradictorily) that when "financial expropriation" continues within an ongoing marriage, it must be the case that "the apparent victim is receiving some compensating financial or nonfinancial benefits from the marriage." Id. Nevertheless, "[t]he availability of exit" means "we need not worry about imbalances in the exchange during the marriage." Id. at 280-81. But it is precisely because of the availability of exit that we *do* need to worry about imbalances of intramarital exchange.

[216] See infra Section IV.C (discussing the "bargaining squeeze"). This point about the application of the bargaining paradigm to marriage is consistent with the lessons of game theory generally, which show that "repeated play can sustain equilibria in which people do very bad things to each other." Andrew Rutten, Anarchy, Order, and the Law: A Post-Hobbesian View, 82 Cornell L. Rev. 1150, 1158 (1997). Indeed,

> the correct statement of the major result in the theory of repeated games is that repeated play allows virtually any payoff to be an equilibrium outcome. In other words, anything can happen in a repeated game. The reason is simple: when people work together, they generate a surplus over what they could

b. *The Shadow of the Market and the Measure of Value*

On a more specific level, the bargaining framework set forth here has the additional virtue of laying bare the hidden importation of market values into the marital bargain. Consider an objection that could be leveled against one aspect of the analysis: the marital pooling condition, which assumes bargaining over all individual assets, net of utility costs. Implicit in this condition is the assumption that unequal sharing or access to monetary income potentially represents a deviation from the egalitarian condition.[217] But men on average earn more than women, and most husbands earn more than their working wives.[218] At the very least, it could be argued, it is fair for wives to work longer hours to obtain access to an equal share of their husbands' greater income.[219] Put another way, perhaps the better method of achieving equality would be for couples to commingle equal amounts of earned income, withholding any excess for their own exclusive use. One spouse would share his or her excess only upon the condition that the other make additional contributions.[220] But to posit a swap of extra earned income for ex-

---

achieve on their own. This surplus is the point of working together. However, there is no natural way to divide the surplus; as long as each player gets more than she would get by working alone, she is better off working with others. Id. (citations omitted).

[217] Of course, the presumption will often be rebutted, since the metric of equality in the model is utility gain, not control over income. Not every instance of deviation from strict equality in income-sharing is inegalitarian. Nor is every deviation from strict equality in time devoted to work activities. Individual couples may have different utility functions for money, just as they have different preferences for work and leisure. But a population-wide pattern of wives' chronic inequality of access to husbands' income (despite wives' equal or greater work hours), like a pattern of wives' chronic inequality of work time, raises suspicions of structural inequality of access to these resources, for there is no reason to expect gender bias *on average* in preferences for control over money and leisure. In "equal power" relationships, the distribution of these resources between the sexes, although subject to variation across relationships, would be expected to balance out in the aggregate.

[218] See supra note 20.

[219] The marital pooling assumption seems especially strained in extreme cases in which husbands hold vast fortunes. If Bill Gates fails to share all his holdings with his wife, does he then fail at egalitarian marriage? Even if he does, can he hope to have an egalitarian marriage on our description? As noted, however, see supra note 54 and accompanying text, this Article concerns itself primarily with marriages that do not represent such extremes.

[220] The evidence that wives do not always have effectively equal control or access to family income, see supra note 11, can be interpreted as reflecting the outcome of bar-

tra hours of domestic service is in effect to abandon a measure of marital balance in terms of individual net utility, and to adopt a market measure of the worth or value of contributions in marriage. A spouse's insistence upon being excused from domestic responsibility because of greater earning power represents the ultimate intrusion of the metric and ethos of the market into the precincts of private marital relations, which are supposed to be sheltered from the market's crass demands. But, as we have seen, the adoption of such a market measure, at least to the extent it influences allocation of the *bargaining* surplus, is a choice, not an economic necessity. To suggest that a man would be justified in refusing to contract, or in calling off, a marriage in which his extra earnings were not matched by his wife's extra domestic effort is to say nothing more than that he will use his superior bargaining power to extract an exchange based on signals from a market that stands outside that relationship. He elects to ground his marital relations in market-based values.

---

gaining over total family income, or it can be viewed as the result of men's violation of the pooling condition by holding back a portion of earnings for their own exclusive use. See supra Section II.D.1 (discussing pooling conditions and "holding back").

There is evidence that working for pay increases women's control and access to marital income although it rarely equalizes it. See, e.g., Alstott, supra note 6, at 2027-28; Marjorie E. Kornhauser, Love, Money, and the IRS: Family, Income-Sharing, and the Joint Income Tax, 45 Hastings L.J. 63, 90 (1993); Lundberg & Pollak, Bargaining and Distribution, supra note 56, at 154-55 (describing evidence for the "kids-do-better" hypothesis, in which women's monetary earnings are correlated with higher family expenditures on women and children). Although this increased access could be viewed as part of a marital exchange in which increased access functions as a side-payment or extra reward to compensate for work overload, see supra Section III.B, the better explanation is that working for pay increases women's bargaining power. But although earning power may provide working women with more potential control over spending than housewives, women's market efforts will not necessarily equal control because, as noted, men have other sources of bargaining power. Indeed, in some cases, a husband's greater bargaining power may translate into a woman's loss of control over her earnings. See Marjorie Kornhauser, Theory vs. Reality: The Partnership Model of Marriage in Family and Tax Law Versus Intra-Household Allocations, 69 Temp. L. Rev. 1413, 1430-31 (1996) (describing a family in which all child related expenses, including "the au pair, baby clothes, baby toys, uncovered medical bills, etc.," were paid out of the wife's smaller income, with money for any additional expenditures to be "requested" from the husband). Moreover, if greater control over income functioned as a "reward" for role overload, one would expect to see women with the greatest role overload exercising more control than women in "sharing" families. Whether this pattern obtains requires empirical investigation.

c. What Does a Woman Want? or From Choices to Preferences Revisited

The insights of bargaining theory, when combined with the working definition of egalitarian marriage adopted here, also reveal a broad set of misconceptions about what lies behind couples' ordering of their affairs and, more importantly, about the relationship between preferences and choices in and outside of marriage.

First, by highlighting the potential influence of external threat advantage on the bargain that is actually struck, the bargaining paradigm shows that observed patterns of marital behavior may have as much to do with women's desire to remain married and to hang onto their husbands as it does with the actual intrinsic tastes and preferences for, and costs and benefits of, the elements of the marital bargain itself. Marriage is widely valued because it is potentially a positive-sum game. There are reasons why women may value playing this game even more than men and why they may be loathe to lose the relationships in which they find themselves. This all-important "threat" factor is often pointedly left out of the highly idealized accounts of divisions of marital responsibility. Those accounts often attempt to explain women's choices as grounded exclusively and straightforwardly in their intrinsic skills and tastes for domestic activities. But that explanation is radically incomplete. That women do not mind shouldering the domestic responsibility as much as men do, or that they do it better, does not explain why they do so much of it, for they would still rather not. Fear of the consequences of doing less completes the account.

The bargaining paradigm helps clarify the true relationship between choices and tastes. The disparity in bargaining power is based in some part on mean differences in men's and women's preferences or tastes. But there is a careless way of discussing those differences, uninformed by bargaining constraints, that provides a highly misleading and radically incomplete account of why women and men do what they do. To tell the truth about men and women, one needs to tell the truth about the way in which marriage forces men and women to engage in bilaterally monopolistic bargaining that differentially circumscribes the option set from which they choose. Simple-minded attempts to link preferences with observed choices do little to explain why responsibilities and privileges are distributed as they are, and they ignore the problems of free riders, holdups, and defection threats that distort the payoffs within a bargaining game.

Recall the Parable of Neat and Slob.[221] Neat likes a clean apartment more than Slob does. Because they are forced to live together, Neat bears all the costs of a clean apartment, while both enjoy the benefits. An outside observer is tempted to reason back from behavior to preferences. He infers that Neat "prefers" to clean and "prefers" a clean room, and that Slob "prefers" to study and "prefers" a messy room. But neither of these statements is true. Slob prefers a clean room to a messy one, just as Neat does. And for his part, Neat would rather Slob clean the apartment. Moreover, Neat's performance of all of the housework cannot be explained as a joint effort to maximize efficiency. That Neat gets more positive utility than Slob from a clean apartment does not necessarily mean that it is more efficient for Neat to do the cleaning. That depends on what Slob does instead; he might be, for example, watching television. Even if the reason Neat cleans *first* is that he gets less disutility from cleaning than Slob (so that having Neat rather than Slob clean increases overall net utility), that does not explain why Neat cleans. He does not clean *because* it is more efficient for him to do so. Rather, he would be quite happy to foist the job on Slob even if that would result in less gain to the unit overall.

So far, the simple story of what Neat and Slob want does not take into account the influence of exit threats. Now suppose that Neat threatens to leave the apartment, sticking Slob with the entire cost of the rent, unless Slob takes on full responsibility for cleaning the apartment. Further suppose both roommates know that it would be impossible for Slob to find another roommate for the balance of the semester. One would not be surprised to learn that, in such circumstances, Neat no longer cleans the apartment. Rather, Slob would do all the work, and Neat would study in a clean apartment. One might say that Neat "prefers" to study, while Slob "prefers" to clean, but that conclusion would be as nonsensical as its converse. To say that one party "prefers" cleaning confuses a desire to gain the benefits of having an activity performed with a desire to perform it. Under the threat and non-threat scenarios, both parties have in common that they benefit

---

[221] See supra Section II.D.3.c.

from the results of cleaning. Both understand that cleaning imposes costs. Both would prefer enjoying the benefits alone to enjoying the benefits while incurring the costs. Who will get his way?

As the Parable of Neat and Slob illustrates, the confusion inherent in the usual way of speaking of men's and women's choices in marriage is compounded by the fact that intrinsic preferences and the allocations forced by the bargaining dynamic (including the extrinsic differential threat of exit) often point in the same direction. Women might value the fruits of domestic labor more and might mind doing it less (although they still mind). They might have more exacting standards for the duration and quality of parental care (although they may be largely indifferent as to which parent provides it). But it does not follow that women would not choose a different bargain—one in which the allocation of costs, benefits, and responsibilities was more favorable to them—if they could only get it. The fact that they often cannot is related to their preferences, but only indirectly. It is related to the manner in which their preferences interact with the structural features of marriage as a bilateral and exclusive monopoly and the rules for exit from, and intervention in, marriage as ordained by law.

Where there are cost-benefit tradeoffs between bargaining partners, there is always another, better bargain that each partner could conceivably procure.[222] Each partner could always get a larger slice of the pie. It follows that there is always another more

---

[222] This situation follows from the most basic structural feature of a bilateral bargain to split a fixed pie. If the bargainers differ in their preferences or utility functions, one party's gains will entail losses for the other. Whether more or less depends on how much those utility functions differ or overlap—which is determined in turn by the degree of mutuality, commonality, and love within the relationship. But none of those can completely abolish the need for tradeoffs or a role for power. See infra Section IV.B.1.d. As Alan Wertheimer explains it:

[T]here is an important sense in which any marginal gain to one party within the zone of agreement is indeed at the other party's expense: while the parties may prefer any outcome within the zone of agreement to the nonagreement solution, they are not indifferent to the distribution of the social surplus within the zone of agreement. Each would prefer a price that is furthest from his or her reservation price. And any movement away from one's own reservation price is, in that sense, at the other party's expense.

Wertheimer, supra note 32, at 21 (footnote omitted). A more piquant observation on the situation is offered by Rebecca West, who stated that "the great enemy of feminism is that men don't like housework and women don't like housework." Leslie Garis, Suburban Classic, Ms., July-Aug. 1987, at 142, 142 (putatively quoting Rebecca West).

favorable bargain that each would like to have, but might lack the leverage to obtain. In the words of Susan Okin, a division more favorable to the other side will be resisted by those who "do not want [it], and are able, to a very large extent, to enforce their wills."[223] Thus, doing what one wants to do in a bargaining situation is always a comparative concept. If the act of providing a benefit imposes costs on one partner, that partner will want to provide less of it. If the result of a benefit being provided favors one partner, she will want more of it to be provided, but preferably by another. As between two partners, the relative magnitude of costs and benefits does not matter as long as the net calculus points in the same direction: Each would rather free ride. That calculus will be reflected in each partner's preferred ordering of bargained-for deals.

The effects of bargaining constraints on bargaining partners' choices are parallel to the effects of tax policy on married women's labor force participation, which have been described by Edward McCaffery.[224] McCaffery accepts that men and women have different exogenous preferences for employment, as revealed by a "greater [work] elasticity among married women" and a greater interest in part-time work.[225] But the choices men and women make, given those preferences, depend critically on a system of taxation that taxes second-earner incomes at a much higher rate than primary breadwinner's earnings. By attaching consequences to work that "push[] men to work more and many women to work less," the tax system "perpetuates social stereotypes" about what men and women really want.[226] Yet, under a different tax system, men and women might make very different choices that provide far less support for those stereotypes.[227] The same can be said about men's

---

[223] Okin, supra note 32, at 153.

[224] See McCaffery, supra note 186; Edward J. McCaffery, Equality of the Right Sort, 6 UCLA Women's L.J. 289, 306-17 (1996).

[225] McCaffery, supra note 224, at 316.

[226] Id. at 317. McCaffery makes a similar although less straightforward point about how women's choices are influenced by the paucity of "quality" part-time work options in the labor market, which he describes as a form of market failure. McCaffery, supra note 186, at 619-22.

[227] McCaffery faults Richard Epstein and others for "repeatedly point[ing] to free 'choices' as being responsible for whatever observed inequalities we see. How can we make men and women change if they don't seem to want to?" McCaffery, supra note 224, at 316. Epstein has commented that "[i]f individuals do have different natural endowments, then the system of voluntary arrangement should reflect those

and women's choices in marriage. Within a very different institution—or outside of the institution altogether—men and women might behave quite differently than they do, and we might speak about "what they want" in very different terms. But the situations in which men and women find themselves militates decisively against different choices.

d. The Ineluctable Role of Power

Feminists are sometimes accused of distorting the "true" nature of marriage by viewing power as a key determinant of relations between the sexes.[228] This recasting of an age-old institution whose guiding principles are supposed to be cooperation and affection is criticized as sinister and destructive. Although no one denies that some actual relationships fall short of the mark, the attainable ideal of a "good marriage" is thought to be one in which the assertion of power has no place and no explanatory role. Power simply falls out of the picture as a meaningful component of a "good marriage" as it is commonly understood.

The modeling of marriage as a bargain teaches that this ideal is hopelessly unrealistic. Feminists who assert that power is an ineluctable feature of marriage may be guilty of subversive demystification, but they are not wrong. When the interests of two individuals fail precisely to coincide, there is potential for conflict. Even the very best marriage is marked by some degree of con-

---

differences," thus implying that tastes and dislikes are the exclusive source of family divisions of labor, and that bargaining leverage has nothing to do with it. Richard A. Epstein, Two Challenges for Feminist Thought, 18 Harv. J.L. & Pub. Pol'y 331, 340 (1995). But Epstein candidly admits elsewhere in the same article that there is a "risk of exploitation . . . present in marital arrangements" because a typical husband is in the position to "extract most of the gains from the marriage, even if the wife is better off than she would have been if the marriage had never taken place." Id. at 344. This concession evinces an understanding of the central insights of bargaining theory. Unfortunately, Epstein does not identify the forces and structures that determine how gains within the family will in fact be allocated. Nor does he expand on the point that those with a better fallback position within and outside of marriage have more power to get their way within their relationships.

[228] Ruth Wisse, a Harvard literature professor critical of feminism, has recently stated: "By defining relations between men and women in terms of power and competition instead of reciprocity and cooperation, the [women's] movement tore apart the most basic and fragile contract in human society, the unit from which all other social institutions draw their strength." Ruth R. Wisse, On the Future of Conservatism, Commentary, Feb. 1997, at 41, 42.

flict—not in the overt sense of acrimonious disagreement, but in the sense that both partners cannot simultaneously maximize the satisfaction of *all* their preferences and desires. When both partners cannot win, what determines who gets his or her way and who gives way? In a bargaining relationship, the answer is bargaining power.

Certainly the participants in a good marriage have many goals, desires, and tastes in common. There are large areas of endeavor in which conflict is absent because the couple is of one mind: Priorities overlap, and agreement is complete and absolute. And then there is love, which can transform the fulfillment of another person's wishes and desires into one's own. But although conflict may be uncommon in some relationships, it is never absent. At some point, individual interests assert themselves. As long as the spouses are *in any way* distinct persons with distinct goals, there will be conflict in marriage.

The bargaining paradigm predicts that conflict will be resolved against women more often then against men. To be sure, women are not wholly powerless within marriage. That they will get their way less often than men does not mean that they never will, nor does it mean that men will never have to relinquish their objectives or do things they do not want to do. Moreover, an individual woman may be very powerful, both absolutely and relative to her husband. The point is that women as a group have fewer of the traits and assets that confer power within private consensual relationships. Their power is idiosyncratic, not structural. Indeed, many individual attributes that confer power within relationships could be expected to balance out between men and women: For every woman who is physically beautiful, gracious, tenacious, or intimidated by displays of emotion, there is a man with similar traits (although those people may not be married to each other).[229] But

---

[229] In measuring marriage against an egalitarian ideal, one can imagine three possible situations: (1) equality case by case for each marriage; (2) a range of more or less lopsided marriages, arrayed on a bell curve that measures imbalance in favor of one or the other sex, but with no clear sex-based skew overall; or (3) a distribution of imbalance in relationships, but with more relationships favoring members of one sex and favoring them to a greater degree (which this Article asserts is the prevailing pattern, in favor of men).

The great diversity among individuals who enter into marriage and the heterogeneity of coupling suggest that the realization of the egalitarian ideal for each individual

when potential sources of power are considered over the population as a whole, a structural advantage emerges over and above the individual variation, and that advantage favors men. Women are, on average, *relatively* powerless, which means that, on the occasions when compromise is called for, it is women who will end up compromising more often.

This conclusion holds regardless of whether women tend to be more deferential than men. Indeed, the point stands even if we indulge every hoary stereotype about "difference" and accept for the sake of argument that the average woman is more deferential, altruistic, and averse to conflict than the average man.[230] Even if we assume that women defer to their partners more often than men because they want or "prefer" to (in the sense that they "get positive utility out of it"),[231] that does not exclude the distinct possibility that women also defer more often than men *even when they do not*

---

couple—represented by the first possibility—is an unrealistic aspiration. The differences between people who marry each other are bound to give rise at the individual level to disparities in the factors that confer power within relationships. Although the elimination of the extremes of such individual disparities is in itself desirable, this Article is centrally concerned with inequalities of bargaining power within relationships that correlate systematically with sex.

A consideration of homosexual unions clarifies the importance of distinguishing sex-based imbalances of power within the population as a whole from any variance in power balance within relationships—either in the aggregate or individually—that is unrelated to sex. For example, lesbian couples may on average be more "equitable" than male homosexual relationships—that is, they may cluster more closely around the center of the bell curve for power disparities between the partners. Yet, by definition, homosexual relationships do not give rise to asymmetries in power within relationships that correlate with sex. See England & Kilbourne, supra note 5, at 172.

[230] This insight about power's ineluctable role in marriage also does not depend on how rich or "loaded" our concept of psychic utility in marriage is. Even if each spouse's utility function is replete with vicarious preferences and second-order desires, all that matters is that, in each marriage, each spouse's elevation of the other's satisfaction over his or her own will at some point run out. The time will come when each spouse will want something on his or her own account. In other words, all that matters is that pure (or even partial) selfishness comes into play once in a while.

The important point is that the conclusions about the role of bargaining power hold even on a fairly straightforward rational choice model. This shows that the model is sometimes quite useful in demonstrating the validity of feminist insights and that the feminist critique of the rational actor model as subversive of feminist goals is not always well-taken. See, e.g., Beyond Economic Man: Feminist Theory and Economics, supra note 36; England, supra note 5; Elizabeth Anderson, Should Feminists Reject Rational Choice Theory?, Address to the APA Eastern Division Meetings (Dec. 30, 1996) (transcript on file with the Virginia Law Review Association).

[231] See discussion supra Section III.C.

want to. The first type of (directly preference-driven) deference, though perhaps the product of undesirable or "oppressive" social conditioning,[232] might still be said to add to the welfare of the actor herself.[233] The second type of (non-preference-driven) deference, in contrast, is a matter of power only. It forces the actor to take steps that do not add to her immediate well-being. Rather, she acts to forestall imminent or future consequences that will work an even greater deprivation. That is, she acts out of fear of consequential harm, not out of an anticipation of immediate personal benefit. The layering of the effects of power upon any preexisting tendencies will make women seem even more deferential than they really are.

The conflict inherent in marriage also sheds light on forms that female sexuality can take both within and outside that relationship. A satisfying treatment of marital sexuality cannot proceed without a fully nuanced anatomy of desire and, perhaps, a normative hierarchy of the consistency of varieties of sexual experience with the dignity and integrity of the person. Even without these tools, however, it is possible to recognize a continuum of sexual encounters: from those accompanied by elemental sexual arousal or sexual desire, to those devoid of sexual feeling but undertaken for distinctly instrumental purposes. On the latter end of the spectrum, a person might decide to have sex without arousal or desire because of the expected negative consequences of refusing or to make it easier to obtain a desirable nonsexual objective. The most extreme example of "instrumental" sex is submission motivated by a fear of physical violence. But that is not the main concern here. Rather, the more interesting category for our purposes is that of women who find themselves having sex, not because they welcome the encounter for its own sake or even simply from a loving desire to give pleasure or to make a partner happy, but because of concerns about conse-

---

[232] See supra note 32.

[233] There are, of course, many who would question a utility model that viewed the satisfaction of all preferences, however formed, as enhancing the welfare of the person holding those preferences. See supra note 32, and sources cited therein; see also Sen, supra note 8 (arguing that an individual's preferences are influenced by exogenous pressures); Sumner, supra note 32, at 66, 160-62 ("[P]ersonal values are also notoriously subject to influence by accustomed social conditions."); Cass Sunstein, Legal Interference with Private Preferences, 53 U. Chi. L. Rev. 1129 (1986) (noting that private preferences are not uninfluenced by legal rules).

quences within and for the relationship. A woman may decide against refusing her husband for a range of reasons: she may anticipate his displeasure or dread his moods or worry that he will renege on a promise. She may recognize that a well-timed sexual encounter will help her to "get her way" in a conflict that lies on the horizon or will simply aid her in procuring day-to-day cooperation. Or she may simply wish to solidify or preserve a valued relationship by minimizing the incremental tensions that can lead to eventual disaffection or abandonment. To be sure, men might occasionally find themselves having sex "without really wanting to" for similar reasons.[234] And there is certainly room for disagreement as to whether all "instrumental" reasons for having sex, as so described, are to be considered suspect or undesirable, especially within an ongoing long-term relationship. Because motives are often mixed, the line between sex provided from anticipation of loss or gain and sex provided out of love can sometimes be very fine indeed. Nonetheless, it must at least be acknowledged that marriage provides a potential setting for sex that has little to do with ardor or affection as such, and much to do with fear of being deprived of the forms of material and social well-being that a partner can provide. Women's weaker bargaining position suggests that the experience of having sex that is "unwanted"—in the sense that it is not undertaken out of an immediate *physical* desire for the other person or from the wish to give or receive *sexual* pleasure, but rather out of a concern for a deprivation the other person might inflict—is a more common one for women than for men. The fundamental insight is that women's experience of sex must be decisively colored by the power men (including husbands) exercise in ordinary marital relationships.

---

[234] Biology ensures, however, that a man—unlike a woman—cannot have heterosexual intercourse in the absence of sexual arousal. If sexual desire is a richer and more complicated psychological state than mere arousal, a man could find himself in a situation in which he would prefer to forgo a sexual encounter despite a level of arousal that makes the encounter possible. In that case, he might go ahead despite his lack of desire for the same reasons a woman might do so: to further some instrumental purpose. Cf. Mary Becker, Women, Morality, and Sexual Orientation, 8 UCLA Women's L.J. (forthcoming 1998) (on file with the Virginia Law Review Association) (recognizing a category of sexual experiences that "one would rather forgo than endure were there no negative consequences").

2. Egalitarian Marriage and Premarital Endowments

Formidable forces are arrayed against the realization of the egalitarian ideal for marriage. Before further exploring the pragmatic implications of this insight, it is necessary to discuss some problematic limitations of the egalitarian paradigm. Every concept of equality must not only answer the question "equality of what?" but also "equality as compared to what?" The latter inquiry requires establishing a baseline against which to measure equality—a baseline that is as free from arbitrary assumptions and "undeserved" credit as possible. How well does the concept of egalitarian marriage employed here satisfy those conditions?

The utility measure and the marital pooling condition seek to minimize "the importation of a market idea of fairness into family life."[235] The measure of entitlement is not an individual's market resources, but the more neutral metric of equality of satisfaction or well-being. That measure strives to be "for internal use only"[236] in two senses. First, it does not rely directly on market price and value in fixing the terms of exchange within marriage. Second, it excludes certain conditions external to the marriage—partners' differential prospects on the remarriage and labor markets, for example—in determining the measure of well-being.

These conditions raise the question of whether, even if spouses are equally likely to get their way within a marital union, they are really equally well off if one spouse, but not the other, could do almost as well within another marriage or outside of marriage altogether. Should the measure of relative position take account of opportunity cost—that is, how well each spouse is doing compared to his or her prospects elsewhere? This question shows that rejecting extramarital opportunities as the basis for assessing equality requires some justification.

The decision to view extramarital prospects as external to the bargain is a decision to reject extramarital well-being as a baseline for gauging marital equality, and equal gain in utility over that baseline as the benchmark for equality. If the latter measure were adopted, the basis for equal division would be the divorce-threat bargaining surplus, and an equal division of that surplus would

---

[235] Bergmann, supra note 7, at 271; supra note 160.
[236] Bergmann, supra note 7, at 272.

spell marital equality. Such an approach would obviously yield a quite different assessment of the degree to which real life bargains deviate from the egalitarian norm, because the potential effects of unequal extramarital prospects between men and women would be rendered invisible by folding these factors into the starting point for equality. Nevertheless, our framework suggests that actual relationships might *still* deviate from this measure of equality, though perhaps not as sharply as under our working model: The free rider effects of different intramarital threats or the sex imbalance in negotiating skills and strength might still operate to allow men to garner a greater share of gains over the extramarital baseline.

The main problem with adopting an extramarital baseline and shares of utility gain over that baseline as the measure of equality is that it "may well prescribe exactly the sorts of distributions that motivated the concern with inequality of bargaining potential in the first place."[237] This does not mean that it is the wrong principle. But it is a less heuristically valuable one. The chosen framework permits clear identification of *more* of the key factors that put women at a real-life disadvantage.

It is nonetheless important to acknowledge that the egalitarian calculus adopted here does not create a division rule that is entirely untainted by fixed traits, market values, or other extrinsic social forces that influence the parties' baseline endowments. Indeed, it would be difficult to come up with a calculus free from these influences that did not wholly flout our intuitive sense of marital benefits and burdens. Partners' endowments (in the form of beliefs, talents, energy, tastes, and skills) help determine how much utility each spouse can and will contribute to the marital pool. Those endowments also determine how much value each spouse draws from the pool (including how much benefit is derived directly from the other spouse's contributions). A paradigm that allows these endowments to affect gains and entitlements—as does ours—can be faulted as arbitrary or unjust[238] in its treatment of the

---

[237] Wertheimer, supra note 32, at 68.

[238] On the supply side, earning power and accumulated wealth inevitably affect the utility calculus because earnings expand the pool of marital assets to be disbursed and generate utility for family members. But earning power and wealth, like other assets and endowments spouses bring into the marriage, can be traced in part to arbitrary advantages that differ by sex, such as better educational, training, or job opportuni-

range of background conditions that may create a debt for one
party in favor of the other.[239]

---

ties for men. Alternatively, sex-correlated preferences for certain kinds of work
might produce supply-side dislocations that depress or enhance the pay for some sex-
stereotyped jobs. Also, men might have a greater "taste" for wealth accumulation.
See Spain & Bianchi, supra note 7, at 90-96, 129-31; Daniel R. Fischel & Edward P.
Lazear, Comparable Worth and Discrimination in Labor Markets, 53 U. Chi. L. Rev.
891 (1986); Richard A. Posner, An Economic Analysis of Sex Discrimination Laws,
56 U. Chi. L. Rev. 1311 (1989). Alternatively, though, great wealth and earning
power may also be the product of great premarital effort or hard work, which is generally costly to the spouse expending that effort. It could be argued that a spouse
should somehow get credit within the marriage for "negative utility" expended in
creating assets that are imported into the marriage, at least to the degree that those
premarital costs exceed the other partner's. Yet our model does not generally permit
such credit, since it nets out from the marital pool only those costs individually incurred during the life of the marriage.

Furthermore, a husband may be able to add value to the marriage through minimal
effort because he is handsome, empathic, or charming. These attributes generate
marital capital, which redounds directly to the benefit of his wife. The wife's gain is a
function of the husband's fixed, passive, and "unearned" characteristics, and not of
his effort or active input. Yet the husband will "get credit" for these contributions in
the marital calculus, if only because they add directly to his wife's satisfaction. The
amount of satisfaction his wife gains from the husband's possession of those attributes is in turn based on her preferences and tastes, which are equally arbitrary and
undeserved. More pertinently for present purposes, it is suggested that men and
women may differ in their degree of distaste for domestic tasks. If a husband hates
doing laundry twice as much as his wife does, is he to be rewarded for this preference
by having to do half as much or getting twice as much marital compensation for doing
it all? The latter case presents the problem posed by a relationship in which one
spouse's preferences threaten to turn him into a type of "utility monster"—that is, a
person who obtains "enormously greater gains in utility from any sacrifice of others
than these others lose." Robert Nozick, Anarchy, State, and Utopia 41 (1968). These
possibilities raise difficult issues that this model does not resolve. But see Wertheimer,
supra note 32, at 216-30 (discussing how the judgment of the fairness of a bargain is
influenced by the sense of justice or the moral significance of the background conditions contributing to the bargainer's endowments and outside opportunities). See
generally Richard H. Fallon, Jr., To Each According to His Ability, From None According to His Race: The Concept of Merit in the Law of Antidiscrimination, 60 B.U.
L. Rev. 815 (1980) (assessing the costs and benefits of merit-based distributive systems);
John Rawls, A Theory of Justice (1971) (describing the arbitrariness of talents);
George Sher, Desert 22-36 (1987) (assessing Rawls's critique of concepts of desert).

[239] There are additional problems with the model's treatment of preferences. For
example, in discussing the influence of the endowment effect in the negotiating process, men's tendency to discount the worth of working wives' monetary income
(because those inputs are seen as coming at the expense of other valuable wifely
services) is viewed as contributing to deviation from an egalitarian relationship because it "distorts" the negotiating process. There is, however, an alternative way to
think about this phenomenon. If men view their wives' paid work effort as imposing
grievous costs as well as benefits, then perhaps it makes sense for women to work
harder at home just to balance out those perceived costs and even up the ledger of

These problematic features cannot be completely avoided if one sticks with subjective, psychic utility as the measure of well-being.[240] Although this exercise by no means requires a larger commitment to the view that preferences are exogenous, the model adopted here by and large takes people as it finds them. We need only be mindful that the working egalitarian calculus has the potential to hide problematic sources of advantage in the marital bargaining game. Nevertheless, the concept of egalitarian marriage, for all its flaws, provides a useful heuristic for identifying and examining a host of forces that push intramarital arrangements in directions that favor men over women and for understanding the consequences of bargaining imbalance.

C. The Bargaining Squeeze

The bargaining approach helps identify the forces that cause the average wife to agree to take on a greater burden of domestic work and responsibility than her husband. If the wife also participates significantly in the paid labor market, she will find herself working harder overall. Moreover, as discussed,[241] power distribution af-

---

effort and reward. In other words, if we take men's perceptions of the worth of women's efforts as given in the utility calculus, then perhaps women's greater domestic effort should be perceived as making the relationship *more* equal, not less.

Moreover, in choosing one baseline among others, the model treats certain elements (like personal tastes or preferences, or labor market prospects) as sometimes internal to the model and at other times external to it. Like earning power, a spouse's professional status, mechanical skill, social graces, and love of children are all incorporated into the measure of an egalitarian relationship, in that each affects the contents of the pool from which the other spouse draws satisfaction within the marriage. In contrast, a man's desire to marry a younger woman is a preference that is viewed as external to the relationship and to the definition of equality. Thus, some differences in preferences and endowments define equality while others are identified as sources of deviation from it. Also, some of the same elements appear on both sides of the equation, as when market earning power figures both in the creation of the marital pool (which fixes the criterion for the ideal egalitarian division) and in the magnitude of the marital threat values (which determines the negotiation set and thus the likely deviation from equality).

[240] For example, in proposing a "sharing ethic," in which each spouse's contribution would be valued "as proportional to the total time the person devoted to the family's economic well-being" and "[e]ach hour would be valued inversely to the pleasure the activity gave," Barbara Bergmann sidesteps the difficult problem of assessing the equitable value of spouses' positive contributions by adopting the metric of hours of work. Bergmann, supra note 7, at 272. She thus obviates the need to consider any subjective measure of the utility spouses generate for themselves or others.

[241] See supra Section IV.A.2.

fects the choices that wives make about whether and how much to participate in the labor market. A wife might work for pay even if she would be better off staying home, or she might stay home even if she would be better off working. A more detailed and dynamic examination of the elements of marital bargaining adds richness to these insights by showing how initial disparities in bargaining power, and other factors that compound those disparities, create a form of "feedback transmission,"[242] or feedback loop, that amplifies behavioral differences between the sexes and, ultimately, gender inequality. The result is a progressive bargaining squeeze that has potentially detrimental consequences for women, for children, and for the marital unit as a whole.

How does feedback transmission work? This Article has suggested that men and women do not start out with equal bargaining power in marriage because marriage is on average more valuable to women than men, and because men and women have different utility functions for the supply of public goods.[243] That initial disparity leads the average woman to agree to take on a greater burden of domestic responsibility than her husband, even if she also works long hours for pay. Initially, she may find herself making a more intensive "active" investment in idiosyncratic marriage-specific capital than her husband. Even if that greater investment does not at first result in greater labor market opportunity costs (i.e., cutbacks at work), she still functions as a first performer of the implicit marital contract: Her greater sunk costs (which necessarily increase her relative costs of exit) will lead to further erosion in her bargaining power. She will also begin to experience a decline in her remarriage options, which will add to the weakness of her position.[244] As her bargaining position slips, her husband is tempted to press for a greater share of marital gains because he has the power to get his way. As a result, she may experience steadily increasing pressure to take on more responsibility. The greater pressure has two possible results. The wife may resist the pressure by shirking and cutting corners at home in order to bring down her total costs

---

[242] The phrase is Amartya Sen's. Sen, supra note 8, at 138 n.25 (noting the tendency to "ignor[e] the role of 'feedback transmission' in sustaining gender asymmetry").

[243] See supra Section II.D.3.c.

[244] This corresponds to the passive first performer component, described above. See supra note 14 and accompanying text.

in the marriage and increase her net share. At the same time, she may increase her investment in paid work, in order to buy "insurance" against the spouse's further reneging or decision to dissolve the relationship altogether. Alternatively, she may withdraw from paid work and specialize more in unpaid work in order to relieve the pressure and costs of greater responsibility. But the latter choice only worsens her bargaining position by introducing significant market opportunity costs as well as deepening her sunk costs (in the form of marriage-specific investment) relative to her "portable" employment market investment. This process can continue indefinitely until the woman withdraws from market work to a significant degree or drops out of the labor force altogether.

This scenario reflects the fact that the inability to enter an enforceable long-term contract to govern a relationship where one party is the first performer is equivalent to inviting inefficient opportunistic renegotiation.[245] Because couples cannot make a premarital contract that is enforceable intramaritally, they must constantly negotiate and renegotiate the marital bargain as the marriage progresses. The position from which women renegotiate the bargain is generally one of progressively declining bargaining strength, in which they stand to relinquish the gains, or "quasirents" that they might have captured if an enforceable, long-term agreement had been negotiated before entering into the relationship.[246] The response to the threat of opportunistic appropriation is some form of suboptimal investment, in which the more powerful party reneges or threatens to renege, and the vulnerable party scrambles to minimize her potential losses by decreasing her total investment as bargaining strength permits (by cutting back at work,

---

[245] See Cohen, supra note 4; supra Section I.B (discussing the first performer problem); see also Brinig & Crafton, supra note 55 (discussing opportunism in marriage under no-fault rules). The first performer problem is a variant of the larger dilemma posed by "sunk costs," or specialized investment in the context of relational contracts in which the parties find it necessary (because of unanticipated contingencies) to renegotiate the terms of the contract midstream. In that case, the parties "have incentives to use strategic or opportunistic behavior in order to secure a larger slice of the enhanced contractual 'pie.'" Goetz & Scott, supra note 107, at 1101. For a discussion of relational contracts, see infra notes 250, 297 and accompanying text.

[246] See Cohen, supra note 4, at 287-89.

at home, or both) or by rechanneling her efforts into "portable" assets (such as labor market human capital).[247]

Consider the hypothetical bargain that a particular couple would strike on the eve of marriage if they possessed perfect information and were guaranteed perfect enforcement of their deal. Even if the couple did not start out from positions of equal outside options and equal extramarital welfare, and thus would be unlikely to negotiate a perfectly egalitarian deal,[248] the ability to negotiate a binding antenuptial agreement would still have salutary effects, because it would arrest the bargaining squeeze and eliminate the potential for opportunism that it presents. If we assume that the couple first settles on some significant level of mutual participation in the paid labor market,[249] then they would likely agree initially to an allocation of unpaid labor that was efficient (Pareto or Kaldor-Hicks), and then would agree on side-payments that reflected their relative bargaining position. This might result in some degree of role division. But because, by hypothesis, their agreement would be both specific and specifically enforceable for the life of the relationship, any role division (which might require one party to make a greater domestic investment) would not contribute to the more domestic spouse's deteriorating bargaining position. There would be no op-

---

[247] Although it may "cost" a woman to combine domestic work with market work during the life of the marriage (as compared to dropping market work altogether), investing in market work is a wise strategy in a climate of uncertainty regarding the contours of the marital deal or the very continuation of the marriage itself. One explanation for why women persist in working for pay despite the relative overload of dual responsibility is that they are purchasing insurance against divorce. See supra Section IV.A.2.

[248] The average premarital positions of men and women—the positions from which they would write a private contract to govern intramarital relations—are probably not the same and thus would not be expected to produce an egalitarian deal for most women on the market. An egalitarian deal might be possible if the woman settled for a much less desirable partner than she could ordinarily obtain on a marriage market in which both matches and marital terms would be determined competitively. For a discussion on the interaction of the marital bargain and the marriage market, see supra Section II.D.3; infra Sections V.C, D.1.

[249] In reality, not all couples would decide on this level of mutual employment, and the decision about just how much paid labor each person would perform would not be made independently of all other decisions about work, leisure, and distribution. Moreover, the couple's commitment to paid employment could not really be independent of bargaining power. But, for simplicity, this discussion takes as its starting point a situation in which both members of a couple engage in significant amounts of paid work.

portunistic renegotiation because the more vulnerable party could refuse to renegotiate the contract or demand compensation for doing so. The deal would be stable and permanent, and an optimal and efficient level of domestic services would be supplied.[250]

But consider what happens when any initial arrangement is not enforceable. Once the marriage is underway, the woman will come under pressure to do an even greater share of unpaid work; her greater sunk costs improve her husband's bargaining position, allowing him to engage in opportunistic shirking of the performance of his initially agreed-upon amount or to renege on promised side-payments. The husband's shirking will in turn induce the wife to shirk: It may not be worthwhile for her to continue to maintain the *total* level of domestic services contemplated in the original agreement by taking over the husband's share in addition to doing her greater agreed-upon share. Rather, she will adopt some level of output of domestic services (probably a level between her own initially bargained-for level and the amount needed to maintain the total—his plus hers—bargained-for output) that is optimal *for her*, given the balance of costs and benefits. Because of the ceiling effects of women's time and effort overload and the steep increase in the negative marginal utility of work near the top of the ceiling, it may be in her interest to reduce her effort significantly. In other words, she will engage in a process of self-help to soften the effect of her husband's refusal to honor the bargain, thus capturing some portion of the benefits of the bargain at his expense. The result may well be an overall undersupply of domestic investment to the unit (by both husband and wife) relative to the optimal amount.

---

[250] See, e.g., Benjamin Klein, Robert G. Crawford & Armen A. Alchian, Vertical Integration, Appropriable Rents, and the Competitive Contracting Process, 21 J.L. & Econ. 297, 301 (1978) (describing the efficiency costs of opportunistic behavior). Of course, a comprehensive anticipatory contract is a virtual impossibility because the parties cannot possibly predict all future eventualities that bear on the relationship between the parties. To posit a fully specifiable contract is, in effect, to read marriage out of the category of relational contracts as they have been described and analyzed. See, e.g., Goetz & Scott, supra note 66; Robert E. Scott, Conflict and Cooperation in Long-Term Contracts, 75 Cal. L. Rev. 2005 (1987). It is nevertheless analytically useful to set out the ramifications of assuming that an anticipatory binding contract could be devised. See infra Section V.D.1.

The unit as a whole would be worse off, and both spouses, as individuals, would be too.[251]

There is another possible consequence of men's shirking from an ideal bargain if that behavior is coupled with direct pressure on wives to take up the full degree of slack: Men's greater bargaining power might result in some husbands' overplaying their hand and pushing women beyond their "reservation price" for the relationship, thus inducing women to initiate divorce. This scenario helps explain how evolving bargaining inequality due to diverging threat alternatives can destabilize marriage. It also helps explain how the data suggesting that women initiate divorce more frequently than men[252] is fully consistent with the bargaining paradigm and with women doing worse by marriage than men. Because of her weaker bargaining position and her smaller surplus share, the typical wife may be squeezed closer to her reservation price than her husband, and the margin for further pressure is smaller. In the give and take of marital negotiation, the person in the weaker position (the wife) is more likely to be pushed past her reservation price to a zero, or negative, share of marital surplus.[253] The husband, in contrast, has a much larger cushion of surplus going into any negotiation, and thus is less likely to be pushed "over the edge" by the other partner's hard bargaining. This explanation for observed patterns of divorce initiation holds good even though what awaits the woman after divorce is less attractive than what awaits her husband. The willingness to divorce is not a function of this interpersonal comparison. Rather, what matters is the *intra*personal difference in how well each spouse can do inside versus outside the marriage. If the woman's bargaining position is so weak that she cannot gain even a minimal share of marital surplus, she will initiate divorce. Wives are more likely to be in that position than husbands.[254]

---

[251] That is because, by hypothesis, the size of the pie would be smaller under the re-negotiation scenario than if an enforceable deal could be made between the same spouses up front. This scenario assumes that there is no marriage market effect from being able to write an enforceable prenuptial agreement. See infra Section V.D.1.

[252] See supra note 175.

[253] This effect can be exacerbated by a woman's sense of the unfairness of being pushed too hard. On the role of the "taste for equity" in fueling marital breakdown, see supra note 174.

[254] But see infra note 268 (suggesting factors going to variations in timing of divorce initiation by men and women).

The real victims of the spousal race to the bottom, however, may be third parties who typically benefit most from investments in domesticity: children. As working couples engage in their rounds of self-protective shirking, children may receive less than an optimal amount of attention and suffer accordingly. Indeed, the scenario shows how women's lesser bargaining power within marriage can hurt children. Women may have strong preferences for children's receiving parental attention and care. If working women could somehow attain greater bargaining power in marriage, they might use it to induce men to relinquish some of their leisure time in order to care for children. If women had the bargaining strength to effect more spousal sharing of domestic responsibility, each unit of women's attention to children would come at lower cost than under conditions of severe maternal work overload. The result might be a greater degree of combined parental time for children overall.[255]

The social science data provide evidence of a dramatic reduction in total household time devoted to both housework and childcare over the past thirty years.[256] To be sure, much of the decline follows women's substitution of paid work for unpaid work, which increases monetary income that can be spent on children. Whether the reduction in parental time represented by the substitution of paid work for domestic work represents a harmful net loss for children in a family is a function of a complex calculus: It depends on whether increased earnings make up for the loss of maternal attention, whether one or both parents have adjusted the quantity or quality of attention paid to children in off-work hours,[257] and

---

[255] This conclusion is of a piece with the "kids-do-better" hypothesis, see supra note 220, which asserts that "children benefit when their mothers control a larger fraction of family resources." Lundberg & Pollak, Bargaining and Distribution, supra note 56, at 155. That control can take the form of initial maternal command over resources brought into the marriage (such as the mother's earnings or child allowances assigned specifically to the mother, see Lundberg & Pollak, Noncooperative Bargaining Models, supra note 56, at 135) or through any measures that give women more bargaining power within the family.

[256] See Blau & Ferber, supra note 16, at 126 tbl.5.3; Robinson & Godbey, supra note 18. For an interesting sociological perspective on the "flight from domesticity," see Arlie Hochschild, The Time Bind: When Work Becomes Home and Home Becomes Work (1997).

[257] As to the issue of "quality time," Steve Nock and Paul Kingston, in their 1981 study of working couples with children, found that children in single breadwinner, two-parent families spend substantially more time with their parents (mostly mothers) than children in dual-earner families, but that the difference with dual-earner

whether there is an important and independent value in a parent's just being present for most of a child's waking hours. It is possible that, in some families, couples work too hard and long to give children the attention they need, even if all of both parents' nonwork hours are devoted to children. Below that level, and at any given level of total commitment to paid work, reductions in parental attention during off-work hours may at some point start to detract significantly from children's well-being. Evidence indicates, as already discussed, that the void at home produced by women's entry into the job market has not been completely filled by men. On the contrary, men seem to have taken full advantage of their bargaining power to minimize the extent to which women's market efforts impinge on their freedom and leisure. This analysis suggests that, by imposing costs on women and pressuring them to engage in self-help, this strategy may have come at children's expense as well.[258]

The foregoing explains how the marital bargaining squeeze might produce suboptimal total investment in domesticity and children. In other cases, however, it might have the effect of exerting downward pressure on a woman's investment in paid work below the level that a woman might select if she bargained from a position of greater strength. Some wives might choose to recapture a greater share of the bargaining surplus not by cutting back on domestic

---

families is "largely accounted for by the lesser time of employed mothers in activities that involve children only peripherally, not in directly child-oriented activities." Steven L. Nock & Paul William Kingston, Time with Children: The Impact of Couples' Work-Time Commitments, 67 Soc. Forces 59, 59 (1988).

[258] This conclusion comports with the observations in one study of working spouses' childcare arrangements, which found that "variation in husband's [sic] hours of work has no statistically significant effect" on men's childcare responsibilities or time with children. Richard R. Peterson & Kathleen Gerson, Determinants of Responsibility for Child Care Arrangements among Dual-Earner Couples, 54 J. Marriage & Fam. 527, 532 (1992). The authors conclude that "[h]usbands' involvement in paid work and relatively low participation in household work appear to be the path of least resistance." Id.

Nock and Kingston found that fathers in dual-earner couples do not generally make up for even a portion of parental time lost to children by mothers' going out to work. Rather, they spend on average *less* time with their children than otherwise comparable men in single-earner couples. See Nock & Kingston, supra note 257, at 74. Much of this effect is the result of couples' practice of engaging in staggered shift work in order to minimize the cost of paid childcare. Moreover, the data suggest that couples tend to arrange shiftwork so that fathers are at work and mothers are at home when children are present and awake (e.g., afterschool and early evening). See id. at 73-76, 81 & tbl.3. These arrangements mean that men can spend more time at home at leisure rather than engaging in childcare.

labor but by reducing the effort expended on paid labor.[259] The pressure to withdraw from paid work is independent of efficiency considerations, since it results from the weaker party's desire to recapture a greater share of the marital surplus by reducing her effort. But the woman who chooses this avenue of cost-reduction further weakens her bargaining position because she effectively specializes in nonmarket work. She thus increases marriage-specific investment and market opportunity costs, which widens the divergence between her expected extramarital utility and her husband's. This strategy creates a vicious cycle in which withdrawal from market work generates fresh pressure to withdraw even more. These pressures operate independently of the famed returns to specialization touted by Gary Becker, which tend to increase role division by enhancing marital surplus.[260] Rather, the increased role division here is a matter of power loss within a bargaining relationship due to the divergence of threat points and has no necessary connection to efficiency gains.

The downward pressure on paid work has far-reaching consequences for women's well-being and social status as a group. First, the prospect of encountering such pressures affects women's long-term incentives to prepare for market work, since women who anticipate that they will be forced to take on a greater share of unpaid work and to withdraw from paid work will underinvest in labor market capital.[261] Since high earning power only alleviates, but

---

[259] This choice between cutting back on domestic work and scaling back paid work might reflect variation in women's tastes for paid work and domestic work. It might also reflect intrasex differences in utilities attached to certain types of risk, since women's market work probably plays an important role as insurance against marital breakdown. See supra notes 191-193 and accompanying text. That there is some range of taste in these matters is suggested by data showing that married women fall into distinct camps based on their labor supply elasticities, and that they differ in the magnitude and direction of income and substitution effects. Some studies indicate that married women with high labor market participation have elasticities close to those of married men, whereas women who work less are generally highly responsive to factors that make work more or less lucrative. See Alstott, supra note 6, at 2018-20 & n.75. In light of these differences, one would expect that some hypothetical "egalitarian" couples might choose to strike quite "equalitarian" deals characterized by similarity in marital roles, see supra Section II.C.1, while others would negotiate for more role division.

[260] For a discussion of Becker's comparative advantage argument, see supra note 187.

[261] See Okin, note 32, at 144; see also Mahony, supra note 16, at 69-71 (describing how a traditional woman "burns bridges" to alternatives to being a homemaker);

does not eliminate, the disparity in bargaining power, this effect will operate apart from any other incentives to engage in labor market capital investment. Second, the logic of disparities in bargaining power dictates that small initial inequalities of responsibility for household work inexorably tend to snowball. Although sex differences in preferences, tastes, earning power, or comparative advantage help to create initial bargaining disparities, those disparities unleash a set of forces that take on a life of their own. The effects of bargaining inequality are then added to the other social, personal, and labor market factors that militate against women's full participation in the workforce, or in any other worldly endeavors—such as politics—that require large commitments outside the home.[262] This contributes to the creation of a caste-like system in which women as a group enjoy less economic and political power and fewer of the benefits that economic and political power bring.[263]

V. IS THERE A CURE FOR BARGAINING IMBALANCE?

Suppose equal bargaining power is defined as the condition that would allow the partners, regardless of sex, to negotiate an egalitarian marriage. What, if anything, could be done to attain that ideal? How might we go about correcting the *sexual* imbalance in bargaining power that marks the institution of marriage as it currently exists?

The sources of women's bargaining disadvantage are threefold: differences in the premarital and evolving divorce threat advantage, differences in the intramarital threat advantage, and differences in factors leading to weakness in the negotiating process. Each of these sources of bargaining imbalance stems from the peculiar interplay of differences between men's and women's prefer-

---

Williams, supra note 3, at 2241 (discussing the rhetoric of choice: "women are really equal, goes the argument, they just make different choices").

[262] See, e.g., Nancy Burns, Kay Lehman & Stanley Verba, The Public Consequences of Private Inequality: Family Life and Citizen Participation, 91 Am. Pol. Sci. Rev. 373, 382-83 (1997) (exploring possible links between spouses' control over family money and free time and involvement in political activities); see also McCaffery, supra note 186, at 623 (noting that women planning to marry may have fewer incentives to pursue education); Okin, supra note 32, at 138-39 (suggesting that women may make themselves more vulnerable by anticipating the division of labor within marriage).

[263] See Cass R. Sunstein, The Anticaste Principle, 92 Mich. L. Rev. 2410, 2411 (1994) (describing castes as resulting from "social and legal practices [that] translat[e] highly visible and morally irrelevant differences into systemic social disadvantage").

ences or social position with key features of the marital regime. The most important features are fundamental to marriage itself: Both legally and conventionally, marriage is understood to be an exclusive, bilaterally monopolistic contract within which spouses are committed to satisfying a host of mutual needs. Two other key features are the legal convention of marital privacy—which gives rise to a strong formal rule against intramarital enforceability of explicit contracts between spouses—and marriage's practical character as a complex relational contract—which makes the creation and enforcement of explicit terms for the conduct of marriage as a going concern highly infeasible. The final feature of the marital regime is the law of exit (or divorce). Divorce is made easy and is accompanied by limited redistribution of resources. The rules of divorce are also sex-blind, in that they take no systematic notice of the structural differences between men's and women's fate following divorce. Consequently, men and women are forced to bargain in the shadow of the markets for employment and for mates, where those markets offer different prospects for men and women.

Any corrective for bargaining imbalance must deal adequately both with men's exit threat advantage and their intramarital advantage. (It would also ideally come to grips with women's potential weakness in the process of negotiation itself—a tall order.) Unfortunately, a measure that may correct or mitigate some sources of imbalance will not necessarily address others, may exacerbate them, or will produce other perverse effects. For this and other reasons, a comprehensive solution to bargaining imbalance is hard to come by.

A. Rules of Marriage and Divorce

The deep structure of marriage and the conditions of exit from marriage appear most critical to the development of the bargaining imbalance. The most obvious corrective is to abolish either marriage or divorce. Although the former has recently been proposed,[264] and the latter actually implemented in the past,[265] neither is a feasible solution. Because a suitable marriage is a positive-sum

---

[264] See Fineman, supra note 3, at 228-30 (proposing that the *legal* institution of marriage be abolished).
[265] See Lawrence Stone, The Road to Divorce: England 1530-1987, at 1-8 (1990).

game, it is safe to predict that people will find a way to play it. Thus, even if legal marriage were abolished, people would continue to couple up, to make relationship-specific investments, and to lose those investments through sex-skewed opportunistic defections under conditions that favor the strong at the expense of the weak, just as they do today.[266] The abolition of legal marriage would at most effect a deregulation of a social practice that would continue without benefit even of the inadequate post-marital safeguards (such as child support and property division laws) that are currently in place.

As for abolishing divorce, the problems of an absolute ban are inherent in any change that makes divorce harder to obtain: Women (and men) who would like to stay married would be favored at the expense of women (and men) who would not. In any event, some spouses would still abandon one another (and withdraw their marital contributions), since no divorce rule can force people to live together. Many more would stay together, but at the cost of the worst type of marital inefficiency: Both partners would be better off divorced.[267] Although the differential value of staying married for men and women might mean that female winners from a ban would outnumber the losers, there would still be a considerable number of women for whom marriage to a particular man would no longer be worthwhile under any feasible bargaining scenario.[268]

---

[266] See Amy L. Wax, The Two-Parent Family in the Liberal State: The Case for Selective Subsidies, 1 Mich. J. Race & L. 491 (1996) (discussing Martha Fineman's proposal to abolish marriage, and predicting the emergence of "virtual" traditional marriages even without legal recognition for marriage).

[267] Cf. Estin, supra note 4, at 534 ("[A]n 'inefficient divorce' is one that occurs even though husband and wife together enjoy a greater gain from marriage than they would from divorce.").

[268] See supra text accompanying notes 174, 252-254 (discussing reasons why women might frequently initiate divorce despite appearing to have more to lose from marital breakup, including dissatisfaction with inequity as such, men's "hard bargaining" pushing women past their reservation price, and the reduction or destruction of a woman's share of "marital capital" by irreconcilable conflict or by the husband's misfeasance, such as abuse, noncooperation, or sexual infidelity). While foreclosing divorce weakens men's bargaining position by precluding exit, it also weakens women's position by depriving them of the strategic advantage of threatening to leave. Even when continuing a particular marriage remains a positive-sum game, a woman may better her bargaining position if her husband believes that she might "call his bluff" by acting on her own threats or forcing him to act on his. On the role of making credible threats in positive-sum games, see supra note 153.

Short of a ban on divorce, rule changes have been proposed that attempt to make exit more difficult. Currently, all fifty states have some variation of no-fault divorce, and the great majority have unilateral no-fault.[269] Although reintroducing fault or universalizing bilateral consent rules would allow women to block or impede male-initiated divorce, it would not equalize intramarital bargaining power. Exit threat is only one component of the imbalance. As the following discussion illustrates, by trapping women within noncooperative or disharmonious marriages, sex-neutral impediments to exit would exacerbate the inequalities that stem from intramarital differences in access to resources.

A rule of bilateral consent would alleviate the bargaining imbalance created by the threat of a husband's defection: Women who wish to remain married despite their husband's desire to divorce would be given an effective property right to the marriage. If the husband gained more from divorce than the wife gained from marriage, the husband could try to induce the wife's consent by effecting a transfer that would make her indifferent between divorce and continuing the marriage.[270] But the buyout tactic is only open if the initiating spouse's gains from divorce exceed losses to the other. If

---

Although there is some data to suggest that women initiate most divorces, see supra note 175, there is a paucity of information about the timing of divorce initiations by men and women. The bargaining model would predict that most early divorces would be initiated by women, since women's bargaining power and remarriage prospects decline during the early years while men's are on the rise. It is especially to a woman's advantage, if things are not going well, to end a marriage before the birth of children. Men, on the other hand, have much to gain from staying with a woman until both have reached middle age (since his position is on the rise relative to hers). Thus, male-initiated divorces might begin to increase and perhaps even dominate as middle age approaches, even though that is when women's bargaining position is weakest. Cf. supra text accompanying note 253 (discussing why women might tend to initiate more divorces as their bargaining position deteriorates).

[269] See supra notes 99-103 and accompanying text.

[270] Ideally, the marriage would then only dissolve if divorce was Kaldor-Hicks efficient (producing enough gains to one or both spouses to allow a Pareto-superior redistribution). See, e.g., Estin, supra note 4, at 541 (discussing Allen Parkman's argument that "mutual consent . . . permits a wife opposed to a divorce to demand compensation for all the nonfinancial losses that result from divorce"); see also Martin Zelder, Inefficient Dissolutions as a Consequence of Public Goods: The Case of No-Fault Divorce, 22 J. Legal Stud. 503 (1993) (explaining that, by compelling a redistribution that leaves both parties better off upon divorce and discouraging divorce unless there are enough gains to improve both parties' positions relative to remaining married, the bilateral consent rule promotes "efficient marriage"). For a discussion of "efficient" alimony rules, see infra text accompanying notes 316-317.

that condition does not obtain—or even if it does—the spouse seeking a divorce might try to induce the other to abandon the marriage by destroying through his or her own conduct much of the unique marital capital that makes the marriage valuable in the first place. There would no longer be a marriage worth saving, or at least the marriage would not be worth nearly as much as before, and it would thus be easier for the disgruntled spouse to persuade the other to grant consent.[271]

This point illustrates why reform of consent or fault rules cannot provide the complete remedy to bargaining imbalance. Rules that regulate exit address only the component of bargaining weakness that is attributable to differential exit threat advantage. They leave untouched other possible sources of bargaining weakness—specifically, the husband's superior intramarital threat position under the "burnt toast" scenario. If, as hypothesized, husbands on average have a greater ability to make their wives miserable within marriage than wives do their husbands, equalizing exit threat advantage alone will not solve the problem.

In any event, a bilateral consent rule will have consequences that could hurt some women. By granting a property right in the marriage to the husband that is symmetrical to the wife's, the rule adds as much to men's bargaining strength as to women's. A woman who wanted to divorce might in turn be blocked by a husband who might be able to extract concessions (such as the relinquishment of property or custody rights) as the price for exit, thus making the woman even worse off.[272] Although combining a bilateral consent rule with a fault regime would discourage some forms of deliberate marital misbehavior, women would still be stuck with undesirable partners who fell short of the fault standard, and would lose protection if they were "at fault" themselves.[273]

In sum, reviving fault or consent rules can only be a partial solution to bargaining imbalance. Indeed, it helps some women at the expense of others. For women whose marriage has lost its value or

---

[271] See, e.g., Cohen, supra note 4, at 300 ("Because the law can do little to enforce the most meaningful and possibly onerous obligations of a marriage, it is possible for a party to breach the contract while remaining nominally married.").

[272] See Mnookin & Kornhauser, supra note 89, at 963-64.

[273] For a review of the general critique of fault rules in divorce, see Estin, supra note 4, at 559-64; see also Ellman, supra note 99 (general review of fault rule).

worse, remaining married is nightmarish. For women who dearly wish to hold onto their husbands and recoup their investment in married life, abandonment is their greatest fear. Fault rules favor the second group over the first, but both need help.

The limitations of fault and consent rules stem partly from trying to find sex-blind and symmetrical solutions to a sex-specific problem. The conservative commentator Irving Kristol has suggested that unilateral no-fault divorce be made available only to women; men would be required to prove wives' misfeasance to obtain a dissolution.[274] Although this regime would give wives considerable leverage, the solution would not be costless. Most notably, it would hurt men whose wives' reprehensible behavior falls short of legal fault. The main drawback, however, is that the rule might not survive a constitutional challenge, since it makes an overt legal distinction between men and women.[275]

B. Child Custody

One area in which the law long tolerated a sex-specific preference (in favor of mothers) is child custody. But the law surrounding divorce shifted from formalistic and rigid rules (such as "maternal preference" or "maternal presumption") to more fluid or egalitarian standards (the "best interests of the child" or "joint custody").[276] The process of shaping the details of custody arrangements, as with other aspects of the law governing family relations, has become increasingly "privatized."[277] Child custody is now determined primarily by interspousal bargaining.

---

[274] Irving Kristol, Sex Trumps Gender, Wall St. J., Mar. 6, 1996, at A20; see also Burggraf, supra note 81, at 136 (discussing Kristol's proposal and responses).

[275] See United States v. Virginia, 518 U.S. 515 (1996); Califano v. Goldberg, 430 U.S. 199 (1977); Craig v. Boren, 429 U.S. 190 (1976); Stanton v. Stanton, 421 U.S. 7 (1975); Frontiero v. Richardson, 411 U.S. 677 (1973); Reed v. Reed, 404 U.S. 71 (1971); see also Alstott, supra note 6, at 2042 n.171 ("Constitutional precedent suggests that the gender-neutral formulation would be necessary in the United States.").

[276] See Maccoby & Mnookin, supra note 18, at 6-7.

[277] See, e.g., id. at 8-10 ("[C]ontemporary divorce law has increasingly recognized the legitimacy of 'private ordering.'"); Mnookin & Kornhauser, supra note 89, at 952-56 (discussing the shift to "private ordering"); id. at 963-77 (discussing the role of parental negotiation in resolving child custody issues); id. at 977-84 (discussing different child custody regimes); see also Jana B. Singer, The Privatization of Family Law, 1992 Wis. L. Rev. 1443.

Mnookin and Kornhauser have explored the effect of negotiated child custody arrangements on the welfare and position of participants following divorce.[278] But, as with all conditions that bear on the spouses' "exit options," the prospect of having to bargain over custody at divorce also influences what goes on within "successful" marriages. The move from a maternal preference rule to negotiable child custody arrangements and joint custody can best be described as having a detrimental effect on women's intramarital bargaining position. By awarding the mother something she is likely to find quite valuable (if only because of her limited reproductive potential and her larger investment in existing offspring), the old-fashioned maternal presumption or preference improved the mother's extramarital position and thus her exit advantage relative to her husband's. To the extent some (if not many) fathers value more than sporadic contact with their children, the maternal preference reduced those men's exit advantage by increasing the price (loss of contact and control over children) attached to divorce.

An understanding of men's and women's respective bargaining positions within marriage points the way to significant (and backward-looking) reform in the law of child custody. Where bargaining power is unequal, as it often is for husbands and wives within marriage and after divorce, private ordering will inevitably cause the weaker party to lose out unless bargaining takes place against a baseline that corrects for this imbalance.[279] Child custody should be at least partly "deprivatized" by reviving a strong presumption for maternal custody. Of course, a mother can always relinquish custody by private agreement, but she would do so against a baseline entitlement that could only rarely be taken away. Moreover, the rule should not take the form of a primary caretaker rule, which looks to which parent provided the most "hands-on" care. Although such a rule would favor women in most instances, it would undermine the bargaining position of working women who are the most likely to share childcare responsibilities with their husbands and paid caregivers but who, as we have seen, still suffer from unequal bargaining power within marriage for other reasons. The purpose of a return to maternal preference would only partly be to compen-

---

[278] Mnookin & Kornhauser, supra note 89, at 951.

[279] For a discussion of "private ordering" solutions to bargaining imbalance, see infra Section V.D.

sate for the loss in bargaining power that results when women take on a disproportionate share of childcare within marriage. The rule would also provide a crucial counterweight for the structural advantage men possess by virtue of their longer reproductive life (which makes their investment in each child, however large, less important to them) and the marriage-market advantages that flow from this biological fact. Moreover, any legally enforceable paternal visitation rights should be conditioned on payment of child support. This condition would strengthen the wife's hand within marriage by taking away a possible bargaining chip from the father in the event of divorce.[280]

As with so much else in divorce law, post-divorce child custody rules are rarely discussed in light of their effects on the conduct of marriages in which divorce is not (yet) an issue. Yet couples conduct their daily married life not just in the shadow of the market but also in the shadow of everything that awaits them after marriage dissolves. The lack of realism about the relationship between married life and divorce, and an ill-advised quest for neutrality, flexibility, and autonomy in divorce law, has resulted in rules that hand men potent bargaining tools and deprive women of what little power they have. Recent "reforms" in child custody rules have increased sex-based disparities in bargaining power within marriage.

C. Informal Social Norms and Self-Help

Traditionally, strong norms regulated many aspects of behavior surrounding marriage and reproduction, ranging from the division of sexual responsibility within marriage to the social consequences of premarital sexual conduct, adultery, spouse abandonment, and divorce. Many of those norms have changed dramatically in recent years.[281] Is it possible to imagine any informal norm changes, under

---

[280] This quid pro quo rule would make it harder for fathers who care little about visitation to use their rights strategically by offering to reduce contact with the children if the mother would accept less money. But cf. Mnookin & Kornhauser, supra note 89, at 980-85 (criticizing a proposed legal rule to deny noncustodial parents visitation rights).

[281] See, e.g., Burggraf, supra note 81, at 112 ("Prior to the late 1960s, nonmarital sex was a strong taboo in American culture ... [and] the social sanctions weren't trivial."); George A. Akerlof, Janet L. Yellen & Michael L. Katz, An Analysis of Out-of-Wedlock Childbearing in the United States, 111 Q.J. Econ. 277, 278 (1996) (noting the erosion of the custom of shotgun marriage in the 1970s); Amy L. Wax, Against

current marriage and divorce regimes, that would help to equalize bargaining power between men and women? In considering this question, it is important to be mindful of the distinction between normative conventions that are enforced by conspicuous external sanctions and mechanisms, which are perhaps resisted by persons expected to follow the norm, and internalized norms, which are not resisted but adopted as values and preferences. In the arena of marital behavior, many conventions may have significant components both of external sanction and internalized taste that are difficult to disentangle. Moreover, some conventions may have an important biological source; if so, they might not be easy to change.[282]

Certainly, some of the problem of sexually skewed bargaining power would go away if women and men shared the same average preferences, tastes, drives, outlook, and utilities respecting all functions internal and external to the family economy. We have so far treated observed preferences as exogenous, fixed, and largely uninfluenced by the very pressures that create bargaining disparities and account for their feedback effects.[283] Although the notion that men's and women's preferences are exogenous and impervious to social expectations and choice-constraining pressures has repeatedly been challenged,[284] and there is evidence that the challenge may in some respects be justified,[285] there is no obvious known method for moving men's and women's preferences—if indeed they are disparate—towards parity.

Nature—On Robert Wright's *The Moral Animal*, 63 U. Chi. L. Rev. 307, 347-48 & n.68 (1996) (book review) (noting erosion of social norms that imposed sanctions for divorce).

[282] See Wax, supra note 281, at 307-08.

[283] See supra notes 32, 233.

[284] See supra notes 32, 233.

[285] A small study of "equalitarian" (role-sharing) married couples is provocative on this score. In describing the experience of her sample, the author wrote:

> The change to a more even sharing of domestic chores was not easy. Not only did the wives have to contend with the husband's disinclination to do chores, they also had to cope with guilt feelings about abandoning their traditional role and with the mixed feelings they had seeing their husbands do nontraditional tasks. As their strong interest in a profession consumed more and more of their mental and physical energy over the years, however, housework seemed increasingly tedious rather than challenging. In addition, the women's movement led them to believe that doing double work is unfair and made them feel better about sharing domestic chores with their husbands.

Haas, supra note 43, at 294.

There is another set of preferences that are external to the marital economy but critically important to family bargaining power: the preferences for partners, which operate on the marriage and remarriage markets. As already discussed, men prefer younger women and are indifferent to parity or mild inferiority of social status. Women marry slightly older men and seem to prefer higher status husbands.[286] These patterns give men more currency on the remarriage market and exacerbate disparities in earning power as between couples.

Two tactics have been proposed to deal with the conditions that create men's superior remarriageability. Concerned with neutralizing the effects of remarriage patterns on women's bargaining weakness within marriage,[287] Rhona Mahony recommends that women adopt a strategy of hypogamy—marrying down in status and earnings.[288] Lloyd Cohen, on the other hand, recommends that women marry much older men, on the theory that those men's value on the marriage market will decrease with age.[289] Both Cohen's and Mahony's recommendations appear to be directed at women only. The assumption seems to be that self-help is superior to politics: People are more likely to change their own conduct to advance their own interests than to get other people to change their behavior to their detriment.

Mahony's proposal necessarily entails women marrying down in age. She suggests that men married to higher-earning women will choose to specialize in marriage-specific capital as readily as women married to higher-earning men, and thus will relinquish the exit threat advantage conferred by better labor market prospects and fewer marriage-specific investments. Mahony's suggestion is unlikely to work very well, for several reasons. First, a sudden shift to a world in which women prefer younger and lesser-status men will do little good so long as men's preferences do not change. It takes

---

[286] Status disparities have been moderated in recent decades by the rise in assortative mating, which tends to match people of similar educational attainment and initial occupational potential. See, e.g., Robert D. Mare, Five Decades of Educational Assortative Mating, 56 Am. Soc. Rev. 15 (1991) (documenting the dramatic rise in educational syngamy, or the tendency to marry another with similar years of schooling, especially among the college-educated).

[287] See Mahony, supra note 16.

[288] See id. at 215-38.

[289] See Cohen, supra note 4, at 293.

two to make a marriage, and the match a woman can make is not simply a function of her own tastes. Rather, it is determined by a process of "pairwise-bargained allocation"[290] in which various supply and demand curves, reflecting men's and women's priorities, meet. If men do not give priority to higher status wives, but continue to seek the traits they have traditionally found desirable (youth, beauty, and conventional femininity), there will be a serious mismatch on the market, and fewer women may be able to find mates at all.

Second, Mahony's suggestion requires a coordinated and uniform change in women's preferences and practices. Even if a particular woman could find a man of lesser status to marry her, there will be a steadily increasing pool of other women willing to marry up to him as he gets older and earns more, and his wife will still face a declining pool of men willing to marry her. Thus, female hypogamy as an individual solution can only delay, but cannot wholly solve, the problem of women's declining currency on the marriage market.

The task of persuading all women to shun hypergamy (marrying up) and embrace hypogamy (marrying down) presents all the formidable collective action problems entailed in trying to change an existing norm, and in maintaining uniformity in the face of incentives to defect from the norm.[291] But even if women could overcome their emotional attraction to men of higher status—which may be just as deeply ingrained and difficult to alter as men's penchant for younger women—they may not gain much by marrying down, for they will give up valuable tangible benefits by choosing lower status men. A smaller piece of a larger pie (in the form of an unfavorable marital bargain with a higher status man) may be worth as much—or possibly more—than a larger piece of a smaller one, in the form of an egalitarian marriage to a lower status man.[292] Whether women as a whole would be better off as more equal

---

[290] See Rochford, supra note 56.

[291] See Sunstein, Social Norms, supra note 32 (discussing the difficulty of a minority faction changing existing norms).

[292] See infra Section V.D.1. Departures from rationality due to information deficits, cognitive distortions, and the tendency to discount the future—which have received little discussion in this Article—probably play an important role in real-life decision-making in this area: The future losses from weak bargaining power are speculative and painful to confront, but the current inadequacies of a marital candidate are vivid and immediately apparent.

partners to lower status men is a complex question that depends on the state of the marriage market, and on whether the far-reaching secondary costs to women of the bargaining squeeze—costs that would not be incurred in an egalitarian relationship—are fully taken into account by women in their selection of mates on the currently unregulated market.[293] The fact that, in the absence of enforceable bargains, the resources a man commands and his wife's leverage over these resources in bargaining would probably continue to bear an inverse relationship suggests that women may not gain much by marrying down.

Cohen's suggestion avoids one flaw in Mahony's plan: Because older men would probably be more than happy to marry much younger women, women's collective decision to choose much older men would not result in severe market mismatch of supply and demand. But, as with the decision to marry younger men, marrying much older ones would entail some loss in utility unless women could overcome their market preferences for only slightly older men (which may be no easier than adopting a desire for younger mates). Even though a husband's death (as opposed to divorce) leaves the surviving wife with an undivided claim on his assets, it is still not clear that the increased bargaining power a woman enjoys because of the reduced risk her husband will divorce her outweighs her projected losses due to the risk of his dying earlier in the marriage. Finally, because intramarital bargains equilibrate with conditions on the marriage market—and, in the absence of enforceable bargains, do so, at least in theory, with no gain in efficiency or increase in the size of the pie[294]—Cohen's ploy may only introduce different tradeoffs rather than create absolute gains. Cohen tries to argue that women's tendency to choose somewhat older husbands already shows that "women realize that they have more reason to be concerned with divorce than widowhood."[295] It appears, however, that women have already balanced the risks of those unfortunate states in favor of husbands only somewhat older than themselves.

---

[293] See Lundberg & Pollak, Bargaining and Distribution, supra note 56, at 152-54 (describing equilibration of marriage market conditions and intramarital bargaining possibilities when binding agreements are not feasible).

[294] See infra Section V.D.1.

[295] See Cohen, supra note 4, at 294.

Mahony's and Cohen's suggestions have this in common: They implicitly recognize that, absent a change in the external rules defining the marital regime, a more balanced marital bargain can be reliably secured only by choosing a man of the type that now has lesser currency on the marriage market. What lies behind the lesser currency, however, is that these men offer fewer benefits to their mates. Even if age and status ceased to be attractive to women as a psychological matter, the sociological fact remains that those traits correlate in men with the ability to bring tangible benefits to a marriage, and women continue to value those tangible benefits. For these proposals to work, women would have to decide they do not care about their husband's material wealth and earning power after all.

The prior discussion suggests that, in the absence of a massive transformation of taste, it is futile to attempt to change the intra-marital balance of power without recourse to an independent, external mechanism for fixing the costs and benefits of marriage—a mechanism that does not depend on self-help by the person in the weaker bargaining position. That self-help is futile under current circumstances can be illustrated by considering another imaginary scenario that relies on changing the social norms surrounding the choice of mate. Suppose all women got together and decided to demand an egalitarian division as a condition of getting married in the first place or continuing in their current marriage. Suppose such an initial coordination were possible. (Clearly, such an ultimatum would have little effect if not issued—and followed—by most women, since men would simply search for women who did not demand such a condition.) This cartel would initially lower men's exit advantage by reducing the leeway for finding a better marital bargain in the division of marital contributions. But the removal from the market calculus of the availability of lopsided marital bargains would still not completely eliminate men's threat advantage: A husband would still be able to look for a younger and more attractive—albeit equally demanding—mate (and find one), whereas a wife could not.

Women's awareness of men's greater ability to procure a rematch would doom the cartel. The temptation to defect would be overwhelming, as individual women viewed bargaining concessions as a way to hold on to what they have (on the view that this is the best they could ever get). That the ultimatum could be issued as a condition of agreeing to get married in the first place would not matter: Women could not take effective advantage of their relative bargaining strength during their youthful period on the primary marriage market because any bargain they struck initially would be subject to endless renegotiation throughout an intramarital period of rapidly eroding leverage. The lack of any external mechanism for enforcing the collective norm of issuing an equality ultimatum is a pivotal defect. Once married, every woman would be on her own, and the temptation to abandon the norm would prove irresistible.

D. Private Ordering: Contracting for Marital Terms and Costs of Exit

1. Antenuptial Agreements

Comprehensive antenuptial contracts to regulate the conduct of the marriage face two formidable obstacles, one legal and one practical. First, as noted, the law will not enforce them during the life of the marriage.[296] Second, the very nature of marriage as a relational contract means that such a fixed document cannot in reality ever be produced; "unknown contingencies or the intricacy of the required responses may prevent the specification of precise performance standards."[297] Thus, the complete, anticipatory regulation of marital relations, without provision for revision or renegotiation, is a chimera.

Nevertheless, the subject of antenuptial contracting is provocative, at least from a theoretical point of view. Suppose we could reverse a key structural feature of the current marital regime: the refusal to enforce contracts between spouses during the life of the marriage. Could privately negotiated antenuptial agreements cor-

---

[296] See supra note 66 and accompanying text.

[297] Goetz & Scott, supra note 66, at 1092; see supra note 250; Scott & Scott, supra note 210 (describing marriage as a paradigmatic relational contract); see also Cohen, supra note 4, at 298 (noting that an enforceable marital contract would have to take into account "the stage in the marriage when the breach occurs, the circumstances of the parties at the time of marriage, and the circumstances at the time of breach"); Oliver E. Williamson, Transaction-Cost Economics: The Governance of Contractual Relations, 2 J.L. & Econ. 233, 238 (1979) (observing the replacement of neoclassical processes by "adjustment processes of a more thoroughly transaction-specific, ongoing-administrative kind").

rect the problems posed by inequality of bargaining power within marriage? The short answer is no. Private bargaining cannot rectify inequality of bargaining power. Rather, the bargains struck will simply reflect that inequality. The long answer is somewhat more complex. Although private antenuptial contracting cannot cure initial disparities in bargaining power due to men's and women's somewhat different average demand for marriage, it could counter the progressive slide of women's bargaining position by cutting off the possibility for renegotiation during the course of the marriage. This should have the effect of reducing shirking, self-insurance, and underinvestment in domesticity. To remedy the principal sources of bargaining power disparity, the contract would ideally specify disposition of value following marital dissolution (to modify exit threats). But it must also regulate *intramarital* behavior and be enforceable during the marriage to keep husbands from capitalizing on their intramarital threat advantage.[298]

The first objection to the use of antenuptial contracts is that they present coordination and collective action problems: One bride's demand for an antenuptial promise is unlikely to be met with assent when the default rule is no deal at all, and most women ask for nothing more. In the absence of a universal norm of premarital contracting, some men will simply search for women who will not demand contractual protection against deteriorating bargaining power.[299]

---

[298] An antenuptial contract might propose the incorporation of post-marital monetary compensation for any imbalances in costs and benefits that resulted during the course of the marriage from one partner's bargaining weakness. Even apart from posing practical difficulties of valuation, such a rule would only compensate for imbalances in the event of divorce. It would not eliminate inequalities in the conduct of an ongoing marriage. Only a rule of redistribution or specific performance that operated intramaritally could be expected to accomplish that goal.

[299] Although courts will generally not enforce contracts intramaritally, antenuptial contracts that specify some intramarital and post-marital conditions will be enforced in many states upon dissolution. See Silbaugh, supra note 17, at 34; see also Laura P. Graham, Comment, The Uniform Premarital Act and Modern Social Policy: The Enforceability of Premarital Agreements Regulating the Ongoing Marriage, 28 Wake Forest L. Rev. 1037 (1993) (detailing implications of approval of the Uniform Premarital Agreement Act). The infrequency with which such contracts are drafted might reflect adverse selection problems. In the absence of a coordinated or uniform custom of prenuptial contracting, women who demand such contracts might be seen as untrustworthy or otherwise undesirable. This problem, and the reluctance of women to relinquish an advantage in competing for desirable spousal traits, which

Even if that objection could be overcome, any attempt to arrest the progressive decline in women's initial bargaining position by private contract will have side-effects on the marriage market. As noted, the marriage market is a complex process of "pairwise-bargained allocation"[300] that matches men and women depending on both the attributes they possess and the ones they are looking for. The marriage market is not perfectly competitive, because people are not perfect substitutes for one another. Two other important factors influence men's and women's currency and their choice of mates on the marriage market: how well men and women do outside of marriage (determining how eager they are to marry), and how satisfactory a deal they can strike within marriage (a function of their bargaining position as the marriage progresses).

As discussed above, men and women may not regard marriage as equally valuable, perhaps because men can obtain more of what they want outside of marriage (and can wait longer for what they want within marriage). This relative value of marriage is reflected in the marriage market price of each person, which in turn determines how desirable a mate he or she can obtain under prevailing baseline conditions—that is, where there are no intramaritally enforceable prenuptial deals. Under these conditions, each person searches for the best mate he or she can get, and each can command a mate with certain qualities. The legal and practical obstacles to binding antenuptial deals effectively allocate to women most of the risk of exploitation through opportunistic renegotiation during marriage and of potential expropriation of quasi-rents through divorce. This allocation of risk is probably "priced into" the market in the form of extra compensation to women for bearing that risk (and a lower "price" for men imposing it). In effect, a woman will demand more compensation up front (in the form of a higher quality husband) because the risk of loss of her marital investment is so high. The man may be willing to pay more up front for the privilege of reserving the potential to exploit. Thus, a particular woman may be able to find a more desirable man, and a

---

might have to be traded off against the security, certainty, and more favorable terms of the marital bargain, combine to impede the development of a society-wide norm in favor of premarital contracting. Newlyweds' refusal to contemplate divorce and women's dim awareness of the structural sources of their bargaining power disadvantage may also lead women to underestimate any benefits of such contracts.

[300] See Rochford, supra note 56.

man may be forced to settle (and will be willing to settle) for a somewhat less desirable woman, in partial compensation for the gender-based allocation of risks imposed by the current marital regime.[301]

Nevertheless, reducing or eliminating those risks contractually by forcing parties to negotiate for binding terms on the semicompetitive primary marriage market should make for more efficient marital agreements. This might allow some women to come out ahead. Eliminating the possibility of opportunistic renegotiation or defection should reduce expensive, inefficient self-protective behavior and underinvestment, which ought to increase the overall size of the marital "pie."[302] Precisely how that extra surplus would be distributed, however, is unclear, because it depends on how a marriage market that has equilibrated in the absence of binding and enforceable contracts would adjust to their widespread adoption. If women could capture some of the increased surplus (and they should be able to), much of the extra payoff would probably come in the form of reduced risk: Although the average woman might have a somewhat less desirable husband, she might be compensated not only by her greater bargaining power but also by enjoying a marriage of greater predictability, stability, and permanence.

Although antenuptial agreements face formidable practical and legal obstacles and might shift the marriage market, this discussion

---

[301] The interaction of the marriage market with the balance of power within marriage suggests that a woman should seek to maximize her marital payoff, in the absence of a binding premarital contract, by finding a man of such high quality (e.g., rich enough, attractive enough) that she obtains sufficient up-front benefits to compensate for the possibility of early defection and the threat of first performer losses. But the fact that a woman wants to find a man whose very desirability insures her against the actuarial risk of early desertion does not mean that she can find one: Her currency on the market is determined by microeconomic forces that fix the "price" of what she is offering, largely determined by her attributes and attractiveness, as well as the market demand for those traits. On the marriage market, you cannot always get what you want. Thus, many women will in fact be underinsured against the bargaining squeeze and undercompensated for the risk of divorce. On the interaction of marriage markets and marital bargaining generally, see Becker, supra note 37; Gary S. Becker, A Theory of Marriage (pt. 2), 82 J. Pol. Econ. S11 (1974); Bergstrom, supra note 56, at 1929-30; Lundberg & Pollak, Bargaining and Distribution, supra note 56, at 152-54.

[302] See, e.g., Klein, Crawford & Alchian, supra note 250, at 301 (describing the costs of opportunistic behavior); see also Jeffrey Evans Stake, Mandatory Planning for Divorce, 45 Vand. L. Rev. 397 (1992) (discussing premarital agreements as a hedge against marital opportunism).

suggests why they might still be a good idea. It is true that some women might have to lower their sights, but that adjustment might bring greater efficiency to marriage markets, with benefits to be shared by women. It is the current marriage market that is distorted by its invitation to opportunism generally, and by the greater potential for opportunism by men. It could be argued that women now marry higher quality men than they rightly "deserve" precisely because they pay on the back end rather than the front. Under the current marital regime, women assume a greater risk of a larger loss than they would if obligations could be fixed ahead of time. As a result, the variance in payoffs is greater. In effect, the current marriage market is a high stakes game for women with big winners (those who manage to hold onto high quality husbands) and big losers (those left relatively destitute when their husbands abscond). To the extent that the remote risk of divorce is notoriously discounted by most people,[303] the current regime seems like a good deal, but it may not be.

2. Dowry and Bride Price

Another variation on the theme of private contracts is the custom of dowry or bride price.[304] Dowry is money or property paid by the husband or his family to the family of the bride to be held in trust for her in the event of the husband's breach of the marriage contract. So long (but only as long) as the marriage endures, the money becomes part of the couple's estate. Dowry therefore functions as a performance bond on the husband. It moves bargaining power towards parity by operating as a kind of tax on the husband's defection, which lowers his effective exit threat advantage.

---

[303] See Baker & Emery, supra note 14, at 443 (noting that while marriage license applicants who were surveyed estimated correctly that half of U.S. marriages would end in divorce, their median response was *0%* when asked to assess the likelihood that their own marriages would suffer this fate).

[304] See generally Cohen, supra note 4, at 292-93 (discussing the role of bride price "to alleviate some of the problems of appropriable quasi rents" in marriage); Ivy Papps, The Role and Determinants of Bride-Price: The Case of a Palestinian Village, 24 Current Anthropology 203 (1983) (applying economic theory to the payment of bride price); Melford E. Spiro, Marriage Payments: A Paradigm from the Burmese Perspective, 31 J. Anthropological Res. 89 (1975) (giving an overview of the customs and economic role of dowry and bride price in southeast Asian communities).

Apart from its inherent imprecision in estimating relative exit threats, dowry has limited usefulness under current social conditions. First, earning power, not property, is the most important source of marital wealth for most couples, and most people do not have enough up-front resources to post an effective bond. (The alternative—permitting the husband to borrow the money against future earnings—is in effect an alimony rule, which is discussed below.[305]) Second, as with all devices that regulate exit threats, the stability of the practice of dowry would depend on its adoption across the board. But its adoption cannot be imposed by fiat. As Lloyd Cohen states, dowry is "a cultural phenomenon that evolves over a period of centuries."[306] Third, the custom would have to incorporate an understanding that even women who do not assume a traditional role and are not overtly financially dependent—and who thus appear to have little labor market opportunity cost of marriage—deserve a bond against the passive depreciation of their marital capital. This would require a revolution in thinking about marital relations.[307]

Finally, dowry shares the limitation of any mechanism that does not rely on intramarital enforcement: The marriage must end before the remedy for unequal bargaining power is triggered. Intramarital free rider strategies that push women to a point short of divorce would continue unabated. If conditions grew poor enough to induce the wife to initiate exit, she could not claim the bond under traditional dowry principles. Moreover, a fault component would be needed to deal with the moral hazard of opportunistic exit by the wife.[308] But traditional concepts of fault are too broad-gauged to protect a wife from all possible efforts by the husband to destroy or appropriate marital capital.

---

[305] See infra Section V.E.2.

[306] Cohen, supra note 4, at 292.

[307] For a comparable discussion of new alimony rules, see infra notes 317-324 and accompanying text.

[308] See Cohen, supra note 4, at 292 (suggesting that dowry cannot work within a no-fault system).

E. Bargaining in the Shadow of the Law: Mandated Payment or Transfer Rules

The foregoing sections suggest that, if the world is to be made safe for egalitarian marriage, the way lies not in self-help but in politics. Women cannot get a better deal by choosing a worse husband, and they cannot rely on other women's voluntarily standing firm with them to insist on a better bargain. Likewise, private ordering cannot be a complete answer to inequality of bargaining power, because an egalitarian deal cannot be expected to result when men and women negotiate from different premarital starting points and when the negotiated deal equilibrates with an unregulated marriage market.

Would external regulation work? There are a number of possible measures that could be adopted.[309] Perhaps the law should alter or control the marriage contract by regulating intramarital relations or by fixing the terms of post-marital distribution. This Section will consider both possibilities.

1. Intramarital Payments or Transfers

Detailed regulation to equalize the precise terms of marital relations would be impracticable for the same reasons that relational contracts for that purpose are infeasible. Nevertheless, the government can selectively intervene to redistribute some forms of marital assets during the life of the marriage. Two proposals are the assignment of a family allowance to the mother or primary caretaker of a child[310] and mandated income sharing within marriage.[311]

---

[309] Various mixed public-private schemes are not discussed here. One example of such a scheme would be taxing single men to try to equalize their premarital bargaining position with unmarried women, and then allowing the parties to negotiate an enforceable prenuptial deal privately. I owe the suggestion to tax single men to George Triantis. Interestingly, proposals for a "bachelor tax," or tax surcharge on single marriageable men, were a staple of Swedish politics at the turn of the century. Their avowed purpose, however, was to stem the precipitous fall in the national birthrate by encouraging men to marry earlier, not to provide women greater marital leverage. See Allan Carlson, The Swedish Experiment in Family Politics 16 (1990).

[310] For an extensive discussion of family allowances, see Alstott, supra note 6, at 2042-55.

[311] See Okin, supra note 32, at 180-83 (proposing income sharing within marriage).

a. Child Allowances

Many European countries now pay a universal family or child allowance to families, prorated according to the number of children. Most countries pay the allowance either to the mother or to a primary caretaker who is defined as the person providing most care for the child within the family.[312] How might a woman's control over this subsidy affect intramarital bargaining power? Under the divorce threat model, the fact that the subsidy was assigned to a mother within an intact marriage would not make any difference because it would not in itself improve the terms of her exit. Moreover, some husbands might continue to have the leverage to bargain away the benefits of a wife's control of extra income by taking control of other valuable resources. Only if single or divorced mothers also received the subsidy—that is, only if the subsidy continued outside of marriage—would a woman's exit threat be enhanced and her bargaining position improved.[313] But the intramarital threat model does predict that intramarital assignment of the allowance to mothers would improve women's bargaining power, because wives' and children's fallback position within a conflict-ridden marriage would improve.[314] The child allowance would be like income to the mother, which could be withheld from her spouse without directly hurting the recipient or her children.

b. Intramarital Income Sharing

It is not clear that legally enforced income sharing during marriage would help to improve many women's position. Like a child allowance, income sharing would at best provide only a partial solution to bargaining power inequality and could not be expected to

---

[312] See Alstott, supra note 6, at 2042. As Anne Alstott notes, a family allowance expressly earmarked for mothers might present constitutional difficulties within the United States. See id. at 2042 n.171.

[313] As Anne Alstott suggests, the exit threat enhancement effect would result from "a system of family allowances paid *only* to single mothers," regardless of whether married women were also paid. Id. at 2052. Note, however, that a system of exclusively intramarital payments would have some effect on the husband's exit threat, because he would lose the ability to share in the allowance if he leaves the family. See id. at 2052 n.213.

[314] See Lundberg & Pollak, Bargaining and Distribution, supra note 56, at 149 (noting that a separate spheres intramarital bargaining paradigm predicts enhancement of women's bargaining power from a child allowance assigned to mothers).

negate all sources of bargaining imbalance. Susan Okin describes income sharing as establishing each spouse's entitlement to an equal share of all earnings coming into the household. She recommends that "employers make out wage checks equally divided between the earner and the partner,"[315] giving each spouse legal title to half of the total family income. Wives would then have a claim on some portion of husbands' earnings and husbands would gain a claim on wives'. The effect would depend on relative earnings contribution. For wives who earn little or nothing, the entitlement would represent a real but hardly egalitarian improvement. It would reduce the husband's intramarital threat of withdrawing access to income, but it would not alter the exit threat generated by the potential for future earnings and other factors (such as remarriage prospects). For working wives who bring in a significant portion of the family income, the effect of income sharing would be more equivocal. The additional bargaining leverage granted by wives' access to husbands' earnings would be partly balanced by the husbands' reciprocal rights over wives'. Other sources of men's superior bargaining power would remain, affecting bargaining over the remaining portions of family income.

2. Post-marital Transfers or Alimony

A rule of income sharing *after* the termination of a marriage—in effect a form of alimony—should be considered in the larger context of extramarital and post-marital payment or transfer rules and their potential effects on intramarital bargaining power. The rules can be divided into those that transfer assets between spouses after divorce, and those that provide for direct government payments (without interspousal redistribution) to divorced custodial mothers or single mothers generally. As the previous discussion of child allowances suggests, extramarital or post-marital payments or transfers can adjust the relative exit threats of the parties. Post-marital transfers from husband to wife generally raise the wife's exit advantage and lower the husband's. Alimony taxes divorce for

---

[315] Okin, supra note 32, at 181. Okin does not recommend that all family income be jointly owned. The reasons are obvious: By granting each spouse legal veto power over all expenditures, this would create intolerable hold-out problems that would favor the spouse with otherwise greater bargaining power.

the man both by depriving him of income and by making him less attractive to future mates. Government payments to ex-wives or mothers (whether previously married or not) raise women's exit advantage but leave men's unchanged.

With respect to the distribution of post-divorce assets between husband and wife, what legal rule would best achieve equalization of intramarital bargaining power? Consider first one key determinant of bargaining power imbalance: exit threat disparity attributable to different prospects outside of marriage. A transfer rule that neutralized that disparity must insure that neither party had more to fear from the other's defection from the marriage. The rule that would accomplish that purpose, assuming perfect information and enforcement, would require that assets be adjusted between parties following divorce such that both parties are, at the very least, indifferent between continuing or terminating the marriage.

Such a rule would operate in a manner similar to a requirement of bilateral consent to divorce. (Unfortunately, as will be discussed below, it also has some of the same drawbacks.[316]) Under this rule, the party who seeks dissolution must transfer enough assets to the party who resists divorce to make that party at least as well off outside the relationship as he or she expects to be within it. If that transfer rule is imposed, no one will ask for a divorce unless the divorce is Pareto efficient. In effect, the rule would force the spouse initiating divorce to internalize the costs of divorce to the unit as a whole by shielding the other from the current and prospective costs suffered from the termination of a relationship. That means that neither party should be unduly influenced in his or her intramarital negotiation strategy by the other's exit threat.

Apart from any practical difficulties,[317] adopting a post-divorce transfer rule expressly designed to correct an imbalance in bargaining power would require thinking about alimony in an entirely new way. The proper measure of post-divorce alimony is a complex subject that has received intense academic attention, in part because of a lack of consensus about the nature of the marital con-

---

[316] For discussions of bilateral consent rules, see supra Section V.A; infra note 331 and accompanying text.

[317] The rule would be plagued by all the problems of valuation, tailoring, and prediction that would mark any scheme for intramarital regulation by private contract.

tract and the duties spouses owe to one another.[318] Any rule that would govern alimony for the purpose of correcting an imbalance in bargaining power must take into account remarriage prospects. That would require a very different rule from one ever seriously proposed. For example, it would mandate some readjustment in favor of the woman—based on the actuarial chance of remarriage—regardless of whether she seemed to assume greater responsibility at home or managed to maintain earnings or career parity with her husband.[319] Under current alimony practice, in contrast, it would be rare for a woman with significant earning power and an uninterrupted work record to receive alimony on her own account.[320] But any rule designed to equalize bargaining power would need to focus as much on the role of passive depreciation in the marital balancing act as on active and measurable opportunity costs.

Such a post-divorce transfer rule has its limitations in addition to difficulties in implementation.[321] A stringent alimony rule, like private prenuptial contracts, leaves the marriage market unregulated. The rule would have the predicted effects of any measure that takes power away from men and reduces the risk of exploitation for women. Some men's unwillingness to marry on those terms

---

[318] See, e.g., Ellman, supra note 63; Elisabeth M. Landes, Economics of Alimony, 7 J. Legal Stud. 35 (1978); Parkman, supra note 40; Symposium on Divorce and Feminist Legal Theory, supra note 4; Symposium on Family Law, 1991 BYU L. Rev. 1; Trebilcock & Keshvani, supra note 4. For a comprehensive review of the subject, see Estin, supra note 4, and Estin, supra note 36. Alimony's possible purposes include holding couples to their long-term promises, promoting efficient investment, compensating for loss of a reliance interest, or deterrence. The measure of alimony consistent with each purpose will have different effects on bargaining power as well as other incidents of marriage, including stability.

[319] The rule could be based on actuarial projections of remarriage prospects (broken down by parameters such as age, sex, income, and education). Alternatively, income and assets could be divided with an upward adjustment upon the remarriage of one spouse to compensate the unmarried spouse for the value of the married spouse's new partner. Such a rule would greatly discourage remarriage and new family formation by *both* men and women.

[320] See Weitzman, supra note 12, at 147-50 (describing the circumstances under which alimony is awarded under the current no-fault system).

[321] Recognizing long-term post-marital claims by one spouse on the other's income, which would be required to make the rule work, would discourage labor market participation and hard work through a substitution effect, or would drive workers into the underground economy. See, e.g., Burggraf, supra note 81, at 133. The most pronounced effects would be felt on the low end of the income scale, where labor market participation is tenuous.

would tend to produce a decline in marriage rates from current
levels and a delay in the age of marriage.[322] Some women might
have to settle for lower quality men. On the other hand, as with
antenuptial contracts,[323] a rule creating a more enforceable long-
term contract should lead to a deeper and more efficient level of
intramarital investment and more stable and predictable marital
relationships. The diminution in the payoff from opportunistic defection should create a larger "marital pie," shares of which compensate the average woman for other marriage market effects. For
persons of both sexes seeking stability and a reliable return on investment, this effect would increase the incentive to get married.[324]
Finally, an alimony rule that seeks to compensate for intangible
losses through monetary transfers would function in a fashion that
discriminated against the poor. Because people at the lower end of
the income scale would be pushed below the subsistence level by
any interspousal transfer of income, they will rarely initiate divorce
under a rule that really takes into account all forms of prospective loss.

Contrast the complete-internalization rule with a regime that has
been proposed by some commentators: post-marital equal sharing
of income.[325] Income splitting has the virtue of simplicity. It does
not require case by case evaluation and adjustment for the tangible
or intangible components of relative contribution, sacrifice, benefit, or opportunity cost during the marriage. But in its very simplicity lies its weakness as an instrument for equalizing bargaining
power. A pure division of partners' income is a very blunt instrument for bringing about equalization of bargaining positions within

---

[322] For a discussion of marriage market effects of private contracts, see supra Section V.D.

[323] For a discussion of the efficiency of antenuptial contracts, see supra Section
V.D.1.

[324] Jana Singer has suggested that a simple post-divorce income-sharing requirement
might have the effect of "encourag[ing] *husbands* to increase their investment in
family care, 'since the financial consequences of such an investment strategy would
not be so devastating in the event of a divorce, and the benefits of investing solely in
one's own career would not be so complete.'" Singer, Alimony and Efficiency, supra
note 187, at 2455 (quoting Jana B. Singer, Divorce Reform and Gender Justice, 67
N.C. L. Rev. 1103, 1121 (1989) [hereinafter Singer, Divorce Reform]).

[325] See, e.g., Burggraf, supra note 81, at 131-33, 254; Martha L. Fineman, Implementing Equality: Ideology, Contradiction and Social Change, 1983 Wis. L. Rev. 789;
Okin, supra note 32, at 180-83; Singer, Alimony and Efficiency, supra note 187, at
2454-60; Singer, Divorce Reform, supra note 324, at 1114-21.

marriage. It fails to take into account the individualized, intangible benefits and costs of a marriage and its alternatives—including average differences by sex. Although this lack of flexibility would help some women by raising their exit advantage to near parity or beyond, it would hurt others (by undercompensating them), and it would also unfairly hurt some men (by overtaxing them).

Moreover, if a background of no-fault divorce is assumed, a rigid income-sharing rule would apply regardless of who initiated divorce and would dictate the same allocation regardless of how much better or worse off each partner would be following divorce. As such, it would often fail to take into account "what, in many cases, may be the most significant loss associated with divorce: the loss of the marital status itself."[326] Such loss is somewhat greater for women and grows with age. The person who can remarry— more often the man—will gain a share of a new marital surplus and perhaps a second income. The income-splitting rule provides no special compensation for this differential in threat advantage, and thus may often (as when earnings are similar) undercompensate the wife. In addition, because the income-splitting rule looks only to earnings disparity and not to the remarriage chances of divorced spouses, such a rule could severely penalize some higher-earning women, imposing even greater pressure on them to make marital concessions to forestall the loss of their husbands.

Finally, adoption of a post-divorce redistribution rule that assigns one partner an enduring share in a former partner's future income regardless of any notion of breach or fault creates an opportunity for strategic behavior on the part of a nonearning or lower-earning spouse. If, for reasons unrelated to her husband's misfeasance or hard bargaining, a lower-earning wife feels she would be better off outside the marriage—perhaps because she has found a better prospective husband—then she gains a windfall by initiating divorce. (This would, at the very least, create a disincentive for men to marry women without independent income or to consent to a wife's withdrawal from paid employment.) Alternatively, if the marriage remains marginally valuable to her absent income redistribution, but is worth leaving if she can gain an equal share of her husband's post-divorce income, the income-sharing rule will induce

---

[326] Singer, Alimony and Efficiency, supra note 187, at 2448.

her to leave even if it would make her husband worse off. Put another way, a rigid income-sharing rule creates a moral hazard by
encouraging divorce in cases in which divorce is not Pareto superior to staying married and thus ends up imposing deadweight
losses on one spouse.[327] That problem bears directly on bargaining
power: The spouse in danger of bearing the costs of divorce will be
at a bargaining disadvantage within the marriage.[328]

The ideal complete-internalization rule suggested above, in contrast, does not present this particular danger. A spouse would not
seek a divorce unless that partner would be so much better off outside the marriage that he or she could afford to transfer enough assets to make the other partner better off as well. There would be
no deadweight loss and no opportunism. Many couples would stay
married rather than divorce when one partner wanted out, because
the mandated transfer would make that partner worse off than he
or she would be by remaining married.

The complete-internalization rule has its own difficulties, however, which are characteristic of all alimony rules that are triggered

---

[327] As Michael Trebilcock and Rosemin Keshvani write:
> In constructing the hypothetical contract at the time of marriage, would the two
> parties agree that the wife should share in the husband's economic returns both
> where there is no marriage dissolution and where there is? ... [N]o insurer
> would write such a policy because the wife may well be rendered largely indif-
> ferent to sustaining or terminating the marriage, given the assumption that her
> entitlements on divorce are not contingent on proof of absence of fault on her
> part for the marriage dissolution.

Trebilcock & Keshvani, supra note 4, at 557; see also H. Elizabeth Peters, Marriage
and Divorce: Informational Constraints and Private Contracting, 76 Am. Econ. Rev.
437, 443-44 (1986) (discussing moral hazard in the context of marital relationships).

[328] Jana Singer argues that the moral hazard endemic in post-divorce income splitting is overstated because "income sharing after divorce is not likely to improve a
lower wage earner's financial position." Singer, Alimony and Efficiency, supra note
187, at 2457. She explains that "given the added expense of maintaining two households, divorce is likely to result in a net decrease in both spouses' financial well-
being," id., and that "a lower wage earning spouse is likely to have invested disproportionately in marriage-specific human capital, ... [thus] reduc[ing] a spouse's incentive to engage in opportunistic behavior during marriage." Id. at 2458.

Although Singer's observations are valid, her analysis suffers from a failure to consider the full range of scenarios that could obtain if income sharing were available. A
"predatory wife" might marry with an eye towards gaining a partial claim on a future
husband's income. Or a fragile but "efficient" marriage might become worth more
dead than alive to a lower earning spouse. By giving one spouse the chance to improve her position at the expense of the other, the sharing rule might result in a decrease in total well-being overall.

by the desire to exit rather than by breach of a well-defined promise or fault.[329] The very scenario that creates the greatest difficulty for an inflexible income-sharing rule—that of the lower-earning spouse who nevertheless would like to leave the marriage—also exposes the practical flaws inherent in the less rigid rule. Once again, the bedrock presumption of the internalization rule is that the party who seeks the divorce has judged that he or she will be better off outside the marriage, taking into account both tangible and intangible benefits, and regardless of any apparent decline in financial well-being. Thus, if a lower-earning wife seeks a divorce and her husband resists, the presumption would apply, and the transfer rule will mandate that, if anything, assets will flow from her to her husband to compensate him for his losses. In practice, the application of the presumption gives rise to the objection already discussed, which stems from the monetization of marital value inherent in any rule of compensation: It favors the party with money or the ability to generate it. A lower-earning wife who has invested primarily in marital capital and who has little labor market value may be so miserable that she feels she is better off without her husband, but she may lack the means to pay for the privilege of exit.[330] This would mean that, as a practical matter, higher-earning spouses (mostly men) would be able to buy their way out of loveless or irksome marriages more often than traditional wives.

The complete-internalization rule is also not free of the potential to elicit strategic behavior. Although it neutralizes the predatory wife problem posed by the income-sharing rule (by barring transfers to the one initiating divorce), it fails to deal adequately with a disturbing alternative scenario: the miserable wife married to the bad or exploitative husband. If the husband makes the marriage undesirable or worthless to the wife through infidelity, misfeasance, or noncooperation—if he uses his superior intramarital threat advantage to destroy or appropriate a large share of marital assets, even to the point of pushing the wife below a reservation price already made quite low by poor extramarital prospects, large marriage-specific investments, and the burden of children—then the husband could effectively sidestep the obligation to pay ali-

---

[329] See, e.g., Ellman, supra note 4, at 6-9, 49-53, 74-81.
[330] See Zelder, supra note 270, at 506 (pointing out that many of the assets of marriage are tied up in children, who are neither liquid nor divisible).

mony through his own misdeeds.[331] In effect, he could use his other sources of bargaining power advantage to torment his wife so much that divorce would entail a net utility gain for her, thus relieving him of the obligation to provide her with any compensation upon exit. A rule that ignores the husband's capacity to engage in this loss-making strategy cannot hope to accomplish a *comprehensive* equalization of marital bargaining power. This is just another way of saying that the alimony rule functions poorly if it allows payment to a spouse despite "fault." A fault conception, however, would only work well if it was sufficiently sensitive to take into account the full range of strategies, from annoying to egregious, for inducing the other spouse to initiate divorce.

The prime strategy for driving the other to initiate divorce is to take advantage of intramarital threat potential. Thus, adjusting exit threats through monetary allocations would not suffice: The rule would have to be combined with some form of direct intramarital intervention or redistribution to neutralize shortfalls from differences in intramarital threat potential and chronic negotiating weakness.[332] But, as we have seen, direct intramarital regulation— whether by contract or by rule—would be infeasible and transform the nature of the institution beyond recognition.

One way to mitigate—if not entirely negate—the perversities of the wealth effect and the potential for strategic appropriation of marital capital would be to supplement an alimony rule based on complete internalization with a requirement like the one proposed

---

[331] See the discussion of parallel problems with the rule requiring bilateral consent for divorce, supra Section V.A. The most extreme example would be physical abuse or the threat of abuse, which is not uncommon. See, e.g., Demie Kurz, For Richer, For Poorer: Mothers Confront Divorce 52-56, 64-75 (1995) (describing the role of physical violence for a sample of divorcing couples). The rule could be written to make an exception for this type of behavior, but that would leave untouched the considerable portion of men's intramarital threat advantage that does not stem from or require resort to physical violence.

[332] An alimony rule, like an antenuptial bargaining term, could be designed to include post-marital monetary compensation for any imbalances in costs and benefits that resulted from intramarital bargaining weakness. As with the antenuptial term, such a rule would only compensate for imbalance in the event of divorce, but would have little effect on the conduct of an ongoing marriage. See supra note 298; cf. Ellman, supra note 4 (rejecting on feasibility grounds any alimony rule that attempts to adjust for inequities during the life of the marriage); Ellman, supra note 63, at 280 (arguing against adopting an alimony rule that provides "a remedy for unfair exchanges during the marriage").

by Ira Ellman, which seeks to compensate the spouse who has invested disproportionately in marriage-specific capital. Ellman proposes that alimony reflect such a spouse's opportunity cost in the form of forgone investment in market human capital or other tangible or clearly quantifiable sources of potential financial gain.[333] In the event an unhappy low-earning wife initiates a divorce that is not mutually agreeable, that supplemental principle would usually have the effect of converting her indeterminate debit into a credit, at least insofar as she could demonstrate that her greater investment in domestic pursuits entailed a personal financial sacrifice. Even a wife with considerable earning power might be able to argue for forgone opportunity and escape having to pay for the privilege of divorce if she could demonstrate a greater in-kind contribution to the maintenance of the household.

3. Welfare payments

An alternative way to increase women's well-being outside of marriage, and thus reduce men's marital threat advantage within marriage, is for the government to make payments to ex-wives or custodial mothers directly. Until recently the United States had AFDC, a means-tested federal family-allowance program.[334] Before the repeal of the program, AFDC paid benefits not just to ex-wives but also to never-married single mothers. Persons qualifying for AFDC often received supplemental benefits such as Medicaid or Food Stamps. These benefits might have had the effect of making some women with low earnings capacity virtually indifferent as between marriage and non-marriage. Because the package of aid was sometimes as or more valuable than full-time wages at the bottom of the income scale,[335] federal poverty programs set women up as the equivalent of non-working wives to phantom husbands. To be sure, some real-life husbands supply extras in the

---

[333] See Ellman, supra note 4, at 49-53.

[334] 42 U.S.C. §§ 601-687 (1994). The program was repealed in 1996 and replaced with a block grant program known as Temporary Assistance to Needy Families ("TANF"). Pub. L. No. 104-193, 110 Stat. 2105, 2112 (1996). Under TANF, however, some states have continued benefits programs similar to those in place under AFDC.

[335] See, e.g., Michael Tanner, Stephen Moore & David Hartman, Cato Institute, The Work vs. Welfare Trade-Off: An Analysis of the Total Level of Welfare Benefits by State, Sept. 19, 1995; Michael Tanner & Naomi Lopez, Cato Institute, The Value of Welfare, June 12, 1996.

form of emotional support and partial sharing of household responsibilities, but other husbands may impose net costs that partially offset the income they provide. AFDC may be more attractive than these husbands by supplying the income without the costs.

These poverty programs would tend to put poor women in a powerful bargaining position with respect to low-earning husbands. But such programs would also probably destabilize existing marriages among eligible populations or deter marriage altogether. Marital instability and low rates of marriage among the most poorly educated and least employable groups are consistent with these predicted effects, although they clearly have other causes as well.[336]

F. Informal Social Norms Revisited

As the previous discussion suggests, there are two important parameters that must be considered when trying to correct bargaining imbalance between husbands and wives: intramarital threats and divorce exit threats. There are in turn two important elements to be considered in any attempt to adjust men's and women's divorce exit threats: each spouse's relative value of leaving the marriage compared to the other's and the absolute value of the exit threat for each spouse. The latter affects the incentive to marry and stay married. If exit threat is to be set equal as between the sexes, there are three possible permutations: raise one spouse's threat point so both are high, lower the other's so both are low, or establish some point between the extremes. Federal poverty programs may have had the effect of raising some women's well-being outside of marriage to a level virtually equivalent to, or perhaps greater than, their well-being within most marriages they potentially could make. Because women could have children out of wedlock without losing welfare benefits, the expected costs to a welfare-eligible woman of remaining or becoming single was brought within the range of the costs to a man, with costs being rather low for both. In effect, the threat advantage for both potential partners was rendered quite high, with a predictable destabilizing effect. A complete-internalization

---

[336] See, e.g., Daniel T. Lichter, The Retreat from Marriage and the Rise in Nonmarital Fertility, *in* Dep't of Health & Human Servs., Report to Congress on Out-of-Wedlock Childbearing 137, 138 (1995) (discussing evidence that recent declines in marriage have been greatest among least-educated women).

alimony rule would, in contrast, adjust one spouse's exit threat upward (the payee) and the other's downward (the payor). The hope is that the adjustment would, at worst, have a negligible effect on marital stability, and at best would decrease instability by forcing the would-be defector to internalize some of the losses imposed on the spouse who would be abandoned.

Perhaps the most pro-marriage rule of all, however, is one that insures that both spouses' exit prospects are similarly unattractive. Before about 1960, divorce carried a stigma in American society that had real reputational and economic consequences. Those included difficulties in remarrying, ineligibility for higher political office, and possible derailment of promising professional or business careers—all consequences with potentially greater impact on men. The informality of the stigma allowed for gradations in response depending on circumstance and perceived fault.[337] To be sure, *all* divorced persons were suspect, and women who abandoned their families or were otherwise thought to have contributed to their own difficulties were judged harshly. But because it was understood that dependent wives had more to lose from divorce than men, a man's defection invited special opprobrium.

The insights of bargaining theory reveal that remarkable wisdom informed the informal customs that made the post-divorce state unpleasant for all concerned. Other defunct social norms that made the unmarried state unattractive for men, such as the taboo against casual premarital sex and the expectation of marriage following out-of-wedlock pregnancy ("shotgun marriage"), also helped even the playing field between men and women within marriage.[338] But those norms, although supplemented by religious

---

[337] See, e.g., Joseph Adelson, Splitting Up, Commentary, Sept. 1996, at 63; Frank F. Furstenberg, Jr., History and Current Status of Divorce in the United States, 4 Future of Children, Spring 1994, at 29; Richard Epstein, Enforcing Norms: When the Law Gets in the Way, Responsive Community, Fall 1997, at 1, 7 ("When divorce was regarded as socially unacceptable, divorcees found it difficult to get jobs, join clubs, or run for public office."). See generally Jonathan Rauch, Live and Let Lie, New Republic, Sept. 22, 1997, at 24 (describing bygone informal social controls surrounding marriage, adultery, and divorce).

[338] See, e.g., Burggraf, supra note 81, at 112; David Popenoe, Modern Marriage: Revising the Cultural Script, *in* Promises to Keep: Decline and Renewal of Marriage in America 261 (David Popenoe, Jean Bethke Elshtain & David Blankenhorn eds., 1996) ("Under the old system . . . if a man wanted regular sex (other than with prostitutes) he had to marry."); see also Akerlof, Yellen & Katz, supra note 281, at 284

scruples, have ultimately proved highly unstable. Greater mobility, women's increasing financial independence, and changing attitudes about the role of sex, relationships, and marriage have contributed

---

tbl.II (noting decline in shotgun weddings from 1965 to 1984). Bargaining theory predicts that the stigma attached to premarital sex would strengthen women's hand within marriage by making sex harder to obtain. The shotgun marriage practice would also tend to have this effect, since it imposed severe penalties on men who abandoned or refused to marry a pregnant girlfriend.

According to Akerlof and his co-authors, shotgun marriages occurred because women customarily elicited a promise of marriage in the event of pregnancy in exchange for agreeing to engage in premarital sex, and men routinely made good on that promise to avoid the social and reputational costs of reneging. Id. at 297-304. With the advent of the birth control pill and legalized abortion, the market was flooded with women who were willing to take contraceptives or abort, and thus these women had less of an incentive to extract a promise of marriage as the price of engaging in premarital sex. This development destabilized the "promise" norm by putting women who insisted on a provisional promise of commitment at a competitive disadvantage in attracting young men. Id. at 307-10.

According to the authors, the increased availability of sex without a promise of marriage led to an increase in the out-of-wedlock birth rate. Id. Some women (mostly those in the lower socioeconomic classes) who found themselves pregnant—and who previously would have been good candidates for shotgun brides—decided to go ahead with their pregnancies even if the fathers refused to marry them. If one of the important reasons men marry is to have their own children, then the reported increased willingness of some women to bear children out-of-wedlock would be predicted to increase their prospective mates' well-being outside of marriage as well. This would not only decrease these men's willingness to marry, but might also increase men's leverage within those marriages that are contracted.

The dramatic recent increase in the age of first marriage for both men and women, see supra note 1, is consistent with the contemporaneous increase in the availability of premarital sex in all social classes. The ease of obtaining sex outside of marriage decreases the costs of delayed marriage for both sexes, but especially for men, who are always faced with greater scarcity of sexual opportunities. See Akerlof, Yellen & Katz, supra note 281, at 309 (noting the erosion over the past three decades of the taboo against premarital sex except as a prelude to marriage). But the lifetime marriage rates among higher socioeconomic classes has not dropped nearly as much as among the less educated. See Lichter, supra note 336, at 138-39. This pattern may be due partly to the practical unavailability to higher status men of having their own children outside marriage. In contrast, out-of-wedlock birthrates have exploded among the relatively poor and less well-educated: More men in those groups can now obtain both sex and children outside the marital union. See Wax, supra note 266, at 493 n.6 (citing statistics on rates of extramarital childbearing, which indicate that rates decline steeply among white women as education and income rise). Interestingly, single motherhood through artificial insemination or adoption does not have the effect of giving identifiable men their own children. To the extent that well-off white women favor those methods, out-of wedlock childbearing (which occurs infrequently in this group anyway) will make little contribution to men's extramarital welfare or their disincentive to marry.

to the erosion of the informal social sanctions.[339] The steep rise in the divorce rate to a near-majority phenomenon has made it more difficult to treat divorced persons as deviant and socially marginal or to impose meaningful reputational costs.[340] As a result, the social stigma that once attached to divorce has all but disappeared in most quarters. Finally, informal sanctions against divorce carried a social price. By imposing additional and onerous transaction costs on divorce, the fear of social disapproval held some people in otherwise negative-sum unions. In addition, spouses were locked into inefficient relationships in which one spouse had more to gain from divorce than the other had to lose—a problem better solved with post-divorce redistribution. On the other hand, the social stigma of divorce was particularly effective in protecting the well-being of third parties—most notably, children—whose interests in the continuation of an unhappy marriage did not precisely coincide with their parents'.

VI. CONCLUSION

While not solving the puzzle entirely, this account of marital bargaining provides an important missing piece in the search for explanations of why women occupy a lower social status and perform the lion's share of less valued work. More specifically, it helps to explain why married women—still the majority of women—appear on average to work harder and longer and for fewer rewards than their husbands. The standard account says that women are doing what they want to do: They like it this way, and would not change it if they could. Alternatively, women just *appear* to do worse. There are hidden compensations and consolations that make them just as well off as men. When different preferences and utilities are factored in, equality reigns.

---

[339] See, e.g., Barbara Dafoe Whitehead, The Divorce Culture (1997) (documenting the recent destigmatization of divorce); see also Toni M. Massaro, Shame, Culture, and American Criminal Law, 89 Mich. L. Rev. 1880, 1916 (1991) (discussing forces of modernity, mobility, and anonymity that contribute to the erosion of social norms).

[340] See Daniel Patrick Moynihan, Defining Deviancy Down, 62 Am. Scholar 17 (1993) (discussing general difficulty of maintaining social stigma against behaviors as they become more common); Sunstein, Social Norms, supra note 32, at 929-30 (discussing the costs of policing social norms); Wax, supra note 266, at 508-25, 533-37 (discussing erosion of norms stigmatizing illegitimacy).

Although bargaining theory cannot definitively refute this account, it shows why there is no reason to credit these stories and good reason not to. Women probably *do not* like it that way and *would* change it if they could. But they cannot, because they lack the leverage to do so. The reasons behind this dilemma lie deep within the structure of marriage itself. The bilateral and monopolistic institutional framework—in which each woman is forced to bargain with one man with little outside help or intervention—is an effective mechanism for turning women's differences to women's disadvantage. To be sure, the scope for "private" bargaining within the marital relationship is affected by baseline rules of domestic law (supplemented by custom), which in turn determine the rights and obligations that spouses have towards each other. These factors can strengthen or weaken women's hand. But domestic law has been increasingly deregulated and privatized.[341] By imposing fewer and fewer specific obligations on spouses and leaving more matters to be worked out between the parties, recent changes have forced women to rely on the not-so-tender mercies of a bargaining game undertaken from a baseline of unequal starting points and bargaining strength. The key structural features of our current marital regime—exclusivity, minimal and sex-blind barriers to exit, no intramarital enforcement of promises or contracts, and little post-marital redistribution of resources—insure that the institution operates very much in men's favor. But even though some of these features represent fairly recent innovations and reforms that could be abandoned, there are limits to what law or custom can do to strengthen women's bargaining position, given marriage's fundamental nature. Conflict and power cannot be wished out of marriage. Nor can the disparity between men's and women's positions. That disparity is not just a contingency of the institution, a superficial cultural gloss that can be discarded in some times and at some places. Rather, it is of the essence: a consequence that springs from the deep and defining nature of marriage as a *monopolistic* institution marked by the expectation of exclusivity, fidelity, and cooperation for living. Marriage has always been a two-person bargain at its core, insofar as many key matters between husband and wife, including divisions of labor and reward, have always been

---

[341] See, e.g., Mnookin & Kornhauser, supra note 89, at 952-58; Singer, supra note 277.

regarded as "something to be sorted out privately rather than made a subject of public intervention."[342] To the extent the spouses must work out the most important terms of their life together and then rely largely on self-help to make those terms stick, marriage must continue to be an institution in which "the balance between freedom of action and security . . . [remains] dependent on shrewdness, negotiating skill, and the preexisting distribution of wealth, power, and legal entitlements."[343]

To be sure, the structure of the marital relationship is not the only culprit responsible for women's disadvantage. Such diverse factors as the rigidities of the labor market,[344] the pro-breadwinner bias in the tax code,[345] the cultural equation of manliness with occupational success,[346] the eroticization of men's dominance over women,[347] the stigma of male domesticity,[348] the "iron law of childcare,"[349] and the residue of job discrimination and sexual harassment all are important. Women's own outlook and aspirations also play a role. Such putative traits as women's greater concern for children, for compromise over conflict, and for caring rather than ruling would put them at a competitive disadvantage in the wider world even if marriage could somehow be radically transformed or even extinguished as a social norm. Women's preferences still might lead to systematic specialization even within a marital institution structured to achieve a more egalitarian balance; in turn, women might hold fewer positions of worldly power, and women's interests might be slighted. There is no simple solution to this problem, and the abolition of all traces of sexual caste would

---

[342] Richard A. Posner, Conservative Feminism, U. Chi. Legal F. 1989, at 191, 200.

[343] Gregory C. Keating, The Idea of Fairness in the Law of Enterprise Liability, 95 Mich. L. Rev 1266, 1302 (1997); see also Tracy E. Higgins, Democracy and Feminism, 110 Harv. L. Rev. 1657, 1674 (1997) (discussing the idea that women's relative lack of power in private relationships—as opposed to the public sphere—is a significant source of women's inequality).

[344] See McCaffery, supra note 186; Williams, supra note 3.

[345] See Edward J. McCaffery, Taxing Women (1997).

[346] See Williams, supra note 3, at 2238-39.

[347] See, e.g., Catherine A. MacKinnon, Feminism Unmodified 127-214 (1987).

[348] See Williams, supra note 3, at 2243; Case, supra note 159.

[349] See Fuchs, supra note 7, at 137 (noting that the labor intensiveness of childcare entails either that most women cannot afford trustworthy care, or that childcare workers will be poorly paid).

clearly require radical and far-reaching changes (which in turn would entail some very real costs).

Nonetheless, marriage as currently structured remains a critical and important component of women's inequality. There is a disparity between the promise of equal partnership that marriage represents and the means to enforce that promise. Neither legalistic measures nor private contracts provide the complete solution to the problem of bargaining imbalance within marriage. Nevertheless, marriage generally performs its social functions best when enduring as a long-term contract in which participants honor their reciprocal obligations. Unfortunately, few marital obligations are effectively enforced either formally or informally. A deliberate decision has been made to give divorcing couples a clean break. Thus, the final accounting ordained by current law and custom does little to make good on the types of long-term promises that are the source of most of the institution's unique social benefits. The failure to enforce the promises implicit in the marital relationship, although certainly not the exclusive source of men's and women's inequality within marriage, contributes to it by opening the way for rampant opportunism that disproportionately harms women and children. Proposals that attempt to make marital promises stick—such as the revival of alimony, fault, and consent requirements—have some potential to strengthen women's hand within marriage. But the sex-neutral form that these proposals most often take undermines that potential by strengthening men's position as well.

There is no panacea for women's age-old dilemma in marriage. It is difficult to redistribute power in relationships that depend, in important part, on voluntary choices and voluntary contributions between unequals, and it is difficult to transform a vital social institution that, in its transformation, would be destroyed. The relative powerlessness of women within marriage that is described in this Article—and the sense of being *overpowered* in a relationship central to human existence and happiness—marks out an important but poorly understood locus of dejection at the heart of feminine experience. The resignation that characterizes women's outlook on relationships with men and the persistence of the "woman question" in general can be traced in large part to the basic intransigence of the problem of marriage as a relationship that aspires to be between equals, but is not. Indeed, it could be argued that the gulf between aspiration and reality (or between aspiration and structure) is a source of frustration for both sexes, since men must also learn to live within an institution rigged to their own advantage but not of their own making.

Finally, the built-in structural inequalities of marriage, which may once have been thought to be a source of strength for the institution, may now have come to represent a fatal weakness. The evidence would suggest that women are increasingly dissatisfied with marriage as it currently exists. More and more women are turning their backs on their marriage, often seemingly at great cost to themselves and their children. One possible explanation for this otherwise puzzling behavior is that women, as weak bargainers, are losing out in the marital give and take to the point where they perceive themselves as better off outside marriage than within it. Or perhaps they are repelled by the imbalance in their "positive-sum" bargain and have come to see that imbalance as fundamentally unfair. Can women's sense of injustice and the desire for a fair deal be suppressed forever, even for their own and their children's sake? Must the chronic imbalance in such a key relationship—one so central to social life and to the fate of individuals—inevitably generate rebellion?[350] Women's growing distaste for marital inequality—coupled with men's unsurprising desire to maintain it—may represent the most potent and ominous threat to the institution of marriage so far.

---

[350] See, e.g., Joshua Cohen, The Arc of the Moral Universe, 26 Phil. & Pub. Aff. 91 (1997) (suggesting that human moral and emotional makeup is such that a group's chronic experience of relative powerlessness within a basic social institution—such as slavery—must inevitably lead to a recognition of injustice and a rebellion against injustice).

Part II
Parenting and Being Married

A
Family and State

[9]

THE FAMILY AND THE STATE*

GARY S. BECKER and KEVIN M. MURPHY

University of Chicago and National Opinion Research Center

I. INTRODUCTION

CHILDREN are incapable of caring for themselves during many years of physical and mental maturation. Since their mental development is not sufficient to trust any contractual arrangements they may reach with caretakers, laws and social norms regulate the production and rearing of children. Laws punish child abuse, the sale of children, and unauthorized abortions. They provide compulsory schooling, welfare payments to families with dependent children, stringent rules about divorce when young children are involved, and minimum ages of marriage.

Trades and contracts are efficient if no deviation from the terms would raise the welfare of all participants. An alternative criterion for efficiency is that the monetary gains to those benefiting from a deviation do not exceed the monetary loss to those harmed. Unfortunately, the immaturity of children sometimes precludes efficient arrangements between children and parents or others responsible for child care.

This difficulty in establishing efficient relations within families provides the point of departure for our interpretation of the heavy state involvement in the family. We believe that a surprising number of state interventions mimic the agreements that would occur if children were capable of arranging for their care. Stated differently, our belief is that many regulations of the family improve the efficiency of family activities. To be sure, these regulations raise the welfare of children, but they also raise the welfare of parents, or at least they raise the combined welfare of parents and children.

* This is the ninth Henry Simons Lecture, delivered by Becker to the University of Chicago Law School on February 25, 1987. We received valuable research assistance from Michael Gibbs and insightful comments on an earlier draft from David Friedman, Richard Posner, and Sam Preston. Our research was supported by National Science Foundation grant SES-8520258 and by National Institute of Child Health and Human Development grant SSP 1 R37 HD22054.

[*Journal of Law & Economics*, vol. XXXI (April 1988)]

2   THE JOURNAL OF LAW AND ECONOMICS

The efficiency perspective implies that the state is concerned with justice for children, if "justice" is identified with the well-being of children, for their well-being is the prime factor in our analysis. The efficiency perspective does not imply, however, that the effect on children alone determines whether the state intervenes. The effect on parents is considered too. The state tends to intervene when both gain or when the gain to children exceeds the loss to their parents.

According to Richard Posner and others, the common law also improves efficiency when transaction costs are large. Richard Posner says, "In settings where the cost of allocating resources by voluntary market transactions is prohibitively high—where, in other words, market transactions are infeasible—the common law prices behavior in such a way as to mimic the market."[1]

We cannot *prove* that efficiency guides state involvement in the family. We will show, however, that state interventions in the market for schooling, the provision of old-age pensions, and access to divorce are consistent on the whole with the efficiency perspective.

The modern theory of regulation and public choice questions whether much government activity encourages efficiency and justice. Section VII sketches an analysis of interest-group behavior that can lead to government intervention to promote efficient family arrangements.

In order to interpret public policies, we develop an analysis of family behavior under different circumstances. The analysis greatly extends earlier work by Becker. His Woytinsky Lecture of more than twenty years ago shows that only parents who give their adult children gifts or bequests make optimal investments in children.[2] Becker and Tomes, and Becker's *A Treatise on the Family* develop this approach further.[3] Thompson and Ruhter reached the same conclusion while apparently unaware of this earlier literature.[4]

Our discussion of the gains from government intervention in family decisions generalizes the analysis of subsidies to schooling and other human capital found in Becker's Woytinsky Lecture and *Treatise*.[5] Thompson and Ruhter have a nice analysis with a similar interpretation of

[1] Richard A. Posner, Economic Analysis of Law 230 (3d ed. 1986).

[2] Gary S. Becker, Human Capital and the Personal Distribution of Income: An Analytical Approach, W. S. Woytinsky Lecture (1967), reprinted in Gary S. Becker, Human Capital (2d ed. 1975).

[3] Gary S. Becker & Nigel Tomes, Human Capital and the Rise and Fall of Families, 4 J. Lab. Econ. S1 (1986); Gary S. Becker, A Treatise on the Family (1981).

[4] Earl A. Thompson & Wayne E. Ruhter, Parental Malincentives and Social Legislation (unpublished paper, UCLA, undated).

[5] Becker, *supra* note 2; Becker, *supra* note 3.

government intervention in families.[6] Also relevant is the discussion of fertility by Nerlove, Razin, and Sadka.[7]

II. ALTRUISM TOWARD CHILDREN

We assume that the large majority of parents are altruistic to their children in the sense that parental utility depends on the number of children and the utility of each child as well as on their own consumption. The altruism assumption is supported by the many sacrifices parents frequently make for children. Parents spend money, time, and effort on children through child care, expenditures on education and health, gifts, and bequests. More or less all parents spend on young children, but only some parents give sizable gifts to adult children or leave bequests.

Plato's *Republic* objects to the rearing of elite children by their parents. It advocates instead that "as soon as children are born, they will be taken in charge by officers appointed for this purpose . . . , while taking every precaution that no mother shall know her own child."[8] Plato's views attracted the attention of philosophers and stimulated experiments that invariably failed. Even the kibbutz movement has returned to giving parents responsibility for the care of children.

Parental altruism is the reason why essentially all societies have shown more common sense than Plato and give parents or other close relatives primary responsibility for child care. Altruistic parents are good caretakers because they consider the effects of their actions on the welfare of children. They sometimes sacrifice their own consumption and comfort to increase that of their children.

Of course, some parents abuse their children, as examples of battered children depressingly illustrate. But even contemporary Western countries display great confidence in parents as caretakers, at least relative to feasible alternatives. Despite the anguish over parental abuse of defenseless children, governments seldom remove children from their parents. Fewer than two children per 10,000 below age eighteen are under state care in either the United States or England and Wales.[9]

Sometimes cited against the importance of parents' altruism is that parents seldom insure the lives of their children. This evidence does not

[6] Thompson & Ruhter, *supra* note 4.

[7] Marc Nerlove, Assaf Razin, & Efraim Sadka, Some Welfare Theoretic Implications of Endogenous Fertility (unpublished paper, University of Pennsylvania 1987).

[8] The Republic of Plato 160 (Francis M. Cornford trans. 1951).

[9] See Robert Dingewall & John Eckelaar, Rethinking Child Protection, in State Law and the Family 99 (M. D. A. Freeman ed. 1984); American Humane Ass'n, Highlights of Official Child Neglect and Abuse Reporting (1984).

speak to the effect of a child's death on the utility of parents, however, because optimal insurance works to equalize the *marginal* utility of income in different states of the world. Even if a child's death enormously reduced parents' utility, it would not be insurable if it hardly raised and perhaps reduced the marginal utility of money to parents. Support for the importance of altruism comes from the time and effort parents devote to lowering the probability of accidents, illness, or other harm to children. These "self protection" activities respond not to the effect of a child's mishap on the marginal utility of parents' income but, rather, to their effect on the *level* of parents' utility.

Our analysis recognizes that frequent contact among family members often raises the degree of altruism. That is to say, altruism may well have some of the properties of an addictive taste that is fostered by its consumption.[10] We believe that addictive aspects of altruism better explain the apparently larger bequests by parents to children who visit them more frequently than does the view that parents use bequests to "buy" visits.[11]

The Rotten Kid Theorem states that, under certain conditions, both altruistic parents and their perhaps selfish children work out efficient relations that maximize the combined resources of the family as a whole.[12] If this theorem applies to most situations, state interventions in the family could not raise efficiency.

The Rotten Kid Theorem fails to hold, however, when parents do not give children gifts or bequests.[13] They may not give because their altruism is weak, but even parents with strong altruism may not give gifts and bequests when they expect their children to be much better off than they are. Children are better off than parents when economic growth is rapid and when their endowments of ability and other qualities are higher than those of their parents.

Bequests are large in rich families, fairly common among the middle class, and unimportant in poor families. One reason is that endowments of children tend to exceed those of their parents in poor families and to be less than their parents' in rich families. But whatever the reason, the evidence on bequests implies that certain types of efficient transactions with children are less common in poorer than in richer families. Never-

---

[10] On addiction, see Gary S. Becker & Kevin M. Murphy, A Theory of Rational Addiction, J. Pol. Econ. (in press).

[11] This view is developed in B. Douglas Bernheim, Andrei Schliefer, & Larry H. Summers, The Strategic Bequest Motive, 4 J. Lab. Econ. S151 (1986).

[12] Becker, *supra* note 3, ch. 8.

[13] Other qualifications are discussed in Theodore Bergstrom, Remarks on Public Goods Theory and the Economics of the Family (unpublished paper, University of Michigan 1984).

theless, bequests may cause other inefficiencies, as we will show in the next section.

III.   INVESTMENTS IN THE HUMAN CAPITAL OF CHILDREN

Since parents must reduce their own consumption (including leisure) to raise the time and resources they spend on child care and children's education, training, and health, even altruistic parents have to consider the trade-off between their consumption and the human capital of children. But altruistic parents who plan to leave bequests can avoid this trade-off by using bequests to help finance their investments in children. In effect, they can force even selfish children to repay them for expenditures on the children's human capital. These parents would want to invest efficiently in children because that raises children's utility without costing them anything.

To make this clear, assume a 4 percent rate of return on assets accumulated over the life cycle to provide either old-age consumption or gifts and bequests. If the marginal rate of return on investments in children exceeds 4 percent, parents who give gifts and bequests could invest more in children without lowering their own consumption by accumulating fewer assets. For example, if the marginal rate on human capital is 7 percent, an additional $1,000 invested in children raises their adult earnings by about $70 per year. If parents finance this investment through reduced savings of $1,000 and by reducing annual gifts by $40, their consumption at all ages would be unaffected by greater investment, while their children's income increases by $30 per year.

Clearly, then, altruistic parents who leave bequests will invest until the marginal rate of return on human capital equals the rate on assets. They are better off with efficient investments because they can trade between bequests and investments.

Some altruistic parents do not leave bequests because they get less marginal utility from consumption by their adult children than from their own consumption when elderly. They would like to raise their own consumption at the expense of their children's, but they cannot do this if unable to leave debts to children. Although children have been responsible for parents' debts in some societies, that is uncommon nowadays. Selfish and weakly altruistic parents would like to impose a large debt burden on their children. Social pressures can discourage this in closely knit societies where elderly parents live with and depend on the care of children, but these pressures are not effective in mobile modern countries where the elderly do not live with children.

Parents who cannot leave debt can substitute their own consumption for their children's by investing less in the children's human capital and instead saving more for old age. Therefore, in families without bequests, the equilibrium marginal rate of return on investments in children must exceed the rate on assets saved for old age; otherwise, parents would reallocate some resources from children to savings. These parents under-invest in the human capital of children.

When the rate of return on savings is less than the marginal rate on human capital, both children and parents could be better off with a "con-tract" that calls for parents to raise investments to the efficient level in return for a commitment by children to repay their elderly parents. Unfor-tunately, young children cannot be a party to such contracts. Without government intervention, social norms, or "guilt" by parents and chil-dren, families without bequests would underinvest in children's human capital.

More generally, expenditures by an altruist are inefficient in the states of the world where he gives to a beneficiary if he does not give in other states. When he does give, an altruist would get the same utility from equally small changes in his own and in his beneficiary's consumption. Therefore, he would be willing to give more in these states in return for a commitment by the beneficiary to give him even a little in the other states. The selfish beneficiary also gains from such an agreement since he would receive much more in some states than he gives up in the others. Unfortu-nately, the beneficiary's promises to give may not be credible, just as children's promises to support elderly parents may not be credible.

State intervention in the provision of education and other human capital could raise investments in children to the efficient levels. Since poor parents are least likely to make efficient investments, such intervention would also reduce the inequality in the opportunities between children from richer and poorer families. The compulsory schooling laws in the United States that began in the 1880s and spread rapidly during the subse-quent thirty years tended to have this effect. A state usually set minimum requirements at a level that was already exceeded by all but the poorest families in that state.[14] These laws raised the schooling of poor children but did not tend to affect the schooling of other children.

Subsidies to public elementary schools in the United States also began to grow in the latter half of the nineteenth century, and subsidies to public high schools expanded rapidly during the twentieth century. These sub-sidies appear to have raised the schooling of poorer families relative to

---

[14] See William M. Landes & Lewis C. Solmon, Compulsory Schooling Legislation: An Economic Analysis of Law and Social Change in the Nineteenth Century, 32 J. Econ. Hist. 54 (1972).

richer ones, for the effect of parental wealth and education on the education of children declined over time as public expenditures on schooling grew.[15]

Strong altruism of parents contributes to efficient investments in children by raising the likelihood that parents give gifts or bequests to adult children. Strong altruism may reduce efficiency in other ways, however, if children recognize that they will be rescued by parents when they get into trouble. For example, children who do not receive gifts now but expect gifts in the future from altruistic parents will save less and borrow more to increase their current consumption and reduce their future resources since altruistic parents tend to increase their gifts when children are poorer.[16] Similarly, children may have fun in school and neglect their studies if they expect greater future support from their parents when their earnings are lower. Or children who receive gifts from altruistic parents may take big risks because they expect large gifts if they fail and yet can keep most of their gains if they succeed since gifts cannot be negative.

Parents will not give children such perverse incentives if they can precommit the amount of future gifts and bequests. With precommitment, children cannot rely on parents to bail them out of bad gambles or other difficulties. Precommitment is unnecessary if parental altruism declines enough when they believe that children caused their own difficulties by gambling excessively, neglecting their studies, and so on.

Parents may choose not to precommit, however, even when it is perfectly feasible. The Rotten Kid Theorem gives one advantage of retaining flexibility in future transfers. Flexibility can discourage children from actions that help children but hurt parents even more. With flexible gifts and bequests, parents would reduce their transfers sufficiently to make children worse off if they take these actions.[17] Parents may choose not to precommit also because they want to help children who get into difficulties through no fault of their own.

When precommitment is either not feasible or not desirable, parents may take other actions to give children better incentives in the future. They would *overinvest* in education and other training if children cannot run down human capital as readily as marketable wealth. They would also invest more in other illiquid assets of children, such as their housing.

[15] David L. Featherman & Robert M. Hauser, Changes in the Socioeconomic Stratification of the Races, 82 Am. J. Soc. 621 (1976).

[16] Neil Bruce & Michael Waldman, The Rotten-Kid Theorem Meets the Samaritan's Dilemma (Working Paper No. 402, UCLA 1986); Asser Lindbeck & Jorgen W. Weibull, Strategic Interaction with Altruism: The Economics of Fait Accompli (unpublished paper, University of Stockholm 1987) develop similar arguments.

[17] Becker, *supra* note 3, at 188–89; and Bruce & Waldman (1986).

8   THE JOURNAL OF LAW AND ECONOMICS

Public policies can also discourage children from inefficient actions. Many countries require parental approval when children want to marry early, drop out of school, get an abortion, or purchase alcoholic beverages. Presumably, one reason is to prevent children who do not anticipate delayed consequences from taking actions that will make them worse off in the future. Another reason, however, is that children may anticipate all too well the future help they will receive from parents if they get into trouble. The state then tries to reproduce the effects on children's behavior of an optimal degree of commitment by parents.

IV. Social Security and Other Old-Age Support

Throughout history, children have been a major help to elderly parents. The elderly frequently have lived with children who care for them when ill and provide food and other support. In the United States a mere thirty years ago, only about 25 percent of persons over age sixty-five lived alone.[18]

Richer families who leave bequests rely less on children because they are insulated from many risks of old age. For example, parents who live longer than expected can reduce bequests to finance consumption in the additional years. The opportunity to draw on bequests provides an annuity-like protection against an unusually long life and other risks of old age. If bequests are not a large part of children's assets, elderly parents get excellent protection against various hazards through the opportunity to reduce bequests, and yet this does not have much influence on children's welfare. In effect, children would help support their parents in old age, although their support is not fully voluntary.

Children in poorer and many middle-level families would be willing to help support parents who agree to invest the efficient amount in the children's human capital. Few societies have contracts or other explicit agreements between parents and children, but many societies have social "norms" that pressure children to support elderly parents. Although little is known about how norms emerge, it is plausible that norms are weaker in modern societies with anonymous cities and mobile populations. Public expenditures on the elderly together with public expenditures on children's education and other human capital can fill the void left by the breakdown in norms.

Expenditures on the elderly in Western countries have grown rapidly in

---

[18] Robert T. Michael, Victor Fuchs, & Sharon R. Scott, Changes in the Propensity to Live Alone: 1950–76, 17 Demography 39 (1980).

recent decades. United States governments now spend more than $8,000 on each person aged sixty-five or over, largely in the form of medical and pension payments. Is the rapid growth in expenditures on the elderly mainly due to the political power of a growing elderly population? The media contains much discussion of generations fighting for a limited public purse.[19] Some economists support a balanced budget amendment to prevent present generations from heavy taxation of children and other future generations.[20] In a widely cited and stimulating presidential address to the American Population Association, Samuel Preston suggested that growing public support for the elderly has been partly at the expense of public expenditures on children.[21]

We would like to suggest the alternative interpretation that expenditures on the elderly are part of a "social compact" between generations. Taxes on adults help finance efficient investments in children. In return, adults receive public pensions and medical payments when old. This compact tries to achieve for poorer and middle-level families what richer families tend to achieve without government help; namely, efficient levels of investments in children and support to elderly parents.

Federal, state, and local expenditures on education, head start programs, welfare, and the like are large: in recent years they exceed $2,500 per child under age 22. Even though real expenditures per capita on the elderly in the United States grew at a rate exceeding 7 percent from 1950 to the 1980s, Table 1 contradicts the impression that expenditures on the elderly grew at the expense of expenditures on children. Per capita public expenditures on the young hardly changed between 1950 and 1983 relative to per capita expenditures on the old.

As Table 1 shows, public expenditures on education in the United States increased long before spending on the elderly did. If public spending on education and the elderly are both part of a social compact, then the first generation of parents taxed to finance investments in children would be the first to receive public old age support. If education taxes start when a person is a young married adult, some thirty to forty years should elapse between the growth in spending on education and the introduction of social security. Perhaps the actual lag in the United States was longer because immigration was not really constrained until the early

---

[19] See, for example, Philip Longman, Justice between the Generations, 85 Atl. Monthly 73 (1985).

[20] See James M. Buchanan & Richard E. Wagner, Democracy in Deficit: The Political Legacy of Lord Keynes (1977).

[21] Samuel H. Preston, Children and the Elderly: Divergent Paths for America's Dependents, 21 Demography 435 (1984).

TABLE 1

REAL PER CAPITA PUBLIC EXPENDITURES IN THE UNITED STATES ON PERSONS UNDER AGE
TWENTY-TWO AND SIXTY-FIVE AND OVER (1980 DOLLARS)

	Children under Twenty-two, Including Higher Education ($) (1)	Persons Sixty-five and Over ($) (2)	Col. 1/Col. 2 (3)
1920	122	*	...
1930	293	126	2.33
1940	393	1,022	.38
1950	557	1,708	.33
1960	922	3,156	.29
1970	1,825	5,447	.34
1980	2,472	7,520	.33
1983	2,515	8,307	.30

SOURCES.—U.S. Dep't of Health and Human Services, Social Security Bulletin Annual Statistical
Suppl. (various years). U.S. Dep't of Education, National Center for Education Statistics, Digest of
Education Statistics (various years). U.S. Dep't of Commerce, Bureau of the Census, Statistical Abstract
of the United States (various years).
* Unable to estimate but apparently a small amount.

1920s. A social security system introduced prior to that time might well
have encouraged substantial immigration of older people.

The much greater per capita spending on the elderly ($8,300 vs. $2,500)
seems difficult to reconcile with a social compact between the young and
the old. But these numbers are deceiving: the young, if anything, actually
do better than the old. To show this, suppose young adults pay $2,500 to
finance public investments in the human capital of each child. When
adults reach age sixty-five they receive $8,300 annually for the remainder
of their lives. These expenditures on children and the elderly continue
until possibly a last future generation. Which generations would be better
off with these expenditures?

Since the net reproduction rate in the United States is now close to
unity, we assume that the representative parent has one child at age
twenty-five. We also ignore offsetting reductions in parents' spending on
children in response to public expenditures on children and offsetting
reductions in children's support of parents in response to social security
payments (our analysis applies directly if reduced parental spending
equals reduced child support). Currently in the United States, a twenty-
five-year-old has a .79 probability of reaching age sixty-five, and a sixty-
five-year-old can expect to live until age eighty-two. Therefore, each adult
member of the initial generation would pay $2,500 annually from ages
twenty-five to forty-six and expects to receive $6,557 (.79 × $8,300) from

ages sixty-six to eighty-two. All subsequent generations receive a per capita government investment in their human capital of $2,500 until age twenty-two. The last generation does not invest in children, but it pays $6,557 from ages forty-one to fifty-seven to support the elderly of the prior generation. Each member of all in-between generations pays $2,500 from ages twenty-five to forty-six to support children of the succeeding generation, $6,557 from ages forty-one to fifty-seven to support the elderly of the prior generation,· and expects to receive $6,557 from ages sixty-six to eighty-two.

Since estimated rates of return on schooling and other types of training exceed 5 percent,[22] and since most public expenditures on children are for schooling and other training, we assume conservatively that these have an average rate of return of 5 percent in the form of equal increases in earnings from ages twenty-three to sixty-five. Then $2,500 invested for twenty-two years would increase earnings each year by $5,939. The after-tax net earnings of each member of the last generation would increase by $5,939 from ages twenty-three to forty; they decrease by $618 ($6,557–$5,939) from ages forty-one to fifty-seven while they are taxed to support the elderly of the previous generation, and they increase again by $5,939 from ages fifty-eight to sixty-five. The present value of this net earnings stream is positive for all nonnegative interest rates. Therefore, the last generation clearly gains from this exchange of child support for old-age support.

Unlike the last generation, generations between the first and the last must also support children of the succeeding generation but receive support when old. The reader can work out the arithmetic of their complicated net earnings stream, but the bottom line is that the present value of this stream is positive for nonnegative interest rates. Therefore, all generations in between the first and the last also unambiguously benefit from the present combination of public spending on the young and old.

The initial generation of adults does the least well. Each member pays $2,500 on child care from ages twenty-five to forty-six and gains $6,557 in old-age support from ages sixty-six to eighty-two. The internal rate of return on this series of gains and losses is a little less than 2 percent. This rate is slightly higher than the average interest rate (1.8) on short-term U.S. government securities from 1948 to 1980 after adjustment for anticipated inflation,[23] but it is considerably lower than the 4 percent average rate of return on tangible business capital in the United States during the

---

[22] See George Psacharopoulos, Returns to Education: An International Comparison (Keith Hinchcliffe asst. 1973).

[23] See Robert J. Barro, Macroeconomics (2d ed. 1987), at ch. 7.

12   THE JOURNAL OF LAW AND ECONOMICS

post–World War II period.[24] This generation does less well because their human capital is not augmented by public spending; however, they may still be better off even if this internal rate of return is less than the appropriate market rate of interest because their utility is higher when the welfare of the next generation is higher (assuming altruism toward children).

Whatever the conclusion about the initial generation, our results sharply contradict the view that government payments to the elderly in the United States are large relative to government spending on the young. Indeed, any generation that benefits from the current level of public investments in children can easily use the higher earnings created by these investments to provide current levels of support for the elderly, and they would still have a considerable profit left over. Therefore, children would be happy to enter into a social compact with their parents whereby the children support their parents when old at current levels in return for a commitment to the current level of public support on children.

Our theoretical analysis implies that an efficient compact between the young and the old raises the human capital of children from poorer and middle-class families in return for contributions to the health and incomes of older members of these families. We indicated earlier that public spending on education favored the poor and middle class. Public spending on medical care also favors poorer families: the rapid growth in public spending on medical care during the past twenty years sharply reduced the effect of family income on medical care.[25] In addition, poor and middle-level older persons are much more likely to live apart from their children than they were before social security became important.[26]

V. DIVORCE

Practically all societies forbid marriage prior to specified ages; many countries have banned marriages between men and women of different races, religions, and social classes; and Christian countries have not allowed polygamy. Regulation of divorce is equally common. The United States and other Western countries essentially did not allow divorce until the mid-nineteenth century. There were fewer than two (!) divorces per year in England from 1800 to 1850.[27] Gradually, divorce laws in the West

---

[24] See Edward C. Prescott, Response to a Skeptic (Quarterly Review, Federal Reserve Bank of Minneapolis 1986).

[25] Victor R. Fuchs, Who Shall Live: Health, Economics, and Social Choice (1975).

[26] Michael *et al.*, *supra* note 18.

[27] Griselda Rowntree & Norman H. Carrier, The Resort to Divorce in England and Wales, 1858–1957, 11 Population Stud. 188 (1958).

liberalized toward allowing divorce when one party committed adultery, abandoned his or her spouse, or otherwise was seriously "at fault." Divorce by mutual consent also began to be possible, especially when there were no young children. About twenty years ago, the United States and other countries started to allow either spouse to divorce without proving fault or getting consent.

Although some divorces badly sear the children involved, little is known about the usual effects of divorce on children. Among other things, the available evidence cannot distinguish the effect of a divorce from the effect of having parents who do not get along.[28] All altruistic parents consider the interests of children and are less likely to divorce when their children would be hurt badly. Nevertheless, even if we ignore the conflict between divorced parents in determining how much time and money each spends on their children,[29] altruistic parents might still divorce when their children are harmed. Parents who do not leave bequests might divorce even when the money value of the cost to children exceeds the money value of the gain to parents. The reason is that children do not have a credible way to "bribe" their parents to stay if they cannot commit to old-age support or other future transfers to parents contingent on the parents not getting a divorce.

The story is different in families with bequests. If divorce does not change the degree of altruism toward children and if a divorce only affects future earnings and the value of other tradable resources, then children would also be made better off if their parents decide to divorce. The reason is that parents raise their gifts and bequests to compensate children for any losses from the divorce. This is an implication of the Rotten Kid Theorem.[30]

On the other hand, children may suffer from a divorce even by parents who give bequests if the divorce reduces the nontradable goods consumed by children. For example, children may be unhappy after a divorce because they seldom see their fathers. Parents cannot directly compensate children for the effect of a divorce on their happiness or other consumption. Indeed, if the effect on nontradables lowers the marginal utility to children of tradable resources, altruistic parents who divorce would *reduce* their gifts of tradables to children and thereby make children still worse off.

---

[28] See Robert E. Emery, Interpersonal Conflict and the Children of Discord and Divorce, 92 Psychological Bull. 310 (1982).

[29] This issue is well analyzed in Yoram Weiss & Robert J. Willis, Children as Collective Goods and Divorce Settlements, 3 J. Lab. Econ. 268 (1985).

[30] Becker, *supra* note 12.

14   THE JOURNAL OF LAW AND ECONOMICS

We claimed earlier that the degree of altruism is not fixed but often responds to the frequency and intensity of contacts with beneficiaries. In particular, over time a divorced father might become less altruistic toward his children as his contact with them declines. This would explain why many divorced fathers are delinquent in child-support payments,[31] and it strengthens our conclusion that a divorce may make children worse off even when their parents are quite altruistic prior to a divorce and even if they continue to give bequests after a divorce.

A divorce may greatly harm a wife who has many children and cannot earn much in the labor force or when her ex-husband fails to meet his financial and other obligations to the children. This is true even when divorce requires mutual consent because in many societies husbands could intimidate wives into agreeing to a divorce under unfavorable terms for them.

It does not seem farfetched to suggest that the state often regulates divorce to mimic the terms of contracts between husbands and wives and parents and children that are not feasible. Such contracts, for example, might greatly reduce the incidence of divorce when families have many children since the aggregate loss to children (and mothers) from divorce would rise with the number of children. Many countries did prohibit divorce when the typical family was large. Moreover, even when a divorce could not be easily obtained, marriages without children often could dissolve—could be "annulled." Divorce laws eased as birth rates began to decline in the nineteenth century. In recent decades, low birth rates and the much higher labor force participation of women stimulated a further easing toward no-fault divorce.

Some parents choose to separate from their children not through divorce but through the sale of their children. The universal ban on this practice strongly suggests that the sale of children lowers social utility. Young unmarried women and poor parents who need money are the two groups most likely to sell their children. Some children sold to prosperous families who want them may consider themselves better off than if they had remained with their parents. But even children who would suffer greatly might be sold because they have no way to compensate their parents for keeping them. Just as a ban on divorce may improve efficiency because certain contracts between parents and children are not feasible, so too may the ban on the sale of children improve efficiency. Nevertheless, Landes and Posner, and Posner could be correct that a very limited right to sell babies is better than the present controlled adoption

---

[31] Weiss & Willis, *supra* note 29, give other reasons.

system.[32] Note that subsidies to poor families with children through Aid to Families with Dependent Children and other programs encourage unmarried and other poor mothers to keep their children rather than give them up for adoption.

VI. Optimal Population

With a heroic amount of additional imagination, we can consider not only the relation between parents and actual children but also contracts between parents and *potential* children. Such a thought experiment provides a new way of determining optimal family size and optimal population. The literature on optimal population has lacked an attractive guiding principle.[33]

Suppose that a potential child could commit to compensating his parents eventually if he is born. This "contract" would be Pareto improving (we assume that third parties are not hurt by births) if the child would still prefer to be born after compensation to parents that makes them better off. Since such contracts are impossible, some children may not get born even when both parents and children could be better off. Both fertility and population growth are too low when compensation from unborn children to their parents would be Pareto improving.

The first-order utility-maximizing condition with respect to number of children implies that parents are indifferent to a small increase in numbers. Unborn children want to compensate parents to change indifference into a positive preference for additional children. All parents might appear to welcome compensation, regardless of their altruism, because compensation lowers the net cost of additional children. This conclusion is correct for parents who do not provide gifts and bequests to children since these parents would benefit from old-age support or other compensation from children (see Section III).

The surprising result is that compensation *lowers* the utility of parents who do provide children with gifts and bequests. Compensation from potential children, in effect, reduces the net gift to these children. But parents do not need compensation to reduce gifts since they may reduce them in any case if they so choose. Therefore, families with gifts and bequests to children do have the Pareto-efficient number of children (ne-

---

[32] Elisabeth M. Landes & Richard Posner, The Economics of the Baby Shortage, 7 J. Legal Stud. 323 (1978); Richard A. Posner, The Regulation of the Market in Adoptions, 67 B. U. L. Rev. 59 (1987).

[33] See the criticisms of this literature in James E. Meade, Population Explosion: The Standard of Living and Social Conflict, 77 Econ. J. 233 (1967); David Friedman, What Does "Optimum Population" Mean? 3 Research Pop. Econ. 273 (1981).

16   THE JOURNAL OF LAW AND ECONOMICS

glecting effects outside the family): compensation from unborn children makes the parents worse off rather than better off.

The seemingly bizarre thought experiment with unborn children has a very concrete implication. We have shown that poorer families are less likely than richer ones to leave bequests. If commitments for compensation from unborn children are not feasible, fertility in poorer families is too low, and fertility in richer families (who give bequests) is optimal. Therefore, our approach implies—with any third-party effects ignored— that the aggregate private-fertility rate is below the Pareto-efficient rate.

A conclusion that poorer families may have too few children will shock some readers because poorer families already have larger families than richer ones. But other factors raise fertility by poorer families, including welfare programs, subsidies to education, and limited birth control knowledge.

Thompson and Ruhter also conclude that parents who do not leave bequests tend to have too few children,[34] but their argument, in contrast to ours, seems to depend on the underinvestment in the human capital of each child by these families. Such an argument is not correct since underinvestment in children may induce families to have too many rather than too few children. The suboptimal expenditure per child "artificially" lowers the effective cost of an additional child through the interaction between the quantity and quality of children.[35]

VII. Political Competition between Generations

Since public policy results from competition among interest groups, how does competition for political favors lead to efficiency-raising state interventions in the family? In this section we sketch out a possible answer when parental altruism is important.

Political competition between adults and children is hardly a contest since children cannot vote and do not have the means and maturity to organize an effective political coalition. If adults use their political power to issue bonds and other obligations, they can help support themselves when old by selling these obligations to the next generation of younger adults. Some economists support balanced government budgets and limits on debt issue to control such exploitation of the political weakness of children and later generations. Of course, this is not a problem if each

---

[34] Thompson & Ruhter, *supra* note 4.

[35] See the analysis in Gary S. Becker & Kevin M. Murphy, Incomplete Markets and Investment in Children (unpublished paper, University of Chicago 1986); Nerlove *et al.*, *supra* note 7.

generation can repudiate debt issues by previous generations. Since the issues involved in debt repudiation are beyond the scope of this article, we will just assume that debt is not repudiated.

Although present generations may be able to exploit future generations, altruism limits their desire to do so. Indeed, if all parents are altruistic and leave bequests, present generations have no desire to exploit future generations. After all, if they want to, they may take resources from future generations by leaving smaller bequests. Although families who do not leave bequests favor debt and other exploitation of the political weakness of future generations, their degree of altruism may greatly affect how they use their political power against future generations.

We showed in Section III that families who do not leave bequests underinvest in the human capital of their children. They can increase the wealth of the children's generation by using their political power to raise education and other training through state schools and subsidies to other investments in children. Then the present generation may, if it wishes, issue obligations to future generations that extract this increase in children's wealth.

Although selfish parents try to extract as much as they can from children, altruistic parents may prefer to share some of the increased wealth with children. This means that future generations may also benefit from the political power of present generations. Therefore, even if the altruism of many parents is not strong enough to lead to positive bequests and efficient investments in human capital, it could be strong enough to ensure that future generations also gain when the present generation uses its political power to issue debt and other obligations to future generations.

This overly simplified analysis of political power and political incentives may help explain why public expenditures in the United States on children are not small compared to public expenditures on the elderly. The discussion in Section IV indicates that the next generation gains enough from public expenditures on children by the current generation to pay social security and other help to the elderly of the current generation, and yet the next generation still has some profit left over from the public investment in their human capital.

VIII. SUMMARY

We have tried to understand the widespread intervention by governments in families. We conclude that many public actions achieve more efficient arrangements between parents and children. Clearly, parents and children cannot always make efficient arrangements because children are unable to commit to compensation of parents in the future.

Families who leave bequests can "force" children to repay parents for investments in human capital by reducing bequests. Therefore, these families do not underinvest in children's human capital. By contrast, families who do not leave bequests, often poorer families, do underinvest in children. The state may subsidize schools and other training facilities to raise investments in children by poorer families to efficient levels.

We consider not only subsidies to education and training but also social security and other old-age support, subsidies to births, laws that limit access to divorce and the sale of children, and laws that require parents' permission for early marriage and other choices of children. It is remarkable how many state interventions in family decisions appear to contribute to the efficiency of family arrangements.

[10]

PARENTS AS FIDUCIARIES

Elizabeth S. Scott *
Robert E. Scott **

TRADITIONALLY, the law has deferred to the rights of biological parents in regulating the parent-child relationship.
More recently, as the emphasis of legal regulation has shifted to
protecting children's interests, critics have targeted the traditional
focus on parents' rights as impeding the goal of promoting children's welfare. Some contemporary scholars argue instead for a
"child-centered perspective,"[1] in contrast to the current regime
under which biological parents continue to have important legal
interests in their relationship with their children. The underlying
assumption of this claim is that the rights of parents and the interests of children often are conflicting, and that greater recognition
of one interest means diminished importance to the other.

One way of thinking about a legal regime that seeks to harmonize this conflict is to imagine that the parent's legal relationship to
the child is shaped by fiduciary responsibilities toward the child
rather than by inherent rights derived from status.[2] Fiduciaries in
law are agents who occupy a position of special confidence, superi-

---

* University Professor and Robert C. Taylor Research Professor, University of Virginia
School of Law.

** Dean and Lewis F. Powell, Jr. Professor of Law, University of Virginia School of
Law.

We are thankful to Clay Gillette, Charles Goetz, Douglas Leslie, Jody Kraus, Saul
Levmore, Steve Sugarman and George Triantis for their helpful comments on prior drafts
and to Eric Graben for excellent research assistance. We also thank participants in a
workshop at the University of Virginia and the Symposium conference.

[1] See, e.g., Barbara Bennett Woodhouse, Hatching the Egg: A Child-Centered
Perspective on Parents' Rights, 14 Cardozo L. Rev. 1747 (1993). Woodhouse argues that
gestational and social parenting should receive legal protection, while the fact of biological
parenthood should have little relevance.

[2] Woodhouse describes parenthood using the model of stewardship. See id. at 1755.
Although commentators have suggested rhetorically that the parental role be defined as
that of a fiduciary, no one has rigorously examined the implications of defining the legal
role in this way. See, e.g., Francis J. Catania, Jr., Accounting to Ourselves for Ourselves:
An Analysis of Adjudication in the Resolution of Child Custody Disputes, 71 Neb. L. Rev.
1228, 1231-32 (1992); Ira C. Lupu, The Separation of Powers and the Protection of
Children, 61 U. Chi. L. Rev. 1317, 1318-19 (1994).

ority, or influence, and thus are subject to strict and non-negotiable duties of loyalty and reasonable diligence in acting on behalf of their principals.[3] Characterizing parents as fiduciaries suggests that the parent-child relationship shares important features with other legal relationships that have been similarly defined, such as trustees and trust beneficiaries, corporate directors and shareholders, executors and legatees, and guardians and wards. Basic structural similarities are apparent. There are information asymmetries in this family relationship that are analogous to those of other fiduciary relationships. Moreover, satisfactory performance by parents, like that of other fiduciaries, requires considerable discretion, and children, like other principals, are not in a position to direct or control that performance. Here, as in other contexts, the challenge for legal regulation is to encourage the parent to act so as to serve the interests of the child rather than her own conflicting interests, and yet to do so in a context in which monitoring parental behavior is difficult.

Particular features of the parent-child relationship distinguish it from most traditional fiduciary relationships, however, and thus present some unique challenges. This relationship is broader in scope than are many other fiduciary relationships. Beyond this, the parental relationship, once established, has intrinsic value for the child that extends beyond successful performance of caretaking tasks.[4] Obviously, the unique characteristics of family relationships

---

[3] "The fiduciary relation may exist wherever special confidence is reposed, whether the relationship be that of blood, business, friendship, or association, by one person in another who are in a position to have and exercise or do have and exercise influence over each other." Dawson v. National Life Ins. Co., 157 N.W. 929, 933 (Iowa 1916); see also Charles J. Goetz & Robert E. Scott, Principles of Relational Contracts, 67 Va. L. Rev. 1089, 1126-30 (1981) (summarizing the strict obligations imposed upon fiduciaries for the benefit of principals).

[4] The loss of the relationship with a parent can inflict serious costs on the child. Research on divorce indicates that reduced contact with fathers is a source of significant harm to many children. See E. Mavis Hetherington, Martha Cox & Roger Cox, The Aftermath of Divorce, *in* Relationships: Mother/Child, Father/Child (Joseph H. Stevens, Jr. & Marilyn Matthews eds., 1978) [hereinafter Hetherington et al., Aftermath of Divorce]; E. Mavis Hetherington, Martha Cox & Roger Cox, Divorced Fathers, 25 Fam. Coordinator 417, 424-26 (1976); E. Mavis Hetherington, Martha Cox & Roger Cox, Effects of Divorce on Parents and Children, *in* Non-Traditional Families: Parenting and Child Development 233 (M. Lamb ed., 1982); see also Judith S. Wallerstein & Joan B. Kelly, Surviving the Breakup: How Children and Parents Cope With Divorce (1980); Judith S. Wallerstein and Sandra Blakeslee, Second Chances: Men, Women, and Children a Decade

necessarily shape legal regulation in idiosyncratic ways. Nonetheless, thinking systematically about parents as agents and fiduciaries is a useful project.[5] By employing this framework, we can draw on lessons learned from the legal regulation of fiduciaries in other contexts, and on the insights of legal and agency theory that have shaped our understanding of how the law can function to optimize these relationships. Such an exercise may illuminate the deep structure of the regime of legal and extralegal norms that shape parental behavior.

Agency theory identifies two means of reducing conflicts of interest between agents and principals. Bonding encourages agents to align their interests with those of their principals, while monitoring facilitates the oversight of agents' performance to detect selfish behavior.[6] Fiduciary law utilizes varying combinations of these mechanisms in different settings to reduce or avoid conflicts of interest. Viewed through this lens, much contemporary regulation of the parent-child relationship can be understood as serving either bonding or monitoring functions. There are, however, some aspects of family law that seem sharply dissonant with this perspective, reflecting in part the lingering influence of traditional legal structures regulating family-state relations.

Part I of this Article begins with a brief account of the growing criticism that legal policy regulating the parent-child relationship is driven excessively by the objective of protecting parents' rights. Critics argue that children's welfare rather than parents' rights

---

After Divorce 143-44 (1989); Judith S. Wallerstein & Joan B. Kelly, Effects of Divorce on the Visiting Father-Child Relationship, 137 Am. J. Psychiatry 1534 (1980) [hereinafter Wallerstein & Kelly, Visiting Father-Child Relationship]; Judith S. Wallerstein & Joan B. Kelly, The Effects of Parental Divorce: Experience of the Child in Later Latency, 46 Am. J. Orthopsychiatry 256 (1976) [hereinafter Wallerstein & Kelly, Parental Divorce: Experience of the Child in Later Latency]. Goldstein, Freud and Solnit argue against state interference with even suboptimal parent-child relationships because of the importance of this bond to children. See Joseph Goldstein, Anna Freud & Albert J. Solnit, Before the Best Interests of the Child 3-25, 75-86 (1979).

[5] The utility of this perspective depends in part on whether the normative premise of the focus on children's welfare is attractive, a point which might be debated. We do not propose to enter this debate. Rather, our purpose is to examine the implications of thinking about family relationships from a fiduciary perspective, *assuming* that the normative goal is to advance the interests of children.

[6] See Michael C. Jensen & William H. Meckling, Theory of the Firm: Managerial Behavior, Agency Costs and Ownership Structure, 3 J. Fin. Econ. 305, 308 (1976).

should define the legal relationship between parent and child. We suggest that the critics' challenge argues for a focus on the instrumental effects of legal regulation on this relationship. This approach asks to what extent the law influences parents to act in ways that promote their children's interests, and to what extent the focus on parents' rights is incompatible with that objective. The answer to those questions is complicated by the dynamics of the parent-child relationship, and especially by the feedback effects between parental performance and parental rights.

In Part II, we develop an informal model of the parent as fiduciary. We use the tools of agency theory to identify the optimal combinations of extralegal and legal arrangements that seem to best reduce conflicts of interest within the parent-child relationship. Owing to the peculiar characteristics of this relationship, the utility of specific mechanisms varies depending on whether or not the parent lives in a family unit with the child. In the intact family, the dominating effects of informal norms reduce the demand for extensive legal regulation. When the family is fractured, the power of extralegal constraints is diminished and more elaborate legal rules are required to ameliorate potential conflicts.

In Part III, we apply this relational model of parents as fiduciaries to contemporary family law. We conclude that, in many respects, current law fits comfortably within the fiduciary paradigm. Indeed, legal rules that are justified (and criticized) in terms of parental rights can be better rationalized as necessary complements to fiduciary obligations. To be sure, some aspects of current law appear to intensify conflicts of interest between parent and child. Many of the rules governing divorce, for example, seem to undermine children's welfare by encouraging parents to exercise their rights selfishly. But the central insight of the relational approach is to focus attention on the feedback effects between parental rights and children's interests. The contract metaphor makes explicit what is implicit in contemporary family law: parental "rights" are granted as ex ante compensation for the satisfactory performance of voluntarily assumed responsibilities to provide for the child's interests.

We conclude, therefore, that the criticism of contemporary family law as being unduly "rights-centered" is misplaced. The paradox of modern family law is the uneasy coexistence of legal outcomes that largely can be explained and justified within a framework of reciprocal rights and responsibilities, together with legal rhetoric that fails to make explicit the nexus between this framework and the normative goal of promoting the welfare of children.

I. RECONCEPTUALIZING THE PARENT-CHILD RELATIONSHIP

A. *The Critique of Parents' Rights*

Legal deference to the claims of biological parents recently has come under attack in the courts, in the academic literature, and in the popular media.[7] Cases such as the highly publicized dispute between the DeBoers and Daniel Schmidt over the custody of "Baby Jessica"[8] contribute to a view that the law, frozen in ancient

---

[7] See, e.g., Lehr v. Robertson, 463 U.S. 248, 259-60 (1983) (observing that a "mere biological relationship" cannot alone establish parental rights); see also Michael H. v. Gerald D., 491 U.S. 110 (1989) (Scalia, J., plurality opinion) (denying challenge of biological father to California statute establishing conclusive presumption that mother's husband at child's birth is legal father of child); Katharine T. Bartlett, Re-Expressing Parenthood, 98 Yale L.J. 293, 295 (1988) (advocating an emphasis on parental responsibilities rather than parental rights); Woodhouse, supra note 1 (placing the child's interests at the center of family law); Nancy Gibbs, In Whose Best Interest?, Time, July 19, 1993, at 44 (relating the pain of couples forced to relinquish an adopted child to its biological parents); Geoffrey Cowley, Who's Looking After the Interests of Children?, Newsweek, August 16, 1993, at 54 (emphasizing the vulnerability of adopted children under current custody laws).

[8] See DeBoer v. Schmidt (In re Baby Girl Clausen), 502 N.W.2d 649 (Mich. 1993); In re B.G.C., 496 N.W.2d 239 (Iowa 1992). "Baby Jessica" was given up for adoption by her mother only hours after birth, without the knowledge of her biological father, Daniel Schmidt, and placed in temporary custody with the DeBoers. A few weeks later, upon learning that he was the father of the child, Schmidt initiated legal efforts to gain custody, on the grounds that he had not consented to the termination of his parental rights. During the pendency of the legal battle, Jessica remained in the home of the DeBoers, who resisted Schmidt's efforts to reclaim his daughter. Despite testimony from experts who warned that return to her father's custody would be emotionally traumatic for Jessica, the Iowa Supreme Court ruled that Schmidt was legally entitled to custody of his daughter. Although a subsequent determination by a Michigan court concluded that transferring custody was not in Jessica's best interests, the Michigan Supreme Court deferred to the jurisdiction of the Iowa courts, enforcing the order to return Jessica to her biological parents. For popular accounts of the case, see Bill Hewitt, The Battle for Baby Jessica, People, May 31, 1993, at 32; Jon D. Hull, The Ties That Traumatize, Time, April 12, 1993, at 48. A more recent example involves "Baby Richard," whose father's parental rights were reinstated almost four years after his placement in an adoptive home. See *In re Petition of Doe*, 638 N.E.2d 181 (Ill.), cert. denied, 115 S. Ct. 499 (1994).

The "Baby Jessica" case has proved an attractive target for scholarly criticism of contemporary family law. See Suellyn Scarnecchia, A Child's Right to Protection from

doctrine, accords unwarranted legal protection to biological parents in ways that are both directly harmful and symbolically corrosive to the interests of their children.[9] For example, recognition of the rights of non-custodial biological parents can undermine a relationship between the child and a more suitable social parent.[10] Further, the latitude given to parents in rearing their children is seen as excessive, allowing some parents to inflict unmonitored and unsanctioned harm on their children.[11] More indirectly, to the extent that the law emphasizes parental rights, it encourages parents' inclination to put their own interests before those of their children, both in the intact family and on divorce or dissolution.

However controversial this issue may be today, the tradition of legal protection of parental rights has deep historical roots.[12] Before the twentieth century, the combined status of biological

---

Transfer Trauma in a Contested Adoption Case, 2 Duke J. Gender L. & Pol'y 41 (1995); Suellyn Scarnecchia, Who Is Jessica's Mother? Defining Motherhood Through Reality, 3 Am. U. J. Gender & L. 1 (1994). Scarnecchia, a professor at the University of Michigan School of Law, physically delivered Jessica from the DeBoers to the Schmidts. See also Wendy A. Fitzgerald, Maturity, Difference, and Mystery: Children's Perspectives and the Law, 36 Ariz. L. Rev. 11, 72-84 (1994) (arguing that the mechanistic legal doctrine governing the "Baby Jessica" case failed to honor Jessica's individual interests as a child).

[9] For general critiques of the emphasis on parental rights in modern family law, see Goldstein et. al, supra note 4, at 54; Bartlett, supra note 7, at 295; Woodhouse, supra note 1, at 1756, 1809-12. Similarly, James Dwyer argues for abandoning parental rights altogether and according parents merely child-rearing privileges, the contours of which are subject to the rights of the children. James G. Dwyer, Parents' Religion and Children's Welfare: Debunking the Doctrine of Parents' Rights, 82 Cal. L. Rev. 1371, 1374 (1994).

[10] Critics charge that policies grounded in parental rights empower unmarried fathers (like Daniel Schmidt) to derail an adoption that is in the child's interest. See supra note 8; see also Bartlett, supra note 7, at 322, 324 n.137 (arguing that the emphasis on parental rights permits fathers to exploit the legal system to the detriment of the child). These policies also devalue the custodial claims of stepparents and other third parties who have functioned as parents, and inhibit the termination of the parental rights of unfit parents to allow permanent placement of children in foster care. See Woodhouse, supra note 1, at 1784-95.

[11] The case of Joshua DeShaney is often cited as demonstrating the law's excessive deference toward abusive parents. See DeShaney v. Winnebago County Dep't of Social Servs., 489 U.S. 189 (1989). Joshua was severely beaten by his father following many episodes of abuse. Although his case was being monitored by a social worker during the period of the abusive treatment, the county failed to intervene and prevent the abuse. See also infra note 111 (comparing *DeShaney* to other cases of parental abuse).

[12] See Martha Fineman, Dominant Discourse, Professional Language, and Legal Change in Child Custody Decisionmaking, 101 Harv. L. Rev. 727, 737-39 (1988); Barbara Bennett Woodhouse, "Who Owns the Child?": *Meyer* and *Pierce* and the Child as Property, 33 Wm. & Mary L. Rev. 995, 1041-50 (1992).

parenthood and marriage signified a legal authority of almost limitless scope. Until the social reform movement at the beginning of this century,[13] the state took little interest in family governance.[14] Parents, particularly fathers as heads of household, had extensive legal authority over the lives of their children.[15] Parental rights were understood to be grounded in natural law and were not dependent on behavior that promoted the child's interest.[16] Parents' interest under traditional law was property-like in many respects.[17] A parent's right to the custody of his children so approximated property ownership that it could be transferred by contract,[18] and lost only by abandonment or unfitness.[19] In the 1920s, the United States Supreme Court elevated parental rights to constitutional stature, restricting the extent to which the state can

---

[13] This movement included the creation of the social work profession, with its mission of promoting the welfare of children, the founding of the juvenile court (characterized by early reformers as an institution that could perform a parental function, when parents failed), and the development of widespread public education. See Murray Levine & Adeline Levine, A Social History of Helping Services: Clinic, Court, School, and Community (1970); Anthony M. Platt, The Child Savers: The Invention of Delinquency (2d ed. 1977).

[14] Indeed, Anthony Platt argues that the reform efforts of the Progressive Era were driven by a desire to create a legal means for state supervision of working class parents. See Platt, supra note 13, at xxii-xxix.

[15] See sources cited supra note 12. Even today, parental rights operate against the state, third parties, and the child herself. These rights include discretion over custody, discipline, education, medical treatment, religious upbringing, and earnings and services. See Katharine T. Bartlett, Rethinking Parenthood as an Exclusive Status: The Need for Legal Alternatives When the Premise of the Nuclear Family Has Failed, 70 Va. L. Rev. 879, 884 (1984).

[16] Bartlett discusses the natural law origins of parental rights. See Bartlett, supra note 15, at 887-90; see also Risting v. Sparboe, 162 N.W. 592, 593-94 (Iowa 1917) (holding that "utter selfishness alone cannot be allowed to cut off the natural claim of parents to the custody of their own offspring").

[17] See sources cited supra note 12. Indeed, before the Industrial Revolution, children were economic assets of their parents in agrarian society, contributing to the characterization of the parents' interest as a property right. See John J. Dempsey, The Family and Public Policy 3 (1981).

[18] This transaction could occur, under ancient English common law, when parents placed children in indentured service or apprenticeship. Lucy S. McGough & Lawrence M. Shindell, Coming of Age: The Best Interests of the Child Standard in Parent-Third Party Custody Disputes, 27 Emory L.J. 209, 210 & n.5 (1978).

[19] See, e.g., Quilloin v. Walcott, 434 U.S. 246, 255 (1978). The loss of parental rights through abandonment is firmly based on property concepts. Unfitness is, of course, a different matter.

override parental authority.[20] Although modern courts vigorously reject the characterization of children as the property of their parents, many argue that this legacy continues to cast a shadow.[21]

In fact, the situation is even more complex than the critics recognize. Although many assume that outcomes such as that reached in the DeBoers-Schmidt dispute result from the failure to reform archaic legal doctrine, the extension of parental rights to unmarried biological fathers is actually a relatively recent development.[22] Historically, unmarried fathers were invisible parents, presumed by courts and legislatures to have no legal interest in their children.[23] This presents an apparent puzzle, given the patriarchal character of traditional family law (although the legal response may reflect, as Mary Shanley has argued, a desire to shield fathers from financial responsibility for children that they produced outside of marriage).[24] In any event, legal policy rested on the very plausible empirical assumption that most unmarried fathers had little interest in having a relationship with their children.[25] Today, the rhetoric of parental rights extends to this group of parents, and consent of the unmarried father to the adoption of his child (either by

---

[20] See, e.g., Meyer v. Nebraska, 262 U.S. 390 (1923) (holding that the fundamental right to control education of one's child is constitutionally protected); Pierce v. Society of Sisters, 268 U.S. 510 (1925) (holding that an Oregon law requiring children to attend public schools was an unconstitutional violation of the fundamental right to control education of one's child); see also Woodhouse, supra note 12, at 997 (arguing that these cases gave a constitutional underpinning to the concept that children are property of their parents).

[21] See, e.g., Woodhouse, supra note 12, at 997, 1113-15; Bartlett, supra note 15, at 882.

[22] Traditionally, unmarried mothers had more robust rights than fathers. For example, before Stanley v. Illinois, 405 U.S. 645 (1972), the mother's, but not the father's, consent to adoption was required under most adoption statutes. The parental rights of unmarried mothers, however, were (and are) more fragile than those of married parents, at least in practical effect. Unmarried mothers are much more likely to be subject to state supervision and intervention as a part of receipt of public assistance.

[23] See John R. Hamilton, Note, The Unwed Father and the Right to Know of His Child's Existence, 76 Ky. L.J. 949, 949 (1987-88) ("Until a few years ago, unwed fathers were ignored by or received virtually no protection from either the United States Constitution or the statutes of most states."); Elizabeth R. Stanton, Note, The Rights of the Biological Father: From Adoption & Custody to Surrogate Motherhood, 12 Vt. L. Rev. 87, 92 (1987).

[24] See Mary L. Shanley, Unwed Father's Rights, Adoption and Sex Equality: Gender-Neutrality and the Perpetuation of Patriarchy, 95 Colum. L. Rev. 60, 66-70 (1995). Shanley contrasts the lot of unmarried fathers ("shielded from financial responsibility for his 'spurious' offspring") with that of mothers ("[A] woman who bore children outside of marriage was 'ruined'. . . ."). See id. at 69.

[25] The exigencies of administrative efficiency in the placement of children supported a policy of presuming that unmarried fathers lacked a legal interest in their children.

strangers or by a stepparent) has become a factor of much greater importance.[26] The outcome in the DeBoers case, vindicating the paternal rights of Daniel Schmidt, fits into this legal framework.

Outside of the adoption context, non-custodial biological parents often win custody contests with stepparents and other third parties who have functioned in a parental role.[27] To the consternation of critics, traditional law gives little legal protection to the relationship between the faithful stepparent and the child if the biological parent is fit.[28] Similarly poignant are cases in which a grandparent or other relative has assumed the care of a child who is neglected or informally abandoned by his parent. Months or even years later, the wayward parent who mends her ways may assert her parental rights and often successfully reclaim custody.[29]

Critics of parental rights also decry the legal response to seriously deficient parental conduct. State agents are constrained from directly monitoring the quality of parental care by policies that support parental authority and family privacy.[30] Many critics view these policies as leaving children vulnerable and without adequate

---

26 Modern doctrine has evolved from the 1972 Supreme Court opinion in *Stanley*, 405 U.S. at 648, which signalled that the claims of at least some unmarried fathers warrant constitutional protection. In the years since *Stanley*, the Court has explored the constitutional scope of parental rights in several cases involving unmarried fathers.

27 Woodhouse, supra note 12, at 1048 nn.245-47, describes several such cases. See, e.g., Harper v. Tipple, 184 P. 1005 (Ariz. 1919) (holding that a child who lived over three years with her grandparents following her mother's death must be returned to the father, absent clear showing of incompetency); In re Salter, 76 P. 51, 52 (Cal. 1904) (directing lower court to award guardianship of a child to his father rather than the child's grandmother if father found competent); Lee v. Lee, 65 So. 585, 588 (Fla. 1914) (ruling that a father had the right to custody of his seven-year-old child despite fact that child had been raised by cousins from the age of nine days); Hernandez v. Thomas, 39 So. 641, 645 (Fla. 1905) (finding a competent father is generally preferred as custodian of his child over other parties, here a grandmother); In re J.P., 648 P.2d 1364, 1374-75 (Utah 1982) (holding that absent a showing of parental unfitness, state may not terminate parental rights, even if such termination would be in the best interest of the child).

28 Traditional law is slowly changing in this area, but courts still generally favor biological parents in these contests. For a discussion of the legal protection of stepparents' rights, see David R. Fine & Mark A. Fine, Learning from Social Sciences: A Model for Reformation of the Laws Affecting Stepfamilies, 97 Dick. L. Rev. 49, 56-57 (1992). For a survey of statutes covering the rights of third parties, see American Bar Association, "Rights of Third Party," 25 Fam. L.Q. 26 app. (1991).

29 See supra note 27.

30 See Carl E. Schneider, Moral Discourse and the Transformation of American Family Law, 83 Mich. L. Rev. 1803, 1835-39 (1985) (discussing the legal tradition of noninterference in the family).

protection from their parents' neglectful or abusive behavior.[31] Even when children are in state custody, the spectre of parental rights casts a shadow. Foster care placement tends to extend indefinitely for a large percentage of these children,[32] who are neither returned to their parents' custody nor available for adoption because parental rights are not terminated. Children get older (and less adoptable) while parents are given expansive opportunities to remedy the conditions that resulted in the removal.[33] Mean-

---

[31] See, e.g., Fitzgerald, supra note 8, at 63-64. A particularly grim and poignant illustration of this point is the case of Lisa Steinberg, who was illegally adopted by New York lawyer Joel Steinberg and his live-in companion, Hedda Nussbaum. In 1987, after years of abuse, Lisa was beaten to death at age six by Joel Steinberg. Steinberg repeatedly beat Nussbaum as well, and police had been to their apartment several times prior to the fatal beating to answer neighbors' complaints. Nussbaum's coworkers had tried unsuccessfully to block the adoption, and Steinberg never formally registered the adoption to avoid investigation. Two complaints of possible child abuse were investigated in 1983 and 1984, but were rejected as unsubstantiated by investigators from the city's Human Resources Administration. See Ken Gross, A Wicked Rage Claims a Child, People, Nov. 23, 1987, at 44.

[32] See Robert H. Mnookin, Foster Care—In Whose Best Interest?, 43 Harv. Educ. Rev. 599, 610-13 (1973) (a classic early account of the problems with the foster care system). Despite efforts to improve the situation of children in foster care, the average stay in foster care in many jurisdictions still exceeds two years. David J. Herring, Exploring the Political Roles of the Family: Justifications for Permanency Planning for Children, 26 Loy. U. Chi. L.J. 183 (1995), cites several studies in support of this assertion:

A New York adoption study revealed that in 1989, a child, on average, spent 4.6 years in foster care before being eligible for adoption. Debra Ratterman, Termination Barriers: Speeding Adoption in New York State Through Reducing Delays in Termination of Parental Rights Cases at iii (1991); see also Permanency Planning Task Force Court Appointed Special Advocates Subcommittee, Demographics of Permanency in Allegheny County, Pennsylvania (1992) (reporting that of the children living in foster care in Allegheny County, Pittsburgh, Pennsylvania, 44% had been in foster care for more than two years); Voluntary Cooperative Information System & American Public Welfare Association, Characteristics of Children in Substitute and Adoptive Care: A Statistical Summary of the VCIS National Child Welfare Database 116-17 (1993) . . . (summarizing statistics showing that by the end of fiscal year 1989, 39.5% of children living in substitute care had been there for more than two years, 15.5% had been in care between two and three years, 13.4% had been in care between three to five years, and 10.6% had been in care five years or more).

Id. at 190 n.50.

[33] Robert Mnookin reported twenty years ago that social workers are often reluctant to terminate parental rights because to do so necessitates a separate legal proceeding, often with more stringent standards than those required for initial removal, and because termination of parental rights is seen as a drastic measure. See Mnookin, supra note 32, at 612-13. The problem has not been resolved. The Adoption Assistance and Child Welfare Act of 1980, Pub. L. No. 96-272, § 471(a)(15), 94 Stat. 500, 503 (codified in scattered

while, children's relationships with foster parents receive little legal protection (and children are moved from one foster family to another) on the ground that a strong attachment might undermine family ties with the biological parents.[34]

Considerable reform efforts, including comprehensive federal legislation, have focused on the problem of foster care "drift," but with few positive results.[35] Policies promoting family reunification have had mixed success, because a large portion of parents are unable to resume care, or fail to do so adequately. Moreover, systemic efforts directed at facilitating termination of parental rights and adoption in appropriate cases have been largely unsuccessful. Terminating parental rights continues to be a costly and cumbersome process, owing to procedural and substantive requirements

---

sections of 42 U.S.C.), imposed a requirement that state welfare agencies make reasonable efforts to avoid removing children from their homes or to return them to their homes after staying in foster care. According to David Herring, social workers generally fear having to prove "reasonable efforts" in court and thus decline to seek termination of parental rights. See David J. Herring, Inclusion of the Reasonable Efforts Requirement in Termination of Parental Rights Statutes: Punishing the Child for the Failures of the State Child Welfare System, 54 U. Pitt. L. Rev. 139, 180 (1992). The Department of Health and Human Services confirms this observation: "Over 75% of the respondents in the State survey indicate that the inability of the child welfare agencies to meet the 'reasonable efforts' standard to the satisfaction of State courts in a timely manner is *the primary barrier* to implementing permanent plans of adoption." Office of Inspector General, Dep't of Health and Human Servs., Barriers to Freeing Children for Adoption 11 (1991), *cited in* Herring, supra, at 180 n.117.

In Santosky v. Kramer, 455 U.S. 745, 768-70 (1982), the Supreme Court held that due process requires proof by clear and convincing evidence of parental unfitness to terminate parents' rights. Some observers argue that after *Santosky*, state agencies increasingly tend to maintain children in foster homes for long periods of time while they accumulate "clear and convincing evidence." See, e.g., Fitzgerald, supra note 8, at 63.

[34] Mnookin, supra note 32, at 612-13, 624-25. The phenomenon of foster care "drift" has been well documented. See Barbara L. Atwell, "A Lost Generation": The Battle for Private Enforcement of the Adoption Assistance and Child Welfare Act of 1980, 60 U. Cin. L. Rev. 593, 595 (1992); Herring, supra note 33, at 140-41.

[35] The Adoption Assistance and Child Welfare Act of 1980, Pub. L. No. 96-272, 94 Stat. 500 (codified in scattered sections of 42 U.S.C.), created a two-prong policy initiative to redress foster care "drift." The first prong emphasizes maintaining the family unit, by discouraging removal of the child and encouraging states to promote reunification of the family through services that would facilitate that end. See 42 U.S.C. §§ 625-27 (1988); see also S. Rep. No. 336, 96th Cong., 2d Sess. (1980), *reprinted in* 1980 U.S.C.C.A.N. 1448, 1450 (describing the purpose of the act). The second prong focuses on efficient monitoring and review procedures, so that if parents cannot resume custody, parental rights can be terminated and adoption facilitated. See 42 U.S.C. §§ 670-73 (1988). There is little evidence that the Act has led to substantial improvements.

directed toward protecting parental interests.[36] For the population of children in foster care, a large gap separates the cases in which parents can resume care of their child from the cases in which parenting is so clearly deficient that state agents pursue termination of parental rights.[37] The interests of the children in this middle category, the critics argue, are poorly served by policies that protect parents' rights.[38]

Advocates invoke child development theory in attacking legal deference toward biological parents' rights. Attachment theory emphasizes the critical importance of the relationship between the child and her primary caretaker for healthy psychological development. Although this caretaker most commonly is the child's biological mother, the biological relationship in itself is unimportant under the theory. Three psychoanalysts, Joseph Goldstein, Anna Freud, and Albert Solnit, have been particularly influential in popularizing this perspective.[39] They argue that the welfare of the child would be promoted if biology were deemphasized, and the law focused on protecting the relationship between the child and her *psychological* parent, the adult who cares for her needs on a day-to-day basis. In the view of Goldstein, Freud and Solnit, the biological parent who does not fill the role of psychological parent becomes a stranger to the child, and should not have a privileged legal status.[40]

The critics of parental rights often focus on cases of horrendous parental conduct,[41] or on contexts in which parents use a legal entitlement to claim (or reclaim) a relationship with their child which

---

[36] See supra note 33; Fitzgerald, supra note 8, at 60-61. Moreover, although the Supreme Court has declined to hold that a parent has a right to an attorney in any termination proceeding, see Lassiter v. Department of Social Servs., 452 U.S. 18 (1981), almost all states provide counsel for parents.

[37] In 1984, only eleven percent of children in foster care were adopted. Edith Fein & Anthony N. Meluccio, Permanency Planning: Another Remedy in Jeopardy?, Soc. Sci. Rev. 335, 340-41 (1992). This statistic is largely attributable to the procedural barriers precluding termination of parental rights. See Mnookin, supra note 32, at 612-13 (identifying the strict legal requirements for termination of parental rights as a deterrent to the initiation of termination proceedings).

[38] See, e.g., Fitzgerald, supra note 8, at 63-64.

[39] See Goldstein et al., supra note 4.

[40] See id. at 16-28, 47-48.

[41] For examples of such cases, see infra note 111 (reviewing the child abuse cases of Joshua DeShaney, Susan Smith, and Elizabeth Steinberg).

in some sense they have not earned.[42] A more subtle critique focuses on the intangible but perhaps more pervasive effects of contemporary "rights talk"[43] on family relationships. A rights framework is grounded in autonomy and protection of individual interests. Thus, it reinforces the parents' tendency to elevate self-interest over the interests of their child.[44] As Carl Schneider suggests, thinking in terms of rights "encourages us to think about what constrains us from doing what we want, not what obligates us to do what we ought."[45] Arguably, the legal emphasis on parental rights (and the cultural rhetoric that it generates) influences parents' behavior in a number of ways. It might affect the allocation of financial resources and parental efforts between family and personal pursuits, as well as the inclination to consider the child's welfare in making family decisions.[46] An incentive to act selfishly can, of course, lead to abuse and neglect in extreme cases. A more subtle but destructive impact on the stability of family relationships

---

[42] See, e.g., Fitzgerald, supra note 8, at 72-84 (recounting the custody dispute underlying the "Baby Jessica" case).

[43] See Mary Ann Glendon, Rights Talk: The Impoverishment of Political Discourse 121-30 (1991) (criticizing excessive emphasis on rights in American society).

[44] Many family law scholars have criticized the law's emphasis on rights in this context as undermining family relationships and failing to express the importance of moral responsibility. See, e.g., Bartlett, supra note 7; Bruce C. Hafen, The Constitutional Status of Marriage, Kinship, and Sexual Privacy—Balancing the Individual and Social Interests, 81 Mich. L. Rev. 463 (1983). Carl Schneider describes the decline of moral discourse in family law. See Schneider, supra note 30. See also Mary Ann Glendon, Abortion and Divorce in Western Law (1987) (comparing the individual rights-based approach to abortion and divorce in the United States with a more responsibility-based approach under Western European laws); Mary Ann Glendon, The Transformation of Family Law: State, Law and Family in the United States and Western Europe 311-12 (1989) (describing the impact of law in shaping how people think and feel about personal commitments and the possibility that law may contribute unintentionally to "dis-integrating" trends in families); Martha Minow, "Forming Underneath Everything That Grows:" Toward a History of Family Law, 1985 Wis. L. Rev. 819 (1985) (arguing that while family law tends to be explained in terms of individual rights, it more properly should be seen as an implementation of relational values).

[45] Carl E. Schneider, Rights Discourse and Neonatal Euthanasia, 76 Cal. L. Rev. 151, 162-63 (1988).

[46] A well-publicized and somewhat bizarre example of parental selfishness involved a couple who spent several days vacationing in Mexico, leaving their elementary-school-age children at home to fend for themselves. For details, see Jennifer Lenhart & Flynn McRoberts, Abandoned Kids' Parents Land in Jail, Chi. Trib., Dec. 30, 1992, at 1; Lindsey Tanner, A Year After Vacationing Couple Left Kids Alone, People Still Ask 'Why?,' Chi. Trib. Evening Update, Dec. 20, 1993, at 2.

results if parents are less motivated to preserve the family in the face of marital stress, or, if the family dissolves, to maintain a relationship with the child and provide financial support.[47]   The regime of no-fault divorce may exemplify the effects of a rights-based conception of the parent-child relationship.[48] By making divorce easy, the law signals that, in making the decision to divorce, parents are not required to weigh the interests of their children.[49]

B. A Relational Approach

Although the critics whose concerns we have articulated concur that beneficial family law reforms would deemphasize parental entitlement, there is no consensus about how best to promote children's welfare. One alternative is to enhance the state's role as *parens patriae* within the traditional paradigm, which purports to balance parental rights against the interest of the state in promoting the welfare of children.[50]   This approach would demand a larger state presence in the family, with increased supervision of parental care and greater readiness to terminate parental rights. While this perspective does not focus directly on the parent-child relationship, its effect is to discount the interests of parents and to reduce parental authority and rights. This is because the interest-balancing approach pits the welfare of children against the interest of parents and presumes that the latter will be diminished if the former is enhanced.

Simply shifting the focus of legal regulation toward greater protection of the needs of children is unhelpful, in our view. This is so

---

[47] Carl Schneider argues that one of the factors behind the recent rise in tolerance of divorce and non-marital relations is the American tradition of liberal individualism. See Schneider, supra note 30, at 1839-42. Barbara Woodhouse refers to the emphasis on parental rights as "[t]his destructive emphasis." Woodhouse, supra note 1, at 1812. Mary Ann Glendon states that "[i]t is still more regrettable when the legal system inadvertently fosters irresponsible behavior, as has been the case with certain aspects of American family law." Glendon, supra note 43, at 105.

[48] See Elizabeth S. Scott, Rational Decisionmaking about Marriage and Divorce, 76 Va. L. Rev. 9, 25-37 (1990).

[49] This is not to say, of course, that parents necessarily or even generally ignore their children's interest in deciding to divorce.

[50] This interest-balancing approach has characterized legal policy and constitutional doctrine toward families since the turn of the century. For a discussion of these countervailing interests, see Fitzgerald, supra note 8, at 37-46.

not because such a perspective misunderstands the social goals that
drive the regulation of parent-child relationships, but rather
because a child-centered approach, standing alone, will not lead
reliably to legal rules that effect those objectives. Presumably, the
social goal at stake in the regulation of the parent-child relationship is to ensure children the care necessary for their development
into healthy, productive adults. This goal is more likely to be
achieved if the law focuses principally on the relationship between
parent and child, rather than on the child's needs per se. Parents
are not fungible child rearers. The link between parent and child
has substantial and intrinsic value to the child; the substitution of
another parent and/or termination of the relationship is accomplished only at considerable cost to the child.[51] Moreover, as a
general matter, the state is not well suited to substitute for parents
in the job of rearing children. If the calculus used to determine the
optimal state role focuses on the child's interest discounted by the
(now less weighty) parental interest, the presumption that these
interests are inherently in tension persists and the central importance of the relationship is likely to be obscured. Moreover,
assuming that we are correct that parents presumptively are the
"first best" child-rearers, an interest-balancing approach offers no
grounding for a regulatory regime that promotes optimal parental
performance.

Other critics of rights-based family law argue that the law should
emphasize parental responsibility, rather than rights.[52] Katharine
Bartlett, for example, emphasizing the law's expressive function,
argues that the law should express a "better view of parenthood,"[53]
one that is grounded in the morality of benevolence and responsibility. In her view, responsibility *is* inherent in relationship, and

51 See Margaret Beyer & Wallace J. Mlyniec, Lifelines to Biological Parents: Their
Effect on Termination of Parental Rights and Permanence, 20 Fam. L.Q. 233, 237-40
(1986); Marsha Garrison, Why Terminate Parental Rights?, 35 Stan. L. Rev. 423, 469-72
(1983); Michael S. Wald, State Intervention on Behalf of "Neglected" Children: Standards
for Removal of Children from Their Homes, Monitoring the Status of Children in Foster
Care, and Termination of Parental Rights, 28 Stan. L. Rev. 623, 672-74 (1976).

52 See, e.g., Bartlett, supra note 7, at 294-95; see also Milton C. Regan, Jr., Family Law
and the Pursuit of Intimacy (1993) (arguing for a communitarian framework that
emphasizes responsibility and relationship).

53 Bartlett, supra note 7, at 294.

describes a connection based on identification.[54] Although parental responsibility is a component of a rights-based conception of family relationships, it serves primarily as a justification for rights. As such, the importance of responsibility and other relationship values is obscured and diminished.[55]

In our view, Bartlett correctly identifies parental responsibility as a core component of a regulatory scheme that will better promote the interests of children. Although in many regards our analysis is compatible with communitarian principles, we propose to explore the issues of parental responsibility through a lens that is quite different from the more philosophically-based critiques developed by Bartlett and others. Our relational approach is more explicitly positive and instrumental in character.[56] We seek to discover the means through which a scheme of legal regulation can best motivate parents to invest the effort necessary to fulfill the obligations of child-rearing. This inquiry leads to another: to what extent and through what means does the current regime function to encourage desired parental behavior?

Even cursory consideration of a relational approach to the protection of children's interests suggests features that pose challenges for legal regulation. The scope of the relationship between parents and children and the range of parenting tasks are very broad. Parenting places substantial demands on the time, energy and resources of those who undertake the job, and good parenting requires giving the role a high priority relative to others in parents' lives. Inevitably, parents experience conflicts between the claims

---

[54] Id. at 299 (citing Thomas Nagel, The Possibility of Altruism 83 (1970)).

[55] As Bartlett puts it: " 'Having rights' means to be entitled to, to be owed, to have earned, or to deserve something in exchange for who one is or what one has done." Id. at 298.

[56] In applying relational theory to family law, we start with analyses that have heretofore been focused principally on more explicitly contractual relationships. See, e.g., Charles J. Goetz & Robert E. Scott, The Mitigation Principle: Toward a General Theory of Contractual Obligation, 69 Va. L. Rev. 967 (1983); Goetz & Scott, supra note 3; Robert E. Scott, Conflict and Cooperation in Long-Term Contracts, 75 Cal. L. Rev. 2005 (1987) [hereinafter Scott, Conflict and Cooperation]; Robert E. Scott, A Relational Theory of Default Rules for Commercial Contracts, 19 J. Legal Stud. 597 (1990); Robert E. Scott, A Relational Theory of Secured Financing, 86 Colum. L. Rev. 901 (1986). Some efforts have been made, however, to apply the principles of relational theory to other, more diverse contexts. See, e.g., Robert E. Scott & William J. Stuntz, Plea Bargaining as Contract, 101 Yale L.J. 1909 (1992).

of parental obligation and other interests that may interfere with the fulfillment of parental duty.[57] It is in the child's interests that these conflicts be resolved without sacrificing parental obligation. Thus, the law's overarching goal is to encourage and reinforce parents' reasonable efforts to fulfill child-rearing duties and to reduce the conflicts of interest that might lead to shirking of their responsibilities.

Regulation directed toward this end must be constrained and shaped by the complexity of the parents' task and by certain qualities of the parent-child relationship. The "performance" of parental obligation in rearing children to adulthood is extraordinarily complex and subject to many uncertainties. Numerous contingencies confront parents in making appropriate choices about health care, safety, nutrition, discipline and education. Narrowly prescribed performance criteria are incompatible with the latitude and discretion that parenting requires. Moreover, the parent-child relationship is uniquely intimate, and presumably requires considerable privacy in order to flourish.[58] Intrusion by state agents may impose peculiar costs for this reason. Any legal supervision of parents that seeks to reduce conflicts of interest between parental and non-parental tasks must be fashioned in a way that does not substitute one set of costs for another.

The task of legal regulation is further complicated by the fact that parents receive no financial compensation for the care of their children; indeed, in financial terms, children are a significant drain.

---

[57] These "other interests" can include a broad range of parental preferences and behaviors that conflict with the child's interest, either because they result directly in harm to the child (physical abuse, abandonment) or because they contribute to inadequate fulfillment of parental responsibility. Parents may pursue career advancement instead of spending time with their children and attending to their needs. They may relieve frustration by hitting their child, rather than exercising self-restraint. They may spend money on alcohol or drugs (or cars, clothes, trips or jewelry) instead of on their children's educational needs. They may satisfy their own personal needs by pursuing extramarital relationships that threaten family stability and ultimately harm their children. They may fail to maintain contact with the child when the family dissolves, because new relationships provide more gratification.

[58] This is the thrust of the argument against state intervention in the family made by psychoanalysts Goldstein et al., supra note 4. The authors argue that undisturbed development of the parent-child bond is essential to healthy child development, insisting that state intrusion is "invariably detrimental." See id. at 9. The child has a liberty interest in privacy and parental autonomy, they argue, which is a part of "family integrity." Id.

2418 *Virginia Law Review* [Vol. 81:2401

The coin in which parents are paid for their work is the nonpecuniary compensation they derive from the role and the relationship. Thus, legal regulation needs to minimize the impact of intervention on parental role satisfaction by avoiding unnecessary burdens and by supporting parents' inherent desires to have and rear children.

In sum, the challenge for family law is to construct a legal apparatus that regulates parental behavior in a complex relational context. The welfare of children and their successful development hinges to a large extent on adequate performance by parents of their child-rearing obligations. At least in theory, the law can encourage parents to act in ways that better serve their children's interests whenever they otherwise might be inclined to pursue self-interested goals. The context, however, also suggests that there will be significant constraints on the types of legal mechanisms that can safely be deployed to reduce conflicts of interest.

II. REGULATING CONFLICTS OF INTEREST BETWEEN PARENT AND CHILD

The analysis in Part I describes a current of dissatisfaction with legal regulation of the parent-child relationship and an emerging sense that the primary objective of state regulation of this relationship should be to advance the interests of children whenever they conflict with those of their parents. This premise in turn suggests that family law could usefully employ analogies drawn from the legal treatment of other relationships similarly subject to substantial conflicts of interest. Because of the asymmetries in information and control between parent and child, fiduciary relationships seem particularly relevant, and on inspection the relationship between parent and child shares many features in common with this category of relationships. Indeed, the fiduciary heuristic seems to capture the essence of the argument for a legal regime that is grounded in parental obligation to serve the child's interests.

Fiduciaries in law, such as trustees, corporate directors and managers, guardians, and executors, carry a heightened moral and legal obligation to serve the interests of a principal/beneficiary, and, within the scope of the fiduciary relationship, to subordinate their own personal interests.[59] This duty is underscored by a requirement of due diligence and unqualified fidelity.[60] In the same vein, a family law regime premised on a fiduciary framework would entrust parents with the duty to raise their children to adulthood, to provide for their physical and psychological needs, and to perform the services of parenthood with reasonable diligence and "undivided loyalty" toward their children's interests.

In many respects, optimal fiduciary behavior as it is described in other contexts seems quite analogous to the ideal of parenting advocated by critics of the parental rights approach.[61] This analogy is typically only casually drawn, without any systematic attention to the implications of treating parents as fiduciaries. Our purpose is to push the analogy beyond rhetoric.

A. The Structure and Control of Fiduciary Relationships

Fiduciary relationships are a subset of agency relationships, a broad category of legal relationships in which one party undertakes to perform a service for another. A key goal in the regulation of agency relationships is to encourage the agent to serve her principal's interests as well as her own. Several characteristics of agency relationships contribute to the risk of self-interested actions. In contrast to performance under a simple contingent contract, the agent's performance is complex and cannot be reduced readily to specific obligations.[62] Satisfactory performance demands consider-

---

[59] In such relationships, where the principal "occupies a position of special confidence, superiority, or influence, a 'special duty' exists to protect the interest of the other." Goetz & Scott, supra note 3, at 1127 (citations omitted). As Goetz and Scott note, "Fiduciaries are required, inter alia, to act 'primarily for the benefit of another, in matters connected with the undertaking.'" Id. (citing Nagel v. Todd, 45 A.2d 326, 327 (1946) (quoting Restatement of Agency § 13, cmt. a (1933)); accord Weisbecker v. Hosiery Patents, Inc., 51 A.2d 811, 813 (Pa. 1947)). For a general discussion of the duties of corporate directors and managers, see Robert Charles Clark, Corporate Law, chs. 3-8 (1986). For a discussion of the trustee's duty of loyalty, see George T. Bogert, Trusts § 95 (6th ed. 1987).

[60] Although the obligation of loyalty and "unqualified fidelity" is mandatory, the parties are free to define by contract the specific duties required of the fiduciary. See Alison Grey Anderson, Conflicts of Interest: Efficiency, Fairness and Corporate Structure, 25 UCLA L. Rev. 738, 760 (1978).

[61] The metaphor of fiduciary responsibility, in different forms, has been used by commentators to emphasize the importance of parental obligation. See supra note 2.

[62] For this reason, Charles Goetz and Robert Scott designate the agent-principal relationship as a relational contract. See Goetz & Scott, supra note 3.

able decisionmaking discretion, and monitoring the quality of the agent's performance may be difficult.

These factors are exaggerated in a fiduciary relationship because the principal will typically be even less able to control or monitor the fiduciary's performance than is the case in an ordinary agency relationship.[63] The problem may be particularly acute if the principal/beneficiary is a minor or is mentally disabled. More typically, beneficiaries—whether shareholders, trust beneficiaries or legatees—are presumed to lack the requisite information or expertise to understand and evaluate the fiduciary's performance, and acquiring such information is very costly.[64] As a result, not only is it difficult to monitor the agent's diligence and effort in performing her assigned responsibilities, but the context carries a heightened risk of self-dealing as well. In general, the law characterizes as fiduciary those agency relationships in which the principal is particularly vulnerable and unable fully to protect and assert his own interests, thus providing the agent a peculiar opportunity and incentive either to shirk or cheat.[65]

Fiduciary law seeks to change these incentives through mechanisms designed to encourage actors to pursue collective rather than personal goals. Legal duties of fiduciaries fall roughly into two categories: a duty of care—the agent must perform her responsibilities with reasonable diligence—and a duty of loyalty—the fiduciary must not place her personal interests above those of her principal.[66] The objective, in either case, is first to encourage the

---

[63] Robert Clark argues that fiduciaries are different from typical agents, because principals control agents and are ready to countermand their agents' decisions. See Robert C. Clark, Agency Costs versus Fiduciary Duties, *in* Principals and Agents: The Structure of Business 55, 56-59 (John W. Pratt & Richard J. Zeckhauser eds., 1985). In our view, fiduciary relationships should be treated as a subset of agency relationships which have many agency characteristics in exaggerated form.

[64] This is often true of trust beneficiaries and shareholders. Alison Anderson discusses the costs to shareholders of acquiring information, each of whom has a small stake in the corporation, and thus may not be motivated to invest enough to acquire adequate information. See Anderson, supra note 60, at 778-80; accord Clark, supra note 63, at 77.

[65] See supra note 3.

[66] In Bayer v. Beran, 49 N.Y.S.2d 2 (Sup. Ct. 1944), the court made this distinction very clear:

> The fiduciary has two paramount obligations: responsibility and loyalty. . . . The responsibility—that is, the care and the diligence—required of an agent or of a fiduciary, is proportioned to the occasion. It is a concept that has, and necessarily so, a wide penumbra of meaning . . . .

fiduciary to take the beneficiary's interests properly into account in making decisions, and second to facilitate detection of her failure to do so.

The means used to achieve the desired goals include both extralegal mechanisms (primarily informal social norms) and legal devices, and are usefully grouped into two broad categories. Monitoring arrangements allow the principal to supervise the agent's actions so as to detect and sanction agent conduct in pursuit of selfish ends.[67] Bonding arrangements align the interest of the agent with that of the principal through self-limiting constraints that serve a precommitment function.[68] Bonding mechanisms, although they constrain agent behavior, will be as desired by agents as by principals to the extent that they substitute for even more costly monitoring efforts.[69] In contractual agency relationships, for example, agents voluntarily accept the imposition of sanctions upon default, thus providing assurance to principals that they will not act contrary to the principals' ends.[70] In fiduciary relationships, legal and extralegal limits on fiduciary conduct serve an analogous bonding function, defining the role in a way that constrains the fiduciary's future conduct through threat of sanction in the event of default.

From an efficiency perspective, the goal of legal regulation of fiduciaries (and other agents) is to reduce conflicts of interest (situations that compromise either the agent's diligent performance or loyalty, or both) at the least cost. In service of this goal, extralegal

---

The concept of loyalty, of constant, unqualified fidelity, has a definite and precise meaning. The fiduciary must subordinate his individual and private interests to his duty . . . whenever the two conflict.
Id. at 5, *cited in* Goetz & Scott, supra note 3, at 1127 n.86.

[67] Jensen & Meckling, supra note 6, at 308.

[68] Id.

[69] Jensen & Meckling established the reciprocal relationship between bonding and monitoring functions. Through bonding, the agent guarantees that she will not take certain actions which would harm the principal or ensures that the principal will be compensated if she does take such actions. Ex ante, these precommitments benefit the agent as well as the principal to the extent that they increase the value of the performance being provided. The enhanced performance is reflected in a higher price paid to the agent for her services. Thus, self-limiting constraints will be voluntarily assumed whenever these precommitments can substitute for more costly monitoring alternatives. See id. at 323-26.

[70] It is useful to think of bonding mechanisms as precommitments that will encourage the agent to pursue the collective long-term interest at times when her short-term interest diverges from the cooperative goal. Id.

and legal mechanisms are substitutes for one another, as are bonding and monitoring devices. Thus, where informal social norms exert a powerful influence on agents' behavior, less extensive legal mechanisms are required.[71] Similarly, insofar as the fiduciary is adequately "bonded" (i.e., she sees her interests as allied with that of the beneficiary), the principal's need to monitor the fiduciary's performance is reduced. Consequently, the optimal scheme of regulation (specifically, the best combination of extralegal and legal incentives and of bonding and monitoring mechanisms) will vary depending on the circumstances and the particular context.

The prohibition against self-dealing, a feature common to the regulation of fiduciaries, is a particularly appropriate illustration of the variable nature of legal regulation. This proscription functions to define a boundary of fiduciary discretion, and it varies in its strictness in different settings. In trust law, the prohibition is absolute; trustees cannot engage in self-dealing, however reasonable the transaction.[72] The beneficiaries can rescind any transaction between the trustee and the trust, and require the trustee to disgorge profits.[73] The duty of corporate managers and directors, however, is less stringent. A corporate director who enters into a contract with the corporation must demonstrate that the deal is fair to the corporation, in the sense that the transaction is as advantageous to the corporation as a comparable transaction in a competitive market.[74]

---

[71] Stewart Macaulay relates the comment of one businessman:

> "[I]f something comes up, you get the other man on the telephone and deal with the problem. You don't read legalistic contract clauses at each other if you ever want to do business again." As an example of how well established this attitude is, Macaulay tells of the large manufacturer of packaging materials who inspected its records and found that it had failed to create legally binding contracts in two-thirds of the orders randomly selected for review.

Scott, Conflict and Cooperation, supra note 56, at 2047-48 (citations omitted) (quoting and citing Stewart Macaulay, Non-Contractual Relations in Business: A Preliminary Study, 28 Am. Soc. Rev. 55, 60-61 (1963)).

[72] Self-dealing is implicated any time the trustee, as trustee, bargains with himself in an individual capacity. It occurs any time the trustee sells his own property to the trust or buys trust property. See Jesse Dukeminier & Stanley M. Johanson, Wills, Trusts, and Estates 851-52 (4th ed. 1990).

[73] Id. at 852.

[74] Clark, supra note 63, at 73-74; see also American Law Institute, Principles of Corporate Governance and Structure: Restatement and Recommendations § 5.02 (Tent. Draft No. 5, 1986) (covering transactions by directors and officers for a corporation), *cited*

The self-limiting constraint is more stringent as applied to trustees then to corporate fiduciaries in part because, as a class, trust beneficiaries have less control[75] and are more vulnerable[76] than are shareholders. For these reasons, trustees may face a greater opportunity and temptation to cheat than corporate fiduciaries, and thus require greater levels of deterrence and constraint. But perhaps more importantly, the more stringent rules that apply to trustees generally reflect the more limited purpose and scope of the trust relationship. In contrast to trustees, corporate directors are engaged in a broad range of activities on behalf of the corporation. Broader discretion and a presumption of good faith and diligence are justified in the corporate context by the broad scope of the agency relationship as well as the importance of encouraging directors willingly to invest effort in service of the shareholders.

In corporate law, the presumption of due diligence is embodied in the business judgment rule, "a presumption that in making a business decision the directors of a corporation acted on an informed basis, in good faith and in the honest belief that the

---

in William L. Cary & Melvin A. Eisenberg, Corporations 591 (6th ed. 1988); Clark, supra note 59, § 5.2 (describing three conditions for the validity of self-dealing transactions involving directors or officers of a corporation). For example, if the corporate president happens to own a gravel pit and sells gravel to the corporation at above market price, the shareholders can rescind the deal or collect damages. As Clark explains, this response is part of a general scheme of rules prohibiting the corporate director/manager from using her positional advantage to the detriment of the corporation. These include prohibitions against corporate directors and managers developing corporate opportunities unless the corporation is unable to do so. See Clark, supra note 63, at 74-75. The prohibition against insider-trading was originally imposed under the Securities Act of 1933 and the Securities Exchange Act of 1934 on the ground that insider trading was wrong. See Henry G. Manne, Insider Trading and the Stock Market 8-10 (1966). Some argue that the insider-trading ban is valuable because it reinforces confidence in the stock market among third parties and avoids the appearance of conflict of interest. If the majority of potential investors fear the market is unfair, they will refrain from investing, leaving the market undercapitalized. See Roy A. Schotland, Unsafe at Any Price: A Reply to Manne, Insider Trading and the Stock Market, 53 Va. L. Rev. 1425, 1440-42 (1967).

[75] Trust beneficiaries cannot terminate the relationship with the trustee, unlike shareholders, who can vote to terminate directors. See William L. Cary & Melvin A. Eisenberg, Corporations 205-07 (6th ed. 1988); Clark, supra note 59, § 3.1.1.

[76] Among multiple shareholders in a corporation, some are likely to be inclined to monitor managerial behavior even if most are not. A given trust will usually have one or a small number of beneficiaries, who may be minors or otherwise incapable of monitoring. Thus, the potential for abuse of power by fiduciaries may be greater in the latter situation.

action taken was in the best interests of the company."[77] The actions and judgments of corporate directors are not protected by the business judgment rule, however, when the judgment in question was tainted by a conflict of interest[78] or by gross negligence.[79] In sum, the business judgment rule assumes that the decision in question reflects reasonable diligence and care, but evidence of a violation of the duty of care (negligence) or of the duty of loyalty (self-dealing) will trigger sanctions. The business judgment rule represents an implicit recognition that the more complex and broad ranging is the fiduciary relationship, the more discretion is needed and the more legal norms must be selectively deployed in concert with other informal arrangements that also align the interests of the parties.

1. *Bonding Arrangements*

The legal rules that support the duties of care and loyalty serve both bonding and monitoring functions. Given the costs of enforcement, however, the bonding function dominates. Bonding restrictions function principally as precommitments; they are undertaken by the fiduciary with the purpose of limiting her future actions in a way that reduces the incidence of conflicts of interest.[80]

---

[77] Aronson v. Lewis, 473 A.2d 805, 812 (Del. 1984); see also Zapata Corp. v. Maldonado, 430 A.2d 779, 782 (Del. 1981) (holding that the business judgment rule is a presumption of good faith and due diligence that requires deference to the expertise of corporate directors); American Law Institute, Principles of Corporate Governance: Analysis and Recommendations § 4.01(c) (Proposed Final Draft 1992) ("A director or officer who makes a business judgment in good faith fulfills the duty under this Section [titled Duty of Care of Directors and Officers; the Business Judgment Rule] if the director or officer: (1) is not interested . . . (2) is informed . . . (3) rationally believes that the business judgment is in the best interests of the corporation."); Clark, supra note 59, § 3.4 (summarizing the business judgment rule).

[78] See Shlensky v. Wrigley, 237 N.E.2d 776, 780 (Ill. App. Ct. 1968).

[79] See Bucyrus-Erie Co. v. Gen. Prod. Corp., 643 F.2d 413, 420 (6th Cir. 1981).

[80] A decisionmaker, wanting to follow a chosen course of action, and fearing that in the future she may be tempted to make choices that are inconsistent with that course, may precommit by taking present actions that make it more difficult in the future to depart from the chosen course. For a discussion of precommitment theory in various legal contexts, see Robert E. Scott, Error and Rationality in Individual Decisionmaking: An Essay on the Relationship Between Cognitive Illusions and the Management of Choices, 59 S. Cal. L. Rev. 329, 342-47 (1986); Scott, supra note 48, at 40-42. For discussions of precommitment theory generally, see R.H. Strotz, Myopia and Inconsistency in Dynamic Utility Maximization, 23 Rev. Econ. Stud. 165 (1955-56) (the pilot work in the field); George Ainslie, Behavioral Economics II: Motivated, Involuntary Behavior, 23 Soc. Sci.

On the margin, the fiduciary will internalize the prohibition and avoid conduct that increases the risk of self-interested actions. Toward this end, fiduciary law explicitly uses informal social norms to influence fiduciary behavior in ways that reduce conflicts of interest. By establishing a standard of performance that emphasizes heightened obligations of loyalty and integrity, and by the use of hortatory moral rhetoric, the law invokes a personal sense of moral obligation in the performance of fiduciary duty.[81] As Robert Clark observes, courts talk about fiduciary duty in a tone that contrasts sharply with that which is used to describe obligation in commercial contractual relationships.[82] The stance of moral neutrality that courts adopt toward efficient breach in other contexts is absent here; fiduciary default is treated as a moral violation with attendant reputational costs.[83] This invocation of morality may compensate partially for the ineffectiveness of market controls in this context, since beneficiaries are presumed less able to protect their interests than are parties in ordinary commercial relationships.[84] In any

---

Info. 47, 54-56 (1984); George Ainslie, Specious Reward: A Behavioral Theory of Impulsiveness and Impulse Control, 82 Psychol. Bull. 463, 476-89 (1975); Thomas C. Schelling, Egonomics, or the Art of Self-Management, 68 Am. Econ. Rev. (Papers & Proc.) 290 (1978); Thomas C. Schelling, Ethics, Law, and the Exercise of Self-Command, *in* Choice and Consequence 83 (1984); Thomas C. Schelling, Self-Command in Practice, in Policy, and in a Theory of Rational Choice, 74 Am. Econ. Rev. (Papers & Proc.) 1 (1984).

[81] Justice Cardozo described fiduciary duty in the following terms:

Many forms of conduct permissible in a workaday world for those acting at arm's length, are forbidden to those bound by fiduciary ties. A trustee is held to something stricter than the morals of the market place. Not honesty alone, but the punctilio of an honor the most sensitive, is then the standard of behavior. As to this there has developed a tradition that is unbending and inveterate. Uncompromising rigidity has been the attitude of courts of equity when petitioned to undermine the rule of undivided loyalty . . . . Only thus has the level of conduct for fiduciaries been kept at a level higher than that trodden by the crowd.

Meinhard v. Salmon, 164 N.E. 545, 546 (N.Y. 1928).

[82] Clark, supra note 63, at 75-76.

[83] Id. The importance of reputational costs and benefits in shaping behavior according to moral prescriptions has been examined in the context of marital and family behavior in Amy L. Wax, Review Essay: Against Nature—On Robert Wright's *The Moral Animal*, 63 U. Chi. L. Rev. (forthcoming 1996) (manuscript at Part II.1, on file with the Virginia Law Review Association).

[84] As Clark points out, a breach of contract is likely to be sanctioned, because the obligee will know of the breach and may seek a remedy. In contrast, moral disapproval is needed in the fiduciary context because ordinary market and legal controls are less effective, either because beneficiaries lack information or because they are incompetent. See Clark, supra note 63, at 78-79.

event, the rhetoric of fiduciary duty is a strong signal that this relationship does not involve "business as usual." The fiduciary who is tempted to defect faces the informal social costs of guilt and moral opprobrium as well as others that the law might impose.

The tradition, often endorsed by law, of appointing family members as fiduciaries is another example of a bonding mechanism that reinforces extralegal norms.[85] Family members are often chosen as trustees, executors, or guardians and as managers in close corporations, because it is assumed that they will be more likely to identify their interests with the interests of their principals, and will be less likely to abuse their discretion. The informal cultural norms of family loyalty reinforce legal standards, thereby encouraging self-limiting behavior by the fiduciary. The family fiduciary anticipates costs of humiliation and social disapproval upon default that exceed those experienced by non-family fiduciaries. These costs may discourage self-interested behavior.

The rhetoric of obligation that characterizes the fiduciary relationship is directed principally toward reducing the heightened risk of disloyalty. Thus, as Robert Scott and Charles Goetz have shown, the extraordinary obligations of fiduciary performance are obligations of loyalty and integrity, rather than requirements of extraordinary effort in pursuit of collective purposes.[86] Fiduciaries are not obliged to attend to their fiduciary duties to the exclusion of other personal obligations and activities. Scott and Goetz argue that the degree of care and effort required of a fiduciary in advancing the principal's interests is analogous to that required in other agency relationships—an amount of diligence and effort that maximizes the joint utility of beneficiary and fiduciary.[87]

---

[85] See Uniform Guardianship and Protective Proceedings Act §§ 2-205, 2-309, 8A U.L.A. 439, 489-90, 509-10 (1982) (establishing priority for appointment of family members as guardian and conservator, respectively). This mechanism is not suitable, of course, for the setting of the public corporation, where there are multiple "beneficiaries."

[86] See Goetz & Scott, supra note 3, at 1126-30. In corporate law, however, sometimes the line is ambiguous between duty of loyalty on the one hand and duty of care on the other.

[87] Id. at 1128-29. The joint maximization hypothesis follows from the reciprocal nature of contractual relationships. Parties enter into contractual relationships in order to pursue individual ends through collective action. The greater the benefits that can be gained from their contractual venture, the greater the individual benefits for each contracting partner, *ceteris paribus*. An assumption that the degree of effort required of a fiduciary or other agent is that necessary to maximize the joint interests of the parties thus provides the most

2. Monitoring Mechanisms

The beneficiary in a fiduciary relationship is generally less well-positioned to monitor the agent's behavior than is the principal in a typical contractual agency relationship.[88] As a consequence, legally prescribed and supervised oversight plays a larger role in monitoring fiduciary conduct. Trustees, guardians and executors are subject to elaborate, judicially supervised reporting requirements obliging them to disclose their activities as fiduciaries, and some fiduciary decisions are subject to court approval.[89] Corporate fiduciaries are legally obliged to report to shareholders;[90] they are

---

rational default rule for specifying standards of performance in the absence of specifically agreed upon alternatives. Id. at 1126-30. Moreover, the joint maximization criterion subsumes other plausible alternatives such as a standard of reasonable diligence and care, since any effort that maximizes the joint product will, by definition, be the effort required of a reasonably prudent agent.

The joint maximization criterion also fits comfortably within the rhetorical tradition of fiduciary law. Such a standard requires the fiduciary to treat the principal's interests fairly, taking both parties' interests into account when determining the appropriate amount of effort to devote to collective as opposed to individual tasks.

Although the joint maximization criterion functions primarily as a default rule in contractual agency relationships, the logic that underlies the criterion would be equally compelling in determining mandatory standards of performance for other fiduciary relationships, including those where the contractual relationship runs from the settlor or the state to the fiduciary insofar as the state or settlor undertook to establish the relationship to advance the interests of the beneficiary.

[88] The creator of the fiduciary relationship (the settlor of a trust, for example) can sometimes monitor the fiduciary's performance. This may be difficult for a trustee, however, and impossible for a testator. Of course, in a guardianship, the state as creator of the guardianship monitors through judicial supervision.

[89] See, e.g., Uniform Guardianship and Protective Proceedings Act, §§ 2-109, 2-209, 2-317-18. Guardians, under some statutes, must seek court approval for extraordinary medical treatment such as psychiatric hospitalization, or sterilization of minors or the mentally impaired. See, e.g., Ark. Code Ann. § 20-49-202 (Michie 1991); Conn. Gen. Stat. Ann. § 45a-698 (West 1993); Kan. Stat. Ann. § 59-3018(g)(8) (1994); N.C. Gen. Stat. §§ 35-36, 35-37 (1990). Some states require court approval for guardians to sell stock or real estate of their minor wards. See, e.g., Ga. Code Ann. §§ 29-2-5, 29-2-6 (Michie 1993).

[90] For example, under the authority of the Securities Exchange Act of 1934, the Securities Exchange Commission requires registered corporations to send an annual report to shareholders along with proxies. The report must include audited balance sheets for the last two fiscal years, information concerning disagreements with accountants or changes in accountants, management's analysis of the corporation's financial condition and the result of corporate operations, the identity of all directors and executive officers, as well as other information. See 17 C.F.R. § 240.14a-3(b) (1995). Many states have similar provisions. California, for example, requires that an annual report containing a balance sheet and income statement for the past fiscal year be sent to shareholders 15 days prior to annual meetings. See Cal. Corp. Code Ann. § 1501(a) (West 1990). Other states merely give

also subject to oversight by the Securities and Exchange Commission.[91]

An important means of controlling misbehavior in most agency relationships is the principal's right to terminate the relationship or to replace the agent.[92] In many fiduciary relationships, however, this right is either not available to or is not easily exercised by beneficiaries.[93] The choice of fiduciary is controlled by the party who creates the relationship, who in many contexts is not the bene-ficiary.[94] Corporate shareholders have the power to remove direc-tors and (indirectly) managers, but in many other fiduciary relationships this power can only be exercised by a court unless otherwise provided by the party creating the relationship.[95] Courts

---

shareholders a right to inspect corporate records upon written request. See, e.g., N.Y. Bus. Corp. Law Ann. § 624 (McKinney 1986).

[91] Publicly-held corporations are subject to periodic reporting requirements imposed under the authority of the Securities Exchange Act of 1934. They must file annual 10-K forms, quarterly 10-Q forms, and 8-K forms when certain events occur. 10-K forms must be filed within 90 days of the end of the fiscal year and must include, inter alia, information on the corporation's financial condition and general business development, disclosures on legal proceedings against the corporation, executive compensation, and conflict of interest transactions. See 17 C.F.R. §§ 240.13a-1, 240.15d-1, 249.310 (1995). For a copy of form 10-K, see Research Institute of America, 4 Securities Regulation ¶ 13,139 (1993). Form 10-Q reports must be filed within 45 days of the end of the quarter, except for the fourth quarter. See 17 C.F.R. §§ 240.13a-13, 240.15d-13, 249.308a (1995). They must include a quarterly financial report, a management report, and disclosures on legal proceedings and defaults on senior securities, as well as other requirements. For a copy of form 10-Q, see Research Institute of America, 4 Securities Regulation ¶ 13,141 (1993). A form 8-K must be filed within 15 days of a change in corporate control, if the corporation experiences a major change in assets (beyond the ordinary course of business), or if there is a change of accountants. See 17 C.F.R. §§ 240.13a-11, 240.15d-11 (1995); For a copy of Form 8-K, see Research Institute of America, 4 Securities Regulation ¶ 13,133 (1993). See generally J. Robert Brown, Jr., Corporate Communications and the Federal Securities Laws, 53 Geo. Wash. L. Rev. 741 (1985) (analyzing corporate disclosure duties). States also have their own reporting requirements. See Cary & Eisenberg, supra note 75, at 269-70.

[92] See Goetz & Scott, supra note 3, at 1130-49.

[93] Termination of the fiduciary relationship (such as the dissolution of a trust) and replacement of one fiduciary with another are, of course, different acts.

[94] Moreover, in trusts and wills, the settlor and testator are often not available.

[95] Compare Clark, supra note 59, § 3.1.1 (noting conditions under which corporate shareholders may remove directors), with Bogert, supra note 59, § 160, at 573-74 (noting conditions under which courts may remove trustees, including, inter alia, insanity, habitual drunkeness, extreme improvidence, conviction of a crime, insolvency, bankruptcy, failure or refusal to act, mingling of trust property with the trustee's individual property, failure to account, conflict of interest, and failure to cooperate with co-trustees). The court has considerable power with respect to trustees:

generally have broad discretion to remove and replace fiduciaries who misbehave.[96] Courts exercising this power typically assume that substituting a new fiduciary imposes only minimal costs on the beneficiary and that fiduciaries themselves have little direct interest (other than loss of income) at stake in the relationship.[97]

3. Rewards of the Fiduciary Role

If the relationship between fiduciary and beneficiary is structured primarily to serve the interests of the beneficiary, why would the role of fiduciary have any appeal? To be sure, some fiduciaries may be altruistic, or motivated by a preexisting sense of duty toward a particular beneficiary, perhaps because of a family relationship. Fiduciaries also receive financial compensation for their work, and in some professions involving fiduciary obligation the compensation is generous. Another important component of role satisfaction for many fiduciaries is reputational reward and correlative self-esteem. The role of trustee, for example, invokes respect in the community, signaling that the individual has assumed an important responsibility, and is trustworthy and morally upright. Community recognition of these attributes carries its own reward, enhancing the nonpecuniary value of the fiduciary role.

In sum, through a scheme of formal and informal bonding and monitoring mechanisms, the fiduciary is encouraged to subordinate self-interest in carrying out her responsibilities and to devote appropriate efforts toward furthering the beneficiary's interests.

If a beneficiary can prove that his financial interests will be seriously endangered by a continued operation of the trust by the trustee, he may be able to secure the trustee's removal by a court of equity.

. . . .

The court has power to remove a trustee and to appoint a successor trustee.
Id. at 571.

[96] See, e.g., Hines v. Brown's Comm., 88 S.W.2d 314, 316 (Ky. Ct. App. 1935); Uniform Guardianship and Protective Proceedings Act, §§ 2-112, 2-211; George G. Bogert & George T. Bogert, The Law of Trusts and Trustees § 527, at 49 & n.3, 52 & n.7 (Rev. 2d ed. 1993) (citing statutes).

[97] Some courts do acknowledge that the fiduciary has a reputational interest at stake in a removal proceeding. See, e.g., IFS Indus., Inc. v. Stephens, 205 Cal. Rptr. 915, 925-26 (Cal. Ct. App. 1984); Heizer Corp. v. Hackbarth, Civ. A. No. 7949, 1988 WL 58272, at *2 (Del. Ch. 1988); In re Estate of Georgiana, 458 A.2d 989, 991 (Pa. Super. Ct. 1983); Dahl v. Akin, 645 S.W.2d 506, 520 (Tex. Ct. App. 1982); see also Bogert, supra note 59, § 160, at 571 (noting that reputational costs deter courts from removal of trustees).

These responsibilities are induced by a quid pro quo: compensation that includes, in addition to financial rewards, broad grants of authority and discretion that enhance reputation and self-esteem.

B. A Relational Model of Parents as Fiduciaries

1. In General

The relationship between parent and child invites comparison to legal fiduciary relationships and poses similar challenges for legal regulation. It is apparent at the outset, however, that applying a fiduciary framework to the parent-child relationship requires accommodation of some peculiar features that distinguish this relationship from many others in the fiduciary category. Given the extensive scope of the relationship, a prescription that parents must systematically subordinate their personal interest to that of the child when the two are in conflict seems unduly burdensome, and ultimately likely to deter prospective parents from taking on the role. Furthermore, enforcement of such an obligation, although theoretically feasible, would require costly and intrusive state supervision of intact families. This effect seems particularly troublesome given the intimacy of the relationship and the presumed importance of privacy to optimal family functioning. Moreover, the substantial costs to children of replacing parents and of severing the filial bond inhibits the imposition of a sanction that is used to discipline fiduciaries in other contexts.[98]

Thus, a model scheme for regulating the parent-child relationship must attend to the unique features of this familial bond, and some adaptation of the conventional regulatory mechanisms is required. The usefulness of this approach is not diminished by these constraints, however, so long as policymakers appreciate the goals of regulation and evaluate legal rules as means to the prescribed ends. Optimal rules that seek to motivate parents to act so as to promote their children's welfare and to encourage parental commitment to the relationship will necessarily weigh the burdens that are placed on parents and the costs of disrupting the relationship. To ignore these costs is counterproductive, and, by definition, suboptimal. Because parents are not fungible actors in their chil-

---

[98] See supra note 4.

dren's lives, and because parents' enthusiasm for their role can be assumed to affect their children's welfare, protecting the child's interest requires particular attention to the effects of regulation on parental satisfaction and commitment. As in all other relationships that are similarly regulated, rules that reduce conflicts of interest and self-dealing are shaped by the character of the relationship being regulated.

Although the parent-child relationship is formally derived from status, its salient characteristics suggest that the relationship is most closely analogous to contract-based agency relationships that carry fiduciary obligations, such as the duties of corporate directors to their shareholders. The role of parents, like that of corporate directors, involves a performance that includes an extensive range of decisions and tasks. Like corporate directors, parents are granted broad discretion in making decisions that affect the interests of their principals. Moreover, as is true in the family context, the ultimate goal of maximizing shareholder value is served by encouraging directors to invest substantial efforts in performing their duties. Many of the rules governing corporate directors—such as the business judgment rule—implicitly recognize the feedback effects between role satisfaction and performance.

2. A Relational Model of the Intact Family

At the outset, we make several fundamental assumptions about state regulation of the parent-child relationship. First, we assume that the overarching purpose of the state is to protect the interests of children in receiving from their parents the care and nurture necessary to enable them to develop into healthy adults. Second, we assume that parents function as "first best" caretakers and are preferred to state agents, *ceteris paribus*. Finally, we assume that a substantial motivation leading parents to procreate is the anticipation of rearing their children in a family unit. Taken together, these assumptions imply that the state, in specifying an optimal scheme of regulation, must attend to the interests of parents in having and rearing children.

One method of analyzing the interplay among these basic assumptions is to imagine a hypothetical negotiation between the state and parents over the appropriate standards of parental responsibility. The state's interest is to achieve its stated goals.

The parents' interest is to maximize the returns from parenthood. We then ask what combination of regulatory provisions would be agreed to by the state and the broadest number of parents engaged in such a bargaining process.[99] In the context of the intact family, both extralegal forces and legal bonding arrangements emerge as attractive candidates.

a. Extralegal Influences: Biological and Affective Bonds and Social Norms

In analyzing the appropriate role that extralegal forces play in encouraging parents to act in their children's interest, we assume that having children represents a voluntary choice on the part of parents,[100] but that in rearing children parents must fulfill the fundamental objective of the state: to provide the care and nurture necessary for children to develop into healthy, functioning adults. Given this assumption, it follows that social norms and other influences that bond parents to their parental obligations serve the interests of both parents and the state. The state's interest is to achieve its objective at least cost, and thus it would always agree to substitute a less costly extralegal arrangement for more costly state supervision.[101] Similarly, parents would accept self-limiting con-

---

[99] Some readers have objected to the use of a contractual model that characterizes parents as agents of the state in the rearing of their children. Stephen Sugarman challenges this characterization, arguing that the agency model does not capture the understanding of the parental role shared by most people. Parents, unlike other fiduciaries, are free to do as they want with their children (above some minimum level of care). Letter from Stephen Sugarman to authors (Mar. 6, 1995) (on file with the Virginia Law Review Association). We are sympathetic to the discomfort that the relational model may cause. However, a model is not tested by how accurately it captures real world experience—which no model purports to do. Rather, the validity of a model turns on how well it predicts results. We believe that the agency model explains much of the peculiar design of the legal regulation of the state-parent relationship. If anything, the relational model exaggerates parental autonomy and deemphasizes the authority of the state to dictate standards of parental performance. As our analysis shows, the freedom of parents to make decisions about child-rearing free of state intrusion (which, as Sugarman observes, distinguishes the parental role from other fiduciary relationships) is entirely consistent with the relational model.

[100] This assumption may be counterfactual in some instances, of course. It is generally sound, however, given that it is relatively easy to avoid having unwanted children.

[101] It is important to remember that the cost of any regulatory mechanism is the sum of two types of costs: the direct costs of enforcement and the "error" costs of a failure to control perfectly the behavior subject to regulation. Thus, a given arrangement is cost-

straints that deter selfish behavior whenever these constraints can substitute for more onerous state controls on child-rearing.

The biological and affective bonds between parents and children together with informal social norms encourage parents to identify their interests with those of their children and to approach their performance as parents with a sense of moral obligation. In such an environment, parents would expect to experience the rewards of social approval and self-fulfillment for good parenting, and would expect both guilt and social opprobrium to follow default. Indeed, in contrast to other fiduciary contexts where the invocation of morality as a means of influencing fiduciary behavior is largely a legal construction, in the family setting these extralegal factors function independently of the law to influence parental behavior. Research and other evidence suggests that most parents are influenced to a greater or lesser degree by biological, psychological and social forces which, in combination, generate a norm of parental obligation.[102]

The most controversial strand of this complex bond is biological. Scholars representing very diverse perspectives and ideologies have emphasized the importance of the biological bond between parents and children as an influence on parental behavior.[103] Evolutionary psychologists argue that biological parenthood inclines

---

effective when the sum of enforcement and error costs is less than the total cost of any available alternative.

[102] See infra text accompanying notes 103-13 for discussion of the relevant research.

[103] As discussed in the text and notes below, evolutionary psychologists and sociobiologists most prominently argue for the importance of biology. See infra notes 104-06 and accompanying text. Legal scholars, such as Richard Epstein, have advocated the importance of sociobiology. See Richard A. Epstein, Gender is for Nouns, 41 DePaul L. Rev. 981 (1992); Richard A. Epstein, The Authoritarian Impulse in Sex Discrimination Law: A Reply to Professors Abrams and Strauss, 41 DePaul L. Rev. 1041 (1992); Richard A. Epstein, Two Challenges for Feminist Thought, 18 Harv. J.L. & Pub. Pol. 331 (1995). Moreover, feminist legal scholars such as Robin West, Mary Anne Case, and Martha Fineman also have focused on the importance of the biological bond between parent and child. West argues that women's identities are importantly shaped by the experience of connection in pregnancy and birth. See Robin West, Jurisprudence and Gender, 55 U. Chi. L. Rev. 1 (1988). Case, in an entertaining and provocative response to the enthusiastic endorsement of sociobiology by Richard Epstein, suggests that if law sought to embrace the lessons of sociobiology, it would protect the mother-child dyad rather than the tenuous marital bond. See Mary Anne Case, Of Richard Epstein and Other Radical Feminists, 18 Harv. J.L. & Pub. Pol'y 369 (1995). Case bases this argument on Martha Fineman's thesis that the mother-child dyad should be legally protected as the core family relationship. See Martha Fineman, The Neutered Mother, the Sexual Family, and Other Twentieth Century

parents to protect and care for their children.[104] By this account, parents nurture their young (and have little inclination to nurture the children of others) in order to protect their genetic heritage and maximize its survival.[105] Researchers point to the much lower rates of violence directed toward biological children than toward stepchildren and non-biological family members as evidence of this biological inclination.[106]

Less debatable is the powerful affective bond between parent and child. At the birth of their child, parents undertake a long-term relationship which usually builds incrementally and involves a deep emotional attachment. This relationship is distinctive among others characterized by emotional attachment, constituting what social psychologists describe as a "crescive bond," which links irreplaceable individuals into a continuing relationship.[107] For these bonds to form, the relationship must be an important component of the parents' personal and social identity and must provide rewards, particularly self-esteem. Research suggests that the role of parent is among the most important in defining personal identity for both men and women.[108]

The affective bond provides powerful grounding for a parental precommitment to care for the welfare of one's children. The force of that commitment does not, however, derive solely from the

---

Tragedies (1995). Fineman does not argue for rights based on biology per se, but on nurturing (a function usually fulfilled by mothers).

[104] See Margo Wilson, Impact of the Uncertainty of Paternity on Family Law, 45 U. Toronto Faculty L. Rev. 216, 222-24 (1987); see also Martin Daly & Margo Wilson, Child Abuse and Other Risks of Not Living with Both Parents, 6 Ethology & Sociobiology 197 (1985) (concluding that children living with one natural parent and one stepparent are dramatically more likely to suffer child abuse than those living with both natural parents); Joy L. Lightcap, Jeffrey A. Kurland & Robert L. Burgess, Child Abuse: A Test of Some Predictions from Evolutionary Theory, 3 Ethology & Sociobiology 61 (1982) (concluding that lack of genetic relationship makes "parent" more likely to neglect or abuse child).

[105] See Daly & Wilson, supra note 104, at 197; Lightcap et al., supra note 104, at 62; Wilson, supra note 104, at 222-24.

[106] See Daly & Wilson, supra note 104, at 205; Lightcap et al., supra note 104, at 64-66.

[107] See Ralph H. Turner, Family Interaction 80 (1970). For a discussion of the parent-child relationship as a crescive bond, see Lynn White, Step Families Over the Life Course: Social Support 4-5 (paper presented at National Symposium on Stepfamilies, Pennsylvania State University, Oct. 14-15, 1993) (on file with the Virginia Law Review Association).

[108] See White, supra note 107, at 4-5. White notes that the role of stepparent is much less salient. Recent research has found the role of parent to be the most salient role. Id. (citing Peggy A. Thoits, Identity Structures and Psychological Well-Being: Gender and Marital Status Comparisons, 55 Soc. Psych. Q. 236 (1992)).

existence of a strong affective bond.[109] Informal social norms play an important part in shaping parents' recognition that their role is defined by serious obligation and subordinated self-interest. Certainly, much of the rhetoric about parenthood in contemporary culture reinforces this sense of obligation, and anecdotal evidence suggests that the message is getting stronger.[110] Several examples make the point. First, public concern about child abuse and neglect has increased in the past generation. Predictable reactions of outrage follow egregious examples of parental misconduct[111] and self-interested behavior.[112] Second, popular media attention has focused on the harmful psychological and economic impact of divorce on children, and negative publicity about "deadbeat dads" has been translated into tough child support enforcement legislation.[113] Examples of fathers going to jail or losing professional

---

[109] The fact that the parent-child relationship is of identity-defining importance to the parent does not mean, necessarily, that parents will understand their role as shaped principally by obligation. The role could also include a sense of entitlement.

[110] A theme of popular psychology in the 1970s and 1980s was that "parents are people, too" and should not feel guilty about pursuing their own interest. Carl Schneider discusses the "rise of psychologic man" as a modern cultural phenomenon in which personal fulfillment and self realization are emphasized. See Schneider, supra note 30, at 1852-60. The enthusiasm for this attitude seems to have waned in recent years, however, perhaps because of concern about the impact of widespread divorce on children and the growing focus on child abuse. See infra text accompanying notes 202-07.

[111] The cases of Susan Smith, Joshua DeShaney, and Joel and Lisa Steinberg are good examples. Susan Smith drowned her two sons in South Carolina in 1994. Bill Hewitt, Tears of Hate, Tears of Pity, People, Mar. 13, 1995, at 76. A national poll revealed that 50% of the public supported her execution for the crime. Id. at 78. Joshua DeShaney was beaten so badly by his father that he will spend the rest of his life in a home for the severely retarded. Most public outrage was focused on the U.S. Supreme Court for not allowing Joshua's mother to sue the social services department that failed to remove Joshua from the custody of his father, her former husband. "Poor Joshua!," Time, Mar. 6, 1989, at 56; Cold Comfort and a Beaten Child, N.Y. Times, Feb. 26, 1989, at E22. Joel Steinberg beat his illegally adopted six-year-old daughter to death. See supra note 31. Even fellow inmates wanted to kill Steinberg. Steinberg, Citing Fear, Misses Court Hearing, N.Y. Times, Dec. 17, 1987, at B5.

[112] A good example is the public outrage that followed an episode in which two parents left two small children home alone for several days over Christmas while they went to Acapulco. See supra note 46.

[113] For examples of popular media articles on the effect of divorce on children, see Barbara Kantrowitz, Breaking the Divorce Cycle, Newsweek, Jan. 13, 1992, at 48; Jennet Conant, You'd Better Sit Down, Kids, Newsweek, Aug. 24, 1987, at 58; Aric Press, Divorce American Style, Newsweek, Jan. 10, 1983, at 42.

For examples of popular media articles on deadbeat dads, see David van Biema, Dunning Deadbeats, Time, Apr. 3, 1995, at 49; Joe Klein, 'Make the Daddies Pay',

licenses for failure to pay child support underscore the lesson that parental default is a moral, as well as a legal, violation.[114] Thus, as is true with other fiduciary relationships, these informal norms can be invoked to reinforce the commitment by parents to limit their future behavior in ways that will serve their children's interest.

The pervasive force of these extralegal influences in shaping parental attitudes distinguishes the parent-child relationship from other fiduciary bonds.[115] The utility of parents' affective bonds and informal social norms in promoting desirable behavior reduces substantially the role for formal legal incentives in mitigating conflicts of interest. Moreover, extralegal norms impose much lower costs on both the state's and parents' interests in procreation and

---

Newsweek, June 21, 1993, at 33; Steven Waldman, Deadbeat Dads, Newsweek, May 4, 1992, at 46.

In recent years, Congress has sought to promote enforcement of child support through tougher legislation, including the Child Support Enforcement Amendments of 1984, Pub. L. 98-378, 98 Stat. 1305 (codified at 42 U.S.C. § 1305 (1988)); the Family Support Act of 1988, Pub. L. 100-485, 102 Stat. 2343 (codified at 42 U.S.C. § 1305) (mandating automatic withholding by employers of legally due child support payments); and the Child Support Recovery Act of 1992, Pub. L. 102-521, 106 Stat. 3403 (codified at 18 U.S.C. § 228 (1994)) (authorizing interstate imposition of fines and imprisonment for non-payment). In March of 1995, the House passed H.R. 4, the Personal Responsibility Act of 1995. Title VII, Child Support, requires state child support agencies to maintain automated child support registries, requires employers to provide information on all newly-hired employees to a central registry and provides for civil penalties for employers that fail to comly, authorizes and encourages states to suspend driver's and professional licenses of parents in default, provides for withholding of wages to satisfy delinquent child support obligations, and expands the authority of the Federal Parent Locator Service. H.R. 4, 104th Cong., 1st Sess. (1995).

State legislatures have also been active. In January 1994, Massachusetts Governor William Weld signed legislation giving the state the power to jail defaulting parents or to revoke their driver's or professional licenses. See Mass. Gen. Laws Ann. ch. 119A, § 16 (West Supp. 1995).

The direction of legal reform regarding parental obligation runs counter to the dominant ethos of moral neutrality in contemporary family law. See Schneider, supra note 30, at 1812.

[114] See Peter J. Howe, New 'Deadbeat Dad' Law, Boston Globe, Jan. 21, 1994, at 18 (summarizing provisions of the Massachusetts law). Several fathers have been jailed or have lost their professional licenses for failure to pay child support under this new law. See Andrea Estes, DOR Nabs 3 Deadbeat Dads Owing $200G Out of State, Boston Herald, June 2, 1994, at 11; Doris Sue Wong, State Pulls Job Licenses of 'Deadbeat' Fathers, Boston Globe, May 19, 1995, at 51.

[115] As we noted, in other settings the informal norms themselves are largely legal constructions, generated from judicial and other legal descriptions of the fiduciary bond. See supra notes 81-84 and accompanying text. Moreover, other fiduciary relationships often do not involve the biological and affective components of the parental bond.

child-rearing. These norms are low-cost/high-benefit instruments for reducing the incidence of self-interested behavior by parents and thus function as substitutes for more intrusive and costly legal constraints.[116]

b. Legal Bonding Arrangements: Conflict of Interest Rules

As we suggested above, the dominant function of conflict of interest rules in fiduciary law is to induce self-limiting behavior by the fiduciary. In the family context, however, blanket rules against self-dealing analogous to those applied to trustees and executors would impose much greater demoralization costs on parents and would undermine the interests of both the state and parents in promoting procreation and child-rearing activity.[117] Parents' and children's interests are extensively intertwined, and many decisions that parents make affect their own lives as well as those of their children. Thus, even the relaxed standard for avoiding conflicts of interest between corporate directors and shareholders would be costly if applied to parents. It is hard to imagine effective self-enforcement of a precommitment under which, for example, a parent would be required to ensure that a proposed move across the country for professional advancement is in the child's interest. Such a restriction would be unsatisfactory both because of the demoralization costs that it imposed and because of the fundamental uncertainty about how and to what extent particular parental choices affect children's interests. These costs, together with the pervasive character of the informal norms that reinforce commitments of diligence and loyalty, imply that the parties to an ex ante bargain would instead contract for a legal presumption of good faith and reasonable diligence in assessing parental performance,

---

116 The distinctive character of family relationships suggests a cautionary note, however. Because of the vulnerable status of children and the emotional quality of public responses to that vulnerability, the use of moral rhetoric and an exalted standard of fiduciary duty as a mechanism to reduce conflicts of interest, see supra notes 81-84 and accompanying text, may carry an offsetting risk of intrusive and oppressive policies driven by a societal zeal to protect children.

117 Of course, the extent of the state's interest in promoting procreation depends on a number of other factors, including rates of population growth and available resources, such as land. The state has an unambiguous interest in adequate parenting of the children who *are* produced.

analogous to the presumption applied to corporate directors.[118] We call this presumption a "parental judgment rule."

Some parental actions and judgments, however, would not be protected by a parental judgment rule. As powerful as are extralegal influences on parental behavior, these normative forces, by themselves, cannot be relied upon to align parents' and children's interests in all instances. Thus, some specific conflict of interest rules would predictably be agreed upon as supplements to a parental judgment rule. Predicting the precise domain of these rules ex ante is a problematic exercise. The significant costs entailed in enforcing legal rules that trump informal norms implies that preemptive conflict of interest rules would be specified only when a societal consensus about the impact of the regulated conduct on children dictates a particular choice. These same concerns argue for retaining parental discretion whenever "reasonable" parents are likely to differ about what choice promotes the interest of children.[119]

By aligning legal rules with prevailing social norms, several of the potential costs of conflict of interest regulation can be reduced. First, the saliency of a clear societal consensus significantly reduces the uncertainties about optimal parental behavior that otherwise would impose costs on both parents and the state.[120] Preemptive rules grounded in consensus are clear signals of the limits of acceptable behavior and are readily enforced by the state. Second, tracking broadly shared societal norms of parental behavior enhances the self-enforcing benefits of the legal rules (and concurrently reduces demoralization costs).

Optimal parental conflict of interest rules, then, announce a social consensus that mandates the legislatively designated approach. Parents who would choose a different course are acting in a way that conflicts with children's interest. Child labor laws and

---

[118] See supra text accompanying notes 77-79 (summarizing the business judgment rule).

[119] For example, it is probable that a societal consensus supports requiring parents to assure that their children are educated. In contrast, no consensus supports the requirement that education need conform to a prescribed curriculum or take place in public school.

[120] In a sense, the existence of a social consensus solves a coordination problem for the parties by offering a default solution to the bargaining game on some issues. The state's initial bargaining stance may generally incline toward regulation and the parents' toward maintaining discretion.

compulsory school attendance requirements, for example, serve as legally-supported announcements that children's welfare is furthered by remaining in school until a designated age, and that any other choice is contrary to their interest.[121] Consensus-driven rules could also establish minimum age restrictions for drinking, driving and marriage.

These sorts of legal preemptions are a close analogue to conflict of interest rules in other fiduciary contexts. In many other settings, of course, the fiduciary obligation primarily involves financial management, and thus conflict of interest rules focus on financial decisions.[122] Because the scope of parental authority is broader and includes decisions affecting every aspect of the child's life, legal rules regulating parents would predictably cover a wider range of issues, from health to education to discipline. By limiting legally-imposed restrictions to only those that reflect a normative consensus about the welfare of children, parents are left with broad discretion to rear their children according to their own values. Thus, a limited domain for legal regulation promotes the shared objective of encouraging investment in the parental role. At the same time, the law reinforces broadly shared social norms in ways that induce parents to internalize an obligation to attend to their children's welfare.

c. The Function of Parental Rights

In an ideal regulatory scheme, extralegal and legal norms function both as complements and substitutes. For example, a parental judgment rule together with narrowly drawn conflict of interest rules will specify only the broad parameters for the exercise of parental discretion. Thus, extralegal norms are a necessary complement to establish the further constraint that discretion does not imply license to pursue selfish interests. In the same vein, the rela-

---

121 The prohibition of corporal punishment by parents under Swedish law is another example. See Greg McIvor, Human Rights: Swedish Parents Demand Right to Smack Children, Inter Press Service, Feb. 5, 1993, *cited in* Robert H. Mnookin & D. Kelly Weisberg, Child, Family & State 333-35 (3d ed. 1995) (describing the policy and suggesting that consensus supporting it may be in question). That corporal punishment by parents is not prohibited in this country suggests the lack of a consensus.

122 Some restrictions on guardians deal with other kinds of decisions, because the scope of guardians' authority encompasses a broader range of decisions.

tional model predicts that the parties would agree to amplify and reinforce informal social norms with pervasive and powerful legal rhetoric of parental fidelity and responsibility.

On first analysis, the conferral of parental rights and the characterization of parents' status in terms of entitlement seems inconsistent with this requirement of complementarity.[123] Legal attention to parents' rights appears to weaken informal normative signals about parental responsibility and to dilute social sanctions. Thus, the functioning of extralegal norms that do much of the work to incline parents toward an attitude of obligation may be undermined by a robust concept of parents' rights. Furthermore, a focus on rights encourages parents to consider their own interests, rather than their child's, in asserting relationship claims. Through this lens, the standard assumption that parental rights count *against* children's interests makes sense.

Despite its apparently corrosive influence, however, the legal recognition of parental rights plays a central role in a fiduciary regime, and its banishment from the family context would entail substantial costs. The absence of pecuniary compensation to parents for capably performing parental tasks necessarily increases the value of nonpecuniary substitutes such as reputation and role satisfaction.[124] On this dimension, parental authority over the relationship with children is offered as the quid pro quo for satisfactory performance. It is unlikely that, in a hypothetical bargain over the terms of their performance, parents would agree to undertake the responsibilities desired by the state without assurance that their investment would receive legal protection. Recognition of these parental claims in some form is an important inducement to encourage investment in children's welfare.

In sum, a regime of parental rights has offsetting effects. To the extent that rights are closely linked to performance, they serve as the ex ante compensation for the satisfactory future performance

---

[123] "Rights" of fiduciaries in other contexts are limited to pre-agreed compensation. Tamar Frankel, Fiduciary Law, 71 Cal. L. Rev. 795, 801 (1983) ("[A]n entrustor [beneficiary] does not owe the fiduciary anything by virtue of the relation except in accordance with the agreed-upon terms or legally fixed status duties.").

[124] We have noted that even in contexts in which fiduciaries are compensated, nonpecuniary reputational attributes of the role increase its attractiveness. See supra Part II.A.3.

of critically important social functions. But the rhetoric of parental rights (especially when it is divorced from the quid pro quo of parental obligation) can also intensify parental inclinations to view the relationship in terms of self-interest. One method of correcting for these negative effects is to clarify the link between rights and responsibilities and to impose substantial sanctions, such as restriction or withdrawal of parental authority, for serious default on parental obligations.

d. Monitoring Mechanisms

The relational model suggests that, within the intact family, bonding arrangements will dominate, and that extralegal influences on parents' behavior will do much of this work. The effectiveness of these norms reduces the relative benefits of monitoring alternatives. Moreover, direct state monitoring of parental performance in the intact family is awkward and very costly.[125] Monitoring rules used in other fiduciary contexts, such as judicial supervision of important decisions and regular reporting requirements, would impose demoralization and uncertainty costs on parents who are presumptively the superior caretakers for their children. Moreover, systematic monitoring by governmental agencies represents an intrusion into family privacy which carries a further relational cost. These arguments together provide strong support for a parental judgment rule which establishes a presumption of reasonable diligence and good faith in the exercise of parental duties.

Nonetheless, some specific devices to detect and discourage deficient parental behavior are cost-justified. For example, mandatory school physical examinations are a low-cost means of evaluating children's health and development. Psychological evaluations would serve a similar function. In addition, teachers, doctors, and baby-sitters can serve as informal, but effective, monitors. More

---

125 For this reason among others, systematic state monitoring is simply not cost-effective in the absence of parental default. The experience with in-home supervision in abuse-neglect cases supports the proposition that such direct state monitoring is awkward and inefficient. If a court opts to leave children in their parents' home, it can order the parents to allow a public health nurse to visit the child, to participate in therapy or alcohol or drug addiction programs, or to bring the child to public daycare. See Wald, supra note 51, at 630. Making sure parents comply requires constant monitoring by public caseworkers who are generally overburdened and underfunded. See Garrison, supra note 51, at 432 n.44 (summarizing the caseload burdens on social workers).

formally, child abuse reporting statutes impose a duty on all professionals dealing with children—as well as an opportunity for neighbors and acquaintances—to bring seriously deficient parental conduct to the attention of child protective service agencies.[126] Parents who receive public welfare support are subject to an additional level of monitoring by social service professionals.[127]

As in any contractual relationship, both parties' interests are served by stipulating sanctions for breach. In the case of the intact family, the principal sanction for deficient parental performance is reduction or withdrawal of parental rights. Upon default by the parent, the presumption of good faith and due diligence gives way to more precise monitoring rules that confine parental discretion. Parents whose children are found to be abused or neglected will be subject to formal judicial and agency supervision. In this way, parents whose precommitments prove unreliable are more carefully monitored until the deficient behavior is cured. If the parents' default is judged to be irremediable, further sanctions can be imposed, including termination of parental rights (after an appropriate judicial proceeding), followed by placement with substitute adoptive parents.

In short, as this somewhat stylized description suggests, state monitoring of parental conduct has limited utility (and higher costs) in the context of the intact family. However, monitoring plays an important role in a scheme of sanctions once evidence of parental deficiencies overcomes the presumption of good faith and diligence.

3. Reducing Conflicts of Interest in Broken Families

The preceding discussion suggests that there will be some significant differences between the optimal means of aligning the interests of parents and children in intact families and those that are best for reducing conflicts of interest between children and non-

---

[126] See, e.g., Cal. Pen. Code § 11,166 (West Supp. 1995). This statute requires not only professionals such as doctors or teachers to report abuse, but also film developers who discover possible sexual abuse of children captured on film.

[127] This form of parental monitoring is controversial, of course, because it focuses on poor families. Some observers believe that the disproportionate number of poor parents who are the subject of abuse/neglect investigations is attributable to the fact that they are subject to greater governmental scrutiny. See Wald, supra note 51, at 629 n.21.

custodial parents. A hypothetical ex ante bargain between non-custodial parents and the state would most likely rely upon a significantly different combination of extralegal norms and legal rules, and of bonding and monitoring arrangements.

Several distinct situations present contexts for regulation of the relationship of children and non-custodial parents. One category of cases involves biological parents (usually fathers) who have never lived in a family unit with the child. In others, the dissolution of the family unit may result from divorce or separation, or from state intervention and removal of the child because of inadequate parental performance. In some sense, it seems curious to conceive of these parents as fiduciaries, and surely a threshold question is whether the law should encourage any involvement with their children. In general, parents not living with their children perform a greatly diminished parental role, and those whose children have been placed in state custody have been specifically found to be deficient as caretakers. In these contexts, if no parent-child bond has developed, the benefit to the child of promoting further parental commitment may be offset by counterbalancing costs. Nonetheless, so long as the state pursues the objective of promoting the interests of children, the model of parents as fiduciaries applies equally to the relationship between the non-custodial parent and the child. Differences in the regulatory regime turn in part on variations in the content of the desired parental performance and in the anticipated conflicts of interest that occur when the child and parents no longer form a family unit.

a. The Importance of the Non-Custodial Parent-Child Relationship

The first question, then, is what are the goals of legal regulation of non-custodial parents, and what kind of parenting performance should be encouraged. The relational model dictates different responses depending on whether or not established family relationships exist.

The case for encouraging involvement by a non-custodial parent rests first on the non-trivial value attached to biological parenthood. First, biological parenthood may be an important influence on behavior. If we accept the lessons of sociobiology, biology inclines parents to care for and protect their children to a greater extent than stepparents or other non-genetically related substitute parents.[128] The genetic link can reinforce and strengthen the crescive bond that defines the relationship as central to personal identity.[129] Second, the bond to the biological parent has value to the child. Children find meaning in their genetic ties as a source of personal identity, a tendency that is evident in the efforts of adopted children to establish a link to their biological parents. The response of children whose biological parents have severed ties reveals the psychological importance to children of this relationship.[130] Thus, the relational model supports encouraging non-custodial biological parents to invest in a relationship with their children absent offsetting costs to relationships with parents filling more substantial functions.

The importance of the biological link justifies providing the non-custodial parent with the opportunity to establish a relationship with his infant child. If a parent fails to act expeditiously, and the child establishes such bonds with other adults, the risk of offsetting costs argues against further parental involvement.[131] The parent who is dilatory in assuming responsibilities may be supplanted by another; at this point further involvement is more disruptive than beneficial.

---

[128] See supra notes 104-06 and accompanying text.

[129] See White, supra note 107, at 4-5.

[130] Judith Wallerstein and Joan Kelly have found that children visited infrequently by their fathers suffered severely diminished self-esteem during the first five years after the separation of their parents. See Wallerstein & Kelly, Parental Divorce: Experiences of the Child in Later Latency, supra note 4. Robert Hess and Kathleen Camara have found that children who maintained positive relationships with both parents demonstrated less aggression and stress and functioned more effectively in work and social relations with their peers. Robert D. Hess & Kathleen A. Camara, Post-Divorce Family Relationships as Mediating Factors in the Consequences of Divorce for Children, 35 J. Soc. Issues 79, 92-95 (1979). Children who have lost or never had fathers yearn for them and feel disappointed by their absence. See Woodhouse, supra note 1, at 1765. Studies show that there is an increase in delinquency and antisocial behavior when the father is absent. This delinquency is much more pronounced when the father is absent because of separation or divorce rather than death. See J.W.B. Douglas, J.M. Ross, W.A. Hammond & D.G. Mulligan, Delinquency and Social Class, 6 Brit. J. Criminology 294, 300 (1966); H.B. Gibson, Early Delinquency in Relation to Broken Homes, 10 J. Child Psychol. & Psychiatry 195, 203 (1969); Michael Rutter, Parent-Child Separation: Psychological Effects on the Children, 12 J. Child Psychol. & Psychiatry 233, 241-42 (1971).

[131] This point will be developed further in the analysis of the rights of unmarried fathers. See infra Part III.A.2.

When the parent and child have an established relationship, usually built through life together in a family, the situation is quite different. Except where parental conduct is so harmful that it warrants severing the relationship or where the parent has had minimal involvement, the continuing importance of this relationship for the child persists even when parent and child are no longer part of a family unit. Parents are not fungible players in their children's lives, and disruption of the parent-child bond is costly to children's psychological health.[132] For these reasons, both child-development experts and policy analysts argue for protecting established parent-child relationships outside of the intact family.[133] Thus, the basic

---

[132] Most child-development experts emphasize the harm to the child of any disruption of the parent-child bond. Joseph Goldstein, Anna Freud and Albert J. Solnit, for example, argue against removal of the child from parental custody except under the most threatening of circumstances, positing that disruption of the bond is almost always extremely destructive. See Goldstein et al., supra note 4, at 4-14. Policies of state intervention and removal are premised on a view that weighs more heavily the harm to children of inadequate parenting and less heavily the harm of disruption.

Researchers have found that adoption is associated with psychological adjustment problems. See Garrison, supra note 51, at 470 & n.218 (citing studies finding that adopted children are disproportionately vulnerable to psychological and emotional problems). Adoptees' emotional problems are generally worse the older they are at adoption. See id. at 471 & n.223 (citing studies finding that the later the age of adoption, the greater the frequency and severity of emotional problems).

[133] See, e.g., studies cited supra note 132; Andre P. Derdeyn, Andrew R. Rogoff & Scott W. Williams, Alternatives to Absolute Termination of Parental Rights After Long Term Foster Care, 31 Vand. L. Rev. 1165 (1978); Garrison, supra note 51; see also infra note 143 and accompanying text (clarifying that the reform movement that favors shared parenting after divorce is predicated in part on the importance for the child's welfare of continued involvement by both parents).

Legal rules governing state intervention in families have been reformulated both to discourage removal of the child from parental custody, and, if the child is removed, to encourage remediation of parental deficiencies so that the child can be returned to parental custody. A primary example of such legislation is the federal Adoption Assistance and Child Welfare Act of 1980, Pub. L. No. 96-272, 94 Stat. 500 (codified in scattered sections of 42 U.S.C.). The Act was designed to change the emphasis of child protection services from centering on foster care to centering on either maintaining the child in her original family or creating a new family through adoption. Thus, the Act, while beginning with the presumption that parents are the first best caretakers, does not seek to maintain the parent-child relationship if parents continue to be deficient. The goal then becomes to provide the child with a new permanent family through adoption. See supra note 35 (summarizing the provisions of the Act). The Act has not been very successful at achieving its goals. For analyses of the success of the Act, see Alice C. Shotton, Making Reasonable Efforts in Child Abuse and Neglect Cases: Ten Years Later, 26 Cal. W. L. Rev. 223 (1990); MaryLee Allen, Crafting a Federal Legislative Framework for Child Welfare Reform, 61 Am. J. Orthopsychiatry 610 (1991).

legal objectives that shape regulation of intact families—encouragement of parental responsibility and commitment to the relationship—are unchanged in this context, even though the parental role is more limited.

b. *Replacing Informal Norms with Legal Regulation*

Within the intact family, extralegal bonds of biology, affection, and crescive attachment, together with internalized informal norms about parenting, are assumed to function effectively, mitigating potential conflicts of interest without extensive legal regulation. When the family is fractured, however, either voluntarily[134] or because the parents' performance has been found to be inadequate, there is greater reason to question the power of extralegal constraints on parents' inclination to act selfishly. A presumption of good faith and reasonable diligence, as reflected in a parental judgment rule, is not warranted. This necessarily increases the demand for more elaborate legal rules to ameliorate potential conflicts.

Parents who lack custody of their children because of divorce or dissolution and those whose children are in state custody are more likely than parents in intact families to choose self-interest over parental responsibility. Selfish behavior by non-custodial parents is more prevalent, even when those parents were unselfish custodians when the family was intact. In a typical example, the divorced father who previously seemed to care about his children's education refuses to contribute to college expenses. Divorced parents defect on obligations that they would have fulfilled before divorce in part because the postulated identity of interests between parent and child erodes over time. For some non-custodial parents, the crescive bond of parenthood grows more attenuated, such that being the child's parent becomes less central to personal identity.[135]

---

[134] Voluntary dissolution occurs most commonly when the parents divorce. Of course, the issues created by divorce would arise whenever the child's parents dissolved their relationship, whether or not they are married.

[135] Several researchers have found that many fathers withdraw from the relationship with their children after divorce. See, e.g., Robert E. Emery, E. Mavis Hetherington & Lisabeth F. Dilalla, Divorce, Children, and Social Policy, *in* 1 Child Development Research and Social Policy 189, 213 (Harold W. Stevenson & Alberta E. Siegel eds., 1984) (citing Furstenburg, Spanier & Rothchild, Patterns of Parenting in the Transition from Divorce to Remarriage *in* Women: A Developmental Perspective 325 (Phyllis W. Berman & Estelle

As the unity of parents' and children's interests dissolves, the risk of conflicts intensifies. Moreover, for many non-custodial parents, the rewards of parenthood diminish after divorce,[136] reducing further the incentive to invest in the relationship with their children. Parent-child interaction is less frequent and is often accompanied by conflicts with the former spouse. Other attachments, perhaps to a new family and different children, substitute for those in the dissolved family, and the fulfillment of previously established parental responsibilities becomes more burdensome.

Parents whose children have been placed in state custody present a somewhat different case for more pervasive legal oversight. Assuming that the state has correctly judged their parenting to be deficient,[137] these parents have revealed themselves to be insufficiently influenced by the informal norms that shape parental behavior. Since informal mechanisms have failed, more formal legal constraints and sanctions are required to reduce the risk of misbehavior.

Encouraging non-custodial parents to act in their children's interest requires translating informal norms into more explicit legal directives. Two examples under current law make the point. Parents whose children have been removed by the state and placed in foster care are subject to explicit directives (usually in a foster care

---

R. Ramey eds., 1982)). See also Hetherington et al., Aftermath of Divorce, supra note 4, at 93; Wallerstein & Kelly, Visiting Father-Child Relationship, supra note 4, at 1534.

[136] Many fathers tend to find this non-custodial relationship artificial and unsatisfactory. See Furstenburg et al., supra note 135, at 331; Mel Roman & William Haddad, The Disposable Parent: The Case for Joint Custody (1978); Judith B. Greif, Fathers, Children, and Joint Custody, 49 Am. J. Orthopsychiatry 311 (1979). Hetherington, Cox & Cox found that some fathers reported that they could not tolerate the artificial relationship permitted by visitation. See Hetherington et al., Divorced Fathers, supra note 4, at 427. See also C. William Briscoe & James B. Smith, Depression in Bereavement and Divorce, 32 Archives Gen. Psychiatry 439 (1975); Briscoe & Smith, Depression and Marital Turmoil, 29 Arch. Gen. Psych. 811 (1973). Hetherington, Cox & Cox describe the stereotypical "Disneyland Daddy" relationships in which fathers see their children occasionally and shower them with gifts but do not develop real relationships. See Hetherington et al., Divorced Fathers, supra note 4, at 425-26; see also Grief, supra, at 315 ("Fathers experiencing greater child absence are more prone . . . to entertain their children with constant activity, despite a repeated disdain for being seen as a 'Sugar Daddy.' ").

[137] We acknowledge that state intervention in families may sometimes be driven by class biases that affect social workers' assessment of adequate parenting, rather than parents' conduct that actually conflicts with the child's interest. For the purpose of this analysis, we set this issue aside.

plan) that define their obligation to their children. Parents may be required to abstain from drinking alcohol, to clean up the house, to participate in therapy, or to terminate a relationship with another adult who abuses the child.[138] In the divorce context, non-custodial parents are subject to court orders directing them to provide financial support to their children, while custodial parents and parents in intact families are not. Parents in family units share their children's standard of living and, through informal influences, can usually be trusted collectively to take their children's needs into account in allocating family resources. Moreover, for reasons discussed earlier, oversight of parents' financial decisions in intact families imposes demoralization costs, and is unlikely to yield significant net benefits for the child. Parents not living with their children, on the other hand, are less likely to give priority to their child's financial needs and may require a formal legal incentive in the form of a child support order.

The status of parents as "joint fiduciaries" further complicates the process of designing optimal rules for non-custodial divorced parents. In the intact family, the issue of disagreement between parents over appropriate caretaking actions is resolved by a pre-

---

[138] The Virginia Code, for example, states that a "foster care plan shall describe . . . the participation and conduct which will be sought from the child's parents and other prior custodians . . . ." Va. Code Ann. § 16.1-281(B)(ii) (Michie Supp. 1995). At periodic reviews, a petition must be filed for each child that "set[s] forth in detail the manner in which the foster care plan previously filed with the court was or was not complied with and the extent to which the goals thereof have been met." Va. Code Ann. § 16.1-282(B)(6) (Michie Supp. 1995). The court may terminate parental rights if parents fail to remedy the conditions which led to foster care placement in the first place. Va. Code Ann. § 16.1-283(C)(2) (Michie 1988). Foster care plans can include a variety of conditions on parents, depending on the conditions which led to foster care placement. See, e.g., Comer v. Virginia Beach Dep't of Social Servs., No. 2103-94-1, 1995 WL 91399 (Va. Ct. App. 1995) (requiring mother to complete an alcohol abuse treatment program, attend weekly Alcoholics Anonymous meetings, and avoid voluntary contact with her abusive husband); Durham v. Alexandria Dep't of Social Servs., No. 2176-93-4, 1994 WL 242442 (Va. Ct. App. 1994) (requiring "home based services" and mental health counseling); Hileman v. Winchester Dep't of Social Servs., No. 0320-93-4, 1994 WL 161390 (Va. Ct. App. 1994) (requiring counseling sessions for paranoid schizophrenic); Hunter v. Commonwealth, No. 2592-92-3, 1993 WL 364736 (Va. Ct. App. 1993) (requiring substance abuse therapy and psychological testing); Edwards v. Fairfax County Dep't of Human Dev., No. 2607-92-4, 1993 WL 302380 (Va. Ct. App. 1993) (requiring mother to receive substance abuse treatment and mental health counseling, stop associating with drug dealers and users, find stable and appropriate housing, obtain employment, maintain weekly visitation with her daughters, and acknowledge the abuse and neglect suffered by them).

sumption that the family unit will generate consensus on the best course of action. But in the case of divorce or dissolution, there is a significant risk of conflict between parents over how best to promote children's interests. This requires more elaborate and formal rules to resolve potential disputes between the fiduciaries. Thus, explicit directives may be required to signal which parent has authority to make particular decisions (such as those regarding religious practice or education) and how the child's time is to be allocated between the parents.[139] Arrangements that would be reached informally and by consensus in the intact family may be prescribed by court order,[140] and in cases of irreconcilable conflict, legal rules must determine which parent is to exercise sole authority as decisionmaker.[141] Predictably, under a relational model, the parent with primary responsibility (physical custody) retains greater decisionmaking authority (legal custody) when parents cannot cooperate. This authority serves as ex ante compensation for the fulfillment of more expansive parental obligations.

In sum, in both the divorce and abuse/neglect contexts, legal rules articulate and reinforce informal social norms regarding parental responsibility, norms which in intact families are presumed adequate by themselves to constrain behavior. The state substitutes formal, legal rules for the informal arrangements that govern the intact family because in this context the informal mechanisms are inadequate. Moreover, re-articulating informal norms

---

[139] Separation agreements and court orders often incorporate a schedule describing when the child will be with each parent, including a schedule for holidays, vacations and birthdays. Experts suggest that the more arrangements for the child can be reduced to precise written terms, the less the potential for future conflict. See Robert Emery, Renegotiating Family Relationships: Divorce, Child Custody, and Mediation 162-67 (1994).

[140] Courts have authority to order parents to cooperate with each other and prohibit each from undermining the child's relationship with the other parent. See Va. Code Ann. §§ 20-124.2, 20-124.3 (Michie Supp. 1995). Courts may threaten withdrawal of custody if a parent fails to cooperate. See Beck v. Beck, 432 A.2d 63, 72 (N.J. 1981).

[141] When parents have joint legal custody, they share legal authority to make decisions regarding education, religious practice, etc. Courts sometimes set aside joint custody orders and give one parent sole legal custody when parents are not able to cooperate about these issues. See, e.g., Schultz v. Elremmash, 615 So. 2d 396 (La. Ct. App. 1993) (awarding sole custody to mother after joint custody arrangement broke down over father's desire to take child for visits to Libya and his desire that daughter be isolated from Catholicism and American political culture).

in legal prescriptions serves to reinforce the independent weight of the informal precommitments.[142]

c. *Rewards of the Parental Role*

If maintaining a relationship with the non-custodial parent is important to the child's welfare, then the ex ante bargain must provide for enhanced role and relationship rewards for the parent as well as encourage responsible conduct. Moreover, enforcement costs will be reduced if parents are inclined voluntarily to meet their parental obligations, and voluntary compliance will increase with greater role satisfaction and relationship rewards. Fiduciaries in other contexts (including custodial parents) are motivated in part by reputational and other nonpecuniary rewards. Non-custodial parents similarly will respond to recognition that they have an important parental role.

From this perspective, joint legal custody after divorce constitutes a symbolic acknowledgment of parental status and authority; it promotes fatherly involvement that may translate into more faithful fulfillment of financial responsibility.[143] Common sense

---

[142] Thus, legal regulation requiring noncustodial parents to provide financial support to their children signals the law's endorsement of one form of parental obligation. Moreover, the extent to which enforcement of this duty is lax or rigorous indicates whether or not this responsibility is an important societal value.

[143] Proponents of joint custody argue that it will promote sharing of parental responsibility and will reduce the tendency of fathers to withdraw from their relationship with their children after divorce. This issue is discussed in Elizabeth Scott & Andre Derdeyn, Rethinking Joint Custody, 45 Ohio St. L.J. 455, 458-62 (1984). Some state codes state this objective explicitly as a legislative purpose. The California Code, for example, was amended in 1979 to facilitate joint custody. It states:

> The Legislature finds and declares that it is the public policy of this state to assure minor children of frequent and continuing contact with both parents after the parents have separated or dissolved their marriage, and to encourage parents to share the rights and responsibilities of child rearing in order to effect this policy, except where the contact would not be in the best interest of the child . . . .

Cal. Fam. Code § 3020 (West 1994).

Eleanor E. Maccoby and Robert H. Mnookin have found that fathers who see their children regularly after divorce are more compliant in paying child support, although they found no correlation between joint custody arrangements per se (as opposed to sole custody with visitation rights) and child support compliance. See Eleanor E. Maccoby & Robert H. Mnookin, Dividing the Child: Social and Legal Dilemmas of Custody 250-57 (1992).

The premise that it is important to recognize the status of non-custodial parents can also be seen in reform measures that affect non-custodial parents in sole custody arrangements.

supports the notion that non-custodial parents are more likely to embrace their responsibilities if the relationship continues to offer emotional rewards. Thus, an optimal regulatory scheme will encourage frequent contact between the non-custodial parent and child after divorce, whatever the formal custody arrangement, unless this contact generates offsetting costs to the child.[144] Moreover, custodial parents are properly encouraged to promote the child's relationship with the other parent.[145] The same point holds for parents whose children are removed by the state. Encouraging meaningful contact between parent and child during the period of state custody and seeking to reestablish the family within a reasonable time serves to increase parental efforts and commitment.

Imagining an ex ante bargain between non-custodial parents and the state focuses attention finally on legal termination of the parent-child relationship. Here, distinguishing features of the parent-child bond complicate the issue. In other settings, beneficiaries and other agents are presumed to be as well served by one fiduciary as another, and fiduciaries who perform poorly are replaced. In contrast, once the parent-child relationship is established, even suboptimal parents have idiosyncratic value to their child. The relational model thus argues against severing this relationship unless it results in greater harm than benefit to the child.[146] This is true even when many of the tasks of parenthood have been assumed by others.

For example, modern law gives non-custodial parents access to their children's school and medical records, a recognition of their parental status. See, e.g., Colo. Rev. Stat. § 14-10-123.5(7) (1987); Fla. Stat. Ann. § 61.13(2)(b)(3) (West Supp. 1995); Idaho Code § 32-717A (1983); Mont. Code Ann. § 40-4-225 (1993). Under traditional law, no such right of access was available, a small but perhaps particularly grating signal that these parents held a diminished legal status as parents.

[144] For example, if the parents have a very conflictual relationship, the costs to the child of being subject to the conflict may offset the benefit of continued contact with both parents. See Robert E. Emery, Interparental Conflict and the Children of Discord and Divorce, 92 Psych. Bull. 310, 313 (1982); Scott & Derdeyn, supra note 143, at 490-92.

[145] See supra note 140. Custody statutes also make the inclination of each parent to support the child's relationship with the other parent a factor in deciding custody.

[146] See Goldstein et al., supra note 4, at 4-14 (advocating a policy of "minimum state intervention" in the family). When the state intervenes in the family to promote the welfare of children, the minimum that can be asked is that it not do more harm than good. See Franklin E. Zimring, The Changing Legal World of Adolescence 62 (1982).

4. Summary

The relational model of parents as fiduciaries suggests the contours of an optimal regime for regulating the parent-child relationship. Informational and control asymmetries generate a significant risk of conflicts of interest in parent-child relationships. The costs of these deviations from the norm of parental responsibility toward children can be efficiently reduced by a legal regime that is constructed around a pre-existing network of informal social norms. By selecting the appropriate mix of extralegal and legal norms and of bonding and monitoring arrangements, a fully integrated regulatory regime can function harmoniously both to encourage parents to approach the tasks of child-rearing with an elevated sense of duty and to detect when parents fail to perform those tasks adequately.

The character of legal regulation will differ depending on whether or not the family is intact. In the intact family, extralegal norms do much of the work to promote desired parental behavior. This is a function of the relatively high cost of monitoring and the correspondingly lower costs of effective bonding alternatives. In this setting, bonding through psychological attachment and informal social norms is an efficient substitute for invasive restraints on discretion and family privacy. Legal directives that function as supplemental precommitments are appropriately limited to issues where a strong societal consensus dictates mandatory behavior. Viewed only from the perspective of legal regulation, such a regime may seem imbalanced: a broad recognition of parental rights and authority, together with a narrowly drawn set of legal responsibilities. This apparent inequality dissipates, however, once the powerful effects of extralegal norms are recognized.

The optimal regulatory patterns change when the subject of legal regulation is the non-custodial parent. Here, legal regulatory prescriptions are necessary substitutes for the informal norms that are relied upon in the intact family. The substitution of more exacting legal standards is justified by the weakening of informal norms, the breach of the obligation to provide satisfactory care, and by the potential for conflict between parents as joint fiduciaries.

III. The Relational Model and Modern Family Law

In this Part, we apply the relational model of parents as fiduciaries to contemporary family law. We will argue that, to a considerable extent, the model explains the deep structure of the legal regulation of the parent-child relationship. Although generally not described in these terms, the parent-child relationship is regulated by a variety of interactive mechanisms that function to encourage parents to serve their children's interests better. Analyzing family law from a fiduciary perspective also reveals particular areas in which legal norms depart from these principles. Certain aspects of contemporary law regulating divorce and termination of parental rights, for example, appear to exacerbate conflicts of interest between parent and child. More generally, the rhetoric of parental rights, unconstrained by any explicit conceptual framework, may undermine informal norms and distort the feedback function of rights in a fiduciary scheme.

A. Contemporary Family Law as a Fiduciary Regime

1. Some General Similarities

The peculiar shape and character of contemporary family law conforms, in large measure, to the predictions of the relational model of parents as fiduciaries. Parental performance in the intact family is shaped largely by extensive extralegal norms and by a correlative presumption of parental authority and discretion. Explicit legal commands are limited largely to a series of preemptive rules that define the boundaries of parental discretion. The array of preemptive rules, including compulsory school attendance requirements, child labor restrictions, curfew laws and vaccination requirements, appears to function principally as a means of reinforcing powerful extralegal influences.

As the model predicts, the set of regulatory mechanisms changes when the family dissolves; informal social norms are replaced by formal prescriptive rules. For example, parents whose children are in foster care are subject to state agency directives regarding their obligations under foster care plans.[147] These parents, having devi-

---

[147] As discussed previously, court orders sometimes direct one parent not to undermine the child's relationship with the other parent, not to involve the child in a particular religious practice, etc. See supra notes 140-41 and accompanying text.

ated from informal normative standards, are provided with explicit performance objectives (at least in theory[148]) that must be met before they can resume custody. The foster care plan functions as a more formal bonding arrangement, creating incentives for parents to avoid parenting practices that conflict with their child's welfare and clarifying the sanctions for breach of the commitment.

The recent trend promoting shared parenting after divorce, either through joint custody or through sanctions against uncooperative parents,[149] is further evidence of the descriptive power of the relational model.[150] As with foster care plans, these require-

---

[148] See Mark Hardin, Legal Placement Options to Achieve Permanence for Children in Foster Care, *in* Foster Children in the Courts 128 (Mark Hardin ed., 1983). Hardin cites the Colorado statute defining "residual parental rights and responsibilities" as:

> those rights and responsibilities remaining with the parent . . . including, but not necessarily limited to, the responsibility for support, the right to consent to adoption, the right to reasonable visitation unless restricted by the court, and the right to determine the child's religious affiliation.

Id. at 181 n.49 (quoting Colo. Rev. Stat. § 19-1-103(24) (1978)). Hardin also cites: Idaho Code § 16-1602(p) (1979); Mass. Gen. Laws Ann. ch. 119 § 26 (West 1975 & Supp. 1981); Utah Code Ann. § 78-3a-49 (1977); Vt. Stat. Ann. tit. 33 § 632(a)(16) (1981); Va. Code Ann. § 16.1-228(S) (Michie 1982); Wash. Rev. Code Ann. § 13.34.160 (Supp. 1981). Id. at 181 nn. 49, 52.

[149] There has been much criticism of the implementation of foster care plans by social service agencies. The criticisms are either that state agencies are dilatory or unclear in setting objectives, or that they don't provide services necessary for parents to comply with requirements.

[150] For a discussion of joint custody, see supra notes 143-45 and accompanying text. Under what have been described as "friendly parent" provisions, judges are encouraged in custody hearings to consider which parent is more likely to support the other parent's relationship with the child. The goal is to foster the relationships of both parents with the child. For examples of friendly parent provisions, see Alaska Stat. §§ 25.20.060, 25.24.150(c)(6) (1991); Ariz. Rev. Stat. Ann. § 25-332(A)(6) (Supp. 1994); Cal. Fam. Code Ann. § 3040(a)(1) (West 1994); Colo. Rev. Stat. § 14-10-124(1.5)(f) (1987); Fla. Stat. Ann. § 61.13(3)(a) (West Supp. 1995); La. Civ. Code Ann. art. 134(10) (West Supp. 1995); Mich. Comp. Laws Ann. § 722.23(3)(j) (West Supp. 1995); Minn. Stat. Ann. § 518.17(13) (West Supp. 1995); Mont. Code Ann. § 40-4-223 (1993); Nev. Rev. Stat. Ann. § 125.480(3)(a) (Michie 1993); 23 Pa. Cons. Stat. Ann. § 5303(a) (1991). Such provisions discourage parents from presenting evidence that joint custody would be against the best interest of the child, because presenting such evidence can make a judge feel that the adversarial parent is unlikely to foster the child's relationship with the other parent. See Scott & Derdeyn, supra note 143, at 476 nn.101-02 (1984) (summarizing the policy imperatives underlying friendly parent provisions); see also Joanne Schulman & Valerie Pitt, Second Thoughts on Joint Child Custody: Analysis of Legislation and Its Implications for Women and Children, 12 Golden Gate U.L. Rev. 539, 554-56 (1982) (noting that friendly parent provisions promote the use of custody as a bargaining chip by parents seeking to minimize child support obligations or to maintain access to a victim of abuse).

ments function to formalize norms of parental cooperation that are implicitly presumed when parents live together. Upon divorce, conflict between the parents may undermine the cooperative norm and promote conduct that conflicts with the child's interest. Viewed in this way, the controversy surrounding joint custody may reflect a dispute about whether the formal requirement of post-divorce cooperation distorts pre-divorce norms and conduct, and whether the law is realistic in assuming that divorced parents can cooperate as joint fiduciaries to the extent that joint custody requires.[151]

As the model predicts, monitoring arrangements are used far more extensively upon family breakdown. In general, parents who are divorced, and to a far greater extent, those whose children are in state custody, are subject to a degree of judicial and state agency supervision that would be deemed violative of family privacy if applied to intact families. Increasingly tough child support enforcement procedures assure that non-custodial parents fulfill their financial duty.[152] Courts may authorize formal agency supervision of abusive or neglectful parents.[153] Moreover, regular judicial supervision is used to determine whether these parents are progressing in remediating performance deficiencies.[154]

Divorce lawyers utilize evidence of what has been designated "parental alienation syndrome" to establish the claim that the opponent has sought to turn the child against the other parent. See Richard A. Gardener, The Parental Alienation Syndrome (1992). For a critical analysis, see Cheri L. Wood, Note & Comment, The Parental Alienation Syndrome: A Dangerous Aura of Reliability, 27 Loy. L.A. L. Rev. 1367 (1994).

[151] For example, a joint custody order can coerce cooperation between a primary caretaker and a formerly uninvolved parent.

[152] See supra notes 113-14.

[153] Such supervision involves mandatory family cooperation with the agency's treatment plan and regular agency monitoring of the family. See supra note 125; see also Bonnie Kamen & Betty Gewirtz, Child Maltreatment and the Court, in Clinical Social Work with Maltreated Children and their Families: An Introduction to Practice 178, 183-84 (Shirley M. Ehrenkranz et al. eds., 1989).

[154] The Adoption Assistance and Child Welfare Act of 1980, Pub. L. No. 96-272, 94 Stat. 500 (codified in scattered sections of 42 U.S.C.), requires the development of a case plan for every child in foster care, a review of the plan every six months, and a "dispositional hearing" no later than eighteen months after a child enters foster care. See 42 U.S.C. §§ 627(a)(2)(B), 671(a)(16), 675(1), 675(5) (1988). For a discussion of these provisions, see MaryLee Allen, Carol Golubock & Lynn Olson, A Guide to the Adoption Assistance and Child Welfare Act of 1980, in Foster Children in the Courts 575, 582-84 (Mark Hardin ed., 1983). Periodic review has been established in a majority of states. For examples of

Even features of contemporary family law that are conventionally understood as serving the interests of parents can better be understood and rationalized as promoting the goal of optimizing the parent-child relationship. Thus, for example, legal restrictions on state supervision of families are commonly thought to reflect deference toward parental authority, and are justified in the rhetoric of parental rights.[155] Some critics assume that this deference to parental authority would be greatly diminished were the law to focus instead on children's welfare.[156] To the contrary, however, our analysis indicates that a fiduciary regime will rely substantially on informal norms to shape responsible parental behavior and that explicit legal directives will not serve the desired ends of enhancing parental performance.[157] Moreover, the relational model suggests that parental authority and discretion are the necessary quid pro quos for parents undertaking the responsibilities of parenthood. Thus, setting aside the *rhetoric* of parental rights, deference to family privacy fits comfortably into a fiduciary framework.

2. *Relationship Claims of Unmarried Fathers*

a. *Parents' Rights in the Supreme Court*

In a series of opinions dealing with the claims of unmarried biological fathers, the Supreme Court has struggled to define the

---

current laws, see Cal. Welf. & Inst. Code § 366, 366.22 (West Supp. 1995); N.Y. Soc. Servs. Law Ann. § 392 (McKinney Supp. 1995).

[155] See Dwyer, supra note 9; Schneider, supra note 30, at 1835-42; Fitzgerald, supra note 8, at 37-45; Woodhouse, supra note 12, at 1112-22; see also Bartlett, supra note 7, at 297-98 (characterizing the rhetoric of parental rights as intrinsic to the modern liberal state); Woodhouse, supra note 1, at 1811 (arguing that the "possessive individualism" underlying parental rights objectifies children).

[156] See, e.g., Bartlett, supra note 7; Dwyer, supra note 9; Fitzgerald, supra note 8; Woodhouse, supra note 1. Some experts have proposed policies of extensive state oversight to protect children. In the 1970s, Henry Kempe proposed a Home Visitor Program to undertake health monitoring of all infants at home. See Richard J. Light, Abused and Neglected Children in America: A Study of Alternative Policies, 43 Harv. Ed. Rev. 556, 567-71 (1973).

[157] Joseph Goldstein, Anna Freud and Albert J. Solnit emphasize the importance for the child's welfare of an undisturbed parent-child bond. See Goldstein et al., supra note 4, at 4-14. Zealous efforts to protect children's welfare in the intact family also run the risk of inefficient use and exhaustion of scarce resources, which are dissipated and not targeted toward situations in which intervention is needed. For a discussion of the difficulties in actually measuring levels of child abuse, see Light, supra note 156, at 560-67; R. Gellas, Demythologizing Child Abuse, Family Coordinator, Apr. 1976, at 135-38.

rights of unmarried fathers, a group of parents who historically were presumed to lack any legally protected interest in their relationship with their children.[158] Under current constitutional doctrine, biology is an important but not sufficient condition for establishing a cognizable parental claim.[159] Under the Court's analysis, legal protection of the biological father's parental relationship is strongly correlated to his investment in and fulfillment of his parental role. Thus, the constitutional analysis conforms to the predictions of the relational model, although it has not been couched in these terms.

In *Stanley v. Illinois*,[160] the Supreme Court extended parental rights to an unmarried biological father who had lived with his children and their mother until her death.[161] *Stanley* invalidated an Illinois statute that established a presumption of unfitness for unmarried fathers and automatically transferred custody to the state upon the death of the mother.[162] The Court recognized Stanley's legitimate interest in a continuing relationship with his children and held that the state could not terminate that interest without giving him an opportunity to demonstrate his fitness as a parent.[163]

Stanley can be understood on one level as simply announcing that formal marriage is not a predicate for legal protection of a father's relationship with his child. The case was described by the Court as presenting an unremarkable father-child relationship in an intact family, except that Stanley and the mother of the children were unmarried.[164] In extending parental rights to Stanley, the Court implicitly recognized that the parent-child relationship is the core value that underlies the legal recognition of parental rights.

---

[158] See supra notes 23-25 and accompanying text.

[159] As the Supreme Court stated in Lehr v. Robertson, 463 U.S. 248, 262 (1983), "the biological connection . . . offers the natural father an opportunity that no other male possesses to develop a relationship with his offspring."

[160] 405 U.S. 645 (1972).

[161] The majority assumed that Stanley performed his parental role adequately. The dissent, and some critics of the opinion, were not so charitable, suggesting that Stanley played an episodic role in his children's lives and was far from the exemplary parent. See id. at 667 (Burger, C.J., dissenting).

[162] See id. at 646-49.

[163] Id. at 649, 658. At the same time, the Court found the state's interest in separating children from fit parents to be de minimis. Id. at 657-58.

[164] See id. at 651-52.

Since *Stanley*, the Court has considered the claims of several unmarried fathers, each seeking to block adoption of their child by a stepparent. The articulated basis for separating successful and unsuccessful parental rights claims in these cases has been evidence that the father established a relationship with his child and filled a parental role.[165] The Court has endorsed protection of the rela-

---

[165] Fathers who do not live with their children are more likely to have their relationship claims recognized if they were once part of a family unit with their children. This factor distinguishes the fathers in two Supreme Court opinions after *Stanley*: Quilloin v. Walcott, 434 U.S. 246 (1978), and Caban v. Mohammed, 441 U.S. 380 (1979). Both Quilloin and Caban sought to block the adoption of their children by the husbands of the children's mothers, under similar Georgia and New York statutes which allowed adoption over the objection of the biological father. See Ga. Code Ann. §§ 74-203, 74-403(3) (1975) (*Quilloin*); N.Y. Dom. Rel. Law § 111 (McKinney 1977) (*Caban*). Caban had lived with the children from their birth until the couple's separation, when the oldest child was four years old, while Quilloin had never shared a home with his son. The Supreme Court rejected Quilloin's due process claim, but upheld Caban's equal protection claim.

Janet Dolgin argues that recognition of fathers' claims under Supreme Court doctrine depends on whether the parent-child relationship was grounded in a shared life with the child's mother in an acceptable family unit. See Janet L. Dolgin, Just a Gene: Judicial Assumptions About Parenthood, 40 UCLA L. Rev. 637, 649-50 (1993). We think that this is important mostly because it serves as a handy proxy for the kind of involvement that is relevant to the judicial determination of parental rights.

The family unit will often be the context in which the kind of bond that receives protection is formed. This factor is not sufficient in itself, however, as evidenced by statutes permitting adoption by stepparents after a period of default by non-custodial parents, regardless of whether the father once lived with the child. See, e.g., Alaska Stat. § 25.23.050 (1991); Cal. Fam. Code § 8604(b) (West 1994); N.Y. Dom. Rel. Law § 111(1)(d) (McKinney 1988).

Moreover, nothing in parental rights doctrine as articulated by the Supreme Court, or in the legal treatment of this matter under state law, supports the claim that the father who fulfills his parental obligations but never lives with the child and her mother will find that this parent-child relationship is unprotected when a stepfather seeks adoption. The biological father who develops a parent-child relationship in which he fulfills the responsibilities of his role by spending time with the child and by providing financial support on an ongoing basis has parental rights that are unlikely to be set aside.

Some courts have recognized the claims of fathers to rights vis-a-vis children with whom they have not lived. Usually there is some uncertainty in these cases as to whether the father sought a relationship with the child but was prevented by the mother from establishing such a relationship. See, e.g., Michael M. v. Giovanna F., 7 Cal. Rptr. 2d 460 (Ct. App. 1992) (awarding to biological father of child conceived out of wedlock, prior to mother's marriage to another man, the right to establish paternity of his child); Sider v. Sider, 639 A.2d 1076 (Md. 1994) (holding that biological father originally unaware of his paternity was entitled to establish paternity and join mother in seeking transfer of custody to mother from mother's husband in pending divorce dispute).

The Supreme Court has yet to deal with the case of a father who has a parent-child relationship and fulfills his fatherly responsibilities by providing financial support to the child, but who has never lived with the child's mother and the child in a family unit.

tionship between the child and the father who "demonstrates a full commitment to the responsibilities of parenthood by 'com[ing] forward to participate in the rearing of his child.' "[166] In *Caban v. Mohammed*,[167] for example, the father had not only lived with his children, but had provided financial support and had spent time with the children after his relationship with their mother had ended.[168] In contrast, the father's efforts in *Quilloin v. Walcott*[169] were sporadic,[170] and in *Lehr v. Robertson*,[171] no parent-child relationship was ever established.[172] In rejecting Lehr's claim that his unsuccessful efforts should be recognized, the Court emphasized that only an actual relationship of parental responsibility is entitled to legal protection.[173] This relationship is important to the parties and to society because of " 'the emotional attachments that derive from the intimacy of daily association, and from the role it plays in 'promot[ing] a way of life' through the instruction of children.' "[174]

---

[166] Lehr v. Robertson, 463 U.S. 248, 261 (1983) (quoting *Caban*, 441 U.S. at 392).

[167] 441 U.S. 380 (1979).

[168] Id. at 382.

[169] 434 U.S. 246 (1978).

[170] Quilloin saw his son now and then and gave occasional gifts and financial support. Moreover, he only came forward to legitimate his son when the child was eleven years old and the stepfather had petitioned for adoption. See id. at 247-51.

[171] 463 U.S. 248 (1983).

[172] Id. at 262.

[173] Id. *Lehr*, however, remains something of a puzzle under this analysis. Why was Lehr, frustrated in his efforts to establish a relationship with his daughter by her mother's resistance, not rewarded for his efforts (albeit unsuccessful), when finally after more than two years he asserted his legal claim? The temporal element may be the key to the puzzle. Genetic fatherhood creates the opportunity, as the Court said, to assert parental rights. The claim, however, must be made in a timely manner, or the right atrophies. Id. at 262. Despite the dissent's account, see id. at 268-69 (White, J., dissenting), Lehr seems at a minimum to have been inept and dilatory in seeking to establish a legal relationship with his daughter. He failed to come forward to establish his claim until very late in the game. See id. at 250-53. (In this regard, he was unlike Daniel Schmidt, who challenged the DeBoers' adoption petition shortly after the birth of Baby Jessica. See supra note 8.) The metaphor of the father's rights as a seed seems particularly apt. If tended, the rights grow into a substantial claim based on a flourishing relationship. If not, they wither away and eventually die.

In *Lehr*, the child was well-situated in a family unit with her mother and stepfather, and with only a hypothetical interest in her relationship with her biological father. The costs of developing the bonds that would generate a legally protected parental relationship might well have disserved the child's interests.

[174] Id. at 261 (quoting Smith v. Organization of Foster Families for Equality & Reform, 431 U.S. 816, 844 (1977) (quoting Wisconsin v. Yoder, 406 U.S. 205, 231-33 (1972))).

2460   *Virginia Law Review*   [Vol. 81:2401

The Supreme Court's treatment of biological fathers fits comfortably into a fiduciary framework. Fathers like Caban who have invested in the relationship with their child are granted legal protection for the relationship. The child benefits when her non-custodial parent works to maintain a relationship previously established within the family unit. In contrast, no protection is extended to fathers such as Quilloin who are sporadic in their attention and who announce a serious commitment only after an established substitute father threatens their paternal status. This dilatory behavior conflicts with the child's interest. Even the outcome in *Lehr* is consistent with the relational model. The failure to initiate a relationship until after a stepfather functionally becomes father to the child justifies treating the biological father's relationship claim as forfeited. Tolerating the father's ineffectual efforts to establish a relationship would encourage strategic behavior and undermine informal incentives to assume the role of parent. In essence, the Court has recognized paternal rights of fathers who act like fiduciaries. Establishing the desired patterns of behavior reduces the risk of conflicts of interest between the father and child and justifies "compensation" in the form of recognized parental rights.

b. *Unmarried Fathers Under State Law.*

The constitutional framework developed by the Supreme Court to define the rights of unmarried fathers has influenced state regulation, which conforms as well to the relational model of parents as fiduciaries. Statutes provide the unmarried father with the opportunity, when his child is born, to acknowledge paternity and accept parental responsibility.[175] Fathers who are ready to assume full

---

[175] In California, for example, an unmarried man is presumed to be a child's father if he receives the child into his home and openly holds out the child as his natural child. See Cal. Fam. Code § 7611(d) (West Supp. 1995). He can also claim paternity by voluntary declaration at the time of the child's birth, Cal. Fam. Code §§ 7571, 7574 (West 1994 & Supp. 1995), or by suit, Cal. Fam. Code §§ 7630-7631 (West 1994). A putative father who is not the presumed father must come forward within 30 days of the birth of the child or within 30 days of receiving notification that he might be the child's father if the mother is seeking to put the child up for adoption. See Cal. Fam. Code §§ 7631, 7664, 7666 (West 1994).

In New York, under the statute upheld in *Lehr*, a father may voluntarily establish paternity at birth by filling out a notarized acknowledgement of paternity form. N.Y. Pub. Health Law § 4135-b(1)(a) (McKinney Supp. 1995). He may also bring suit to establish

parental responsibility can acquire custody of the child, blocking adoption by third parties even when the mother consents to the adoption. The law assumes that the biological parent who steps forward to act as parent will fill this role better than other candidates. On the other hand, biological fatherhood alone is not sufficient to establish a substantial parental claim. Adoption placement in most jurisdictions will not be defeated by the father who is dilatory in assuming responsibilities or who is not ready to accept full responsibility as a custodial parent.[176]

State law responses to the efforts of stepparents to adopt and to sever paternal rights is similarly explained by a model that links parental rights with responsibility. The father who fails to maintain contact with his child or who is seriously delinquent in providing financial support may lose his parental status when a stepfather seeks to adopt the child.[177] Statutes of limitation in some states

---

paternity anytime before the child reaches age 21. N.Y. Fam. Ct. Act § 517 (McKinney Supp. 1995).

[176] See, e.g., Adoption of Christopher S., 242 Cal. Rptr. 866, 870 (Ct. App. 1987) (denying biological father the right to veto adoption because he had not supported children while he was in prison and prior to imprisonment); In re Raquel Marie X., 559 N.E.2d 418, 424 (N.Y.) (observing that "the biological father not only must assert his interest promptly . . . but also must manifest his ability and willingness to assume custody of the child") (citations omitted), cert. denied, 498 U.S. 984 (1990); In re Stephen C., 566 N.Y.S.2d 178, 179 (App. Div. 1991) (holding that readiness to assume full custody is threshold criterion for right to veto adoption and thus denying father's attempt to block adoption because he wanted child's mother or paternal grandmother to care for child rather than himself); In re Adoption of Kyle, 592 N.Y.S.2d 557, 560-61 (Surrog. Ct. 1992), aff'd 601 N.Y.S.2d 902 (App. Div. 1993) (holding that father who had acknowledged paternity and provided financial support in past could not veto adoption because of present, lengthy incarceration).

[177] In California, the consent of a presumed father is required for adoption unless he has failed to communicate with and pay support for his child for one year. Cal. Fam. Code § 8604 (West 1994). If the child has no presumed father, only the consent of the mother is required. Cal. Fam. Code § 8605 (West 1994).

In New York, a father of a child over six months old must maintain "substantial and continuous or repeated contact" with his child, by paying support and either visiting the child at least monthly or communicating with the child regularly, in order to veto adoptions. N.Y. Dom. Rel. Law § 111(1)(d) (McKinney 1988). The father loses his rights if he fails to communicate with the child for six months. Id. § 111(2)(a). See also In re J.J.J., 718 P.2d 948, 954 (Alaska 1986) (holding that biological father who failed to provide support for at least 12-month period could not block stepfather adoption); Adoption of Christopher S., 242 Cal. Rptr. at 870; Hergenreder v. Madden, 899 P.2d 1155, 1160-61 (Okla. 1995) (upholding Oklahoma statute allowing adoption without consent of father who fails to pay court-ordered child support for one year).

specify forfeiture of parental rights following extended parental absence and default.[178] On the other hand, the stepfather's efforts to adopt will be unsuccessful if the father has maintained a relationship based on sustained commitment, contact, and financial support. By promising legal protection of the relationship, the law encourages unmarried non-custodial fathers to undertake a limited, but nonetheless important, parental role.[179]

3. Explaining the Contours of Legal Regulation

Existing legal regulation of the parent-child relationship is broadly consistent with the model of parents as fiduciaries. This is not surprising, despite critics' claim of excessive deference to parents' rights because promoting the welfare of children is an explicit goal of modern family law. Indeed, legal regulation of the parent-child relationship is the one area of contemporary family law where the modern trend toward pursuit of self-interest is categorically modified.[180] Principles of parental obligation increasingly shape regulation and constitute strong themes in political and scholarly commentary.[181] It follows that the law would discourage

---

[178] See supra note 177 (discussing the California and New York statutes); see also Alaska Stat. § 25.23.050(a) (1991) (providing that consent is not required from a parent who has abandoned the child for at least six months or from a non-custodial parent who has failed to communicate meaningfully with the child or failed to provide support for at least one year); Okla. Stat. Ann. tit. 10, § 60.6 (West Supp. 1995) (providing that consent is unnecessary from a parent who has failed to pay child support for one year) (upheld in *Hergenreder*, 899 P.2d at 1160-61). These statutes seem to be applied only in cases in which a stepparent seeks to adopt and to provide a substitute for the defaulting biological parent. We found no cases in which the custodial parent alone successfully effected termination of the rights of the defaulting parent.

[179] Only because the child's basic needs are met by her custodial parent is a limited fatherly role in her interest. In this regard, this context differs significantly from that of adoption placement.

[180] Modern family law is increasingly based on principles of liberal individualism, a trend which has been criticized as promoting selfish behavior. In the mid-1980s, Carl Schneider observed that moral discourse in family law has declined in the past generation. See Schneider, supra note 30, at 1805-08; see also Elizabeth S. Scott, Rehabilitating Liberalism in Modern Divorce Law, 1994 Utah L. Rev. 687, 708-17 (discussing the trend toward liberal family law and the communitarian critique of the trend). In the regulation of the parent-child relationship, however, reforms in family law have placed increasingly forceful emphasis on parental obligation. This has been particularly true in the enforcement of non-custodial parents' financial obligations. See supra notes 113-14.

[181] Certainly, the political climate today is one in which more stringent enforcement of parental obligation is favored. The polemical tone of Republican critiques of welfare

selfish behavior in parents and encourage them to align their child's interests with their own.

The law's purpose in promoting the alignment of parent-child interests, for unmarried fathers and for other parents, is a central insight of the relational model. As our earlier analysis indicates, role satisfaction is a key component of successful performance by parents. Thus, any regime directed toward discouraging selfish parental conduct requires a means of rewarding good parenting and encouraging commitment. Legal protection of parental rights and authority serves as an important form of compensation for fulfillment of parental obligations and thus functions to serve the child's interest in receiving good care from her parents. The conventional analytic model that balances parental rights *against* the child's interest misperceives this function. The problem with parental rights is not the grant of authority to parents but rather the failure to recognize the instrumental function of rights and authority as an inducement to satisfactory parental performance. The claim that parental rights are a license to engage in selfish behavior ignores the function of rights as a mechanism for aligning conflicting interests.

B. Rules that Exacerbate Conflicts of Interest

Although much of contemporary family law conforms to the relational model of parents as fiduciaries, the correspondence is not complete. Some aspects of the legal regulation of parents appear to exacerbate inherent conflicts between the self-interest of parents and the interests of their children. To the extent that this observation is accurate, the descriptive power of the model is incomplete. This argues for a continuing search by family law scholars for a more complete explanatory theory. It also provides the basis for a normative critique of those provisions that appear to reinforce selfish behavior by parents.

---

policy in the 1994 congressional elections had a flavor of moral outrage at parents who produce children for whom they cannot care. Newt Gingrich has argued for removal of welfare children from their homes and placement in orphanages. See Mary McGrory, Orphanage Idea Has Many Parents, Wash. Post, Dec. 13, 1994, at A2; Excerpts from Speaker Newt Gingrich's Opening Remarks, Wash. Post, Jan. 5, 1995, at A12. In a more thoughtful voice, Katharine Bartlett and others have argued that the parent-child relationship be recast as one of parental obligation. See Bartlett, supra note 7, at 295-306.

1. Conflicts of Interest in Divorce Law

Parents negotiating with the state over the terms of their future performance and seeking to maximize their own interests would predictably bargain for the right to dissolve a truly unhappy marriage which renders cooperative parenting within a family unit untenable. The state would likely agree to such a term because the informal norms that are relied upon to shape parental behavior are vulnerable to breakdown if the parents are in serious conflict. Thus, the law governing availability of divorce (without the necessity of proving fault against the spouse) is fully compatible with the model of the parent as fiduciary.

Some dimensions of contemporary no-fault divorce law, however, appear to intensify the conflicts of interest between parent and child. Modern marriage is often characterized as an "at will" relationship between the spouses. Thus, either spouse can terminate the relationship at any time for any reason (or no reason) upon notice to the other.[182] The goal of modern divorce law is to facilitate a "clean break," so that the parties will be free to pursue their personal ends, including new intimate relationships, unencumbered by an unhappy marriage.[183]

This approach, grounded in norms of short-term, rational self-interest, ostensibly does not affect parents' obligation toward their children. In at least two ways, however, the recent understanding of marriage and divorce as a means of self-actualization discounts the importance of parental obligation and encourages self-interested behavior by parents. First, divorcing parents receive no encouragement to consider the impact of family dissolution on their children. The law presumes that if either spouse is dissatisfied with the marriage, then termination is appropriate. Further, the dominant "clean break" norms of modern divorce law may obscure

---

[182] Indeed, the freedom of spouses to terminate marriage with no sanction for breach goes beyond any bases for termination under contract law. See Scott, supra note 180, at 720-25.

[183] Modern divorce law at one level reflects the application of principles of liberal individualism to the regulation of family relationships, a broad trend in family law in this century. In some regards, however, modern no-fault divorce law distorts liberal principles in discounting the possibility of binding, enforceable, voluntary commitments between spouses. See id. at 725 (arguing that legal recognition of binding contractual commitments between spouses are consistent with liberal principles); see also Scott, supra note 48, at 21.

the incompatible norm that obligation to children continues even though the marriage is dissolved.

a. The Right to Divorce and Children's Welfare

Divorce is a major disruption of children's lives. The negative effects on psychological adjustment and financial security for many children have been well documented.[184] Although parents (and policymakers) may find comfort in the assumption that divorce is better for children than is being raised in an unhappy family, the empirical evidence offers little support for this view. As a general matter, except in families in which children experience serious conflict between their parents,[185] divorce has more costs than benefits for children.

Nevertheless, parents contemplating divorce face few legal incentives to subordinate their individual interest to that of their children or even to take children's interests into account. This is evidenced most strikingly by the fact that children, whose interests are profoundly affected by divorce, have no standing to object to the dissolution of the family and no right to be represented in the proceeding in which their future is determined. Nor can a spouse object to the divorce on the ground that the children of the marriage will be harmed. Current law sanctions "quickie" divorces, permitting spouses to exit the marriage without requiring any period of reflection on the impact of divorce on their children.[186]

The relational model of parents as fiduciaries would suggest, to the contrary, that legal oversight of parental choice is warranted under these circumstances. In the context of spousal conflict and dissatisfaction, extralegal factors that otherwise align the interests of parent and child in the intact family may no longer function to constrain parental choices. The model would predict provisions in divorce law that reduced the risk that the child's interest would be

---

[184] For a detailed description of the psychological and economic research examining the impact of divorce on children, see Scott, supra note 48, at 25-37.

[185] It is well-established that the most destructive aspect of divorce for children is exposure to serious interparental conflict. See Scott & Derdeyn, supra note 143, at 490-92 (citing studies).

[186] See Scott, supra note 48, at 26.

2466 *Virginia Law Review* [Vol. 81:2401

subordinated.[187] To be sure, legal impediments to divorce impose costs on parents by constraining parental authority and autonomy.[188] Nevertheless, the relational model suggests that such costs are more than off-set by reductions in the ex ante risk of potential conflicts of interest. A legal rule that constrained parental choices about divorce would function as a substitute for extralegal norms rendered less effective by the prospect of family dissolution.

b. Clean Breaks and Child Support

Once parents divorce, their future actions are influenced by a "clean break" policy that dominates modern divorce law. This norm, which, for example, supports a preference for short term rehabilitative alimony and lump sum property settlements, promotes efficient disentanglement of divorced couples.[189] It signals that former spouses should be free of financial and other ties so

---

[187] Several plausible reforms would be consistent with the model. For example, a mandatory waiting period before divorce is granted increases the likelihood that long-term rather than short-term goals will be pursued. Such a "cooling-off" period is premised on the assumption that most parents are inclined to consider their children's interest over the longer term, but that short-term preoccupation with marital conflict or alternative relationships may distort decisionmaking. A period of mandatory delay before divorce also encourages parents, in a general way, to make careful, thoughtful (and thus more accurate) decisions. See Scott, supra note 48, at 76-78. Distortion caused by deviation between long-term and short-term preferences could also be mitigated by increasing parents' access to information concerning the child's interests through counseling, mediation, and the like. Further, mandatory mediation of custody disputes encourages parents to shift their attention from their selfish separate interests to their mutual interest in planning for post-divorce arrangements that serve their children's interest. Finally (and most radically), a court-appointed guardian ad litem could be charged with representing the child's interests in the divorce proceedings and advising the court regarding the costs to the child of awarding divorce.

[188] The costs of reducing the conflict of interest when parents consider divorce are modest by comparison with the costs of more intrusive monitoring of parental behavior after divorce, when the assumption that extralegal factors constrain the conflict of interest becomes far weaker. See infra text accompanying notes 134-42.

[189] Short-term rehabilitative alimony allows the dependent partner to obtain education or skills so that she can support herself. Permanent spousal support is virtually a thing of the past in many states. See, e.g., Del. Code Ann. tit. 13, § 1512(d) (1993) (providing that alimony shall generally be limited to a period not to exceed 50% of the duration of marriage). The trend toward rehabilitative alimony is based in part on the assumption that men will remarry and have new family responsibilities. See Turner v. Turner, 385 A.2d 1280, 1281-82 (N.J. Super. Ct. Ch. Div. 1978).

that they can enter new relationships and form new families.[190] This message contributes to an attenuated sense of financial responsibility toward the children of the prior marriage.

The clean break policy supports reductions in child support payments—on the ground of "changed circumstances"—when an obligor parent has a new spouse and/or child to support.[191] This "changed circumstance" criterion is complicated because the rule is driven in part by parental obligation to children in the new family. Nonetheless, the rule exacerbates conflicts of interest by encouraging parents to pursue their interest in creating a new family, thereby marginally undermining their pre-existing parental obligation. By weakening the informal norms that serve to align the interests of parents and children, the clean break policy pits the financial security of children against the personal fulfillment of parents.[192] Harmonizing the "clean break" norm with the notion of

---

[190] See *Turner*, 385 A.2d at 1282 ("The law should provide both parties with the opportunity to make a new life . . . . Neither should be shackled by the unnecessary burdens of an unhappy marriage.").

[191] See Berg v. Berg, 359 A.2d 354, 356 (R.I. 1976) ("It is recognized in . . . [many] jurisdictions that the expenses incurred by a divorced father's remarriage may be considered in determining whether child support payments should be reduced, terminated, or, increased."); accord Cagwin v. Cagwin, 245 P.2d 379, 380 (Cal. Dist. Ct. App. 1952); LaBove v. LaBove, 503 So.2d 670, 674 (La. Ct. App. 1987); Belke v. Belke, No. 0749-93-2, 1994 WL 369718, at *2 (Va. Ct. App. 1994); see also Ira M. Ellman, Paul M. Kurtz & Katharine T. Bartlett, Family Law 482-85 (2d ed. 1991) (considering the rule that remarriage may justify reduction in child support); C.P. Jhong, Annotation, Remarriage of Parent as Basis for Modification of Amount of Child Support Provisions of Divorce Decree, 89 A.L.R.2d 106, 115-18 (1963) (citing cases). But see Dorgan v. Dorgan, 571 N.E.2d 325, 326-27 (Ind. Ct. App. 1991) (holding that father's remarriage and adoption of new wife's children did not warrant reduction in child support); Young v. Young, 762 S.W.2d 535, 536 (Mo. Ct. App. 1988) (holding that birth of father's child of second marriage did not require reduction of child support); State v. Reed, 658 So.2d 774, (La. Ct. App. 1995) (same); McCarthy v. McCarthy, 610 N.Y.S.2d 619, 620 (App. Div. 1994) (same).

Statutes are often written to give courts broad discretion. See, e.g., N.Y. Dom. Rel. Law § 240(1-b)(g) (McKinney Supp. 1995) ("Where the court finds that the non-custodial parent's pro rata share of the basic child support obligation is unjust or inappropriate, the court shall order the non-custodial parent to pay such amount of child support as the court finds just and appropriate . . . ."); N.Y. Dom. Rel. Law § 240(1-b)(f) (McKinney Supp. 1995) (providing that court may adjust child support if non-custodial parent must provide for other children not involved in the case at hand); Cal. Fam. Code. § 3651(a) (West 1994) (providing that, with certain exceptions, "a support order may be modified or terminated at any time as the court determines to be necessary").

[192] It should give one pause to consider how improbable such a rule would seem in a commercial context. Consider the response to a debtor who, outside of the context of

fiduciary responsibility requires giving priority to the claims of children of the dissolved marriage over later-in-time obligations. As with any precommitment, parents understand that future opportunities for self-fulfillment are limited by their responsibility to existing children.

2. Termination of the Parent-Child Relationship

We have argued that the Supreme Court's recognition of the rights of unmarried fathers adheres to fiduciary principles in its encouragement and protection of fathers' efforts to fulfill parental responsibilities. In other contexts, however, legal deference toward parental rights can undermine the interests of children. In the case of parents whose children are removed due to abuse or neglect, legal regulation of the termination of the parent-child relationship has lacked conceptual coherence. In practice, if not in design, the legal process for terminating the rights of deficient parents reflects an unresolved tension between what are understood to be the conflicting goals of protecting parental rights and promoting the child's welfare. Courts also show curious tolerance of absentee non-custodial parents if no substitute parent has formally adopted the child. Viewed from the perspective of the relational model of parents as fiduciaries, the results are often inconsistent and counterproductive.

a. The Inadequate But Involved Parent

Current policy requires that an abused or neglected child removed from the custody of a parent should either be returned quickly upon remediation by parents or placed permanently in an adoptive home following termination of parental rights.[193] In prac-

---

bankruptcy, has incurred additional financial obligations and, on that basis, seeks to reduce her outstanding debt to her original creditor.

[193] This is the fundamental goal of the Adoption Assistance and Child Welfare Act of 1980, Pub. L. No. 96-272, 94 Stat. 500 (codified in scattered sections of 42 U.S.C.). The Senate Finance Committee Report stated this objective at the outset:

> In particular, the incentive structure of present law is modified to lessen the emphasis on foster care placement and to encourage greater efforts to find permanent homes for children either by making it possible for them to return to their own families or by placing them in adoptive homes.

S. Rep. No. 336, 96th Cong., 2d Sess. (1980), *reprinted in* 1980 U.S.C.C.A.N. 1448, 1450. For detailed analysis of the provisions of the Act, see Allen et al., supra note 154.

tice, however, courts are reluctant to terminate the rights of parents despite their inability competently to assume full responsibility for their children. This leaves children in limbo, as parents' probationary period is extended indefinitely and permanent placement is postponed.[194] The standard criticism is that this judicial distortion of stated policy is driven by excessive deference toward the rights of biological parents.

We think the issue is more complex. The current regime, through the threatened sanction of termination of parental rights and the reward of regained custody, creates powerful incentives for those parents who both desire custody of their children and are able to remediate. It does not, however, seek to motivate less able parents to maintain a relationship with their children, although the bond may have substantial value to the child. Many parents whose performance is suboptimal have a substantial relationship with their children and make efforts (albeit unsuccessful) to remediate the conditions that led to their children's removal. A continued relationship may in fact serve the child's interest.[195] This intuition contributes to a reluctance by some courts to sever the parent-child relationship, a response which, in the current legal framework, leaves the child's status uncertain. Further, the signals to parents are confusing and blurred; the threat of termination always hovers, but is rarely carried out.

Under this scheme, the law's instrumental function of encouraging parental commitment is surely diluted. Straightforward legal reinforcement of the efforts of suboptimal parents, together with permanent custodial placement of the child with adequate substitute parents, might better serve the child's interest than the current ambivalence. To be sure, in some cases continuing a relationship is harmful to the child. In general, however, the older the child and the greater the duration of the parent-child relationship, the more

---

[194] See supra notes 32-38 and accompanying text.

[195] Psychological research supports the claim that severing the biological parent-child bond can be costly to children, even if the child has a tenuous relationship with the parent and the alternative placement is independently desirable. See Garrison, supra note 51, at 461-67 (citing studies).

costly is the decision to terminate parental rights.[196] A sensible legal rule would capture this insight.[197]

b. The "Enoch Arden"[198] Parent

Courts routinely terminate the parental rights of the biological parent who has not maintained any relationship with the child, so as to allow adoption by stepparents. When substitute social parents have not formally established parental status, however, non-

---

[196] Common sense argues that termination is less costly if the child is young or if the parent has failed over an extended period to maintain meaningful contact. Moreover, for older children with a substantial filial bond, the probability that a substitute parent can or will fill the parental role is not great. Older children are less likely to be adopted at all and more likely to face a series of foster placements.

Marsha Garrison extensively analyzes the clinical literature on the need of older adopted children and children in foster care for continued contact with their parents. See Garrison, supra note 51, at 461-72. Garrison concludes that the earlier a child is adopted, the less likely the adoptee is to have emotional problems, citing the following studies:

> Humphrey & Ounsted, Adoptive Families Referred for Psychiatric Advice, I: The Children, 109 Brit. J. Psychiatry 599, 604-05 (1963) (children adopted after six months of age are more likely to exhibit symptoms of disturbed social behavior, stealing, cruelty, destructiveness, and lying); Jameson, Psychiatric Disorder in Adopted Children in Texas, 63 Tex. Med. 83 (1967) (greater incidence of severe psychiatric illness in children adopted after infancy); Offord, Aponte & Cross, Presenting Symptomatology of Adopted Children, 20 Archives Gen. Psychiatry 110, 116 (1969) ("[t]he later the age of adoption, the greater the frequency and severity of the antisocial behavior."); See also S. Wolff, Children Under Stress 107-08 (2d ed. 1981) (a child's age is a main factor associated with the adoption outcome). But cf. Schwam & Tuskan, [The Adopted Child, in 1 Basic Handbook of Child Psychiatry 342, 345-46 (Joseph D. Noshpitz ed., 1979)] (it is unclear whether these studies can be generalized throughout adopted population).

Id. at 471 n.223.

[197] A more tailored two-tiered scheme that might better reduce conflicts of interest could be rationalized within a fiduciary framework. Under such an approach, termination of parental rights would be ordered in cases of serious harmful impact or abandonment of the relationship—the failure to maintain meaningful contact. In other cases, parents' failure to remediate deficiencies adequately would lead to denial of the child's return to parental custody, substituting instead permanent state (or third party) custody with parental visitation rights. The parent who cares about continuing her relationship would understand that preserving the bond with her child requires effort, and that efforts will be rewarded. Moreover, under a regime that offers permanence to the child without termination of parental rights, courts would likely be prepared to make the decision regarding permanent placement more expeditiously than under the current regime.

[198] This term describes a person who suddenly returns after a long absence from which he was not expected to return at all. It comes from Tennyson's poem, "Enoch Arden." See Alfred Lord Tennyson, Enoch Arden (1864), *reprinted in* The Poetic and Dramatic Works of Alfred Lord Tennyson 227 (Cambridge ed., Houghton, Mifflin & Co. 1898).

custodial biological parents are far more likely to succeed in asserting parental rights. Thus, stepparents, grandparents and others who have functioned as parents can have their claim trumped when the absent biological parent returns and claims custody.[199] In other cases, the custodial parent dies, and the non-custodial biological parent seeks custody, often prevailing over the faithful grandparent or stepparent who has not adopted the child, but who has functioned in a parental role.[200] Finally, cases in which the custodial, single parent objects in vain when the defaulting parent petitions for visitation rights. In a typical case, the custodial mother is raising the child alone (or with a female partner) when the non-custodial parent appears to claim visitation rights.[201] In all of these cases, a haphazard interest-balancing approach vindicates parental rights without promoting responsibility and commitment—often at the cost of the child's relationship with a functional parent.

To the extent that the law affords parents an indefinite opportunity to develop a relationship with their child, it fails to motivate them to accommodate other interests to the responsibilities of parenthood. The relational model argues instead for sanctioning fundamental failures to assume parental responsibilities by denying

---

[199] See, e.g., Scarpetta v. Spence-Chapin Adoption Serv., 269 N.E.2d 787 (N.Y. 1971); In re Ronald FF v. Cindy GG, 511 N.E.2d 75 (N.Y. 1987).

[200] See, e.g., Collins v. Gilbreath, 403 N.E.2d 921 (Ind. Ct. App. 1980) (awarding custody to the biological father, rather than stepfather, after mother's suicide); In re S.B.L., 553 A.2d 1078 (Vt. 1988) (awarding custody to the biological father, rather than maternal grandfather, after the mother was killed in a car accident); see also Margaret M. Mahoney, Support and Custody Aspects of the Stepparent-Child Relationship, 70 Cornell L. Rev. 38, 74-78 (1984) (discussing the "natural parent preference" in custody disputes between biological parents and stepparents).

Today, the law has evolved to the extent that stepparents have a reasonable chance of winning custody against seriously defaulting biological parents. See In re Osborne, 21 Fam. L. Rep. (BNA) 1478 (Kan. Ct. App. August 22, 1995) (holding that wife of deceased custodial father may intervene in divorce action versus former wife to seek custody of stepchildren); Mahoney, supra. For proposed reforms, see Fine & Fine, supra note 28, at 78; Janet L. Richards, The Natural Parent Preference Versus Third Parties: Expanding the Definition of Parent, 16 Nova L. Rev. 733, 765-66 (1992).

[201] See Thomas S. v. Robin Y., 618 N.Y.S.2d 356 (App. Div. 1994) (granting an order of filiation to the father to confer standing upon him to seek visitation rights); see also Jhordan C. v. Mary K., 224 Cal. Rptr. 530 (1986) (granting sperm donor visitation rights, rejecting claim to right of family autonomy by mother and female partner). In a case with which we are familiar, the unmarried father left after the child's birth and the mother alone cared for the child until she was six years old. At this point, the father returned and was granted visitation rights over the mother's objections.

the absent parent a subsequent opportunity to develop the relationship. The benefits of such an approach are obvious when the stepparent has established a parental relationship and the contesting biological parent is a remote figure. When the single custodial parent protests, the prospect of increased financial support might seem to argue against a sanction for material breach (indeed, the child may benefit from a relationship with the absent parent). Relational theory suggests, however, that the judgment to forego financial support as well as other possible benefits is properly left to the custodial parent, whose interests are presumptively better aligned with the child's. The underlying theme of this analysis is that parents should be encouraged to create and maintain a parent-child relationship which represents their "best efforts," given their circumstances and capacities. This goal requires sanctions for parents' default and rewards for efforts to invest in the relationship with the child.

3. Informal Norms of Responsibility and Parental Rights

The relational model points to the centrality of extralegal social norms that function to align parents' and children's interests in the intact family. Indeed, in contrast to other fiduciary contexts, these norms are imbedded in the culture and are not primarily legal constructions. A variety of cultural influences reinforce the common belief that the role of parent is intrinsically desirable, socially important and imbued with responsibility.[202] For many people, personal fulfillment is linked to having children and rearing them successfully. Parents who default on their responsibility meet intense social disapproval, as is evidenced by public outrage over child abuse and neglect.[203]

---

[202] A 1986 Roper phone poll of 1654 American adults found that 95% of the respondents felt "being a good parent" was "very important" to their "idea of success." Roper Center for Public Opinion Research, Feb. 1987, available in Westlaw, Poll database.

[203] Examples include the angry public response to crack-addicted mothers exposing their infants to the dangers of addiction, Anastasia Toufexis, Innocent Victims, Time, May 13, 1991, at 56; Tom Morganthau, The Orphanage, Newsweek, Dec. 12, 1994, at 28; fathers who fail to pay child support, supra note 113; and evidence of the harmful psychological impact of divorce, Pamela Lansden, Going Home Alone, Too, Newsweek, Dec. 28, 1992, at 7; all seem particularly intense because of a sense that there has been a breach of a fiduciary obligation.

Some evidence suggests that interwoven with this conception of the parental role is a distaste for legal norms of parental entitlement. There is a persistent public perception that the law grants to biological parents a property-like interest in their children, and that this often results in legal outcomes that are harmful to the child's interest.[204] The sense that social norms and legal rules are divergent is reinforced in the popular culture by cases such as "Baby Jessica" and "Baby Richard," in which courts have ordered the removal of young children from their adoptive families and returned them to their biological parents.[205] While public response in both cases is based perhaps on a distorted view of the legal situation,[206] the reaction indicates a powerful disquiet with a legal regime that speaks in the language of parental rights.

The paradox of contemporary family law, as the preceding analysis reveals, is the uneasy coexistence of legal outcomes that largely fit within a fiduciary framework together with legal rhetoric that continues to emphasize parental rights without responsibility. The divergence of legal outcomes and legal language is commonplace in the common law tradition, but even divorced from results, rhetoric grounded in parental rights can undermine the effects of social norms in subtle but pervasive ways. Conflicting signals are sent by a legal regime that emphasizes parental rights as well as the welfare of the child, but links the two by balancing the one against the other. It is not suprising that this is understood to mean that when parental rights are vindicated, children's welfare is sacrificed.

---

[204] See supra note 9. Many family law scholars have criticized the rhetoric of rights in family law. See, e.g., Glendon, supra note 43; Glendon, supra note 44; Minow, supra note 44; Bartlett, supra note 7.

[205] See supra note 8.

[206] Few critics focused on the fact that Daniel Schmidt asserted his interest soon after the birth of Baby Jessica, and that much of the delay was due to the DeBoers' pursuit of appeals. See DeBoer v. Schmidt (In Re Baby Girl Clausen), 502 N.W.2d 649, 652-54 (Mich. 1993) (recounting the procedural history of the case). Similarly, Otakar Kirchner made efforts to find his child despite the mother's claim that the baby had died, and when he was finally successful 57 days after the birth, he immediately petitioned for custody. See In re Petition of Doe, 638 N.E.2d 181, 182 (Ill. 1994) ("When the father entered his appearance in the adoption proceedings 57 days after the baby's birth and demanded his rights as a father, the petitioners should have relinquished the baby at that time. It was their decision to prolong this litigation through a lengthy, and ultimately fruitless, appeal."), cert. denied, 115 S. Ct. 891 (1995). Moreover, in the latter case, the adoptive parents' attorney knew that the mother was withholding the father's name, but made no effort to identify him. Id.

Virginia Law Review   [Vol. 81:2401

The central insight of the fiduciary heuristic is to focus attention on the reciprocal relationship between parental rights and children's interests. The contract metaphor makes explicit what is implicit in social norms: parental "rights" are granted as compensation for the satisfactory performance of voluntarily assumed responsibilities to provide for the child's interests. It follows that substantial default on those responsibilities leads to the loss, in whole or in part, of the instruments of parental authority. We have argued that the outcomes (as distinct from the rhetoric) of modern family law are substantially consistent with this relational model of parents as fiduciaries. The dissonance lies in the use of an inapt doctrinal framework to regulate a dynamic relationship. Unlike the "law of rights," a fiduciary framework consistently underscores and reinforces norms of parental responsibility and obligation as conditions to the reciprocal obligation of the state to provide compensation for satisfactory performance.

The changing legal response to non-custodial divorced parents suggests that the evolution of family law doctrine may be underway. Pre-reform child support enforcement was lax, encouraging parents to assume that pursuit of their own interests to the detriment of their children's welfare was acceptable behavior. Over the last decade, tough enforcement measures have been enacted which function to require parents to consider their child's interest together with their own.[207] These measures send strong signals that the law requires parents to fulfill their obligations. At the same time, legal reforms have expanded the relationship claims and the role of non-custodial parents.[208] Laws that encourage shared cus-

---

[207] See supra notes 113-14 (summarizing contemporary child support enforcement measures).

[208] See David J. Miller, Joint Custody, 13 Fam. L.Q. 345, 364-65 (1979); Scott & Derdeyn, supra note 143. In addition to joint custody, some states require custodial parents to give non-custodial parents access to medical and school records. See, e.g., La. Rev. Stat. Ann. § 9:351 (West Supp. 1995); Utah Code Ann. §§ 30-3-33(11) (1995); McDougal v. McDougal, 422 S.E.2d 636 (W. Va. 1992) (denying father joint custody but granting access to medical and school records). Custody law encourages parents to cooperate and to support the child's relationship with the other parent. See supra note 150 (discussing friendly parent provision and parental alienation syndrome).

Courts also may require custodial parents to give non-custodial parents some latitude in sharing their religious beliefs with their children. Courts have enforced prenuptial agreements providing for the religious upbringing of the child when the custodial parent seeks to change the child's religious training. See Spring v. Glawon, 454 N.Y.S.2d 140, 142

tody and offer increased participation and authority to non-custodial parents are often justified on the ground that parents who have
a strong relationship are more likely to fulfill their financial
responsibilities.[209]

Modern child custody and support doctrine thus links responsibility and rights much more explicitly than previously and underscores the instrumental function of rights.[210] This approach
presumes that parental role satisfaction is tied to successful performance, and that the noncustodial parent's commitment to act in
ways that reduce potential conflicts of interest are, to a degree,
contingent on relationship rewards.

CONCLUSION

The relational model of parents as fiduciaries provides a
purchase from which to evaluate the evolution of contemporary
family law on issues relating to the state's role in the family. This
perspective differs from the traditional interest-balancing approach
that pits the state's interest in protecting children against parents'

(App. Div. 1982); Gluckstern v. Gluckstern, 220 N.Y.S.2d 623, 624 (Sup. Ct. 1961); see also
Gruber v. Gruber, 451 N.Y.S.2d 117, 122 (App. Div. 1982) (holding that father must fulfill
promise to enroll children in yeshivah as per separation agreement). But see Lynch v.
Uhlenhopp, 78 N.W.2d 491, 496 (Iowa 1956) (holding antenuptial agreement on child's
religious upbringing void for vagueness). Courts will also sometimes uphold a non-
custodial parent's right to have the child participate in religious activities different from
those of the custodial parent when with the non-custodial parent. See, e.g., Murga v.
Murga, 163 Cal. Rptr. 79, 82 (Ct. App. 1980); Felton v. Felton, 418 N.E.2d 606, 607 (Mass.
1981). But see Andros v. Andros, 396 N.W.2d 917 (Minn. Ct. App. 1986) (granting
exclusive control over religious education of children to custodial parent); Morris v.
Morris, 412 A.2d 139, 147 (Pa. Super. Ct. 1979) (holding that Jehovah's Witness non-
custodial father could not take daughter along on door-to-door solicitations).

[209] See supra note 143 and accompanying text.

[210] An emerging issue that is being reexamined in this light is the relationship between
visitation rights of the non-custodial parent and the obligation to pay child support.
Traditionally, these were not interdependent—at least not in doctrine. Failure to pay child
support did not result in loss of visitation rights, and the custodial parent's (or child's)
undermining of the ability to exercise visitation rights did not absolve the obligor parent of
the duty to pay child support. The trend is to link visitation rights and child support
obligations. For an overview of the doctrine and the split amongst the different states, see
Karen Czapanskiy, Child Support and Visitation: Rethinking the Connections, 20 Rutgers
L.J. 619 (1989); Carolyn E. Taylor, Note, Making Parents Behave: The Conditioning of
Child Support and Visitation Rights, 84 Colum. L. Rev. 1059 (1984); Greg M. Geismann,
Comment, Strengthening the Weak Link in the Family Law Chain: Child Support and
Visitation as Complementary Activities, 38 S.D. L. Rev. 568 (1993).

rights. A relational perspective clarifies the core objective of legal regulation: to function in concert with extralegal influences so as to encourage optimal parental behavior. In turn, this objective focuses attention on the reciprocal relationship between parental obligation and parental role satisfaction. The filial bond is central to the lives of both parents and children, is intense and intimate, and requires privacy to flourish.[211] This, rather than any notion of entitlement, is the justification for the initial deference to parental judgments about children's interests. Maintaining the filial bond, however, requires arrangements to guard against conflicts of interest as well as means of compensating parents for avoiding such conflicts. In a very real sense these arrangements confer on parents the status of fiduciaries with the corresponding rights and obligations that such a relationship necessarily implies.

---

[211] Privacy may be important in some other fiduciary relationships, such as that of attorneys and clients and possibly guardians and wards. Given the important role of judicial supervision as a monitoring mechanism in most fiduciary relationships, however, the value of privacy does not seem to be given a great deal of weight.

[11]

THE DEVELOPMENT OF THE CHILD
PREPARED FOR THE LIBERTY FUND SYMPOSIUM
THE FAMILY, THE PERSON AND THE STATE

BY JENNIFER ROBACK MORSE
GEORGE MASON UNIVERSITY
MARCH 1995

I am endebted to James Buchanan and David Levy for comments on previous drafts. The students in my doctoral level Microeconomics class helped me work out a few of the technical details in the model. My husband, Robert Morse, drew the figures.

PART 1. AN EXPANDED MODEL OF THE HUMAN PERSON
INTRODUCTION

Persons enter this world as helpless infants. This readily observed fact has not been fully or satisfactorily incorporated into ordinary economic analysis or into political economic analysis. Economics assumes that persons maximize their utility functions, subject to a set of constraints. But economics has no theory about how a person's utility function comes into being. Economic analysis has assumed either that a person is fully formed, with a completely specified utility function, or that the child is essentially a commodity from the parents' viewpoint. Political economy, especially of the liberal, contractarian variety, typically assumes that persons are fully rational, competent contracting agents. The fact of childhood helplessness is considered incidental to the social order as constructed within these theories.

The present paper is an initial attempt to explore just how the fact of childhood matters in the economic and political order. I maintain that the fact of childhood, and the helplessness of the child are not peripheral facts, but are central to the social order. Any theory that neglects these facts will be defective and incomplete in significant ways.

My ultimate concern is to understand the development of the preferences, the development of the self, and how the relationship between a child and other people influences that development. But, in order to make any progress in this area, it is first necessary to open up the economists' notion of the person. For economic analysis treats the person as if it were fully described by the utility function. Indeed, it is not an exaggeration to say that to an economist, a person is a utility function.

Moreover, we need to note that the calculating man of economics is not really a choosing person in any meaningful sense. The person is defined by the utility function. This utility function, given a priori, confronts the relative prices of various choices that are given to him from the outside. This person then calculates which of the choices maximize his utility.

In this process, there is only calculation, no real choice. For under the standard assumptions about preference orderings, there is only one possible outcome to the confrontation of a given utility function with a given set of relative prices. There is no room for deliberation, regret, or indecision, experiences that are familiar to everyone. My purpose is to extend the standard model to offer an explicit account of these phenomena.

Another way of interpreting my purpose is that I am trying to introduce genuine agency into the economists' model. The economists' view of the person, as it now stands, is that the person is a pure, stimulus-response machine. The preferences are given; the relative prices are given. The person is completely reactive. We might say that the person's behavior is perfectly predetermined, or predestined, once the utility function has been formed, however it might have been formed. There presently is no scope within economics for the genuinely creative act, for the uniquely personal contribution. These things flow from deep within the interior of the person, and have an impact on the external world, rather than the person being exclusively the object of action. In my account, the person will have the capacity to be a subject, as well as an object, an initiator, as well as a reactor.

THE APPETITES AND THE LONGINGS

My initial assumption is that every human person is born with both Appetites and Longings. We might generalize by saying that the Appetites are common to many animals, while the Longings distinguish us from animals. The Longings are desires for ultimate goods, such as Truth, Beauty,

Goodness, Justice, Existence, Love, Friendship. The Appetites correspond to the bodily goods, nourishment, physical comfort, sleep, amusements, sexual gratification and the like. These are pleasurable in themselves, and may also instrumental in achieving the Longings.

We expand the familiar setup of consumer demand theory to assume that utility is a function of the Appetites and the Longings. The Longings have a greater intrinsic weight than the Appetites. But, the Appetites have some value as instruments in achieving the Longings. At the same time, we assume that sometimes, the Appetites may hinder the achievement of the Longings. Examples would include the excessive indulgence in most any of the Appetites. (Six of the Seven Deadly Sins are excesses of things that are surely acceptable in some context: Anger, Pride, Lust, Gluttony, Sloth, and Greed. The only one of the Seven Deadly Sins that does not have a moderate counterpart is Envy.)

We assume that people have identical arguments in their initially endowed utility functions. Everyone has the same set of Appetites, and the same set of Longings. People will differ among themselves in the relative weights they place on the various goods within each category, and the relative weights they place on Appetites versus Longings generally.

Not only do people have a desire for both Appetites and Longings, but people also have some idea about how to obtain them. In particular, people initially have some notion of the relative prices of the goods they can purchase on the market. They also have some notion of the method by which they can obtain the Longings.

People can satisfy their Longings by using their time and some of their goods. In analytical terms, we might say that there is some technology for the production of Longings. A person might pursue Beauty, for instance, by using some of his own time, together with purchased goods such as art classes, music lessons, concert tickets and the like. It is in this sense that we may say that the Appetites can be inputs into the Longings. For it is necessary to remain alive in order to enjoy the Longings, so the bodily needs for food and sustenance and good health must be met. And beyond this most basic requirement, the person needs some material goods with which to pursue Beauty, so that the Appetite for money may become an instrument by which the Longing is met.

But, the pursuit of the Appetites can become a hindrance to the pursuit of the Longings. While a moderate amount of material goods might be necessary for the pursuit of Longings, we can readily conceive of the possibility that one can detract from the pursuit of the higher goods by overindulging the Appetites. If we conceive of the Appetites as inputs into the production of the Longings, we may say that there is a technological optimal amount of the Appetites. Consumption of the Appetites beyond this optimal amount will actually decrease the amount of the Longing produced.

Traditional consumer theory is entirely subjective, in the sense that values are whatever the consumer chooses. Economic analysis typically draws no distinction between good or bad preferences, between virtuous or vicious actions. The present model departs from this custom in one important particular: the preferences remain subjective, but the production of the Longings is objective. That is, there is a specific technology for achieving the Longings, that exists independently of anyone's choice. If a person wants Friendship, there are things must be done and other things that must be avoided. If one wants Truth, whether the knowledge of Truth or the experience of Truth, there are things to do and refrain from doing.

We continue the assumption of subjective preferences, which means that people may assign different relative values to the Longings and the Appetites. Indeed, people may assign different relative values to some of the Longings over others. This assumption allows a wide scope for individual variation, and for individual choice and self-expression. I do insist upon two things, however. I insist that everyone is born with the Longings. And, I insist that the Longings can only be produced in specific ways.

The model so far is a straight-forward extension of standard consumer demand theory. Including self-produced goods called Truth and Beauty is a simple application of Gary Becker's theory of household production. Hypothesizing a region of negative marginal product is not an extraordinary assumption either. But with these modest modifications of consumer theory, we can account for some consumption patterns that are not ordinarily examined in economics. But before we do that, let us turn to an expanded behavioral model of the rational person.

THE TWO COMPONENTS OF THE RATIONAL PERSON

For analytical purposes, I separate the person into two components: the rational person as calculator and the rational person as philosopher. The first component, the rational person as calculator, corresponds roughly to homo economicus as traditionally understood. The rational person as calculator acts on the basis of given preferences. That is, the person acts as if he knows his own preferences, how much pleasure and pain he will receive from each possible action. The second component of the rational person realizes that his knowledge of his own preferences is incomplete, in that he may inaccurately anticipate how a good or activity will make him feel. Because of this imperfect knowledge, the person must periodically reconsider his conception of his own preferences. The person must do more than calculate: the person must reflect upon his own experience, and upon the experience of others. This is the rational person as philosopher.

1. The Calculating Person

Calculating man acts as if his preferences are given, and then confronts relative prices in the environment. These prices include the components customarily considered in economic analysis: monetary prices of market goods, the cost of time, the opportunity cost of foregone alternatives. But our discussion of prices given in the environment must also include some consideration of the reactions of other people. One component of price includes the costs of disapprobation by people who matter. Other people can impose costs or confer benefits on the person in response to his actions. And these reactions must be considered as a component of the relative price. In some cases, particularly for the helpless infant, these responses will form the most significant part of the cost.

The rational person as calculator acts as if he knows what will give him pleasure and pain, that is, as if he knows his utility function. The rational person as calculator also acts as if he knows the relative prices of his actions. But of course, he may be mistaken on both counts. That is, he may not have accurately anticipated the direct impact of the good or activity on his own feelings of pleasure and pain. And he may have miscalculated the external costs and benefits that he would face as a result of his actions. In either of these cases, the person will not receive the level of utility that he expected. This divergence between expectations and reality will provide the motivation for the person to reflect.

2. The Reflecting Person

At this point, the second component of the rational person comes into play. I hypothesize that the person periodically ceases the usual process of calculating costs and benefits, to reassess the internal relative prices. The person adjusts those relative prices to reflect new data.

During this period of adjusting the prices, the person is doing something other than calculating, something that might be called "meta-processing." The person is reviewing his previous actions and their consequences. He is considering whether his relative valuations on activities really met his deeper needs. In short, the person is reflecting. This is the process that makes us most fully human. We are reflecting upon what we in fact value, what kinds of persons we want to be, and how we might become those persons. This is the rational person as philosopher, rather than as calculator.

This division of the person into a calculating part and a reflecting part correspond roughly to James Buchanan's division of politics into ordinary political play, in which the rules of the game are taken as constraints, and constitutional choice, in which the rules of the game are selected. In Buchanan's analytical division, people first choose the rules of the political process under which all future political activity will take place. This is the constitutional choice phase. In the second phase, people actually play out the political game, according to the rules chosen in the constitutional moment.

In Buchanan's setup, the two phases are separated, not only in time, but more importantly, by procedure. Buchanan requires unanimity in the constitutional phase. For Buchanan, this unanimity requirement confers legitimacy upon the constitutional process. At the same time, some sets of bad outcomes are ruled out by a unanimity procedure, as each person can block a procedure or rule that is potentially exploitive.

By contrast, Buchanan places no constraints on the content of the rules that might be chosen. The polity may chose to conduct its ordinary business by simple majority, or by a dictator for life, or by any other procedure, as long as it is unanimously agreed to at the constitutional stage. The experience of ordinary political play becomes data for consideration in the constitutional stage. That is, when people are trying to decide what political rules they want to use, they certainly consider their own experience, and the experience of other polities, under the operation of various kinds of rules.

My framework is in some ways analogous to Buchanan's. Calculating man is conducting business as usual, operating under a given set of preferences, assumptions about technology, and information about prices. But reflecting man is deciding whether these preferences and assumptions are truly the ones he wants to operate under. If he does not obtain the results he expected, he may want to alter some of the ways in which he makes decisions.

We place no external constraints on the person's choice process. We simply note that he may, by his own standards, believe that he needs to make some adjustments. Like the actors in the political game, our individual may come to believe that he can do better under a different decision-making regime. And, in that spirit, he will alter his own, internal, relative valuations of Appetites and Longings, as well as his understanding of the technology for producing the Longings.

In Buchanan's framework, the unanimity rule does all the analytical work. We have nothing quite comparable to that readily observable, though rarely observed, rule. However, we may hypothesize something similar for the individual. We may argue that the person's ultimate goal, his highest Longing, if you will, is Peace. That is, the person wants to be at peace with himself, rather than at war with himself. When his operational utility function is too far out of line with the data he receives about his actual response to his own actions, he knows then, that it is time for reflection. It becomes rational for him to question his beliefs about what gives pleasure and pain, and to adjust his internal valuations accordingly. And while this condition of internal peace is not readily observable in another person, it is something that we know from experience, both in its absence and in its presence. We know Peace when we have it. Sometimes, we can recognize it, or its absence, in others, although we might have a difficult time proving it.

There are several classes of errors that the person needs to reflect upon and correct. The person may incorrectly perceive relative prices, in the strictly material sense. The person may incorrectly anticipate other people's reactions. In some sense, this error could be combined with a misunderstanding of relative prices. However, the misunderstanding, and misinterpretation of other people's reactions will play a significant role in the analysis which follows. The person may be mistaken in his understanding of how an action or good contributes to the production of the longings. In other words, the person may have a defective understanding of technology. Finally, the person may incorrectly anticipate his actual feelings about the outcomes of his choices. That is, the person may have a disordered understanding of the utility function itself.

One important aspect of the problem throughout will be a confusion among these different types of errors. For a person may be confused about the source of his dissatisfaction. He may believe that his dissatisfaction arises from a mistaken judgement about prices, when in fact he has misunderstood the technology for producing the Longings. If this happens, his adjustment process may take several iterations of experience and reflection.

Or, a person's actions may create consequences for, and reactions from, other people that he did not anticipate. The question then becomes whether the person wants to modify his behavior in accordance with the other person's wishes. And if he does, an additional question arises: will he retain that new behavior pattern, even if the other person no longer knows about his actions? That is, will the person change his behavior because he modifies his own internal evaluation of the action? Or will he treat the other person's reactions as something external to himself, and behave as if it were just another component of the cost he must pay?

This issue of confusion of types of errors arises in the context of parent and child in a significant way. For a parent may impose costs on a child to divert him from destructive behavior. The parent believes a child's action to be potentially harmful, and believes further that the child does or can not realize this fact. The parent can prevent the child from taking the action, simply by raising the immediate, readily observable cost to the child. But the child may interpret his parent's bad reaction to his conduct as information solely about the parent and his preferences. The child may not realize that the parent hopes to teach him something about what I have called the technology of the Longings. The child may prefer to believe that his unpleasant experience is caused solely by his parents, and not by the underlying reality of the situation. This kind of conflict is quite common between parents and teenagers. And, the confusion between the costs imposed by the parent and those imposed by reality may take the young person many years of independent living to sort out.

A person may believe that certain things will make him happy, and upon consuming them, discover that they had been mistaken. The process of adjusting one's internal valuations of goods and activities is something quite different from the traditional economic analysis. The person discovers who he is, internally, by a process of reflection. "How did consuming this good really make me feel? How did I really feel about acting this way, as opposed to how I expected to feel?" The person is reacting to events to be sure, in that without the occurrence of the events, he would have no basis for reevaluation. But, the person is reacting not solely to external costs and benefits. Rather, the person is reflecting upon his internal state.

Let us initially hypothesize that young people do these readjustments more often than older people. I offer the following justifications for this hypothesis. First, young people have more to learn, by definition. They are more apt to act on the basis of incorrect data, simply because they have had less experience. They frequently act upon the assumption that they will receive a certain amount of pleasure from a particular action, and then find that they were mistaken. They may confront reactions of other people to their behavior that they did not expect. In short, they may completely miscalculate the consequences of their choices. Indeed, they are likely to so miscalculate on a regular basis.

Besides the primitive groping for accurate data that is so much the feature of childhood, young people need to discover the meaning of their experience. Young adults and adolescents typically spend a great deal of time and energy reflecting upon themselves, their lives, their values, their goals and their plans. Those of us who work with young adults on a daily basis notice this, of course. Indeed, we find there is something rather sad about a young person who does no reflecting, no soul-searching. They may appear to be completely sure of themselves in every dimension. But, we often wonder whether they really mean it, or whether they are kidding themselves.

Adults, by contrast, do relatively little adjusting of their basic value system. Certainly, they do not reorder their priorities as readily as a child or a young person. Sometimes, of course, this is because their efforts in this area were sound during their earlier years. Because they have generated a set of preference orderings that they can truly live with, they do not need to do much reordering during the course of their adult years. They can live off the moral or preference capital they accumulated during their early years of reflection.

On the other hand, we sometimes observe middle-aged people who seem to need a major adjustment in their consumption priorities. And this process can be so unusual, so dramatic, and perhaps, so traumatic, that we have special names for it. We might call it a "mid-life crisis", or a "conversion", or a "recovery experience". In any event, there can be no doubt that the readjustment of priorities after many years of use is more difficult that a readjustment of similar magnitude of preferences that have been in use a short time. Part of our purpose in the sequel will be to explain why this might be so.

In this section, we have expanded the familiar economist's model of the human person. The rational person reflects on his experience, in addition to calculating costs and benefits. The person is born with both Appetites and Longings, and the Appetites are inputs into the production of the Longings. But the person can consume too much of the Appetites in relation to their productivity of the Longings. We have reviewed the kinds of errors that a person might make. The disappointment created by these errors in turn creates the motivation for reflection, and possible readjustment of perceptions about prices and technology, or adjustment of preferences. In the sections which follow, we explore the developing person, beginning with the helpless infant, and moving all the way through adolescence. Throughout, we will consider the interaction between the parents, who are more fully formed, and the child.

PART II: THE DEVELOPMENT OF THE CHILD

In the previous section, we expanded the economists' view of rational human behavior to include a capacity for reflection, as well as for calculation. We also gave some substance to the utiltity function, by hypothesizing that persons receive utility from the satisfaction of Appetites and Longings. Most of that discussion concerned adults. Specifically, the persons were capable of independent action, they had definite preferences, they were capable of learning from their experience, and they had the use of language.

In this section, we discuss the development of persons from infancy toward adulthood. In particular, we begin with persons of minimal capacities for action, for discernment, and for language. We try to analytically separate these features, and capture them in a simple model. We then try to show how the person's behavior changes, as they develop in their various capacities. We also can show how the person's relationships with others changes as their capacities develop.

In particular, I shall begin by assuming that the person in infancy has no capacities, but only needs. In the first stage of his development, I will focus on his need to develop trust in other people, so that these others can helpful to him at the more complex stages of development. During this initial period, the baby learns trust, and is also learning something about his preferences.

The second stage of development I will analyze, I will call childhood. In this phase, the person has already developed some idea of what he likes and does not like. He has some experience with consumption, and so can be said to have some genuine preferences. But, at this slightly more advanced stage, the child now needs to develop a capacity for independent action. The child can learn and needs to learn, how to meet some of his needs for himself. Our goal in this section, is to show an interaction between parent and child that allows the child to learn from the parent. The parent will not immediately satisfy the child's needs, but rather, attempt to teach the child how to do for himself. A part of this process is that the parent deliberately frustrates the child's immediate needs. In the process, the parent will have to draw upon the stock of trust accumulated during infancy.

In the final developmental stage that I will discuss, the adolescent develops a capacity for discernment. That is, the child now knows something about how to do things for himself. He knows how to satisfy his needs. But now the child must learn to distinguish between his real needs and apparent needs. He must learn the difference between the pleasure generated by the satisfaction of the Appetites, on the one hand, and the satisfaction of the deepest Longings on the other.

At this stage, the parent often allows the child to indulge himself and to do for himself. Sometimes, the child will experience disappointment. That is, the child will not receive the level of satisfaction that he expected from a set of activities. This disappointment is distinct from frustration, in the following sense. We use the term frustration to indicate the difficulty the child has simply in the doing of activities. We use the term disappointment to indicate the thwarted expectations the child experiences from an activity that they have the capacity to perform. The parent must then guide the child through the process of interpretting his experience. Again, the parent draws upon the accumulated stock of trust. For it is the child's trust in the parent, the parent's love, the parent's judgement, that allows the child to consider the parent as a credible source of guidance.

Throughout the entire process, the child is developing two other capacities: the capacity for language, and the capacity for abstract thought. Both are relevant to all the developmental stages, and to economic man, generally. The capacity for language is what allows the person a low cost, compact means of summarizing his experience. When a child learns a new activity, he initially talks himself through the activity, using the verbal instructions given by a more experienced person. When an adolescent learns discernment, he alters his beliefs about what will please him through the use of such verbal tools as precepts, rules of thumb and the like. In other words, the person's learning is largely, though not exclusively, carried by language. (This is part of the reason non-verbal persons are difficult to teach.)

The person is also developing his capacity for abstract thought throughout the various stages. Abstract thought allows the person to generalize from his particular experience. He need not approach each decision as if he had never seen anything like it before, even if he has never seen anything exactly like it before. He learns how and when to apply past experience to current decisions. He learns how to determine which feature among his experiences are truly the salient and relevant features to apply to the problem he currently faces. Which differences are the relevant differences? Which similarities are the relevant similarities? On the basis of past experience, what can I reasonably expect from the decision now before me? These are the questions that a person grows more skillful in answering over the course of his life.

Having laid out this basic plan for this section, I want to mention one warning. I will be decomposing persons and their devlopmental stages. It should be obvious that many of these developmental processes are in fact going on simultaneously, at all chronological ages. It should also be obvious that other processes may be at work at the same time. Every child is different, every family is different. I will be abstracting from many complicating factors, for the sake of illustrating processes that I believe to be crucial, and overlooked.

But I hope this abstraction will not blind the reader to the richness and complexity of each individual's development. I hope the abstraction is powerful enough to be useful, but not so powerful that it dominates one's entire vision of the personal process. For sometimes an abstraction of a process takes over the process itself, and gives it all its meaning ever after.

I am particularly aware of this because I believe this is part of what has happened in economics. Our powerful tools have overwhelmed us, have filled up our vision so completely, that we are in danger of overlooking the reality that these abstractions are meant to represent. I believe that much harm has been done by omission. Economics has been correct as far as it has gone, in its analysis of human nature. But the fact that so much has been overlooked has been the source of much error. I mention this warning before I begin decomposing the developmental process. Even though I believe my decomposition will be helpful and useful in understanding some key features, I do not want to mislead anyone into thinking that the model of reality is a perfect substitute for reality.

A. INFANCY: DEVELOPING TRUST

Consider the infant, the helpless, tiny infant, who enters the world attached to an umbilical cord. Who is this little being? Only the most obtuse economist would claim that this small creature possesses the capacity for rational choice, in the usual sense. How shall we characterize the person in his initial condition?

First, let us note that the infant has no capacity for independent action. The child at birth is completely dependent upon others for the satisfaction of his most basic needs. Moreover, the child cannot have developed preferences, for he has had no experience of consuming anything. He cannot know what will please him. Even if he did know, in advance, what will please him, he has no capacity to bring it about. Hence, we can say that the infant initially has no capacity for choice in any meaningful sense. It is the development of such a capacity that we seek to understand.

So, let us not begin with a utility function. For the infant does not yet know even the arguments of a utility function, much less have the capacity to compute marginal rates of substitution. Rather, let us hypothesize that the infant experiences episodes of neediness. The infant does not know exactly what he needs, only that he needs something. Even if he did know what he needed, he could not satisfy the need himself. And even if he knew, and had someone on hand to satisfy his need for him, he can not directly communicate what he wants.

So, the infant, in a very real sense, does not have an economic problem at all. The infant is not allocating scarce resources among competing goods. Someone else must solve that problem on the infant's behalf. The infant will experience the results of that person's decisions, and those results have life and death consequences for the infant. How shall we then, characterize the infant's condition? What is the problem that someone must solve for the infant?

We will hypothesize that the infant is born with both Appetites and Longings. But, of course, distinguishing between these two is well beyond the capacity of the infant. Nonetheless, we know, and the adults in the child's life can know, that the child needs material goods, as well as goods of a more intangible nature. The child experiences neediness; it is the adult's problem to determine what the child actually needs. Initially, the needs are simple and few: food, a clean diaper, a place to sleep. All of these needs readily correspond to the adult appetites. There is one more need that is evidence of a primitive longing: sometimes, infants just want to be held, for no particular reason that anyone can detect. They just want to be held; they seem to crave contact with other persons.

We know that this longing to be held can have physical consequences. For some infants cared for in impersonal settings such as orphanages or maternal hospitals develop the "Failure to Thrive" syndrome. All of the obvious material needs of the children are met; they are fed and changed; they receive medical care. But some of them, for no apparent reason, fail to thrive. They do not gain weight. They may even die, from no identifiable illness. The best of the thinking on the subject is that these children waste away from lack of human contact.

In any event, whatever might be contained in the set of needs, it is certain that the infant experiences neediness. And, the infant experiences a need for other persons, just to satisfy his needs. So, we might say that a need for other persons is experienced jointly with any other needs the child has. At the very least, the child has an instrumental need for other people. We can imagine time in the infant's world as being measured by episodes of neediness. That is, the child experiences his life in short bursts of neediness, each defined as one period long.

The child experiences a need which he can not satisfy by himself. The child cries out for help. Help arrives. And the help actually produces two things for the child. First, the help produces a satisfaction of the need itself. Second, the help may also produce trust. His needs can be met by some combination of time and market goods. Trust, on the other hand, is produced only by the input of adult time.

The adult must solve the infant's problem. Let us hypothesize two different ways that an adult might frame the infant's problem. First, the adult might conceive of the problem as one of meeting the infant's need at minimal cost to himself. The adult ignores the impact of his or her time upon the production of trust on the infant's part. The adult simply tries to satisfy the infant at minimal inconvenience.

The alternative framework for the adult's understanding of the infant's problem is that the adult may place some value on both the satisfaction of the infant's needs, and on the production of trust in the infant. The adult in this case will chose to spend relatively more time and less money on the care of the child, than if the production of trust were ignored. Time with the adult person produces jointly both trust and the satisfaction of the need. Therefore, the inputs of adult time are more productive and valuable than they would be if the production of trust was ignored. The adult who understands this will chose to spend more time than they otherwise would with the child. And the adults will make this choice at any set of prices and wages.

A relatively low choice of adult time, and hence lower production of trust, can come about for several different reasons. First, the adults may be unaware that Trust is being produced jointly with the Needs. In this case, they may simply ignore the impact of their time on the production of Trust. Second, the parents may realize that their time affects Trust. But, the value of their time may be so high, that is, their wages may be so high, that they find it optimal to select a low level of time with the infant.

Finally, adults with few resources may be constrained by necessity to satisfy the Needs at a very low level. In that case, the amount of time and market goods devoted to the infant may both be low. Perhaps the child is taken to a minimal care daycare center. Perhaps the child is left at an orphanage in which the staff props the bottle into the crib, and changes diapers once a day. Or perhaps the child is left on the street to fend for himself as best he can. In all of these cases, for any of these reasons, the input of adult time is low. And the result of this will be a low level of Trust being produced.

This observation that sometimes the needs will be met in only the most minimal way raises an additional issue. If the child's needs are not satisfied, the child may develop something other than trust in adults. Every episode of neediness has the potential to increase either trust or rage within the infant. The production of Trust can be conceptualize in two parts. First, the adequacy of the need has an impact on the child's trust in the parent. If the child's needs are ignored, the child experiences negative trust, which for our purposes, we will call, rage. Secondly, if the need is met adequately, more trust is produced the more personally the need is met. In other words, more trust is produced if the need is met by persons, rather than by commodities. Each episode of need can be met and satisfied, at various levels of satisfaction. The child's hunger can be satisfied by being nursed at his mother's breast, or by having a bottle propped into the crib. The hunger can be fully satisfied, or only partially satisfied, or even poorly satisfied, if insufficient or inappropriate food is provided.

Thus, we expand our production function for trust to include two arguments. In addition to time, we include the difference between the infant's perception of his need, or his target level of need, and the level of need actually provided. If the parent provides as much or more of the need than the child originally demanded, Trust increases. If the parent provides less than the child demanded, the Trust decreases and Rage increases. ~

This formulation allows us to capture the fact that some children are highly indulged by their parents, who give them more than they ask for. Other children are actively abused by their parents, especially around the issue of their needs. A child might be completely neglected, or actively harmed. We capture the ill effects of this interaction by saying that the child's stock of trust can be exhausted down to nothing, and even converted into rage, if the neglect and abuse are serious and systematic enough.

The reader might wonder at this point: What is the economic significance of trust? Why is an economic model of the person including a discussion of the development of trust, a subject that seems to be the domain of psychology? The technical answer is that we will later use the stock of trust as an input into other interactions between the child and other people. But this begs the question in a sense. What reason do we have to believe that a person's stock of trust has consequences for their interactions with other people? And are these consequences of a type and magnitude to be of interest to economists?

Trust is the foundation of reciprocity. For the normal infant, the satisfaction of their needs in a personal way leads to the development of trust, and then to the capacity for reciprocity. The infant can provide something of value and pleasure for the mother: the first smile. And in this exchange of smiles for satisfactions, the child begins to learn the value of reciprocity, of give and take, in human relationships. The child's continued existence depends not only on the presence of adults, but also on their willingness to give to and provide for the child. Being cute, making people laugh, and engaging other people, make it easier for adults to provide help. Or, as an economist would say, adults find it less costly to give to a cute infant than to an obnoxious one. This is the normal path of social development.

Reciprocity is the foundation for exchange. Trade is a reciprocal behavior. Experimental economists have observed that rats behave like homo economicus, if this is defined as having downward sloping demand. That is, experimental economists can show that rats will demand fewer food pellets when the cost of obtaining them is higher. In this very limited sense, rats are rational economic actors.

But what the experimentalists can not induce the rats to do, is to trade. That is, rats will not exchange food, or anything else with each other. Demand is the economic action of an individual in isolation. Exchange is the economic interaction among individuals. Rats compute price. Rats do not trade. They appear to be incapable of reciprocal behavior.

The significance of trust and reciprocity for human interactions, including economic interactions, can be clearly seen in two pathological cases of infant development. In the case of autistic or other unresponsive children, the child does not or can not learn to engage other people. For reasons that are not understood, these children do not learn to be cute, do not learn to engage. Some of them resist being held, and will even arch their backs to escape their mother's embrace. These children have only limited capacity to give benefits to those who care for them. Parenting these children is exhausting in part because the child is giving nothing.

The second pathological case occurs when the child has no one to whom to give. The unattached child is sometimes observed in several different settings. Orphanage children sometimes have little human contact, apart from the satisfaction of their bodily needs. Street children may have little interaction with adults that is not exploitive or abusive. Finally, attachment disorder sometimes develops in children who are removed from their original families because of abuse, and then subsequently moved among various foster care and adoptive arrangements.

In disproportionate numbers, these children continue to be unconnected with other people, even after their periods of isolation have ended. They may be adopted by loving and competent families, and never attach to them. They may not develop the capacity for reciprocity in relationships. Indeed, they may not develop relationships in any meaningful sense. These children become difficult to parent, because, like the unresponsive child, the unattached child is giving nothing.

The prevailing thinking is that children who do not develop attachments in the first eighteen months of life will have grave difficulty in forming attachments later. And if the parents of such children do not intervene by the time the child reaches twelve years of age, the prospects for successful future intervention are thought to be gravely diminished, to the point of hopelessness.

The classic case of attachment disorder is a child who does not care what anyone thinks of him or her. The disapproval of significant others is not a sufficient deterrent from bad behavior, because there is no other significant enough to matter to the child. The child does whatever he or she thinks they can get away with, no matter the cost to other people. They do not monitor their own behavior, so authority figures must constantly be wary of them and watch them. They respond to physical punishments, and to suspension of privileges, but not to disapproval of significant others. They lie if they think it is advantageous to lie. They steal if they can get away with it. They may go through the motions of offering affection, but people who live with them sense a kind of phoniness. They show no regret at having hurt another person, or may offer perfunctory apologies. They may find it fun to torture animals.

As they grow into adolescence, these children may become sophisticated manipulators. Some authors refer to them as "trust bandits," because they are superficially charming, in their initial encounters with people. They can charm people for short periods of time, only to betray the person's trust by using them. They can con people for long enough to use them. In the meantime, their parents, and anyone else who has long term dealings with them, grows increasingly frustrated, frightened and angry, over their child's dangerous behavior, which may include lying, stealing, violence, and firesetting.

As the parents try to seek help for their child, they may find that the child is able to "work the system." They can charm the therapists, the social workers, the counselors, and later, perhaps even the judges and parole officers. This child is unwilling to consider others, or even to inconvenience himself for the sake of others.

Who is this child? Why, it is homo economicus. The person who considers only his own good, who is willing to do anything he deems it in his interest to do, who cares for no one. All of his actions are governed by self-interested calculation of costs and benefits. Punishments matter, loss of esteem does not. He does not self-monitor; so he can always find some opportunity to evade the rules. As to his promises, he behaves opportunistically on every possible occasion, breaking promises if he deems it in his interest to do so. Plainly, this is a person who is not fit for social life.

Most normal people would just call this person a sociopath, and not dignify this character by calling him homo economicus. While it is a stark picture, deliberately drawn, I believe it illuminates a valuable point. The very starkness of this completely unattached person shows us that we economists have been, all along, counting on some feature of human nature other than pure self-interest to hold society together. Even the purely economic realm itself cannot be held together with purely, self-interested, unattached people.

Consider, for instance, the Prisoners' Dilemma, which is, for many social scientists and philosophers, a paradigm for problematic cooperation. The Prisoners' Dilemma analyzes situations in which it is collectively beneficial for people to cooperate with each other, even while it is in their individual and private interest to be uncooperative. In this context, we can see that the ability and willingness to rely upon others has vast social significance.

Game theorists and experimentalists alike have shown that it is privately rational to play tit-for-tat in a prisoners' dilemma game, as long as the game has been started with a cooperative first move. We can conceptualize the parent is the first mover in the child's life. The child receives from the parent, in an unrequited way.

The child does not and indeed, cannot reciprocate in kind. But, the child does learn to participate in reciprocity. The child learns give and take: the child learns to trade smiles with his parents. Sometime between the age of three months and six months, the child learns the cognitively trivial, but socially complex task of playing peek-a-boo. Looking, with anticipation for another person: delighting in the moment of eye-contact. The only reward for the game is laughter and eye-contact. Ultimately, the child learns to take turns in a conversation.

Still later, the child learns to suppress some of his immediate desires, for the sake of the comfort of others. He learns not to scream out for anything and everything he wants. He learns to wait his turn. He learns to share toys. These are all primitive forms of cooperative behavior. All these behaviors have elements of regard for others, elements of reciprocity, elements of mutual benefit and pleasure.

And yet, it would be a mistake, a grave distortion of the situation to describe these behaviors as contracts. Some social scientists and lawyers have a tendency to model every human relationship with reciprocity as a contract, and every interaction of mutual benefit as an exchange. But the persons in question here are far too primitive in their development to be offering consideration in exchange for promises. The mutuality and reciprocity is far deeper than contract, the trust is far more profound than a contractual promise.

The capacity to participate in these profound and subtle relationships with intimates sets the stage for a capacity to engage in more limited trust relationships with strangers. It would not be reasonable to trust a stranger to the same extent that one trusts one's most intimate family members and friends. And at the same time, if one never has the opportunity or develops the capacity to trust the most intimate family members, it is difficult to see how one would ever conclude that trusting more distant people could be beneficial.

This is why a discussion of trust and reciprocity belongs in a discussion about the economists' view of the person. For our traditional description of homo economicus assumed persons with particular capacities: for independent action, for definite preferences, for learning from their experience, and for the use of language. Infants do not fit this description. But, while the infant is developing these capacities that prepare him for economic life, indeed for any social life, he is also developing the capacity for trust and for reciprocity. The person who comes to the economic realm has already mastered these elementary skills.

Under normal developmental circumstances, persons learn these skills so automatically, so effortlessly, so painlessly, that we scarcely notice the process at all. I believe this is part of the reason why this aspect of the human person has been neglected by economists. Trust and reciprocity are so much a part of the human condition that we take them for granted. We notice them only in their absence.

But now, there are coming into society larger numbers of children who have never developed the capacity for trust and reciprocity. Some have experienced neglect and abuse from adults. Some have been through numerous foster care placements. Some have come from orphages run by socialist governments. People with these experiences are few, but significant because of the severity of the problems they cause for any social order. We can hardly afford to take the preferences of people like these as givens. Somewhere along the line, someone, somehow, must take responsibility for the development of preferences and behaviors that will allow these individuals to be full participants in the social order.

B. CHILDHOOD: DEVELOPING CAPACITY

In this section we turn to a discussion of the child. We distinguish the child from the infant in two different ways. First, the child, unlike the infant has has developed some capacity for independent action. The child also has had enough experience with consumption to have developed some preferences over the limited set of goods with which he is familiar.

The child, thus, can have a rudimentary form of the economic problem. The child has competing wants. The child has some limited ability to satisfy those wants. The child must allocate his scarce resources to the satisfaction of competing ends.

What are the child's resources? The child has his own time, and whatever that time can produce in the way of his own satisfaction. The child has access to adults, typically, first to his parents. He has access to some of the material resources of these adults, and more importantly, he has access to some assistance from those adults. Obviously, children with wealthy or able parents have potential access to more resources than do children with poor or foolish parents.

How does a child obtain resources from his parents? Some resources flow automatically and effortlessly to the child. Most children obtain the basic material necessities from their parents without any negotiation or effort on their own part. These automatic resources are a part of the background of the child's economic problem, but not part of the problem itself. The child does not have to exert any effort, or spend any of his scarce resources to obtain this fixed set which flows directly from his parents' bounty. The child can take these resources, and the level of well-being they imply, for granted. But strictly speaking, these resources are not part of the child's problem: they are part of the parents' economic allocation problem.

Our central concern here is how the child allocates his scarce resources among his competing wants. The child will still experience episodes of neediness, defined as bursts of need or desire that are beyond his capability to satisfy. So, the initial problem of infancy will still, in some part, remain with the child. That is, the child will experience need, cry out for help, and continue to be completely dependent on others for the satisfaction of his needs. And the process of accumulating trust or its opposite, rage, will continue, as the adults respond to the child's demands.

But here is the new element to even this primitive problem, as it develops in a child with some capacity for action. The child gradually becomes more able to meet his own needs. If the adults continue to rush to his assistance, the child will be less inclined to learn to do things for himself. If the parent refuses to solve the child's problem for him, the child's initial reaction may well be to become enraged.

So, with the new abilities of the child, the parent now has a new problem. The parent must decide how much to do for the child, how much to give to the child, in response to the child's demands. It is no longer in the child's best interest for the parent to satisfy every demand, even though the child may become just as enraged when his demands are frustrated. The only way for the child to learn to do for himself is for the adult to stop doing for him. So, the parent must balance the increased rage from failing to satisfy the child, against the increased learning and capability that the child will gain. The tradeoff between the costs of frustration and the benefits of increased independence generates what we might call the optimal level of frustration for the child.

But the optimum for the child has some different properties for the adult. For the adult may actually find it less time-consuming and difficult to meet the child's needs himself, rather than to take the time to teach the child to do it. It is much more convenient for the parent, at least in the short run, to do the dishes, make the bed, ties the shoes herself, rather than take the time to provide instruction to a demanding, and already frustrated child. But, at some point, the parent will find it worthwhile to make this investment of time and effort, in the interests of the child's development and independence, not to mention in the interests of her long-run convenience.

So, childhood brings a new pair of problems. The child, for the first time, has a primitive form of the economic problem, in the decision of allocating his scarce resources among competing wants. The parent has a new investment problem, in determining the optimal level of frustration of the child's immediate demands. Our task is to specify each of these problems, and then to specify an equilibrium concept that seems sensible to this interaction.

THE CHILD'S PROBLEM

The child's problem can be understood as the decision of how much assistance to request from the parents. The child would like to conserve his own, very limited resources of time, effort and material goods. On this account, he would prefer that the parent continue to meet his needs for him, so that he can consume his own stock of resources. We can, in the initial stages of the problem, safely assume that the child does not know, as the adults do, that by doing for himself, he will come to have a greater capacity for doing things.

So, we might say that the child obtains utility both from having his needs met, and from consuming his own, limited resources. At the same time, the child's utility may depend upon the help he receives from the adults, independently of its impact on the satisfaction of the needs. That is,

$$U = U(N, H, x_c)$$

where $N = Nc(H, x_n =$ the production function of the child's needs, as understood by the child

H = adult help

x_c = the resources the child consumes

x_n = the resources the child uses to satisfy his own needs and

x = the child's total resources,

divided between x_c and x_n

$$x = x_c + x_n.$$

The child may get positive pleasure from obtaining help, just because he enjoys seeing the parent pick up the toy from that he threw off the high chair for the fifteenth time. Or, the child may get disutility from parental assistance, as when the child insists, "I can do it myself!" We include this term to capture either possibility.

The novel assumption that we make here, is that the price of obtaining help, from the child's point of view, depends on the amount of trust he has in the parent. In particular, the child who trusts his parents feels freer to ask for assistance, than a child who trusts no one, or than a child who fears he may be attacked for asking. So, from the child's point of view, the stock of trust built up in the parent determines the price that he will use in choosing how much assistance to request, and how much to attempt to do on his own.

This formulation of the problem captures some features of the unattached or abused children mentioned earlier. We hypothesize that these children have a low stock of trust. Therefore, they consider the price of asking for help to be very high. This hypothesis is consistent with frequently observed characteristics of these kids. They do not ask for help; they attempt to do everything on their own. They attempt to be self-sufficient at a very early age.

Some abused children become very withdrawn. They seem to be trying to disappear. They do not make their needs known, even to people who are in fact safe. It takes them a long time to believe that it is safe to trust enough to ask for help. These children sometimes appear as model foster or adoptive children, because they are appear undemanding. But under that cooperative exterior, they are not necessarily attaching to the people around them. All is not necessarily well in their interior lives.

Other neglected or abused children give a more hostile appearance. They may be very demanding about trivial tasks which they could easily accomplish for themselves. It is as if they need to continually check out whether the new parent will in fact come through for them. This type of child may test the parent contintually.

On the other hand, this same type of child is often extremely vulnerable around the learning and performance of new or unfamiliar tasks. They do not want to admit that they are anything but completely self-sufficient. They do not trust anyone enough to ask for help with something at which they might fail. The consequence of this set of choices is that the child has great difficulty learning anything new. The child becomes instantly frustrated, and would rather stick with the old, familiar behavior, rather than taking the risks involved in learning something new. This child's world can become extremely small and limited, unless the adults intervene in a very definitive way. If these children are permitted to do only what is comfortable for them, they will not learn much, and will inhabit a very narrow world.

THE PARENTS' PROBLEM

This brings us to the parents' problem. The parents have different objectives than the child. We assume that the parents are not trying to maximize the child's current utility. At this point in the analysis, we also do not assume that the parent is getting utility from his own consumption of goods and leisure. Instead, we focus solely on the parents' problem of trying to improve the child's future well-being.

To do this, we assume that the parents' utility function on the child's behalf has arguments that are not present in the child's utility function. The utility of the parent does depend on the level of satisfaction of the child's needs. But the parental utility function also depends on the child's stock of resources or capacity to do things for himself. The parent realizes that the child's future ability to do for himself, that is, his future stock of resources, which have called X, depends on how much of his resources he uses to satisfy his needs now. The child will not learn how to dress himself, or tie his own shoes, unless he invests some of his current resources in trying.

At the same time, the child's increase in capacity will depend on the amount of time the parent invests in helping him. It takes time to teach a child how to do things, indeed, often much more time initially, than it would take the parent to do it herself. But the wise parent views this process as an investment. Some of the time, the parent will find it optimal to make the investment

of their own time and effort to teach the child how to accomplish tasks for themselves.

So, from the parental viewpoint, we can express the production function for the child's needs

as

$N = N_p(\ t, x_p, x)$ where

t = adult time

x_p = other parental resources

x = child's resources.

We can see that this production function of the child's needs is rather different from the production

function we described as the child's. It is not that the parent and child have different technologies,

or that one is mistaken about how the needs can be addressed. The difference lies in what each

person considers the choice variables of the problem.

From the child's viewpoint, the needs are satisfied by some combination of his own effort and

other people's effort. The child simply wants help, and does not, at least initially, have strong

preferences about the form the help takes. The child just wants the adults to do something for him.

From the parent's viewpoint, however, the form the help takes makes all the difference. The

parent could just satisfy the child, and demand nothing of the child in the process. This, it is safe to

say, is the kind of help the child initially has in mind. But the parent, some of the time, will choose

to take a longer time, and perhaps more other resources as well, to teach the child how to do for

himself. The time and resources the parent spends in this process is not valued in itself, by the child.

The child just wants his needs satisfied at the lowest possible cost to himself.

We can see already a conflict brewing between the parent and child. The optimal choice for

the parent will not be the same as the optimal choice for the child. When it is not, the child will be

frustrated. The child choose to invest a certain amount of effort in asking for help. Instead of getting the job done, promptly and efficiently by the more experienced parent, he gets a lecture, or an instruction manual. And the combination of his frustrated need and the increased demand on him, may cause the child to become enraged.

This leads us to discuss the final element of the parental utility function. The parent also cares about the amount of trust the child has. As we have already noted, the stock of trust is decreased by episodes of frustrated neediness, which may result in rage. The parents know that they may enrage the child by frustrating his plans. They are willing to run down the child's stock of trust, in order to acheive an increase in the child's capacity. But to do this, there must be some trust in place to begin with. And, the parent does not want to frustrate the child needlessly, or frivolously.

The parent knows that the child has some basic trust in her, enough to be willing to ask for help. But the parent frustrates the child's plans, knowing that doing so will consume some of the child's trust in her. The parent faces tradeoffs between satisfying the child's needs, building the child's capacity, and using up the stock of trust.

EQUILIBRIUM

How shall we characterize the equilibrium between parent and child? In most economic problems, equilibria are described as a correspondence between planned outcomes and realized outcomes. The equilibrium in a market occurs when the price at which the quantity the buyers planned to buy to equal to the quantity which the sellers planned to sell. But in the duet between parent and child, inconqruent plans are a necessary part of the child's development.   The child chooses a level of his own effort that is lower than the parent chooses. The parent provides a different type of help than the child had in mind. All the consequences flow from these two disappointments. The child has his needs satisfied differently than he expected. The child experiences rage rather than an increase in trust. And the child acquires an increase in capacity that he did not expect. It is quite possible that the child will eventually come to value this increase in capacity, and be grateful to the parent for this episode of temporary frustration. Indeed, this is the parents' hope.

We characterize the child's initial frustration as a disappointed expectation of the price of obtaining help. The child, knowing the amount of trust that exists between himself and the parent, assumed that he would have to pay a relatively low price of obtaining parental assistance. But the parent, in effect, replies, "if you want my help, you must put forth more effort, of a particular kind, than you had planned." The child faces a higher price of help than he expected.

For his part, the child has some choices about how to respond. The child may pay the higher price of struggling a bit himself to get his shoes tied. On the other hand, the child may resist paying the higher price. He can resist by withdrawing his request for help and going without shoes. Or, he can resist by imposing costs on the parent. He might have a tantrum, or kick off his shoes, or otherwise cause chaos, all the while hoping that the parent will relent, and tie the shoes.

Now, the parents' plans are frustrated. They anticipated perhaps, some resistance. Maybe they overestimated, maybe they underestimated. (There is a large random element to these interactions, as every parent knows.) They face a choice: do they relent and tie the shoe? Or, do they stand firm, and possibly impose some new costs on the child for this reaction?

No matter what the parent chooses to do next, there is always some chance that this particular episode of neediness will continue to go badly. The child may continue to be frustrated. The parent and child may escalate the costs they impose on each other. Ultimately, the episode is resolved and ends one way or the other. We would hesitate to characterize every completed episode of neediness as an equilibrium.

Instead, let us define an equilibrium interaction as one in which the child both learns something, and appreciates it. That is, the child's capacity increases as a result of the parents' deliberate frustration of his plans. And, the child's trust in the parent increases, as a result. The increase need not be back to its initial level or above. But, at the very least, the child trusts the parent more than he did at the height of his frustration.

Why characterize equilibrium in this way? The full satisfaction of the child's plans would not be an acceptable definition. And the complete satisfaction of the parents' forecast of the whole sequence of the interaction would be an excessively stringent requirement to place on the equilibrium concept.

Under this definition of equilibrium, the child actually gains at least knowledge and maybe trust as well. Such a definition corresponds to the idea that there have been some mutual gains to the interaction. The child learned a tangible skill. The child perhaps appreciated the usefulness of the costs the parent imposed him. And the parents, at the end of the day, can feel as if they have done their job. Not perhaps as smoothly or painlessly as they might have hoped, but they have done their job.

With enough of these duets between parents and child, the young child can move beyond the rudimentary tasks of life, and progress to the more complex tasks necessary for independent living. This child can, more and more, make independent decisions, for he has the capacity to carry out the satisfaction of his own needs. He is acquiring, in effect, more and more resources. In the process of acquiring both the experience of doing and of consuming, his preferences are becoming more and more defined. He is developing the capacity to address the economic problem.

His next task is to develop some discernment about which are truly preferences. Now the fun really begins, for the child, and for the parents.

C. ADOLESCENCE: DEVELOPING DISCERNMENT

In this section, we consider the problem of the adolescent. These young people are old enough to have some volition, and some capacity for independent action. But they may not be old enough to have good information about the Longings, and how to obtain them. We attempt to model the very familiar conflicts between teenagers and parents.

In this section, we bring our analysis of the Appetitess and the Longings to the forefront. The person is born with both Appetites and Longings. The Appetites are instrumental in producing the Longings, and the Appetites also give some utility independently of their impact on the Longings. At the same time, the production of the Longings is dependent on the Appetites.

We denote by A* the quantity of the Appetites that achieves the maximal production of the Longings. Consumption of A in amounts up to A* increases the output of the Longings, but consumption beyond A* actually diminishes it. For some consumption level higher than A*, the pure consumption value of the Appetite continues to outweigh the negative impact of A on the production of the Longing. But at some point, the impact of A on the production of the Longing becomes so negative that it outweighs the beneifts received from the pure consumption value of A. At consumption levels beyond this critical amount, A-, the indifference curves begin to slope upward.

For example, the Longing might be for good health, and the Appetite might be for food. In this case, the consumption of food up to some point is necessary and beneficial to good health. But excessive consumption of food might lead to worse health. The fact that the person values A independently of its impact on Health means that one might still consume food, even beyond the point where it is healthy to do so.

Now, we know that persons who face positive prices would never consume in the region beyond A-. So, what is the significance of this region for our analysis? We can use these indifference curves as a benchmark to analyze what would happen to a person who placed no weight on the Longings. We can also use them to analyze what might happen to persons who made certain types of errors in either prices or technology.

Let us consider then, a simple case in which a person might consume more than A-. Consider a person who places no weight on the Longings. Such a person would not consider the upward sloping region of the indifference curve. This person could readily end up consuming at a level beyond A-, especially at low prices of A, or at a high income level. While this person ostensibly

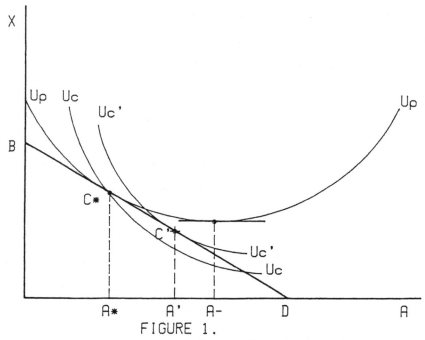

FIGURE 1.
THE CONFLICT BETWEEN PARENT AND CHILD.

suffers no utility loss from doing this, since the marginal utility of health is zero at all levels of health, his health will nonetheless deteriorate. And, when it does, he may decide that it is time for some reflection, and some reordering of the arguments of his utility function.

This, obviously is an extreme case. The person initially places no value at all on his health, and makes consumption decisions accordingly. He experiences some consequences of these decisions, decisions that were rationally made, by the usual economic criterion. Perhaps he has had a heart attack; perhaps he has become grossly over-weight. Or, perhaps someone close to him has experienced one of these consequences. After these experiences, he may shift into the mode of rational person as philosopher, and decide that his preference ordering may need adjustment.

We can use these indifference curves to model the conflict between teenagers and parents in the following way. Let us assume that the parents possess better information about the production of the Longings, or that they place a greater weight upon the Longings than do their teenage children. Perhaps the parents have experienced some of the disappointments associated with receiving less utility than they expected from their consumption decisions. Perhaps the teenagers regard themselves as immortal, and do not take seriously the possibility that their life can end, or that their health can fail, or that truly devastating things can happen to them. For whatever reason, we will proceed on the assumption that the parents place a greater weight on the Longings than does the teenager.

Figure 1 illustrates the conflict. We begin by noting that overconsuming A, relative to the standard of the production of the Longing is more likely when income is high, or the price of A is low. U'_p represents the parents' indifference curve on the child's behalf, while U'_c represents the child's indifference curve for himself. Note that in this figure, the indifference curves are shown intersecting at A*. The production of the Longing begins to be adversely affected by consumption levels beyond A*. The parents know this, and want the child to choose A*. At this combination of

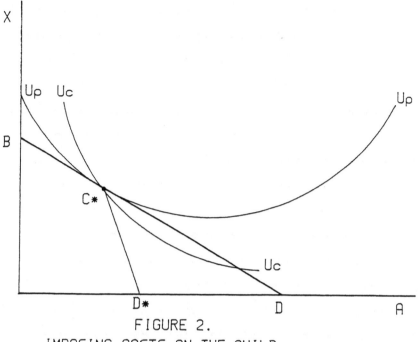

FIGURE 2.
IMPOSING COSTS ON THE CHILD.

prices and income, however, it is evident that the child will chose a larger amount of A. The child receives more utility from consuming A' at point C'.

This figure might illustrate the conflict over consumption of junk food. The parents want the child to consume a modest amount of greasy and sugary foods, while the child wants to eat every meal at McDonald's or Dairy Queen. The conflict might concern the amount of time spent in recreation rather than study. The parents want the child to limit partying to the weekends, and restrict the amount of T.V. that can be watched during the week. The child prefers to do more of both. Or, the conflict might arise over appropriate sexual conduct. The parents think dating is fine, but they do not want their teenager to be sexually active.

The parents realize what their child's preferences are, and attempt to set relative prices such that their child will choose A*. (Fig. 2) They can do this by imposing costs on the child, or imposing sanctions on the child for consumption beyond A*. Instead of allowing the child the full range of options indicated by the budget line BC*D, the parents impose costs for consumption beyond A*, so that the child's opportunity set becomes BC*D*. With this kink in the budget set, the child will chose to consume A*, just as the parents wish.

In the story we have told thus far, the child's optimal consumption is greater than is good for him, given the parents' relative weighing of the Appetites and the Longings. But, the child's preference for his Appetites are not so great that, at these prices and income, he chooses to consume beyond A-. And so, the child, if left unconstrained, might experience some negative consequences from his behavior. And from that experience, the child might conclude to make some alterations, either in his weighting of the Appetites and the Longings, or in his beliefs about the production of the Longings.

In particular, suppose the child, through experience, concludes that his parents were correct in their relative weighing, or in their information about the production of the Longings. In Fig. 3, we redraw Figure 1, with different labels. The parents permit the child to indulge himself, and consume

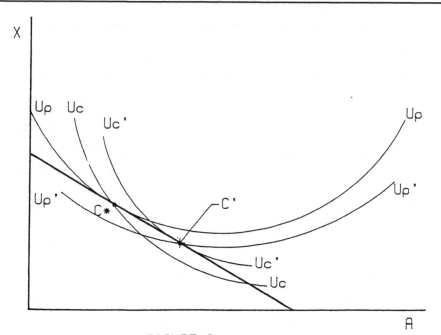

FIGURE 3.
FATHER AND MOTHER KNOW BEST.

at C'. The child expects to obtain utility level U'_b associated with this consumption level, given his preferences and beliefs about how consumption of these commodities will affect him. But, instead of experiencing U'_c he experiences something less.

His problem now, is a different class of problem from the sort economics usually considers. For, he knows that he did not get U'_c but he is not sure how to interpret what he did get. If he trusts his parents, he might conclude that he had obtained U'_p, which is the amount of utility that would be generated by his parents' utility map at the point C'. In that case, he might conclude that their utility map, with all its embedded information about values and technology, is one that he ought to adopt as his own.

If he does not trust his parents, he is not sure what to conclude from his disappointment. First of all, he might not be sure whether his disappointment was created by something specific about this particular experience, or whether the problem is more universal. If he concludes that his experience was not a fluke, and therefore that he ought to revise his beliefs, he still does not know very much.

Let us suppose that he actually knows both his actual utility level, U'_p, and marginal rate of substitution that he actually experienced, instead of the one he expected. He still would not know much about the whole utility map. He would know that the slope of the indifference curve was flatter than he expected, but he would not know by how much. In any case, he would be rational to attempt to incorporate this new information, somehow, into his preference ordering.

This discussion of learning from experience suggests that there might be a case for parents allowing children to "make their own mistakes". That is, there is a case for the parents not imposing costs on the child for consumption beyond A*, so the child can have the experience of finding for themselves just how much trouble they can create. There are at least two caveats to this as a general conclusion. First of all, the parents may not know for sure exactly what the child's utility function is. The graph as draw shows the child creating negative consequences that are nonetheless not completely devastating. But the parents may fear that the child would actually choose to consume beyond A-, where no rational person would ever go, at any price. That is, the parents may fear that the child would indulge themselves to such an extent that he would experience life-shattering consequences. And of course, they do not want that for their child. So, they may impose the costs as shown in Figure 2, simply to keep their child out of the most dangerous outcomes.

The second caveat is that, even if the parents do allow the child to learn from making some mistakes, the child still will not be fully sure what to conclude from his mistakes, as we have already discussed. If a person is trying to -infer the technology of the Longings, solely from his own experience and without any guidance from others, it make take many iterations, a long time, and a lot of anguish. It is not reasonable to suppose that the young person is born with all necessary information about how to achieve the Longings. Therefore, the parents will want to offer some guidance and information about a reasonable interpretation of the child's experience.

How much weight the child will give to this input will depend on how much he trusts his parents. If he does not trust them, he may completely discard all their information, no matter how intrinsically sound it may be. And, of course, parents are aware of the possibility that their counsel and advice may completely backfire.

If the child trusts his parents, he may adopt their utility function as his own, especially after a bit of negative experience. But, if the child does not trust the parents, he will not automatically do so. In fact, the child may conclude that the negative consequences he is experiencing come solely from his parents and not from the intrinsic reality of the situation. "My dad is being a jerk" is a very different conclusion from, "this is bad for me."

There is one last case that can be mentioned before we leave this section on the conflict between parents and children. While the child lives at home, his parents have some capacity both to monitor his behavior, and to impose sanctions on him. When the child moves out, the parent has much less input. We might model this situation from the child's point of view as being a substantial fall in the price of indulging the Appetites.

Figure 4 illustrates the problem. We suppose that the child continues to place little or no weight on the Longings. Now that the child is away from home, the price to him of indulging himself falls. And, he may indulge himself in ways that take him not only beyond A*, but even beyond A-. The child consumes at A', well beyond A-, the point at which the harm from overconsuming would normally outweigh the intrinsic pleasure of the Appetite.

There may be considerable variation in the amount of negative experience needed to convince the now independent child to alter his preferences. Often, the first midterm is a rude awakening to the freshman who spends all his time partying. But other disappointments may be more difficult to process. Perhaps the child was accustomed to having most of his food choices made for him. And now, living in a dorm, he can eat dessert first and ignore the vegetables. It may take a long time for him to either gain weight, or develop health problems. And by the time this happens, he may have created eating habits that will be difficult to break. A young person may be hurt and feel used by a sexual encounter. A young woman might conclude that particular young man was a creep, and try again with someone else. She might conclude that all men are creeps, and give up. It might take her many iterations of believing that the Appetite of sex will lead to the Longing of Love, before she realizes that she had the sequence reversed.

And, even at these new, lower prices, the person who places some weight on the Longings would consume more than before, but still, not beyond A-. That is, the point A_p represents the parents' new optimal point, given the lower prices. A_p is greater than A*, so there is some overindulgence taking place relative to the original standard. But, the choice of the parent even at lower prices, is to consume less than A-.

This diagram thus accounts for two important phenomena. First, we see how a person could be led to consume beyond A-, at least for a while. Second, we see that lower prices could lead a person to consume more of the Appetites than is good for them, relative to the production of the Longings. We might describe this additional income, or lower relative price of the Appetite, as

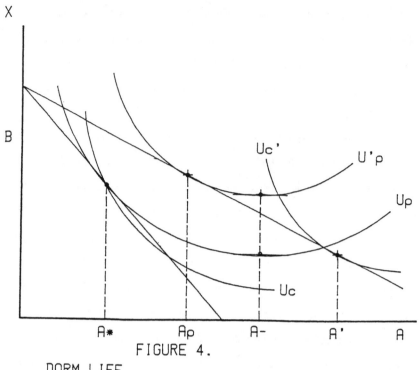

FIGURE 4.

DORM LIFE.

creating temptations. And so, we are led to ask whether it is possible that a person can have too much income, or whether relative prices can become too low.

CONCLUSION

This last observation, that even an adult might experience temptations to consume things which he knows to be not good for him, will lead us well beyond the scope of this paper and this conference. Nonetheless, we might want to consider the implications for the developmental process taking place within the family. The process of re-evaluating one's beliefs and preferences is one that can continue for a lifetime. If the rational person encompasses not only calculation based upon given preferences, but also reflection and reconsideration of those preferences, then rationality actually requires this lifelong process.

One of the most remarkable facts of childhood, is the amazing pace at which the child learns. It is an awe-inspiring sight for us academics, who are "professional learners." For we can be aware that if we kept learning at the pace of childhood, throughout our lives, our knowledge would be so vast that we would be known the world over.

And yet one of the attributes of childhood that makes this pace of learning possible is the child's willingness and capacity to change. The child abandons old behaviors, ideas and strategies, without the slightest hint of defectiveness, shame or loss. The child gives up crawling and baby talk for walking and adult conversation, without feeling as if they had lost something. But as we grow older, we become more invested in our ideas and activities. We find it more difficult to change, even in the face of overwhelming evidence of better life strategies. We think it an admission of defeat, or wrongness, or mistakenness.

And so, taking preferences as given throws out many babies with the bathwater. The whole interior process of reflection and change is one that ought to continue throughout life. The fact that some people can admit mistakes easily, while others seem to never change is surely an important fact, one that can not be readily detected within a theory that takes preferences entirely as given. A theory of rational behavior ought to encompass the possibilty of making, detecting and correcting errors. Otherwise our theory of rationality becomes a theory of omniscience. And it would not be reasonable for a theory of rational behavior to be a theory of omniscience.

B
The Family Firm

[12]

Weak men and disorderly women: divorce and the division of labor

Steven L. Nock and Margaret F. Brinig

> There are people in Europe who, confounding together the different charac-
> teristics of the sexes, would make of man and woman beings not only equal
> but alike. They would give to both the same functions, impose on both the
> same duties, and grant to both the same rights; they would mix them in all
> things – their occupations, their pleasures, their business. It may readily be
> conceived, that by thus attempting to make one sex equal to the other, both are
> degraded; and from so preposterous a medley of the works of nature nothing
> could ever result but weak men and disorderly women. . . . The Americans have
> applied to the sexes the great principle of political economy which governs
> the manufactures of our age, by carefully dividing the duties of man from
> those of woman, in order that the great work of society may be the better
> carried on.
>
> (De Tocqueville, 1835, ch. XII)

De Tocqueville's observations about the political economy of gender relations
at the beginning of the nineteenth century reflected the prevailing patterns of
employment; husbands were gainfully employed for pay, and wives cared for
home and family (see also Brinig and Carbone, 1988). In the new millennium,
this pattern no longer describes most American couples.[1] Some writers have
surmised that the divorce rate has increased because the modern marriage deal
is unfair to women (Parkman, 1998), who must do "two shifts" – their labor
force hours plus the hours of housework that remain (Hochschild and Machung,
1989). Certainly, spouses who feel their marriages are unfair may feel that divorce is a better option. The traditional marriage, which exploited each spouse's
comparative advantage, is arguably more efficient than the two-earner couple
where housework is shared (Becker, 1991). But no research considers whether
specialization can be equated not just with efficiency but with marital stability.
That is the project of this chapter.

According to economist Gary Becker, even though a man and a woman
have functioned quite similarly prior to marriage, they will begin to specialize

---

[1] The most recent statistics from the US Department of Labor suggest that 61.0 percent of women
aged 15–44 are employed, compared with 73.6 percent of men of the same ages (Bureau of Labor
Statistics News, April 2001, Table A-1; http://www.bls.gov/news.release/pdf/empsit.pdf).

172   *Steven L. Nock and Margaret F. Brinig*

once the marriage begins (Becker, 1991, ch. 2; Grossbard-Schechtman, 1993; Allen, 1992). Specialization will occur as the couple realize gains from each partner's "comparative advantage" in one or more functions. Husband and wife will engage in two kinds of labor, which Becker calls market production and household production. The spouse involved in market production divides time between labor (earning money to purchase goods) and leisure activities (spending money, or at any rate not earning more). The spouse engaged in household production divides time between the production of household (or "Z" goods) and leisure (Becker, 1991: 32–41). In "Z" good production, the spouse transforms purchased goods into ultimate consumption goods (Gronau, 1980).

It is because one spouse may have even a tiny comparative advantage at household production that Becker predicts efficient spouses will specialize (Becker, 1985). He argues that, because only women can bear children, they have the comparative advantage when it comes to household production. This advantage will increase because growing girls will invest in human capital that enhances their efficiency at producing household goods (Becker, 1973), which creates a likelihood that they will follow a traditional path (Becker, 1974). Their husbands, on the other hand, will specialize in market production. They will choose human capital investments before marriage to maximize production in the labor force. Pre-marriage specialization will also make each a more attractive mate (Becker, 1991; Duncan and Duncan, 1978). This investment in human capital can produce gendered differences in comparative advantage even without biological differences (Hadfield, 1999).

Becker and others (Parkman, 1992) assume that there is specialization between husband and wife, but not among women. They apparently believe it is less "efficient" to hire someone else to do the wash or clean the house. This view has been criticized in the literature (Brinig, 1994; Brinig and Carbone, 1988) on the ground that it does not make sense to tout specialization in the labor force generally while making an exception for tasks that are commonly performed for the household.

In related work, many critics of the specialization model advocate a more modern notion of marriage as a partnership (Smith, 1990). This alternative assumes individualism within the marriage, equality among spouses, roughly equivalent earning capacity between the spouses, and a need for flexibility over the life cycle. Those who advocate a more egalitarian marriage presume that, as married women enter the labor force, their husbands will pick up a fair share of household tasks.

Since World War II, women have markedly altered their labor force participation profiles. Men, however, have not. Prior to 1970, women typically left the labor force shortly after marriage and/or childbirth, and they maintained lower

Divorce and the division of labor 173

Table 10.1 *Hours spent on housework*

	1960s	1970s	1978	1988
Women			26.7	21.3
Nonmarried			17.2	13.4
Married			29.1	23.6
Not employed	38.0–43.0	23.0–34.0	37.1	33.0
Employed	20.0–26.5	11.5–20.0	24.3	20.8
Men			6.1	7.4
Nonmarried			8.2	7.0
Married			5.8	7.5
Not employed	5.0–8.0	3.0–9.0	5.0	6.4
Employed	5.5–8.0	3.0–9.5	6.4	7.8

Sources: table derived from Blau (1998); data are drawn from the Panel Study of Income Dynamics, Institute for Social Research, University of Michigan, Ann Arbor.

rates of employment thereafter throughout the life course. But in recent decades, there has been growing convergence of life-course patterns of employment, and there is no longer a typical drop in married women's labor force participation rates when children are born (Spain and Bianchi, 1996).

Though married women have steadily increased their labor force activity, they continue to do the bulk of the housework. In table 10.1 we present summaries of time spent on housework by women and men since the 1960s. As these figures indicate, there has been little change in the relative commitment to household labor by men and women. Minor reductions in women's and minor increases in men's household labor are evident, though the magnitude of change is remarkably small.

Sociologists Goldscheider and Waite conclude their *New Families, No Families* by suggesting that Becker-style "old" families will not be possible for much longer.

Why can we not return to the old balance of men's and women's work and family roles, which were "fair" to each in terms of hours, and which provided children with mothers who cared for them intensively and fathers who supported them adequately? . . . The major problem for women posed by "old families" is demographic. With the increase in life expectancy and the decline in fertility, homemaking is no longer a lifetime career for women as a group. Either there has to be a division within their adult lives, with about half their time devoted to raising two or so children to adulthood and half spent in other occupations, or women have to be divided into mothers and workers, or "real" workers and "mommy track" workers. (Goldscheider and Waite, 1991, 202–3)

And what of "new" more egalitarian and sharing families? Although Goldscheider and Waite believe that this must be our future, they are less confident about the implications.

> We have suggested that such families have the potential to solve critical problems facing families today. But what do we really know about them? What effects does this pioneer family form have on marriages and families and on the men, women, and children who live in them? Are more egalitarian and sharing families possible? This is largely uncharted territory. (Goldscheider and Waite, 1991, pp. 204–5)

The current research attempts to navigate some of that unknown terrain. We show how husbands' involvement in *women's* tasks and wives' involvement in *men's* tasks affect the chances of marital disruption. We also explore the extent to which attitudes, as opposed to the fair division of labor, matter for marital stability.

1   Data and methods

Data

The National Survey of Families and Households (NSFH) was first administered in the United States in 1987–8 and included personal interviews with 13,007 respondents from a national sample. The sample includes a main cross-section of 9,637 households plus an oversampling of blacks, Puerto Ricans, Mexican Americans, single-parent families, families with stepchildren, cohabiting couples, and recently married persons. One adult per household was randomly selected as the primary respondent. Several portions of the main interview were self-administered to facilitate the collection of sensitive information and to ease the flow of the interview. The average interview lasted one hour and forty minutes. In addition, a shorter self-administered questionnaire was given to the spouse or cohabiting partner of the primary respondent. We use identical questions asked of the primary respondent and his or her spouse.

The second wave of the NSFH was conducted in 1992–4, five years after the original interview. The second wave included an interview of all surviving members of the original sample via face-to-face personal interview ($N = 10,007$) and a personal interview with the current spouse or cohabiting partner almost identical to the interview with the main respondent ($N = 5,624$). The second wave included a detailed marital history sequence that we used to determine changes in marital status since the first wave.

Our sample is restricted to *couples* who were in their first marriages at wave 1. Neither partner had been previously married. This restriction was imposed to avoid problems associated with remarriages, stepfamilies, and ex-spouses.

Divorce and the division of labor   175

Marital disruption

Our primary concern is marital disruption in the course of five years. We determined whether the couple divorced or separated after the initial interview. If they did, we recorded the month when the divorce or separation occurred. Of the 4,273 couples who met our criteria for inclusion in the first wave, unambiguous information about the subsequent status of their marriage was available for 3,592. Of these, 275 (6.3 percent) divorced and another 105 (2.9 percent) separated (where one spouse permanently moved out of the dwelling) in the course of the study. We treat divorce or separation as marital disruptions, and our equations combine the two. We have investigated divorces separately, and the results are essentially the same as those including separations.

Before considering the role of household labor, we control for the well-known determinants of divorce and separation (Bumpass and Sweet, 1995). Specifically, we include the following factors as controls in our equation:

1. age at first marriage for husband,
2. age at first marriage for wife,
3. the couple cohabited (with each other) before marriage,
4. number of children born to the couple,
5. husband's wage/salary income last year,
6. wife's wage/salary income last year,
7. race (of husbands, and whether the wife is the same race),
8. husband's years of schooling,
9. wife's years of schooling,
10. husband's parents are divorced, and
11. wife's parents are divorced.

To this basic set of predictors, we then add two measures of paid labor (husband's hours at paid work last week, and wife's hours at paid work last week) and four measures of household labor. In a third step, we add four related measures of perceived fairness. In a final equation, we investigate the possible interactions of perceived fairness and measures of household and paid labor.

Household labor

Our measures of household labor are intended to distinguish between those tasks traditionally performed by men and those traditionally performed by women. We relied on earlier studies (for example, Berk, 1995) to make this determination, though there was little question about the gendered nature of household labor. To verify our allocation scheme, we contrasted male and female commitments to each task with paired t-tests. All were statistically significant, and most showed large differences.

Table 10.2 *Average hours spent on household tasks by husbands and wives*

Household task	Husbands	Wives	N	Sig. *t*
1. Preparing meals	2.05	9.75	4.377	.001*
2. Washing dishes	1.76	6.07	4.377	.001*
3. Cleaning house	1.59	8.13	4.379	.001*
4. Outdoor tasks	4.96	1.81	4.380	.001*
5. Shopping	1.39	2.81	4.380	.001*
6. Washing, ironing	0.57	4.29	4.379	.001*
7. Paying bills	1.36	1.60	4.378	.001*
8. Auto maintenance	1.84	0.18	4.379	.001*
9. Driving others	1.15	1.39	4.372	.001*
Male tasks (4 + 8)	6.80	1.99	4.375	.001*
Female tasks (1 + 2 + 3 + 5 + 6 + 7 + 9)	9.87	33.98	4.381	.001*

Note: *paired samples *t*-test (2-tailed) is significant at $p < .001$.

Each spouse was asked to complete a page with the following questions:

The questions on this page concern household tasks and who in your household normally spends time doing those tasks. Write in the approximate number of hours per week that you, your spouse/partner or others in the household normally spend doing the following things:

1) Preparing meals
2) Washing dishes and cleaning up after meals
3) Cleaning house
4) Outdoor and other household maintenance tasks
5) Shopping for groceries and other household goods
6) Washing, ironing, mending
7) Paying bills and keeping financial records
8) Automobile maintenance and repair
9) Driving other household members to work, school, or other activities

For most household tasks, there is little question about which partner typically does most of the work. There are, however, two tasks for which there are only minor differences: Driving (#9) and Paying bills (#7). Husbands do slightly less of each than wives do (see table 10.2) and we treat both as female tasks. Given that husbands and wives commit roughly equal numbers of hours to these two responsibilities, considering them one way or the other has virtually no consequence for the analysis.

We created two summary measures of household labor. The first, *male tasks*, is the simple sum of hours spent on Outdoor and other Household Maintenance Tasks (#4) and Automobile Maintenance and Repair (#8). The second, *female tasks*, is the simple sum of hours spent on all other activities. Men and women spent significantly different amounts of time in each activity (even when the magnitude of such differences was minimal, as with Driving and Paying Bills), although none was the exclusive domain of only one gender. We calculated the number of hours husbands spent in "male" and "female" tasks, as well as the corresponding figures for wives. These four variables are our primary concern in the following equations.

The average hours spent in each of the activities is shown in table 10.2. There are clear differences between husbands and wives in their allocation of time to household tasks. Yet such efforts must be balanced against other commitments of time, especially paid labor. As others have shown (Shelton, 1992; Berk, 1995; Hochschild and Machung 1989), the aggregate (total) amount of both paid and unpaid labor by married spouses is roughly comparable because differences in unpaid labor are compensated for by differences in paid labor. Husbands in this study report spending an average 34.3 hours in paid labor weekly compared with wives, who report an average of 18.5 hours. When both paid and unpaid labor are considered together, therefore, husbands report spending a total of 51.2 hours per week compared with 54.8 hours by wives.

Fairness

The division of tasks and responsibilities is known to be a source of tension for many married couples. It is also quite likely that any consequence of time spent in tasks is conditioned by how fair the allocation is seen to be. We include four measures (two each for husbands and wives) to capture the individual spouse's assessment of the fairness of things. Each spouse was asked:

How do you feel about the fairness in your relationship in each of the following areas?

1) Household chores
2) Working for pay

Answers were: 1 = Very unfair to me, 2 = Somewhat unfair to me, 3 = Fair to both, 4 = Somewhat unfair to him/her, and 5 = Very unfair to him/her. We use the original 5-point scoring of these variables. We explored many alternative specifications, including dummy variables for each value. Despite changes in the magnitude of some coefficients, the pattern of results was invariant over different specifications. This was so even for the middle category (3 = fair to both) and indicates that respondents interpreted the questions and answers as tapping increasing levels of unfairness to their partners.

Others (Smith, Gager, and Morgan, 1998) have suggested that this question actually taps two dimensions: a relative fairness dimension, and the quality of the marriage. Their research found that couples in happy marriages are less likely than those in unhappy marriages to answer this question. However, like most researchers who have considered issues of fairness in the household (for example, Lennon and Rosenfield, 1994; Thomson, 1991), Smith et al. did not consider fairness evaluations in other domains (for example, paid labor). As we show, considering both types of fairness is essential, and failure to do so produces different results than are found when both types of evaluations are considered. Moreover, to our knowledge, we are the first to include both spouses and both types of fairness evaluations in our models.

2   Method of analysis

Cox Proportional Hazards regression is used to determine the risk of divorce associated with each variable in the equation. In the hazards model, there is a risk of marital disruption at each month of duration until the disruption occurs. The risk may be affected by other variables included in the model. The Cox procedure first determines a baseline risk that is associated with months married (every marriage has a calculable risk of dissolution that changes monthly). Then each variable is assessed for how it alters this baseline risk. Our primary question is how allocations of household labor affect the risk of marital disruption.

Specifically, the Cox regression estimates the influence of the independent variables (X) on the hazard (h) of marital disruption as:

$$h(t) = [h_0(t)]e^{(BX)},$$

where $h_0(t)$ is the baseline hazard function when the independent variables, X, are set to zero (similar to the intercept in an OLS equation, or the expected risk of marital disruption when X is zero). B is the regression coefficient – the predicted change in the log hazard for a unit increase in the independent variable.

We present the Cox regression coefficient and its exponentiated (e^B) value in our results. The latter coefficient is labeled *RISK* in the tables, and is helpful for interpreting the magnitude of the effect of a variable. For dichotomous variables such as whether a couple cohabited before marriage, *RISK* indicates the increase (or decrease) in the risk of marital dissolution associated with cohabiting. If this coefficient were 2.0, for example, it would indicate that cohabiting doubles the (baseline monthly) risk of marital disruption. If it were 0.5, it would indicate that the risk is only half as great for those who cohabit as for those who do not. For continuous variables such as the hours spent at paid labor, *RISK* indicates the percentage change in risk with each additional hour worked. Were it to be 1.02 for example, it would mean that each additional hour worked increases the (baseline) risk of marital disruption by two percentage points. Were it 0.97, it would mean that each additional hour of work is associated with a 3 percent lower risk of disruption.

Summary statistics for all variables in the Cox regression equation are reported in table 10.3. We report the results of the Cox regressions in table 10.4. The equation is developed in four steps. In the first, we enter the known

Divorce and the division of labor   179

Table 10.3 *Summary statistics for all variables*

Sample characteristic	Average/percentage	Standard deviation
Years in current marriage	18.99	15.74
Percent who separated/divorced	10.58%	
Husband age at marriage	24.47	5.41
Wife age at marriage	22.26	4.87
Percent of couples who cohabited before marrying	18.34%	
No. of children born to couple	2.12	1.79
Husband wage/salary Wave I ('000)	20.76	26.81
Wife wage/salary Wave I ('000)	8.59	27.69
Husband White	78.97%	
Husband Black	10.45%	
Husband Hispanic	7.24%	
Husband Asian	1.13%	
Husband American Indian	0.36%	
Spouses different races?	13.61%	
Husband years of schooling	12.84	3.43
Wife years of schooling	12.74	2.91
Husband's parents divorced	9.26%	
Wife's parents divorced	9.15%	
Husband hours at paid work last week	34.30	21.82
Wife hours at paid work last week	18.52	19.80
Husband's hours on "men's" tasks last week	6.80	8.75
Husband's hours on "women's" tasks last week	9.87	13.71
Wife's hours on "men's" tasks last week	1.99	4.17
Wife's hours on "women's" tasks last week	33.98	23.73
Husband's fairness: household	3.21	0.56
Wife's fairness: household	2.71	0.64
Husband's fairness: paid work	3.01	0.48
Wife's fairness: paid work	2.99	0.50

Note: $N = 2,892$.

predictors of marital disruption. In the second, we add the summary measures of hours spent on men's and women's tasks by husbands and wives as well as hours spent at paid employment. In the third model, we enter the assessments of the fairness of the division of household and paid labor to determine whether they operate independently of the allocation of time committed to these tasks. In the final model, we add interactions between the measures of fairness and involvement in paid and household work. Our objective in entering these terms is to investigate whether perceptions about fairness condition the consequences of household or paid labor commitments.

The interaction terms added in the fourth model are created by multiplying each of the four fairness questions (husband's and wife's evaluation of household and paid labor) by hours in each of the three types of labor (paid, male, and female tasks), resulting in twelve terms. This strategy produces both similar and dissimilar types of task-and-fairness evaluation interactions. That is, men's evaluations of the fairness of *paid labor* are multiplied by men's involvement in *paid labor*. But men's evaluations of the fairness of paid labor are also multiplied by men's involvement in *household labor*. By investigating both types of possible interactions, we are able to determine whether one type of task spills over into another type. It is possible, for instance, that both types of interactions just described might be associated with higher or lower divorce rates. Were this so, it would suggest that the effect of hours in paid labor is conditioned by men's sense of fairness in *both* paid and unpaid tasks. On the other hand, were we to find that only the second interaction affected divorce rates, this would suggest that men's involvement in paid labor spills over into the household labor project, where men's hours at paid work matter more when household tasks are viewed as unfairly divided.

3   Findings

The first model confirms well-known results. Those who cohabit before marrying, for example, have dissolution rates that are much higher than those who do not cohabit. As table 10.4 shows, the relative RISK of dissolution is 5.88 times higher for those who cohabited prior to marriage. This value is obtained by exponentiating the value of the regression coefficient, $B = 1.7717$. In this case, $e^{1.7717} = 5.88$. Other factors found to influence marital disruption include the presence of children (reduces RISK), being Black (increases RISK), young age at first marriage (significant only for wives, owing to the high correlation between spouses' ages at first marriage), and experiencing one's parents' divorce.

In Model 2, the six measures of time allocation are added. Husband's time at paid labor increases the risk of disruption by about 1.5 percent for each additional hour worked per week. There is no corresponding effect for wife's paid employment.

Our primary interest is in the effects of household tasks performed by husbands and wives. The first such variable shows the effects of hours that men spend on traditionally male tasks. Each hour in such pursuits is associated with about 2.4 percent *reduction* in risk of dissolution. On the other hand, when men do traditionally female tasks, dissolution risks are *increased* by about 1.3 percent for each additional hour spent in such efforts. In short, for husbands who do those tasks normally done by men, the chances that their marriages will end through divorce or separation are reduced. When men venture into less traditional, more female tasks, however, the chances their marriages will dissolve are increased.

Table 10.4 Cox regressions predicting marital disruption

Variable	Model 1		Model 2		Model 3		Model 4	
	B	RISK	B	RISK	B	RISK	B	RISK
Control variables								
Cohabited	1.7717	5.8808**	1.6776	5.3528**	1.6677	5.2998**	1.6651	5.2863**
Number of children	−0.6076	0.5447**	−0.6187	0.5387**	−0.6291	0.5331**	−0.6475	0.5234**
Husband's wages	−0.0019	0.9981	−0.0047	0.9953	−0.0046	0.9954	−0.0050	0.9951
Wife's wages	−0.0101	0.9899	−0.0130	0.9870	−0.0108	0.9893	−0.0103	0.9898
Husband Black	0.4167	1.5169*	0.3728	1.4519*	0.3759	1.4562*	0.4213	1.5239*
Husband Hispanic	0.3080	1.3607	0.2441	1.2765	0.2716	1.3120	0.3054	1.3572
Husband Asian	0.3517	1.4215	0.2471	1.2804	0.2455	1.2783	0.2506	1.2848
Husband American Indian	0.5910	1.8058	0.4515	1.5707	0.3698	1.4475	0.3338	1.3962
Different races	0.0184	1.0186	0.0492	1.0505	0.0402	1.0410	0.0396	1.0404
Husband's education	0.0017	1.0017	−0.0141	0.9860	−0.0164	0.9837	−0.0219	0.9783
Wife's education	0.0017	1.0017	−0.0083	0.9918	−0.0154	0.9847	−0.0142	0.9859
Husband age marriage	0.0002	1.0002	0.0041	1.0041	0.0039	1.0039	0.0055	1.0055
Wife age marriage	−0.0757	0.9271**	−0.0689	0.9334**	−0.0700	0.9324**	−0.0745	0.9282**
Husband parents divorced	0.6762	1.9665**	0.6231	1.8648**	0.5941	1.8115**	0.5326	1.7033**
Wife parents divorced	0.6771	1.9681**	0.6203	1.8594**	0.6096	1.8396**	0.6080	1.8368**
Division of labor								
Husband hours paid work			0.0154	1.0155**	0.0154	1.0155**	0.0090	1.0091
Wife hours paid work			0.0019	1.0020	0.0015	1.0015	0.0360	1.0367*
Husband hours male tasks			−0.0244	0.9759**	−0.0253	0.9750**	−0.0926	0.9115
Husband hours female tasks			0.0133	1.0134**	0.0150	1.0151**	0.1142	1.1210*
Wife hours male tasks			−0.0417	0.9592	−0.0386	0.9621*	−0.2882	0.7496*
Wife hours female tasks			0.0065	1.0065*	0.0066	1.0066*	0.0497	1.0509**

continued overleaf

Table 10.4 (*cont.*)

Variable	Model 1		Model 2		Model 3		Model 4	
	B	RISK	B	RISK	B	RISK	B	RISK
Sense of fairness								
Husband household					-0.1558	0.8557	0.1775	1.1942
Wife household					-0.2478	0.7805**	-0.4391	0.6446*
Husband paid work					-0.3753	0.6871**	-0.6066	0.5452*
Wife paid work					-0.0176	0.9825	0.7369	2.0895**
Fairness–hours interaction								
Husband fairness paid × hours male tasks							0.0201	1.0203
Husband fairness paid × hours female tasks							-0.0218	0.9784
Husband fairness household × hours paid							-0.0054	0.9946
Wife fairness paid × hours male tasks							0.0884	1.0925*
Wife fairness paid × hours female tasks							-0.0141	0.9860**
Wife fairness household × hours paid							0.0092	1.0093*
Husband fair household × hours male tasks							0.0029	1.0029
Husband fair household × hours female tasks							-0.0017	0.9883*
Wife fair household × hours male tasks							-0.0079	0.9922
Wife fair household × hours female tasks							-0.0002	0.9997
Husband fair paid × hours paid work							0.0083	1.0084
Wife fair paid × hours paid work							-0.0199	0.9803**
N	2,858							
–2LL	778.310							
Change (–2LL)	443.766**		44.070**		20.076**		24.066**	

*Note: *p* < .05, **p* < .01 for coefficient or for –2LL change over prior model.

Doing female tasks appears to increase the likelihood of disruption regardless of who does them. Wives' investment in traditionally female tasks leads to marginally higher risks of breakup. Though very small in magnitude (about 0.7 percent per hour), this effect was also found among husbands. Each additional hour that *wives* spend on *male tasks* is associated with a reduction of about 4 percent in the risk of dissolution. In sum, when wives do tasks typically done by husbands, their marriages appear to have lower chances of disruption. When wives increase their involvement in tasks typically done by women, however, their marriages may have higher chances of disruption.

Before interpreting the results already presented, it is necessary to consider the perceived fairness of the division of tasks. In Model 3, the coefficients for two of the four measures of fairness are statistically significant: the wife's sense of fairness in household tasks, and the husband's sense of fairness in paid labor. Both are negative, meaning that, when wives believe the division of household labor or when husbands believe the division of paid labor is *unfair to the other partner,* disruption rates are lower (alternatively, when things are seen as unfair to oneself, disruption rates are higher). These results suggest that perceptions of fairness play a role in how time spent in household and paid labor matters for marital stability. In the final model, we address this issue directly.

The final equation (Model 4) adds twelve interaction terms to investigate how perceptions of fairness moderate the various effects of household labor just described. Five interaction terms are statistically significant, indicating that household and paid labor have differing implications depending on how spouses view the fairness of their arrangements. Four of the five significant interaction effects involve wives' evaluations of fairness. Since there are so many interaction terms, and several pertain to the same variables, the results are difficult to summarize without an illustration.

The interaction effects indicate that similar investments in paid and household labor have different consequences for marital stability depending on how they are perceived (that is, on the evaluation of fairness). To summarize these results, we present the combined effects of the relevant variables in table 10.5. The entries in this table are the changes to the baseline risk of marital disruption associated with each combination of the four questions about fairness. To compute the *RISK* values reported in the table, we evaluated couples at the average (mean) level of involvement in all types of paid and unpaid labor (and at the mean of every other variable except those pertaining to fairness and interactions). Then we added the relevant fairness variables and the interaction terms to produce the change in the baseline risk of dissolution that would result. For example, the first entry in table 10.5 is 4.43. This value indicates that, when time in paid and household labor (and all other variables in Model 2 of table 4) are at the averages, the baseline risk of dissolution is 4.43 times greater when both spouses see each type of labor as "very unfair" to themselves. The

Table 10.5 *Combined effects of interactions of fairness and hours of work on risk of marital disruption*

	Husband's sense of fairness about paid work								
	Very unfair to me Husband fairness household work			Fair to both Husband fairness household work			Very unfair to her Husband fairness household work		
Wife's sense of fairness about paid work	Very unfair to me	Fair to both	Very unfair to her	Very unfair to me	Fair to both	Very unfair to her	Very unfair to me	Fair to both	Very unfair to her
Very unfair to me Wife fairness household work									
Very unfair to me	4.43	3.10	2.17	2.06	1.44	1.01	0.96	0.67	0.47
Fair to both	2.55	1.79	1.25	1.19	0.83	0.58	0.55	0.22	0.16
Very unfair to him	1.47	1.03	0.72	0.68	0.48	0.34	0.32	0.22	0.16
Fair to both Wife fairness household work									
Very unfair to me	8.48	5.93	4.15	3.94	2.76	1.93	1.83	1.28	0.90
Fair to both	8.48	3.42	2.39	2.27	1.59	1.11	1.06	0.74	0.52
Very unfair to him	2.82	1.97	1.38	1.31	0.92	0.64	0.61	0.82	0.30
Very unfair to him Wife fairness household work									
Very unfair to me	16.22	11.35	7.95	7.54	5.28	3.69	3.51	2.45	1.72
Fair to both	9.35	6.55	4.58	4.35	3.04	2.13	2.02	1.42	0.99
Very unfair to him	5.39	3.77	2.64	2.51	1.75	1.23	1.17	0.82	0.59

value 4.43 was obtained by calculating the baseline risk of marital disruption from Model 2, with all variables at their averages. Then values for the four fairness and the twelve interaction terms were varied and their effects were added to the baseline risk. The value for all questions about fairness in this example was 1.0 (very unfair to me). Other cells were computed by changing the values for all fairness questions and the associated interaction terms.

Table 10.5 highlights a central, yet simple, finding of our work: the investment of time in male or female household tasks, or in paid labor, must be understood in connection with perceived fairness when evaluating the consequences for couples. The results in table 10.5 may be summarized by comparing "best" and "worst" cases. The "worst" outcome (that is, the highest *RISK* of 16.22) is found among couples who disagree in an interesting way. Both partners think that paid work is unfair to the husband. They disagree over housework. He sees paid and household work as unfair to him. She also sees paid work as unfair to him. But she sees household work as unfair to herself. The best outcome (that is, the lowest *RISK* of 0.16) is found when the husband sees both paid work and household tasks as very unfair to his wife. She agrees about paid work (very unfair to her), but thinks housework is fair to both, or very unfair to her husband.

Perhaps the most surprising result is found in the case of agreement that paid and household tasks are fair to both partners. The middle cell of the table has a value of 1.59, indicating that this combination is associated with higher risks of divorce. Complete agreement that both spouses are treated fairly, in other words, may not be the best situation.

To gain a sense of the relative importance of the various types of fairness perceptions, we can compare the values of risk in the table. To do so, focus on blocks of nine cells defined by paid-work evaluations. The first such block consists of the nine cells defined by the husband's report that paid work is very unfair to himself, and the wife's report that paid work is very unfair to herself. Generally, the values in table 10.5 decline as one moves from left to right (that is, as husbands report that paid work is increasingly unfair to wives). Further, values increase as one moves from the top to the bottom of the table (that is, as a wife reports that paid work is increasingly unfair to herself). Thus, marriages in which husbands believe their wives bear an unfair burden for paid work and in which wives share that view are at lower risk of dissolution than other combinations. When it comes to perceptions about the fairness of household tasks, another pattern appears. At any combination of values for paid work (for example, the first block of nine cells) agreement by both partners that the arrangement is unfair to the *other person* produces the best outcomes (that is, the lowest risk of disruption). For example, when both partners feel that paid work is unfair to themselves (the first nine-cell block in the table), the risks of disruption range from 4.43 to 0.72. The highest risk obtains when partners each feel household tasks are unfair to themselves. The lowest value obtains when both feel such tasks are unfair to their partner.

Focusing first on how perceptions of fairness about *paid work* influence disruption risks, we compare comparable cells from any two blocks. Men's evaluations of the fairness of paid work alter the risks of disruption by a factor of 2.15 (e.g. 4.43 versus 2.06). Women's evaluations of the fairness of paid work, similarly, alter disruption risks by a factor of 1.91 (e.g. 8.48 versus 4.43). Men's sense of fairness about paid work, in short, is minimally more consequential than is women's.

By focusing on the cells within any block, it is possible to assess the relative importance of perceptions of fairness about *household tasks*. Doing so shows that husbands' sense of fairness about household work changes the risk by a factor of about 2.04 (moving left to right in any block of cells, such as 4.43 versus 2.17) and wives' by a factor of about 3.01 (moving from top to bottom in any block of cells, such as 4.43 versus 1.47). Women's sense of fairness about household work is considerably more consequential than is men's, and more consequential than either partner's concerns about the fairness of paid work.

4   Discussion

We sought to provide a rudimentary answer to the question asked by Goldscheider and Waite (1991): What effect does an egalitarian division of household labor have on marriages? The simplest answer is that marriages are strained when either partner does more traditionally female housework. At the same time, marriages are strengthened by time spent in traditionally male tasks. But this simple conclusion ignores the complexity of the social psychology of the household. At a minimum, "efficiency" (specialization) does not mean "stability." Doing more traditionally male tasks, such as home and auto maintenance, increases marital stability *no matter who does them* and no matter whether the worker is employed or not. This is not consistent with Becker's analysis.

What might explain the difference in the impact of "men's" and "women's" work? Traditionally male jobs, when done outside the household, are better paying than are traditionally female jobs, and tend to be (psychologically) valued more highly. Particularly for the middle-class couples at the mean of our sample, who together were earning roughly $40,000 a year in 1987–8, doing such work for the household may not seem degrading (and may actually seem rewarding). For example, the Bureau of Labor Statistics (United States Department of Labor, 1988) reports weekly earnings of $444 for carpentry and floor work, $385 for plumbing and heating, and $332 for auto repair. In contrast, for either spouse (and particularly men), doing the lower-paying, lower-status "female" work apparently lowers the value of the marriage. The same Bureau of Labor Statistics data show weekly earnings of $210 for residential care, $146 for miscellaneous personal services, $206 for laundry-dry cleaning and garment services, and $159 for retail bakeries. In 1985, men employed as repairers and mechanics earned an average of $400 weekly, compared with the $130 women earned in private household service (United States Department of the Census, 1998, table 698).

There are other, and related, explanations for the difference between the effects of "men's" and "women's" work on marital stability. "Men's work" tends to contribute directly to the value of the couple's tangible assets. For example, building an addition on a house or installing thermally efficient windows will increase the home's resale value. (It will also increase the share of the property allocated to whoever did or financed the improvement, should the couple divorce). Doing work on an automobile may save costly repairs and may increase the car's resale or trade-in value. On the other hand, ironing shirts or keeping a spotless home enhances assets in a much less direct and tangible way.

With higher possible wages, better household technology (Cohen, 1995), and fewer children, late-twentieth-century American women no longer typically dropped out of the paid labor force (Bianchi and Spain, 1996). But the answer to Hochschild's "second shift" problem is not (at least not yet) more sharing of typical homemaking tasks. Our research shows that such a solution would probably increase marital instability. It will not be possible for most couples to eliminate such tasks by, for example, hiring domestic servants. Nor is it likely that American society will suddenly begin to value "women's work" by increasing the wages of those who are engaged in such pursuits. So long as housework is devalued (Silbaugh, 1996; Hadfield, 1993), we can predict that greater sharing of such work will probably contribute to marital instability. But this gloomy assessment must be tempered by the significant role played by assessments of fairness. As our findings showed, such perceptions are critically important, and may trump any particular combination of hours committed by either partner to any particular task.

When married partners share the belief that paid work is unfair to wives and that housework is unfair to the other person, the risks of dissolution are lowered significantly. Whether such marital dynamics are sufficient to overcome any particular division of tasks, of course, cannot be answered with our results. But our results suggest that we may err by paying too much attention to the actual division of tasks and too little attention to how people understand such arrangements.

Though we cannot explain why particular combinations of fairness evaluations are associated with different risks of marital disruption, we are prepared to offer some thoughts about why perceived (mutual) fairness may be incompatible with marital stability. Why would perceived fairness in all matters by both spouses not be the best arrangement? The question is both provocative and central to our thinking about marriage and the household division of labor. As spouses, we worry about fairness or rights at times when our affections for each other or our commitment to the marriage ebb to a low point (Waldron, 1988, p. 628). When we contribute to marriage with an expectation of direct return or reward, we get less from it. Law deals with the tendency to contractualize marriage by making it unattractive. Thus cases, even relatively recent ones, consistently deny enforcement of wives' contracts to receive wages in exchange for their housework (Silbaugh, 1996). As a California case reports,

The dissent maintains that mores have changed to the point that spouses can be treated just like any other parties haggling at arm's length. Whether or not the modern marriage has become like a business, and regardless of whatever else it may have become, it continues to be defined by statute as a personal relationship of mutual support. Thus, even if few things are left that cannot command a price, marital support remains one of them.[2]

[2] *Borelli v. Brusseau*, 16 Cal.Rptr.2d 16, 20 (Cal. Ct. App. 1993).

The psychological literature reveals that spouses who see marriage in exchange terms have lower levels of satisfaction with marriage than other spouses do (Hansen. 1991). Sociological research also shows that marriages are more stable when the spouses depend upon one another (Nock, 1995). When husbands and wives are able to look beyond immediate fairness and to act for the benefit of the other, the children, or the marriage, they take what Milton Regan calls an internal stance (Regan, 1999, p. 24) which "is central to a meaningful interpersonal relationship and the growth of love" (Rempel. Holmes, and Zanna, 1985, p. 110). And this is what the very low values in the upper right-hand block of table 10.5 show. But why marriages benefit when husbands and wives agree that wives are treated unfairly, but suffer when they agree that husbands are treated unfairly (the block at the lower left of table 10.5), is still unclear. Perhaps wives are, in some fundamental sense, more unfairly treated in marriages. Possibly, the contemporary arrangement of American marriages casts women and men in asymmetrical relationships that are inherently unfair in some way. If so, then our results are easily understood. An appreciation for such unfairness, that is, apparently contributes to marital stability. Men and women, it seems, derive some benefit (in marital stability) for acknowledging this issue. Lack of appreciation for the unfair burden may cause women to file for divorce, and it is primarily they who do so (Brinig and Allen, 2000).

Can we have egalitarian marriages? Is it possible to envision a pattern of housework and paid labor that is fair to both partners and that does not undermine the stability of the union? Our results suggest that mutual perceived fairness or an exchange-type relationship may not be the most desirable situation if stable marriages are the desired outcome. *Stable marriages, that is, may not be experienced as fair marriages*. And, although stable marriages are possible with greater sharing of housework. such sharing may not produce desirable outcomes unless both partners understand that wives bear an unfair burden.

REFERENCES

Allen, Douglas (1992), "What Does She See in Him? The Effect of Sharing on the Choice of Spouse," *Economic Inquiry*, 3(1). 57–67.
Becker, Gary S. (1973). "A Theory of Marriage, Part I," *Journal of Political Economy*, 81(4), 813–46.
    (1974), "A Theory of Marriage: Part II," *Journal of Political Economy*, 82(2). S11–26.
    (1975), *Human Capital: A Theoretical and Empirical Analysis, with Specific Reference to Education*, 2nd edn., New York: National Bureau of Economic Research. Columbia University Press.
    (1985), "Human Capital, Effort, and the Sexual Division of Labor," *Journal of Labor Economics*, 3, S33–58.
    (1991). *A Treatise on the Family*, Cambridge, MA: Harvard University Press.

Becker, Gary, Elisabeth M. Landes, and Robert T. Michael (1977), "An Economic Analysis of Marital Instability," *Journal of Political Economy*, 85(6), 1141–87.

Berk, Sarah Fenstermaker (1995), *The Gender Factory: The Apportionment of Work in American Households*, New York: Plenum Press.

Bianchi, Suzanne M. and Daphne Spain (1996), "Women, Work, and Family in America," *Population Bulletin*, 51(3), 2–48.

Blau, Francine W. (1998), "Trends in the Well-Being of American Women, 1970–95," *Journal of Economic Literature*, 36, 112–65.

Brinig, Margaret F. (1994), "Comment on Jana Singer's Alimony and Efficiency," *Georgetown Law Journal*, 82, 2461–79.

Brinig, Margaret F. and Douglas W. Allen (2000), "These Boots Are Made for Walking: Why Most Divorce Filers are Women," *American Law and Economics Review*, 2, 126–69.

Brinig, Margaret F. and June Carbone (1988), "The Reliance Interest in Marriage and Divorce," *Tulane Law Review*, 62, 853–905.

Bumpass, Larry L. and James A. Sweet (1995), "Cohabitation, Marriage and Union Stability: Preliminary Findings from NSFH2," NSFH Working Paper No. 65, Madison, Center for Demography and Ecology.

Bumpass, Larry, Teresa Castro, and James A. Sweet (1990), "Recent Trends in Marital Disruption," *Demography*, 26(1), 37–52.

Cohen, Lloyd (1995), "Rhetoric, the Unnatural Family, and Women's Work," *Virginia Law Review*, 81, 2275–305.

Duncan, Beverly and Otis D. Duncan (1978), *Sex Typing and Social Roles: A Research Report*, New York: Academic Press.

Goldscheider, Frances K. and Linda J. Waite (1991), *New Families, No Families? The Transformation of the American Home*, Berkeley: University of California Press.

Gronau, Reuben (1980), "Home Production – A Forgotten Industry," *Review of Economics and Statistics*, 62(3), 408–16.

Grossbard-Schechtman, Shoshana (1993), *On the Economics of Marriage: A Theory of Marriage, Labor, and Divorce*, Boulder, CO: Westview Press.

Hadfield, Gillian K. (1993), "Households at Work: beyond Labor Market Policies to Remedy the Gender Gap," *Georgetown Law Journal*, 82, 89–107.

(1999), "A Coordination Model of Sexual Division of Labor," *Journal of Economic Behavior and Organization*, 40, 125–53.

Hansen, Gary L. (1991), "Moral Reasoning and the Marital Exchange Relationship," *Journal of Social Psychology*, 131, 71–81.

Hochschild, Arlie and Anne Machung (1989), *The Second Shift*, New York: Viking Penguin.

Lennon, Mary Clare and Sarah Rosenfield (1994), "Relative Fairness and the Division of Housework: The Importance of Options," *American Journal of Sociology*, 100, 506–31.

Nock, Steven L. (1995), "Commitment and Dependency in Marriage," *Journal of Marriage and the Family*, 57, 503–14.

Parkman, Allen W. (1992), *No-Fault Divorce: What Went Wrong?* Boulder, CO: Westview Press.

(1998), "Why Are Married Women Working So Hard?" *International Review of Law and Economics*, 18, 41–9.

Regan, Milton C. (1999), *Alone Together: Love and the Meaning of Marriage*, Oxford: Oxford University Press.

Rempel, John K., John G. Holmes. and Mark P. Zanna (1995), "Trust in Close Relationships," *Journal of Personality and Social Psychology*, 49, 95–120.

Shelton, Beth Ann (1992), *Men, Women, and Time: Gender Differences in Paid Work, Housework and Leisure*, New York: Greenwood Press.

Silbaugh, Katharine (1996), "Turning Labor into Love: Housework and the Law," *Northwestern University Law Review*, 91, 1–86.

Smith, Bea (1990), "The Partnership Theory of Marriage: A Borrowed Solution Fails," *Texas Law Review* 68, 689–743.

Smith, Herbert L., Constance T. Gager, and S. Philip Morgan (1998), "Identifying Underlying Dimensions in Spouses' Evaluations of Fairness in the Division of Household Labor," *Social Science Research*, 27, 305–27.

Spain, Daphne G. and Suzanne M. Bianchi (1996), *Balancing Act: Motherhood, Marriage, and Employment Among American Women*, New York: Russell Sage Foundation.

Thomson, Linda (1991), "Family Work: Women's Sense of Fairness," *Journal of Family Issues*, 12, 181–96.

Tocqueville, Alexis de (1835), *Democracy in America*. New York: Vintage Books, ed. 1954.

United States Department of Labor (1988), Bureau of Labor Statistics, *National Employment, Hours and Earnings*, Series ID: EEU80729004, etc.

United States Department of the Census (1998), *Statistical Abstract of the United States*, Rockville, MD.

Waldron, Jeremy (1988), "When Justice Replaces Affection: The Need for Rights," *Harvard Journal of Law and Public Policy*, 11, 625–47.

[13]

HOW TO PLOT LOVE ON AN
INDIFFERENCE CURVE

Brian H. Bix*

FROM PARTNERS TO PARENTS: THE SECOND REVOLUTION IN FAMILY LAW. By *June Carbone*. New York: Columbia University Press. 2000. Pp. xv, 341. Cloth, $49.50; paper, $18.50.

INTRODUCTION

In *From Partners to Parents: The Second Revolution in Family Law*, June Carbone[1] offers nothing less than a whirlwind tour of the current doctrinal and policy debates of Family Law — an astounding feat in a book whose main text (excluding endnotes and appendices) does not reach 250 pages. There seem to be few controversies about which Carbone has not read widely and come to a conclusion, and usually a fair-minded one: from the effect of no-fault divorce reforms on the divorce rate,[2] to the long-term consequences of slavery for the African-American family (pp. 67-84), to whether the Aid to Families with Dependent Children ("AFDC") program (prior to the recent reforms) influenced the number of nonmarital children (pp. 32-33, 96), just to name three. As it seems impossible to give a faithful overview in a few pages of a text which is already a remarkable work of concision, this Review will focus on three themes highlighted or implicated by the book: (1) the title theme — the way family law has changed its focus from the behavior of adults within a marital or nonmarital relationship ("partners") to the behavior of adults towards their children ("parents");[3] (2) the problems for legal reform when our choices are so deeply affected, and perhaps determined, by history and social norms; and (3) how an attention to history and culture can be used

---

* Frederick W. Thomas Associate Professor of Law and Philosophy, University of Minnesota. D. Phil., Oxford University; J.D., Harvard University. — Ed.

I am grateful to Katharine K. Baker, Margaret F. Brinig, Stephen G. Gilles, Robert W. Gordon, Leonard J. Long, Eric A. Posner, Warren F. Schwartz, Katharine B. Silbaugh, Adam Tomkins, Elizabeth Warren, Jamison Wilcox, and those who attended a workshop at Quinnipiac Law School for their helpful comments and suggestions.

1. Professor of Law, Santa Clara University School of Law.

2. Pp. 86-90. In the course of her discussion, Carbone points to data showing a surprisingly constant increase in divorce rates over the last 140 years, with slight drops for marriages begun in the 1950s and 1980s. Pp. 86-87.

3. In the language of the subtitle, this is the "second revolution," with the change from a fault system of divorce to one that is largely no-fault being the first. P. xiv.

both to deepen and to oppose an economic approach to domestic relations. In connection with this third theme, this Review will also offer some brief comments on the modern hybrids of law and economics and family law scholarship.

I.   FROM PARTNERS TO PARENTS

There was a time when the common law (and society) created severe legal and social handicaps for children born outside of wedlock, with this being justified as a reasonable way to encourage marriage.[4] Starting in the late 1960s, the United States Supreme Court decided a series of cases holding that legal distinctions grounded on legitimacy were to be subject to heightened scrutiny.[5] Constitutional Law courses do not spend much time on this issue any more due to the fact that it is rare to come across cases,[6] in large part because the states have removed many of the laws that discriminate facially between what we now call "marital" and "nonmarital" children.[7] As a related matter, the Uniform Parentage Act, adopted by eighteen states,[8] has the pur-

---

4. The traditional perspective was well summarized by James Fitzjames Stephen:

> Take the case of illegitimate children. A bastard is *filius nullius* — he inherits nothing, he has no claim on his putative father. What is all this except the expression of the strongest possible determination on the part of the Legislature to recognize, maintain, and favour marriage in every possible manner as the foundation of civilized society? . . . It is a case in which a good object is promoted by an efficient and adequate means.

James Fitzjames Stephen, *Liberty, Equality, Fraternity*, in LIBERTY, EQUALITY, FRATERNITY AND THREE BRIEF ESSAYS 156 (University of Chicago Press 1991) (1873).

   Even more telling, if also more strange to modern sensibilities, there was a time when regulating access to marriage was considered sufficient to control (or at least, to affect strongly) population. *See, e.g.,* DANIEL J. BOORSTIN, THE CREATORS 674 (1992) ("Under the Austro-Hungarian laws designed to curb the Jewish population, only the eldest son in any Jewish family was allowed a marriage license.").

5. *See, e.g.,* Weber v. Aetna Cas. & Sur. Co., 406 U.S. 164 (1972) (invalidating a state rule which prohibited illegitimate children from recovering under a worker's compensation law when their fathers died); Levy v. Louisiana, 391 U.S. 68 (1968) (striking down a Louisiana statute excluding illegitimate children from recovery for the wrongful death of a parent). *See generally* LAURENCE H. TRIBE, AMERICAN CONSTITUTIONAL LAW § 16-24, at 1553-58 (2nd ed. 1988) ("Discrimination Against Illegitimates"). Like discrimination on the basis of sex, discrimination on the basis of illegitimacy has been held to warrant "intermediate" scrutiny, somewhere between rational basis review and strict scrutiny. Clark v. Jeter, 486 U.S. 456, 461 (1988).

6. By way of example, one current constitutional law casebook devotes less than four pages, out of over 1500, to "Illegitimacy and Related Classifications." WILLIAM B. LOCKHART ET AL., CONSTITUTIONAL LAW 1308-11 (8th ed. 1996).

7. What few cases there have been in the last twenty years have mostly arisen not from laws which directly discriminate against nonmarital children by denying them some right or benefit, but which discriminate indirectly, for example, by making it difficult to bring a paternity action. *See, e.g.,* Mills v. Habluetzel, 456 U.S. 91 (1982) (striking down a highly restrictive rule for bringing paternity actions on behalf of illegitimate children).

8. UNIF. PARENTAGE ACT, 9B U.L.A. 287 (1987 & Supp. 2000).

pose and effect of "providing substantive legal equality for all children regardless of the marital status of their parents . . . ."[9]

The removal of most legal disabilities for nonmarital children exemplifies the basic theme of Carbone's text: Within American family law there has been a growing doctrinal disconnect between the parents' relationship with one another and their rights and obligations regarding their children.[10] There was a time when one's rights and obligations towards one's children were defined in a large part indirectly, by one's relation to the children's other parent. Married parents had rights and obligations that unmarried parents lacked (p. 164), and one's chances of gaining custody after divorce (or even after the other parent's death)[11] depended on one's relationship with and behavior towards the other parent. Marital misbehavior, for example, would be "punished" by denial of custody (p. 181). The rights of nonmarital children, and the rights and obligations of unwed parents (especially unwed fathers)[12] to those children, are only the sharpest examples of this theme. Another prominent piece of evidence for the change of focus is the growing trend of courts to hold allegations of immorality by a parent irrelevant to a child custody decision unless and only to the extent that this alleged immorality affects the fitness of that person *as a parent*.[13] That approach has two apparent advantages: (1) it changes

---

9. *Id.* at 289.

10. Pp. xi-xiv, 40-41, 131-32, 154-79, 227-41. Ironically, though the legal treatment of nonmarital children is a good example of the point Carbone is making, the topic is treated only briefly in the book, p. 35, and there primarily as an example of the state regulation of sexual morality.

11. See, for example, *Stanley v. Illinois*, 405 U.S. 645 (1972), where the Court considered, and invalidated, a state statute that conclusively presumed that unmarried fathers were unfit parents, whose children should be taken from them; the case involved an unmarried father whose children were taken from him under the statute after the mother, with whom he had cohabited, had died.

12. *See, e.g.*, Lehr v. Robertson, 463 U.S. 248 (1983) (holding that unwed fathers have constitutionally protected rights in their relationship with their children, but only if they act to create a connection with those children); Stanley v. Illinois, 405 U.S. 645 (1972) (invalidating on equal protection grounds a state statute that presumed conclusively that unwed fathers were unfit parents, when no similar presumption was made for unwed mothers). As Carbone points out, pp. 164-79, the Supreme Court's jurisprudence on unmarried fathers' rights is not easy to rationalize, and may be explicable in part on the basis of an unstated preference for unwed fathers who have maintained some sort of connection with their children's mothers. (This usually unstated preference is connected to, but goes beyond the more frequently expressed preference for marriage. *See, e.g., Lehr*, 463 U.S. at 263 ("The most effective protection of the putative father's opportunity to develop a relationship with his child is provided by the laws that authorize formal marriage and govern its consequences.").)

13. *See, e.g.*, Hassenstab v. Hassenstab, 570 N.W.2d 368 (Neb. App. 1997) (refusing to modify custody based on the custodial parent's homosexuality and alcohol consumption); Sanderson v. Tryon, 739 P.2d 623 (Utah 1987) (holding that an initial custody award could not be made based solely on one parent's continued participation in polygamous practices); Judith R. v. Hey, 405 S.E.2d 447 (W. Va. 1990) (reversing a court order that conditioned continued custody on that parent's either marrying the man with whom she was cohabiting or ending that relationship). Not all courts have followed this trend. *See, e.g.*, Roe v. Roe, 324 S.E.2d 691 (Va. 1985) (reversing the award of custody to a parent, the reversal based

the focus more prominently to the interests of the child, rather than using the children as rewards for complying with societal norms; and (2) it reduces the number of times when courts must make controversial judgments about what is sometimes called "personal morality."[14] This approach, however, can also lead to problem cases: As Carbone notes (pp. 186-87), courts sometimes seem predisposed to ignore even bad acts that *should* be seen as evidence of parental unfitness — most egregiously, domestic violence.[15]

The growing legal disconnect between behavior to one's partner (the decision to marry, followed by proper marital behavior) and one's parental rights and obligations exemplifies a more basic shift in the way family life is structured, perceived, and regulated. There was a time when a combination of social norms and economic circumstances meant that a woman who was pregnant would either marry the father or give up the child for adoption; in an earlier era, such marriages lasted because divorce was difficult and often (especially for marital wrongdoers) expensive,[16] and because women, with limited prospects in the workplace and the legal disabilities under coverture, could rarely afford to leave a bad marriage (pp. 88-90, 95). Today, a man who gets a woman pregnant is less likely to feel obligated to marry her, and a woman will frequently be willing either to raise the child on her own or get an abortion (pp. 90-95).

---

solely on that parent's active homosexual relationship); *cf.* Lynn D. Wardle, How Children Suffer: Parental Infidelity and the "No-Harm" Custody Presumption (1999) (unpublished manuscript) (arguing that a parent's adultery *should* be a factor against that parent's receiving custody).

14. There is an ongoing debate about the extent to which the government should be concerned, through criminal prohibitions or otherwise, with adult actions which affect only the actors themselves. *See generally* John Stuart Mill, *On Liberty, in* ON LIBERTY AND UTILITARIANISM 1-133 (Bantam ed., 1993) (1859); Stephen, *supra* note 4; H.L.A. HART, LAW, LIBERTY, AND MORALITY (1963). For an overview of the debates, see BRIAN BIX, JURISPRUDENCE: THEORY AND CONTEXT 145-54 (2nd ed. 1999).

15. *See, e.g.,* Collinsworth v. O'Connell, 508 So. 2d 744 (Fla. App. 1987) (affirming a decision granting both parents shared responsibility for their child, despite evidence of the father's violence against the mother). As Carbone also observes, however, p. 187, more recent court judgments, abetted at times by legislative directives, *have* considered evidence of domestic violence in making custody decisions. *See, e.g.,* Custody of Vaughn, 664 N.E.2d 434, 438 (Mass. 1996) (holding that in custody decisions the court must consider "the special risks to the child in awarding custody to a father who had committed acts of violence against the mother"); *see also* ARIZ. REV. STAT. ANN. § 25-403 (West 2000) (prohibiting the awarding of joint custody where there has been domestic violence).

16. Divorce was expensive in the sense that the former husband's obligation to pay alimony would likely turn on whether he or his wife was at fault in the marriage — the "fault" of one party (and the innocence of the other party) had to be shown before a court would dissolve the marriage. *See, e.g.,* GLENDA RILEY, DIVORCE: AN AMERICAN TRADITION 15, 38, 48, 50 (1991) (discussing alimony during the fault-divorce period). It may be, though, as one historian has recently suggested, that for some unhappy spouses, "leaving was a possibility, even where legal divorce was not." HENDRIK HARTOG, MAN AND WIFE IN AMERICA: A HISTORY 1 (2000).

Carbone's attitude towards such changes in family life is implied more than expressed; it is a mixture of resignation and approval: resignation, in that the changes seem the result of our reaction and adaptation to other societal changes (for example, the greater equality of women, including greater workplace opportunities; and the greater availability of contraception and abortion);[17] and approval, in that the author, tacitly, seems to favor the greater autonomy and lower level of moral supervision and criticism of people's romantic, sexual, and marital lives. There is also a note of regret: however problematic the former approach to family life may have been in many ways (not least in its exploitation of women), it appears to have been largely successful in ensuring that children generally had the care of two parents, and that resources were passed from one generation to the next. Carbone raises reasonable doubts that our current approach to marriage, family, and children can work nearly as well (pp. 49-52, 126-27, 132).

II. THE IMPLICATIONS FOR REFORM

Carbone gets to the heart of questions about family law reform and policy: "With the dismantling of the fault system [of divorce] that had championed the sexual division of marital labor, neither law nor feminism supplied what should be the core of family regulation — the identification of the distinctive *family* values for the law to promote and protect" (p. 27). She is not referring to the "family values" of conservative political rhetoric, but simply the sense of having some vision of an ideal regarding how intimate and family life should be structured (and regulated) within society.

In his dissent in *Bowers v. Hardwick*, Justice Blackmun wrote: "We protect the family because it contributes so powerfully to the happiness of individuals, not because of a preference for stereotypical households."[18] While that may be an accurate characterization of what the Constitution does or should protect, as a matter of policy it is dubious at best. We *do* have some notion as to the *social* benefits of marriage and families, even beyond their undoubted role in the happiness and fulfillment of individuals. Stable marriages and families may be valuable to society, not only as a good context in which to raise children, but also for the same reason that other intermediate institutions (whether volunteer organizations, social organizations, or religious institutions) are valuable to society's flourishing (pp. 38-40). However, even were we to have a clear sense of where we wanted to go — which social institutions and family structures to strengthen and which to discourage — it is far from clear how we can get there. As Carbone ac-

---

17. Pp. 53-66, 85-110. Carbone's general approach to historical analysis and social change will be discussed in the next section.

18. Bowers v. Hardwick, 478 U.S. 186, 205 (1986) (Blackmun, J., dissenting).

knowledges, there are difficulties in "linking public policy concerns to individual behavior at a time when older norms have given way, and there is no consensus on their replacement" (p. 42).

Carbone brings light and insight to many current family law debates by placing them in their larger historical context. She effectively uses history to undermine the arguments for certain current reform proposals, and to alter the way many family law issues are perceived.[19] However, her way of presenting our current social situation as the, perhaps inevitable,[20] result of long-term factors, factors largely beyond our control and more or less impervious to manipulation through law, works equally to undermine her own suggestions regarding legal and social reform.[21]

If one goes back not just decades, but generations, even centuries, one comes across a family structure quite different from the one that predominates today: where the married couple and their children were very much a part of the larger community, and under the constant supervision of that community (pp. 100, 123-24). "The household was the basic unit of production *and* reproduction in a hierarchical society in which church, community, and family overlapped. Without clear boundaries between public and private, the individual never escaped supervision."[22] That family structure changed over time into one more recognizable to modern eyes. Borrowing a term from Milton Regan, Jr.,[23] Carbone speaks of the "Victorian family" and describes it as developing around the eighteenth century in both England and America (pp. 99-100). Married couples gained separation from the community, with significant consequences: (a) the raising of children became the main responsibility of and, increasingly, the primary focus of, individ-

---

19. Looking at the longer term can clarify how we may be seeing current phenomena against a false "baseline." Carbone is effective in reminding us that we seem constantly to be comparing our current situation to the actual or imagined situation in the 1950s, when that period was, over the longer historical view, the anomalous period. P. 88.

Attention to history can also lessen the tendency to speak of "the nature of marriage," for history shows how the institution has changed radically over previous centuries, and even in the course of the most recent decades. See Brian Bix, *Reflections on the Nature of Marriage, in* REVITALIZING THE INSTITUTION OF MARRIAGE FOR THE 21ST CENTURY (Alan J. Hawkins, Lynn D. Wardle & David Coolidge eds., forthcoming, 2001).

20. In Carbone's discussions, as in much historical work, it is hard to distinguish explanations that society changed in a certain way, from more ambitious claims that these changes were *inevitable* given the prior conditions.

21. Carbone's inconsistency on the efficacy on legal intervention is set out insightfully and at length in Katharine Silbaugh's review. Katharine B. Silbaugh, *Accounting for Family Change*, 89 GEO. L.J. 923, 964-66 (2001) (reviewing *From Partners to Parents*).

22. P. 100. One might add that, especially prior to the industrial revolution, one's marriage partner was often also a partner in one's business, a needed extra hand in one's work, whether one was working on the farm or as an artisan; this fact had obvious and important implications for the way people thought about marriage and divorce. See E.J. GRAFF, WHAT IS MARRIAGE FOR? 11-16 (1999) (describing the historical "working marriage").

23. MILTON REGAN, JR., FAMILY LAW AND THE PURSUIT OF INTIMACY 4 (1993).

ual families; and (b) there were growing demands on and greater expectations for marriage, as the haven from commercial and public life, and as the source of intimacy and emotional support (pp. 100-10).

Carbone portrays domestic life as being produced by broad ideas regarding the family, combined with (related) ideas regarding gender roles and sexuality. The Victorian family contained the earlier-mentioned isolation from the larger community and the separation of public and private spheres, along with a strong sense of gendered roles, both within and outside marriage (p. 101). The structure of domestic life was also strongly influenced by the sexual mores, as already discussed[24] (for example, that it was understood that when premarital sex resulted in pregnancy, the couple married, and this understanding was reinforced by strong social norms and sanctions (p. 91)).

The Victorian family has been transformed (or, if one prefers, "undermined") by a series of societal changes in attitude and opportunity: greater emphasis on individual fulfillment, higher levels of premarital sex combined with the greater availability of contraception and abortion, greater opportunity for women in the workplace, and more social acceptance of nonmarital cohabitation, nonmarital births, and divorce (pp. 93-110). The result has been significantly higher levels of divorce,[25] nonmarital births, and children raised by single parents (pp. 88-90, 118-27).

There is currently much talk about, and some action toward, reforming family law, often to try to bring us back to the allegedly better, more moral, and more responsible past. Many recent enacted and proposed reforms in the family law area have been driven at least in part by the general belief that children are harmed by current trends in family structure, and that these trends can and should be fought. AFDC benefits were modified in part because of the belief that the prior benefit structure discouraged marriage and encouraged the birth of nonmarital children;[26] and various divorce reforms, including the "covenant marriage" laws enacted in Louisiana, Arizona, and

---

24. *Supra* text accompanying note 16.

25. Where marriages were once held together by dependence, the stigma of divorce, or strongly internalized feelings of duty and role, marriages now grounded on intimacy and companionship are more fragile, for they have little reason to continue when those values have faded. Pp. 104-05.

26. P. 94; *see also* Tonya L. Brito, *From Madonna to Proletariat: Constructing a New Ideology of Motherhood in Welfare Discourse*, 44 VILL. L. REV. 415, 425-27 (1999) (summarizing the pro-marriage, anti-illegitimate birth rhetoric related to welfare reform).

Arkansas[27] were justified in part by the harm allegedly being done to children by divorce.[28]

While there are studies that seem to show that the children of single parents or divorced parents do less well than the children of intact two-parent homes,[29] Carbone argues that all this may show is that they fare less well *in this society*, a society that is arguably built around the "traditional" two-parent family (p. 49). Martha Fineman has argued that our society does not do enough to support "inevitable dependency" (those who cannot care for themselves – the very young, the very old, and the seriously ill) or "derivative dependency" (those, usually women, who cannot support themselves because they are devoting most or all of their time to caring for the "inevitably dependent").[30] Fineman suggests shifting the state subsidization of the traditional family to those providing the care, be they single parents, divorced parents, or married parents.[31] Carbone returns again and again to the fictional character "Murphy Brown" because that character (and many real-world counterparts with similar resources) has the wealth to protect her child(ren) from many of the usual effects of not having a second parent.[32] If the problem of single parenthood is (only or primarily) that there is no one to support the caregiver, then (a) single parents who *have* sufficient resources should not be criticized; and (b) we should consider creating greater community and/or government support for single caregivers who do not already have such resources (pp. 51-52).

---

27. *See* ARIZ. REV. STAT. ANN. §§ 25-901 to -906 (West 2000); LA. REV. STAT. ANN. §§ 9:272-275.1 (West 2000); 2001 Ark. Acts 1486.

28. *See, e.g.*, Katherine Shaw Spaht, *Louisiana's Covenant Marriage: Social Analysis and Legal Implications*, 59 LA. L. REV. 63, 63-72 (1998) (summarizing the child-focused justifications of the covenant marriage proposal).

29. These studies are complicated by related findings: The children of widowed parents do not seem to be harmed (relative to the children of two-parent families) the way the children of unmarried single parents and divorced parents are, and the children of step-parents do less well than those in other two-parent households. Pp. 111-14.

30. *See* MARTHA ALBERTSON FINEMAN, THE NEUTERED MOTHER, THE SEXUAL FAMILY AND OTHER TWENTIETH-CENTURY TRAGEDIES 161-66 (1995) (discussing the inadequate societal responses to inevitable and derivative dependencies).

31. P. 28 (quoting FINEMAN, *supra* note 30, at 233).

32. Pp. 44-47, 51. One can and should ask about the social forces and circumstances that encourage the belief, including among many of the caretakers themselves, that taking care of children is normally or ideally seen as primarily the responsibility of an isolated parent (usually a mother) for whom caretaking is that parent's exclusive or predominant job. *See* Katharine K. Baker, *Taking Care of Our Daughters*, 18 CARDOZO L. REV. 1495 (1997) (reviewing FINEMAN, *supra* note 30) (suggesting that it is important for caretaking to be degendered).

While Carbone has her doubts about most of the current crop of reform proposals,[33] she has her own ideas for change. For example, she is concerned that the nuclear family can no longer work effectively for the welfare of children because it can no longer shield children, especially teenagers, from the dangers and temptations of the larger world (pp. 221-26, 241). She calls, therefore, for some way of re-establishing the ties between family and community that might bring in societal resources for helping to protect and raise those children (p. 241). Additionally, she promotes a model of a generally egalitarian "supportive partnership" in marriage (pp. 235-38). Far less clearly expressed is what should or could be done in either case (by way of legal or social action) to get there from here.

This "black box" in Carbone's analysis, the mystery element that explains the changes in family life over time and why certain reforms have succeeded or failed, seems to be the same as the "black box" in many economics-driven discussions of law: the internalized beliefs/attitudes/values that some call morality, others sentiment (pp. 99, 235), and others "social norms."[34] What is crucial for change is that people's values and attitudes change. When such changes occur, parallel legal reforms tend to follow (Carbone's example is no-fault divorce following a more individual- and autonomy-focused attitude towards marriage and a more tolerant attitude towards divorce (pp. 89-90)). However, when proposed reforms act *against* such values and attitudes, they are bound to fail. The question, then, is how to get people to adopt desirable values and attitudes. For this most basic question, Carbone offers no answers.[35] This is neither surprising nor the justification for criticism; if we *did* know how to change "hearts and minds," we would have the key to political (and utopian) change, which politicians, reformers, and philosophers have sought for millennia.

III. Engagement with Economics

Beyond its clear merits as a guide to the current theoretical, empirical, and policy debates within family law, Carbone's book is important in the way it exemplifies the current engagement between family

---

33. She writes: "It is possible to demonstrate conclusively that children have suffered from family instability without uncritically embracing proposals to restrict divorce or nonmarital births." P. 118.

34. *See infra* note 53.

35. At one point, Carbone summarizes Stephanie Coontz's work on the connection between women's increasing autonomy and the divorce rate by saying, "changes in behavior preceded the changes in attitudes." P. 90. This only leads to the question, however, "what (changes in values or attitude) caused the changes in behavior?" There is no obvious stopping point to such explanatory regresses.

law and law and economics.[36] Economic analysis, understood broadly to include public choice, game theory, and other variations of rational choice analysis, has become dominant, or at least highly influential, in nearly every area of (American) legal scholarship.[37] Family Law has been one of the areas most resistant to the encroachment of economic analysis,[38] but in recent years the emphasis has been more on how to co-opt, adapt, or modify economics analysis than on how to avoid or refute it. Efforts to apply or adapt economic analysis to family law have come from both directions: from economically minded theorists trying to explain domestic relations (and domestic relations law), and from family law scholars considering the value and limitations of economic analysis.[39] Standard economic analysis as applied to domestic relations starts from the assumption that individuals are trying to maximize their self-interest (even) in that part of their lives; decisions

---

36. "Engagement" may be just the right word, as its two primary meanings show the contrary aspects of the current connection between family law and law and economics: (1) (romantic engagement) as a close connection, in contemplation of an even closer one; and (2) (military engagement) as an event that is part of a larger struggle.

37. Some things are lost when "law and economics" is defined this broadly, with the implication that it is a monolithic whole. In fact, there are important debates and disagreements *within* this large category. For example, game theory entails a sharp critique of traditional economic analysis, *see infra* note 43, and the approach of "new institutional economics" used in Margaret Brinig's work, *see* MARGARET F. BRINIG, FROM CONTRACT TO COVENANT 6 (2000) also deviates from and criticizes the traditional approach, *see* Thráinn Eggertsson, *Neoinstitutional Economics*, *in* 2 THE NEW PALGRAVE DICTIONARY OF ECONOMICS AND THE LAW 665, 665 (Peter Newman ed., 1998) (describing how this approach varies from "neoclassical economics"). Many of the modern economic writers on "social norms" also argue that traditional economic analysis is subject to basic criticisms. *See, e.g.*, ERIC A. POSNER, LAW AND SOCIAL NORMS 4 (2000) (criticizing "[t]he positive branch of law and economics" for assuming that individuals are "unaffected by the attitudes of others" when they make choices).

38. The first important contribution to the economic analysis of family law may be GARY S. BECKER, A TREATISE ON THE FAMILY (enlarged ed., 1991) (1981). Economic attention to domestic relations is relatively recent. As Becker observes, "[a]side from the Malthusian theory of population change, economists hardly noticed the family prior to the 1950s . . . ." BECKER, *supra*, at 3.

39. The first group would include Gary Becker, BECKER, *supra* note 38; Allen Parkman, *e.g.*, ALLEN M. PARKMAN, NO-FAULT DIVORCE: WHAT WENT WRONG? (1992); Eric Posner, POSNER, *supra* note 37, at 68-87 ("Family Law and Social Norms"); and Eric Rasmusen and Jeffrey Stake, *e.g.*, Eric Rasmusen & Jeffrey Evans Stake, *Lifting the Veil of Ignorance: Personalizing the Marriage Contract*, 73 IND. L.J. 453 (1998). The second group would include Margaret Brinig, *e.g.*, BRINIG, *supra* note 37; June Carbone, *e.g.*, CARBONE, FROM PARTNERS TO PARENTS: THE SECOND REVOLUTION IN FAMILY LAW (2000); *see also* Margaret F. Brinig & June Carbone, *The Reliance Interest in Marriage and Divorce*, 62 TUL. L. REV. 855 (1988); Ann Estin, *e.g.*, Ann Laquer Estin, *Love and Obligation: Family Law and the Romance of Economics*, 36 WM. & MARY L. REV. 989 (1995); Rhona Mahony, *e.g.*, RHONA MAHONY, KIDDING OURSELVES: BREADWINNING, BABIES, AND BARGAINING POWER (1995); Milton Regan, *e.g.*, MILTON C. REGAN, JR., ALONE TOGETHER (1999); Katharine Silbaugh, *e.g.*, Katharine B. Silbaugh, *Turning Labor into Love: Housework and the Law*, 91 NW. U. L. REV. 1 (1996); Amy Wax, *e.g.*, Amy L. Wax, *Bargaining in the Shadow of the Market: Is There a Future for Egalitarian Marriage?*, 84 VA. L. REV. 509 (1998); and Joan Williams, *e.g.*, JOAN WILLIAMS, UNBENDING GENDER: WHY FAMILY AND WORK CONFLICT AND WHAT TO DO ABOUT IT (2000).

whether and whom to marry, how to structure marital life, whether to have children and how many, whether to divorce, etc., are all treated as explicable in terms of preferences, incentives, and disincentives.[40] (A core insight of law and economics, the Coase theorem, states that in cases of incompatible rights or activities, it is the individuals' preferences and valuations that determine what occurs; law, the effect of legal rules, is reduced to near irrelevance[41] — though the application of this claim to family law has been, strangely, relatively muted.[42])

---

40. *See, e.g.*, ALLEN M. PARKMAN, GOOD INTENTIONS GONE AWRY: NO-FAULT DIVORCE AND THE AMERICAN FAMILY 4 (2000) ("Economists view the decision to marry and, sometimes, to divorce as based on the benefits and the costs associated with those choices.... Over time, the costs and the benefits of marriage and divorce can change, and then the incentives to marry and to stay married also change.").

41. The Coase theorem states that in a world without transaction costs, the initial distribution of entitlements (for example, whether one party has the right to pollute or the other party has the right to enjoin the pollution) will have no effect on the eventual distribution of entitlements: entitlements will end up with the parties who value them the most. *See* Ronald Coase, *The Problem of Social Cost*, 3 J.L. & ECON. 1 (1960), *reprinted in* R. H. COASE, THE FIRM, THE MARKET, AND THE LAW 95-156 (1988). Among the many efforts to summarize Coase's Theorem are RICHARD A. POSNER, ECONOMIC ANALYSIS OF LAW 55-61 (5th ed. 1998), and BIX, *supra* note 14, at 183-87. Thus, whether, for example, *A* pollutes *B*'s land or not depends entirely on whether *A* values the right to pollute more than *B* values the right not to be subject to pollution, and depends *not at all* on whether *A* or *B* starts with the right. If *A* values the right more than *B*, but does not start with the right, *A* will simply pay *B* for the right. *See* COASE, *supra*, at 97-114. The Market trumps the Law. Of course, and this is Coase's point as well, our world is one of pervasive and often substantial transaction costs, and under such conditions, the initial distribution of entitlements *can* affect the eventual distribution. The extra costs of transacting (contacting the relevant parties, negotiating, drafting the contract, etc.) may mean that *A* will not be able to buy out *B*'s right, even though, transaction costs aside, *A* values the right more than *B*. *See id.* at 114-19.

42. The most obvious and prominent battleground for the application of the Coase theorem to family law is the question of whether the move to no-fault divorce caused the recent rise in divorce rates. Some economic commentators, following the Coase theorem (or a close analogue), and purporting to have data to back up the theorem's predictions, *do* claim that the move to no-fault ("unilateral") divorce laws has had *no* effect on divorce rates. *See, e.g.*, H. Elizabeth Peters, *Marriage and Divorce: Informational Constraints and Private Contracting*, 76 AM. ECON. REV. 437, 437, 452 (1986) (arguing that data supports a Coase theorem-like model: "empirical results show that the divorce rates are not significantly different in unilateral and mutual consent states"); *cf.* BECKER, *supra* note 38, at 15, 324-41 (modifying the conclusion of an earlier edition, that the change in divorce laws should have *no* effect on divorce rates, but only to the conclusion that the change of divorce laws explains *a small part (only)* of the change in divorce rates). On the other hand, many commentators, also apparently supported by empirical data, argue that no-fault *has* made a difference. *See, e.g.*, BRINIG, *supra* note 37, at 153-58; BECKER, *supra* note 38, at 15. One might argue that the latter position is consistent with the Coase theorem on the basis that the theorem allows for legal rules to have effects when there are significant transaction costs. *See supra* note 41. "There is, however, little evidence that such problems [transaction costs] are more pressing in the context of divorce than in other bargains. Even under fault-only regimes, the great majority of divorcing couples resolved their differences before litigation through a separation agreement." BRINIG, *supra* note 37, at 154 (footnote omitted); *see also id.* at 157 (summarizing an empirical study by Martin Zelder which concluded that "transaction cost barriers do not prevent the parties from bargaining around the divorce regime").

An interesting development is a shift towards using game theory in family law scholarship.[43] Game theory, with its emphasis on strategic behavior and imperfect and asymmetric information, seems particularly apt for discussions of "negotiations" between partners before, during, and after marriage.[44] The application of game theory to family law appears promising in many ways, but it is still at an early stage, so its strengths and limitations remain difficult to discern.

One point of tension between (many) family law scholars and (many) law and economics scholars is the idea, assumption, or contention that people acting in love, within marriage, or with their immediate family are best understood as attempting to maximize their self-interest.[45] (One must be careful about terminology: "self-interest should not be confused with selfishness; the happiness (or for that matter the misery) of other people may be a part of one's satisfactions."[46]) The reason family law has always seemed a good candidate to resist law and economics (rational choice theory) is that our actions in the context of love and family seem to be among the actions *least* likely to correspond to the "rational self-maximizer" model. Milton

---

43. Game theory has been defined as the study of the question: "How do, or should, individuals conduct themselves when each realizes that the consequences of his individual acts will depend in part on what other independent actors do?" Stephen W. Salant & Theodore S. Sims, *Game Theory and the Law: Ready for Prime Time?*, 94 MICH. L. REV. 1839, 1846 (1996) (reviewing DOUGLAS G. BAIRD ET AL., GAME THEORY AND THE LAW (1994)) (footnote omitted). The advantages of game theory over traditional neo-classical economic analysis are well summarized by Kenneth Dau-Schmidt:

> Under traditional analysis, you have a variety of basic assumptions: people act rationally, perfect information, zero transaction costs. Under game theory, you can relax some of those assumptions. In fact, the point of game theory is to examine problems of imperfect information, strategic behavior or transaction costs. Where transactions costs and strategic behavior are important, game theory can provide a superior model.

Kenneth Dau-Schmidt et al., *On* Game Theory and the Law, 31 L. & SOC'Y REV. 613, 616 (1997) (reviewing DOUGLAS G. BAIRD ET AL., GAME THEORY AND THE LAW (1994)).

44. *See, e.g.*, Wax, *supra* note 39 (showing how differences in bargaining power and bargaining position between men and women can lead to inequalities within marriage); *cf.* MAHONY, *supra* note 39 (using a negotiation-based analysis of domestic life that approximates game theory); POSNER, *supra* note 37, at 68-87 (discussing family law issues using a "social norms" analysis that is in turn built in large part on game theoretical notions, like "signaling").

45. Becker writes: "In this book I develop an economic or rational choice approach to the family. . . . The rational choice approach . . . assumes that individuals maximize their utility from basic preferences that do not change rapidly over time . . . ." BECKER, *supra* note 38, at ix.

46. POSNER, *supra* note 41, at 4. Becker is similarly careful to note that people can be, and often are, altruistic, altruism being defined as when an individual's "utility function depends positively on the well-being of" another person. BECKER, *supra* note 38, at 278. Becker does not deny that individuals have altruistic feelings towards their close relatives; to the contrary, he goes to some length to consider the (economic) effects of pervasive altruism within the family. *Id.* at 277-306.

Regan's work[47] picks up one aspect of that claim, by arguing that married individuals are (and often should be) thinking basically in "we" terms rather than "I" terms. Regan argues that spouses move back and forth between an "external stance" towards their marriage — a critical and reflective stance that can be roughly equated with that of economic analysis and utility maximizing — and an "internal stance," within which the marriage is part of a universe of shared meaning, a starting place quite different from that of individual utility maximization.[48] Thus, Regan's response to a comment like "spouses will stick with a marriage only if it produces a marital surplus — in the form of potentially utility-enhancing gains for each party — and only if each spouse receives some share of the surplus,"[49] is that it misses the extent to which married people do[50] think in terms of the couple or the family as the agent whose interests are to be maximized, and not each person as an individual agent.[51]

The problem of bounded rationality offers another basis for resisting law and economics[52] — in general, but especially in the area of domestic relations. There are certain kinds of choices most individuals do not make in a rational fashion, as "rational" is defined in economic analysis.[53] These types of choices would seem to include many of those

---

47. *See* REGAN, *supra* note 39. For an insightful critique of Regan's book, see Katharine B. Silbaugh, *One Plus One Makes Two*, 4 GREEN BAG 2d 109 (Autumn 2000).

48. On the difference between "internal" and "external" stances, see REGAN, *supra* note 39, at 5-6, 15-30; on the equation between the economic perspective and the external stance, see *id.* at 33-86.

49. This is Amy Wax's summary of the rational choice approach to marriage. Wax, *supra* note 39, at 529 (footnote omitted). Wax expressly indicates that she is not affirming the validity of the rational choice model and that she is aware of the problems bounded rationality may create for that model. *Id.* at 526-27 n.32.

50. And, Regan might add, "should."

51. *See* REGAN, *supra* note 39, at 62-73 (arguing that economic analysis cannot account for the "internal perspective"). Such a claim goes beyond, and is more complicated than, a Beckerian concession that individuals can be altruistic. *See supra* note 46. Under Regan's analysis, spouses do not merely altruistically desire good things for their partners and children; they *identify* themselves with marriage or the family. *See* REGAN, *supra* note 39, at 5-6, 22-30, 62-73.

52. *See generally* JUDGMENT UNDER UNCERTAINTY: HEURISTICS AND BIASES (Daniel Kahneman et al. eds., 1982) (collecting articles about bounded rationality); BEHAVIORAL LAW & ECONOMICS (Cass R. Sunstein ed., 2000) (collecting articles discussing the implications of bounded rationality for law and economics). It should be noted that some more recent variations of economic analysis do try to take account of bounded rationality. *See, e.g.,* OLIVER E. WILLIAMSON, MARKETS AND HIERARCHIES: ANALYSIS AND ANTITRUST IMPLICATIONS 7 (1975) (describing the importance of bounded rationality to Williamson's approach to new institutional economics).

53. When people do not act as they might be expected to under a rational choice model, economic theorists would once have looked only to high transaction costs, or to some other sort of identifiable "market failure." *See* ROBERT COOTER & THOMAS ULEN, LAW AND ECONOMICS 40-43 (3rd ed., 2000) (discussing "market failure"). More recently, the law and economics theorists have looked towards "social norms" to explain the deviation from "rational" behavior — but this has only led to efforts to explain and predict the development of

central to family law: the decision to marry, the decision to divorce, the decision to sign a premarital agreement, and so on.[54] To the extent that the central model of law and economics significantly distorts the decisionmaking process it purports to represent, there are reasons to doubt the efficacy of the approach. Law and economics theorists might reasonably respond, to this criticism and to other similar challenges, that even if their approach falls short of a full explanation, it *can* explain some phenomena that might otherwise seem mysterious, and therefore should be kept as a tool, even as we recognize that this tool is inadequate for offering a *complete* explanation of domestic and intimate relations.[55]

Carbone's contributions to this ongoing dialogue include her ability to synthesize — concisely and in understandable prose — a vast amount of work by economists, the critics of economics, and people working in other fields. More pointedly, she shows how economic analysis in the domestic relations area has sometimes fallen short because of insufficient attention to culture and history.[56] She favors theories that "pay attention not just to financial incentives ... but [also] to the psychological and cultural factors that underlie decision-making ..." (p. 95). Carbone's summary of the historical work on the development of the family shows how explanations grounded solely or primarily on economics have failed,[57] while simultaneously showing how attention needs to be paid to economic class *within* work about the family (pp. 55-110, 124-26, 308 n.1).

---

social norms in rational choice terms. *See, e.g.*, Conference, *Social Norms, Social Meaning, and the Economic Analysis of Law*, 27 J. LEGAL STUD. 537-823 (1998) (discussion by a number of prominent scholars of the law and economics approach to social norms).

54. *See, e.g..* Lynn A. Baker & Robert Emery, *When Every Relationship Is Above Average: Perceptions and Expectations of Divorce at the Time of Marriage*, 17 LAW & HUM. BEHAV. 439 (1993) (using survey data to show that couples about to marry tend to be overly optimistic about the chances that they will be able to avoid divorce, or if divorced, that the child support obligor will pay the full amount owed); Brian Bix, *Bargaining in the Shadow of Love: The Enforcement of Premarital Agreements and How We Think About Marriage*, 40 WM. & MARY L. REV. 145, 193-200 (1998) (discussing the rationality problem in the context of premarital agreements); Melvin Aron Eisenberg, *The Limits of Cognition and the Limits of Contract*, 47 STAN. L. REV. 211, 254-58 (1995) (describing how "bounded rationality" can explain the restrictions on the enforceability of premarital agreements); Ziva Kunda, *Motivated Inference: Self-Serving Generation and Evaluation of Causal Theories*, 53 J. PERSONALITY & SOC. PSYCH. 636, 636 (1987) (describing how people generate self-serving theories to convince themselves that their chance of divorce is far less than the general divorce rate).

55. *Cf.* DANIEL A. FARBER & PHILIP P. FRICKEY, LAW AND PUBLIC CHOICE: A CRITICAL INTRODUCTION 4-5 (1991) (making a similar claim for public choice theory).

56. As Carbone recognizes, economists have not entirely ignored history. *See, e.g.,* BECKER, *supra* note 38, at 85 (discussing some historical aspects of polygamy); pp. 55-57 (summarizing Friedrich Engels' historically based economic analysis).

57. Pp. 58-59, 90-99. Purely economic explanations that seem to have been rebutted by more careful study of the data include purported connections between industrialization and the development of the nuclear family, pp. 55-59, and between welfare benefits and nonmarital birth rates, p. 94.

While economic explanation might be adequate (and more) for "snapshot" analyses — given people's preferences, how will they react to a particular choice, or how will the sum of choices within a population be affected by a change in incentives caused by (say) a new law? — it is often less useful in explaining and predicting over the longer term. That is, economics is better at discussing how people will act given their preferences, and less good at predicting how and why people's preferences will change. There are a number of examples in Carbone's book of longer-term explanation and the shortfalls of economic analysis there. For example, there is currently a divergence in expectations between men and women regarding marriage roles, differences that in turn vary as one moves from class to class, and among different ethnic and racial groups (p. 19). In subgroups where women generally expect or demand a relatively egalitarian division of roles and men generally expect or demand a relatively traditional/hierarchical division of roles, the result has been a lower rate of marriage.[58] The question then becomes: if people value marriage (and the benefits that can be received from it) significantly, why do they not "renegotiate" the terms of marriage (and adjust their attitudes accordingly) in order to marry?[59] If the answer is because the individuals in question value those terms of marriage and attitudes towards marriage so much higher than the benefits of marriage that there is no point where the trade-off would be worthwhile,[60] then one can ask, how did the individuals come to value these attitudes or terms of marriage so highly? While the change in values *might* have an economic explanation, most of the evidence to date seems not to support that conclusion.[61]

---

58. P. 19. The most extreme example may be in the African-American community, which once had marriage rates far higher than that for whites, but now has much lower rates. Pp. 78-80. While the explanation of this change is controversial and likely reflects a multitude of factors, at least one commentator has attributed the change in large part to differing attitudes among African-American men and women to marriage roles. ORLANDO PATTERSON, RITUALS OF BLOOD: CONSEQUENCES OF SLAVERY IN TWO AMERICAN CENTURIES 93-132 (1998).

59. Pp. 18-19. Carbone indicates that just such a "renegotiation" took place in the nineteenth century, after "women's greater economic independence, however minimal in today's terms, corresponded with a greater degree of family instability." P. 230.

60. There are other factors and explanations worth considering. As Eric Posner reminded me (in commenting on an earlier draft), the state, through its laws, puts some limits on the renegotiation, for example by prohibiting polygamy and (in most jurisdictions) same-sex marriage. Robert Gordon (also commenting on an earlier draft) speculated that men and women sometimes view marriage as a bundle of goods, and when those bundles overlap very little (as might be the case between an egalitarian/romantic view of marriage and a traditional/hierarchical view) and the parties are unwilling to unbundle the goods, fewer people might reach negotiated arrangements.

61. *See supra* note 57; *see also* PATTERSON, *supra* note 58, at 93-132 (offering a largely non-economic explanation for attitudes within the African-American community).

The current generation of family law theorists and law and economics theorists have shown that there is much that rational choice analysis can offer to the understanding of the domestic life and law, but they have also shown this approach's limits. The areas that interest many family law scholars the most — explaining familial and intimate behavior on one hand, and trying to predict, control or reform such behavior on the other hand — may be the areas where law and economics has the least to offer.[62]

CONCLUSION

While it seems a truism that every generation believes it is living at a crucial moment, and that change is occurring at unprecedented levels, when Carbone makes claims of this kind about the modern family — and family law and policy — it is hard to disagree. As she writes: "In the [last] twenty years . . . there is very little about the family that has not changed, and few verities that remain unchallenged" (p. 48). *From Partners to Parents* gives an excellent field guide to these changes, offering perspectives from history, economics and political theory.[63] Carbone shows how both family law doctrine and social thought have focused on the care of children but have unmoored that concern from any focus on the parents' behavior toward one another. The result has been a confused drifting in family law policy in general, and the regulation of marriage in particular. Additionally, Carbone's text, not always intentionally, leaves one cautious, even pessimistic, about the ability of government (or anyone else) to do much about the problems relating to the family. However, such caution may not be entirely a bad thing.

---

62. Which, of course, is not to say that any other single school or approach has done significantly better in this area.

63. Three small corrections and amendments should be offered:

(1) The reference to "Carl MacIntyre," p. 38, is an unintended conflation of the family law scholar Carl Schneider and the moral philosopher Alasdair MacIntyre.

(2) A footnote, p. 295 n.40, misstates the holding of *Ireland v. Smith*, 547 N.W.2d 686 (1996). That decision — an appeal from a highly publicized lower-court custody decision that seemed to punish a young woman's decision to put her child in day care while she went to university — did not "uph[o]ld an award of custody to a father whose own mother planned to care for the child." P. 295 n.40. In fact, the decision upheld an intermediate appellate court, which had *reversed* and remanded the lower court award of custody to the father. *Ireland*, 547 N.W.2d at 692.

(3) The reader should be told that the (initially startling) 1646 Colonial Massachusetts statute, p. 296 n.1, for the *execution* of recalcitrant children, simply restates (almost verbatim) Biblical language. *See Deuteronomy* 21: 18-21. As Carbone writes, there is no evidence that any child was ever actually executed under this statute. P. 296 n.1.

[14]

LOVE IT OR LEAVE IT: PROPERTY RULES, LIABILITY RULES, AND EXCLUSIVITY OF REMEDIES IN PARTNERSHIP AND MARRIAGE

SAUL LEVMORE*

I

INTRODUCTION

The traditional rule in partnership law is that a claim for "final accounting" is a partner's exclusive remedy. Under this rule, withdrawal from a partnership must precede or accompany legal actions against one's partners. A partner must "love it or leave it," with judicial attention available only after leaving the relationship. Rather plainly, this rule can be unfair and inefficient. At the same time, there is something attractive about the idea of encouraging private compromise by limiting the availability of courts to parties that are unable to continue their relationships.

Part II of this article introduces this tension by discussing the evolution of the rules of partnership law away from the love-it-or-leave-it, or "exclusivity," tradition and by comparing traditional partnership law first to domestic relations law, where the love-it-or-leave-it character of remedies is even more striking, and then to corporate law, where the structure of remedies is almost reversed. Parts III and IV connect this exploration of remedies to a familiar framework in the law-and-economics literature that compares property rules and liability rules. The connection reveals new ways of thinking about the remedies in partnership law and casts light on the occasional attractiveness of love-it-or-leave-it rules. Part V compares the selection of remedies in business and in marriage, with some reference to other relationships as well. Part VI offers some concluding comments about love-it-or-leave-it strategies and the evolution of our legal system.

II

LOVE-IT-OR-LEAVE-IT RULES IN PARTNERSHIP AND OTHER LAW

Imagine that A and B are partners in a business and B believes that A has wrongfully exploited B or otherwise breached the partnership agreement. The

Copyright © 1995 by Law and Contemporary Problems

* Brokaw Professor of Corporate Law and Albert Clark Tate, Jr., Professor, University of Virginia.

I am grateful for comments received from Chris Akin, Jim Bowers, Peggy Brinig, Glen Robinson, Bill Stuntz, and especially Larry Ribstein, as well as participants at a University of Virginia Law School faculty retreat.

traditional rule is that if B seeks damages from A or from the AB partnership for the alleged wrong, B will be required first to ask the court for a final accounting, which in turn often requires the dissolution of the partnership.[1] On its face, the rule denies B the power to sue the ongoing partnership enterprise while simultaneously avoiding the costs of dissolution, the most important of which may be the value of B's share of the ongoing concern.[2] It is easy to imagine that this exclusivity (of remedies) rule can leave wrongs uncorrected and in this way permit an unhealthy degree of exploitation of a minority partnership interest. A related intuition is that when the future prospects of a partnership look promising, one partner may be especially tempted to exploit another unless there is reason to fear external legal intervention. This intuition, however, is difficult to pin down.

There are at least three strategies for understanding the traditional exclusivity, or all-or-nothing, rule and the steady migration away from this seemingly strange, anachronistic, unfair, and inefficient rule.[3] First, we might examine partnership cases in order to identify the inevitable exceptions to the rule. Most harsh or striking rules have numerous exceptions, and this one is no different.[4] As the exceptions grow in number and importance, the original rule is more likely either to appear in retrospect to have reflected some evolutionary or legal accident or be otherwise anachronistic. Either way, surging exceptions can be taken as evidence of healthy evolution away from the rule. If we focus on either of two straightforward explanations of the origin of this particular exclusivity rule—with no attention to similar rules in other areas of law—evolution and abandonment of the rule seem predictable. One explanation suggests that the rule arises out of a formalist conception of the "aggregate theory" of partnerships.[5] Courts in an earlier era might have had trouble imagining a lawsuit going on within a partnership, much as we would find it bizarre to imagine or to allow one division of a corporation to sue another

---

1. *See, e.g.*, Goff v. Bergerman, 50 P.2d 59, 61 (Colo. 1935) (the exclusivity rule requires both a final accounting and a settlement of partnership affairs); *see also* 2 ALAN R. BROMBERG & LARRY E. RIBSTEIN, BROMBERG AND RIBSTEIN ON PARTNERSHIP § 6.08(b) (1988) ("Prior to the [Uniform Partnership Act], the action for an accounting was generally denied except incident to dissolution.").

2. This assumes that the going concern value will not always be salvaged by a purchase and refinancing on the part of a surviving partner. If going concern value (partnership value) is never lost—which under some rarefied economic assumptions is the case—then most of the rules discussed in this paper make no difference at all. But there are reasons to think that withdrawals can sink profitable enterprises. For example, outsiders, including creditors, may have difficulty discerning which enterprises have going concern value. Moreover, there are arrangements where continuity can be threatened because of legal or other institutional hurdles. Thus, partners may bring unique skills or legal licenses to a venture—all of which may be inalienable—so that dissolution can be mutually threatening and not simply overcome by a buyout.

3. *See infra* notes 8-14 and accompanying text.

4. *See infra* note 8.

5. When treating partnerships as aggregates of individuals, "suing a partnership would be characterized [by the common law] as being on both sides of the case." BROMBERG & RIBSTEIN, *supra* note 1, at §§ 1.03(b), 6.08(c). The exclusivity rule survived a gradual shift toward an "entity theory" of partnerships. *Id.* § 6.08(c); *see also* Sertich v. Moorman, 783 P.2d 1199, 1201 (Ariz. 1989) (noting that earlier courts did not view the partnership as separate entity).

division of the same firm.[6] The second explanation for the origins of the exclusivity rule can be drawn from the distinction between law and equity.[7]

As for the evolution of the exclusivity rule in partnership law, there are in fact modern cases that virtually dispose of the rule.[8] The Uniform Partnership Act encourages the demise of the rule, although there is some reason to think that the rule lives on despite what a casual reading of the Act would first suggest.[9] The "Revised" Uniform Partnership Act seeks to bury the exclusivity rule by allowing almost any cause of action by a partner against the partnership or against other partners without a final accounting or dissolution.[10] Further

---

6. JOHN COLLYER, PRACTICAL TREATISE ON THE LAW OF PARTNERSHIP § 264 (5th ed. 1861) ("useless for one partner to recover what, upon taking a general account amongst all partners, he might be liable to refund").

Another explanation for the exclusivity rule is that it saved judicial resources. *See infra* note 71.

7. The exclusivity rule on its face is about the distinction between law and equity. The rule precludes suits at law until after the equitable remedy of a full accounting has been had. *Sertich*, 783 P.2d at 1201-02 (describing the exclusivity rule as an anomaly that arose from the common law distinction between law and equity).

8. *Id.* at 1201-05 (abandoning the exclusivity rule in Arizona). For more limited exceptions, see Hanes v. Giambrone, 471 N.E.2d 801 (Ohio Ct. App. 1984) (action to collect partnership contributions with no accounting); Fulton v. Baxter, 596 P.2d 540 (Okla. 1979) (fiduciary breach suit in absence of accounting). More generally, courts have made an exception for situations in which "by some special agreement the particluar matter has been withdrawn from the partnership account." Kunneke v. Mapel, 53 N.E. 259, 261 (Ohio 1899). Similarly, courts have allowed the equitable remedy of a constructive trust without requiring accounting and dissolution. BROMBERG & RIBSTEIN, *supra* note 1, § 6.08(c)(8). *See generally* Susan Swinson, *Partner v. Partner: Actions at Law for Wrongdoing in a Partnership*, 9 GA. ST. U. L. REV. 905 (1993).

9. As noted below, any reference to the Uniform Partnership Act, or UPA, risks ambiguity because the "current" Uniform Partnership Act (1994) is commonly but not officially referred to as the Revised Uniform Partnership Act, or RUPA. The 1914 Act (with the usual changes over the years) is commonly referred to as *the* Uniform Partnership Act. In any event, the immediate reference in the text is to the better known Uniform Partnership Act (1914). In terms of the issues discussed here, its basic structure is as follows: (1) Any partner can force dissolution unless there is an agreement to the contrary, including an express or implied agreement to continue the partnership for a specified term. *See* UNIF. PARTNERSHIP ACT § 31 (last amended 1914), 6 U.L.A. at 376 (1969). Moreover, any partner can terminate a partnership, although doing so may breach the agreement. *Id.* §§ 31, 38, 6 U.L.A at 376, 456. Any partner has a right to formal accounting (without dissolving the partnership) when (a) wrongfully excluded from the business, (b) if the partnership agreement provides for the right, (c) a partner has appropriated an unauthorized benefit, or (d) whenever it is just and reasonable. *Id.* § 22, 6 U.L.A. at 284.

The UPA (1914) thus encourages evolution away from the exclusivity rule by allowing courts to describe claims (that include claims for full accounting but do not call for dissolution) as "just and reasonable." Nonetheless, because the claimant must obtain an accounting (even without dissolution), there is still an element of an all-or-nothing choice because the cost of an accounting (and the added animosity arising from a legal action that imposes serious costs on the partnership) will discourage actions in profitable partnerships. BROMBERG & RIBSTEIN, *supra* note 1, § 6.08(b) (noting that predissolution accounting actions are rare for these reasons).

10. The Uniform Partnership Act (1994), previously and commonly known as the Revised Uniform Partnership Act, or RUPA, abandons the exclusivity rule by allowing a partner to sue the partnership or other partners for almost any cause of action without seeking an accounting. RUPA § 405(b) (last amended 1994), 6 U.L.A. 280, 316 (Supp. 1995). Dissolution or, in the language of this Act, "dissociation," remains something that can always be done, rightfully or wrongfully. *Id.* § 602, 6 U.L.A. at 325. The Official Comment to the new (model) statute notes that the abolition of the exclusivity rule "reflects a new policy choice that partners should have access to the courts during the term of the partnership to resolve claims against the partnership and other partners, leaving broad judicial discretion to fashion appropriate remedies." RUPA § 405(b), 6 U.L.A. at 316 n.2 (Supp. 1995).

focus on this first approach is unnecessary; a healthy evolution away from a suboptimal and dated rule may be optimistic, lawyerly, and plausible, but it is perhaps limited in relationship to partnership law. Moreover, the most sophisticated commentators already follow this strategy.[11]

A second approach to understanding the exclusivity rule, and the evolution away from it, is to have some confidence in the lawmakers of earlier eras and explore the possibility that the evolution from one rule to another reflects the fact that reasonable observers might be uncertain which of several rules is superior.[12] The exceptions that materialize in the shadow of a rule might provide hints as to the perceived disadvantages of that rule.[13] The discussion below suggests that it is not obvious how to choose between conflicting strategies for motivating peaceful compromise while discouraging strategic exploitation among quarreling parties. The exclusivity rule in partnership law might be one strategy aimed at this end, but it is difficult to evaluate, and, therefore, it is an approach that might give way to permitting piecemeal litigation and anticipating legal intervention in ongoing partnerships. In turn, this latter approach might itself be displaced over time, when a return to exclusivity is possible.

Finally, a third, though not necessarily unrelated strategy is to generalize the problem and to ask when similar all-or-nothing rules are found in law. Much as the traditional partnership rule tells a potential complaining partner that he or she must love-it-or-leave-it, which is to say simply end the relationship or not litigate at all, there are other areas of law where litigants must elect between such extremes. The most familiar example is in domestic relations law.[14]

---

11. *See* Larry E. Ribstein, *The Revised Uniform Partnership Act: Not Ready for Prime Time,* 49 BUS. LAW. 45, 61 (1993).

12. *See* Saul Levmore, *Variety and Uniformity in the Treatment of the Good-Faith Purchaser,* 16 J. LEGAL STUD. 43 (1987).

13. Thus, there is evidence that courts imply agreements as to limited terms where no such explicit agreements existed, in order to impose liability on a partner who ends a partnership with going concern value. *See* Robert W. Hillman, *The Dissatisfied Participant in the Solvent Business Venture: A Consideration of the Relative Permanence of Partnerships and Close Corporations,* 67 MINN. L. REV. 1, 20-27 (1982)[hereinafter Hillman, *The Dissatisfied Participant*]. Professor Hillman, it should be noted, disapproves of this judicial practice. *Id.* Foreign jurisdictions, interestingly enough, do not allow partners to leave and pay damages if their partnership is for a specified term. *See* Robert W. Hillman, *Indissoluble Partnerships,* 37 U. FLA. L. REV. 691, 694-95 (1985). In unusual cases, U.S. courts may do the same, perhaps in order to force bargaining. *See* Infusaid Corp. v. Intermedics Infusaid, Inc., 739 F.2d 661 (1st Cir. 1984). The apparent choice for courts between damages and prohibitions is the subject of parts IV and V below.

The second approach described in the text differs from the "healthy evolution" described in the first approach, in that the second approach anticipates a resting point with multiple equilibria rather than a sense that less exclusivity is generally if not always better than more. Moreover, there is the possibility that courts develop schemes in which love-it-or-leave-it rules are used for some cases and not others, with the courts enjoying some flexibility when it comes to determining partnership liabilities. It may be that the constructive trust exception to the exclusivity rule, *see supra* note 8, provides one useful judicial tool.

14. The most familiar examples to lawyers may be the love-it-or-leave-it rule regarding attorney-client litigation and the treatment of joint tenants and cotenants in property law. As for the first of these, an attorney may not be on the opposite side of any litigation from his or her client. MODEL RULES OF PROFESSIONAL CONDUCT Rule 1.7(a) (1983); *see* Lake County Bar Ass'n v. Gargiulo, 404

Indeed, if this article were not part of a symposium organized around partnership law, it might have been most sensible to focus first on family law, and especially on the normal exclusivity of the divorce remedy as a means of asking why other areas of law evolved away from, or in some cases never adopted, the all-or-nothing judicial attitude that is found where complaints about marriage are concerned.

In the law of domestic relations, we do not expect a court to award contract damages to a plaintiff who complains about a spouse's misconduct or laziness or breach of an interspousal promise. Such a remedy might accompany or be a part of a divorce settlement, or might simply be unavailable because of the exclusive character of the divorce remedy.[15] The judicial practice is not simply the result of adhering to a nonmarket conception of a woman's traditional work as wife and mother; a husband would also have trouble collecting damages from a wife who broke a promise concerning the maintenance of hearth and home (and had property with which to pay a judgment).[16] And either spouse would

---

N.E.2d 1343 (Ohio 1980) (lawyer disciplined after filing in same action claims on his own behalf against each client and by each client against the other). Thus, an attorney may not even sue a client for unpaid fees—until the entire attorney-client relationship comes to an end. Disclosure does not free the attorney of this constraint. There is, of course, sometimes the option of ending the relationship and forcing (which may be to say threatening) the client to seek other counsel and pay twice for some work. *See* 7 AM. JUR. 2D *Attorneys at Law* § 306 (1980). This love-it-or-leave-it rule does not, however, seem to have much to do with other love-it-or-leave-it rules. It appears to reflect the special concern of the law for conflicts or appearances of conflict between lawyer and client. The law worries that lawyers may seem to root against their own clients if they are also seen to be in open conflict with these clients. This concern may be misplaced, for it is arguable that uncollectible fees or unresolvable conflicts may in fact lead to greater agency problems, but it is probably safe to set aside this love-it-or-leave-it rule as a special case.

In the case of multiple ownership of property, there is a striking love-it-or-leave-it rule when courts will not intervene in disputes among joint tenants or cotenants until one asks for a partition. *See* JOHN E. CRIBBET & CORWIN W. JOHNSON, PRINCIPLES OF THE LAW OF PROPERTY 113 (3d ed. 1989). The law in this area can also be explained as minimizing valuation tasks. *See infra* part V.B (valuation tasks may explain difference between marriage and business partnership); Saul Levmore, *Explaining Restitution*, 71 VA. L. REV. 65, 70 (1985) (valuation considerations may explain rule permitting joint tenant to recover for improvements to property only in partition). It goes almost without saying that a common feature of many joint tenancies, cotenancies, and business partnerships (and all marriages) is that the parties have familial ties. In these settings, courts may think either that it is especially likely that compromises will eventually be reached or that it will be difficult to unravel the numerous interactions and identify the initial or true wrongdoer.

15. Following, or along with, dissolution, courts may pass on claims for conduct during the marriage. Remedies may be reflected in the division of property at divorce or in separate judgments. *See, e.g.*, Henriksen v. Cameron, 622 A.2d 1135 (Me. 1993) (allowing action following a no-fault divorce by former spouse for intentional infliction of emotional distress during marriage); Roland v. Roland, 519 So. 2d 1177 (La. Ct. App. 1987) (finding wife's intemperance constituted independent contributory cause of marital breakup thus precluding permanent alimony). But it appears that as state legislatures move toward no-fault divorce, legislatures and courts are less inclined to look back, or at least give less weight to, behavior within the marriage in dividing property. HOMER H. CLARK, JR., THE LAW OF DOMESTIC RELATIONS IN THE UNITED STATES § 1.1 (2d ed. 1988).

This explanation does not include tort claims between spouses because the evolution away from the spousal tort immunity is easily linked to the desire to mesh tort claims with typical insurance coverages. The movement toward allowing these claims within marriage thus does not seem like much of an exception to the larger love-it-or-leave-it rule.

16. Reva Siegel, *The Modernization of Marital Status Law: Adjudicating Wives' Rights to Earnings, 1860-1930*, 82 GEO. L.J. 2127 (1994).

find it impossible to collect damages or gain specific performance from a spouse who for selfish reasons failed to maximize his or her earnings.[17] Whether courts aim to encourage compromise with a love-it-or-leave-it rule or simply refuse to monetize or otherwise become entwined in ongoing spousal relations, there is little doubt that this is an area of law where the expected outcomes are limited to self-help, private negotiation, or the extreme step of dissolution.

In contrast, a shareholder of a corporation can pursue a claim against an agent, or fiduciary, while continuing to own stock in the corporation.[18] Somewhat similarly, an employee can sue her employer (and, conversely, the employee can be sued) without severing the employment relationship. To be sure, it may be awkward to sue one's boss, but the point is that love-it-or-leave-it in these cases is a private, rather than a legally imposed, constraint on one's options. Other fiduciaries can also be sued while their services continue.[19] There is, therefore, the general question of when love-it-or-leave-it rules are attractive.[20]

One indication that this question is unlikely to yield simple answers is that closely allied areas of law (which is to say similar transactions and relationships) sport sharply divergent rules. Thus, while marriages and business partnerships might seem similar—if only because partnerships are often formed among

More generally, an explanation of the love-it-or-leave-it rule in marriage might build on the idea that women were relatively disadvantaged by a rule that made divorce a prerequisite for other interspousal claims. The point in the text, however, is that the law might have disadvantaged women still more by allowing men (and not women) to bring suits in marriage when their expectations were disappointed. The law was not above such a facially nonneutral rule.

17. Indeed, it would be no simple task to collect explicitly promised amounts. *See* Miller v. Miller, 42 N.W. 641 (Iowa 1889) (refusing to enforce written agreement between husband and wife promising fidelity and $200 per year for wife's personal use despite husband's breach by "wasting his money on other women").

18. In derivative actions in Delaware, for example, the plaintiff *must* remain a stockholder throughout the litigation. Lewis v. Anderson, 477 A.2d 1040 (Del. 1984); *In re* Resorts Int'l. Shareholders Litig., C.A. No. 9470, slip op. at 31 (Del. Ch. Sept. 7, 1988), *aff'd*, 570 A.2d 259 (Del. 1990). *See generally* ROBERT CHARLES CLARK, CORPORATE LAW 650-52 (1986) (contemporaneous ownership rule normally requires shareholder who brings derivative suit to allege that he was a shareholder at time of transaction of which he complains—and also to hold shares when bringing suit and throughout the suit).

19. The remedies available to the beneficiary of a trust, for example, generally include declaratory judgments interpreting the trust, UNIF. DECLARATORY JUDGMENTS ACTS § 2 (1922), injunctions against wrongful acts, GEORGE T. BOGERT, TRUSTS § 154 (1987), specific performance, *id.* § 155, and money damages, *id.* § 157. These actions need not result in the removal of the trustee. *Id.*

20. There is a normative and a positive angle to the question, but for the present there does not seem to be a reason to separate these inquiries. The present inquiry can also be thought of as asking the positive question of why, if in some areas of law love-it-or-leave-it rules are found attractive, such rules are not more commonly used. I have tried to ask similar questions about other rules we do not often find, with the hope that we can learn a good deal about the law that we do experience by exploring the laws we do not. *See, e.g.*, Saul Levmore, *Gomorrah to Ybarra and More: The Puzzle of Immoderate Group Liability*, 81 VA. L. REV. 1561 (1995) (puzzle of failure of law to experiment with extreme form of group liability in order to extract confessions from rational wrongdoers); Saul Levmore, *Obligation or Restitution for Best Efforts*, 67 S. CAL. L. REV. 1411 (1994) (contractual acquaintances rarely recover for apparently wealth-maximizing precautions); Saul Levmore, *The Case for Retroactive Taxation*, 22 J. LEGAL STUD. 265 (1993) (exploring general hostility to retroactive taxes even though such taxes have certain attractive qualities).

relatives—so that their once-analogous love-it-or-leave-it rules suggest consistency, it is not the case that employer-employee law, or principal-agent law more generally, has insisted on such exclusivity. For example, in the principal-agent context, if B contracts with A to sell A's products and to earn a commission on all sales, B and A may sue one another regarding explicit or implicit violations of their agreement, even while they continue to enjoy the going concern value of their relationship by respectively supplying and selling products as before.[21] The exclusivity tradition in partnership law is therefore especially remarkable because partnerships are easily and most often described as mutual agency arrangements.

The occasional attraction of love-it-or-leave-it rules is particularly intriguing because in many cases rules about the exclusivity of remedies are not merely default rules but are instead virtually mandatory. It can be difficult, if not impossible, for parties to modify or otherwise escape love-it-or-leave-it rules through private bargaining. Thus, partnership law has generally permitted a partner to force a dissolution, but, as we have seen, the traditional rule did not permit most litigation outside the context of a final accounting. One way to contract out of the first half of this love-it-or-leave-it rule is to specify that the partnership is for a set period of time or for a distinct project. In that case, there is no right to a "free" dissolution but rather an explicit agreement to give up the right to withdraw for a set period of time.[22] However, this strategy for private ordering does not solve the problem of the partner who seeks judicial intervention or enforcement of an agreement without separation. Thus, the love-it-or-leave-it rule may have forced a kind of bundling on some unwilling players.[23] Similarly, potential partners might wish to prevent untimely

---

21. E. ALLAN FARNSWORTH, CONTRACTS § 8.15 (1982).

22. *See supra* note 9; UPA §§ 31, 38, 6 U.L.A. at 376, 456. The rule continues under RUPA § 602, 6 U.L.A. at 553 (dissociation is within power of partner but is wrongful if prior to expiration of definite term or completion of particular undertaking). The general rule is that every partner has the power to dissolve a partnership at any time, even though a partnership agreement may try to limit or deter that power. In particular, the exercise of this power before expiration of a specified term may make the partner liable for damages. McCall v. Frampton, 415 N.Y.S.2d 752 (1979); Woodruff v. Bryant, 558 S.W.2d 535 (Tex. Civ. App. 1977).

23. Similarly, spouses might wish to precommit never to get divorced, but the law does not provide for this option and makes bargaining around the default rules and in favor of this precommitment strategy very difficult. In the case of business partnerships, it is preferable to say that the law disfavors some packages, rather than that it makes them impossible, because it is difficult to know how courts would react to clever schemes. Thus, parties might use nested partnerships in order to dissolve one partnership while continuing to do business together in a successor partnership, but with the intention of using the "dissolution" as a means of getting into court with their claims. It is difficult to know whether courts, operating under the traditional rules, would be willing to allow such a strategy, and the most noteworthy thing may be that parties apparently have not tried this route around the love-it-or-leave-it norm.

The mandatory nature of some of these rules does not make it impossible to describe the love-it-or-leave-it rules discussed in this article as examples of precommitment strategies. Investors might occasionally wish to precommit to all-or-nothing rules (no litigation short of dissolution), and this is indeed what is meant by the possibility of traditional partnership and corporate law offering different default rules. Similarly, spouses may wish to precommit to be unable to litigate short of divorce, and it is even remotely possible that nations would want to precommit to ban conventional weapons. *See*

dissolution (or threats of dissolution) and also to allow claims within the ongoing relationship, but under the traditional rule they find it difficult to do so. Analogously, spouses cannot successfully contract around their love-it-or-leave-it relationship.

III

EXCLUSIVITY RULES AND BARGAINING

A. Two Kinds of Exclusivity

The domestic relations example suggests that an important aspect of love-it-or-leave-it rules is the impetus they might give to private bargaining. It is at least plausible that the threat of withdrawal, be it from marriage or from a business partnership, facilitates settlement by jeopardizing the value of a going concern. The law might impose a love-it-or-leave-it framework on parties—who might themselves be thought of as precommitting to this set of choices or to this strategy—because of a conviction that they will choose to iron out their differences in the shadow of destructive dissolutions. The most obvious alternative regime is one that permits and perhaps even encourages midstream appeals to judicial authority. One implicit question is whether a love-it-or-leave-it rule generates more or less private bargaining or compromise than a scheme that permits ongoing appeals or judicial intervention. Another question is whether the choice between these schemes is likely to influence the outcome of private bargaining in an important way.

Consider the relative desirability of two opposing exclusivity schemes. The first, resembling the traditional partnership rule—and in some respects the law governing marriages—promises liquidity by offering every participant the right to exit with the net value of that participant's share in the enterprise, but allows no other remedy. The threatened coventurers may bargain, especially if the withdrawal of this participant makes it difficult for those who wish to continue on to do so, but they instead may think it unlikely that the threat will be carried out inasmuch as the threatening partner risks losing his share of the going concern value of the partnership.[24] Put differently, the right to exit or dissolve invites a kind of "chicken" game that almost surely reduces litigation but occasionally invites the baby to be thrown out with the bath water. This love-it-or-leave-it strategy may lead to accommodation rather than separation, although

---

infra part V.D.1. But some of these love-it-or-leave-it strategies seem like unlikely precommitment strategies. We are accustomed to love-it-or-leave-it precommitments where coalitions are malleable and voting paradoxes flower, as in Congress agreeing to vote up or down (love-it-or-leave-it) the proposals of a military base closing commission, but such precommitments would seem unusual or even counter-intuitive where two parties were concerned. Put differently, it is the (at least somewhat) mandatory quality of these rules that makes them different and more interesting.

24. All partners may know that the value of the firm exceeds that which a suspicious outsider would pay. *See* Hillman, *The Dissatisfied Participant, supra* note 13, at 35 (potential loss of going concern value discourages liquidation).

it is surely an empirical question whether such an extreme rule leads to less or more dissolution than alternative remedy regimes.

The second remedy scheme, resembling the traditional situation in closely held corporations, allows a participant (shareholder) to bring suits, based on fault or contractual agreement, against fiduciaries or the ongoing enterprise. Because courts rarely go so far as to dissolve corporations, one might think of there being an exclusivity rule of the opposite kind in this arena: "Litigate but do not leave it."[25]

B. Choice of Form

One way to think about the comparison between the traditional partnership-chicken scheme, which anticipates only dissolution (and the threat of it), and the close-corporation scheme, which encompasses suits for fiduciary breach and other invitations to judicial monitoring but anticipates no serious threat of dissolution, is from the perspective of the choice of form. There is a large body of literature on the choice between the partnership and corporate forms, but surprisingly little attention is given to the different remedy regimes. If potential joint venturers believe that threats generate bargains, that judicial monitoring is costly, time consuming, and prone to error, and that the threat of destruction of going concern value will only rarely need to be exercised, then they might well prefer the traditional partnership form with its exclusivity of remedies rule. Other investors, however, may have greater faith in judicial monitoring or greater fear of the chicken game created by the love-it-or-leave-it approach associated with the exclusivity rule of traditional partnership law. In short, an interesting snapshot of bygone law reveals different default rules associated with the corporate and partnership forms. Although the choice between these forms is often described as based on limited liability, governance, or tax consider-ations, the choice may also be based on the stark contrast in available remedies regarding internal disputes.

One problem with this view is the mandatory nature of these default rules. Another problem is that the most natural default rule providing for a right to exit would seem to be one that guaranteed exit *and* also allowed litigation in an ongoing relationship. As suggested below, this may be where both partnership and corporate law are heading, but the important point for present purposes is

---

25. In contrast to the partner's right to dissociate, a shareholder cannot demand to be permitted to exit with a proportional share of the firm's value, unless an appropriate and specific buy-out, appraisal, or other right has been bargained for or legislated. There is, of course, important commentary suggesting that there be a right of ready exit from close corporations. *See, e.g.*, J.A.C. Hetherington & Michael P. Dooley, *Illiquidity and Exploitation: A Proposed Statutory Solution to the Remaining Close Corporation Problem*, 63 VA. L. REV. 1 (1977). It is interesting that Hetherington and Dooley recommend that their rule be itself love-it-or-leave-it; partnership law is mimicked with the idea that an investor can force exit or even dissolution if there is otherwise no agreement to buy the offered shares, but the shareholder who seeks to sell or part ways cannot force partial dissolution. *Id.* at 50-51. More generally, the trend in close corporation cases is toward granting exit rights, so that partnership and corporate law are converging. *See* WILLIAM L. CARY & MELVIN A. EISENBERG, CASES AND MATERIALS ON CORPORATIONS 542-44 (7th ed. unab. 1995).

that the two different default rules associated with traditional partnership and corporate law can be seen as providing, or perhaps as having once provided, a conspicuous choice to coventurers.[26]

C. Love-It-or-Leave-It and Bargaining Space

A recurring question in the law and economics literature is whether bargains are more or less likely when there is more uncertainty and more at stake. On the one hand, parties would not want to expend resources going through trials, weathering shutdowns and labor strikes, or enduring any of a variety of other costly skirmishes if there were relatively little to be gained compared to the costs of conflict. But, on the other hand, risk aversion might lead parties to settle more readily where the risk of not settling is more substantial. The obvious analogy is to the variety found in fee-shifting rules.[27] The British rule, which requires the losing litigant to pay the winner's reasonable attorney's fees, has something in common with the love-it-or-leave-it rule in that both raise the stakes for those who insist on proceeding to litigation. One novel but perhaps simplistic way to think about love-it-or-leave-it rules generally is to recognize that to the extent they raise the stakes in a dispute by allowing only claims for final accounting, the law reflects an intuition that settlements (including the simple decision not to complain) are more likely when there is more uncertainty.[28] Of course, this intuition may be wrong. Settlement will also depend on the parties' relative optimism.[29] And settlement may have more to do with the information that parties find worthwhile to share than with the bargaining space

---

26. For more on the idea of these exclusivity rules as historical default rules and on their future convergence, see *infra* part V.D.2.

27. John J. Donohue III, *Opting for the British Rule, or If Posner and Shavell Can't Remember the Coase Theorem, Who Will?*, 104 HARV. L. REV. 1093 (1991) (accepting inherited wisdom that fee-shifting encourages risk-averse parties to settle but questioning claims regarding settlement differentials when risk effects are ignored).

28. One implication of this perspective is that we might expect to find different love-it-or-leave-it rules in a jurisdiction with more or less fee-shifting than ours. The simplest form of this suggestion is that our love-it-or-leave-it rules may be substitutes for fee-shifting rules.

One potential example comes from the law of estates. United States law permits no-contest provisions in wills so that a testator can force a beneficiary to love it or leave it. If a beneficiary challenges a will with a no-contest clause, then the beneficiary forfeits his benefits under the will, unless the challenge has probable cause or likelihood of success, or unless the suit is determined to be one for the construction of the will. We might expect the British rule to be different because the well-known fee-shifting in Britain might serve much of the purpose of a no-contest clause. Unfortunately, this expectation is too difficult to assess. One problem is that rules in both countries are difficult to pin down. For U.S. law, compare Porter v. Baynard, 28 So. 2d 890 (Fla.) (suit to strike provision as against rule against perpetuities not a contest of the will), *cert. denied*, 330 U.S. 810 (1946), with Smithsonian Inst. v. Meech, 169 U.S. 398 (1898) (giving effect to clause despite contest brought in good faith); Cocklin's Estate, 17 N.W.2d 129 (Iowa 1950) (holding suit to invalidate codicil did not trigger no-contest clause); Barry v. American Sec. & Trust Co., 135 F.2d 470 (D.C. Cir. 1943) (clause effective absent allegation of forgery or subsequent revocation); UNIF. PROBATE CODE § 3-905 (last amended 1969), 8 U.L.A. 383 (1983). The British, in turn, appear willing to ignore no-contest clauses when there is "probable cause." An optimist might say that the British de-emphasize the love-it-or-leave-it strategy inasmuch as they already have fee-shifting, but the context-specific nature of many of these applications makes it difficult to compare the British and U.S. rules.

29. *See* Donohue, *supra* note 27.

between them.[30]   However, rather than pursuing this matter, this article suggests that the choice of an exclusivity rule can be usefully situated in the larger literature on the choice between "property rules" and "liability rules." A discussion of this literature—and some additions to it—now follows.

IV

PROPERTY RULES AND LIABILITY RULES IN NUISANCE AND PARTNERSHIP

A. Introduction

Inasmuch as most readers will be familiar with the literature just referred to, it may be useful to begin with a quick explanation of how love-it-or-leave-it rules, in partnership or elsewhere, tie in to the choice between property and liability rules. A serious exclusivity rule in partnership law, by way of example, gives a partner the right to exit and, at least in some sense, the right to bring a halt to the partnership. Similarly, a property rule in nuisance law might allow a party to halt the activity of an offending neighbor. The power to stop an activity—and not simply to collect damages for the injuries it generates—is thus common to both settings.[31]   Correspondingly, the settlement value to a partner of the threat to withdraw capital and to inflict a suit for final accounting is much like the endowment effect enjoyed by one who obtains, or might obtain, injunctive relief against a neighbor's nuisance.

When the property-rule character of the love-it-or-leave-it practice in traditional partnership law is put this way, it obscures the fact that the most striking thing about the partnership rule is not that it equips a partner with the right to stop an activity, or force a dissolution, but rather that it denies a partner the right to bring liability claims unless dissolution is sought. It is this feature, often all, that distinguishes (traditional) partnerships from agency and other arrangements involving personal services which can always be withdrawn. At the same time, the exclusivity tradition in partnership law raises the question of whether "property rights" in other areas of law always encompass "liability rights." This article's strategy, therefore, will be to suggest not only that partnership, domestic relations, and other law can be understood by thinking of their remedies in property-liability rule terms, but also that the exclusivity traditions encountered in these areas of law reflect some light on nuisance law and other areas where the choice between property and liability rules is already celebrated—but perhaps not entirely understood.

The next few sections of the article begin with a quick review of Calabresi and Melamed's property-liability framework and then explore some extensions

---

30. Ian Ayres & Eric Talley, *Solomonic Bargaining: Dividing a Legal Entitlement to Facilitate Coasian Bargaining*, 104 YALE L.J. 1027 (1995).

31. Thus, much as an injunction might permit B to stop A's factory, a dissolution right permits B to stop A's partnership or marriage. On the possibility that a true property right always includes a "lesser" liability right, see *infra* text accompanying notes 50-53.

Economics of Family Law I

of this framework in order to prepare for a return to a discussion of love-it-or-leave-it rules and an attempt to situate these rules and their competitors in the expanded property-liability framework. Although this is surely not the place to rethink the Calabresi-Melamed framework, the extensions reported and developed here may be independently interesting.[32]

B. The Calabresi-Melamed Four-Rule Framework

In the classic setting, one or more residential neighbors, collectively called B, seeks relief from a neighboring factory, A. In their famous work, Calabresi and Melamed taught us to consider four options available to a court hearing a claim by B against A.[33] First, the court can decide that A is indeed a private nuisance, and it can enjoin A. A may be able to bargain around this rule by buying B's property or simply paying B for permission to do what the court has agreed to allow B to halt,[34] but the court will have established the property rights, or starting point, of this bargaining process. Second, the court can use a liability rule, requiring A to pay damages to B. Third, the court can do the opposite of the first rule, permitting A to continue as before. Fourth, the court can start with the first rule, allowing B to stop A, but it can also require B to compensate A.

On inspection, this fourth and most celebrated option is conceptually interesting but unlikely to be terribly appealing except in a very weak form. In the very circumstances in which it is tempting—perhaps because there is some fear that B has "come to the nuisance" in order to extort and could just as well have located elsewhere or perhaps because the defendant enjoys the court's sympathy for having done nothing actively antisocial—the defendant will often enjoy increased property values. Specifically, a previously unobjectionable use or activity is just the sort of enterprise courts will enjoin when there is an influx of residents.[35] Thus, although B complains and wishes to stop A, B has also enriched A. Put differently, we can imagine that the owner of a feedlot or dog-breeding enterprise rejoices rather than frets when residential development approaches. Litigation may of course ensue; however, when this legal conflict ends, the first property owner, A, is almost certain to enjoy increased wealth, for development tends to increase property values. Inasmuch as A's land may be more profitably developed in the future than in the present, it is possible that A's land will actually fall in value when the court enjoins the current use, but it is plain that A's property's value has not fallen if measured from some point

---

32. *See* Saul Levmore, Rethinking Remedies: Property Rules, Liability Rules, and Elastic Rules (draft manuscript, on file with author).

33. Guido Calabresi & A. Douglas Melamed, *Property Rules, Liability Rules, and Inalienability: One View of the Cathedral*, 85 HARV. L. REV. 1089 (1972).

34. *Id.* at 1105-06.

35. A well-known example, where coming-to-the-nuisance proves to be no bar to complaints, is Ensign v. Walls, 34 N.W.2d 549 (Mich. 1948) (residents in conflict with preexisting dog-breeding operation).

before B's arrival on the scene. It is no accident that the notable case of *Spur Industries*,[36] which Calabresi and Melamed anticipated with their fourth rule, simply held that B must pay A's *moving or relocation costs*.[37] Whatever one's intuition about the injury A "causes" B, it is also the case that B has caused A's land to appreciate. The disinclination to award more than relocation costs reflects either a sense that justice does not call for a double payment from B to A or a fear of moral hazard.[38]

C. Novel Rules

1. *The Post-Calabresi-Melamed Literature.* If one takes the Calabresi-Melamed framework to suggest that a variety of mixtures of original endowments, liability rules, checks on moral hazards, and incentives can produce behaviorally similar, efficient results, then other rules can also be anticipated. The three extensions offered below illustrate the plasticity of the property-liability framework in thinking about a wide variety of judicial and other legal moves. They also illuminate the set of plausible rules in partnership law and other legal fields where love-it-or-leave-it and exclusivity rules have blossomed.

Students of the torts literature will hardly be surprised by the idea that Calabresi-Melamed missed some rules. There is, for example, Professor Polinsky's provocative exploration of "partial property rules," with which courts might grant injunctive relief to the extent that they are confident and promise damages where they are not.[39] Rather than allowing B to stop A, courts could allow B to stop A from engaging in some level of operation and award damages for operation below that level. Inasmuch as this particular extension of the Calabresi-Melamed framework has no special application to partnerships or love-it-or-leave-it questions, this article will not dwell on it. One might think of it as fitting in between Calabresi-Melamed's first and second rules.[40]

Professors Krier and Schwab, with imagination rivaling that of Calabresi and Melamed, have suggested another extension of the four-rule framework.[41] They offer as a fifth rule the idea that B stops A, but also pays to A, not A's

---

36. Spur Industries, Inc. v. Del E. Webb Dev. Co., 494 P.2d 700 (Ariz. 1972).

37. *Id.* at 708.

38. If A collects more than its relocation costs, A may decline to convert the use of its property until litigation takes place. Of course, there is still a more limited moral hazard when A collects bare relocation costs, because A may defer relocating until such time as a court awards these costs.

39. A. Mitchell Polinsky, *Resolving Nuisance Disputes: The Simple Economics of Injunctive and Damage Remedies*, 32 STAN. L. REV. 1075 (1980).

40. This characterization ignores the question of how often there really is the kind of second rule (B collects damages from A) that Polinsky, *supra* note 39, for example, builds on. In many settings it is likely that if a party continued its activity, and anticipated paying damages, a court would eventually allow punitive damages, criminal law, or even property rules to control the defendant's behavior. In other circumstances, however, where judges are genuinely uncertain about the relevant costs and benefits, the attraction of the second rule may be real enough for judges to maintain it. In any event, when the second rule comes in the form of a strict liability rule (which I will leave unnumbered), there is no reason to think that the defendant cannot continue its activity as before.

41. James E. Krier & Stewart J. Schwab, Property Rules and Liability Rules: The Cathedral in Another Light (Dec. 1994) (unpublished manuscript, on file with author).

costs of moving or some other amount keyed to A's circumstances, but *B's* alleged damages.[42] The idea behind this fifth rule is that when A's activity causes B $X in harm, B ought to be willing to pay $X in return for A's ceasing the harmful activity. Because Krier and Schwab structure the rule as an option given to A,[43] this fifth rule might be classified as a property rule.[44] In any event, the idea of working with B's enrichment from A's cessation rather than with A's costs of cessation or conversion to another activity may be attractive if there is cultural or political sympathy for A or where B's claim is difficult to verify.

Unfortunately, this fifth rule comes with its own problems. The first of these problems suggests immediately why one is unlikely to find this rule applied to partnership disputes. Although the rule may combat the moral hazard of B's coming to a nuisance and exaggerating damages, because B may be required to pay that which B claims to have lost while A's activity was in progress, the mirror-image risk arises that A will create problems for B in order to extract payments equal to B's damages but far in excess of A's avoidance costs.[45] Second, an offer-asking problem, or endowment effect, may prevent B from paying the amount required by this fifth rule, even where A would be unable to bargain for the right to continue as before if B had been awarded the property right (as suggested by the first Calabresi-Melamed rule).[46]

Note also that this fifth rule is not as strange as it first seems. It is true that we regularly encourage citizens to do X rather than Y by taxing or forbidding Y, but it is hardly unusual to subsidize X instead. Both the fourth and fifth rules reward or subsidize A's switching to another activity; one simply looks for the minimum amount necessary to encourage the switch, while the other asks

---

42. One could imagine two versions of this rule. In one, B pays if A stops, and in the other, A must stop and B must pay. Krier and Schwab favor the first, *id.* at 30-31, perhaps because they like the idea that misestimation of B's damages need not lead to an inefficient cessation of A's activity. In contrast, the advantage of the second version is that it controls B's claim. Indeed, the second version of the rule can be seen as an example of the kind of self-assessment scheme that our legal system could probably resort to more often.

43. Of course, it could also be seen as an option offered to B to bring suit against A, where such suit gives A an option to stop and collect damages from B.

44. The fact that B's damages define the amount of the subsidy or incentive to A does not necessarily turn this into a liability rule, because we normally think of liability rules as compensatory.

45. In some sense the fifth rule is therefore nothing new but rather a clever way of describing the extortion fear that accompanies too firm a belief in private bargaining. Thus, in a Coasian world, we can ask why intentional torts need to be actionable, inasmuch as B can always pay A not to kick B, and so forth. The answer presumably relates to the problem of separating credible from "mere" extortionary threats.

46. Thus the fifth rule is not of much help in cases like Rodgers v. Elliott, 15 N.E. 768 (Mass. 1888) (no liability for extrasensitive plaintiff's alleged injuries from defendant's ringing of church bells). An extrasensitive person might not have the means with which to buy relief (quietude, for example) from a noisy neighbor, even though the noisemaker might have been unable to buy the right to make noise if the right to tranquility had been allocated to the sensitive person in the first place.

the beneficiary to pay over what it would gain. A bargain might have materialized anywhere in between these two poles.[47]

2. *Forward-Looking Rules.* The remaining extensions of the Calabresi-Melamed framework draw attention both to temporal flexibility and to the fact that such flexibility sometimes seems to be kept deliberately out of judicial bounds. Consider a sixth rule, under which a judge gives no damages for past injuries suffered by B, but specifies the rate at which, or simply hints that, damages will be assessed for future injuries if A's behavior continues. Free of the property-liability framework, one recognizes this strategy as a fine, and is accustomed to legislative and administrative moves of this sort. Moreover, it is easy to imagine the occasional attraction of such a rule. Liability seems more attractive where there is notice, and forward-looking liability has this feature. More interestingly, when liability is only forward looking, the defendant has a chance to cease the offensive behavior with no liability at all. The knowledge that courts are likely to use only forward-looking remedies (of the property or liability rule type) in some settings may therefore avoid the problem of chilling activity in the face of uncertainty about what courts will find to be wrongful or otherwise actionable.

This sixth rule (A pays B's future damages) reveals that the more familiar second rule (B collects damages from A) is less pliant than it first seems. A party is unlikely to give up the right to collect past damages without appropriate consideration. It is one thing to say that if a court uses the second rule, A can still bargain with B so as to allow A to continue its activity while paying less than a court's liability rule decrees (and A's payment for past harm should not affect A's marginal decision about future behavior), but it is quite another for A to anticipate and then bargain preemptively regarding the likelihood of future retrospective liability. The prospect of a liability rule may thus be much more like that of a property rule than it initially seems, because, to the extent that liability rules encompass damages for past behavior, potential defendants will wish to bargain in advance before putting themselves in a position where they can be held liable for past practices. This description of the utility of fines, or the sixth rule (A pays B's future damages), raises the question of why judges do not issue exclusively forward-looking liability decisions and why Calabresi-Melamed miss this option. For now, I note simply that it is not within our legal culture for judges to do this. Property rules but not liability rules—which is to say injunctions but not damages—often come in exclusively forward-looking forms.[48] Courts can of course come very close to this sixth rule (A pays B's

---

47. And as for comparing the fourth (B stops A but pays A's net loss) and fifth (B stops A but pays B's enrichment) rules, it may be useful to note that we often fear subsidies more than taxes, because the former can be exploited in a way that comes close to moral hazard concerns. However, we do see a role for subsidies—especially if they must be financed by interest groups that bring about the policy (favoring the activity that is encouraged by the subsidy) in the first place.

48. *See infra* text accompanying note 53.

future damages) without levying fines; for example, they can find that something was a nuisance only in the very recent past, awarding minimal damages but promising larger future damages if A's behavior continues. Similarly, they can begin with the first rule (B stops A) but then sanction the violation of this injunction with damages. The first of these strategies (or low-level subterfuge) may be unsuitable where juries are in control of factfinding.[49]

By focusing on the ability of law to separate the past and future, the question of the relationship between Calabresi-Melamed's first and second rules becomes yet more interesting—and suggests still another missing rule. If a court chooses the first rule and issues an injunction stopping A on behalf of B, does such a property rule necessarily promise damages for past losses suffered by B at the hands of A? There is no doubt that a court can and often will provide injunctive relief along with damages for the past, but the Calabresi-Melamed analysis implies a separation of the two remedies. Thus, the claim that a property rule can be superior to a liability rule when the latter involves damages that are difficult to assess virtually assumes that the property rule listed by Calabresi-Melamed does not itself include damages for past injuries.[50] Nevertheless, let us consider their first rule to be the stronger version of a property rule, so that B stops A and also collects from A for past injuries. This version is strengthened by the idea that "property" is a bundle of rights normally thought to include the lesser right of bringing liability suits. In any event, under this version of the first rule, the second rule (B collects damages from A) becomes a subset of the first (B stops A and collects from A).

There is, then, room for another rule, which we can label the seventh rule, under which B stops A but collects no damages for A's past behavior. Note that both the sixth rule (A pays B's future damages) and the seventh rule (B stops A but collects no damages) are forward-looking in that they offer no damages for past injuries. It is easy to see how the seventh option might empower courts in public law and even in private law cases to take progressive or even radical steps. Indeed, it is possible that *plaintiffs* would argue for the seventh rule (B stops A but collects no damages) over the first (B stops A and collects from A), if the two were mutually exclusive, although they are not, because the first may often be too powerful to gain currency. This choice is examined in terms of plaintiffs' preferences because, as a matter of practice, it may often be the case that the first and seventh rules are not choices available to courts so much as to plaintiffs who can decide whether to ask for the seventh rule.[51] In asking for the seventh rule (B stops A but collects no damages),

---

49. There are, therefore, interesting comparative law implications as to the mix of property and liability rules found in different legal systems.

50. Calabresi & Melamed, *supra* note 33, at 1092 (commenting on property rule with the point that once "the original entitlement is decided upon, the state does not try to decide its value"). *But see id.* at 1119 (comparing entitlement protected by property rule to one protected "only" by a liability rule).

51. This is hardly the place to explore the question of when courts will give relief that no party has quite requested, or when a party must elect among the available remedies. The point in the text is simply that when the plaintiff, for example, asks for less rather than more, a court might be more willing

plaintiffs may preclude their own later claims for damages, but they may make it easier for courts to give them what they request. By asking for the first rule (B stops A and collects from A), plaintiffs may create some awkwardness for courts, which will need to find reasons to give equitable relief but not damages if giving both seems unwise or unjust.[52] In any event, this seventh rule (B stops A but collects no damages) rings familiar in many areas of public law where judicially imposed changes in criminal procedure and in the operation of public facilities such as prisons and schools come about in part because courts do not feel compelled to apply new law retroactively.[53] And we can surely imagine private law courts giving themselves a choice between the first and seventh rules (along with others)—even if it is normally the case that plaintiffs can limit the courts' options by asking for *either* the second rule (B collects damages from A) or the seventh rule (B stops A but collects no damages) or by merging two claims together and thus forcing courts to choose between the first rule (B stops A and collects from A) and no relief, which may be to say the third rule (A is unstoppable).[54]

D. The Property-Liability Framework and Partnership Law

This article has cultivated more theory than can possibly be directly relevant to understanding love-it-or-leave-it and liability rules in partnership law, and this is not the place for a full exploration of these rules and their temporal features. The immediate suggestion is that there are useful connections between partnership law, or even love-it-or-leave-it rules generally, and the property-liability rules framework. As previously noted, there are joint ventures where participants can sue for damages but not necessarily exit, others where the right to exit and gain one's fair share is the exclusive remedy, and still others where one can have both the exit option and the right to sue for damages without

---

to comply.

52. If the plaintiff requests "too much" of an injunction and does not request damages, a court can tailor the injunction.

53. One method of retrospective application is to permit (or even automatically grant) claims for damages for past actions.

If Calabresi-Melamed intend for their first rule (B stops A) to exclude retrospective damages, then I should have numbered as seventh the option of a powerful property rule that included liability rights. In any event, there are three rules (first, second, and seventh) where Calabresi-Melamed count only two. Moreover, this counting itself ignores Polinsky's rule. *See supra* notes 39-40 and accompanying text.

54. The choice between giving courts or plaintiffs these menu-setting choices is part of what I must leave for another project. My intuition is that a clever court can virtually always give itself a choice between the first and seventh options. It can, for example, use the seventh option where the first was requested by deciding that there is a nuisance to enjoin but that it has only risen to the level of nuisance (or negligence) in the very recent past.

Note also that the third rule can itself be thought of as a love-it-or-leave-it rule where the party's option is to stop or leave the relationship with no possibility of damages for what has occurred. In situations where a party's options are limited to exit and voice, one might think of the third rule as in effect.

exiting.[55] If the right to exit, or dissolve an arrangement, is recharacterized as the right to stop the joint venture, then there is the equivalent of the following: B stops A but collects no damages, B collects damages from A, and B stops A and collects from A. These are the seventh, second, and first rules discussed above.

Remarkably, partnership law also adopts the fourth Calabresi-Melamed rule (B stops A but pays A's net loss). As discussed earlier, when a partnership agreement is for a specified period or project, or even where it is not but where courts regard a party's exercising the power to force dissolution as exploitative, the doctrine of wrongful dissolution can be used to extract damages from the partner who insisted on stopping the venture.[56] There is, therefore, a set of cases where B can stop A but must pay A damages. The "relocation and moving costs" referred to in the lone celebrated case noted earlier[57] have a direct counterpart in the damages paid by the wrongful dissolver. And partnership law, explored in the manner just suggested, reveals at long last a practical side to Calabresi-Melamed's theoretical ingenuity.

As for the extensions developed here, the fifth rule (B stops A but pays B's enrichment) would allow a court in a wrongful dissolution case to have the dissolver pay the partnership not the damages suffered by the partnership or remaining partners but rather the gain to the dissolver. In cases where the underlying problem is that partners have a fundamentally different view of how best to earn profits or what level of risk in which to engage, however, the wronged partner cannot possibly believe that his damages are less than the dissolver's gain.[58] In all these cases, the advantage of the fifth rule (B stops A but pays B's enrichment) is absent; its strong point is that it serves as a check on the damages claimed by a plaintiff, but in the partnership context the

---

55. *See supra* part III.A (contrasting corporate rule with traditional partnership rule); *supra* note 10 ("Revised" Uniform Partnership Act rule allowing dissociation but also permitting other claims).

56. *See supra* note 23 and accompanying text (rightful and wrongful power to dissolve); *supra* note 13 (courts finding wrongfulness in order to prevent perceived exploitation).

Note that we might not expect Calabresi-Melamed's third rule (A is unstoppable) in partnership law because courts would need to force personal services in many cases. *See* UPA § 31, 6 U.L.A. at 376 ("The relation of partners is one of agency. The agency is such a personal one that equity cannot enforce it even where the agreement provides that the partnership shall continue for a definite time."). *But see supra* note 13 for the point that foreign jurisdictions do not allow a partner to force dissolution of a partnership for a specified term. Of course, many of these jurisdictions are more generally inclined toward remedies in the specific performance family.

57. Spur Industries, Inc. v. Del E. Webb Dev. Co., 494 P.2d 700, 708 (Ariz. 1972).

58. The dissolver may be wrongful either because he breaks an agreement as to the term of the venture or because he drastically destroys synergy. Either way, the very nature of the complaint against this dissolver is that there is loss, not gain, in dissolution.

Put quite differently, the fifth rule (B stops A but pays B's enrichment) imitates the worst bargain that the plaintiff or dissolver, B, would agree to, for it aims to capture his gains from stopping A or the venture. In the nuisance context, these gains are known because the plaintiff can be asked to claim damages before the court decides whether to go with the second (B collects damages from A) or fifth (B stops A but pays B's enrichment) rule. But in the partnership context, the fifth rule would present a valuation task where none existed before.

dissolver need not normally self-assess the damages from continuing on with the venture.[59]

Finally, the sixth rule (A pays B's future damages) suggests that forward-looking damages, or judicial fines, are sometimes useful and that a party subject to this remedy will occasionally find it worthwhile to continue the offensive behavior and pay the forward-looking damages, fines, or taxes, which the court has specified or simply threatened in the past. In other settings, the defendant will prefer the option of ceasing the offense and owing nothing at all. In one weak sense, partnership law may exhibit this rule as well. If B brings a suit against her partner A, then, as discussed earlier, it is traditional or possible for a court to refuse to explore the claim unless a claim for final accounting is brought at the same time. A, however, is generally free to change his behavior or to force dissolution himself, so that if A is fearful that one day in a final accounting B will collect for the matter complained about (but not judicially decided), A is able to avoid this liability. Moreover, it is at least plausible that if in a final accounting B complains for the first time about past wrongful behavior by A, having never expressed this objection to A (by direct communication or through a rejected lawsuit), a court might discount or even ignore B's claim. It is thus possible that courts feel quite free subtly to apply the sixth rule (A pays B's future damages) in partnership law. Unfortunately, it is difficult to test this hypothesis, if only because courts could not possibly feel *limited* to the sixth rule.[60] But without the property-liability rules framework—and the extensions suggested here—there would have been no clue to suggest looking for this explanation of partnership cases.

---

59. Some of these issues arise in cases where a partner has usurped a business opportunity. But in these cases valuation problems can normally be entirely avoided by the imposition of a constructive trust. Indeed, this explains the fact that constructive trust cases form a common exception to the traditional exclusivity rule in partnership law. *See supra* note 8; *infra* note 71 (constructive trust as an exception that does not implicate serious factfinding resources). Note also that when the offended partner objects to an alleged usurpation of opportunity, the time that passes between learning about the usurpation and objecting (or simply bringing a lawsuit) provides an opportunity for one party's expected gain to exceed the other's losses, because the plaintiff may be able to engage in "strategic delay" in order to see whether the competing business is something to be envied. *See generally* Saul Levmore, *Strategic Delays and Fiduciary Duties*, 74 VA. L. REV. 863 (1988).

60. If B turns up evil behavior by A, a court would surely be empowered to use the second rule, though it may defer action until a final accounting.

V
SELECTING REMEDIES

A. Bargaining Costs, Error Costs, and Moral Hazards

The literature on why and when judges might, or might be encouraged to, embrace one or the other of the Calabresi-Melamed rules, or for that matter choose among remedies in general, is murkier than the framework itself.[61] Conventional wisdom is that property rules are appropriate "shortcuts"—that is, decisions in the presence of, and in an attempt to economize on, transaction costs—when the likely results of hypothetical bargains are fairly clear.[62] For example, rather than allowing a nuclear weapon to be constructed in A's backyard, requiring A to pay damages if something goes awry, and expecting A's neighbors to bargain for A to switch hobbies, a property rule allowing neighbors (or the state) to stop A provides a convenient shortcut. Theoretically, a liability rule ought to produce the same result. Therefore, the advantage of property rules where the hypothetical bargain is clear is either that judges and especially juries might underestimate damages or that defendants like A might occasionally be undeterred by damage awards, if only because they anticipate a judgment-proof future. There might also be some benefit in encouraging future parties to bargain rather than await official damage assessments.

Liability rules, in contrast, are regarded as superior when the hypothetical bargain is less clear, because judicial error as to negligence can be overcome by the defendant continuing as before while paying damages.[63] There may also be moral and political advantages in allowing judges to balance some of the wealth effects at stake by requiring the winner in property-rights terms to pay something to the loser.

In short, liability rules provide judges with flexibility, but the very nature of these remedies requires time and effort by the factfinder.[64] Property rules are said to be preferable where the parties can bargain better than judges can assess damages, but this seems to undervalue the point that parties can always bargain

---

61. There is also the question of when to structure rules with enrichment rather than injury in mind. *See* A. Mitchell Polinsky & Steven Shavell, *Should Liability Be Based on the Harm to the Victim or the Gain to the Injurer?*, 10 J.L. ECON. & ORGANIZATION 427 (1994).

62. Krier & Schwab, *supra* note 41, at 13.

63. Calabresi & Melamed, *supra* note 33, at 1119. *But see* Krier & Schwab, *supra* note 41, at 15; Polinsky, *supra* note 39, at 1111. *See also supra* note 40 (question of whether parties could really continue as before and pay damages).

64. In theory, judges could choose wildly high approximations after expending very little time and effort, and such liability rules might dominate property rules because the defendant would be left with some room to continue its activity while over-paying for nonnegligently imposed harms. But our notions of due process make such a low-cost version of a liability rule difficult to fathom. Moreover, in some settings the wrongdoer can "choose" the liability remedy by destroying the property in question—unless the law further deters such self-help.

around liability rules as well.[65] As such, the choice seems to depend on the question of whether the benefit from flexibility, in mitigating wealth effects and in allowing deadlocked parties to continue as before while paying damages, exceeds the cost of assessing damages and the danger of behavioral insensitivity.[66]

The preceding paragraph summarizes a bargaining-based view of the choice between property and liability rules. A somewhat different perspective discounts the differences sketched above and emphasizes instead the moral hazard problems. Property rules would seem rather generally to create graver moral hazard problems because the winning party is in a position to extract payment from the loser whenever the court errs and the value of business-as-before to the winner exceeds the real costs of injury-as-before to the loser. It may therefore be profitable to come to a nuisance or to bring a complaint where no serious harm is really suffered. A liability rule creates a comparable moral hazard only where there is misassessment and damages are set too high. Thus, the common preference for liability rules over property rules in tort law conflicts may reflect an instinct for avoiding moral hazard problems. As already intimated, the fifth rule (B stops A but pays B's enrichment) may be unappealing to real judges for the same moral hazard-related reason that subsidies are often ridiculed in public policy debates. In short, one way to think about these rules is not as liability versus property, but rather as whether or not a moral hazard problem is present.

This article has already suggested that the superiority of liability rules on moral hazard or activity-level grounds becomes even more pronounced when liability rules can be structured as purely forward-looking.[67] But, as also noted, our legal culture appears to encourage legislators and regulators—but not judges—to use forward-looking liability schemes. Courts will often find it awkward to use forward-looking liability rules without also assessing damages for past conduct and harms. In contrast, they can probably enjoin future activity without awarding past damages.[68] A reasonable observer might in the end think that liability rules are superior because they raise fewer moral hazard

---

65. *See* Krier & Schwab, *supra* note 41, at 24-29. Put this way, the analogy to love-it-or-leave-it issues is again helpful. Consider, for example, the well-known idea that courts ought to be more willing to dissolve close corporations if only because, when there is going concern value, the parties can be expected to salvage this value by bargaining (for an exit price) in the wake of the dissolution decree. Hetherington & Dooley, *supra* note 25, at 27-29. In theory, the same ought to be true where courts refuse dissolution, so that there is only a liability right and no property right. The going concern value ought once again to be preserved by rational bargainers, although the exit price for the dissident will almost surely be lower than under a property rule assignment which guarantees exit or makes dissolution more likely. The argument for or against dissolution thus seems to be more about perceptions of ex post fairness than efficiency.

66. For example, a party's judgment-proof status can enfeeble liability rules.

67. *See supra* part IV.C.2.

68. *See* text accompanying notes 50-54 (discussing seventh rule). Some readers might think it the other way around, that exclusively forward-looking damages are more likely (less awkward for courts to carry out) than exclusively forward-looking injunctions (which is to say property rules with no damages for the past).

dangers, but that courts nevertheless occasionally choose property rules in order to economize on their own decision costs. In any event, it is likely that parties themselves behave in the shadow of backward-looking liability rules very much as they might be expected to in the face of anticipated property rules.

B. Valuation Tasks and Liability Rights in Partnership but Not in Marriage

Returning to partnership disputes, consider again the idea that the ability to force dissolution and a final accounting be regarded as a property right while the ability to bring suit for wrongful behavior, fiduciary breaches, and so forth be thought of as a liability right. As previously noted, the love-it-or-leave-it tradition in partnership law reflects the kind of property right that includes the lesser right to a liability rule because courts will permit the parties to bring other complaints to their attention once a final accounting is underway.[69] Indeed, under the traditional partnership rule, the very point of bringing a claim for one's "property right" of final accounting and dissolution may be to get a hearing on a liability matter that the complaining party would in fact have preferred to bring without severing the relationship.

The previous section of this article reviewed the idea that one strategy for choosing between property and liability rules (assuming for the moment that these are the only two choices) is to favor the less flexible property rules when liability is particularly difficult for courts to assess. This perspective offers a quick insight into partnership remedies once one recognizes that, in dissolution, judges will be required to undertake the very same valuation tasks that can be avoided by refusing liability rights. If the usual advantage of property rules is that judges need not assess damages, then it is critical to see that this very advantage is absent here because a final accounting requires these very valuation exercises. Put slightly differently, property rules may sometimes be preferred over liability rules in order to avoid the explicit valuation tasks associated with the latter,[70] but this distinction evaporates in the partnership setting because a party's property right of exit requires an evaluation of the worth of the partnership—not to mention an assessment of deferred claims among partners that could not be brought before the property-right trigger was pulled.

One cannot go so far as to say that property rules necessarily dominate liability rules in this setting. After all, the valuation task is deferred and may ultimately be avoided when a love-it-or-leave-it (or property) rule scheme is used.[71] The argument for a love-it-or-leave-it rule on these grounds must

---

69. *See supra* text accompanying notes 50-54 (comparing first and seventh rules).

70. There are implicit valuation tasks associated with most property rules, as when a judge must assess whether a factory is a nuisance or not.

71. And, indeed, one conventional explanation for the exclusivity rule in partnership law was that it economized on judicial resources. *See, e.g.,* Schuler v. Birnbaum, 405 N.Y.S.2d 351, 352 (N.Y. App. Div. 1978) (exclusivity rule promotes judicial economy by preventing piecemeal litigation). The exception in which the court could impose a constructive trust obviously fits this explanation.

therefore be based on the likelihood of private bargaining and its ability to avoid the costs associated with the litigation (or separation) that a liability right might generate. The traditional love-it-or-leave-it rule was hardly ridiculous, for it is surely possible that it encouraged private ordering and economized on judicial valuation tasks. Nevertheless, the move toward a liability rule can be understood as attractive because the valuation tasks associated with the liability claim were not necessarily avoided by the property rule in the first place.

The comparison with the law of domestic relations is instructive. The love-it-or-leave-it rule governing marriage[72] might be regarded as economizing on valuation work, among other things, because, even when parties proceed to divorce, courts can often avoid performing the valuation tasks that would be necessary if married persons had liability rights. It is, after all, often the case that decisions about divorce, child custody, support payments, and so forth can be made without assessing the harm imposed earlier by implicit or explicit breaches of the marriage arrangement.[73] For this reason alone, it is not surprising that the law of partnership remedies has moved further and more quickly toward a liability rule than has the law of marriage and divorce. The contrary view is that many divorces do involve courts in difficult decisions, so that the preference for a love-it-or-leave-it rule requires one to consider cultural factors or to face the fundamental question of whether love-it-or-leave-it rules can be expected to lead to more rather than less compromise.[74] Inasmuch as this article next turns to a different argument about love-it-or-leave-it rules for marriage, it is useful to assume that valuation tasks are indeed avoided by a love-it-or-leave-it rule in the law of domestic relations.

The focus on valuation tasks suggests less early intervention in marriages. At the same time, the role of moral hazard dangers in choosing among remedies suggests that in both marriage and business partnership settings, if there is to be judicial intervention, there might be a greater range of available remedies than in much of tort or other law. The reason is that parties would seem less likely to enter, or to be able to enter, marriage or partnership arrangements simply to profit from exit. For example, a court that hesitated to invoke the fifth rule in a nuisance case, for fear that the prospect of payment to A of B's alleged damages might cause A to engage in an activity that is likely to be injurious to B, might be more likely to experiment with a partnership (or even a marriage) case where such very ex ante moral hazard seems unlikely.[75]

---

72. *See supra* notes 14-17 and accompanying text.
73. *See* CLARK, *supra* note 15, § 1.1.
74. For the sake of argument, this analysis assumes that the law regards more compromise as a good thing.
75. Once there is conflict in a partnership or marriage, the moral hazard problem returns. Partners and spouses are surely capable of engaging in offensive behavior and thus imposing costs on their partners, in order to gain bargaining advantage, even where there is no intrinsic gain to the actor. But the fact that the relationship itself is relatively unlikely to be entered into in order to gain this sort of advantage suggests that there may be more room for some moral hazard-prone remedies here than in standard tort cases.

A comparison of nuisance and partnership claims emphasizes the idea that one way to think about the evolution of partnership law is to focus on the valuation tasks peculiar to dissolution conflicts in that area of law. When B seeks to shut down A, the injunction or property rule sought by B requires no explicit valuations by the supervising judge; a rough calculation might be needed in order to decide whether this property rule is the appropriate shortcut, but no precise measurement is required.[76] In contrast, when a partner moves to "shut down" a partnership, the final accounting that must be undertaken includes the very same valuation tasks as the liability suit that was shunned earlier because of the traditional love-it-or-leave-it rule.

C. Property Rules and Not Liability Rules for Domestic Relations

This article has suggested in passing that a love-it-or-leave-it rule for parties to a marriage contract may be superior, at least from a court's perspective, to a liability rule because the former may first postpone and then entirely avoid difficult valuation tasks. The property-liability framework points to a much stronger explanation for love-it-or-leave-it rules in marriage law.

It is easy to regard the love-it-or-leave-it rule for marriage as anachronistic. There is some irony to the claim that parties to a marriage should not litigate but should work out their problems. First, the same might be said of most other parties in conflict; if courts think that peaceful settlement is promoted by a love-it-or-leave-it rule in marriage, then it is not entirely obvious why courts do not extend that intuition to parties to other contracts.[77] Second, and more important, it is precisely in the area of domestic relations, where the love-it-or-leave-it rule is most robust, that a substantial industry of counseling and mediation has arisen. Private parties can be said to react to the mandatory love-it-or-leave-it rule by "litigating" in the shadow of the courthouse and turning to pastors, psychologists, and other counselors. The demand for these nonjudicial services might be regarded as a clamor for a liability remedy where none is offered by law.

Put differently, when there is conflict in marriage and dissolution is a risk, the parties' friends normally appear to think that third-party intervention promotes, rather than threatens, compromise and long-term peaceful, pleasurable coexistence. It is no accident that mediation has blossomed most in the very context in which the love-it-or-leave-it rule stands most firm in the courtroom. Why then do judges not supply law where it is apparently sought?

The question returns us to the nature of property and liability rules in different settings. It is useful to think of the remedies available to courts in business and then in marriage arrangements. Monetary relief is of course common in shareholder-corporate disputes, and it is easy to use in partnership cases where the traditional love-it-or-leave-it rule has fallen. Specific

---

76. Calabresi & Melamed, *supra* note 33, at 1120.
77. Parties might agree that any suit for breach releases the other party from further performance.

performance is less common if only because it will often require postjudgment supervision. Such supervision is especially difficult and distasteful where personal services would be required from one who does not wish to perform. Injunctive relief is, of course, a kind of specific performance, and some structural injunctions do involve a great deal of monitoring (for example, prisons and school systems that do not wish to perform as required by courts). These exceptional examples make clear why courts would not wish to supervise decrees regarding married persons. Yet in most marriages, assets are commingled. It is thus hard to imagine most courts agreeing to use liability rules without a divorce decree because the judgment would have little effect if the spouses did not have separate financial lives. The alternative of specific performance would require enormous judicial involvement. Although courts do need to undertake some involvement after divorce, as when parties do not live up to their judicially imposed responsibilities regarding the payment of child support or facilitating visitation rights, the love-it-or-leave-it rule is unsurprising when one realizes the enormous tasks courts would be required to undertake were there in-marriage remedies.[78] Finally, courts are simply not in the business of counseling or issuing advisory opinions to private parties.

This analysis suggests that the valuation idea does explain a great deal of the love-it-or-leave-it pattern. Even if marriage is an exception rather than another example of this theme, the use of the love-it-or-leave-it rule in marriage is best explained by the observation that a liability rule is essentially unworkable in a world where most spouses commingle their financial resources.

D. Love-It-or-Leave-It Revisited

1. *Intuitions about Love-It-or-Leave-It Rules in Disparate Settings.* What, then, explains the exclusivity rule as embodied in the first and seventh property rules in traditional partnership law? One possibility is that private bargaining is more likely if liability suits are unavailable. But, as already noted, if the parties can bargain, it should often make little difference whether they are bargaining around a property rule or a liability rule.[79] It is plausible, however,

---

78. Note that, consistent with the analysis in the text, there is room for in-marriage remedies of the property-rule kind. Where there is a fear of violence, for example, one spouse may get a restraining order against another. More generally, when courts chip away at the love-it-or-leave-it rule, we should expect them to do so where there are modest valuation tasks and property-rule like remedies. Thus, it would not be shocking if a court came to the assistance of a spouse who wished to stop another from undertaking an imprudent investment. Still, such interventions are not to be expected outside of community property jurisdictions. *Compare* Kirchberg v. Feenstra, 450 U.S. 455 (1981) (holding unconstitutional Louisiana statute that allowed husbands, but not wives, to execute mortgages on jointly owned property without spousal consent), *with* McGuire v. McGuire, 59 N.W.2d 336 (Neb. 1953) (insisting that "public policy" requires rejection of wife's complaint about insufficient financial support).

One should recognize that when these rules were developed, spouses were regarded by the law as having separate financial assets and lives. Put differently, 50 years ago courts could have required one spouse to pay damages to the other, but they did not. The story in the text is thus incomplete, but might be enriched by adding the reality of limited liquid assets.

79. *See supra* part V.A.

that with more at stake under a love-it-or-leave-it rule, parties may shy away from going to court with their conflicts.[80]

Imagine, as a first example, a labor law rule that barred litigation either in court or through the National Labor Relations Board unless the union was on strike or locked out. Under such a rule, the two sides to a collective bargaining agreement would have a "property right" to stop work but no stand-alone liability rule as a remedy. My intuition is that most observers would think that such a love-it-or-leave-it rule would generate more strikes and social costs than the present regime, which is more permissive of litigation including a kind of forced arbitration. The love-it-or-leave-it rule might, of course, also stimulate additional compromises (because not all disputes need trigger strikes), but the point is that there might be greater rather than smaller social and private costs under such an extreme rule.

Consider, by way of comparison, the now-familiar love-it-or-leave-it rule regarding conflicts between spouses. The parties are unable to bargain around this rule; a prenuptial contract regulating responsibilities within a marriage and in the event of divorce may carry weight in the event of a divorce, but it is most unlikely to open up the courthouse doors during a marriage. Courts treat marriage as a rather extreme love-it-or-leave-it arrangement. Here, most observers may sense that the love-it-or-leave-it rule does not increase the social costs and likelihood of divorce. There is obviously much to be said about strategic behavior and cultural norms in both the marriage and collective bargaining contexts. The narrow point is that these contrasting intuitions reflect the idea that it is by no means obvious whether love-it-or-leave-it rules, which is to say property rules, or "cliffs,"[81] promote compromises or hostile separations.

To use one more example, consider the role of mutually assured destruction in game theory about warfare.[82] It is plausible that there is less war where there is mutually assured destruction, much as it is possible that there is less litigation (and dissolution) with love-it-or-leave-it rules. But the more telling comparison is whether a nation or a pair of nations would be better off armed with nuclear weapons and capable of mutually assured destruction—while possessing no conventional weapons at all. Is it plausible that superpowers would be better off giving up their conventional weapons in order to have only the threat of nuclear weapons? My intuition is that most of us think that

---

80. This is the argument set aside in part III.C, *supra.*

81. The idea is that when rules present actors with the prospect of serious liability if they step over a thin, uncertain line, these actors might be overdeterred and stand back from the line or "cliff." *See* SAUL LEVMORE, FOUNDATIONS OF TORT LAW 99 (1994) (suggesting that the kink or cliff or overdeterrence effect generally assumes that full rather than incrementally caused damages will be assigned to the negligent tortfeasor); John Calfee & Richard Craswell, *Some Effects of Uncertainty on Compliance with Legal Standards*, 70 VA. L. REV. 965 (1984). Love-it-or-leave-it rules would seem to have this feature as well.

82. Of lasting value is THOMAS C. SCHELLING, THE STRATEGY OF CONFLICT 119-61, 230-54 (1960).

conventional weapons, and their liability rule counterparts, reduce the opportunity for exploitation and even the likelihood of mutual destruction.[83]

Nevertheless, it is plausible that parties would benefit from a choice between a property rule and a liability rule, or between mutually assured destruction alone and conventional weapons along with mutually assured destruction. Different intuitions about games of chicken or different reactions to different settings could easily lead to a preference for one scheme or the other.

2. *Explaining the Traditional Rule in Partnership.* The exclusivity rule in partnership[84] might also be explained by returning to the earlier discussion about the choice of business form.[85] Once upon a time, coventurers could choose between a love-it-or-leave-it and a liability rule by selecting either the partnership or corporate form. But in a world in which this choice is dominated by tax and governance considerations, there is no room for an exclusivity rule of the kind once found. It is therefore not surprising that the corporate and partnership rules have drifted closer to one another.

At the same time, the remedies have not quite converged. The evolved partnership law norm approximates the first rule[86]- a right to dissolution along with a right to sue for damages in an ongoing relationship. The evolved corporate norm is closer to the second rule (B collects damages from A), with a hint, and not a guarantee, of an exit right, except where an appraisal remedy or other developments creep in. It would not be surprising if the convergence trend continued. Thus, one might expect courts more often to imply agreements for partnerships of specified terms in order to withdraw the claim-free, or untaxed, right to exit.[87] Alternatively, corporate law might increasingly grant requests for dissolution (or appraisal), in which case that body of law will become more like contemporary partnership law.[88] If there is convergence, and a shared default rule materializes, there will be some room for debate as to whether the shared rule is efficient or instead supplants what had been useful, alternative default rules.[89] In any event, one aim of this article is to draw attention to the idea that the law of remedies in partnership and corporate law

---

83. To the extent that it *is* plausible that nuclear deterrents *alone* would make sense if there were only superpowers, and no smaller enemies to fear, an interesting observation is that we are most inclined toward the love-it-or-leave-it-like extreme where peers are involved. Partnerships, marriages, and superpowers can be said, at least ideally or in theory, to be bargaining as equals, unlike principals-agents, corporations-shareholders, and many other areas where love-it-or-leave-it can be said to have been rejected (such as states-citizens). Because there are important counterexamples, where "peers" have ongoing litigation, this article does not pursue this theme. These counterexamples include employers-unions and, more generally, parties to most contracts.

84. *See supra* notes 5, 7 and accompanying text.

85. *See supra* part III.B.

86. The labels refer again to the first through seventh rules, sketched *supra* in parts III.B, IV.C.

87. *See supra* note 13.

88. *See supra* note 25.

89. *See generally* Jody S. Kraus, Legal Design and the Evolution of Commercial Norms (unpublished manuscript, on file with author).

once offered alternative and very different default rules but is narrowing over time.

Finally, it is noteworthy that the evolution of partnership law has not only been from the mold of the seventh rule (B stops A but collects no damages[90]) to that of the first (B stops A and collects from A), but also may have shifted toward nonmandatory default rules. The traditional exclusivity rule was substantially mandatory.[91] The question is whether the modern trend toward allowing actions while the partnership continues without an accounting[92] anticipates letting partners opt out of this permissive rule into a love-it-or-leave-it scheme.[93] If so, which is to say that agreements not to bring actions will be enforceable or will at least provoke claims all their own, then the Calabresi-Melamed framework is all the more appropriate. That framework, after all, anticipates private bargaining around the rules, except for unusual cases of inalienability.[94] Put in more negative terms, one drawback to thinking about the traditional partnership remedy and other love-it-or-leave-it rules in property-liability terms is that the property-liability framework too easily obscures the mandatory nature of some of these remedy rules.

E. The Survival of Love-It-or-Leave-It in Domestic Relations Law

The love-it-or-leave-it rule in domestic relations has come to look rather lonely. This article has suggested that its survival can be explained more by the disinclination of courts to deal with the enforcement of liability rules in the family setting than by the advantages of love-it-or-leave-it rules.[95] It is possible, of course, that the love-it-or-leave-it rule in marriage will yield, as it did in business partnerships, to other rules. But the trend in the law of domestic relations can be described as heading toward yet stronger love-it-or-leave-it rules, in that courts seem less interested than before in assigning "fault" during marriage.[96] At the same time, the level of judicial supervision required post-divorce regarding child custody and support payments may soon persuade courts that their jobs might in fact be easier if there were more intervention during marriages.

---

90. That is, unless there were wrongs that can now be assessed at the time of final accounting.
91. *See supra* text accompanying note 22.
92. *See supra* note 23.
93. Although we are accustomed to courts supporting precommitments to go to arbitration rather than formal litigation, courts will surely be troubled by some agreements to forgo litigation. On the other hand, courts might be inclined to allow private agreements for love-it-or-leave-it rules where the parties are seen as bargaining equals.
94. Calabresi & Melamed, *supra* note 33, at 1123-24, note the possibility of giving a polluter an inalienable right to pollute in some specified amount. This can be seen as a love-it-or-leave-it rule.
95. Approximately one-third of the states have adopted "no-fault" statutes regarding the granting of divorce. WALTER WADLINGTON, CASES AND OTHER MATERIALS ON DOMESTIC RELATIONS 1033 (2d ed. 1990).
96. *See supra* note 15.

VI
CONCLUSION

Contract law itself has evolved away from a love-it-or-leave-it rule and toward ongoing liability rules. There was a time when to bring a claim against one's supplier, for example, was to terminate the supply contract.[97] Over time it appears that most parties, and therefore judges, came to prefer an expansion of remedies and, in particular, the possibility of legal intervention in a continuing contractual relationship. A sensible explanation of this and other evolutionary examples is probably that our culture, both legal and general, prefers more rather than fewer remedies and is generally disinclined to adopt a strategy of encouraging compromise and peace by denying the opportunity for modest skirmishes. It is, of course, also conceivable that this evolution is efficient. There seems to be no evidence that parties or lawmakers systematically learned that love-it-or-leave-it rules generated greater social costs (or even private costs[98]) than alternative remedy schemes, but it is possible that the law improves in mysterious ways.

If the story of these love-it-or-leave-it rules and their demise (outside of domestic relations law) reflects evolution in the direction of additional remedies, it becomes yet more important to learn to match specific remedies with particular circumstances. This article has suggested that we pay more attention to the remedies that we still struggle to imagine. Love-it-or-leave-it rules, forward-looking damage rules, and subsidies as substitutes for taxes have something in common, for they seem less unusual when closely examined and, once investigated, they look like plausible candidates for new roles in the future.

---

97. The rule was that a partial claim often precluded a later claim, because only one action was permitted. *See* E. ALLAN FARNSWORTH, CONTRACTS 635 (2d ed. 1990).

98. It is possible that additional remedies transform the private costs of bargaining into externalized costs for the court system. However, this effect is likely to be limited. Litigation may involve large costs that the parties do not bear, but litigation itself appears to generate very substantial private costs, if only because private bargaining is less constrained by formal rules.

C
The Unhappy Family

[15]

Separate Spheres Bargaining and the Marriage Market

Shelly Lundberg and Robert A. Pollak

University of Washington

This paper introduces the "separate spheres" bargaining model, a new model of distribution within marriage. It differs from divorce threat bargaining models (e.g., Manser-Brown, McElroy-Horney) in that the threat point is not divorce but a noncooperative equilibrium within marriage; this noncooperative equilibrium reflects traditional gender roles. The predictions of our model thus differ from those of divorce threat bargaining models; in the separate spheres model, cash transfer payments to the mother and payments to the father can—but need not—imply different equilibrium distributions in existing marriages. In the long run, the distributional effects of transfer policies may be substantially altered by changes in the marriage market equilibrium.

I. Introduction

The expectation that family policies will affect distribution within marriage is implicit in much popular discussion. For example, child care subsidies and child allowances are often regarded as women's issues. Women's groups are outspoken advocates of such programs, and women are expected to be among their primary beneficiaries. This linking of women's and children's welfare with child-based sub-

This paper is a revised and retitled version of "Gender Roles and Intrafamily Distribution." We would like to thank our respective spouses for their cooperation and the Rockefeller Foundation for financial support. Neither our spouses nor the Rockefeller Foundation is responsible for the views expressed here. We are grateful to the anonymous referees, to Laurie Bassi, Gary Becker, David S. Johnson, Andrew Postlewaite, Mark Rosenzweig, Pepper Schwartz, and Amartya Sen, and to seminar participants at Chicago, Georgetown, Harvard, Indiana, Pittsburgh, Penn, Penn State, Texas, and Washington for useful comments.

[*Journal of Political Economy*, 1993, vol. 101, no. 6]

sidies is rooted in the gender assignment of child care: mothers expect and are expected to assume primary responsibility for their children.[1] Yet the distributional implications of these policies are far
from clear. Child-conditioned subsidies would certainly transfer resources to the heads of single-parent families, who are predominantly
women. But what effect, if any, would such programs have on distribution between women and men in two-parent families?

Using a new model of marital bargaining, we analyze the distributional effect of such programs in two-parent families, focusing on an
analytically tractable special case. We compare two child allowance
schemes: in the first, a cash transfer is paid to the mother; in the
second, it is paid to the father. In the event of divorce, we assume
that under both schemes the mother becomes the custodial parent
and receives the child allowance. The comparison we propose is sim-
pler than those involving more familiar programs such as child care
subsidies because the alternative policies we consider involve neither
price effects nor tax incentive effects.

The two leading economic models of intrafamily allocation imply
that these alternative child allowance schemes have identical implications for distribution in two-parent families. In the altruist model
(Becker 1974a, 1981), the equilibrium is the point in the feasible
consumption set that maximizes the altruist's utility; that point is independent of which parent receives the child allowance because the
feasible consumption set is identical under the two child allowance
schemes. In the bargaining models of Manser and Brown (1980) and
McElroy and Horney (1981), the equilibrium is determined by the
feasible consumption set and a threat point that is interpreted as the
utility of remaining single or of getting divorced. The equilibrium is
independent of which parent receives the child allowance because the
feasible consumption set and the well-being of single and divorced
individuals are identical under the two child allowance schemes.

Many participants in the public debate concerning actual government transfers take it for granted that intrafamily distribution will
vary systematically with the control of resources. When the British
child allowance system was changed in the mid-1970s to make child
benefits payable in cash to the mother, it was widely regarded as a
redistribution of family income from men to women and was expected to be popular with women: "Indeed so convinced did some
Ministers become that a transfer of income 'from the wallet to the

---

[1] As Crawford and Pollak (1989) point out, it is often asserted that mothers are
primarily responsible for child care in three senses: first, it is mothers who find a child
care provider and make the arrangements; second, it is mothers who take time off
from work when a child is sick or when child care arrangements collapse; and third,
it is mothers who "pay" child care expenses from their discretionary incomes.

purse' at a time of wage restraint would be resented by male workers, that they decided at one point in 1977 to defer the whole child benefit scheme" (Brown 1984, p. 64).

In this paper we propose the "separate spheres" bargaining model, a new model of distribution in two-parent families. The separate spheres model differs from the divorce threat model in two ways. First, the threat point is not divorce but a noncooperative equilibrium defined in terms of traditional gender roles and gender role expectations. Second, the noncooperative equilibrium, although it is not Pareto optimal, may be the final equilibrium because of the presence of transaction costs. We show that in the separate spheres bargaining model, cash transfer child allowance schemes that pay the mother and those that pay the father can—but need not—imply different equilibrium distributions in existing marriages. The separate spheres model is thus not inconsistent with the view, popular among noneconomists, that distribution between women and men in two-parent families will depend on which parent receives the child allowance payment.

In the long run, the redistributive effects of child allowances depend on the feasibility of making contractual arrangements in the marriage market. The marriage market will wholly undo any redistributive effects if prospective couples can make binding, costlessly enforceable, prenuptial agreements to transfer resources within the marriage; dowry and bride-price can, under certain circumstances, be interpreted as examples of practices that facilitate such Ricardian equivalence. If binding agreements cannot be made in the marriage market—and we think that this is the relevant case for advanced, industrial societies—child allowances may have long-run distributional effects.

The analysis of alternative cash transfer child allowance schemes is analytically tractable because it does not require us to consider policies that affect prices (e.g., subsidizing child care) or policies that affect the well-being of single or divorced individuals (e.g., Aid to Families with Dependent Children and other welfare programs). Cash transfer schemes such as child allowances are the policies most likely to be undone in the short run by bargaining within existing marriages and in the long run by adjustments in the marriage market. The effects of other policies, such as child care subsidies, on distribution between women and men in two-parent families are thus likely to be greater than our comparison of alternative child allowance schemes suggests.

In Section II we provide an overview of the problem of intrafamily distribution, and in Section III we develop several versions of the separate spheres bargaining model. Section IV shows that in the long run the marriage market can completely undo any redistribution effects of child allowances if binding, costlessly enforceable, prenuptial agreements can be made. In Section V we consider the case in which individuals cannot make binding, costlessly enforceable agreements in the marriage market; we show that in this case the redistributive effects of child allowances may induce changes in the equilibrium number of marriages, as well as changes in distribution within particular marriages. Section VI is a brief conclusion.

II. Models of Intrafamily Distribution

Economic models of household behavior have generally ignored distribution within the family. Samuelson's (1956) consensus model provided the first formal justification for this neglect. Samuelson was concerned not with explaining distribution within the family but with identifying the conditions under which consumer demand analysis could proceed without doing so. In the consensus model, each member of the family behaves as though there were a family utility function that all attempt to maximize; this assumption allows the family to be analyzed as a single unit. Because the incomes of individual family members are pooled in the joint budget, the effect of lump-sum payments (e.g., property income or government transfers) is independent of which family member receives the payment. As Samuelson made clear in his original article, as a theory of distribution within the family, the consensus model is a nonstarter.

The economist's standard model of distribution within the family is Becker's (1974a, 1981) altruist model. Becker postulates that the family contains one "altruistic" individual—the husband, father, patriarch, dictator—whose preferences reflect his concern for the welfare of other family members. Becker argues that the presence of one altruist who makes positive transfers to each member of the family is sufficient to induce purely selfish but rational family members to maximize family income. The resulting distribution is the one that maximizes the altruist's utility function subject to the family's resource constraint. Becker's "rotten kid theorem" (Becker 1974b, 1981) embodies this result; Pollak (1985), Bergstrom (1989), and Johnson (1990) articulate the conditions under which the conclusion of the rotten kid theorem holds. The source of the altruist's power in Becker's model is not his concern with the welfare of others but rather his assumed ability to confront others with "take-it-or-leave-it" choices; altruism in the sense of caring about the welfare of others is required only to explain why the altruist chooses a distribution that allows other members of the family a positive surplus (i.e., more than their reservation levels of utility). The altruist model implies that an increase in family resources, within certain limits, will have the same effect on intrafamily distribution regardless of which spouse receives the resources. It therefore implies that a government program of child allowances would have identical effects on distribution regardless of whether the payments went to mothers or to fathers. According to both the altruist model and the consensus model, the family behaves as though it were maximizing a single utility function. This implies restrictions on observable outcomes that the data fail to support.[2]

Bargaining models of marriage (Manser and Brown 1980; McElroy and Horney 1981) treat marriage as a cooperative game: spouses with conflicting interests or preferences are assumed to resolve their differences in a manner prescribed by the Nash or some other explicit bargaining solution. A distinguishing feature of bargaining models is that family demand behavior depends not only on total family resources but also on the resources controlled by each spouse individually. Individual control of resources matters because bargaining outcomes depend on threat points as well as on the feasible consumption set. The threat point in a cooperative game is usually described as reflecting the outcome that would obtain in the absence of agreement. Manser and Brown (1980) and McElroy and Horney (1981) specify the threat point as the individuals' maximal levels of utility outside the family, that is, the value of divorce. The more attractive an individual's opportunities outside the family, the more strongly that individual's preferences will be reflected in the intrafamily distribution of resources.[3]

The dependence of intrafamily distribution on the well-being of divorced individuals provides a mechanism through which government policy can affect distribution within marriage in divorce threat bargaining models. An increase in the child allowances paid to *divorced* mothers will increase the expected utility of divorced women and cause a reallocation of family resources in two-parent families toward goods and services more highly valued by wives. An increase in child allowances paid to *all* mothers would affect distribution in two-parent families through the divorce threat effect and through an income effect. Under our assumption that, in the event of divorce, the mother gets the children and the child allowance, both husbands

---

[2] A survey by McElroy (1981) concludes that there is little empirical support for these restrictions. Lundberg (1988) empirically rejects a simple version of the consensus model as a foundation for the labor supply behavior of husbands and wives.

[3] As McElroy (1990) emphasizes, this dependence of household demands on the external alternatives available to individual family members is a testable implication of the bargaining framework. Empirical evidence consistent with family bargaining has been accumulating. For example, unearned income received by husbands and wives has been shown to have different effects on outcomes such as time allocation and fertility (Schultz 1990) and child health and survival (Thomas 1990).

and wives would be indifferent between a child allowance scheme that paid mothers and one that paid fathers: an increase in child allowances paid to married mothers and a decrease in child allowances paid to married fathers create neither divorce threat effects nor income effects.

While divorce may be the ultimate threat available to both spouses and is a possible destination for marriages in which bargaining has failed, it is not the only possible threat point from which bargaining could proceed.[4] Following a suggestion by Woolley (1988), we consider a noncooperative Cournot-Nash equilibrium within marriage as an alternative threat point.[5] Within an existing marriage, a noncooperative equilibrium corresponds to a utility-maximizing strategy in which each spouse takes the other spouse's strategy as given. Under some circumstances, this equilibrium more accurately represents the outcome of marital noncooperation than does the costly and time-consuming alternative of divorce.

What distinguishes a noncooperative marriage from a pair of independently optimizing individuals? Joint consumption economies are an important source of gains to marriage, and even noncooperative family members enjoy the benefits of household public goods. If individual family members can supply public goods consumed by the entire household, then the noncooperative family equilibrium is analogous to the voluntary provision of public goods model analyzed by Bergstrom, Blume, and Varian (1986). As one might expect, public goods are undersupplied in this noncooperative equilibrium, and there are potential gains to cooperation. Additional gains can be expected if coordination of individual contributions is required for efficient household production. In the absence of cooperation and coordination, the effective quantity of public goods and services such as meals and child care will be less than the amounts that could be produced from the individual contributions. Specialization in the provision of such goods reduces the need for complex patterns of coordination, and traditional gender roles serve as a focal point for tacit division of responsibilities.

Specialization by gender is a pervasive aspect of family life. In the United States, though market work by married women has increased enormously in recent decades, men continue to carry most of the responsibility for earning income in two-parent families, and women continue to carry both the responsibility for and the actual work of

---

[4] We ignore the threat and the actuality of family violence, although we think that the relationship between family violence and intrafamily distribution deserves more attention. For an interesting discussion, see Tauchen, Witte, and Long (1991).

[5] Because Nash's name is associated with both the cooperative and the noncooperative equilibrium concepts we use, we have tried to avoid the phrase "Nash equilibrium."

supplying household services. Carried to extremes, the traditional division of labor and responsibilities suggests a "separate spheres" equilibrium in the family. When husband and wife each bear the responsibility for a distinct, gender-specific set of household activities, minimal coordination is required because each spouse makes decisions within his or her own sphere, optimizing subject to the constraint of individual resources. If binding, costlessly enforceable agreements regarding transfers can be made prior to marriage, such agreements may involve a "housekeeping allowance" for the wife or "pocket money" for the husband.[6] If binding agreements cannot be made, the level of transfers may be zero, or it may be determined by custom or social norms.

In a noncooperative marriage, a division of labor based on socially recognized and sanctioned gender roles emerges without explicit bargaining. In the separate spheres bargaining model, this voluntary contribution equilibrium is the threat point from which bargaining proceeds. Cooperative bargaining is distinguished by the ability of the players to make binding agreements within marriage.[7] The negotiation, monitoring, and enforcement of such agreements give rise to transaction costs, which may vary over husband-wife pairs. The noncooperative default allocation avoids these costs; the voluntary contribution equilibrium is maintained by social enforcement of the obligations corresponding to generally recognized and accepted gender roles.[8] It will be optimal for couples with high transaction costs or low expected gains from cooperation to remain at the stereotypical noncooperative solution.

The distributional implications of the separate spheres bargaining model differ from those of the divorce threat bargaining model. As Warr (1983) and Bergstrom et al. (1986) have shown, the control of resources among the potential contributors to a public good in a

---

[6] Pahl (1983) describes four types of financial management in husband-wife households, three of which are consistent with the "separate spheres" equilibrium. Under the "whole-wage" system, one partner, usually the wife, manages all family income and is responsible for all expenditures, except for the personal spending money of the other partner. This system is characteristic of low-income families in Britain and other European countries. Under the "allowance" system, the husband pays the wife a set amount, and she is responsible for specific items of expenditure. With "independent management," separate incomes are used to finance expenditures within each partner's "sphere of responsibility." In all empirical studies cited, these three systems are together more prevalent than the fourth—"shared management."

[7] Caution: We are concerned here with the ability of the spouses to make binding agreements *within* marriage. Their ability to make binding agreements *before* marriage plays a crucial role in determining long-run effects.

[8] This is, of course, a cop-out. By appealing to the social enforcement of gender roles, we beg the question of how "norms" of any type are established and maintained. Elster (1989) and Sugden (1989) discuss this issue and provide references to the literature.

voluntary provision model affects neither the equilibrium level of
the public good nor the equilibrium utility levels of the potential
contributors, provided that each potential contributor makes a strictly
positive contribution. These invariance properties do not hold, however, at corner solutions. In the noncooperative, voluntary contribution equilibrium in the family, gender specialization generates corner
solutions, and hence the equilibrium distribution may depend not
only on total family resources but also on who controls those resources.

III. Household Public Goods and Bargaining

We first consider distribution within a particular marriage. The preferences of the husband, h, and the wife, w, are represented by the
von Neumann–Morgenstern utility functions $U^h(x_h, q_1, q_2)$ and $U^w(x_w,
q_1, q_2)$, where x_h and x_w are private goods consumed by the husband
and wife, and q_1 and q_2 are household public goods jointly consumed
by the husband and wife. Thus we assume that interdependence in
the marriage operates only through consumption of the public goods:
there is no "altruism" in the sense of interdependent preferences,
although it would be a straightforward extension to allow i's utility to
depend directly on j's private consumption or j's utility.[9] Cooperative
solutions to the family's distribution problem have been extensively
analyzed elsewhere. With Nash bargaining, the equilibrium values of
x_h, x_w, q_1, and q_2 are those that maximize the product of the gains
to cooperation; these gains are defined in terms of a threat point
representing the utility each spouse would achieve in the absence of
agreement. Figure 1 depicts the threat point, the feasible set, and
the Nash bargaining solution in the utility space.[10] An alternative
characterization of the Nash bargaining solution is as the point in the
feasible set that maximizes a "social welfare function" that depends
on the threat point. More precisely, the Nash social welfare function
is a symmetric Cobb-Douglas function, where the origin has been
translated to the threat point: $N = (U^h - T^h)(U^w - T^w)$. It follows
immediately that the utility an individual receives in the Nash bar-

---

[9] Although child allowances may affect fertility, we ignore this complication. Instead
we assume that all marriages produce the same number of children, thereby avoiding
the issues of endogenous fertility and stochastic fertility.

[10] Nash (1950) shows that a system of four axioms uniquely characterizes the Nash
bargaining solution: Pareto optimality, invariance to linear transformations of individual von Neumann–Morgenstern utility functions, symmetry (i.e., interchanging the
labels on the players has no effect on the solution), and what Sen (1970) calls "property
α." Luce and Raiffa (1957) call this property "independence of irrelevant alternatives"
(except the so-called threat point), but Sen points out that this is not equivalent to
Arrow's condition of that name.

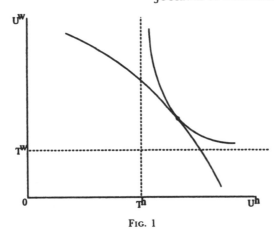

FIG. 1

gaining solution is an increasing function of the utility the individual receives at the threat point: thus, for example, an increase in the threat point utility of h and a decrease in that of w will cause an increase in the Nash bargaining solution utility of h and a decrease in that of w. We write the threat point as $\{T^h(p_1, p_2, I_h, I_w), T^w(p_1, p_2, I_h, I_w)\}$, where $T^i(p_1, p_2, I_h, I_w)$ is the indirect utility function, p_1 and p_2 are the relative prices of the public goods (we assume that the prices of x_h and x_w are equal and we normalize them to one), and I_h and I_w are the exogenous incomes received by husband and wife.[11]

To derive the demand functions for the public and private goods, we maximize the Nash social welfare function

$$N = [U^h(x_h, q_1, q_2) - T^h(p_1, p_2, I_h, I_w)][U^w(x_w, q_1, q_2) - T^w(p_1, p_2, I_h, I_w)]$$

subject to the constraint that joint expenditure equal joint income:

$$x_h + x_w + p_1 q_1 + p_2 q_2 = I_h + I_w.$$

This yields the demand functions

$$x_i = g^{x_i}(p_1, p_2, I_h, I_w), \quad i = h, w,$$

$$q_k = g^{q_k}(p_1, p_2, I_h, I_w), \quad k = 1, 2.$$

Incomes received by the husband and wife enter these demand functions separately because they affect not only the feasible set but also the threat point. If the threat point depends on other parameters representing the extramarital environment, then these parameters

---

[11] Instead of treating income as exogenous, we could treat wage rates as exogenous and focus on labor-leisure choices, with leisure as a private good.

will also enter the demand functions of two-parent households. So far we have been silent about the interpretation of the threat point: it could correspond to divorce, to violence or the threat of violence, or to a noncooperative equilibrium within marriage.

A noncooperative marital equilibrium provides an interesting alternative to divorce as a specification of the threat point. If divorce involves substantial transaction costs or can be dominated by sharing public goods within an intact but noncooperative marriage, then the voluntary contribution equilibrium offers a more plausible alternative to divorce as the threat point from which bargaining may proceed. Replacing an "external" threat point with an "internal" one and introducing transaction costs will affect final household allocation in two ways: it will influence cooperative bargaining outcomes via the threat point for each spouse, and it may be an equilibrium allocation in marriages for which transaction costs outweigh the potential gains to cooperation. Until otherwise noted, we assume that divorce is impossible or prohibitively expensive so that the relevant threat point is the noncooperative, voluntary contribution equilibrium within marriage.

We begin with a simple Cournot equilibrium in the provision of public goods by husband and wife, assuming that socially prescribed gender roles assign primary responsibility for certain activities to the husband and others to the wife. The implications of household separate spheres are straightforward; they generate corner solutions and thus nonneutrality in the provision of public goods. We show below how these results are modified when we allow cash transfers or binding premarital agreements between husband and wife.

Suppose that the public good, q_1, falls within the husband's traditional sphere so that, in the absence of a cooperative agreement, the husband decides unilaterally on the level of q_1 consumed by the household. Similarly, suppose that q_2 falls within the wife's sphere. In a noncooperative marriage, husband and wife decide simultaneously on the levels of q_1 and q_2 they will contribute to the household. This exclusive assignment of public goods reflects a socially sanctioned allocation of marital responsibilities and is independent of preference or productivity differences between husband and wife in a particular marriage.[12]

---

[12] Household production models, on the other hand, explain specialization by gender as a response to pervasive and persistent differences in home and market productivities of the husband and wife in a particular marriage, while recognizing that these individual productivity differences may reflect past investments in specific human capital. Average differences in preferences or productivities may help to explain the evolution of gender roles, but individuals take gender roles and gender role expectations as given.

The husband chooses x_h and q_1 to maximize $U^h(x_h, q_1, \bar{q}_2)$ subject to $x_h + p_1 q_1 = I_h$, where $\bar{q}_2$ is the level of public good chosen by the wife. This decision leads to a set of "reaction functions,"

$$x_h = f^{xh}(p_1, I_h, \bar{q}_2),$$

$$q_1 = f^{q_1}(p_1, I_h, \bar{q}_2).$$

Similarly, the wife's demand functions for (x_w, q_2) will depend on $\bar{q}_1$. The Cournot equilibrium is determined by the intersection of the public goods demand functions. For a simple example, consider the Klein-Rubin-Stone-Geary utility functions:

$$U^h = \alpha_h \log(x_h - x_h') + \beta_h \log(q_1 - q_{1h}') + (1 - \alpha_h - \beta_h)\log(q_2 - q_{2h}'),$$

$$U^w = \alpha_w \log(x_w - x_w') + \beta_w \log(q_2 - q_{2w}') + (1 - \alpha_w - \beta_w)\log(q_1 - q_{1w}').$$

Because these utility functions are separable, the reaction functions are independent of the quantity of the public good provided by the spouse, and demands take a very simple form:

$$x_h = x_h' + \alpha_h I_h^*, \quad q_1 = q_{1h}' + \frac{\beta_h}{p_1} I_h^*,$$

$$x_w = x_w' + \alpha_w I_w^*, \quad q_2 = q_{2w}' + \frac{\beta_w}{p_2} I_w^*,$$

where I_h^* and I_w^* are the husband's and wife's supernumerary or discretionary expenditures, which are defined as

$$I_h^* = I_h - x_h' - p_1 q_{1h}',$$

$$I_w^* = I_w - x_w' - p_2 q_{2w}'.$$

Substituting the reaction functions into the direct utility functions yields indirect utility functions of the form $V_0^h(p_1, p_2, I_h^*, I_w^*)$ and $V_0^w(p_1, p_2, I_h^*, I_w^*)$. The husband's utility depends on the resources of his wife through his consumption of "her" public good, and vice versa.

In the separate spheres model with a Cournot threat point, the alternative child allowance schemes imply different household allocations: the noncooperative equilibrium depends on the individual resources of husband and wife and, thus, on which parent receives the child allowance payment. A change in child allowance policy that affects the threat point will also affect the cooperative equilibrium. Thus distribution between men and women in two-parent families can be affected by policy changes that have no effect on the relative well-being of divorced men and women.

This nonneutrality result is sensitive to our assumptions. If the model is altered by removing the separate spheres assumption, then household allocation will be invariant to changes in the child allowance policy whenever positive contributions to each public good are made by both husband and wife. If the model is altered by allowing additional mechanisms for reallocation between spouses, such as cash transfers or binding premarital agreements, then household allocation will be invariant under some conditions. We examine these two modifications in the next version of the model, in which the wife specializes in the provision of a single household public good, q, which we describe as child services, and the husband specializes in the provision of money income, some portion of which he may transfer to his wife.

In the model with transfers, we assume that the process determining the distribution of the marital surplus occurs over two periods. In period 1, marriage contracts are made. When these contracts are made, the parties do not know the actual values of individual incomes, I_h and I_w, though the distributions from which they are drawn are common knowledge to all marriage market participants. We assume that prospective couples can make binding, costlessly enforceable, prenuptial agreements that specify a minimum transfer, t, which will be paid from husband to wife in period 2. The agreed minimum transfer cannot be contingent on future income realizations;[13] it may be voluntarily augmented by the husband in period 2 or may be superseded by cooperative bargaining. If binding agreements are not possible, then all marriages that form will be based on a contractual transfer level of zero, although all marriage market participants recognize that voluntary supplementary transfers may be made in period 2. We discuss marriage market effects in Sections IV and V.

In period 2, husband's and wife's incomes are realized and the husband may voluntarily make a supplementary transfer, $s > 0$, in order to increase his consumption of q. We suppose that the husband acts first, choosing x_h and s to maximize $U^h(x_h, q)$ subject to the budget constraint $x_h = I_h - t - s$ and the wife's reaction function $q(s)$. The wife takes the husband's supplementary transfer as given and chooses x_w and q to maximize $U^w(x_w, q)$ subject to $x_w + pq = I_w + t + s$, where p is the relative price of child services. Consider the case of Klein-Rubin-Stone-Geary utility:

$$U^h = \alpha_h \log(x_h - x'_h) + (1 - \alpha_h)\log(q - q'_h),$$

$$U^w = \alpha_w \log(x_w - x'_w) + (1 - \alpha_w)\log(q - q'_w),$$

---

[13] There will be no marital bargaining in period 2 if complete contingent contracts can be made in the marriage market.

where, to simplify the algebra, we assume that $q'_h = q'_w = q'$.[14] The discretionary expenditures of each spouse are given by

$$I^*_h = I_h - x'_h,$$

$$I^*_w = I_w - x'_w - pq'.$$

The supplementary transfer to the wife will be positive when

$$I^*_h - t > \alpha_h(I^*_h + I^*_w).$$

When $s > 0$,

$$x_h = x'_h + \alpha_h(I^*_h + I^*_w),$$

$$x_w = x'_w + \alpha_w(1 - \alpha_h)(I^*_h + I^*_w),$$

$$q = q' + \left[\frac{(1 - \alpha_w)(1 - \alpha_h)}{p}\right](I^*_h + I^*_w),$$

yielding indirect utility functions (and threat points) of the form $V^i(p, I^*_h + I^*_w)$. If the equilibrium is one in which positive supplementary transfers are made from husband to wife, then the value of the noncooperative solution to each spouse depends only on the total resources of the family, and not on the separate sources of income. Redistributions from husband to wife will be offset dollar for dollar by adjustments in the supplementary transfer, s.

If the realizations of I_h and I_w are such that the condition for positive supplementary transfers is not met, however, individual incomes affect the noncooperative equilibrium. If $s = 0$, the husband spends his entire uncommitted income, $I_h - t$, on his private good, x_h, and the wife allocates her total income, $I_w + t$, to her private good and child services. The utilities corresponding to this voluntary contribution equilibrium are

$$V^h_0(p, I^*_h - t, I^*_w + t), \quad V^w_0(p, I^*_w + t).$$

In the separate spheres bargaining model with transfers, the alternative child allowance schemes have identical effects if supplementary transfers are positive when the child allowance is paid to the mother. But if the family is at a corner solution—that is, if $s = 0$ when the child allowance is paid to the mother—then the threat point will be affected by which parent receives the payment.[15]

---

[14] Allowing q'_h and q'_w to differ complicates the algebra but does not substantially alter the results.

[15] Nonneutrality at corner solutions also occurs in Becker's altruist model, although corner solutions in the two models have different interpretations.

It is straightforward to apply the separate spheres bargaining model in a household production framework and to allow husband and wife to have different productivities in producing the public good. With constant returns to scale and no joint production, this is equivalent to assuming that the husband can purchase the public good at a different (presumably higher) price than the wife. Ignoring coordination problems, let the total amount of child services consumed by the couple be $q = q_h + q_w$, where q_h is purchased by the husband at a price p_h and q_w is purchased by the wife at a price p_w. There are now two ways in which the husband can influence his own consumption of child services in a noncooperative household: he can influence his wife's resources through supplementary transfers and he can purchase child services directly.

Under our assumptions about the wife's utility function, the husband faces a constant "price" of purchasing the public good via supplementary transfers, namely $(1 - \alpha_w)/p_w$. Hence, except in a razor's edge case the husband will not simultaneously make positive supplementary transfers and direct purchases of the public good, but will choose the method with the lower price. If the noncooperative equilibrium is such that $q_h > 0$ and $q_w > 0$, redistribution between husband and wife will be neutral only if they face the same price for the public good. In a cooperative household, all child services will be purchased by the wife at the lower price.

We can relax our earlier assumption that divorce is impossible or prohibitively expensive and modify our analysis to recognize that, for some marriages, divorce is the relevant threat point. When both divorce and noncooperative marriage are possible outcomes, the relevant threat point will depend on the utility possibilities associated with these states and on the institutional rules governing divorce.[16] The separate spheres model can be interpreted as the case in which the voluntary contribution marriage is Pareto superior to divorce, so that neither spouse can convincingly threaten divorce; hence, the voluntary contribution equilibrium is the relevant threat point for the bargaining game. On the other hand, if both spouses prefer divorce

---

[16] One approach would be to assume that, at the beginning of the cooperative bargaining game, both spouses recognize that if they fail to reach an agreement, they will play a noncooperative game. Institutional rules must specify the outcome of the noncooperative game when one spouse prefers the voluntary contribution equilibrium within marriage. If unilateral, no-fault divorce is permitted, then divorce is the outcome unless both parties choose a voluntary contribution marriage. If, on the other hand, the rules permit divorce only with the consent of both spouses, then a voluntary contribution marriage will eventuate unless both spouses choose divorce. The expected utility for each spouse in this noncooperative postgame is the threat point for cooperative bargaining.

to any noncooperative marriage, then divorce is the relevant threat point. In general, the recognition that divorce is the relevant alternative for some marriages attenuates the link between child allowances and intrafamily distribution. When divorce is the threat point, the two child allowance schemes we consider have identical distributional effects.

IV. Marriage Markets with Binding Agreements

As Becker has emphasized, the marriage market is an important determinant of intrahousehold distribution. Bargaining within a marriage is limited to the "surplus" generated by that marriage and thus depends on the alternatives available outside the marriage. If there are no information, search, or contracting problems, then a continuous distribution of preferences and traits in the population implies that distribution within marriage will be completely determined in the marriage market; there is no surplus to be bargained over in any particular marriage, because the next-best marriage is just as good. Stapleton (1990) provides a careful analysis of this extreme case.

If marriage market participants are heterogeneous, surpluses depend on the matching of men and women. Matching models (see Mortensen 1988; Roth and Sotomayor 1990) provide an analytical framework for investigating equilibrium or stable assignments of men to women in the marriage market, and such models typically possess multiple equilibria. Search costs further complicate the analysis of marriage market equilibria (see Mortensen 1982a, 1982b, 1988). Becker (1973, 1974a, 1974b, 1981) was among the first to recognize the relationship between distribution within marriage and "assortative mating" in marriage markets. Lam (1988) analyzes the effect of household public goods on marriage patterns and shows how different assumptions yield results very different from those predicted by Becker.

The noncooperative distribution of household resources described in the previous section will depend on the value of the transfer, t, determined in the marriage market. To analyze the short-run effects of a new child allowance scheme (i.e., its effect on distribution in existing marriages), it was appropriate to take the value of this transfer as predetermined. In the long run, however, new marriages will form taking the new policy into account. In this section we show that, when prospective couples can make binding, costlessly enforceable prenuptial agreements about the minimum level of transfers, a "Ricardian equivalence" result emerges: new marriages will completely offset the effects of any change in the child allowance scheme.

In our model, a marriage contract specifies a transfer that is not contingent on the realized values of income. We denote the marriage of female i to male j by the pair (i, j) and the transfer that the male is obliged to make to the female by t_{ij}; a negative value of t_{ij} thus implies a transfer from female i to male j. We denote a marriage contract by (i, j, t_{ij}).

A marriage market structure is a set of marriage contracts: $S = \{(i, j, t_{ij})\}$. Both female i and male j evaluate a prospective marriage contract (i, j, t_{ij}) in terms of the expected utility associated with it; this utility can depend on attributes of the spouse as well as on consumption of the private good and the public good. To calculate expected utility, the expectation is taken over the joint distribution of incomes and transaction costs facing the pair (i, j). The reduced-form expected utility functions can be written as $V^i(i, j, I_{0i} + t_{ij}, I_{0j} - t_{ij})$ and $V^j(i, j, I_{0i} + t_{ij}, I_{0j} - t_{ij})$, where I_{0i} and I_{0j} are the noncontingent components of female and male income.

Child allowances can be easily introduced into the model. If a child allowance, a, is paid to the husband, then the reduced-form utility functions are $V^i(i, j, I_{0i} + t_{ij}, I_{0j} + a - t_{ij})$ and $V^j(i, j, I_{0i} + t_{ij}, I_{0j} + a - t_{ij})$. If the child allowance is paid to the wife, then the reduced-form utility functions are $V^i(i, j, I_{0i} + a + t_{ij}^*, I_{0j} - t_{ij}^*)$ and $V^j(i, j, I_{0i} + a + t_{ij}^*, I_{0j} - t_{ij}^*)$, where t_{ij}^* is the transfer from the husband to the wife when the wife receives the child allowance.

In the long run the marriage market can undo any short-run distributional effects achieved by paying child allowances to wives rather than to husbands. That is, the set of equilibrium marriage market structures is independent of the child allowance scheme. When the child allowance is paid to wives rather than to husbands, the marriage market structure with the same pairing of women and men, but with transfers from men to women reduced by the amount of the child allowance, is an equilibrium. With binding transfers, therefore, the distributional effect of a policy changing the recipient of child allowances will persist only within marriages in existence at the time of the policy change. For subsequent generations of marriages, adjustments in prenuptial transfers will exactly offset the shift in child allowances. This Ricardian equivalence result, of course, depends on the assumption that prospective couples in the marriage market can make binding, costlessly enforceable agreements.

V. Marriage Markets without Binding Agreements

Even without binding agreements, the requirements of equilibrium in the marriage market can generate substantial differences between the short-run and the long-run effects of child allowances. In this section we focus on a simple special case to illustrate the range of long-run outcomes that are consistent with our model. We assume that all individuals live as adults for two periods. In the first period everyone participates in the marriage market. Those who do not marry in the first period remain unmarried in the second period. Those who marry in the first period remain married in the second period; divorce is impossible or prohibitively costly. We assume that the only differences among individuals are differences in the utility associated with remaining unmarried: all men have identical (nonstochastic) incomes, and all women have identical (nonstochastic) incomes. Distribution within marriage is determined by bargaining, and since divorce is ruled out, the threat point is a noncooperative marriage. We assume that the representative marriage is at a corner solution with respect to supplementary transfers, so that a change from the child allowance scheme that pays fathers to the scheme that pays mothers will increase the utility of married women and decrease the utility of married men.

Under our assumptions that all women are identical except in the utility of remaining unmarried and that all men are identical except in the utility of remaining unmarried, the utilities associated with a particular marriage—say (i, j)—are independent of i and j. Individuals contemplating marriage can compare the utility of the representative marriage with the utility of remaining unmarried. Since all marriages are identical, the only function of the marriage market is to determine which individuals marry and which individuals remain unmarried.

To analyze equilibrium in the marriage market, we introduce a function $G^w(U^w)$ showing the number of women for whom the utility of being unmarried is less than or equal to the utility of being married, U^w; $G^h(U^h)$ is the corresponding function for men. The value of the function $G^w(U^w)$ is, of course, the number of women willing to marry when the utility of married women is U^w.

Instead of focusing on just two child allowance schemes—one paying fathers and the other paying mothers—we can consider a continuum of child allowance schemes in which a portion of the child allowance is paid to mothers and the remainder to fathers. We denote the child allowance payment to mothers by γa and the payment to fathers by $(1 - \gamma)a$. Thus if $\gamma = 0$, the entire child allowance, a, is paid to the father; if $\gamma = \frac{1}{2}$, the child allowance is divided equally between the parents; and if $\gamma = 1$, the entire child allowance is paid to the mother.[17]

---

[17] Values of γ outside the interval [0, 1] correspond to imposing a lump-sum tax on one spouse and paying the child allowance plus the lump-sum tax to the other spouse. To avoid invoking lump-sum taxes, we confine ourselves to values of γ in the interval [0, 1].

We now use γ to reparameterize the "willingness to marry" functions, $G^w(U^w)$ and $G^h(U^h)$. Because U^w is an increasing function of γ, we can define a new function $G^{*w}(\gamma)$ by $G^{*w}(\gamma) = G^w(U^w(\gamma))$; $G^{*w}(\cdot)$ is an increasing function of γ (more precisely, a nondecreasing function of γ). Similarly, $G^{*h}(\cdot)$ is a decreasing (more precisely, nonincreasing) function of γ. The number of marriages corresponding to various values of γ is given by $N = \min\{G^{*w}(\gamma), G^{*h}(\gamma)\}$.

There are three interesting cases, illustrated in figure 2A, B, and C, distinguished by whether women or men are in short supply in the marriage market at various values of γ. In case A, $G^{*w}(\ )$ is less than $G^{*h}(\ )$ for all γ in the interval [0, 1], so that more men than women wish to marry. A change from the child allowance scheme that pays fathers to one that pays mothers will increase the utility of married women and decrease the utility of married men; such a change will also increase the number of marriages, because the number of women willing to marry is the binding constraint under both child allowance schemes. Individuals who were unmarried under the old scheme and marry under the new scheme experience a welfare gain.

In case B, $G^{*h}(\ )$ is less than $G^{*w}(\ )$ for all γ in the interval [0, 1]. In this case, the number of men willing to marry is the binding constraint at both endpoints of the interval. Shifting the child allowance payment toward mothers will increase the utility of married women and decrease the utility of married men; such a shift will also decrease the number of marriages. Individuals who were married under the old scheme but remain unmarried under the new scheme will experience a welfare loss.

In case C, the curves $G^{*h}(\ )$ and $G^{*w}(\ )$ intersect at some value γ^* in the interval [0, 1]. There is, however, no mechanism to drive γ to γ^* because individuals cannot make binding agreements in the marriage market. In case C, the effect on the number of marriages of a change from the child allowance scheme that pays fathers to the one that pays mothers is indeterminate: as we have drawn the curves, the number of marriages is the same under both child allowance schemes.

This section has analyzed long-run implications for distribution between spouses when binding agreements cannot be made in the marriage market in a very restrictive special case. Even when all individuals of the same gender are perfect substitutes in the marriage market and differ only in the reservation utility for marriage, the range of possible outcomes is very wide. This suggests to us the impossibility of obtaining strong general results. Although there is much to be said for models that allow additional heterogeneity among individuals and, hence, assortative mating, such models are likely to be consistent with an even wider range of possible outcomes.

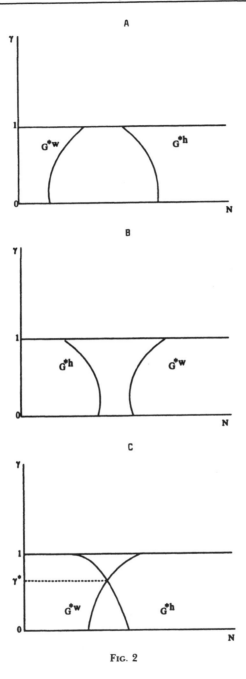

FIG. 2

VI. Conclusion

In this paper we have introduced the separate spheres bargaining model, a new model of distribution within marriage. To compare the separate spheres model with the leading economic models of distribution within marriage—Becker's altruist model and the Manser-Brown/McElroy-Horney divorce threat bargaining model—we have emphasized the distributional implications of alternative child allowance schemes that differ only in their treatment of two-parent families. Under one scheme, payments go to the father; under the other, they go to the mother; under both schemes, in the event of divorce, the mother gets the children and the child allowance. In the altruist model and the divorce threat bargaining model, these alternative child allowance schemes imply identical distributions between mothers and fathers in two-parent families. In the separate spheres bargaining model, these schemes can imply different distributions.

The separate spheres bargaining model, like the divorce threat bargaining model, views marriage as a cooperative game. The separate spheres model differs from the divorce threat model in its specification of the threat point. In the separate spheres model, the threat point is a noncooperative equilibrium within marriage defined in terms of traditional gender roles and gender role expectations. Because the child allowance schemes can imply different noncooperative equilibria, they can imply different distributions in two-parent families.

Any redistribution between women and men resulting from the choice of one child allowance scheme rather than the other may be transitory. If binding, costlessly enforceable, prenuptial agreements can be used to specify transfers within marriage, then the marriage market will undo any redistribution. If, on the other hand, binding prenuptial agreements are impossible, then the choice of one child allowance scheme rather than the other can have long-run effects on distribution in two-parent families. We show, however, that even without binding agreements, the requirements of equilibrium in the marriage market can generate long-run results that differ substantially from short-run results.

Bargaining models of marriage have almost invariably treated marriage as a cooperative game, and our separate spheres bargaining model follows this tradition. Recent advances in noncooperative bargaining theory provide an alternative approach: specifying the bargaining process as a sequence of moves and a corresponding information structure, and analyzing it as a game in extensive form. Rubinstein (1982) analyzes a bargaining game in which the players take turns making offers and shows that a class of alternating offer games have unique, subgame perfect equilibria. Binmore, Rubinstein, and Wolinsky (1986) show that the Nash bargaining solution, a standard axiomatic solution concept for cooperative games, can be reinterpreted as the solution to a noncooperative alternating offer game if the threat point is suitably interpreted. On the basis of these results, we might reinterpret the Nash bargaining solution to our separate spheres bargaining model as the solution to a specific noncooperative bargaining game.[18]

We have two reservations regarding this approach. First, we doubt that marriage is best formulated as an alternating offer game. Solutions to extensive form games are sensitive to the details of their specifications, and this particular extensive form game does not seem to capture the essential features of marital bargaining. Second, we have doubts about whether marriage is best formulated as a noncooperative game: cooperative game theory may provide a more fruitful framework for analyzing distribution between spouses. Discussing cooperative games, Shubik (1989, p. 103) writes as follows:

> The game in extensive form provides a process account of the detail of individual moves and information structure; the tree structure often employed in its description enables the researcher to keep track of the full history of any play of the game. This is useful for the analysis of reasonably well-structured formal process models where the beginning, end and sequencing of moves is well-defined, but is generally not so useful to describe complex, loosely structured social interaction.

It is difficult to think of many better examples of a "complex, loosely structured social interaction" than marriage.

References

Becker, Gary S. "A Theory of Marriage: Part I." *J.P.E.* 81 (July/August 1973): 813–46.
———. "A Theory of Marriage: Part II." *J.P.E.* 82, no. 2, pt. 2 (March/April 1974): S11–S26. (*a*)
———. "A Theory of Social Interactions." *J.P.E.* 82 (November/December 1974): 1063–93. (*b*)
———. *A Treatise on the Family.* Cambridge, Mass.: Harvard Univ. Press, 1981; enl. ed., 1991.
Bergstrom, Theodore C. "A Fresh Look at the Rotten Kid Theorem—and Other Household Mysteries." *J.P.E.* 97 (October 1989): 1138–59.

---

[18] Kanbur and Haddad (1994) apply the results of Binmore et al. (1986) to the analysis of intrahousehold allocation.

Bergstrom, Theodore C.; Blume, Lawrence; and Varian, Hal. "On the Private Provision of Public Goods." *J. Public Econ.* 29 (February 1986): 25–49.

Binmore, Ken; Rubinstein, Ariel; and Wolinsky, Asher. "The Nash Bargaining Solution in Economic Modelling." *Rand J. Econ.* 17 (Summer 1986): 176–88.

Brown, Joan C. *Family Income Support Part 2: Children in Social Security.* Studies of the Social Security System, no. 3. London: Policy Studies Inst., 1984.

Crawford, David L., and Pollak, Robert A. "Child Care Policy." Manuscript. Philadelphia: Univ. Pennsylvania, 1989.

Elster, Jon. "Social Norms and Economic Theory." *J. Econ. Perspectives* 3 (Fall 1989): 99–117.

Johnson, David S. "Team Behavior in the Family: An Analysis of the Rotten Kid Theorem." Manuscript. Washington: Bur. Labor Statis., 1990.

Kanbur, Ravi, and Haddad, Lawrence. "Are Better off Households More Unequal or Less Unequal: A Bargaining Theoretic Approach to 'Kuznets Effects' at the Micro Level." *Oxford Econ. Papers* (1994), in press.

Lam, David. "Marriage Markets and Assortative Mating with Household Public Goods: Theoretical Results and Empirical Implications." *J. Human Resources* 23 (Fall 1988): 462–87.

Luce, R. Duncan, and Raiffa, Howard. *Games and Decisions: Introduction and Critical Survey.* New York: Wiley, 1957.

Lundberg, Shelly. "Labor Supply of Husbands and Wives: A Simultaneous Equations Approach." *Rev. Econ. and Statis.* 70 (May 1988): 224–35.

McElroy, Marjorie B. "Appendix: Empirical Results from Estimates of Joint Labor Supply Functions of Husbands and Wives." In *Research in Labor Economics*, vol. 4, edited by Ronald G. Ehrenberg. Greenwich, Conn.: JAI, 1981.

———. "The Empirical Content of Nash-Bargained Household Behavior." *J. Human Resources* 25 (Fall 1990): 559–83.

McElroy, Marjorie B., and Horney, Mary Jean. "Nash-Bargained Household Decisions: Toward a Generalization of the Theory of Demand." *Internat. Econ. Rev.* 22 (June 1981): 333–49.

Manser, Marilyn, and Brown, Murray. "Marriage and Household Decision-making: A Bargaining Analysis." *Internat. Econ. Rev.* 21 (February 1980): 31–44.

Mortensen, Dale T. "The Matching Process as a Noncooperative Bargaining Game." In *The Economics of Information and Uncertainty*, edited by John J. McCall. Chicago: Univ. Chicago Press (for NBER), 1982. (*a*)

———. "Property Rights and Efficiency in Mating, Racing, and Related Games." *A.E.R.* 72 (December 1982): 968–79. (*b*)

———. "Matching: Finding a Partner for Life or Otherwise." *American J. Sociology* 94 (suppl., 1988): S215–S240.

Nash, John F. "The Bargaining Problem." *Econometrica* 18 (April 1950): 155–62.

Pahl, Jan. "The Allocation of Money and the Structuring of Inequality within Marriage." *Sociological Rev.* 31 (May 1983): 237–62.

Pollak, Robert A. "A Transaction Cost Approach to Families and Households." *J. Econ. Literature* 23 (June 1985): 581–608.

Roth, Alvin E., and Sotomayor, Marilda A. Oliveira. *Two-sided Matching: A Study in Game-Theoretic Modeling and Analysis.* Cambridge: Cambridge Univ. Press, 1990.

Rubinstein, Ariel. "Perfect Equilibrium in a Bargaining Model." *Econometrica* 50 (January 1982): 97–109.

Samuelson, Paul A. "Social Indifference Curves." *Q.J.E.* 70 (February 1956): 1–22.

Schultz, T. Paul. "Testing the Neoclassical Model of Family Labor Supply and Fertility." *J. Human Resources* 25 (Fall 1990): 599–634.

Sen, Amartya. *Collective Choice and Social Welfare.* San Francisco: Holden-Day, 1970.

Shubik, Martin. "Cooperative Games." In *The New Palgrave, Game Theory,* edited by John Eatwell, Murray Milgate, and Peter Newman. New York: Norton, 1989.

Stapleton, David C. "Implicit Marriage Markets with Collective Goods." Manuscript. College Park: Univ. Maryland, 1990.

Sugden, Robert. "Spontaneous Order." *J. Econ. Perspectives* 3 (Fall 1989): 85–97.

Tauchen, Helen V.; Witte, Ann D.; and Long, Sharon K. "Domestic Violence: A Nonrandom Affair." *Internat. Econ. Rev.* 32 (May 1991): 491–511.

Thomas, Duncan. "Intra-Household Resource Allocation: An Inferential Approach." *J. Human Resources* 25 (Fall 1990): 635–64.

Warr, Peter G. "The Private Provision of a Public Good Is Independent of the Distribution of Income." *Econ. Letters* 13, nos. 2–3 (1983): 207–11.

Woolley, F. "A Non-cooperative Model of Family Decision Making." Manuscript. London: London School Econ., 1988.

[16]

ELSEVIER

Why Are Married Women Working So Hard?

ALLEN M. PARKMAN

Anderson Schools of Management, University of New Mexico
E-mail: parkman@unm.edu

I. Introduction

Recent developments might cause one to conclude that the welfare of women has been improving. Certainly, their relative wages and labor force participation have increased.[1] However, one disconcerting development has been the increase in the total number of hours worked by married women at home and on a job. Victor Fuchs found that between 1960 and 1986, married women increased the total number of hours that they worked per week by 4 hours, while their husbands were decreasing theirs by 2.5 hours.[2] Sarah Fenstermaker Berk notes, "Thus, the practical effects of employment on wives' household labor are limited primarily to the 'shortcuts' that wives can apply to their work; a reapportionment of domestic chores among household members is very unlikely."[3] A similar pattern has been observed by other researchers.[4]

This paper provides an explanation for some of this increase based on the introduction of no-fault divorce. In the first section, the change in the divorce grounds from fault to no-fault is discussed. Then the impact of this change on the allocation of married women's time is discussed, and a hypothesis about the impact of no-fault divorce is developed. This hypothesis is tested using data from the *Time Use Longitudinal Panel Study, 1975–1981*. The empirical results suggest that the introduction of no-fault divorce has increased the hours worked by married women. If hours worked are a measure of their welfare, no-fault divorce has made married women worse off.

II. The Divorce Laws

During most of the history of the United States, divorce, to the extent that it was allowed at all, was based on fault with the grounds being adultery, cruelty, and desertion.

This research was funded by a summer research grant from the Anderson Schools of Management Foundation. I am grateful to Micha Gisser and Ron Johnson for valuable comments.

[1] See Robert T. Michael, "Consequences of the Rise in Female Labor Force Participation Rates: Questions and Probes," (1985) 3 J. Lab. Econ. S117; and Kevin M. Murphy and Finis Welsh, "Inequality and Relative Wages," (1993) 83 A. E. R 104.

[2] Victor Fuchs, *Women's Quest for Economic Equality*, Harvard (1988), p. 77.

[3] Sarah Fenstermaker Berk, *The Gender Factory*, Plenum (1985), p. 8.

[4] For example, see Joseph H. Pleck, *Working Wives/Working Husbands*, Sage, (1985) and Beth Anne Shelton, *Women, Men and Time*, Greenwood (1992).

Because of the gains from specialization during marriage, essentially all adults benefitted from being married, with marriages usually lasting until the death of one spouse. The increase in the employment opportunities for women and domestic labor-saving devices for men eventually reduced the gains from marriage for some adults, increasing the attraction of divorce.[5] The divorce rate rose gradually during the 20th century as it became more common for the spouses to agree—not necessarily enthusiastically—to divorce, using fabricated testimony to establish the fault grounds. Because most spouses who wanted to dissolve their marriage did not have evidence to support the fault grounds, they had to obtain their spouse's cooperation. This process usually required concessions by the party who more strongly wanted the divorce as an inducement for the other spouse to be the plaintiff in the divorce action. Eventually, public concerns about the hypocrisy of the perjured testimony along with the self-interest of some divorced men and career women led to the introduction of no-fault divorce based on incompatibility, irretrievable breakdown, or separation for an extended period.[6] Between 1969 and 1985, all the states either replaced or augmented their fault grounds for divorce with no-fault grounds. In most cases, the no-fault grounds for divorce permitted a spouse to obtain a divorce unilaterally.

The laws controlling the financial and custodial arrangements at divorce, which often had been ignored in the prior negotiated divorces, were not addressed in any systematic way during these deliberations. Because a no-fault divorce usually did not require the agreement of the spouses, the need for concessions from a divorcing spouse were reduced and the settlements shifted from those based on negotiations—which often ignored the applicable laws—to ones based on those legal standards.[7] These laws usually have not been generous to individuals who have increased their specialization in domestic work during marriage. The property settlement usually consists of a return of any separate property and an equal division of the marital property—generally ignoring the largest source of the couple's wealth, human capital. In addition, a divorced spouse could expect short-term spousal support along with child support for and joint custody of any minor children.

Gradually, it was recognized that the no-fault grounds for divorce reduced the negotiating power and, therefore, the settlements of spouses who did not want to divorce.[8] Often these individuals were women who had increased their specialization in domestic work during marriage. These women were particularly vulnerable because the contributions of men and women to marriage can be asymmetric.[9] The primary child-

---

[5]See June Carbone and Margaret F. Brinig, "Rethinking Marriage: Feminist Ideology, Economic Change, and Divorce Reform," (1991) 65 Tulane L. R. 953; and Lloyd R. Cohen, "Rhetoric, the Unnatural Family, and Women's Work," (1995) 81 Va. L. R. 2275.

[6]Allen M. Parkman, *No-Fault Divorce: What Went Wrong?* Westview (1992).

[7]Under both the fault and the no-fault grounds for divorce, private negotiations have been important as negotiations are often an attractive alternative to litigation. George L. Priest and Benjamin Klein, "The Selection of Disputes for Litigation," (1984) 13 J. Legal Studies 1. This is especially true in divorce cases. Robert H. Mnookin and Lewis Kornhauser, "Bargaining in the Shadow of the Law: The Case of Divorce," (1979) 88 Yale L. J. 950. Under fault divorce, approximately 90% of divorces were uncontested. Max Rheinstein, *Marriage Stability, Divorce, and the Law,* University of Chicago (1972), p. 248. A similar outcome was observed after the introduction of no-fault divorce. Mnookin and Kornhauser, *supra* p. 951. Therefore, the major change with no-fault divorce was not the percentage of cases settled but the reduction in the concessions that the divorcing spouse was willing to make to obtain the agreement of the other spouse, because it was easier for spouses to dissolve their marriage.

[8]Lenore J. Weitzman, *The Divorce Revolution,* Free Press (1985).

[9]Lloyd Cohen, "Marriage, Divorce, and Quasi Rents: or 'I Gave Him the Best Years of My Life,'" (1987) 16 J. Legal Studies 267.

rearing obligations often assumed by wives occur before the peak earnings period of the husbands, making divorce especially attractive to middle-age husbands.[10]

III. The Impact of No-Fault Divorce on Work by Married Women

As these effects of no-fault divorce were recognized, married women started taking steps to protect themselves from the potentially adverse consequences of divorce. Before 1970, much of the increase in the labor force participation rate of women can be explained by the increase in real wages.[11] That pattern stopped in the 1970s as the labor force participation rate of women accelerated as the real wage growth rate slowed. No-fault divorce has provided an explanation for some of the recent increase in women working outside the home during marriage.[12] The labor force participation rate of women has increased dramatically since World War II, with the rate of married women rising from 23.8% in 1950 to 58.5% in 1991. This increase was particularly evident for the women who traditionally had the strongest attachment to the home, mothers with young children. The labor force participation rate of married women with children less than 6 years of age rose from 11.9% in 1950 to 30% in 1970, the year in which no-fault divorce was introduced in California. It continued to rise to 59.9% in 1991, having accelerated after 1970.

Not only have married women increased their labor force participation, they also have increased the total number of hours that they work. The decision by married women to work outside their home should not necessarily result in their working more total hours. Gary Becker asserts that married couples benefit from an increase in their specialization of labor based on comparative advantage, with women normally increasing their specialization in domestic work and men in income earning.[13] This arrangement is in the best interests of the spouses, so they agree to it voluntarily. Labor market conditions may change, increasing the opportunity cost of domestic work either because real wages have risen or because the marginal productivity of some labor in the home has declined because of domestic labor-saving devices. Under those circumstances, it is attractive to families for wives to shift more time to employment. These women only would volunteer to make the shift if the benefit to them exceeded the cost. Some of their benefit may come from other family members who agree that the shift is also in their best interests and assume responsibility for some goods and services that

---

[10]Although more divorces are initiated by women than men, the greatest injustices tend to occur when middle-aged women in long-duration marriages are divorced. For a discussion of who initiates a divorce, see Sanford L. Braver. Marnie Whitley, and Christine Ng, "Who Divorces Whom? Methodological and Theoretical Issues," (1993) 20 J. Divorce Remarriage 1.

[11]James P. Smith and Michael P. Ward, "Time-Series Growth in the Female Labor Force." (1985) 3 J. Lab. Econ. S59. The increase in the labor force participation of women reduced the gains from marriage for some adults by decreasing the gains from specialization during marriage. As marriage became less attractive, support for easier divorce processes developed that contributed to the introduction of no-fault divorce. See Parkman, *No-Fault Divorce, op. cit.* note 6, p. 58.

[12]H. Elizabeth Peters, "Marriage and Divorce: Informational Constraints and Private Contracting." (1986) 76 A. E. R. 437 and Allen M. Parkman, "Unilateral Divorce and the Labor-Force Participation Rate of Married Women, Revisited," (1992) 82 A. E. R. 671 reach this conclusion with slightly different frameworks using 1979 data. Using data from 1972, William R Johnson and Jonathan Skinner. "Labor Supply and Marital Separation," (1986) 76 A. E. R. 455 found that the probability of divorce increases the labor force participation rate of married women, but they found that living in a no-fault divorce state had a negative effect on a married woman's labor supply. However, 1972 was probably too early in the no-fault divorce era to provide a reasonable test of its effect.

[13]Gary S. Becker, *A Treatise on the Family,* Harvard (enl. ed.–1991).

had been provided by the women in the home.[14] The husband or children might assume some responsibility for cooking or cleaning. Overall, the total number of hours worked by married women should not necessarily increase.

Alternatively, married women might pursue employment due to the decline in the net benefit from increasing their specialization in domestic work during marriage. When divorce essentially required a negotiated settlement that could include favorable financial and custodial arrangements for the party who did not want the divorce, women could anticipate that the sacrifice of human capital to increase their specialization in domestic work had some protection. The no-fault grounds for divorce and the resulting reduced transfers at divorce provided by the law reduced this protection and, thereby, reduced the expected net benefit from specialization in domestic work during marriage. The likelihood increased that decisions by married women to become employed outside the home were based on the women's desire to protect themselves from the potentially adverse effects of no-fault divorce rather than to improve their family's welfare.[15] The value of the goods and services available to their families due to the women's employment might be less than that of those produced during a corresponding period of domestic work. A shift of hours from household production to employment could reduce the families' welfare. Under those circumstances, the other family members would be less likely to assume the responsibility for providing the goods and services that had been provided by the wives and mothers.

Although women might feel compelled to take steps to protect themselves from the potentially adverse effects of divorce, their marriage will continue only as long as it is attractive to both spouses. In additional to physical and emotional attraction, their marriage should continue to be attractive to many wives because their husband's earnings have usually increased during their marriage.[16] Meanwhile, if wives' transfers of hours from domestic work to employment would lower their family's welfare, they have to reduce their domestic work by less than the increase in their hours of employment to continue to make this marriage attractive to their husband. Consequently, we

---

[14]Becker has argued that people do not maximize their utility by just buying goods, but instead that they accomplish that goal by combining the goods that they buy with their time to produce "commodities." Their budget constraint is their "full" income that would be realized if all time were devoted to market work. Gary S. Becker, "A Theory of the Allocation of Time," (1965) 75 Econ. J. 493.

[15]Needless to say, this is not likely to be an explanation given by wives, especially to their spouse. The common rationale for the recent increase in the employment of married women, at least in the popular press, is financial necessity. Victor R. Fuchs, *How we Live*, Harvard (1983) p. 130 and Sam Ward, "Why Women Work," *USA Today* (June 22, 1990) p. A1. Before no-fault divorce, necessity provided an explanation for married women's labor force participation because the highest rate was for those married to low-income men (Fuchs, *id.*) It is less convincing for other women, because it is difficult for them to increase family income significantly, inasmuch as most married couples file joint federal and state individual income tax returns. As a result, there are no exemptions or deductions available to the second income earner plus their income is taxed at a high marginal rate. In addition, their social security contributions may not provide a pension that exceeds the spousal benefits for which they have already qualified. Last, there can be substantial employment-related expenses such as travel, clothing, meals, and child care that reduce disposable income. It is noteworthy that the largest increase in the labor force participation rate of married women since the advent of no-fault divorce has occurred among wives of middle- and high-income men. Marina Whitman, "Do women work because they have to?", *Detroit News* (February 16, 1997) p. B7. These women generally have higher education levels and, therefore, would sacrifice important investments in on-the-job training that would increase their human capital, if they limited their career to providing domestic work. Gary S. Becker, *Human Capital*, Chicago (3rd ed.—1993) p. 228. As noted above, these women would not be compensated in any systematic way at divorce for these sacrifices.

[16]Another reason may be that women have a stronger attraction to their children than their husbands, and they feel that an intact family is a preferred environment for raising those children. Fuchs, *Women's Quest, op. cit.*, note 2.

Table 1. Variable definitions and mean values

Variable	Definition	Married women	Married men
Regular work	Minutes per week associated with employment in 1981	1,106.2	2,283.8
Housework	Minutes per week associated with housework in 1981	2,173.3	1,180.9
Child care	Minutes per week in child care in 1981	260.1	104.1
Leisure	Minutes per week spent in leisure in 1981	6,535.2	6,507.1
Total work	Minutes per week in regular work and housework in 1981	3,279.5	3,464.7
Age	Age in 1981	47.9	51.2
Assets	Assets owned in 1981 in thousands of dollars	69.1	70.8
Catholic	1 if Catholic	0.24	0.24
Children 0–3	Number of children in the household age 0–3 in 1981	0.11	0.11
Children 4–18	Number of children in the household age 4–18 in 1981	1.36	1.30
White	1 if white	0.9	0.9
Years of education	Number of years of education completed by 1981	12.3	12.8
SMSA	1 if the person lived in a standard metropolitan statistical area in 1981	0.35	0.36
Husbands earnings	Husband's earnings in 1981 in thousands of dollars	20.2	NA
Wive's earnings	Wive's earnings in 1981 in thousands of dollars	NA	4.7
No-fault	1 if a divorce can be obtained in state within two years based on no-fault grounds in 1978	0.66	0.68
West	1 if the person lived in the West geographic division	0.14	0.13
North central	1 if the person lived in the North Central geographic division	0.37	0.36
South	1 if the person lived in the South geographic division	0.22	0.23
Sample size		172	159

Note: The sample consists of married men and women who lived in the same residence in 1981 as in 1975. Source: *Time Use Longitudinal Panel Study, 1975–1981,* Survey Research Center, University of Michigan.

would expect the total number of hours worked by married women to be greater in no-fault divorce states, in which they had little protection, than in fault divorce states, in which they had some protection.

IV. Empirical Analysis

The hypothesis developed above has been tested using 1981 data from the *Time Use Longitudinal Panel Study, 1975–1981.*[17] In 1975 and 1981, individuals were asked to complete diaries detailing their time spent in 223 activities during 4 days over a 1-year period. In addition, these individuals responded to demographic and financial ques-

---

[17]The data used in this paper were made available by the Inter-university Consortium for Political and Social Research. The data for *Time Use Longitudinal Panel Study, 1975-1981,* were originally collected by F. Thomas Juster, Martha S. Hill, Frank P. Stafford, and Jacquelynne Eccles Parsons of the Survey Research Center, Institute for Social Research, the University of Michigan. Neither the collector of the original data nor the Consortium bear any responsibility for the analyses or interpretations presented here. For other uses of time budget surveys, see Jonathan Gershuny and John Robinson, "Historical Changes in the Household Division of Labor," (1988) 25 *Demography* 537 and F. Thomas Juster and Frank P. Stafford, "The Allocation of Time: Empirical Findings, Behavioral Models, and Problems of Measurement," (1991) 29 J. Econ. Lit. 471.

TABLE 2. Activity regression equations: Married women

Variable	Regular work	House work	Child care	Leisure	Total work
Intercept	2675.84***	1607.20**	458.72**	5336.89***	4283.04***
	(3.11)	(2.54)	(2.30)	(7.88)	(6.03)
Age	−40.95***	10.42*	−8.36***	38.91***	−30.53***
	(4.83)	(1.83)	(4.26)	(5.84)	(4.37)
Assets	0.15	0.02	0.05	0.21	0.16
	(0.24)	(0.03)	(0.31)	(0.43)	(0.32)
Catholic	155.41	−113.69	−26.71	−15.18	41.72
	(0.71)	(0.71)	(0.53)	(0.09)	(0.23)
Children 0–3	−648.09***	167.70	343.68***	135.82	−480.39**
	(2.81)	(0.99)	(6.43)	(0.75)	(2.53)
Children 4–18	−144.69*	102.20*	49.09***	−6.85	−42.49
	(1.89)	(1.82)	(2.77)	(0.11)	(0.67)
White	−256.38	216.88	141.04	−102.96	−39.49
	(0.54)	(0.63)	(1.29)	(0.28)	(0.10)
Year of education	72.61*	−15.05	−2.44	−55.32*	57.56*
	(1.96)	(0.55)	(0.29)	(1.90)	(1.89)
SMSA	−122.63	−3.26	−10.35	136.57	−125.89
	(0.61)	(0.02)	(0.22)	(0.87)	(0.77)
Husband's earnings	−12.35***	3.65	0.70	9.41**	−8.71**
	(2.62)	(1.06)	(0.64)	(2.54)	(2.24)
No-fault	392.52**	−122.42	1.74	−271.94*	270.10*
	(2.01)	(0.85)	(0.04)	(1.77)	(1.68)
West	−325.77	−155.42	101.22	379.56	−481.19*
	(0.99)	(0.64)	(1.33)	(1.46)	(1.77)
North central	78.15	−105.80	−56.14	83.62	−27.65
	(0.32)	(0.59)	(0.99)	(0.43)	(0.14)
South	−109.75	−24.71	4.26	130.14	−134.46
	(0.38)	(0.12)	(0.06)	(0.57)	(0.57)
Adjusted R^2	0.16	0.03	0.45	0.26	0.14
N	172	172	172	172	172

T = statistics are in parentheses.
*Significantly different from zero at the 10% level.
**Significantly different from zero at the 5% level.
***Significantly different from zero at the 1% level.

tions. The 1981 survey consisted of 620 respondents and 376 spouses, although not all of them completed all four diaries. This survey is particularly attractive because it provides a cross-sectional sample of individuals living in both fault and no-fault divorce states. Less detailed demographic information was collected in 1981 than in 1975, so the only way to identify the state of residence in 1981 was to restrict the sample to the individuals who had not moved since 1975. This sample also had the advantage that it was more likely to consist of people familiar with that state's laws than new residents in a state. To provide for a lagged effect of the switch from fault to no-fault grounds for divorce, the sample was restricted to fault divorce states and the no-fault divorce states that had adopted no-fault divorce grounds by 1978. Observations from the states that switched from fault to no-fault divorce between 1978 and 1981 were eliminated from the sample.

A.M. PARKMAN

TABLE 3. Activity regression equations: Married men

Variable	Regular work	House work	Child care	Leisure	Total work
Intercept	3971.34***	626.77	175.96	5306.07***	4598.11***
	(41.3)[a]	(1.13)	(1.33)	(6.12)	(5.28)
Age	−53.14***	10.71*	−3.42**	45.85***	−42.43***
	(5.55)	(1.93)	(2.59)	(5.30)	(4.89)
Assets	−0.03	−0.23	−0.01	0.27	0.26
	(0.04)	(0.58)	(0.13)	(0.43)	(0.41)
Catholic	121.08	48.06	−50.20	−119.54	169.14
	(0.49)	(0.33)	(1.47)	(0.53)	(0.75)
Children 0–3	−218.60	88.00	118.88***	11.33	−130.61
	(0.94)	(0.66)	(3.73)	(0.05)	(0.62)
Children 4–18	49.73	−1.56	10.83	−59.00	48.17
	(0.57)	(0.03)	(0.90)	(0.75)	(0.61)
White	69.70	285.11	116.83*	−472.64	354.81
	(0.15)	(1.03)	(1.78)	(1.10)	(0.82)
Year of education	46.45	−14.50	1.84	−33.97	31.95
	(1.40)	(0.76)	(0.40)	(1.14)	(1.06)
SMSA	−21.37	−190.17	−15.28	226.96	−211.53
	(0.10)	(1.52)	(0.51)	(1.16)	(1.08)
Wive's earnings	16.86	−3.99	2.48	10.44	12.86
	(1.13)	(0.46)	(1.21)	(0.78)	(0.95)
No-fault	127.32	−65.21	−40.73	−21.22	62.11
	(0.56)	(0.50)	(1.31)	(0.10)	(0.30)
West	−131.26	156.69	17.48	−43.88	25.43
	(0.37)	(0.77)	(0.36)	(0.14)	(0.08)
North central	189.14	56.81	−31.02	−215.85	245.95
	(0.66)	(0.34)	(0.79)	(0.84)	(0.95)
South	53.70	76.63	−34.06	−97.01	130.33
	(0.17)	(0.41)	(0.76)	(0.33)	(0.44)
Adjusted R-square	0.28	0.02	0.22	0.28	0.23
N	159	159	159	159	159

[a]T = statistics are in parentheses.
*Significantly different from zero at the 10% level.
**Significantly different from zero at the 5% level.
***Significantly different from zero at the 1% level.

The primary focus of this study is on married women. Still, a concern was whether all married individuals worked more hours in no-fault divorce states. Regressions were also estimated for married men to address that concern. The sample consists of 172 married women and 159 married men.

Five regression equations for married women and men were estimated.[18] Table 1 contains the definitions of the variables used in the regressions and their means. The dependent variables used in these regressions are the minutes per week spent in four activities: regular work, housework, child care, and leisure, plus total work that is the

---

[18]Because the property division at divorce varied among states based on legal standards such as community property and equitable distribution and on the amount of judicial discretion, equations were estimated that included those variables. None of those variables were significant, so they are not reported here.

sum of regular work and housework. Domestic work was separated into housework and child care, because the former was viewed as more onerous than the latter. The independent variables consist of variables associated with labor force participation: age, family assets, religion, number and age of children, race, education, spouse's earnings, whether the family lived in a Standard Metropolitan Statistical Area (SMSA), and regional variables for the western, north central and southern United States. The influence of no-fault divorce was introduced by a dummy variable for states that in 1978 permitted unilateral divorce within 2 years.[19]

V. Results

The results of the regression analysis for married women are presented in Table 2. Four of the no-fault divorce coefficients have the anticipated signs, and they are statistically significant in three of the five equations. The coefficient in the regular work equation is positive and significant, corroborating the earlier research that living in a no-fault divorce state tends to increase the employment of married women. The coefficient in the housework equations is not statistically significant, but it has the anticipated negative sign, and the sum of it and the child-care coefficient is substantially less than the increase in regular work implied by its coefficient. The no-fault coefficients in the leisure and total work equations are statistically significant at the 10% level, suggesting that living in a no-fault divorce state results in married women having 4.5 hours less leisure time and approximately the same amount of additional time devoted to work. These results support the hypothesis that married women in no-fault divorce states have been forced to take steps to protect themselves from the potentially adverse effects of no-fault divorce.[20]

It is particularly noteworthy that the 4.5-hour change in the total work of married women in no-fault divorce states noted in this study is very similar to the change observed by Victor Fuchs in the total work of married women between 1960 and 1986, before and after the no-fault divorce became the norm in the United States. Although this study investigates the effect of living in a no-fault divorce state, by 1986 all states had some form of no-fault divorce, so all married women were affected by no-fault divorce, thereby providing an explanation for the change observed by Fuchs.

Among the other variables that are statistically significant, the signs are usually the ones we would expect—total work decreases with age and increases with education. However, there is a substantial reduction in total work for married women with young children that probably does not conform to our usual expectations. This is probably due to child care not being treated as work and the fact that many leisure activities such as reading a newspaper, talking on the telephone, or walking can occur when someone is caring for children, but not when they are at regular work.

Table 3 contains the results from the regression analysis for married men. The no-fault divorce term is not statistically significant in any of the equations. Because these regression equations imply that living in a no-fault divorce state does not affect the number of hours worked by married men, one has to conclude that the greater

---

[19]In these states, a divorce could be obtained based on incompatibility, irretrievable breakdown, or living separately and apart for up to 2 years. The key to these grounds is the availability of a divorce based on the desires of one spouse and over which the other spouse has little or no control.

[20]It is noteworthy that the no-fault divorce coefficient for the child-care equation is trivial and that its *t*-statistic is essentially zero, implying that whereas married women are willing to cut corners with housework, they are not willing to reduce the time spent with their children.

diligence of married women in those states is not likely to be due to all adults working harder in those states.

VI. Conclusion

This paper investigates the reasons why the hours worked by married women have increased. The introduction of no-fault divorce that caused a decline in married women's net benefit from specialization in domestic work provides an explanation. Because of these laws, an increase in employment by married women often is motivated by a desire for personal insurance against the potential costs of divorce rather than by an increase in their family's welfare. Consequently, the other family members have been reluctant to assume responsibility for the goods and services produced by the women in the home. Still, to continue to make their marriage attractive to their husband, they have to continue to provide a substantial number of hours of domestic work. The result has been an increase in the total number of hours worked by married women.

Name Index

Economic Approaches to Law